Developmentally Appropriate Curriculum
Best Practices in Early Childhood Education

Marjorie J. Kostelnik
Anne K. Soderman
Alice Phipps Whiren

Michigan State University

Merrill,
an imprint of Prentice Hall

Upper Saddle River, New Jersey   *Columbus, Ohio*

Library of Congress Cataloging-in-Publication Data
Kostelnik, Marjorie J.
    Developmentally appropriate curriculum : best practices in early
childhood education / Marjorie J. Kostelnik, Anne K. Soderman, Alice
Phipps Whiren.
        p. cm.
    Rev. ed. of: Developmentally appropriate programs in early
childhood education. c1993.
    Includes bibliographical references and index.
    ISBN 0-13-080407-X
    1. Early childhood education—United States.   2. Early childhood
education—United States—Curricula.   3. Child development—United
States. I. Soderman, Anne Keil. II. Whiren, Alice Phipps.
III. Kostelnik, Marjorie J. Developmentally appropriate programs in
early childhood education.   IV. Title.
LB1139.25.K67   1999
371.21'0973—dc2l

98-30845
CIP

Cover photo: © Simpson, Steven/FPR International
Editor: Ann Davis
Production Editor: Julie Peters
Production Manager: Laura Messerly
Design Coordinator: Diane C. Lorenzo
Text Designer and Production Coordination: Custom Editorial Productions, Inc.
Cover Designer: Tanya Burgess
Photo Researcher: Sandy Lenahan
Director of Marketing: Kevin Flanagan
Marketing Manager: Suzanne Santon
Marketing Coordinator: Krista Groshong

This book was set in Garamond by Custom Editorial Productions, Inc., and was printed and bound by
R.R. Donnelley & Sons Company. The cover also was printed by R.R. Donnelley & Sons Company.

© 1999 by Prentice-Hall, Inc.
Simon & Schuster/A Viacom Company
Upper Saddle River, New Jersey 07458

Earlier edition, entitled *Developmentally Appropriate Programs in Early Childhood Education,* © 1994 by
Macmillan Publishing Company.

Photo Credits: pp. 15, 202, Anne Vega/Merrill; p. 48, Todd Yarrington/Merrill; pp. 77, 331, 396, 467,
Barbara Schwartz/Merrill; pp. 116, 124, Barbara Rohde; p. 354, Anthony Magnacca/Merrill p. 427,
Dan Floss/Merrill; p. 453, Bruce Fox/Michigan State University; all other photos by David Kostelnik

Printed in the United States of America

10 9 8 7 6 5 4 3 2 1

ISBN: 0-13-080407-X

Prentice-Hall International (UK) Limited, *London*
Prentice-Hall of Australia Pty. Limited, *Sydney*
Prentice-Hall of Canada, Inc., *Toronto*
Prentice-Hall Hispanoamericana, S. A., *Mexico*
Prentice-Hall of India Private Limited, *New Delhi*
Prentice-Hall of Japan, Inc., *Tokyo*
Simon & Schuster Asia Pte. Ltd., *Singapore*
Editora Prentice-Hall do Brasil, Ltda., *Rio de Janeiro*

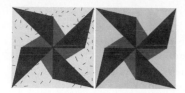

Preface

Every adult needs a child to teach. It's the way adults learn. —Anonymous

❏ What are developmentally appropriate practices, and how effective are they?

❏ How can we create the very best programs for young children?

❏ As early childhood educators, what is our role in shaping children's educational experiences? What is the child's role? What is the role of the family and community?

❏ How can we tell if children are really learning?

Questions such as these are typically posed by early childhood professionals-in-training as well as by seasoned practitioners in the field. Our work with students and increasing numbers of educators probing for answers indicated the need for a comprehensive guide to support the exploration, planning, and implementation of developmentally appropriate programs. Thus, our goal in writing *Developmentally Appropriate Curriculum: Best Practices in Early Childhood Education* was to bring together the best information currently available for developing an integrated approach to curriculum and instruction in the early years. We also hoped to bridge the worlds of childcare and early education, as well as those of preprimary and primary programs. The resulting volume addresses *early childhood professionals-in-training and professionals working in formal group settings with young children from three to eight years of age.* We realize that early childhood edu-

cation spans birth to age eight; however, we see infancy and toddlerhood as unique ages within this period, requiring specialized knowledge beyond the scope of this text. For this reason we have not focused on infants or toddlers in our discussions.

We believe the information in this book will be *valuable to both novices and master practitioners.* The ideas here have been extensively field tested and found to be effective. All are designed to give you a cohesive view of the *"what," "why," and "how" of developmentally appropriate practices.*

Finally, you should know that the authors have had many years of experience working directly with young children and their families and with educators in preprimary and primary settings. We have been in urban, suburban, and rural programs; large-medium and small classes; public, private, not-for-profit, and profit-seeking organizations; half- and full-day programs; preschool classes; and the elementary grades. Currently, all of us are actively engaged in educating young children and the professionals who work with them.

Distinctive Features of This Text

Developmentally Appropriate Curriculum: Best Practices in Early Childhood Education offers instructors and readers several unique features that increase reader understanding and skill development:

❑ The text addresses the classroom as an ecosystem that includes contributions of children and adults, characteristics of the physical and social environments, and the contextual factors leading to learning.

❑ The concept of developmentally appropriate practices is pervasive throughout the volume. Each chapter addresses principles of age appropriateness, individual appropriateness, and social and cultural appropriateness.

❑ This book spans the early childhood years from 3 to 8 in a comprehensive, cohesive approach that results in greater continuity for children and practitioners.

❑ Each chapter progresses clearly from theory/research to practice.

❑ The authors use developmental domains to address early childhood curriculum. This helps practitioners better understand the link between child development and program implementation.

❑ Every curriculum chapter includes sample activities.

❑ The text address both individual curricular domains and curriculum integration.

❑ Detailed directions facilitate the implementation of developmentally appropriate practices.

❑ We demonstrate the interaction of developmentally appropriate practices, developmental goals, and relevant curriculum content.

❑ Readers learn a comprehensive approach to conceptualizing, planning, implementing, and evaluating curriculum.

❑ Chapter-end activities provide readers the opportunity to extend their understanding of chapter content to their professional lives. *Discussion questions* focus on essential information in each chapter and give readers an opportunity to explore ideas with classmates and colleagues. *Journal recommendations* enhance readers' reflective thinking. Sample *observations* help readers to recognize developmentally appropriate practices in operation. *Classroom activities* enable readers to apply chapter content and processes in interactions with children, families, or professionals in the field. Finally, if readers complete the *portfolio entries* in each chapter, they will create a comprehensive portfolio including artifacts (things generated in class and then used in a portfolio), reproductions (things reproduced by camera, video, or audio for use in the portfolio), productions (things specifically produced for placing in the portfolio), and testimonials (others attesting to their abilities), all centered around developmentally appropriate practices.

Format and Chapter Sequence

Developmentally Appropriate Curriculum: Best Practices in Early Childhood Education is divided into four parts. Part 1, Foundations of Early Childhood Education, consists of the Introduction as well as Chapters 1 and 2 and addresses the philosophy of developmentally appropriate practice, which has been the driving force in early childhood education over the past ten years. Characteristics of the field, principles associated with developmentally appropriate practice, and critical issues in early childhood education are outlined in Part 1. "Setting the Stage for Learning" is the focus of Part 2, Chapters 3 through 7. In these chapters we describe the preliminary understandings and skills you must have to create an effective program for young children. These include planning, implementing, and organizing small-group and whole-group activities and the physical space and materials used in the classroom; creating a schedule for the day; and determining how to group children to achieve certain aims. Child guidance and family involvement are addressed as fundamental to effective teaching. In Part 3, Chapters 8 through 13, the curriculum has been explained in terms of six developmental domains, rather than by subject or materials. Within this segment we focus on aesthetic, affective, cognitive, language, physical, and social development. Each of the domain chapters has a discussion of theory, research, and educational issues related to children's development and learning in that particular arena, a suggested outline of ultimate goals and intermediate objectives, teaching strategies that undergird the domain, and examples of classroom activities. The curriculum domains are presented in alphabetical order to underscore the idea that no one domain is more important than any of the others. However, it may be useful for you to know that each domain refers to five kinds of knowledge: physical, logical-mathematical, representational, social-conventional, and metacognitive. If you are familiar with these terms, reading Chapters 8 through 13 in order will make sense. However, if you are unfamiliar with them, it will be useful to first read

Chapter 10, in which the terms are explained. The last section of the book is Part 4, Integrating Curriculum. This part includes Chapters 14 through 16, all focused on integrating the content and processes in Parts 2 and 3 to create a cohesive whole. This includes classroom-based methods such as pretend play and construction, theme teaching, and authentic assessment.

Structural Features

Each chapter begins with a series of questions that pique readers' interest in the material and provide a framework for reflecting on the chapter's content following an initial reading. In addition, a series of culminating activities enables readers to review and apply the material in their professional lives. Thus, every chapter ends with discussion questions, potential observations to make in early childhood settings, application activities, guidelines for journal entries, and suggested items to add to a portfolio. These learning aids will hone readers' understanding and skill and serve as resource materials for the future.

What's the Same About This Volume

Among the popular elements we transferred from the first edition was our focus on developmental domains, a strong research basis for the information provided, and an emphasis on practical applications. Because readers liked the clear link between theory and practice provided by the "Implications" sections in the early chapters, those have remained. The curriculum chapters still include rationales and sample teaching strategies specific to each domain, objectives, issues practitioners face, and illustrative activities. Examples featuring children, families, and professionals from a variety of backgrounds continue to be a feature of the chapters that compose the end of the book.

Significant Changes

Title Change   Instructors and students familiar with our previous book, *Developmentally Appropriate Programs in Early Childhood Education,* will note our newly revised title, *Developmentally Appropriate Curriculum: Best Practices in Early Childhood Education.* This change more clearly indicates the curricular focus of the text and highlights the research support for the practices that are included.

Content Changes   This edition has been extensively updated. Based on feedback from our readers, we have added several new segments to the book. What constitutes high-quality early childhood education is addressed in the Introduction. Chapter 1 includes the most recent definition of developmentally appropriate practice (DAP), research supporting the principles of DAP, criticisms aimed at DAP, and examples of various approaches to DAP, including Reggio Emilia, High/Scope, and Glasser's Quality Schools. Chapter 2 now is devoted solely to principles of development and learning and their implications for program implementation. This highlights more powerfully the link between development and appropriate practices.

Chapters 3 and 4 are entirely new. The basic steps in planning effective small-group activities for young children are presented in Chapter 3, as are teaching strategies most commonly associated with DAP. Although teaching children in small groups is the backbone of DAP classrooms, whole-group instruction is important as well. For that reason, Chapter 4 focuses on planning and implementing effective group times, organizing successful field trips, and working with visitors. We have combined the skills of organizing space, materials, time, and children's groups in one place (Chapter 5) to help readers more easily recognize how these curriculum elements work together. Learning centers are incorporated in this chapter along with very specific guides for setting up core centers. Because readers have indicated that child guidance is critical for setting the stage for learning, we have moved that chapter to an earlier place in the book (Chapter 6). Chapter 7, "Strengthening Developmentally Appropriate Programs Through Family Involvement," now emphasizes that not only parents but also other family members may significantly influence young children's development and learning. We also place greater emphasis on the notion of an integrated approach to family/program partnerships.

The domain chapters retain many of the features readers found useful the first time around. However, new material has been added to each one. Elements of dance and expanded teaching strategies are included for the aesthetic domain (Chapter 8). Readers will find new sections on children's development of emotional awareness and emotional intelligence in Chapter 9, covering the affective domain. Chapter 10, on the cognitive domain, has been completely reworked and now strongly emphasizes both Vygotsky and multiple intelligences. The intermediate objectives in this chapter are now more manageable, and additional activities for children in first and second grade have been incorporated. The language domain is covered in Chapter 11, now entirely rewritten, providing much more material on literacy, written language, and phonological awareness. The Physical Domain, Chapter 12, has also been rewritten, and now includes new material on fitness, health, safety, and perceptual awareness. New antibias activities have been added to Chapter 13, which addresses the social domain.

We have taken pretend play and construction out of the curriculum segment of the book and combined them into one chapter (Chapter 14). Our aim is to highlight the integrative nature of play and its importance at all levels of early childhood education. The chapter on themes (Chapter 15) has been enlarged to include more information on the Project Approach. Defining and focusing more attention on authentic assessment is the major change in Chapter 16.

All of these revisions address current issues in early childhood curriculum development and implementation. Their inclusion should better prepare readers to face the realities of teaching young children on a day-to-day basis.

Acknowledgments

We would like to recognize the major contributions to this text by seven of our colleagues in early childhood education: Barbara M. Rohde, Director, Developmentally Appropriate Practices, Owasso Public Schools, contributed Chapter 8; in addition, she supplied artwork for the classroom floor plans and the pictograph that appear in Chapter 12. Laura C. Stein, Specialist and Head Teacher, Department of Family and Child Ecology, Michigan State University, produced Chapter 13. Patricia Weissman, Research Associate and Reggio Project Coordinator, Merrill Palmer Institute of Wayne State University, contributed the section on the "Reggio Emilia Approach to Early Childhood Education"; Mary Hohmann, Senior Consultant, Program Division, High/Scope Educational Research Foundation, wrote the portion entitled "The High/Scope Approach to Early Childhood Education"; and, Kaye Mentley, principal of Huntington Woods Elementary School, authored the information on the "Quality School Approach to Early Childhood Education." All of these segments appear in Chapter 1. Judy Harris Helm, of Best Practices, Incorporated, wrote the material describing the "Project Approach," featured in Chapter 15. The work of these individuals has broadened the scope of the text and has enabled us to present multiple voices describing developmentally appropriate curriculum.

We appreciate the generous assistance of David Kostelnik, photographer, who provided excellent images taken at a number of preschool and elementary sites. We are also indebted to the teachers in the Child Development Laboratories at Michigan State University for their early and continuing work on the curriculum, for providing continuous and easy access to their classrooms for observation, and for inspiring many of the ideas represented here. Thanks to Stephanie Perentesis, Reference Librarian, College of Human Ecology, for assistance in finding sources and references vital to our work. An-Sook Kim and Delene Lautigar helped with the library work as well. We are grateful to Deborah Sharpe, Haslett Public Schools, and Grace Spalding, Department of Family and Child Ecology, for the group times described in Chapter 4; and to Donna Howe, Department of Family and Child Ecology, for materials related to learning centers (Chapter 5) and theme-related material (Chapter 15). Dr. John Haubenstricker, Department of Physical Education and Exercise Science, graciously shared his research and the figures that illustrate gross motor skills (Chapter 12).

We also appreciate the help of the following colleagues who read revised chapters, making numerous suggestions to improve them: Kara Gregory, Holly Brophy-Herb, Donna Howe, Barb Meloche, Unhai Rhee, Barbara Rohde, Laura Stein, and Grace Spalding. Mary Faloon, Deborah Porter, Ruth Sedelmeir, Karen Tkaczyk, Susan Zutaut, and Andrew Konkle provided able technical assistance and support throughout the project. We are grateful for the gifts of time and expertise each person offered.

We would like to thank the following reviewers for their comments and suggestions: Gloria Boutte, University of South Carolina; Jeri A. Carroll, Wichita State University; and Pat Hofbauer, Northwest State Community College.

Ann Davis, our editior at Merrill/Prentice Hall, was a tremendous support as were all members of the production team. During the preparation of this manuscript, we discussed our ideas with and received feedback from a number of Michigan State University students as well as Head Start, Chapter 1, childcare, nursery school, and elementary school teachers and administrators. We heard the concerns of many parents of young children and listened to the children themselves as they responded to diverse program practices in their classrooms. We are especially grateful for all these contributions in shaping our vision of appropriate practices and in motivating us to share that vision with others.

Marjorie Kostelnik
Anne Soderman
Alice Whiren

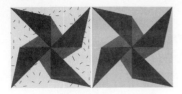

About the Authors

Marjorie J. Kostelnik, Ph. D., is Chairperson of the Department of Family and Child Ecology, College of Human Ecology, Michigan State University. For 13 years, she served as program supervisor of the Child Development Laboratories on campus. In this facility she worked daily with students-in-training and with 250 children and their families. The population served included families from many different socioeconomic and cultural backgrounds as well as children whose developmental abilities varied widely. A former childcare, Head Start, and nursery school teacher, as well as elementary school specialist, Dr. Kostelnik has been actively involved in helping early childhood programs explore the implications of developmentally appropriate practices. Whether in the United States or abroad, much of this exploration has focused on how teachers can translate their understandings into practical strategies they can use immediately. Dr. Kostelnik has just completed a four-year term as Vice-President of the National Association for the Education of Young Children.

Anne K. Soderman has had 14 years of classroom experience working with children in both public and nonpublic educational settings prior to joining Michigan State University, where she is currently Professor of Family and Child Ecology. In addition to carrying out teaching assignments in a number of international settings, she consults with public school systems in early childhood curriculum, instruction, and evaluation, with a particular focus on early literacy for at-risk children. She has also recently coauthored *Creating Phonological and Print Awareness in the Early Years: Developmentally Appropriate Practices* with Kara M. Gregory and Louise T. O'Neill.

Alice Phipps Whiren is a professor and Program Supervisor of the Child Development Laboratories, Department of Family and Child Ecology, College of Human Ecology, Michigan State University. She teaches curriculum in early childhood and child development to undergraduate and graduate students. Early in her career, she taught young children in an inner-city public school in Michigan. She also served as a Head Start assistant director and has provided a variety of training sessions for preprimary teachers nationally and internationally. Most recently she has been a consultant to public school systems as their staffs implement more developmentally appropriate programs for children.

CONTRIBUTORS

Barbara Rohde is the Director of Developmentally Appropriate Practices for the Owosso Public Schools in Owosso, Michigan. A former nursery school teacher, Laboratory School supervisor, and elementary school art teacher, she has an art education degree, which has informed her interests in vocal and instrumental music, drawing, printmaking, and illustrating.

Laura C. Stein is a Head Teacher in the Child Development Laboratories at Michigan State University. Her role includes training teachers as well as teaching 4- and 5-year-old children. She has coauthored a textbook on children's social development, has contributed numerous chapters and articles to books and journals, and speaks extensively to professional audiences.

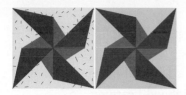

Contents

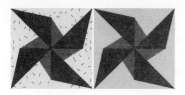

Introduction

If you are a practicing teacher, you probably know the joy of getting a love note from a child. If you are an aspiring early childhood educator, you might receive a letter like this someday, a hug, a smile, or some other sign that you have become an integral part of a young child's life. Knowing you make a difference to children and families is one of the best things about being an early childhood professional. Another is knowing that you are helping children at the start of life, a time of amazing potential and tremendous opportunity.

A GOOD BEGINNING IS ESSENTIAL

You know that the beginning is the most important part of any work, especially in the case of a young and tender thing.—Plato

During the early years, children develop the dispositions and attitudes toward education and themselves as learners that will stay with them their whole lives. Educators report that, by the end of second grade, many children have reached one of the following conclusions (Kostelnik, 1989, 24):

School is exciting/challenging/fun, and I am a good learner.

or

School is boring/difficult/painful, and I can't learn.

Youngsters whose conclusions are positive have a strong foundation for subsequent life success. However, the future for children whose school- and self-evaluations are negative is bleak. These are the children most likely to require extensive remedial assistance, encounter mental-health problems, endure academic failure, and drop out of school (Doyle, 1989; Elkind, 1987). The particular opinions children form are greatly influenced by their education experiences in the first few years of life.

As an early childhood professional, you play a major role in shaping those experiences. The more you know about the field you are entering, the better prepared you will be to create effective early childhood programs. This introduction provides an overview of early childhood education today. We define the profession and talk about its significance now and in the future. In addition, we describe the children, families, and professionals who learn together in early childhood settings. Let us begin.

WHAT IS EARLY CHILDHOOD EDUCATION?

Which of the following programs would you label as early childhood education?

> Nursery-school classroom.
>
> Second-grade classroom.
>
> Family-childcare home.

If you answered "All of the above," you were correct. Early childhood education involves any group program serving children from birth to 8 years of age that is designed to promote children's intellectual, social, emotional, language, and physical development and learning (Bredekamp & Copple, 1997; NAEYC, 1995). This translates into a wide array of programs attended by children of many different ages. Early childhood education includes programs for infants and toddlers, as well as preschool, kindergarten, and primary programs. These programs may be half-day or full-day, public or private, enrichment or remedial in focus, targeted at low-, middle-, or high-income families, and administered by a variety of institutions in the community.

At one time, our view of early childhood education and its focus group was quite limited. In the not-too-distant past, the term *early childhood* was used only in reference to children 5 years old and younger. Parents and educators alike recognized that such youngsters differed significantly from older children. Under this traditional interpretation, entry into primary school (usually first grade) divided early from later childhood. Thus, preschoolers and kindergartners were

categorized as one group, and school-age children as another (Smart & Smart, 1972). Following this line of reasoning, you might assume that first and second graders would be more like fifth graders than like kindergartners. However, research and practical experience refute this. Evidence related to children's intellectual, social, and physical powers suggests that significant shifts in young children's development more likely occur around 7 or 8 years of age than age 5 (Brewer, 1998; Safford, 1989). Consequently, psychologists and educators have conceptualized early childhood as extending through the eighth year of life. This period crosses traditional programmatic boundaries, including preschool children, kindergartners, and students in the early primary grades. Currently, more children than ever are involved in early childhood programs.

EARLY CHILDHOOD EDUCATION IS A GROWING ENTERPRISE

You are entering a field that is in high demand. Peter Francese, president of *American Demographics* magazine, says that "Early childhood professionals are in the right profession at the right time. I have never before conducted a market analysis of any trade where the demographic indicators pointed so strongly in the right direction" (Neugebauer, 1994, 80). Three factors in particular indicate that the demand for early childhood education in the United States will accelerate in the coming years:

❏ The population of children from birth to age 8 will reach record highs in the next several years.
❏ The number of families wanting formalized care and education for their young children is rising.
❏ Strong evidence indicates that early childhood education yields positive outcomes for poor children and children described as at risk for potential school failure.

In summarizing these trends and predictions, James Hymes (1991, 2) notes that "the field of early childhood has moved from the fringes of the education 'establishment' to center stage." As you become involved in this movement, you will find it useful to understand more about the children and families with whom you will be working.

CHILDREN AND FAMILIES IN EARLY CHILDHOOD EDUCATION

Mary Hughes was making nametags for the children in her class: Juan, Un-Hai, Rachel, Steven, LaTanya, Clarissa, Heidi, Mohammed, Molly, Sally, Keiko, Mark, LeRoy, Indira, Jennifer, and Sasha. As she finished each nametag, she thought about how different each child was. The youngsters represented many racial, ethnic, and cultural backgrounds. They varied greatly in terms of how much education their parents had and in the socioeconomic status of their families. Some children spoke English, and several spoke languages other than English at home. Some had prior preschool experience, and some had none. Some children lived at home with two parents, some were living in single-parent households, and one youngster was a foster child, newly arrived in her foster home. The children also functioned at varying developmental levels. Mary marveled at the diversity of the group.

Early Childhood Programs Serve a Diverse Population of Children and Families

Like Mary, you will likely work with a diverse array of children and families throughout your career in early childhood education. This is because the United States is becoming more diverse each year. For instance, racial and ethnic diversity has increased substantially in the United States over the past 20 years and is projected to increase even more as we move into the twenty-first century. The U.S. Census Bureau expects the proportion of white children to decline steadily from 69 percent in 1990 to about 50 percent in 2030. Conversely, the proportion of all children who are of a nonwhite population group is expected to grow from 31 percent to 50 percent (Hernandez, 1995). In addition, within the next five years, perhaps up to one third of the children between the ages of 3 and 8 will speak home languages other than English. Such linguistic diversity means the mix of languages present in early childhood classrooms will be greater than it is now. Family structures are also shifting. Today children may live in a variety of family arrangements—two-parent families, single-parent families, blended families, interracial families, families in which parents are of different genders and families in which parents are of the same gender, adoptive families, and foster families. Family income is another differentiating variable. You might work with children whose families have limited financial resources as well as with children whose families have large financial reserves. Some programs serve families whose income levels are within the same range; other programs serve families whose socioeconomic circumstances vary widely. Another factor that has influenced diversity in early childhood classrooms is inclusion. Since the passage of Federal Law 94–142

Early childhood education programs are inclusive, enhancing the development and learning of all the children enrolled.

in 1976, children with disabilities have been provided access to free public education in the least restrictive setting. In 1987, Public Law 99–142 extended such services to children 3 to 5 years of age. The Americans with Disabilities Act of 1990 provided additional protections to people with disabilities, including freedom from discrimination as well as equal access to public programs. All of these laws underscore a U.S. commitment to educate all children, to the maximum extent appropriate, in regular classrooms on a full-time basis. Support services are brought to children as needed, rather than removing children from the early childhood setting to receive the services. Thus, children with disabilities are not clustered into groups of persons with similar disabilities. They are no longer served only in separate classrooms labeled "learning disabled" or "emotionally impaired" (Miller, 1996). This "mainstreaming" has led to increased numbers of children with handicapping conditions being served in regular early childhood classrooms.

These trends mean that early childhood educators have to create responsive early childhood programs that treat all people with respect. Rather than viewing one set of life experiences or demographics as "appropriate" and others as "inappropriate," we must integrate children's beliefs, history, and experiences into our programs in ways that make sense to children and enable them to flourish as learners (Garcia, 1993).

Families Are Children's First Teachers

During early childhood, the immediate context of the family has the greatest influence on the child. The family is responsible for meeting children's physical needs as well as for socializing the younger generation. Family members provide children with their first social relationships, models for behaviors and roles, a framework of values and beliefs, and intellectual stimulation (Bobbitt & Paolucci, 1986). All of these functions take place through direct and indirect teaching, in constructive and sometimes destructive ways, more or less successfully. In addition, most environmental influences are channeled to some extent through the family. For instance, it is via the family that children gain access to economic resources and learn the customs of their cultural group. The first attitudes toward education, work, and society that children encounter are in the family. Parents arrange for out-of-home care and

make the initial entrée into a school for their children. They also promote or inhibit opportunities for peer and community contact. If parents are stressed by the hardships of poverty, the uncertainty of losing a job, or the prospects of marital dissolution, their ability to meet the needs of their young children is jeopardized. If such parents receive help or support from relatives, friends, or social institutions, the home environment they create for their children may be enhanced.

EARLY CHILDHOOD PROGRAMS VARY IN STRUCTURE AND SCOPE

During your years as an early childhood professional, you will most likely work in a variety of settings and programs. Education programs for young children come in all forms. Programs for young children operate under different funding sources (public or private) and vary in location and size (private home, church, small-group center, or large school). They encompass a wide range of educational philosophies and curricula. Early childhood education programs also vary in their target audience, their scope (full-day to half-day; full-year to partial-year; every day to some days), and the training background of key personnel. An overview of the vast array of services currently available is offered in Table 1.

These variations in programs serving young children have evolved from distinct needs and traditions. For instance, modern childcare programs have come about in response to societal demands for protected childcare environments during parents' working hours. Historically, they have emphasized the health and safety of the children enrolled, and, although some involve government subsidies, many rely on corporate or private sponsorship and/or parent fees. Supplementing the learning experiences children have at home has long been the function of the nursery-school movement. Usually financed through parent fees, nurturance, enrichment, and school readiness have been its primary aims. More recent early intervention programs, such as Head Start and Chapter 1, are the result of federally mandated and supported efforts to remediate unfavorable developmental or environmental circumstances. These compensatory education programs focus on a particular segment of the population—disadvantaged children. They are designed to change such children's life opportunities by altering the course of

TABLE 1
Early Childrhood Education Programs for Children Ages 3–8 Years

Program	Children Served	Ages	Purposes	Funding
Nursery schools	Mostly middle class	2–5 years	Enrichment experiences aimed at whole-child development	Parent tuition
Parent cooperative preschools	Children of participating parents	2–5 years	Enrichment experiences aimed at whole-child development and parent education	Parent tuition and support services
Religious preschools	Children of church/temple/mosque members and the religious community	2–5 years	Enrichment experiences aimed at whole-child development and spiritual training	Church subsidies and parent tuition
Group childcare programs	All	6 weeks–12 years	Comprehensive care of children covering all aspects of development	Varies. Sources include employer subsidies, parent tuition, state agencies, and the federal government via Title XX funds, USDA Child Care Food Program, childcare tax credits, and private and charitable organizations.
Famility childcare homes	All	6 weeks–12 years	Comprehensive care of children covering all aspects of development	Varies. Sources include employer subsidies, parent tuition, state agencies, and the federal government via Title XX funds, USDA Child Care Food Program, childcare tax credits, and private and charitable organizations.
Head Start	Children from low-income families, children with disabilities	3–5 years	Comprehensive development program addressing children's educational, nutiritional, and medical needs, also parent education	Federal funds

(continued on the next page)

TABLE 1
(continued)

Program	Children Served	Ages	Purposes	Funding
Even Start	Children and parents from low-income families	1–7 years	Integration of early childhood education and adult education of parents	Federal funds
Follow Through	Children from low-income families	5–8 years	Continuation of educational support for former Head Start participants	Federal funds
Chapter 1	Educationally de-prived children (migrant, disabled, neglected, and delinquent children)	4–12 years	Supplemental educa-tion for children and parents	Federal funds
State-sponsored 4-year-old programs	Children identified as at risk for economic, develop-mental, or environ-mental reasons	4–18 years	Development of readiness skills for future schooling	State taxes and special allocations
Developmental kindergarten	Children identified by school or parents as not ready for regular kindergarten	5 years	Development of readiness skills	State and local taxes or, in the case of private schools, parent tuition
Kindergarten	All	5–6 years	Introduction to formal schooling	State and local taxes or, in the case of private schools, parent tuition
Transitional rooms (pre- or junior first grade)	Children identified by school as not ready for first grade following a year or more of kindergarten	6–7 years	Development of readiness skills (most likely related to reading)	State and local taxes or, in the case of private schools, parent tuition
First, second, and third grade	All	6–8 years	Transmission of society's accumulated knowledge, values, beliefs, and customs to the young	State and local taxes or, in the case of private schools, parent tuition

their development for the better. Primary education, on the other hand, reflects a history that emphasizes the commitment of public funds to mass education.

The goals of primary education have focused on trans-mitting society's accumulated knowledge, values, be-liefs, and customs to youngsters of all backgrounds and educational needs. Compulsory in some states, not required in others, but available in all, kindergarten straddles the two "worlds" of early childhood. Long considered a transition into formal schooling, kindergarten programs have been the center of much current controversy. Should they be structured more like nursery school or more like the upper elementary grades? Traditionally more similar to the former than to the latter, today's kindergarten programs have experienced a shift in emphasis. Awareness that many children have previously attended early education programs and concern over children's subsequent school success have resulted in increasingly adult-centered, academic kindergarten programs (Morado, 1990). This trend has ignited renewed debate, not yet resolved, over the real function of kindergarten and its role in children's lives. It has also spawned new early childhood programs like developmental kindergartens and transition rooms.

The program variations just described are implemented by a wide array of practitioners trained to work with young children. Let us briefly take a moment to consider how people become early childhood professionals and what distinguishes a professional from an amateur.

EARLY CHILDHOOD PROFESSIONALS

When Scott arrived at Lakeland College, he majored in business administration. After taking some classes, he realized business was not for him but had no clear idea of what he wanted to do. One afternoon he went with some friends to help supervise a Halloween party for kindergartners at the local YMCA. He had a great time with the children. They were fun and so smart. After several more experiences with children at the Y, Scott decided to talk to his advisor about the major in early childhood education.

Jackie is the mother of three children. When she began working in a Head Start classroom as a parent volunteer, she became intrigued with preschoolers' development and learning in the classroom. She vowed that someday she would earn her associate's degree in child development. Today she is close to fulfilling that dream—just one class to go!

Lourdes knew she wanted to have a classroom of her own from the time she was a little girl. She played teacher with her friends and took a child development course in high school. Every chance she got, Lourdes found ways to work with children. She tutored at the local elementary school and participated in the Big Sister program in her town. During her freshman year, Lourdes signed up for courses in early childhood education, determined to make her lifelong dream come true.

What Makes Someone an Early Childhood Professional?

As evidenced by Scott, Jackie, and Lourdes, early childhood educators come to the field in a variety of ways. Some begin their training on the job; others start in a two- or four-year institution. Some are hoping to fulfill a long-held goal; others "discover" the field as a result of different life experiences. Whatever their motivation and point of entry, there comes a time when individuals decide to move from layperson status to the professional world of early childhood education. This shift is the result of education and training, not simply desire. Thus, certain characteristics differentiate the professional early childhood educator from the layperson.

Access to Knowledge   Professionals have access to specialized knowledge and skills that are unavailable to amateurs and that are acquired as a result of prolonged education and specialized training (Katz, 1988). The Association of Childhood Education International (ACEI) and the National Association for the Education of Young Children (NAEYC) have made recommendations for the training of professionals at all levels of early childhood education. Content and skills include general studies (humanities, mathematics, technology, social sciences, biological and physical sciences, the arts, physical health and fitness), child development and learning, curriculum development and implementation, family and community relationships, assessment and evaluation, professionalism, and field experiences with young children under appropriate supervision.

Although valuable, life experience alone is not sufficient to provide the full range of technical know-how and professional skills necessary for maximum effectiveness on the job.

Demonstrated Competence   Professionals also differ from amateurs in having to demonstrate competence in their field in order to enter the profession. The most formalized evidence of mastery requires earning a license or certification, which is usually governed by state or national standards. Slightly less formal monitoring involves having to take tests, pass courses, and demonstrate proficiency either in a practicum setting or on the job. All of these experiences take place under the supervision of qualified members of the profession (Kostelnik, Stein, Whiren, & Soderman, 1998).

Standards of Practice   Professionals perform their duties in keeping with standards of excellence generally accepted for the field. Such standards come about through research and professional reflection (Kostelnik et al., 1998). Some standards are enforced through self-monitoring within the profession, whereas others are maintained through governmental regulation. Whatever the case, professional standards provide a gauge by which early childhood practitioners assess their own performance as well as the overall quality of the services they offer children and families.

Lifelong Learning   To keep up with the standards in their field, early childhood professionals constantly upgrade their knowledge and skills both informally and formally. Such efforts include attending workshops, consulting with colleagues, participating in professional organizations, reading professional journals as well as pursuing additional schooling. Regardless of the means, professionals treat learning as a lifelong process.

Code of Ethics   Although useful, the personal moral code most people bring to their work is not enough to govern professional behavior. What makes common sense to an individual may or may not be congruent with agreed-upon standards within the profession. Thus, professionalism requires adoption of an ethical code of conduct that has been formally approved within the field. Such codes provide guidelines for determining acceptable and nonacceptable behavior on the job. Specific ethical codes govern professionals whose work involves children. Although the particulars may vary, all ethics codes focus on ensuring confidentiality, providing safe and beneficial experiences, and treating people with respect regardless of sex, race, culture, religion, or ability.

THE QUALITY DIMENSION OF EARLY CHILDHOOD EDUCATION

How will you know if the program in which you are participating benefits young children? According to materials prepared for prospective clients, all early child-

hood programs claim to be outstanding. Is this true? Let us look at some examples.

> Brochure describing the early childhood program at the Westover Child Development Center:
>
> *Here at the Westover CDC, we offer a high-quality early childhood program for children from three to five years of age. Our teachers all have degrees in child development or early education. We focus on all aspects of children's learning using a play-based curriculum.*

> Advertisement posted on the community bulletin board of a local grocery store:
>
> *High-quality child care in my home. Loving environment. Lots to do. Fun, safe, reliable. References available.*

> One student intern to another:
>
> *The quality of the program was really poor. The children were running around with nothing to do. No one seemed to be in charge. There were too many kids and not enough adults. I couldn't wait to get out of there.*

> Headline of an editorial in a local newspaper:
>
> *Blue Ribbon Panel Outlines Criteria for High-Quality Schools*

Although each of these examples focuses on a different early childhood program, they all mention quality. People who talk about "high quality" are referring to excellence. When something is described as having "high quality," we understand that it represents more than the minimum standards and has value above the ordinary. "Poor quality," on the other hand, suggests an image of substandard conditions and negative outcomes. These variations in quality are particularly important in relation to early childhood education.

Quality Makes a Difference

Quality is a term early childhood professionals often use in describing their programs. Parents, too, are concerned about the quality of their children's education and care. This is true for families across the board, regardless of background or income level. In a recent national poll, 97 percent of the parents surveyed cited quality as their top priority in determining which early childhood programs they wanted their child to attend (Smith et al., 1997). Yet there is a difference in the quality of education and care children receive. Some children are in high-quality early childhood programs, but many have poor-quality experiences. High-quality programs benefit children and their families; poor-quality programs are detrimental to them.

Poor-Quality Programs   Every day, thousands of children are subjected to program practices that threaten their immediate health and safety as well as their long-term development and learning (Cost, Quality, and Child Outcomes Study, 1995; Whitebook, Sakai, & Howes, 1997). For instance, poor-quality experiences lead to increased behavior problems and poorer academic progress in children. Such children are also more likely to have poor social skills (Howes, 1988; Vandell & Corasanti, 1990). These negative effects appear to be long lasting, with evidence of poor quality still apparent up to five years later. To make matters worse, families may not be able to compensate for the negative impact of poor-quality programs, at least for children who spend 20 or more hours a week in such circumstances (Doherty-Derkowski, 1995). Because high-quality care and education may be more expensive, low-income children are the most likely to be enrolled in poor-quality programs at both the preprimary and primary levels. In this way, poor-quality programs compound the challenges such children face.

High-Quality Programs   Children whose education and care are described as high quality enjoy a variety of benefits. Such children demonstrate higher levels of language development, greater social competence, a better ability to regulate their own behavior, and better academic performance than do their peers in poor-quality programs (Doherty-Derkowski, 1995). Additional evidence indicates that children who have high-quality early childhood program experiences outperform peers who have no such experiences prior to entering school. These results hold true in the short-term and over time. Obviously, our aim as early childhood professionals is to create high-quality early childhood programs for children and families. To do this, we must have a better picture of what such programs involve.

What Do High-Quality Programs Look Like?

With so much at stake, it is critical to ask, "What do high-quality programs look like?" Fortunately, there is a growing research base we can draw upon for the answer. The essential components of high-quality early child-

hood programs are given in the following list (Doherty-Derkowski, 1995; Shimoni, Baxter, & Kugelmass, 1992; Smith et al., 1995; Whitebook, Sakai, & Howes, 1997):

Practitioners are well prepared and well compensated.

❏ Adults have specific training in child development and early childhood education.

❏ Adults vary their teaching strategies and expectations based on what they believe is age-appropriate, individually appropriate, and socially and culturally appropriate for each child.

❏ Adults in higher-quality programs are paid higher wages and receive satisfactory benefits.

Staffing is stable.

❏ Teachers remain with the program and the same group of children long enough for children to develop a trusting relationship with an adult outside the home.

Group sizes are small, and there are few children for each practitioner.

❏ The group size and adult-child ratios are small enough that children can engage in first-hand interactions with adults, receiving individualized instruction and personal feedback about their learning experiences.

❏ At least two adults are present (achieved through the use of paid staff as well as volunteers) in each group.

Warm, attentive relationships are established between adults and children.

❏ Adults are warm, respectful, understanding, affectionate, and friendly toward children.

❏ Adults listen to children, comfort, support, and guide them in ways that make sense to children and help them become more successful in their social interactions.

Environments are safe and healthy.

❏ Health and safety provisions are in place to support children's well-being.

Environments are stimulating.

❏ Adequate, appropriate materials are available to support children's explorations and development of more advanced knowledge and skills.

❏ The curriculum is designed to support and enrich children's aesthetic, affective, cognitive, language, physical, and social development and learning.

Family involvement is evident.

❏ The program is designed to support and complement families in their child-rearing role.

❏ Family members are welcome to observe, discuss, and recommend policies and to participate in the program's activities.

Links to comprehensive community services are made.

❏ Families are referred and/or have access to a wide array of services necessary to support their child-rearing responsibilities.

All of these quality indicators set the stage for the best possible interactions between children and the early childhood professionals who will help prepare them for the twenty-first century.

LOOKING TOWARD THE FUTURE

The children with whom you are now working will be adults in a world we have yet to know. If we focus all our energy on today's demands (i.e., getting children ready for the 4-year-old classroom, preparing them for kindergarten, or concentrating solely on the transition to first or second grade), we will be short-sighted and negligent in our responsibility to help them navigate the future. Instead, we must help children learn the knowledge and skills they will need to prosper in the world of tomorrow. Although specific details are diffi-

Successful citizens of the twenty-first century will have to know how to work together and be flexible thinkers.

cult to predict, there is general agreement that, to function successfully in the twenty-first century, people will have to demonstrate the following core abilities, (Bredekamp & Copple, 1997; Resnick, 1996; Smith et al., 1995):

Possess a solid education and be able to apply what they know and can do in relevant situations: Demonstrate knowledge and skills in the areas of literacy, numeracy, science, social studies, music and the visual arts, physical education, and health.

Work well with others: Communicate well, respect others, engage with colleagues to resolve differences of opinion and function well as members of a team.

Act as problem solvers: Analyze situations, make reasoned judgments, and solve new problems.

Utilize skills broadly and engage in flexible thinking: Apply knowledge and skills across multiple areas, generalize knowledge and skills from one situation to another, regroup and try alternate approaches when standard solutions fail.

Function as information seekers: Access information through various modes, including spoken and written languages, and intelligently employ complex new tools and technologies.

Envision themselves as lifelong learners: Continue to learn new approaches, skills, and knowledge as conditions and needs change.

As early childhood educators, we are becoming increasingly aware that, in addition to *what* children learn, we must consider *how* children learn in order to best promote the development of these core abilities (Smith et al., 1995). In trying to describe how to achieve programs that enhance this kind of learning, educators have created the concept of developmentally appropriate practice. The remainder of this book is devoted to exploring that concept as a means for achieving high quality.

Chapter 1 describes a definition of developmentally appropriate programs and the rationale that drives decision making in such programs. Chapter 2 examines principles of development and learning and the implications those principles have for developmentally appropriate practices. Setting the stage for learning in developmentally appropriate ways is the focus of Chapters 3 through 7. Chapter 3 discusses how to plan small-group activities for children and the typical teaching strategies you will use daily. Planning whole-group activities is the subject of Chapter 4, including circle times, field trips, and visits to the classroom by outside resource persons. In Chapter 5 you will learn how to organize indoor and outdoor space, classroom materials, and groups of children to promote optimal learning. Appropriate child guidance is fundamental to all other forms of instruction and provides the foundation for a developmentally appropriate classroom. This critical topic is addressed in Chapter 6. Chapter 7 focuses on integrating home/ school perspectives through family involvement. The curriculum itself is highlighted in Chapters 8 through 13. Each chapter centers on one developmental domain: aesthetic, affective, cognitive, language, physical, or social. They all provide an overview of content and developmental processes related to the domain, relevant issues, sample goals for children, developmentally appropriate teaching strategies, and activities you might use to reach the goals of the domain. Although the curricular domains are presented separately, in practice they are integrated throughout the

day and across the entire early childhood program. Integrating the curriculum, therefore, is the focus of Chapters 14 through 16. Chapter 14 describes how you might use pretend play and construction activities to help children synthesize what they learn in a holistic way. Themes and projects are an additional strategy you might use and are described in Chapter 15. Chapter 16 focuses on the integrative nature of assessment and program evaluation.

We designed this book to help you develop the knowledge base you will need to function as a professional in the field. While you are reading, we encourage you to reflect on the content in terms of your own experiences with children and early childhood programs. We hope you will select some topics to explore further and that you will ask questions and challenge things you have doubts about. Most important, we urge you to use the material provided here to develop your own ideas about how to create and implement high-quality programs for children. You are the emerging generation of early childhood educators. We are looking to you to add to our store of knowledge about best practices in early childhood education.

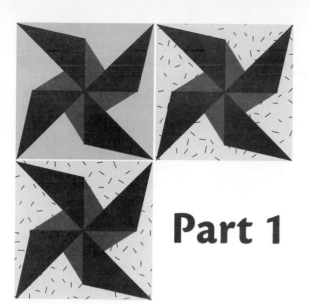

Part 1

Foundations of Early Childhood Education

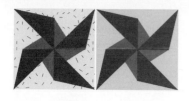

Chapter 1

Developmentally Appropriate Practice: An Evolving Framework for Teaching Young Children

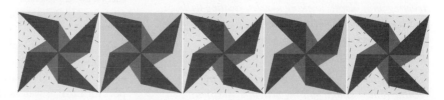

You may wonder:

Exactly what do people mean when they refer to developmentally appropriate practice?

How well do developmentally appropriate practices work?

Is Developmentally appropriate practice an approach everyone should use?

What do developmentally appropriate practices look like in action?

How do your own experiences with young children support or challenge the idea of developmentally appropriate practice?

In this chapter on developmentally appropriate practice in early childhood education, we present information to help you answer these questions.

A visitor asked, "How will I know good teaching practices when I see them?"

The principal replied, "Basically look for action in the learning environment."

Good practice is children in action: children busy constructing with blocks, working puzzles, creating with multimedia, enjoying books, exploring, experimenting, inventing, finding out, cooking, and composing throughout the day.

Good practice is teachers in action: teachers busy holding conversations, guiding activities, questioning children, challenging children's thinking, observing,

drawing conclusions, and planning and monitoring activities throughout the day (Paciorek & Munro, 1995).

This action-based approach to teaching and learning is described as developmentally appropriate practice.

Developmentally appropriate practice (DAP) has had a powerful influence on people's ideas about early childhood education. In less than a decade, DAP has moved to center stage in the discussion of what constitutes a good program for young children. This chapter explores DAP and what it means for you as an early childhood educator. The chapter is divided into four parts: The first part looks at the origins of DAP, defines the philosophy, and outlines the general practices associated with it. This part also describes empirical support for DAP as well as critics' opinions of its universal application. In the second part, you will read about three model programs, the High/Scope approach, the Reggio Emilia approach, and the Quality Schools approach, all of which illustrate DAP in their operations. These models are just three examples of how the general practices associated with DAP can be combined to create effective programs for children and families. The third part of the chapter reviews some of the myths and half-truths associated with DAP. More accurate interpretations of the concept provide an answer to each one. The chapter ends with an outline of the implications for professional practice prompted by the material in the three parts. This makes the link between theory and practice the central feature of the fourth part. Taken altogether, the chapter will increase your understanding of an idea that has strongly influenced the field you will be entering. Now, let us look at how and why DAP was created.

THE NEED FOR DEVELOPMENTALLY APPROPRIATE PRACTICE

The Edgewood School Board voted last night to eliminate morning recess for kindergarten and grades 1, 2 and 3. Board member Roger McPherson says "this will give us more time for classroom instruction. That's really necessary if the Edgewood Schools are going to improve their math and reading scores on the state assessment."
—*The Edgewood Schools Weekly Register*

Kindergarten teachers are reminded there will be a meeting after school to review the new math workbook series we will be using next year. Refreshments will be served.
—*Morning announcement, Spring Arbor Elementary*

The children look like they're having fun. But when do you get down to the real learning?—*Prospective parent observing the program for 3- and 4-year-olds at the Spartan Nursery School*

These real-life events illustrate a continuing trend in the United States—the "pushing down" of curriculum from the primary grades into the kindergarten and preschool. Practices that only a decade ago were not encountered until first grade or later—such as whole-class instruction, teacher-directed instruction, formal reading instruction, written instruction out of workbooks, and frequent grading—have become commonplace in kindergarten and some preschools (Stipek,

Feiler, Daniels, & Milburn, 1995). First and second graders, too, are expected to do things previously reserved for the upper grades such as taking standardized achievement tests and dealing with possible retention. Parent demands for more academics and a "back to the basics" philosophy have supported such practices.

These trends came about due to society's increased recognition that the early years are significant and that early intervention can have beneficial outcomes. They also resulted from our desire to remain competitive with other nations and to help our children "get ahead." The unfortunate result of this competitive urge was reinforcement of the belief that "earlier is better" (Elkind, 1987). Consequently, more and more young children find themselves sitting at desks, filling out ditto sheets, and taking tests to get into kindergarten and first grade. Teachers feel pressured to engage in classroom practices they believe are not in the best interests of young children. Child advocates are alarmed at what they view as an erosion of childhood and the "miseducation" of the youngest members of society (Elkind, 1989). Physicians report a dramatic increase in the numbers of young children who visit them for stress-related illnesses and conditions. Nationwide, people who understand child development warn that children are being hurried into functioning in ways that do not match their natural modes of learning (Elkind, 1981; Gardner, 1991).

A Professional Response

In response to these circumstances, the National Association for the Education of Young Children (NAEYC) developed a position paper in 1986 defining the concept of developmentally appropriate practice (DAP). This paper was quickly followed by an NAEYC–sponsored statement describing examples of appropriate and inappropriate practices for programs serving children ages birth to 8 years (Bredekamp, 1987). "The goal of DAP was to 'open up' the curriculum . . . and move away from the narrow emphasis on isolated academic skills and the drill and practice approach to instruction" that was dominating many programs for young children (Bredekamp & Rosegrant, 1992, 4). Several important education associations such as the National Council for the Social Studies, the National Council of Teachers of Mathematics, the Association for Childhood Education International, and the

Association for Supervision and Curriculum Development endorsed the NAEYC papers. Within a few years, other organizations such as the National Association of State Boards of Education (1988), the National Association of Elementary School Principals (1990), and the National Education Association (Gullo, 1992) published papers and reports corroborating the basic principles associated with DAP. Today

> the DAP guidelines have been widely embraced by many early childhood practitioners who view them as formalization of practices they have long advocated. Increasing numbers of school districts in the United States have instituted policies which recognize DAP guidelines as the source of instructional principles for kindergarten and the primary grades. In addition, child care and preschool settings in a wide range of contexts (e.g., employee-sponsored child care, nonprofit, and Head Start) have begun to revise curricula to meet these expectations. (Klein, Murphy, & Witz, 1996, 144).

This has led thousands of practitioners to use DAP as a basis for examining their own practices and that of the programs for which they are responsible.

WHAT IT MEANS TO BE DEVELOPMENTALLY APPROPRIATE

Practitioners who utilize developmentally appropriate practice make decisions about the well-being and education of young children based on three important kinds of knowledge (Bredekamp & Copple, 1997):

> What they know about how children develop and learn.
>
> What they know about the strengths, needs, and interests of individual children.
>
> What they know about the social and cultural contexts in which children live.

Using this knowledge to guide their thinking, early childhood educators ask themselves, Is this activity, interaction, or experience age appropriate? Is it individually appropriate? Is it socially and culturally appropriate?

Age Appropriateness

Although age is not an absolute measure of a child's capabilities and understandings, it does help establish reasonable expectations of what might be interesting, safe, achievable, and challenging for children to do (Bredekamp & Copple, 1997). To address age appropriateness, we first think about what children are like within a general age-range. Next, we develop activities, routines, and expectations that accommodate and compliment those characteristics. Mrs. Omura, the teacher in the 4-year-old class, is thinking about age appropriateness when she selects wooden puzzles that contain 8 to 15 pieces for the fine-motor area of her classroom. She makes her selections based on her observations of the number of pieces 4-years-olds typically find doable but challenging to complete. Mr. Allison, the second-grade teacher, also makes an age-related choice when he chooses jigsaw puzzles consisting of 40 to 50 pieces for the youngsters in his group. He is aware that children 8 and 9 years old find the more complex puzzles stimulating and fun to try. In both cases, teachers made decisions about age appropriateness based on their understanding of child development gleaned through study and observation.

Individual Appropriateness

All children within a given age group are not exactly alike. Each child is a unique person with an individual pattern and timing of growth, as well as an individual personality and learning style (Bredekamp, 1987). Certain children are more verbal than others; some enjoy solitude; others crave company; some children are skillful readers at 5 years of age; others may achieve proficiency two years later. All of these variations must be considered in the design, application, and evaluation of activities, interactions, and expectations. Both Mrs. Omura and Mr. Allison chose puzzles that ranged in complexity, knowing that some children would need simpler ones to match their current levels of functioning and that others would benefit from more challenging versions. In addition, individual children bring certain levels of previous knowledge and skill to each new experience they encounter. Obviously, children with little or no exposure to a particular situation should not be expected to perform at the same level of competence as children whose backlog of experience is greater. Thus, Josh, a 6-year-old newly arrived in North Dakota from Florida, might take more time than his same-aged peers to put on winter gear because it is entirely new to him. His teacher allows him that time based on the notion of individual appropriateness. To ignore his lack of experience and expect Josh to "keep up" with his classmates in the first few days is inappropriate according to this principle.

Social and Cultural Appropriateness

We have to look at children and families within the context of their community and culture in order to create meaningful, supportive early childhood programs. Consider the following examples:

❑ Kyoko eats rice for breakfast at home. During a nutrition activity at school, some children insist that rice is only a dinner food. The teacher points out that people eat rice sometimes at breakfast, sometimes at lunch, and sometimes at dinner. Later she reads a story called *Everybody Cooks Rice,* which describes people eating rice prepared in various ways and at different meals.

❑ In Nathan's family, children are taught to cast their eyes downward to show respect for their elders. Knowing this, the teacher does not demand that Nathan look her in the eye when she talks to him about why he and another child were arguing.

❑ Mrs. Richards comes from a family in which money matters are strictly private. With this in mind, the director asks her to step into her office, and then closes the door before discussing the parent's unpaid bill. With other families, the director might have discussed the bill quietly at the car, after the parent had dropped off her child for the day.

In each of the preceding situations, early childhood practitioners demonstrated respect for children or their family members by taking into account the social and cultural contexts in which they live.

Understanding social and cultural contexts requires early childhood professionals to recognize differences among children as well as characteristics children have in common with others in a cultural group (Phillips, 1991). Culture is defined by values, traditions, and beliefs that are shared and passed down from one generation to the next. Groups of people develop common bonds based on their ethnic or linguistic heritage, geography, custom, social class, income, lifestyle, or particular life events (Berns, 1996). Thus, people may share certain values, traditions, and beliefs because they have one or more of the following characteristics:

> Are Mexican American.
>
> Can trace their roots to Lebanon.
>
> Live in the hollows of Appalachia.
>
> Speak Mandarin.
>
> Consider themselves middle-class.
>
> See themselves as part of the baby-boomer generation.
>
> Are family members of a child with a disability.
>
> Grew up in a single-parent home.

> Growing up as members of a family and community, children learn the rules of their culture—explicitly through direct teaching and implicitly through the behavior of those around them. Among the rules they learn are how to show respect, how to interact with people they know well as compared to those they just met, how to organize time and personal space, how to dress, what and when to eat, how to respond to major life transitions and celebrations, how to worship, and countless other behaviors that humans perform with little apparent thought everyday. Individual children may be members of more than one cultural group and may be embedded in their cultures to different degrees. (Bredekamp & Copple, 1997, 42)

Because there is so much variation among people, there is no one "correct" set of cultural beliefs. Instead, adults who work with children must recognize the legitimacy of multiple perspectives including ones very different from their own. For example, "it is important to know the family's view of child rearing and their expectations, both personally and culturally. . . . To set up programming that promotes independent functioning and adaptive skills with a family that values dependency is almost sure to fail" (Deiner, 1993, 333). Similarly, home visits may be welcome by some families but perceived as intrusive by others. Based on the community context in which they live, young children in an urban neighborhood might find a class project on public transportation very useful, whereas children in a rural community (where no such transportation is available) might find the same content less relevant. The more strategies and content build on what is familiar to children and families, the more comfortable they feel. The more congruent expectations are between home and the early childhood environment, the more productively children learn.

When we ignore these contexts, the very least that happens is that we lose access to the rich background children bring to the classroom from home. As a result, we fail to take advantage of the full range of children's interests and abilities to help them achieve the learning goals of the program (Bredekamp & Copple, 1997). At worst, such oversights damage children by communicating to them that they are unacceptable or deficient in the eyes of the program (Chipman, 1997; Hale, 1994). In every case, lack of sensitivity and respect for social and cultural contexts leads to negative results for children and programs alike. Thus, understanding what may be interpreted as meaningful to and respectful of children and their families is a key element in determining developmental appropriateness.

The Essence of Developmental Appropriateness

Weaving the strands of age appropriateness, individual appropriateness, and sociocultural appropriateness into a cohesive philosophy requires deliberate effort and continuous reflection by early childhood practitioners. *First*, we must take into account everything we know about how children develop and learn and match that to the content and strategies planned for them in early childhood programs. *Second*, we must think of children as individuals, not as a cohort group. This means recognizing that even children who share many similar characteristics are still singular human beings. *Finally*, we must treat children with respect. This involves appreciating children's changing capabilities and having faith in their capacity to make self-judgments. It also requires us to learn about and value the families, communities, and cultures that shape children's lives. At the same time, we must recognize the unique ways in which children are children, not miniature adults. Experiences and expectations planned for children should reflect the notion that early childhood is a time of life qualitatively different from the later school years and adulthood. These beliefs and intentions form the essence of developmentally appropriate practice. As you read the next section of this chapter, consider how these strands are apparent in the practices described.

GENERAL PRACTICES TYPICALLY ASSOCIATED WITH DAP

Developmentally appropriate practice provides a resource for thinking about, planning, and implementing high-quality programs for young children. It informs our decision making and gives us a basis for continually scrutinizing our professional practices. Within the NAEYC document, examples of appropriate and inappropriate practices are outlined for infants and toddlers, children ages 3 to 5, and children 6 through 8. (Refer to Figure 1.1 for an example.)

As you can see from Figure 1.1, *inappropriate* practice sometimes reflects errors of omission (ignoring parent concerns) as well as errors of commission (communicating with parents only about problems and conflicts). *Appropriate* practices are often defined between these extremes (working in partnership with parents and listening to and talking with parents about children's strengths as well as concerns). Although the NAEYC document contains many examples of appropriate and inappropriate practices, ten fundamental practices

These children are learning by doing.

FIGURE 1.1
Examples of Appropriate Practices and Inappropriate Practices Related to Establishing
Reciprocal Relationships With Families

Reciprocal Relationships with Families		
	Appropriate Practices	**Inappropriate Practices**
Infants and Toddlers	Caregivers work in partnership with parents, communicating daily to build mutual understanding and trust and to ensure the welfare and optimal development of the infant. Caregivers listen carefully to what parents say about their children, seek to understand parents' goals and preferences, and are respectful of family and cultural differences.	Caregivers communicate with parents only about problems or conflicts, ignore parents' concerns, or avoid difficult issues rather than resolving them with parents.
3–5-Year Olds	Parents are always welcome in the program, and home visits by teachers are encouraged. Opportunities for parent participation are arranged to accommodate parents' schedules. Parents have opportunities to be involved in ways that are comfortable for them, such as observing, reading to children, or sharing a skill or hobby.	Teachers view parents' visits to the program as intrusive and discourage parents from visiting. Parent participation is so limited that visits rarely disrupt the classroom. Parent meetings or other participation opportunities occur only during the day when many employed parents are unavailable.
6–8-Year Olds	Educators and parents share decisions about children's education. Teachers listen to parents and seek to understand their goals for their children. Teachers work with parents to resolve problems or differences of opinion and are respectful of cultural and family differences.	School personnel do not involve parents in decisions about how best to handle children's problems or support their learning. They see parents in a negative light, complaining that they have not raised their children well or blaming children's poor school performance on the home environment. Teachers make only formal contacts with parents through report cards and one yearly conference.

characterize the DAP philosophy overall (Gullo, 1994; Hart, Burts, & Charlesworth, 1997; Miller, 1996).

Developmentally appropriate practice emphasizes the following:

❏ *The "whole child."* Early childhood professionals address child development and learning from a holistic perspective, creating curricula to meet children's emotional, social, cognitive, and physical needs.

❏ *Individualizing the program to suit particular children.* Program planning and implementation are adapted to meet the different needs, levels of functioning, and interests of children in the group.

❏ *The importance of child-initiated activity.* Children are active decision makers in the learning process. Teachers accept a wide range of constructive child responses.

❏ *The significance of play as a vehicle for learning.* Play is valued and facilitated both indoors and outside.

❏ *Flexible, stimulating classroom environments.* Teachers actively promote children's learning, using direct and indirect instruction as appropriate.

❏ *Integrated curriculum.* Program content and curriculum areas (e.g., science, math, literacy, and social studies) are combined in the context of each day's activities.

❏ *Learning by doing.* Children engage in concrete experiences with real materials. The activities in which they participate are relevant and meaningful to them.

❏ *Giving children choices about what and how they learn.* Teachers provide a wide range of activities and materials from which children may choose and within which children pursue educational goals in many different ways.

❏ *Continuous assessment of individual children and the program as a whole.* Practitioners use a variety of assessment strategies, including formal and informal techniques. Standardized assessment is deemphasized in favor of performance-based documentation.

❏ *Partnerships with parents.* Parents are valued as partners and decision makers in the education process. Their involvement in their children's education is viewed as desirable and essential.

Practices that negate those just described are often characterized as "developmentally inappropriate." These include the following:

❏ Focusing on limited aspects of child development and learning (e.g., cognitive or social) to the exclusion of all others.

❏ Expecting all children to learn the same things at the same time in the same way.

❏ Creating programs dominated by teacher-centered activities in which the children's role is passive and only one response is judged acceptable.

❏ Treating play as superfluous or unacceptable.

❏ Creating rigid, uninteresting classroom environments.

❏ Fragmenting and compartmentalizing curricula into isolated lessons that have no relation to one another.

❏ Expecting children to learn mostly through listening and engaging in abstract activities that have little meaning or relevance to them.

❏ Denying children opportunities to make choices or to function as active decision makers in the learning process.

❏ Assessing children's learning sporadically and in ways that are unrelated to their actual experiences in the classroom.

❏ Treating parents as adversaries or as inconsequential.

THE ROLE OF JUDGMENT IN DETERMINING DEVELOPMENTAL APPROPRIATENESS

Referring to the practices just outlined, can you determine which of the following situations are developmentally appropriate and which are not?

Twenty 4-year-olds have been in circle time for 40 minutes—DAP or not DAP?

Suzanne wants the easel all to herself. Bianca wants a turn. The provider helps the girls develop a timetable for sharing over the next several minutes—DAP or not DAP?

Jamie, a kindergartner, laboriously copies a series of words onto lined paper—DAP or not DAP?

At first glance, you might have said that a 40-minute circle time is too long for most 4-year-olds and that copywork is not the best way to teach children to write. If so, you probably decided these were examples of developmentally inappropriate practices. You may also have assumed that helping two children learn to share clearly illustrates DAP. Closer scrutiny, however, may prompt you to reassess your original judgments. For instance, you might revise your opinion about the circle time after learning that the children are enthralled by a storyteller who actively involves them in the storytelling process and that the group has been prolonged in response to children's requests to "tell us another one." Likewise, helping children to share is usually a worthwhile aim. But, in this case, Suzanne's aunt, uncle, and cousins recently lost most of their belongings in a household fire. They are staying with Suzanne's family, and Suzanne is having to share many things for the first time—attention at home, her room, and most of her things. Knowing this, we might determine that making her share the easel on this occasion is unnecessarily stressful. Helping Bianca find an alternate activity that will satisfy her desire to paint could be a better course of action for now. A second look at Jamie reveals that he is working hard to copy the words "I love you" for a present he is making for his mom.

He is using a model created by another child and is writing on paper he selected himself. Within this context, it no longer seems questionable for Jamie to be engaged in copywork (Kostelnik, 1993).

Scenarios such as these illustrate that determining what does or does not constitute developmentally appropriate practice requires more than simply memorizing a set of do's and don'ts or looking at children's activities in isolation. It involves considering every practice within the context in which it is occurring and making a judgment about what is happening to a particular child in a particular place at a particular time (Kostelnik, 1998). The best judgments are those you make consciously.

Faced with having to determine the extent to which their actions are developmentally appropriate, early childhood educators find it useful to ask the following questions:

1. Is this practice in keeping with what I know about child development and learning?
2. Does this practice take into account children's individual strengths and needs?
3. Does this practice demonstrate respect for children's social and cultural lives?

These queries can address immediate concerns or serve as the basis for long-term deliberations. They can stimulate individual thinking or consideration of program practices by an entire staff. In every circumstance, the answer to all three questions should be yes. If any answer is no, it is a strong sign that the practice should be reconsidered, revamped, or discarded. If there is uncertainty about a question in relation to a certain practice, that practice is worth examining further. Your response will depend on your interpretation of what is age appropriate, individually appropriate, and socioculturally appropriate in terms of specific children. Your knowledge of child development and learning, your understanding of curriculum development and implementation, your awareness of family and community relationships, your knowledge of assessment and evaluation, and your interpretation of your professional role will also influence what you do (NAEYC, 1996b). All of these things in combination with an understanding of developmentally appropriate practice guide early childhood decision making.

DEVELOPMENTALLY APPROPRIATE PRACTICE HAS HISTORIC ROOTS

The practices associated with developmental appropriateness did not emerge all at once, nor were they the product of any one person's thinking. Although strongly influenced by the theories of Jean Piaget, Lev Vygotsky, and Eric Erickson, certain ideas such as whole-child teaching and hands-on learning evolved over hundreds of years. Table 1.1 gives a brief description of 12 early philosophers and advocates for children whose contributions laid a foundation for general practices that characterize DAP classrooms. This is not a complete list, but it gives an overview of some significant people who have shaped practices in early childhood education today.

Now that we have considered the basic components of developmentally appropriate practice, it is time to explore the effectiveness of this approach. For any framework to stand the test of time, it must be supported by demonstrable results.

Children in developmentally appropriate classrooms are excited about school and eager to learn.

TABLE 1.1

People Whose Work Contributed to Current Practices

Person	Contribution
John Amos Comenius (1592–1670) Moravian philosopher "All material of learning must be divided according to age levels."	Wrote that multisensory learning was more relevant than verbal learning alone. Maintained that learning progresses from general to specific and from easier to more difficult. Urged parents to become involved in their children's education.
John Locke (1632–1704) English philosopher "None of the things children are to learn should be made a burden to them."	Discussed individual differences among children. Believed that education should begin early and be enjoyable to children. Suggested that teaching was best accomplished through modeling, praise, providing opportunities for children to practice what they learned, and adapting to each child's current capacity.
Jean Jacques Rousseau (1712–1778) French philosopher "A child should neither be treated as an irrational animal, nor as a man, but simply as a child."	Recognized individual patterns of development within children. Promoted the idea that children's natural curiosity was a strong source of learning. Believed that the school should fit the child, not that the child must fit the school.
Johann Heinrich Pestalozzi (1746–1827) Swiss philosopher and teacher "Success depends upon how well what is taught to children commends itself to them as true, through being closely connected with their own personal observation and experience."	Emphasized child-initiated activities and sensory learning. Advocated specialized teacher training that was focused on children, not just subject matter.
Robert Owen (1771–1858) Scottish industrialist and social reformer "Physical punishment in a rationally conducted infant school will never be required and should be avoided as much as giving children poison in their food."	Created an employer-sponsored infant school that was a forerunner of the North American preschool. Favored multiage groupings among children 2, 3, 4, and 5 years of age. Focused on hands-on learning and field trips to observe how real things existed in the world. Emphasized the importance of positive discipline. Advocated relevant assessment based on children's individual progress.

TABLE 1.1
(continued)

Person	Contribution
Friedrich Wilhelm Froebel (1782–1852) German philosopher "The prime purpose throughout is not to impart knowledge to the child but to lead the child to observe and think."	Father of the kindergarten. Stressed the significance of play and the value of childhood as a time of importance for its own sake, not simply as preparation for adulthood. Created the first curriculum—including a planned program for children to follow, routines (songs, finger plays, and circle time), and specialized objects for learning (called *gifts*—objects for children to handle). Encouraged women to receive special training to become teachers.
Margaret McMillan (1860–1931) British reformer and teacher "Every slum child is a power-house of energy, once given a chance to grow."	First used the term "nursery school." Focused on whole-child learning through play, sensory experience, and open-air classrooms. Featured daily health checks and teaching children self-care as ways to combat health problems brought on by poverty. Emphasized working with parents, and suggested doing home visits.
Maria Montessori (1870–1952) Italian physician and educator "I differed from my colleagues in that I instinctively felt that mental deficiency was more an educational than medical problem."	Promoted an attitude of respect for children. Demonstrated the value of sequential learning using materials specially designed to be self-correcting. Wrote about children's spontaneous interest in learning, their rights to develop at their own rate, their need for independence, and children making choices about what to learn. Noted for the creation of child-sized furnishings. Recognized the potential learning abilities of children with handicapping conditions.
John Dewey (1859–1952) American educator "Education therefore is a process of living and not a preparation for future living."	Advocated children learning by doing through hands-on activities, projects, units of study, and a child-centered, integrated curriculum. Highlighted the value of play. Promoted respect for children's individuality. Founded the first "laboratory" school for the study of child development and teaching methods through systematic research and practice.

(continued on the next page)

TABLE 1.1
(continued)

Person	Contribution
Harriet M. Johnson (1867–1934) "The play activity of children is a dynamic process, stimulating growth and the integration of the entire organism as no system of training however skillfully devised could do."	Identified a master list of hands-on learning materials to foster a whole-child approach to teaching. Emphasized the importance of play and the integrative nature of learning. Promoted development of child-initiated activities, flexible classroom environments, and children learning by doing.
Patty Hill Smith (1868–1946) American educator "Observe the children and follow their lead."	Emphasized the importance of the kindergarten experience in children's lives. Promoted hands-on learning, experimentation, and self-discovery. Wrote the song "Happy Birthday." Wrote a kindergarten manual that attempted to systematically define best practices for young children. Founded the National Committee on Nursery Schools (1926), which eventually became the National Association for the Education of Young Children (NAEYC).
Lucy Sprague Mitchell (1878–1967) "With adults as well as with children, interests and attitudes are not built up through words but through direct experiences."	Promoted whole-child teaching and hands-on learning. Pioneered the idea of demonstration teaching as a means of teacher training.

EMPIRICAL SUPPORT FOR DEVELOPMENTALLY APPROPRIATE PROGRAMS

Facts, Watson. We must have facts.
—The Adventures of Sherlock Holmes (1939)

What began as a "feeling" for many people is becoming a documented reality. The evidence is mounting that flexible curriculum models, which incorporate principles of developmentally appropriate practice into their programs, lead to positive educational outcomes. In contrast to programs that ignore such principles, they are more likely to produce long-term gains in children's intellectual development, social and emotional skills, and life-coping capabilities (Dunn & Kontos, 1997; Hart, Burts, & Charlesworth, 1997). Children's curiosity and creativity are also enhanced

(Hirsch-Pasek, Hyson, & Rescoria, 1990; Walberg, 1984). Although there is much yet to learn, here are the facts about developmentally appropriate practice as we currently know them.

Cognitive Outcomes

Creativity and divergent thinking are both enhanced when children participate in developmentally appropriate preschool or primary classrooms (Hirsch-Pasek et al., 1990; Hyson et al., 1990). Equally important, children recognize their cognitive competence, accurately perceiving themselves as having the "know-how" to solve intellectual problems (Mantzicopoulos, Neuharth-Prichett, & Morelock, 1994). Worry that children in DAP classrooms may not be learning their numbers and letters is unfounded. On the contrary, children come away from high-quality, developmentally appropriate classrooms demonstrating these important skills (Marcon, 1992; Sherman & Mueller, 1996). Children in classrooms described as less developmentally appropriate learn basic academic skills, too. However, such learning may be accompanied by stress levels twice as high as children experience in DAP-based programs (Burts, Hart, Charlesworth, & Kirk, 1990, 1992; Love, Ryer, & Faddis, 1992).

Children participating in developmentally appropriate reading programs (ones that are process oriented and individualized) demonstrate better comprehension of something read to them and better understanding of what they have read themselves than do youngsters who participate in classrooms in which DAP is not evident (Palincsar & Brown, 1989). Children whose teachers embrace developmentally appropriate practice also demonstrate better listening skills and are more verbally adept (Dunn, Beach, & Kontos, 1994; Marcon, 1992). Reading achievement tests have yielded mixed results about what strategies are most generally effective. Some studies indicate that didactic teaching leads to higher scores in letter recognition at the preschool and kindergarten levels (Stipek et al., 1995). Other research shows that children who were in DAP classrooms for at least three years outscored other children in reading achievement by the second grade (Sherman & Mueller, 1996). Such results may indicate that didactic methods have short-term effects but do not sustain these benefits over time. They may also demonstrate that certain teaching methods are better suited for certain skills and that a mix of strategies will ultimately be necessary to get the best results. Obviously, more research is needed before any final conclusions can be made. However, DAP-oriented strategies now appear to have many long-lasting benefits for children who are learning to read.

When compared with children taught mathematics via traditional methods, children in developmentally appropriate classrooms have been found to be more involved in the process of understanding mathematics. They display a better grasp of concepts and are more adept at generalizing computation skills across a variety of situations (Nicholls et al., 1991). Interestingly, children in DAP-focused classrooms have been found to know significantly more number facts than children who endure drill and ditto-style practice, even when the latter's teachers spend twice as much time on the material (Peterson et al., in press). In other re-

search, second graders who had been in DAP programs since kindergarten scored significantly higher on mathematics achievement tests than did youngsters who were not (Sherman & Mueller, 1996).

Social Outcomes

Children enrolled in developmentally appropriate classrooms exhibit fewer negative social behaviors, better social problem-solving skills, and more cooperation than their counterparts in more traditional classrooms (Fry & Addington, 1984; Mantzicopoulis et al., 1994; Marcon, 1992). Data also show that children whose teachers act in developmentally appropriate ways exhibit significantly fewer stress-related behaviors than children whose teachers rely on strategies described as developmentally inappropriate (Burts, et al., 1990, 1992; Love et al., 1992). Although children in the former group are not completely stress free, both the number of incidents and the total amount of stress they display are far less than that exhibited by children whose time in school is dominated by whole-group instruction, paper-pencil tasks, and oral drills. Children's self-esteem is influenced for the better when teachers treat them in ways congruent with developmentally appropriate practice (Curry & Johnson, 1990; Fry & Addington, 1984). Student attitudes toward school and teachers are apt to be more favorable as well (Hyson, Hirsch-Pasek, & Rescorila, 1990; Walberg, 1984).

Long-Term Effects

"Post-kindergarten follow-up studies into the early and middle elementary school years . . . suggest that less developmentally appropriate preschool and kindergarten classroom experiences are linked to: poorer academic achievement; lower work habit grades; more distractibility; and less prosocial/conforming behavior during the early grade school years. In contrast, attendance in DAP programs appears to be linked to overall positive benefits in terms of later achievement and behavioral outcomes in elementary school for children from varying backgrounds" (Hart, Burts, & Charlesworth, 1997, 7).

As a case in point, consider a five-year study of traditional versus developmentally appropriate classrooms conducted in the Scarborough, Maine, public school district. Evaluators report that the children involved in developmentally appropriate classrooms outshine their peers in more traditional classes in many ways (Belle-mere, 1991). Teacher observations reveal that children in the former group are highly cooperative, confident, and self-motivated learners. They display excellent problem-solving and decision-making skills and are flexible in adapting learning strategies across settings and situations. Anecdotal records and portfolio materials support the conclusion that these youngsters are highly interested in reading, fluent in expressive writing, and knowledgeable of the resources available to them for gathering information and finding answers (including, but going beyond, asking the teacher). Parents report that children in the developmentally appropriate classes are more apt to be excited about reading and writing and better able to make connections between what they are learning in school and the real-life problems they encounter at home and in the community. Standardized tests given at the end of second grade elicited scores that correspond to the favorable outcomes just outlined. Children in both the traditional and developmentally appropriate classrooms scored equally well in general reading skills. However, although traditional classes yielded students who scored higher on tests of spelling and reading mechanics in isolation, youngsters in the developmentally appropriate groups scored significantly higher in vocabulary, reading comprehension, expressive language, and reading and writing mechanics in context. Likewise, the two groups showed similar scores in overall mathematic skill. But children participating under developmentally appropriate conditions scored significantly higher in conceptual understanding and problem-solving skills than pupils not assigned to those classrooms. A statewide assessment of fourth graders (in their fifth year of developmentally appropriate practice) indicated that the positive second-grade trends continued. In addition, children in developmentally appropriate classes scored significantly higher in reasoning and problem-solving skills than did children experiencing more traditional teaching practices. Perhaps the most telling data of all involved children's self-assessments of their progress and themselves as students. Children in developmentally appropriate classrooms reported great enthusiasm for school and high involvement in the learning process. That kind of excitement is in contrast to a second grader in another district who was overheard to tell a kindergartner angrily, "Stay in kindergarten!

Don't go to first grade. First and second grade is awful. All we do is work, work, work. We never get outta our seats. It's awful!" (McKee, 1986, 24).

Beyond the elementary years, researchers report that developmentally appropriate preschool programs produce children who continue into their teens to have high achievement in language, reading, and arithmetic (Schweinhart & Weikart, 1980). Such effects result not only in children's improved scholastic performance but also in lower delinquency rates and lower unemployment rates for those individuals in later adolescence and adulthood (Schweinhart, Barnes, & Weikart, 1993; Schweinhart, Weikart, & Larner, 1986).

Issues of Diversity

An important question is how well developmentally appropriate practice contributes to the positive development, learning, and academic success of diverse children. Many people speculate that DAP is well suited for some youngsters but not appropriate for others. In response to these concerns, current evidence indicates that developmentally appropriate practice has the potential to "provide strong foundational experiences for males and females from different racial and socioeconomic backgrounds" (Hart, Burts, & Charlesworth, 1997, 8). For instance, the positive program results associated with DAP described earlier are evident for boys and girls, for children from higher-income and lower-income families, as well as for European American and African American youngsters. No significant differences in achievement among the children in DAP programs were identified regarding gender, socioeconomic status, or race. This seems to support the idea that children benefit from developmentally appropriate practice even when their backgrounds are not all the same. On the other hand, real inequities apparently do exist for children in classrooms categorized as developmentally inappropriate. In such programs, females, children of higher socioeconomic status, and Caucasian children all perform better and report less stressful experiences than males, children of lower socioeconomic status, and African American children (Burts et al., 1992; Charlesworth et al., 1993; Dunn & Kontos, 1997).

Initial results indicate that DAP is a promising approach for working with diverse populations of children. However, additional studies specifically structured to answer questions of diversity are necessary before we can comfortably say it is a fact that DAP meets the needs of all the children and families early childhood educators serve.

Criticisms of DAP

It would be a misrepresentation of the facts to imply that DAP has met with universal approval and acceptance within the field. Over the past decade, thoughtful criticisms have suggested that DAP fails to meet the needs of diverse children and families in defining what constitutes "appropriate practice." Many of these criticisms question the theories that underpin DAP as well as gaps in the knowledge base upon which DAP is founded. The most common concerns are summarized here:

❑ Early childhood professionals have been cautioned that DAP's focus on child-centered teaching supports middle-class values, while negating the more didactic programs frequently preferred by lower-income families (Powell, 1994).

❑ Many critics believe the DAP philosophy is too narrow to support the optimal development and learning of ethnic, racial, and linguistic minority children and families (Delpit, 1995; Lubeck, 1994).

❑ Special educators warn that although there are many points of congruence between DAP and special education practices, DAP alone is not sufficient to address the wide-ranging problems faced by children with disabilities (Carta et al., 1993; Wolery, Strain, & Bailey, 1992).

❑ Concern has been expressed that DAP's emphasis on child development as a foundation for practice is flawed. This criticism hinges on two points. First, critics point out that much of the current knowledge base related to child development relies on data dominated by European American biases. Evidence from cross-cultural investigations of child development conducted over the past two decades challenges current beliefs regarding normative child development and processes as well as optimal child development settings (New, 1994). Second, early childhood professionals are reminded that child development theory and research is part but not all that is necessary to design comprehensive education programs (Katz, 1996; Spodek & Brown, 1993). Factors such as learning theory, research on teaching, subject-matter content, and cultural, political, and economic factors are also essential to consider.

❑ Theoretically, DAP has been criticized as emphasizing the role of maturation in children's learning more than it has emphasized the social environment (Cross, 1995; Fleer, 1995). Critics protest that teachers assume they have no direct input into children's learning. Educators and researchers who express this concern believe that children do not experience enough intellectual challenge in DAP-oriented programs.

❑ As DAP has become more widely implemented, educators say that it is often used in too prescriptive a fashion. When this happens, DAP becomes a rigid set of criteria rather than a tool for guiding teachers' judgments and decision making (Kessler, 1991; Kostelnik, 1993).

❑ Scholars outside the United States have voiced concern about transplanting the child-centered focus of DAP to other cultures such as South Korea, Australia, or China (Fleer, 1995; Jackson, 1997).

Criticisms such as these have fostered vigorous debate and much reflection regarding early childhood education. The exchange of views that has resulted has vitalized the field and broadened the conversation. It has also led to new research and deeper understandings, which in turn have stimulated greater refinements in DAP and the theories and practices that support it. In response to input from many sources, NAEYC recently published *Developmentally Appropriate Practice in Early Childhood Programs* (Bredekamp & Copple, 1997). The revised document maintains the fundamental principles of the original version but includes new emphases that address many of the concerns just listed. These new focus points are as follows:

❑ Whereas the original document spoke primarily to age appropriateness and individual appropriateness, the revised edition of DAP more clearly stresses the role of culture in children's development and learning. The idea of social and cultural appropriateness is equal in importance to the first two criteria in defining Developmentally Appropriate Practices.

❑ The significance of families in early childhood education is discussed in greater detail.

❑ Emphasis on the social environment and its relation to childhood learning has increased. Also, the importance of teachers as active participants in children's development and learning is more fully described.

❑ The need for multiple sources of information (beyond child development theory) to inform practice is underscored in the revised edition of DAP.

❑ Examples of appropriate and inappropriate practices are presented along a continuum, not as polar opposites. The hope is that the document will less likely be used "cookbook" fashion. Instead, the new edition of DAP emphasizes decision making based on principles that take into account the varying needs of children, families, and communities.

It is still too early to tell how well the revised edition of developmentally appropriate practices will satisfy concerns elicited by the original concept. Theoretical arguments aside, the "proof of the pudding" will be in whether the diverse population of children and families is better served. It is also not possible to clearly identify what new issues may arise as people use the revised DAP guidelines in their daily work with children and families. What we know for sure is that the concept of developmentally appropriate practice will continue to evolve over time. People will still debate and discuss professional practice. These discussions will play a significant part in the forward progress of the field.

WHAT DOES THE DAP DEBATE MEAN FOR EARLY CHILDHOOD PRACTITIONERS?

The debate over DAP is not simply a philosophical argument being carried out by a few academicians in the field. Every day, people at all levels of the profession are engaged in discussions about DAP—what it is, how to enact it effectively, and how to revise it to better support their work with children and families. This ongoing discussion is important for three reasons.

First, it tells us that we are part of a "thinking" profession. As early childhood educators, we face many challenges. Some are economic (how to obtain better wages); some are political (how to move children up on the political agenda); and others are physical (how to get through the day without being totally exhausted). However, our work poses intellectual demands as well, requiring clear, creative thinking. Thus, we must continually asks ourselves, Is our current understanding of DAP comprehensive and inclusive? Does it provide a useful framework? How can DAP be adapted to accommodate the differences among us while maintaining the integrity of its guiding principles? These critical issues remain open to question and will require our very best efforts to answer.

Second, the DAP debate reminds us that the knowledge base undergirding the field is continually changing. We can never sit back and assume that what we know now is all we will ever need to know. Instead, we must approach our profession as lifelong learners— examining, revising, and expanding our thinking over time.

Finally, the debate has made clear that a one-size-fits-all approach to teaching is neither functional nor desirable. There is no one set of strategies that is automatically best for every situation. A strategy appropriate for one child may be less appropriate for another child in another circumstance. Instead, we must adapt our methods to fit the strengths and needs of the children and families we serve. Keeping these ideas in mind, let us examine how programs that exemplify developmentally appropriate practice are similar and how they sometimes differ from one another.

DAP PROGRAMS VARY IN STRUCTURE AND CONTENT

LaJoya Gatewood and her husband are looking for an early childhood program in which to enroll their 3-year-old son and 7-year-old daughter. During their search, they visit three facilities, all of which describe themselves as using developmentally appropriate practice.

The literature for the Burcham Hills Child Development Center states, "We offer a developmentally appropriate array of activities for children designed to foster the development and well-being of the whole child. With the support of caring teachers, children play and experiment, making their own discoveries about the physical and social worlds in which they live. Children learn indoors and outside, in the classroom, at home, and in the neighborhood. Fieldtrips are an integral part of the program as are visits to the classroom by parents and other family members. Parents receive suggested home activities related to what is happening in the classroom on a weekly basis. Every September the staff conduct home visits. During these times, teachers and parents talk about and then develop relevant goals for each child. The staff keep careful records of children's progress and share these with parents throughout the year."

During a visit to the Christian Children's Center they are told, "The philosophy that guides the program at CCC is based on Christian values and developmentally appropriate practice. One of the obvious distinctions of our center is the Christian atmosphere we strive to maintain. Strong efforts are made to incorporate the loving presence of Jesus Christ throughout our program. This includes saying a short prayer before meals, having Bible stories in our book corner and at story times, and teaching children simple Bible verses. We also stress, as Jesus did, the importance of loving and caring for one another. In addition, we appreciate that children develop at varying rates and create programs that allow children to progress at a comfortable pace in learning the skills and concepts necessary for later success in school."

The brochure for the Rosa Parks Community School says, "At the Rosa Parks Community School, children experience a dynamic infusion of African American culture into the early childhood curriculum. Framed within the context of developmentally appropriate practice, children come away with a love of learning and positive self-esteem gained through meaningful activity. Hands-on learning is central to the program. Children learn about Africa and their rich cultural heritage; they learn about African American and African heroes and heroines, music, arts and crafts, and folktales. Teachers come from

Africa as well as the United States, and all have first-hand knowledge of African culture."

All of these programs have features the Gatewoods like, but each is distinct from the others. The family wonders, "How can programs that differ so greatly in focus all be described as developmentally appropriate?" The answer to their question lies in the fact that developmentally appropriate practice *is* a philosophy, a framework, and an approach to working with children. It *is not* a single curriculum (Bredekamp & Rosegrant, 1992). Consequently, early childhood programs that incorporate developmentally appropriate practices into their overall design vary in structure and content. At the same time, they share a common commitment to the principles that are a hallmark of the philosophy.

We asked early childhood educators highly involved in the design of three program models to summarize the key elements of their work. The three models they describe are the High/Scope approach, the Reggio Emilia approach, and the Quality School approach. As you read these descriptions, consider how each program demonstrates principles of developmentally appropriate practice in its operations.

The High/Scope Approach to Early Childhood Education

Mary Hohmann

High/Scope Educational Research Foundation

Origins

The High/Scope educational approach currently used in settings serving the full-range of preschool-aged and early elementary-aged children, was originally developed to serve "at-risk" children in Ypsilanti, Michigan. In 1962, David P. Weikart, now president of the High/Scope Educational Research Foundation, initiated the Perry Preschool Project to see if early education could counteract the persistent school failure of high school students from Ypsilanti's poorest neighborhoods. During this project, teachers worked with three- and four-year-old children in a classroom setting for three hours a day, conducted daily staff meetings, and made weekly home visits. The basic framework of the High/Scope approach emerged with a plan-do-review process and small-group activities as its core. A longitudinal study of the students in the Perry Preschool Project found that at age 27 the preschool students, compared to a group of children from the same neighborhood with no preschool experience, were less likely to have been arrested or receive social services, and more likely to be high school graduates, to earn at least $2,000/month and to own a home.

Central Principles

Five basic principles—active learning, supportive adult-child interactions, a materials-rich learning environment, a consistent daily routine, and ongoing child assessment—form the framework of the High/Scope approach. Through *active learning*—having direct and immediate experiences and deriving meaning from them through reflection—young children construct knowledge that helps them make sense of their world. The power of active learning comes from personal initiative. Young children act on their innate desire to explore; they ask and search for answers to questions about people, materials, events and ideas that arouse their curiosity; they solve problems that stand in the way of their goals; and they generate new strategies to try. As they follow their intentions, children engage in key experiences—creative ongoing interactions with people and materials that support children's mental, emotional, social and physical growth. A brief summary of the High/Scope key experiences is available in Figure 1.2.

Active learning depends on *supportive adult-child interactions.* Mindful of the importance of providing a psychologically safe climate for young learners, adults using the High/Scope approach strive to be supportive as they converse and interact with children. Throughout the day, guided by an understanding of how young children think and reason, adults practice supportive interaction strategies—sharing control with children, focusing on children's strengths, forming authentic rela-

FIGURE 1.2
High/Scope Key Experiences

The areas of key experiences for preschool children are as follows:

Creative representation	Classification
Language and literacy	Seriation
Initiative and social relations	Number
Movement	Space
Music	Time

The areas of key experiences for elementary children related to language and literacy, mathematics, and science are as follows:

Language and Literacy
  Speaking and listening
  Reading
  Writing

Mathematics
  Collections of objects   Measurement of continuous quantity
  Number and numerical operations   Movement, time, and speed
  Geometry and space   Language, symbols, and graphing

Science
  Observing   Designing, building, fabricating, and modifying
  Classifying and ordering materials   Structures or materials
  Measuring, testing, and analyzing   Reporting and interpreting data and results
  Observing, predicting, and
    controlling change

tionships with children, supporting children's ideas, and adopting a problem-solving approach to social conflict. For example, when a child talks, an adult listens attentively, makes related comments and observations, asks open-ended questions directly related to what the child is doing, thinking and saying. This interaction style enables the child to confidently express thoughts and feelings, construct an understanding of concepts, and experience partnership in dialogue. Adults rely on encouragement and use a problem-solving approach to deal with everyday classroom situations rather than a child-management system based on praise, punishment and reward.

Because the *physical setting* has a strong impact on the behavior of children and adults, the High/Scope approach places a strong emphasis on planning the layout of the classroom or center, selecting appropriate materials, and making them accessible to children. An active learning environment provides children with ongoing opportunities to make choices and decisions. Thus, adults organize the learning space into specific interest areas well stocked with natural, found, commercial, and homemade materials which provide many opportunities each day for children to engage in the key experience in creative purposeful ways.

In addition to arranging the setting, adults also plan a *consistent daily routine* that supports active learning. The routine enables young children to anticipate what happens next and gives them a great deal of control over what they do during each part of their day. The High/Scope daily routine includes the plan-do-review process, which enables children to express their intentions, carry them out, and reflect on what they have done. Small group times (for younger children) and workshops (for older children) encourage children to explore and experiment with materials and concepts adults have selected based on their daily observations of children's interests, abilities and the key experiences.

In the High/Scope approach, *assessment* includes a range of tasks teachers undertake to ensure that observing children, interacting with children, and planning for children receive full adult energy and attention. Each day, teachers gather accurate information about children by observing and interacting with children and taking anecdotal notes based on what they see and hear. Periodically, they use the child observations they have noted to complete a key-experience based child assessment for each child—the High/Scope Child Observation Record (COR).

Where Readers Can Find Out More

The High/Scope approach is described in *Educating Young Children* by Mary Hohmann and David P. Weikart, *Foundations in Elementary Education: Overview* by Charles Hohmann and Warren Buckleitner, available from the High/Scope Press, 600 North River, Ypsilanti, MI 48198–2898; telephone 800/407–7377. For up-to-date information about High/Scope training, research, publications, and videos, visit the High/Scope Home page at www.highscope.org.

The Reggio Emilia Approach to Early Childhood Education

Patricia Weissman

The Merrill Palmer Institute of Wayne State University

Origins

The origin of the Reggio approach began after World War II in the northern Italian town of Reggio Emilia. A volunteer group of parents and teachers got together to build a preschool for young children in order to affect positive change after suffering the destruction of the war and Mussolini's fascist regime. This new social experiment in education was designed to help the town's youngest citizens develop in ways that counteract the forces that lead to fascism and war. Through the experience of the Reggio Emilia preprimary schools, children learn to engage in dialogues and debates with others in a nonviolent and constructive manner, as well as to develop critical thinking skills. Children are also encouraged to express and discuss ideas in open-democratic meetings and to form close, long-term relationships with others in the school.

Goals

The Reggio Emilia approach embraces several goals that are based on what has been termed by Reggio educators, "the three protagonists of education"—children, teachers and parents. Each of the protagonists is endowed with rights, and it is the goal of the school to support those rights.

Children have the right to be active participants in the construction of their learning and identity, their sense of autonomy and the development of their capabilities. This construction takes place through relationships and interactions with children, adults, ideas and objects. It is equally important that children feel assured of an effective alliance with adults who are ready to give help and understanding which favors more than the simple transmission of knowledge and skills, but rather children's ability to research constructive strategies of thinking and action.

Teachers and others who work in the school have the right to contribute to widening and deepening those conceptual frameworks which define the content, the goals, and the practices of education . . . always with an eye toward harmony with the rights of children and parents.

Parents have the right to participate freely and actively in the elaboration of the founding principles and in their children's experiences of growth, care and learning.

Content/Focus

The focus of the Reggio Emilia approach stems from the set of interrelated educational principles summarized here:

❐ *The image of the child:* Adults see each child as competent, full of potential and active in constructing his or her own knowledge through interactions with others. Adults try to understand as fully as possible the child's viewpoints and abilities, seeing the child as full of strengths rather than full of needs.

❐ *Education based on relationships:* Education is experienced as continuous interaction within the community of the school. As much as possible, children and teachers stay together in the same group for three years, changing classrooms each fall. Deep, long-term relationships are formed among children, teachers and families so that a strong link is formed for the child between home and school.

❐ *The role of the environment:* Through careful use of space, color, natural light, displays of children's work, attention to nature and aesthetic detail, the environment serves as another teacher. It conveys to children, parents and teachers that their presence is valued and respected.

❐ *The importance of time:* Children have time to explore their ideas and hypotheses fully and in-depth. Projects and themes follow the children's ideas and development of concepts. Projects, activities and experiences such as field trips and celebrations are not "one-shot deals," rather they build upon one another over time. Children "revisit" their original work and ideas, refining them further through new experiences, activities and forms of expression.

❐ *The hundred languages/symbolic representation:* Children are seen as having a hundred (or more) "languages" with which to express their feelings, ideas and understandings of the world. Drawing, painting, clay, wire, collage, murals, welding, building, dance, theater and puppetry are just some of the hundred languages supported in the Reggio approach.

❒ *The role of families and community:* In the Reggio approach early childhood education is seen as an integral part of the community at large. Strong linkages are forged between school and community, and school and families. Families are welcome and extremely active participants in the schools, collaborating with teachers regarding both curriculum and administrative decisions.

Methods

The methods used in the Reggio approach are flexible and allow for input and decision making on the part of all participants. These include the following:

❒   Careful Observation of Children

Teachers actively solicit children's ideas and thoughts, listen carefully and base classroom plans and projects on their observations.

❒   Documentation

Documentation techniques are highly developed in the Reggio approach. These include recording and transcribing children's discussions, photography, examples of children's work, videotaping and so on. The documentation is displayed throughout the schools for children, parents, and teachers to reflect on and "revisit" the educational experience.

❒   Collaboration Among Educators

There are usually two teachers in a classroom. In addition, each school has an *atelierista* (artist/studio teacher) and a *pedagogista* (pedagogical specialist or education coordinator). Educators meet frequently to discuss observations of the children, their development and how the school can best support them.

❒   Small-Group Project Work

Collaboration is encouraged among children through the use of small groups working together in common pursuit of an investigation or project. These can last for a couple of days, weeks, or months depending on the interest level of the children.

Role of the Teacher

The teacher is viewed as a "co-researcher" along with the children. The teacher's role is not to *fill up* the children with information but rather to *draw out* children's ideas and support their interests. Reggio teachers "provoke" children by offering challenges, suggesting new ways of looking at the topic, or providing related experiences and materials. Another important role of the teacher is to support and develop relationships with each child and family.

Role of the Child

Children are seen as active participants in their learning. Children make many choices throughout the day, including where to go in the building and what to work on. In addition to on-going projects, children engage in pretend play, singing, group games, storytelling, reading, cooking and outdoor play. During large-group meetings children discuss their ideas about what to study and how. Great importance is also placed on the joys of friendship and interaction with others. Children develop social responsibility, respect for others and care for one another through dialogue and small-group collaborative work.

Assessment

There are no checklists of skills, tests or diagnostic evaluations in a Reggio Emilia program. It is felt that standard assessment tools limit children by focusing on their shortcomings or lack of skills—not their strengths and potential. Instead, children are "assessed" through their long-term relationships with their teachers. Teachers carefully observe the children and document their observations. Notes, photographs, and examples of the children's work are organized in portfolios shared with the child's family at the end of the year. Teachers also meet frequently with parents to discuss developmental issues.

Where Readers Can Find Out More

The Reggio Emilia approach is described in *The Hundred Languages of Children: The Reggio Emilia Approach to Early Childhood Education,* edited by G. C. Edwards and G. Forman, published by the Ablex Publishing Corporation and available from Redleaf Press, 800/423–8309. Reggio Children USA Office for Publications (c/o Council for Early Childhood Professional Recognition, 1341 G. Street, NW, Suite 400, Washington, D.C. 20005–3105, 202/265–9090) maintains a free bibliography of Reggio resources and offers many Reggio publications for sale. The Merrill-Palmer Institute publishes a quarterly newsletter, *Innovations in Early Education: The International Reggio Exchange,* which includes articles conference listings, study tour dates, recommended resources, lists of Reggio networks in the United States, and the Hundred Languages of Children exhibit tour. The address is The Merrill Palmer Institute, Wayne State University, 71-A E. Ferry Avenue, Detroit, MI 48202. Phone 313/872–1790.

The Quality School Approach to Early Childhood Education
from the work of William Glasser, M.D.

Kaye Mentley

Huntington Woods Elementary School

Imagine teaching students who enjoy the challenge of doing their very best. Imagine a school filled with children and adults who are happy to be there, who know that each of them is an important part of the community of people who treat each other with respect, affection and support every day. Imagine working with children who take responsibility for their own learning, and willingly participate in classroom planning and management. This is a Quality School, which we have created at Huntington Woods Elementary.

Goals/Beliefs

Huntington Woods is a School of Choice in the Wyoming Public Schools district. Our goals/beliefs as a Quality School are these:

- ❏ Learning adds quality to each student's life. Through learning children gain value, meaning, empowerment, a sense of belonging, freedom and fun.
- ❏ Students do quality work in school. All students can demonstrate competence in each subject area, and each student does some work that is the highest quality she or he can achieve.
- ❏ The school is a joyful place. We believe quality education is a joyful process.
- ❏ There are no discipline problems. There will be occasional incidents, but no significant, ongoing problems with behavior.

Origins

The Quality School model was originated by Dr. William Glasser, now president of the William Glasser Institute, based on his Choice Theory psychology, Reality Therapy techniques, and his study of the management concepts of W. Edwards Deming. *Choice Theory* explains that human behavior is internally motivated, intended to produce desired experiences. People want a particular experience (such as interaction, self-perception, doing or having something) because it will satisfy one or more of their *basic needs*—survival, belonging, recognition and worth, freedom and fun. Learning is intrinsically need-satisfying, and children continue to value learning experiences when their school environment helps them, rather than frustrating them, in their attempts to meet basic needs. *Reality Therapy* is a practical, adaptable process of communication and problem solving that helps individuals gain effective control over their lives by self-evaluating their behavior. This approach takes place in a climate of supportive involvement, such as the trust relationship students have with teachers who care about them and can be trusted not to punish or criticize. Facilitators help children look at their behavior, evaluate how well the behavior is working to get their wants fulfilled, then try better behavioral choices to met those needs effectively and responsibly. As Dr. Deming maintained, the way to achieve high-quality performance (whether producing a product or learning in school) is to improve the system in which people work, rather than trying to force people to conform to an inadequate system. Therefore Huntington Woods has chosen to design the systems of our school to create the best conditions for student learning.

Methods

We develop strategies and relationships to fulfill the *conditions for quality,* which follow:

❏ A warm, supportive environment free of coercion.
❏ Learning that is perceived by students as meaningful, relevant and useful.
❏ Self-evaluation of their own work by students and adults.

A *warm, coercion-free environment* is one in which students can meet their needs for safety, survival, love and belonging, power, freedom and fun. We group students in full-time, inclusive, multiage learning families, each consisting of about 54 students (grades K, 1, and 2, or 3, 4, and 5) and two teachers. There is also a teacher assistant with each team. These groups stay together for three years, enabling us to develop very close relationships among teachers, students and parents. Class meetings, cooperative learning, and student-to-student tutoring enhance learning and also strengthen interpersonal acceptance and friendships. Each learning family flexibly schedules its recess and lunch periods. Classrooms are open to parents at all times; parents participate in all aspects of the school, and are our strongest supporters.

We have also designed a calendar and schedule that are advantageous for learning and professional development. Our students attend school from August 27 to July 22 each year. Spread out within that extended calendar are six weeks of Intersession, themes enrichment classes that are optional for students to attend. We have altered the traditional weekly schedule by lengthening the students' day Monday through Thursday and shortening it on Friday, when students are dismissed at noon (after-school child care is available). This provides the time necessary for our teacher teams to learn, grow and plan together.

To meet the second condition for quality *useful learning,* instruction must be meaningful for students and relevant to their lives. As advocates of developmentally appropriate instruction, we do not use textbooks, but instead rely on teacher-designed lessons and units. We frequently ask students what they would like to learn; it is then the teacher's job to determine how to teach the state and district curriculum objectives within the topics the children want to study.

In our Reality Therapy-based discipline program, we solve all problems by talking them through. No punishments or rewards are used; rather students learn to evaluate what they want and plan the most effective, responsible way to get it. This method, integrated with strong, need-satisfying relationships within a supportive system, is very successful in eliminating major discipline problems.

Teacher and Child Roles

The role of the teacher is that of lead-manager who facilitates learning. The role of the child is that of active, self-directed learner. Because all students are taught Choice Theory and understand the school's philosophy, they become responsible for their own learning.

Content

Content focuses on the skills of speaking, reading and writing, math calculations and problem solving. We use Owens Literacy Learning strategies, an intensive whole language approach to reading and publishing, which originated in New Zealand. We also employ technology for self-directed learning through our networked computers using the software programs of the Integrated Learning System. Students are assessed over basic skills then given appropriate lessons based on the assessment result.

Assessment

We offer a comprehensive assessment program that includes the Michigan Education Achievement Program test (MEAP), a statewide examination for 4th, 7th, 9th and 11th graders, required of all school districts in Michigan. Other assessment strategies include portfolios for each child, performance assessments, and student self-evaluation. The process of *self-evaluation* is, we believe, one of the most important skills we can offer our students. Students are taught from the earliest grades to look at what they do (in both school work and behavior), judge its quality, and decide how they can improve it. Teachers involve children in developing goals and setting criteria for high quality achievement, and teach them that if they wish to improve their work at any time, any grade can be raised. All students are involved in directing their own parent conferences to report on academic progress.

Adults at Huntington Woods also use self-evaluation extensively rather than being evaluated by supervisors. All staff members support the Quality School Philosophy and have received extensive training in Choice Theory and Reality Therapy.

Where Readers Can Find Out More

Quality Is the Key: Stories from Huntington Woods School, by Kaye W. Mentley and Sally A. Ludwig, Wyoming, MI: KWM Educational Services, 1997, and *Building a Quality School,* videotape by National Professional Resources, Inc. Both are available through the Huntington Woods Family Council at 4334 Byron Center Avenue SW, Wyoming, MI 49509; telephone 616/530–7537. Books by William Glasser, published by Peter H. Wyden and Company, are *Reality Therapy* (1989), *The Quality School: Managing Students without Coercion* (1992), *The Quality School Teacher: Specific Suggestions for Teachers Who Are Trying to Implement the Lead Management Ideas of the Quality Schools in Their Community* (1993), and *Choice Therapy: A New Psychology of Personal Freedom* (1998).

❁ ❁ ❁ ❁ ❁ ❁

The High/Scope approach, the Reggio Emilia approach, and the Quality Schools approach, along with the approach presented in this textbook, offer a wide range of ways DAP might be translated from theory to practice. Examples like these give readers a sense of DAP in action. However, for a complete understanding, you must also know what are not accurate reflections of DAP. That information is covered in the following myths associated with developmentally appropriate practice.

MYTHS ASSOCIATED WITH DEVELOPMENTALLY APPROPRIATE PRACTICE

As DAP has become more widely known, it also has been subject to misinterpretation. This is especially true as people try to translate the DAP philosophy into actual classroom practices. As a result some early childhood educators implement practices they consider to be developmentally appropriate, which in fact are not. Others reject DAP because what they believe to be true about the philosophy is really false. Here are some typical examples.

Dennis Avery read an article about developmentally appropriate practice and asked his principal to allow him to purchase a variety of hands-on learning materials. He decided to give the youngsters in his class a two-hour period for self-directed learning while he prepared lessons for the next day. However, things were not working out as he had hoped. Children wandered aimlessly around the room, arguments over materials and who could play with whom were frequent, and the noise level grew worse each day. After the teacher in the next room complained for the third time about the chaos in Dennis's class, he decided to give up on the idea and go back to his traditional way of teaching.

The third-grade teachers were angry. Over the summer, an early childhood committee, consisting of kindergarten, first- and second-grade teachers, had put together a document entitled "Developmentally Appropriate Practice in Early Childhood." The third-grade teachers already knew about DAP—they knew there would be no phonics instruction, and children would not be required to spell correctly. They complained that their workload would certainly increase because they would have to make up for everything the early elementary teachers neglected to teach in the new "watered down" curriculum.

After observing a preschool classroom in a program espousing developmentally appropriate practice, a parent was overheard to say, "It was all very nice. But I'm not sure the children were learning much. All they did was play all day. I never saw anyone teach them anything."

Carla Jones, a student teacher, was interacting with a small group of children. One of them pointed to his green sweater, describing it as blue. Amanda said, "You think that's blue. That color is green. Let's see what else we can find that is green." Later her cooperating teacher said, "Never correct children. It's developmentally inappropriate. Always let them discover answers for themselves."

These real-life happenings illustrate some of the erroneous ideas people have about developmentally appropriate practice. For instance, Dennis Avery was under the mistaken impression that DAP does not require teachers to do anything more than put out a variety of "manipulatives" for children to use each day. The third-grade teachers erroneously believed that academic subjects are ignored in DAP classrooms. The parent observer misunderstood what she saw and assumed the teachers were not teaching. Carla Jones's cooperating teacher mistakenly presumed that teacher-led interactions are always inappropriate. Such misinterpretations have led to tremendous confusion about what developmentally appropriate practices really are. In the absence of true understanding, myths have sprung up representing popular opinions based on false assumptions or faulty reasoning. Some have evolved from people's attempts to oversimplify a complex idea to the point of inaccuracy. Others have resulted from people's intuitive interpretations of child behavior or superficial understanding of child development and learning-related theories and research (Kostelnik, 1992). Still more myths have been created as people try to make finite and absolute a concept that is in fact open ended and responsive to many variations. Unfortunately, these myths are rampant, causing widespread misapplications, resistance, and anxiety among practitioners and the public. What follows is a selection of the most common misunderstandings we have encountered.

Myth   There is one "right" way to implement DAP in the classroom.

As you have already seen via the High/Scope model, the Reggio Emilia model, and the Quality Schools model, developmentally appropriate practices can be combined in varying ways to create different programs to enhance children's learning and development. This openness to variation is also true for individual practices within the classroom. However, when talking about developmentally appropriate practice with any group of educators, it is not unusual to hear statements like "You always use learning centers," "You never use whole-group instruction," "You always let children determine the content of the lesson," "You never correct children," "You always let children figure out their own spellings for words," and "You never use lined paper." Likewise, teachers and administrators may ask, "Is it ever OK to show children how to hold a pencil?" "Is it wrong to spell words for children when they ask?" "Exactly when should we introduce cursive writing?" These kinds of pronouncements and questions represent efforts to establish a single, correct approach to instruction. They are based on the belief that one method of teaching suits all children and all situations.

Unfortunately, the reality is that teaching is complex; there is no *one* solution that fits every circumstance. Actually, individual teaching episodes can and should be qualified by "It depends" (Newman & Church, 1990). It depends on variables such as the child's current level of comprehension, experiences, and previous knowledge and skills. Contextual elements including time, human resources, the physical environment, material resources, parental expectations, and the values and expectations of the school and community must also be considered. The goals, strategies, and standards early childhood personnel finally choose are all affected by these constraints as well as the requirements of developmentally appropriate practice.

This means practitioners must continually assess their actions in relation to their knowledge about how children develop and learn. To translate that knowledge into actual teaching strategies, they must be willing to explore a variety of practices in the classroom and allow themselves to make mistakes. Moreover, teachers must continually examine their assumptions and learn from the children as they evaluate the effectiveness of their teaching. What meets the needs of several children in a group may not be appropriate for others. What was optimal for last year's class may not be so this year. Your search, then, is not simply for "right" answers but for the best answers to meet the needs of children representing a wide range of abilities, learning styles, interests, and social and cultural back-

grounds. Finally, practitioners also differ from one another and require a flexible approach to teaching that is compatible with their beliefs and comfortable for them as well as for their students. These variations in both children's and teacher's needs necessitate different strategies. As mentioned earlier in this chapter, every educational decision requires judgment, made on the spot or over time, but always with certain children in mind. Perpetuation of the "one way" myth ignores the important role such judgments play in determining what is appropriate and what is not.

Myth **All you need to create developmentally appropriate programs are the right materials.**

Some people mistakenly believe that DAP simply involves trading one set of materials (workbooks, basal readers, and lined paper) for other materials (manipulatives, picture books, and unlined paper). They assume nothing more is necessary. If this myth were true, then the guidelines for developmentally appropriate practice would consist solely of an equipment list supplemented by the names of several early childhood materials catalogs. Although equipment does enrich the educational environment, research shows that the teacher is the essential ingredient in determining the quality of education received by children. In turn, program quality is directly linked to the teacher's knowledge of and ability to apply developmentally appropriate principles in his or her classroom (Bredekamp & Copple, 1997; Snider & Fu, 1990). Thus, the proper equipment must be accompanied by having trained staff who know how to use that equipment to enhance child development and learning.

Myth **Developmentally appropriate classrooms are unstructured and chaotic.**

This myth is perpetuated by people who mistake the active learning of DAP classrooms for chaos and disorganization. They sometimes describe what they see as "unstructured," assuming that structure requires silence and lack of movement. That is a misinterpretation of the term (Kostelnik, 1998). Structure refers to the extent to which teachers develop an instructional plan and then organize the physical setting and social environment to support the achievement of educational goals. (Spodek et al., 1991).

By this definition, developmentally appropriate classrooms are highly structured. Both teachers and children contribute to their organization. Teachers generate educational goals for students based on programmatic expectations tempered by their understanding of individual children's needs, abilities, and interests. All of the day's activities and routines are planned to promote these goals. Keeping their instructional plan in mind, teachers determine the arrangement of the furniture, which specific materials to offer children, the nature and flow of activity, the approximate time to allocate to various instructional segments, and the grouping of children throughout the session. As teachers interact with children, they observe, listen, instruct, guide, support, and encourage them. Consequently, while teachers carefully consider long-range objectives, their moment-to-moment decision making remains fluid in order to capitalize on input from the children (Newman & Church, 1990). Children ask questions, suggest alternatives, express interests, and develop plans that may lead the instruction in new directions. In this way, overall instructional goals are merged with more immediate ones, thereby creating a flexible, stimulating classroom structure.

Developmentally appropriate classrooms are active ones in which both teachers and students learn from one another. Such learning requires a constant interchange of thoughts and ideas. As a result, there are times during the day when many people are talking or moving about the room at one time. To the untrained eye these conditions may appear chaotic, but a closer look should reveal children on task, constructively involved in their own learning.

Myth   In developmentally appropriate classrooms, teachers are not teaching.

This myth stems from the stereotypical idea that teachers are people who stand up in front of a group of students, telling them what they need to know, and that the teacher's most important duties consist of assigning work to children and checking for right and wrong answers. According to this scenario, teachers are always at center stage. People who envision teachers this way may not recognize all the teaching that is going on in developmentally appropriate classrooms. For example, teachers create physical environments and daily schedules that enable children to engage in purposeful activity. Curricular goals are frequently addressed through pervasive classroom routines such as dressing to go outside, preparing for snack, and

cleaning up. Although whole-group instruction does take place, teachers spend much of their classroom time moving throughout the room working with children individually and in small informal groups. During these times, they influence children's learning indirectly through the provision of certain activities in which the focus is on children's self-discovery and exploration. They also teach children directly, using a variety of instructional strategies. Teachers initiate learning activities as well as respond to children's initiatives. They pose questions, offer procedural suggestions, suggest explorations, and provide information. As opportunities arise, teachers present children with challenges that help them move beyond their current understandings and strategies (Bodrova & Leong, 1996). Additionally, teachers constantly reflect on what is happening in the classroom. They make judgments about children's progress and introduce variations or changes in focus as children's needs warrant. All of these activities are essential teaching behaviors.

Myth   DAP requires us to think about all educational practices in "either/or" terms.

This misunderstanding has come about because of people's natural tendencies to polarize concepts in order to make them easier to define and talk about. Also, we sometimes overgeneralize the notion of appropriate and inappropriate practices to include a whole range of

Teachers in developmentally appropriate classrooms are often down on the floor with the children.

variables that are more useful to think about in terms of "more or less" or in combination with one another rather than as polar opposites (Kostelnik, 1998). For instance, some people think that

> Programs for young children must be either *process focused* or *product focused.*
>
> Teaching strategies must be either *child initiated* or *adult initiated.*
>
> The curriculum must be either *socially oriented* or *cognitively oriented.*
>
> Learning must be either *constructed* or *instructed.*

Such dichotomies are some of the ones people typically refer to when talking about DAP. Within each statement, the item listed first tends to be defined as "good," "desirable," and "appropriate"; the ones listed second are sometimes described as "bad," "undesirable," and "inappropriate." Furthermore, because either/or items are treated as mutually exclusive, the implication is that developmentally appropriate programs are 100 percent process focused, with no thought given to products; that children initiate all learning episodes and adults initiate none; that social development is more important than cognition; that discovery is the sole means by which children learn; and that direct instruction has no place in a developmentally appropriate program. None of these assertions are true.

Developmentally appropriate programming is not an all-or-nothing proposition. For example, process learning is very important to children and should be highly valued by teachers. The satisfaction a child gains from painting is more important than the degree to which his or her picture represents the adult's notion of reality. However, anyone who has watched young children proudly show off their work knows that products are important, too. Likewise, many, many activities in the developmentally appropriate classroom come about through child exploration and initiation, whereas others can be introduced by the teacher as a way to spark children's interest in something new. And, although social development cannot be ignored, neither can cognitive pursuits. To elevate one above the other denies the integrative nature of child development. Finally, children learn a great deal through self-discovery, but some things—like how to wash one's hands properly, what a certain plant is

called, and what to do during a fire drill—are best learned through modeling and direct instruction.

Consequently, it is more accurate to envision variables such as these along continuums. Rather than calling to mind issues of all or none, yes or no, good or bad, a continuum suggests that educational planning is really a matter of more or less—degrees and balance. In addition, if we no longer treat such ideas as mutually exclusive, we can find ways to combine them to create the best possible programs for young children. Some examples of what these combinations might look like are cited in *Developmentally Appropriate Practice in Early Childhood Programs* (Bredekamp & Copple, 1997, 23):

> Children (benefit from opportunities to) *construct* their own understanding of concepts and they benefit from *instruction* by more competent peers and adults.
>
> Children benefit from opportunities to *see connections across disciplines* through integration of curriculum and from opportunities to *engage in in-depth study* within a content area.
>
> Children need to develop a positive sense of their own *self-identity* and *respect for other people* whose perspectives and experiences may be different from their own.
>
> Children benefit from opportunities to make *meaningful choices* about what they will do and learn and from having a clear understanding of the *boundaries* within which choices are permissible.

If we believe the preceding statements are true, we will create programs that include both open-ended learning opportunities for children and more structured ones; both integrated study as well as in-depth study. We will design curricula in which the self and others are both addressed. We will provide children with many choices while at the same time creating boundaries to help children feel secure. These combinations of strategies make developmentally appropriate programs both varied and comprehensive. They enable children to engage in the kinds of experiences they need at a given time. Such experiences will fall in different places along the continuum, depending on the child and the circumstances at the time.

Myth   Academics have no place in developmentally appropriate programs.

Academics represent the traditional content of the schools. In most people's minds this means reading, writing, and arithmetic. People who *wish* this myth were true believe young children are not ready for academics. They proudly announce that students in their programs are not expected to read, use numbers, or write. People who *fear* this myth is true express concern that children who participate in developmentally appropriate programs are not learning the essentials. They worry that such children will lack critical skills necessary for achievement. Both claims are based on an overly narrow interpretation of academic learning. They equate academics with technical subskills (e.g., reciting the alphabet or writing out numerical equations) or with rote instruction (e.g., emphasizing worksheets and drills). Each of these definitions is too narrow in scope. They confuse concepts with methods and ignore how reading, writing, and number-related behaviors and understandings emerge in young children's lives.

Children do not wait for elementary school to demonstrate an interest in words and numbers. They manifest literacy-related interests as infants when they mouth a book or pat the bunny and again as toddlers when they beg, "Read it again." Likewise, young children count one cookie, two shoes, and three candles on the birthday cake. They compare: "Which has more?" "Who still needs some?" Children calculate: "Will it fit?" "Now I have two; I need one more." These kinds of activities form the beginnings of literacy and mathematical thinking—the true essence of academics.

Children continue on in this manner as they mature, seeking new knowledge and skills as their capacities to know and do increase. Thus, there is no specific time when such learning is either appropriate or inappropriate. These evaluative labels are better applied to the parameters within which academics are defined and the strategies teachers use to address academic learning. Programs that focus on isolated skill development and rely on long periods of whole-group instruction or abstract paper-pencil activities do not meet the needs of young children. Those that emphasize concepts and processes and utilize small-group instruction, active manipulation of relevant, concrete materials, and interactive learning provide a solid foundation for academics within a context of meaningful activity.

Using children's interests and ways of learning as guides, early childhood teachers do four things to promote academic learning. First, they understand the broad nature of literacy and mathematics and are familiar with the concepts, processes, and content that

compose them. They recognize that reading is more than reciting the alphabet or making letter-sound associations out of context, that writing is not the same as penmanship, that mathematics goes beyond rote memorization of number facts. Second, they recognize manifestations of academic interest and exploratory behavior in the children they teach (e.g., "Teacher, what does this say?" "How many do we need?" "Look what I made!"). At the same time, they recognize the importance of phonics or number facts as part of the learning process and incorporate these elements in their teaching in ways that make sense to children. Third, teachers provide concrete materials and relevant experiences to enhance children's academic learning. They read to children often and invite them to respond to and interpret the story. They sing songs, read poems, and play rhyming games in which sound associations are addressed. They give children materials to sort, sequence, count, combine, or divide and make estimations about. They offer children many ways to express themselves both orally and in writing. Fourth, teachers introduce new information, materials, and problems that stimulate children to make observations and comparisons, question, experiment, derive meaning, make predictions, and draw their own conclusions. In this way academics become an integral part of classroom life.

Myth   To be developmentally appropriate, elementary teachers and administrators have to "water down" the traditional curriculum; children will learn less than they have in the past.

This myth is based on two assumptions: that all learning is hierarchical in nature and that the curriculum offered in many elementary schools today is sufficient in scope. Neither is correct.

Learning can be characterized as occurring in two directions, vertically and horizontally. Vertical learning is hierarchical. It can be likened to climbing a ladder. A person starts at the base and gradually moves upward, pausing now and then or even vacillating between rungs but with little veering off to the sides. This kind of learning piles one fact or skill on top of another. As the learner proceeds higher and higher, the result is an increase in the number and complexity of the facts and skills he or she has attained.

Horizontal learning, on the other hand, is conceptually based. An analogy that illustrates the concept is that of casting a net in all directions and then drawing it back in. Within this framework, experiences occur more or less simultaneously, and the role of the learner becomes that of making connections among them. It implies a deepening understanding of the world through the development of increasingly elaborate concepts.

Both vertical and horizontal learning are essential to human understanding. The former expands one's quantity of knowledge and skills; the latter contributes to their quality. Neither should be emphasized to the detriment of the other. Yet the lockstep nature of the curriculum in many primary schools promotes vertical learning to the exclusion of concept development. Curriculum guides delineate a vertical scope and sequence for every subject. Children are continually pushed upward, even when they show signs of inadequate comprehension. If youngsters need more time to consolidate their understandings (an example of horizontal learning), they are identified as "falling behind" or "at risk" for failure. Conversely, when children complete the scope and sequence for a given subject in a particular grade, they are encouraged to continue their vertical climb into the next grade level rather than spending time on strengthening the linkages among the bits of knowledge they have acquired.

The fundamental flaw in all this is that children in the early years are establishing the conceptual base from which all future learning will proceed. Their need for a solid, broad foundation of horizontal learning is great. The breadth of the conceptual base children form influences how well they eventually perform in school. The narrower the base, the fewer connections children are able to make among the pieces of knowledge they encounter over time. The broader the base, the more comprehensive their learning. More of a balance in the curriculum, with both kinds of learning being addressed and valued, is a fundamental tenet of developmentally appropriate programs. This would result not in children learning less but in children learning better.

The past decades have witnessed a narrowing of the elementary curriculum. Many schools have gone from a holistic approach to learning that included social, physical, cognitive, and aesthetic aims to one that focuses almost solely on isolated academic skills such as tracing letters and memorizing number facts (Peck et al., 1988). The beliefs underlying developmentally appropriate programs are that the curriculum needs to be expanded to include experiences related to all aspects of child development. Again, this is not a cry to limit children's learning but to broaden it. The result will not be a watered-down program but a richer, more comprehensive one.

Myth DAP fails to support family values.

Some people assume this myth is true because they disagree with NAEYC's stance of universal respect for children and families regardless of family composition and lifestyle (Kostelnik, 1998). Such individuals have strongly held beliefs about what constitutes an "acceptable family" and think that DAP should incorporate the same definition. They equate the NAEYC position with advocating family lifestyles that are in conflict with these views. Other people believe this myth out of an incomplete understanding of what DAP involves. For instance, many opponents to DAP have never read the position statement itself. Instead, they have read isolated bits of an NAEYC publication, *The Anti-Bias Curriculum: Tools for Empowering Young Children,* and have treated the two works as if they were the same. Because they disagree strongly with antibias tenets, they reject everything associated with Developmentally Appropriate Practice. (A description of the antibias philosophy is presented in Chapter 13 of this text.) Even more people have been aroused by media reports that misrepresent DAP in the ways described earlier. In each of these circumstances, DAP has elicited powerful negative responses from some portions of the public-at-large and certain public decision makers over the issue of family values.

NAEYC's stated mission is to "serve and act on behalf of the needs, rights, and well-being of ALL young children and the professionals who work with them." Every family has values regardless of the composition or structure of the family unit. Such values emerge from the cultural, historic, ethnic, and social milieu in which the adult family members have been raised. Such values are transmitted to the next generation through daily family life and are modified by the experiences of that generation. Because there is no one set of family values that represents all the children and families enrolled in early childhood programs across the United States, NAEYC must find ways to support the varying values families espouse. Thus, NAEYC has taken a values stand based on respect for individual children and their families. Toward this end, NAEYC has made public its commitment to: (1) appreciate and support the close ties between children and their families, (2) recognize that children are best understood in the context of family, culture, and society, and (3) respect the dignity, worth, and uniqueness of each individual child and family member (Bredekamp & Copple, 1997; Feeney & Kipnis, 1992). The organization has also formulated a code of ethics that designates ideals for "respecting the dignity of each family, its culture, customs and beliefs" as well as "respecting families' childrearing values and their right to make decisions for their children." Backed by these commitments, one of the foundational principles of DAP is that of social and cultural appropriateness. As you recall from the early portions of this chapter, that principle requires early childhood educators to incorporate "knowledge of the social and cultural contexts in which children live to ensure that learning experiences are meaningful, relevant and respectful for the participating children and their families" (Bredekamp & Copple, 1997, 9). In a free and democratic society predicated on the premise that its members are created equal, the organization is obligated to ensure that every child and every family is treated with respect. For this reason, NAEYC is constantly deliberating about how to support family values. The DAP document reflects this continuing process.

IMPLICATIONS FOR PROFESSIONAL PRACTICE

Now that you have become familiar with developmentally appropriate practice as well as some people's reactions to DAP, take a moment to consider the implications this educational philosophy could have for your work with children and families. Also, ask yourself, "How will the issues that surround developmentally appropriate practice affect my development as a professional in the field?" Then read the implications we thought of and see how they match your own ideas.

Implications

As early childhood professionals in training or as practitioners in the field, we should do the following:

1. Have a thorough knowledge of what developmentally appropriate practice is and what it is not.

2. Continually examine our practices, reflecting on our work with children and families and revising our actions in accordance with new knowledge and understandings.

3. Combine our understanding of DAP with knowledge of child development and learning, curriculum goals and content, instructional practices, family and community relationships, assessment, and professionalism to create high-quality programs for children and families.

4. Become adept at articulating the rationale behind our practices and connecting what we do in the classroom to the fundamental principles of DAP.

5. Share information about developmentally appropriate practice with parents and colleagues.

6. Listen thoughtfully to questions raised and concerns expressed about DAP and strive to clarify points of agreement and disagreement.

7. Challenge people who make blanket statements or inaccurate overgeneralizations about DAP.

8. Respond to misinformation about DAP with accurate facts and relevant information.

9. Recognize that early childhood education is a vital profession where new ideas are constantly being explored as practitioners and researchers attempt to optimally support children's development and learning.

SUMMARY

This chapter has chronicled an evolving concept in early childhood education: developmentally appropriate practice. Developmentally appropriate programs match how children develop and learn with how they are taught. They are founded on faith in children's capacity to learn as well as respect for children as individuals and people who are shaped by the social and cultural contexts in which they live. Educators working with youngsters between the ages of 3 and 8 recognize that young children's learning differs significantly from that of older children and adults and approach their work with that understanding in mind. Thus, the application of DAP places the nature and well-being of children as the central focus of professional practice. Research supports the idea that developmentally appropriate programs represent positive educational experiences for young children. Not only do children perform well academically, but their attitudes toward school remain enthusiastic and optimistic. That is not the case for many children enrolled in classes that ignore their unique educational needs. However, DAP has not been without its critics. Concern has been expressed that the approach may not meet the needs of all children and that the basic premises underlying the approach are flawed. These concerns led to a revised version of DAP, which was published in 1997. It will take some time to determine how well the ideas presented in the second edition of the NAEYC document will satisfy the concerns expressed. In addition to these concerns, the misinterpretations that sometimes arise from people's efforts to understand

DAP were discussed, as were the realities associated with each one. The entire focus of Chapter 1, therefore, has been to establish the foundation on which developmentally appropriate programs are based. As you explore the ramifications of this concept in the chapters that follow, you will encounter the ideas expressed here again and again. There is no element of early childhood education they do not touch. Activities and routines, materials, the physical environment, classroom management, methods of family involvement, and assessment procedures are all influenced by these principles.

Applying What You Read in This Chapter

1. Discuss

  a. Based on your reading and your experiences with young children, discuss each of the questions that open this chapter.

  b. Describe the materials and routines you would expect to see in a *preschool classroom* advocating DAP. What materials and routines would you expect to see in an *elementary classroom* in which DAP was practiced? Explain your choices.

  c. How would you respond to a parent who is concerned that DAP will lessen his or her child's chances to do well in school?

  d. Read through the examples provided by the High/Scope approach, the Reggio Emilia approach, and the Quality Schools approach to early childhood education. Find examples of how these approaches utilize strategies associated with DAP.

  e. Review the myths associated with DAP. Have you seen or heard any of these in your conversations with colleagues or parents? If you have, what misunderstandings were expressed? How did you respond? How would you respond now? If you have not encountered these misunderstandings, select one, and craft your own response based on what you have learned as well as your experiences in the field.

2. Observe

  a. Observe a teacher who has adopted a philosophy of developmentally appropriate practice. Identify concrete examples of this philosophy in the classroom.

  b. Observe a preschool classroom and a classroom for children older than 5 years. Describe ways the adults have used the principle of age appropriateness in terms of materials, activities, and routines in each classroom. Find the similarities and the differences between the two rooms based on the notion of age appropriateness.

3. Carry out an activity

  a. Talk to an early childhood practitioner about how he or she tries to make the children's program age appropriate, individually appropriate, and socioculturally appropriate. Write a summary of what she or he tells you.

  b. Read a journal article about developmentally appropriate practice. Is the author in favor of the concept or opposed to it? Describe how convinced you are by his or her position.

  c. Select one of the program models described in this chapter. Gather additional information about the approach. Summarize what you find out.

  d. Review written information describing an early childhood program in your community. Based on the program's written philosophy and program description, discuss to what extent the program reflects principles of DAP.

4. Create something for your portfolio

  a. Provide three examples of your work with children: one in which you address the idea of age appropriateness, another in which you demonstrate individual appropriateness, and a third that illustrates your efforts related to sociocultural appropriateness.

5. **Add to your journal**
   a. What is the most significant thing you have learned about developmentally appropriate practice based on your readings and experience with children?
   b. Reflect on the extent to which the content of this chapter corresponds to what you have observed in the field. What is your reaction to any discrepancies you perceive?

   c. In what ways have you utilized Developmentally Appropriate Practices in your work with children? What goals do you have for yourself in this regard for the future?

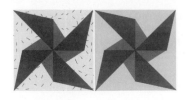

Chapter 2

Principles of Development and Learning: Implications for Effective Teaching

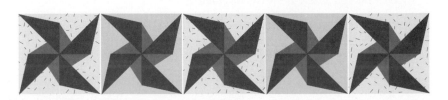

You may wonder:

Why do so many early childhood teacher preparation programs include child development as a significant part of the curriculum?

What difference do child development and learning make in the design of effective early childhood programs?

How might programs for children ages 3 to 8 look similar to or different from programs designed for adolescents or adults?

Is having knowledge about child development and learning enough to ensure high-quality programs for young children?

In this chapter on principles of child development and learning: implications for effective teaching, we present information to help you answer these questions.

Imagine you are interviewing for an early childhood teaching position. The interviewer asks you the following questions:

What kinds of activities will you design for the children in your classroom?

How will you meet the needs of children who vary in age and ability?

When should children stop playing and concentrate on learning?

What role will families play in your classroom?

What will you do if an activity is too simple or too difficult for a particular child?

How will you answer? Although there is no *one* correct response to any of these queries, the answers you give will reflect your ideas about how young children develop and learn. Such knowledge is the hallmark of the early childhood professional and a major factor in the delivery of high-quality programs for children.

EDUCATORS NEED TO KNOW ABOUT CHILD DEVELOPMENT AND LEARNING

Zeal without knowledge is like fire without light.
—Thomas Fuller (1608–1661)

Many adults enjoy working with young children. However, those who have specialized knowledge about child development and learning are the most likely to engage in developmentally appropriate practices

(Andersson, 1992; Gestwicki, 1995a; Goffin, 1989; NAEYC, 1996; Snider & Fu, 1990). Instead of treating their interactions with children as wholly intuitive, they bring factual information to bear on how they think about children and interact with them in the classroom. Thus, early childhood education, like all education, demands well-prepared personnel who appreciate the unique characteristics of the children they serve. Knowledge of child development and learning contributes to that preparation and appreciation.

Child development principles help us to recognize commonalities among children and characteristics typical within age-ranges. Although no two children are alike, we know that 4-year-olds are more like other 4-year-olds than they are like 10-year-olds. Likewise, we recognize that certain behaviors emerge at fairly predictable times. For instance, most children begin to talk somewhere between 12 months and 2 years. Four- and five-year-olds typically engage in various forms of verbal humor. Around age 6 children develop the auditory abilities necessary to discriminate consonant blends such as *sp* (*sp*ace) or *tr* (*tr*ain). Losing their front teeth is a common experience for most 6-, 7-, and 8-year-olds. Such developmental milestones are a natural part of growing up. When teachers know about child development, they gain insights into how and why children behave as they do. These insights make it easier to understand typical variations among children as well as to accurately recognize potential problems that may require specialized intervention (Kostelnik et al., 1998). Familiarity with child development also offers clues about the order in which activities might be presented to children and the degree of developmental readiness children must demonstrate to achieve program goals (Spodek, 1986). Knowledge of child development, therefore, helps adults predict strategies, materials, interactions, and experiences that will be safe, healthy, interesting, achievable, and challenging to children (Bredekamp & Copple, 1997).

Theory and research related to childhood learning yields additional information. Although we are far from having unanimous agreement on every aspect of learning, increasing evidence indicates that young children think and acquire knowledge in ways that differ significantly from those used by older children and adults (Berk & Winsler, 1995; Kamii, 1985; Seigler, 1991; Sulzby & Barnhart, 1990). Awareness of these differences helps us to create programs that support rather than undermine children's natural ways of acquiring new knowledge and abilities. The physical environments we design, the methods we use, and the routines, activities, and assessments we create can all be made better by taking into account principles of childhood learning.

Simply knowing about child development and learning, however, is not enough to ensure that early childhood programs will be high-quality ones (Dunn & Kontos, 1997). *Practitioners must link what they know with what they do.* This connection between theory and practice is essential if children are to actually experience positive outcomes. Keeping this in mind, let us review some basic development and learning principles and then explore their implications for action.

PRINCIPLES OF CHILD DEVELOPMENT

Children Develop Holistically

Aesthetic, affective, cognitive, language, physical, and social development are all interrelated. No one facet of development exists independently from the others, nor is any one the *most* valuable. For example, adults observing children engaged in a vigorous game of dodgeball might categorize their activity as purely physical. Yet the children's ability to play the game is influenced by many developmental processes:

Aesthetic—appreciating the grace of another player's movements, enjoying the rhythm of the game

Affective—coping with the disappointment of being "out," accepting compliments and criticism from other players, expressing anger over a disputed call

Cognitive—figuring out the sequence in which the game is played, determining how many children can fit in the space available, remembering who has had a chance to be "it" and who has not, analyzing the best angle for hitting a fleeing player

Language—determining what "scripts" to use to get into or out of the game, using words to describe the rules, responding to the teacher's directions

Physical—catching, dodging, and throwing the ball; developing stamina

Social—negotiating the rules of the game, signaling others about a desire to have a turn, making way for a new player, working out disagreements over boundaries and teams

Likewise, reading and computing are both intellectual functions that have social, affective, aesthetic, language, and physical elements as well. The same is true for any task children encounter. Social processes shape cognitive ones, cognitive processes promote or restrict social capabilities, physical processes influence language and cognition, and so on. Consequently, when thinking about children, it is best to remember that they are whole human beings whose development is enhanced when educators concern themselves with *all* aspects of their development. This orientation is referred to as focusing on the "whole child" (Hendrick, 1996; Krogh, 1997).

In support of the whole-child philosophy, researchers have found that serious problems arise when one facet of development is emphasized to the exclusion of *all* others. For instance, children who participate in classrooms where academic achievement is the only priority suffer from lack of attention to social and emotional development (Spodek, 1986). For children whose poor social skills lead to rejection by peers, the results can be devastating. Such youngsters are very likely to engage in delinquent acts or succumb to mental health problems (Bierman, 1987; Goleman, 1995; Parker and Asher, 1987).

Equally negative effects occur when physical development is neglected. Children exhibit increasingly poor fitness and health-related behaviors over time (Payne & Rink, 1997; Reuschlein & Haubenstricker, 1985). This is a problem both in the short term (children fail to develop optimal cardiovascular functioning, physical strength, endurance, and physical skills) and in the long run (children grow up to be sedentary adults at risk for heart disease and other physical ailments). So important is the notion of whole-child teaching that in early childhood education, the curriculum and the whole child tend to be seen as indivisible (Williams, 1987). This has important implications for early childhood programs.

Implications

1. Activities and routines are designed so that all aspects of child development are addressed each day.

A sample of developmental processes associated with whole-child learning is offered in Table 2.1.

2. Educators think of subject matter (e.g., spelling or reading) in terms of how it relates to child development. For example, reading is viewed within the context of overall language development. This means it is considered in relation to listening, speaking, and writing, not in isolation. Likewise, handwriting is treated as a product of fine motor development and visual perception. Writing instruction and expectations for children's writing are created with those developmental processes in mind.

3. Daily time allocation is an important consideration. Because all facets of child development are important, huge amounts of time are not devoted to some areas (e.g., reading or art and crafts) to the preclusion of others (e.g., science or social studies, problem-solving activities or games).

4. Classroom activities and routines are designed so children have opportunities to participate in integrated, rather than isolated, experiences. This includes integration across developmental domains, subject matter, and traditional lines of responsibility. For example, children participate in activities that incorporate language, physical, and social processes simultaneously. They have experiences that combine reading, science, and math. The adults with whom they come in contact often work in teams. The responsibility for creating an effective learning environment is shared among students, teachers, specialists, administrators, and parents.

Child Development Occurs in an Orderly Sequence

Try putting these developmental milestones in the order in which they tend to appear during childhood.

> *Fear of ghosts.*
>
> *Fear of animals.*
>
> *Fear of being embarrassed in front of others.*
>
> *Stranger anxiety.*

What did you decide? Sample progressions like these illustrate the notion of developmental sequence.

Development is sequential, and changes over time occur in a relatively predictable fashion. Scientists worldwide have identified typical sequences of behavior

TABLE 2.1
Developmental Facets of Whole-Child Learning

Aesthetic	Affective	Cognitive

Developing sensory awareness
Imagining and visualizing
Exploring
Creating
Responding
Interpreting
Developing critical awareness
Expressing and representing
   through a variety of forms
	Developing a positive, realistic
	   self-concept
	Accepting and expressing
	   emotions in socially
	   appropriate ways
	Coping with change
	Developing decision-making
	   skills
	Accepting challenge
	Developing independence
	Feeling pride in
	   accomplishments
	Increasing instrumental
	   know-how
	Enjoying living and learning
		Developing thinking processes
		   (observing, recalling,
		   comparing, patterning,
		   classifying, generalizing,
		   integrating, and evaluating)
		Constructing knowledge
		Developing memory skills
		Acquiring facts

Adapted from *Kindergarten Curriculum Guide and Resource Book*, 1985, Victoria. British Columbia: Ministry of Education; and *Teaching Young Children Using Themes*, M. Kostelnik (Ed.), 1991. Glenview, IL: Good Year Books.

or understanding related to language: social, emotional, and personality development; graphic and symbolic representation; problem solving; logical-mathematical understanding; moral development; and physical development (Berk, 1997; Sroufe et al., 1996). For instance, before they walk, children first learn to lift their heads, then sit up, then stand with assistance, then crawl, and then stand on their own. Eventually they toddle, then run. Similarly, children's earliest attempts to write messages are the creation of scribbles. In cultures in which the alphabet is used, scribbles gradually give way to letterlike forms, then to single consonants representing entire words, then to combinations of letters in phonetic attempts at spelling, until eventually more and more standard spelling is used. When it comes to childhood fears, they tend to emerge in the following order: stranger anxiety, fear of animals, fear of ghosts, and fear of potential embarrassment.

Such changes are often uneven rather than smooth. Individual children spend more or less time on each step; they may move forward a bit, back a little, then forward again. Some children may even skip some phases that are less relevant to them. However, the sequences tend to remain predictable, with the incre-

ments for each one emerging in the same order. Applying this principle implies the use of certain early childhood practices.

Implications

1. Educators read about development and observe young children carefully so they are familiar with relevant developmental sequences in every domain.
2. Practitioners use their knowledge of developmental sequences to determine reasonable expectations for individual children.
3. Teachers use their understanding of child development to determine what new understandings or behaviors might logically expand children's current levels of functioning. This enables them to challenge youngsters appropriately in the classroom.
4. Teachers avoid unduly pressuring children to accelerate their progress through certain developmental sequences such as those associated with spelling, number recognition, or handwriting.

Child Development Proceeds at Varying Rates Within and Among Children

Emahl is 5; so is Lawrence. Emahl was walking at 1 year and talking in complete sentences by age 2. He still

Language	Physical	Social
Responding and communicating through listening, speaking, writing, and reading Experimenting with language Representing through language	Developing competence in using large and small muscles Taking care of and respecting one's body Being aware of and practicing good nutrition habits Developing physical fitness Appreciating and enjoying human movement	Developing internal behavior controls Helping Cooperating Respecting and accepting others Learning from others Seeking and giving companionship Developing friendships Becoming a responsible citizen Appreciating and respecting the cultural identity and heritage of others Respecting the environment

has a hard time sharing people and toys. Lawrence did not walk until he was 14 months old and only began talking fluidly at 3 years of age. He knows several strategies for sharing, which he uses well. Emahl and Lawrence, alike yet different—both developing normally.

As illustrated by Emahl and Lawrence, every child develops according to his or her own "biological clock" (McKee, 1991). No two children are exactly alike. Differences in development manifest themselves in two ways: intrapersonally and interpersonally.

These second graders share the same birthday but vary in their rates of physical, language, cognitive, and socioemotional development.

Within every individual, various facets of development are dominant at different times throughout childhood. For instance, infancy is a time of rapid physical growth; although language development is also progressing, it is at a relatively slow pace. The same trends reverse themselves as children enter the preschool and elementary years; physical growth slows down, while at the same time children make spectacular strides in using language. These are examples of *intrapersonal* variations in development. Such internal variations explain why the same child may be easily moved to tears, have difficulty with verbal expression, climb nimbly to the highest part of the jungle gym, recite the alphabet backward, and have moderate success cutting with scissors. Such unevenness in development is to be expected.

Interpersonal variations in rates also occur. Even though the typical sequences still apply, the pace at which youngsters move through them differs. Hence, children of the same age may exhibit behaviors and understandings quite unlike one another. And, if you were to chart the normal development of an entire classroom of children, the time at which each child reached certain milestones would vary considerably. For instance, you could expect some first graders to come to school in September reading words and phrases. Other children might just be starting to make the association between various letters and sounds. At the same time, certain children in the class may group objects by function only, others by more than one property at a time, and still others may be exploring how to regroup objects in different ways. All of these variations are normal, and similar differences could be found across all domains.

Readers familiar with age-level expectations or norms may be wondering how those correspond to the variation-in-rates principle. Profiles of typical age expectations for certain skills such as walking, speaking, counting, and participating in games are commonly available for the early childhood years. However, readers are cautioned that the ages identified do not represent exact points in time. Such figures are based on averages. So, even though skipping may be listed at age 6, sometimes this capacity emerges later, say, at age 8, whereas occasionally it can be seen as early as age 5. Norms guide us in understanding the *order* in which certain behaviors appear and approximately when they may occur. They are not meant to be used as absolute standards or rigid timetables for growth and development. There is always a range of variation in human development. Also, when a milestone is achieved it is not necessarily predictive of proficiency over time. By age 10, there may be little difference between children who began skipping at 5 and those who mastered this skill later. Likewise, children who began talking early in their second year do not necessarily talk more or less or with greater or lesser skill than youngsters for whom age 30 months marked the beginning of fluent verbal communication. Understanding the wide-ranging variations among children is a key consideration in the creation of developmentally appropriate educational programs.

Implications

1. Teachers expect that children in early education classrooms will exhibit a wide range of abilities.
2. Early childhood professionals avoid focusing on a single index (e.g., IQ, reading test score, child's ability to draw a person, etc.) as a measure of children's overall potential or achievement.
3. Teachers carefully observe children to discover patterns of behavior for each child within various developmental domains. They use this knowledge to individualize their instruction rather than expecting all children to learn the same thing in the same way at the same time.
4. Educators create daily schedules in which children have opportunities to pursue activities at their own pace. Children are seldom required to rotate from activity to activity on a predetermined schedule. Practitioners adjust or change their plans to meet the current needs of individuals in the group.
5. Developmental norms are not used as rigid standards against which children are labeled "ahead" or "behind" others in the group.
6. Classroom activities are designed to encompass multiple learning objectives, not just one. These allow children more than one opportunity to be challenged and to experience success.
7. Teachers repeat activities more than once during the year so that children can gain different benefits from the activity according to their changing needs and capabilities.
8. Practitioners document children's individual patterns of progress. They keep continuous records based on observations of children's movement from one phase of a developmental sequence to another.

New Development Is Based on Previous Development

If you plant a haycorn, it will grow up into an oak-tree. But it doesn't follow that if you plant a honeycomb, it will grow up into a beehive.
—Piglet to Pooh (Milne, 1995)

Development is based on a foundation; past, present, and future are related and build on each other in succession. New capabilities and understandings arise out of and elaborate on what is already there. The idea that children develop a sense of independence only after establishing an adequate sense of trust illustrates this principle. Similarly, children's writing evolves from scribbling, expressive language is founded on earlier babbling, and children's understanding of numbers is based on their first achieving such milestones as object permanence and one-to-one correspondence. In all of these instances, certain developmental threads are carried forward over time, providing continuity from one phase of development to the next. The implications of this principle for practitioners are obvious but essential.

Implications

1. Practitioners interact with children and observe them to discover what children know and can do.
2. Educators plan instruction based on each child's level of performance and understanding.
3. Ample opportunities are made available for children to explore and practice what they have learned prior to expecting them to learn something new.
4. Teachers help children make connections between new and past experiences and support children's progress toward more elaborate concepts or skills as they exhibit interest, mastery, and understanding.
5. Concepts and skills are not addressed in isolation or out of a context relative to children's experiences.
6. Educators do not expect children to exhibit behaviors and understandings that are *far* beyond the current developmental foundations on which they are building.

Development Has Both Cumulative and Delayed Effects

What we live through is who we become.
—Oprah Winfrey (1996)

Beginning at birth, children accumulate a history of repeated, frequent experiences that may have positive or negative effects on their development depending on the circumstances. How this happens is illustrated by infants who usually have their needs met and so develop a sense of trust in themselves and the world. Youngsters whose needs are often ignored develop mistrust. These outcomes result from not one or two incidents but rather a long-term pattern of interactions that children come to view as typical (Seligman, 1995). Likewise, children who occasionally see a violent television program may not experience long-term damaging effects. However, children who spend hours, weeks, and years watching violence depicted on television eventually demonstrate increased levels of aggression in their daily interactions (Friedrich & Stein, 1973; Schaffer, 1995). Along similar lines, Lillian Katz and Sylvia Chard (1987, 1989) have made an eloquent case for considering the long-term negative effects of such typical school practices as flash-card drills and daily worksheet sessions. They point out that the sporadic use of such techniques is probably harmless. However, the cumulative result for children who receive a steady diet of such experiences seems to be lack of intellectual confidence and an erosion of inquiry and problem-solving strategies. Their concerns are echoed by other educators who fear that practices such as these undermine children's conceptual development, participatory skills, grasp of essential meanings, breadth of knowledge, and interest in school (Cummings, 1991a; Kamii, 1985; Parker, 1991; Steinberg, 1990). Cumulative effects like these are difficult to reverse.

In addition to accumulated impacts, developmental outcomes may be delayed. That is, early experiences may influence children's functioning in ways that become obvious only later in life (Kohn, 1993; Wieder & Greenspan, 1993). For instance, some children of abusive parents may appear remarkably well adjusted while growing up but experience serious mental health problems in adolescence and adulthood as a result of their tumultuous past (Ney, 1988). On the positive side, the benefits of reasoning with children as a way of teaching them how to behave is not always immediately apparent. However, when adults consistently provide reasons for rules and prohibitions, children eventually become better able to reason on their own. This increases their ability to exercise self discipline (Kostelnik et al., 1998).

Implications

1. Professionals consider the long-range implications of their practices as well as short-term outcomes. When current strategies undermine long-term goals, they are revised in favor of the long term. In this way, teachers are careful to ensure that their methods support their goals.
2. Researchers conduct longitudinal studies of children's learning. Program evaluators assess children's progress and program effectiveness over time.
3. Developmentally appropriate practices are explained to parents, colleagues, and decision makers in terms of how they support children's learning over the life span.

Optimal Periods of Child Development

You want to say that it is never too late. But there seems to be something very special about the early childhood years . . . [Through about age 10] there are windows of opportunity that nature flings open, starting before birth, and then slams shut, one by one with every additional candle on the birthday cake.—Begley (1996)

Throughout early childhood, there are opportune times during which significant changes occur in children's development. These changes are related to complex interactions between children's internal structures of body and brain and their experiences with the physical and social environment. During optimal periods, children are more receptive to environmental influences than at other times (McKee, 1991). If they are denied the kinds of experiences that enhance development when such windows of opportunity appear, they may be unmotivated or unable to reach potential later in life.

As one example, preschoolers and children in the early elementary grades are biologically inclined to develop fundamental motor skills such as catching, throwing, hopping, and running that they can later combine into more complex skills. During this phase of their lives, most children are open to instruction and willing to spend hours engaged in physical activity, thereby increasing their skills. However, youngsters for whom such opportunities are unavailable become less willing to initiate and practice fundamental motor skills in the later elementary grades. By middle childhood, many conclude that they do not possess the talent necessary to succeed. Lack of skill and reluctance form a proficiency barrier that causes children to shy away from further involvement in physical activities and games. The cumulative effects of these reactions often last a lifetime. This makes the early childhood years an optimal period for children's achievement of motor proficiency (Gallahue, 1995; Haubenstricker, 1991b). It is then that children's basic attitudes and skills related to their physical selves are either enhanced or discouraged.

Increasing evidence indicates that early childhood marks an optimal period for a variety of developmentally based processes and capacities (Begley, 1996; Berk, 1997; Hendrick, 1996). In addition to motor skills proficiency, some of these include prosocial attitudes and behaviors, affiliation skills, self-esteem, general problem-solving strategies, logical-mathematical thought processes, coping strategies, emergent literacy, verbal language development, second language development, musicality, aesthetic awareness, attitudes toward authority and rules, attitudes toward work, and attitudes toward oneself as a learner.

This list is not meant to be exclusive or exhaustive but to give the reader an idea of the importance of the

FIGURE 2.1

Windows of Opportunity for Development and Learning

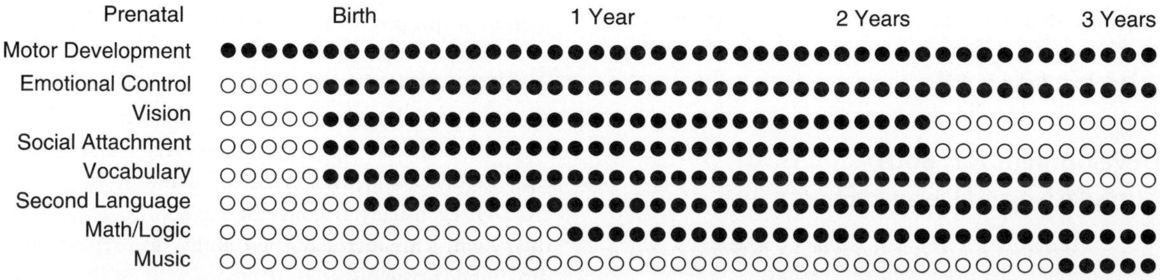

early childhood years and areas that deserve particular attention in early childhood education. A few common "windows of opportunity for development and learning" are illustrated in Figure 2.1.

Implications

1. Educators explain to others the critical nature of the early childhood years in relation to all aspects of child development.
2. Early childhood programs make sure to address the developmental tasks for which the early years represent the optimal time for development and learning.

PRINCIPLES OF CHILDHOOD LEARNING

Children are learning all the time. They learn to say things like "Excuse me" when they bump into someone; they learn to count, catch a ball, play bingo, recognize letters and numerals, find ways to solve problems, and derive pleasure from sharing with a friend. True learning in each of these instances occurs only when children make a relatively permanent change in their thinking or behavior as a result of the interaction between maturation and experience (Shaffer, 1995). Children who clean up, even when no one else is around, have learned. Children who remember a telephone number for 5 minutes and then forget it, have not. Certain universal principles describe children's learning throughout the early childhood years.

Children Are Active Learners

Sung Won is talking to herself as she works on a three-dimensional puzzle. "Gee!" "How can I do it?" "That's really funny." "How come . . .?" "Wait! Wait!" "Oh, I know!" Surprise, puzzlement, struggle, excitement, anticipation, and dawning certainty—those are

the (elements) of intelligent thought. As virtues, they stand by themselves—even if they do not on some specific occasion lead to the right answer. In the long run, they are what count.—Duckworth (1987)

When we say children are active, it is important to recognize the multidimensional nature of their activity. First, young children are motoric beings. They are genetically programmed to reach out, pull up, stand upright, move forward, and move about (Haubenstricker, 1991b). As children move, they seek stimulation, which increases their opportunities for learning.

Second, children use their whole bodies as instruments of learning, taking in data through all their senses. Young children are compelled to taste, touch, hear, look at, and smell objects and spaces in order to find out about them—what their properties are, how they function, and how they fit in with the rest of the world. In this way children connect thought with action.

Third, children are active participants in their own experiences. They are not empty vessels passively waiting to be "filled up" with information and experiences determined by others (Bredekamp, 1991; Sroufe et al., 1996). On the contrary, they energetically seek ways to achieve their maximum potential in both structure and function. Children do this by observing, acting on objects, and interacting with people (Bredekamp & Copple, 1997).

Finally, if the usual avenues are unavailable, children search for substitute sources of satisfaction (Smart & Smart, 1982). Consequently, youngsters find alternate ways of satisfying their needs when ordinary paths are blocked. A child who is deprived of approval from adults may seek it from peers instead; a student who finds seatwork boring may rush through it, heedless of accuracy, in order to gain satisfaction from moving on to another kind of task.

Implications

1. Practitioners provide children with many multisensory opportunities to explore and handle objects directly every day. This kind of hands-on learning dominates the teaching strategies implemented.
2. Substantial segments of time are planned during which children can move about the classroom freely.
3. Teachers create schedules for the day in which quiet times are followed by active times and in which times when children are to be passive are kept to a minimum.
4. Opportunities for gross motor activities are made available to children each day, both indoors and outside.
5. Educators observe children carefully to see if some of children's "unacceptable" behavior may be the result of blocked goals. If such is the case, teachers and administrators work with the child to determine better alternatives for meeting his or her needs. These strategies sometimes involve assisting the child in adopting new behaviors or restructuring some aspect of the classroom that is developmentally inappropriate.

Children's Learning Is Influenced by Maturation

Suppose you have a friend with a 6-month-old son who is just learning to sit up on his own. She wants to impress her mother-in-law, who will be visiting in a few weeks. She decides the way to do this is to teach her baby to walk and asks your advice about the best exercises to use.

Chances are you will tell your friend that no matter how much exercise she provides, her 6-month-old will not be walking in the next few weeks because he is too immature to accomplish the task. His legs cannot support his body, and he lacks the balance and strength necessary to hold himself upright. Practice as they might, her son is simply not ready to walk on his own. Just as it is inappropriate to expect a 6-month-old to walk independently, other demands can be equally unrealistic if suitable maturation has not occurred. For instance, most young children lack the eye control to accurately shift from a near focus (e.g., the paper on their desk) to a far one (e.g., words or numerals on a blackboard). Such coordination tends to mature sometime after the seventh year. This makes the task of copying work from a blackboard generally inappro-

priate for kindergartners and many first graders (Soderman, 1997).

On the other hand, through maturation, new possibilities for learning are created that could not have been realized earlier. This is illustrated by children's increasing ability to understand other people's emotions over time. Between 2 and 5 years of age, children identify someone else's emotional state based on how that person looks—crying equals sadness, and laughter equals joy (Russell & Bullock, 1989). They have little idea that the context of the situation also contributes to people's feelings. However, as their cognitive skills expand, 6- and 7-year-olds take into account situational circumstances, too. Children this age recognize that Sonia could be sad because her dog is lost. They also know that Sonia might feel happy again if the dog returned. By age 9 or 10 many youngsters are aware that memories may produce feelings even though the original event is long past. When 10-year-old Raymond says, "Yoko is sad. She's lonesome for her dog she used to have," he is demonstrating an increasingly mature concept of how and why emotions occur (Kostelnik et al., 1998).

In all of the previous examples, the process of maturation established a general timetable for the emergence of new capabilities and understandings. These timetables could be retarded by environmental insults such as malnutrition or accelerated through environmental stimulation. However, maturation is not completely elastic, and stimulation can accelerate development only within the parameters dictated by each child's biological blueprint (Kaplan, 1986). This was illustrated by the scenario that introduced this principle. As you can see, maturation plays an important role in deciding the appropriateness of certain tasks for young children.

Implications

1. Early childhood professionals learn about how children mature and what might reasonably be expected of children over time. They communicate this understanding to other significant adults in children's lives.
2. Teachers simplify, maintain, or extend activities in response to children's demonstrated levels of functioning and comprehension.
3. School curriculum is designed so that there is some flexibility in the grade placement of learning objectives. For example, no single grade level encompasses

both the introduction and mastery of particular knowledge or skills. Instead, these are spread out over more than one grade. Also, the accomplishment of certain milestones such as counting to 100 or being able to carry out a forward roll fit into the expectations for multiple grades. Restructuring school schedules and grade configurations to allow children to progress at a more self-determined rather than calendar year-determined rate also supports flexibility.

Children's Learning Is Influenced by the Environment

Although they cannot profit from certain experiences without the appropriate neurological and physical structures, *children do not gain knowledge and skills from maturation alone.* Environment plays a critical role in the learning process. The environment runs the gamut from the biological environment of nutrition, medical care, physical exercise, and drugs to the physical environment of clothing, shelter, materials available, and climate to the social environment of family, peers, schools, community, media, and culture (Santrock, 1994). Such environmental variables either enhance or detract from children's ability to learn.

We know, for instance, that children who are well rested, physically comfortable, and generally healthy get more out of early childhood programs than children for whom these basic needs are not fully met (CDF, 1997). Also, children are better able to acquire new understandings when they are free of strong biological urges such as hunger or having to go to the bathroom (Maslow, 1954).

Children learn best when they feel psychologically safe and secure (Bredekamp & Copple, 1997). This translates into knowing that they are in a place where routines and rules/expectations are predictable and suited to their capacities. Being in the company of adults who respect and like them, tolerate mistakes, teach them constructive ways to satisfy their aims, and support children's efforts to explore and experiment helps children feel secure. Thus, children who have positive, consistent relationships with adults at home and in the early childhood program feel more at ease and confident than children who are denied such relationships.

In a like manner, the design of indoor and outdoor spaces and choices of materials and equipment encourages or restricts children's experiences, affecting their behavior and even their emotions (Anziano et al., 1995). For instance, positive peer interactions are facilitated when children have ample (but not too much) space to move around and when play spaces are arranged so small numbers of peers can work together rather than in isolation (Weinstein & Mignano, 1997). As another example, children display better problem-solving skills when classrooms have a large variety of age-appropriate materials from which to choose. Poor variety prevents children from combining materials and exploring new problems to solve (Hayes, Palmer, & Zaslow, 1990).

Optimal learning also requires a stimulating social environment. Because young children develop new understandings from observing and participating with other children and adults, they need numerous opportunities to interact with others in stimulating, satisfying ways.

Implications

1. Teachers and administrators highlight the importance of the environment on learning by making sure that the program facility is safe and secure and complies with the legal requirements of the appropriate licensing or accrediting agency.

2. Early childhood programs are structured to ensure that children's biological and physical needs are addressed. For instance, children may use the toilet whenever they need to, they may rest when they are tired, and they receive snacks and meals as appropriate. Classrooms and outdoor areas offer ample space for safe, unencumbered movement. Adequate ventilation is provided, and room temperatures are maintained at a comfortable level. Children's wet or soiled clothing is changed promptly.

3. A daily schedule is established that is relatively stable and predictable to children. Changes in routine are explained in advance so that children can anticipate what will happen next.

4. Educators design activities, transitions, and routines in keeping with children's attention span, physical development, and needs for activity, social interaction, and attention from caring adults.

5. Consistent adult supervision is provided so that children can readily identify a specific adult from whom to seek help, comfort, attention, and guidance.

6. Children are treated with warmth, respect, and caring (regardless of socioeconomic, cultural, ethnic, or family background, appearance, behavior, or any disabling condition).

7. Early childhood professionals use positive discipline techniques aimed at enhancing children's self-esteem and self-control.

8. Practitioners create classroom environments that support and challenge children's abilities.

Children Learn Through a Combination of Physical Experience, Social Interaction, and Reflection

"Teacher, am I first on the story list?" Maria asks.
"So far you are the only one on the list."
"I'm first," Mollie says.
"You can't be first if I'm first, Mollie.
You have to be called next." Maria says.
"Okay then, Maria. I'm next-first."—Paley (1988).

Physical Experience   Children have a powerful need to make sense of everything they encounter. From birth, their efforts focus on organizing their knowledge more coherently and adapting to the demands of the environment by directly manipulating, listening to, smelling, tasting, and otherwise acting on objects in order to see what happens (Kamii, 1986; Shaffer, 1995a). From such investigations children generate a logic or knowledge of the properties of things, how

they work, and how they relate to one another. This knowledge comes about not simply from the passive act of observing but also from the more complex mental activity of interpreting and drawing conclusions about what happens (Beilin, 1989; Thomas, 1995). Such conclusions either add to children's existing ideas or cause children to reformulate their thinking.

Social Experience   Children's experiences with physical objects are further influenced by their interactions with people (Bodrova & Leong, 1996; Vygotsky, 1978). As youngsters play, talk, and work with peers and adults, they exchange and compare interpretations and ideas. They generate hypotheses, ask questions, and formulate answers (Bredekamp & Copple, 1997). In doing so, they often face contradictions in the way people or objects respond, and those discrepancies force children to extract new understandings from what has occurred. Through such experiences *children construct knowledge internally,* continually shaping, expanding, and reorganizing their mental structures. Dominating the preschool and elementary years, constructed learning like this encompasses all the *operations and conceptual knowledge* children require to get about in the everyday world (Beilin, 1989; Berk, 1997; Katz & Chard, 1989).

Social experiences also provide children with *factual information* they cannot construct solely on their own. Through their interactions with others, children are *instructed* in culturally determined knowledge and skills necessary for successful functioning in society. Examples include the following:

Names of things (door, window or porte, fenêtre).

Historical facts (Martin Luther King's birthday is January 20; you were born in St. Louis).

Customs (when some children are 7 years old, they make their first holy communion; some children who lose a tooth hide it under their pillow).

Rules (wash your hands before eating; walk with the scissors).

Skills (such as how to form the letter *A* or how to throw a football correctly).

Children learn this body of knowledge through observation, imitation, memorization, and reinforcement.

Whether constructed or instructed, "research shows that children need to be able to successfully negotiate

Physical experiences and social interaction enhance children's learning.

learning tasks most of the time if they are to maintain their motivation to learn. Confronted by repeated failure, most children will simply stop trying" (Bredekamp & Copple, 1997, 14). At the same time, there is increasing evidence that children are highly motivated to adopt concepts and skills that are slightly beyond their current level of independent mastery (Bodrova & Leong, 1996). That is, children are eager to learn what they nearly, but do not quite, comprehend, what they can almost do but not quite carry out on their own. Thus, children learn best when teachers provide experiences just beyond what children can do on their own but within what they can do with assistance from someone whose skills are greater. This is sometimes called teaching within the child's *zone of proximal development* (Berk & Winsler, 1995; Vygotsky, 1978). For instance, Irma is speaking in two-word phrases (e.g.,"Big cookie"). In conversations with Irma, her childcare provider expands the child's sentences, adding more language and grammar than Irma is currently capable of producing ("You have a big cookie" or "You like that big cookie."). If the provider's "lesson" is too complex or beyond Irma's understanding, she will not take it in. However, if Irma can simply "stretch" her thinking to encompass the new language, higher-order learning is possible. Under these conditions she will gradually expand her language skills to a higher level of mastery than she would have been able to manage independently. More about the zone of proximal development will be discussed in Chapter 10. For now what is important to recognize is that simply giving children access to a variety of experiences is not enough to foster optimal learning. Adults must monitor such situations to make sure they are manageable for children. They must also provide the assistance necessary to prompt higher-order learning. A youngster who is overwhelmed may be unable to understand or apply knowledge gained regardless of how potentially useful it may be. On the other hand, children who experience no challenge beyond their current level of functioning will fail to progress in their understandings and abilities. Thus, learning is most likely to flourish when children feel both successful and stimulated.

Reflection

"How did you decide this bridge was longer than that one? "

"What do you want to know about insects? How will you find that out?"

"You thought that container had more. What do you think now?"

Questions such as these are aimed at helping children reflect on what they have done or how they know what they know. Such strategies support increased self-awareness and recognition of potential learning strategies. Children who make a plan of how they wish to proceed with an activity, then later recall and analyze how closely their actions matched the original plan, deepen their knowledge and understanding (Elkind, 1976; Hohmann & Weikart, 1995). So, too, do children who generate ideas for how to remember a list of items (e.g., chunking, making associations, and using imagery) and then use one or more of those strategies to aid their memory at another time. Although this kind of learning emerges most prominently during the later elementary years, there is evidence that all children benefit from reflective opportunities to think about their own thinking (Perkins, 1995).

Educators demonstrate an understanding of the importance of physical experience, social interaction, and reflection in relation to children's learning when they do the following things.

Implications

1. Support learning by encouraging children to explore and act on the environment as well as by providing experiences that stimulate children to discover and construct knowledge for themselves.
2. Interact with children, posing questions, and introducing new elements to challenge children's current thinking.
3. Provide daily opportunities for children to interact with their peers.
4. Offer information, ask questions, demonstrate, point out, and explain in an effort to help children acquire knowledge or skills they cannot discover on their own.
5. Provide experiences that enable children to link new information with what they already know and understand.
6. Give children opportunities to reflect on their experiences and help children develop strategies for doing so.

Children's Learning Styles Differ

Sarah likes to work on her own.
Consuelo prefers working with a friend.
Wilma has been interested in numbers since toddlerhood.
Carlos has a way with words.
Jerome seems to have a special feel for the out-of-doors.
Steve enjoys the thrill of competition.
Different children—different ways of approaching the world.

If we adults were trying to get directions to a place we had never been, some of us might prefer using a map, others would like to hear the directions several times aloud, and certain others of us would need physically to go through the motions of orienting our bodies to the left or right as we went over the directions in our minds. These differences in how each person might best process the directions are due to the fact that every human being has a preferential modality that works best for him or her (Kovalik, 1997). Modalities are the sensory channels (visual, auditory, kinesthetic, and tactile) through which people perceive the world. People who are primarily visual learners, for example, respond best to what they see. Often they envision things in their mind as a way to recall them. Youngsters who rely on hearing and talking as their primary means of learning are referred to as *auditory learners.* For them, sound is the message. These youngsters sometimes move their lips or talk themselves through tasks. Kinesthetic/tactile learners are children who must move and constantly touch things in order to grasp concepts. It is not unusual for them also to have to touch themselves in some way to remember or process information. All people use all four modalities to learn; however, all people also function more effectively in the context of their preferred modalities.

Howard Gardner of Harvard University has taken the idea of preferred modalities further than the four modalities described here by expanding the construct beyond simple perceptual processing. He believes that everyone possesses at least seven intelligences, or "frames of mind," and that a person's blend of competencies in each area produces a unique cognitive profile. The seven[1]

---

[1] In recent writings, Gardner speculates about the existence of an eighth intelligence, called the naturalist's intelligence—focused on recognizing flora and fauna (Gardner, 1995). However, he has not yet officially added that intelligence to the original seven he described.

intelligences are linguistic, logical-mathematical, musical, spatial, bodily-kinesthetic, intrapersonal, and interpersonal. Gardner's theory suggests that "each of these (intelligence/competency) areas may develop independently (in the brain). Individuals may be 'at promise' in some areas, while being average or below average in others" (Hatch & Gardner, 1988, 38).

How these intelligences influence children's learning is summarized in Table 2.2. Gardner (1993a) emphasizes that people possess varying degrees of know-how in all seven categories. Yet there are certain ones that eventually dominate, which makes those the ways in which a specific person learns best.

In addition to the learning style variations described so far, further differences among children may exist as a result of cultural factors. Research exploring variations in learning style among Euro-American, African American, and Mexican American children suggest the existence of two basic styles: field dependent and field independent (Anderson, 1988). Field-dependent learners are socially oriented and so work best cooperatively and in groups. Collaboration among peers and between children and teachers are common ways in which these needs are satisfied. Such learners are most attuned to verbal tasks and appreciate figurative learning that has social content characterized by fantasy and humor. Their attention is captured by general principles rather than minute facts. Field-independent learners, on the other hand, value individual achievement and enjoy competition. They are goal-oriented learners who do best on analytic tasks and most easily learn figurative content that is inanimate and impersonal (Reed, 1991).

Studies across cultures indicate that many Western cultural groups of mainly European descent tend to be field-independent learners, whereas non-Western groups are more likely to be field-dependent learners (Anderson, 1988; Gilbert & Gay, 1985; Little-Soldier, 1989). Such results suggest that educators must be careful not to handicap children by demanding that they accommodate a learning style that is foreign to them. Furthermore, when considering these cultural characteristics, one must use qualifying terms such as *may, many,* and *most* and *tend* to indicate that not all children of a particular cultural group possess these characteristics and to avoid stereotypes. Children are at all times individuals and must always be regarded as such (Reed, 1991).

TABLE 2.2
Children's Frames of Mind: Corresponding Learning and Teaching Practices

Type of Intelligence	Child Enjoys	Child Excels in	Child Learns Best by	The Classroom Should Provide Opportunities for
Linguistic Learner "The Word Player"	reading, writing, telling stories.	memorizing, names, places, dates, and trivia.	seeing, saying, and learning language.	many language-based materials, which should be print rich.
Logical-Mathematical Learner "The Questioner"	doing experiments, figuring things out, working with numbers, asking questions, exploring patterns and relationships.	math, reasoning, logic.	looking for patterns and relationships.	handling objects, exploring new ideas, and following the scientific process naturally.
Spacial Learner "The Visualizer"	drawing, building, designing, and creating things	imagining things, sensing changes, doing mazes/puzzles.	visualizing, dreaming, using the mind's eye.	children to work with art and construction materials and to create "projects."
Musical Learner "The Music Lover"	singing, humming, whistling, listening to instruments, responding to music.	picking up sounds, remembering melodies, pitches/rhythms, keeping time.	rhythm, melody	information to be presented via rhythm and melody.
Bodily-Kinesthetic Learner "The Mover"	moving around, touching and talking, using body language.	physical activities (sports/dance/acting), crafts.	touching, moving, interacting with space, processing knowledge through bodily sensations.	role playing, drama, creative movement, gross motor, and other whole-body activities.
Interpersonal Learner "The Socializer"	having lots of friends, talking to people, joining groups.	understanding people, leading others, organizing, communicating, manipulating, mediating conflicts.	sharing, comparing, relating, cooperating, interviewing.	cooperative, collaborative activities and projects; children to express selves to others.
Intrapersonal Learner "The Individual"	working alone, pursuing own interest, self-imagery.	understanding people; focusing inward, on feelings/dreams; following instincts; pursuing interests/goals; being original.	working alone, individualized projects, self-paced instruction, having own space.	self-paced activities, individualized projects, private space, and time for children to work on own.

Adapted from *Frames of Mind: Theory of Multiple Intelligence.* H. Gardner, 1993a. New York: Basic Books; and Seven Styles of Learning, September 1990, *Instructor Magazine*, p. 52.

Implications

1. Educators should provide activities that represent a variety of modalities and address the same concept or skill in more than one modality.
2. An array of activities is provided each day, from which children may choose, so that students can self-select ones that best suit their learning needs.
3. The value of each different learning style is highlighted in various ways rather than focusing on the importance of some (e.g., music or math) and ignoring others (e.g., intrapersonal or kinesthetic).
4. A variety of experiences that suit the learning styles of both field-dependent and field-independent learners is offered, with particular care not to utilize methods characteristic of only one style.

Children Learn Through Play

Play is fun,	It is pleasurable.
not serious,	It is not constrained by reality.
meaningful,	It connects and relates experiences to one another.
active,	Children are doing things.
voluntary,	No one has to force children to play.
intrinsically motivated,	Curiosity, the desire for mastery or affiliation, are some reasons children play.
rule governed.	Rules may be implicit or explicit and are created by the children.

Play is the primary medium through which children learn.

Children play at home, at school, and everywhere in between. They play with people, things, and ideas (Whiren, 1995). When more fundamental needs are met—when children are not sleeping, eating, or seeking emotional support from others—children choose to play and can remain occupied that way for hours at a time (Sutton-Smith, 1971). Play is the province of children from the time they are born throughout the elementary school years.

All areas of development are enhanced through children's play activities. Play is the fundamental means by which children gather and process information, learn new skills, and practice old ones (Spodek, 1986; Sroufe et al., 1996). Within the context of their play, children come to understand, create, and manipulate symbols as they take on roles and transform objects into something else. Children explore social relationships, too—experimenting with various social roles, discovering points of view in contrast to their own,

working out compromises, and negotiating differences (Spodek, Saracho, & Davis, 1991). Play enables children to extend their physical skills, language and literacy capabilities, and creative imaginations (Fromberg, 1987). The safe-haven play provides for the release of tensions, the expression of emotions, and the exploration of anxiety-producing situations has also been well documented (Santrock, 1994). Furthermore, there is convincing evidence that children's general social, communicative, and cognitive functioning in play tends to exceed the level expected of the same children in academic subjects in school (Chance, 1979; Fromberg, 1987). In fact, the research touting the value of play in children's lives is substantial, and most scientists agree that play is central to children's learning. Why, then, is there such resistance to letting children play in some early childhood programs, especially in elementary school?

Some educators suggest that the problem comes about because adults in our society have traditionally considered play the opposite of valuable work and therefore the opposite of learning (Fields & Spangler, 1995). Others believe adults are unaware of play's benefits and so categorize this essential activity as "just playing," equating it with frivolous or extraneous endeavors (Eiferman, 1971). Still others claim that adults confuse educational play (supported by the teacher with educational aims in mind) with random activity (which results when teachers fail to support play properly) (Spodek, 1985). The first two misconceptions are best addressed through better communication about how play helps children develop and learn. This means early childhood professionals who already believe that play is essential for children have to become more knowledgeable and eloquent in defending play to colleagues, parents, administrators, and other program decision makers (Fields & Spangler, 1995). The third misperception will be rectified only when teachers and administrators understand the ways play can vary in the classroom and ways they can support educational play.

Bergen (1988b) has developed a schema of play and learning consisting of four categories depicted along a continuum. These categories progress from play to nonplay, child centered to adult centered, from discovery learning to rote learning. Briefly, the four categories are as follows:

1. *Free play* This is the most child-centered, discovery-oriented category of play. Children choose whether to play, how to play, what to play, and when to play. Such play requires the teacher to provide a safe environment, supported by a variety of props, and minimal restrictions regarding how the play will proceed. Children's creating a grocery store out of a refrigerator box or turning the outdoor climber into a spaceship could illustrate this type of play. Making up their own card game or playing with language sounds are other possibilities.

2. *Guided play* This kind of play has many of the elements of the preceding category, but the experiences are carefully structured by the teacher so that certain discoveries are more likely to occur. Thus, guided play has more rules, fewer alternatives, and closer adult supervision than free play. Examples might include play at the workbench or computer or in a pretend grocery store in which the teacher asks questions or

models behaviors aimed at helping children focus more closely on the roles of customer and employee.

3. *Directed play* When the adult designates that children may choose one of three board games or asks all the children to play "duck, duck, goose," he or she is directing the play. The children's participation is required, and the means by which the children play is often adult determined. The primary kind of learning that takes place within this mode of play is receptive, with the emphasis on verbal instructions and explanations.

4. *Work disguised as play* This category describes task-oriented activities that the teacher attempts to transform into directed- or guided-play episodes. Playing a spelling game or conducting an addition facts race are typical examples. Most work disguised as play involves rote learning. Although it may be a more enjoyable way to engage in practice and drill, it is no longer play because it contains none of the elements of play described at the onset of this section.

Bergen (1988b) points out that the school day for preschoolers and children in the lower elementary grades should include many opportunities for free play and guided play. There are limited benefits to devoting much time to directed play and even fewer for the fourth category. Teachers who transpose these desired emphases by focusing on the last two categories to the exclusion of free play and guided play are not promoting the kind of play from which children benefit the most. The same is true for teachers who take an entirely hands-off view of play (Whiren, 1995). This happens when they allow play but do nothing to enhance or facilitate it. Practitioners who fail to provide a rich background of experiences as a foundation for play, who neglect to rotate props, ask questions, or provide information periodically to enlarge children's perceptions, are depriving children of valuable opportunities to develop and extend their play. Neither overcontrolling the play nor failing to support it altogether are consistent with developmentally appropriate practice.

Implications

1. Early childhood professionals support children's play when they talk to parents and colleagues about the value of play and its relationship to children's development and learning.

2. One or more long blocks of time are devoted during the school day for children to become engaged in

play. Some educators suggest no less than 60 minutes at a time (Cummings, 1991a, 1991b; Michigan State Board of Education, 1992).

3. Classroom space and materials are organized to enable children to engage in both solitary and collaborative play.
4. Play is integrated into all curricular domains.
5. A variety of props and other materials are available with which to play.
6. Adults are joyful and playful as they work with children and stimulate children's play by modeling, taking roles, offering information, asking questions, playing with language, and avoiding interrupting the play when they are not needed.
7. The sound and activity levels within the classroom reflect the quality of children's play—high-quality play is often noisy and active.

Children's Learning Is Influenced by Early Dispositions and Perceptions

The whole time children are acquiring knowledge and skills, they are also developing dispositions toward learning. Dispositions are the typical reaction patterns people develop toward various life events. Penchants, traits, tendencies, or attitudes are other words that describe such reactions. For example, when confronted with a new idea, a child might have the disposition to be curious or apathetic, open minded or rejecting. Whichever of these reactions the child habitually displays, one may infer that he or she has developed a disposition in that direction.

Dispositions have their foundations in early childhood and last a lifetime. As children see certain dispositions modeled by the people around them and as they are reinforced for displaying like behaviors, they adopt those dispositions as their own (Katz & Chard, 1989). Dispositions are not taught directly, nor do they come about as the result of a single incident. Instead, they emerge through accumulated experiences. Consequently, dispositions can be strengthened or weakened by the educational practices children encounter each day.

To illustrate, let us consider a classroom in which children's questions are treated as interruptions, the pursuit of one right answer is emphasized, and a strict timetable governs children's activities. These kinds of strategies detract from children's disposition for

curiosity. On the other hand, to strengthen that disposition, the teacher could provide children with intriguing materials to examine, encourage questioning and other investigative behaviors, allow children to pursue self-determined projects, modify the classroom schedule in line with children's interests, and promote students' search for multiple solutions to problems. Likewise, the disposition to be cooperative is weakened when competition is used to spur children's performance but promoted when teachers encourage group problem solving and implement group rewards.

In addition to dispositions, children form perceptions about themselves and about school. These perceptions are subjective, personal evaluations children make regarding their sense of competence, worth, and security. Interactions with others at school and the overall school climate are major contributors to the conclusions children make. Depending on whether such experiences are predominantly positive or negative, children may perceive themselves as secure or insecure, capable or incapable, or belonging or not belonging. In addition, they may come to perceive school as worthwhile or useless, rewarding or punitive, enjoyable or tedious.

Like dispositions, perceptions evolve gradually. Initially, they are difficult to discern from children's outward behaviors. For instance, youngsters required to master isolated skills prematurely may willingly perform as desired while simultaneously formulating a negative perception of school and themselves as learners. Only after such perceptions are well grounded do they become evident. By that time, they have become relatively enduring. Consequently, we can surmise that the early childhood years are an optimal period for the development of dispositions and perceptions. This is why early childhood educators must exercise particular care to create program environments in which children's favorable dispositions and perceptions are enhanced.

Implications

1. Teachers and administrators strengthen positive dispositions and perceptions among children when they carefully consider the dispositions and perceptions they hope children will develop in their programs (e.g., enthusiasm for learning, curiosity, absorption in tasks, deriving pleasure from effort and mastery, friendliness, generosity, honesty, cooperation, self-confidence).

2. Early childhood educators model the dispositions they wish to strengthen in children.

3. The early childhood program climate promotes children's feelings of competence, worth, and security.

4. Personnel consider to what extent program procedures and structures may undermine the dispositions and perceptions they hope children will develop. Such analyses take into account both direct and indirect strategies, intended and unintended outcomes. When incongruities are discovered, practices and routines are restructured to promote more favorable results.

CONTEXTS OF CHILDHOOD DEVELOPMENT AND LEARNING

Rules of development are the same for all children, but social contexts shape children's development into different configurations.—Bowman (1994)

Children are born and carry out their lives within many contexts. This includes the *biological* makeup bestowed on them by their parents and the *environment* in which they develop. That environment is made up of the immediate and extended family; extrafamilial settings such as neighborhood, childcare center, or school; and the culture and society. These contexts often overlap and are embedded within one another (Bronfenbrenner, 1989). They can be depicted as a series of concentric rings as shown in Figure 2.2, with each system influencing and being influenced by the others.

The Biological Context

At the core of everything is the child. Each youngster is born possessing a unique biological heritage. Genetic givens include gender, temperament, and a timetable for the emergence of intellectual, emotional, and physical capacities. In addition, young children are born with a predisposition to act on the environment, learn, and seek social stimulation as well as form bonds with other people (Sroufe et al., 1996). These traits in combination provide the biological boundaries within which development and learning take place.

The Immediate Context

Development and learning are further influenced by the immediate environment—all the people, objects, settings, and resources with which the child has direct contact. At birth, this context is dominated by the family. Eventually, additional settings (e.g., family childcare home, childcare center, school, playground, neighborhood, or 4-H group) become increasingly influential.

The Socioeconomic Context

All the immediate settings in which children sometimes find themselves are further embedded in a broader socioeconomic context. The impact of social and economic factors on children's development is frequently indirect but profound. For instance, the materials provided in a classroom and the curricula children encounter at school are shaped by educators, parents, and school boards using resources within a particular community. General economic factors and community-based beliefs also contribute to the educational program offered students. Indirectly, all these factors have an impact on each child even though the parties may have no direct contact with one another or the children.

The Sociocultural Context

Individuals, families, schools, and communities exist within a society and a culture and are greatly influenced by these, the broadest of all environments. The sociocultural context, the outermost ring in Figure 2.2,

FIGURE 2.2
The Ecological Context of Child Development and Learning

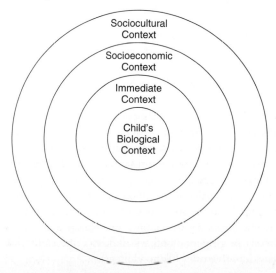

is defined by the belief patterns shared by groups of people. These beliefs shape the structure of various societal institutions (e.g., legal, economic, religious, and political systems) and other social structures such as social class. In addition, within and across societies there exist cultural groups who share more narrowly defined beliefs, norms, and values and who differ from one another in their basic approaches to living. Essential cultural variations exist regarding the way human beings relate to one another, the significance of time, personality types most valued, how humans relate to nature, and fundamental notions of whether human beings are innately good or bad (Berns, 1996). As a result of how different groups approach these issues, some children learn that cooperation is more highly valued than competition, and others learn the reverse. One cultural group might interpret a child's assertive behavior as a positive sign of independence, whereas another would be dismayed at the child's lack of deference. In some groups children are encouraged to revere nature; in some they are taught to control it. Which belief system prevails for children is a function of the cultural context in which they find themselves.

Contextual Relationships and Impacts

None of the contexts described here exists in isolation or exerts its influence apart from the rest. They are all interdependent, both influencing and being influenced by the others. For instance, children are not passive recipients of environmental impacts. They actively contribute to their own development and to the creation of the contexts in which they live and learn. Knowing this, for example, we may observe that a "resistant" child frequently elicits rule-related confrontations from adults and that such behavior, in turn, prompts the child to become increasingly resistant. Similarly, the family environment may be strengthened or weakened by changes that occur in the socioeconomic context surrounding it. However, because influence is bidirectional, families also affect socioeconomic forces, demanding alterations in services and community organizations to support their changing needs. This interdependence among contexts makes it clear that intervention with the child will have an impact on the other contexts within which he or she functions, such as the family. Also, what goes on in the family or neighborhood will influence the child's behavior in the early childhood program.

Finally, the significance that biological variables, other immediate environments, socioeconomic, and sociocultural factors have for young children is always mediated by decisions and interactions within their families (Sroufe et al., 1996). As discussed in the introduction, families are children's first teachers. The interrelationships among contexts and the dynamic nature of their influence on child development and learning suggest important implications for early childhood educators.

Implications

1. Professionals must take into account many dimensions when considering children's early education and determining appropriate methods of intervention.
2. The collective influence of all the contexts referred to in Figure 2.2 is unique for each child. Although some effects may be shared among a group of children, the total milieu for one youngster is unlike that of any other. This means each child is distinct from all others and requires individual consideration at all times.
3. Early childhood programs not only influence children and families but are themselves influenced by the contexts within which they operate. It is neither possible nor desirable to try to work with children in isolation.
4. Because children function within a variety of social settings, communication among those settings is essential. This means continuity among the programs children attend simultaneously (e.g., child-care center and elementary school) is natural and well planned. The same is true as children move from one setting one year (e.g., Head Start) to another the next year (e.g., kindergarten.)

THE OVERARCHING PRINCIPLE OF DEVELOPMENTAL DIRECTION

Both development and learning proceed in predictable directions. In other words, there is a beginning point from which development and learning progress. The principle of developmental direction defines that forward progress. For instance, in the body, maturation proceeds from top to bottom (head to tail) and midline to outer extremities, which is why infants are born with large heads and proportionately smaller lower bodies. The head region, containing the brain, on which all life depends, is more developed than the posterior region, which is not immediately necessary for survival. For the same reason, babies gain control of their head and neck muscles (lifting, turning, and holding up the head) prior to mastering control of their legs and feet. Likewise, the heart and other internal organs are fully coordinated in the newborn, whereas coordination of the hands takes place much later. These outward manifestations of developmental direction are obvious to even the casual observer, but other, more subtle, examples of internal change are equally important for educators to know about. Such changes influence child development and learning throughout the preschool and elementary years.

Development/learning proceeds from simple to complex, known to unknown, self to other, whole to part, concrete to abstract, enactive to symbolic, exploratory to goal directed, inaccurate to more accurate, and impulsive to self-controlled.

Simple to Complex

There are literally hundreds of examples of how this facet of developmental direction influences children's lives. To conserve space, let us consider just one—how children develop categories. At first, toddlers may categorize all fuzzy living creatures into one simple category, "doggies." Gradually as they gain experience and their cognitive powers expand, children differentiate among fuzzy creatures, thereby creating multiple categories, "doggies" and "kitties." Over time, these categorizations will become increasingly complex as children differentiate breeds of cats and dogs, friendly versus unfriendly characteristics of each, real and pretend examples.

Complexity increases as numbers of variables multiply and as the discriminations among those variables become less acute. Also, combining elements is more complex than dealing with them separately. This is why it is more complicated for a child to put together a puzzle containing eight large pieces than one containing four and why it is easier to put together puzzles in which the color and shape of the pieces are extremely different as opposed to ones in which pieces are varied in color but shaped alike. Teachers have this principle in mind when they gradually introduce challenge to children by increasing numbers of elements,

offering finer discriminations for children to consider, and asking children to group and regroup objects and events in different ways.

Known to Unknown

Children base what they learn and do on what is familiar. They build skills on previously learned behaviors. More sophisticated concepts grow out of those that already exist for them. When children can make connections between their prior knowledge and new experiences, those experiences become meaningful. When they cannot, the experiences are irrelevant. This is why it is necessary for teachers to discover what children know and can do prior to introducing brand-new material. It also provides the rationale for addressing concepts within a context that makes sense to the children. Thus, a teacher would introduce mammalian characteristics using as examples animals common in the children's environment, not ones they had seen only in pictures.

Self to Other

The young child's world revolves around him- or herself. All new experiences are considered within this sphere. It is not surprising then that among children's first words are *me* and *mine*. This preoccupation with the self is the child's way of learning about what is closest to him or her and of relating new experiences to familiar ones. At first, children's egocentric interpretations result from an erroneous assumption that all views of the world are identical and so must resemble their own. As experiences occur in which that perspective is challenged and as children develop greater cognitive sophistication, their interpretations expand. They eventually recognize that multiple perspectives are possible and those perspectives might differ. As this understanding takes hold, children become more adept at recognizing, valuing, and accommodating the needs, reactions, and experiences of others. This principle further underscores the importance of relating knowledge and skills to children in ways that have personal meaning. Explanations and experiences that make sense to adults but not to children do not enhance children's development and learning. This principle should also serve as a reminder that children's egocentric world view is a function of their development, not an aberration.

Whole to Part

Children perceive and experience the world in integrated, unified ways, moving from wholes to parts and general to specific understandings. Something like this happens to adults when they go to a movie for the first time. They usually come away with a basic understanding of the plot and sensory impressions of color, sound, and feelings. On seeing the same movie again, people often perceive things they missed initially because they are moving from the holistic sensation of the first experience to paying more attention to detail. A third or fourth trip could reveal even more specifics, contributing to better comprehension of subtle plot nuances as well as the mechanics of filmmaking.

Children take in experiences holistically in much the same way. Only after they have grasped the essentials of that experience do the details become meaningful to them. Hence, children might hear a song several times over before actually differentiating some of the words. Likewise, the value of paying attention to letter-sound associations develops only after children have formulated a concept of print and how it relates to their daily lives. Introducing the specifics prematurely or out of context renders them meaningless. Much the same result would occur were people shown a brief clip of movie dialogue and then asked to analyze it. This mechanical exercise would not lead to substantive gains in their understanding of the story or increase its personal relevance. In fact, if it happened often enough, it might promote a perception of films as boring or purposeless, thereby decreasing their appeal.

Teachers who think about the whole-to-part principle offer children a broad array of rich, multisensory experiences. They repeat activities often, giving children plenty of time to explore and formulate their own impressions and conceptualizations. As children express interest and understanding, teachers draw children's attention to relevant details that enlarge youngster's perceptions and challenge them to try alternatives or reconsider old ideas. Conversely, teachers are careful not to teach children skills or facts in isolation. They work from the general to the specific rather than the other way around.

Concrete to Abstract

The most concrete experiences are tangible ones that involve physical contact with real objects. They are ones in which children taste, touch, and smell as well as see and hear. The further removed an experience is from this tangible state and the fewer senses children are required to employ, the more abstract it becomes. Providing children with real leaves to look at, handle, take apart, smell, and taste are concrete ways to enhance children's interest in and knowledge about leaves. Giving children pictures to explore or having them cut leaves from magazines is a step removed from the real thing and so is more abstract. Even further removed is having children watch the teacher point to leaves in a book or on the bulletin board. The most distant and therefore most abstract activity involves having children think about leaves as the teacher talks about them.

Children throughout the preschool and elementary years benefit from concrete experiences in all developmental domains and across all subject areas. The more unfamiliar the object or phenomenon, the more this is true. Even adults who are learning something for the first time do better when given opportunities for real-life experiences rather than just seeing something modeled or having it explained. The danger in ignoring this principle is that children may parrot what the adult wants to hear but not truly understand essential concepts. For this reason teachers provide children with many firsthand experiences and tangible objects on which to base their learning.

Enactive to Symbolic

Enactive Representation   Children begin representing the world enactively. They use their bodies to reconstruct or act out events and roles using objects, gestures, sounds, and words. This is a very tangible, concrete way to think through an experience and the most basic form of representation (Lawton, 1987). Teachers observe enactive representation when, after taking a field trip to feed the ducks, the children return to the classroom imitating duck sounds, waddling, and making "quacking" gestures with their hands. Such representations duplicate and preserve many of the distinctive qualities one associates with the actual phenomenon, ducks.

Iconic Representation   A somewhat more abstract mode of representation involves children making pictures or constructing three-dimensional images of what they see and think about. These are iconic representations. Youngsters who reproduce or create their own interpretations of objects and events using art or construction materials such as blocks are demonstrating iconic representation. Thus, following the duck field trip, some youngsters might paint what they saw, and others might sculpt ducklike shapes in clay. Although these pictorial representations share many of the same characteristics as real ducks (e.g., color and shape), other concrete cues such as sound and motion are less obvious.

Symbolic Representation　The ultimate and most abstract means of representation is symbolic. In this mode, children manipulate words and symbols, such as letters and numerals, to interpret and represent particular objects and events. Youngsters coming back from a field trip could represent what occurred by dictating or writing descriptions of the trip. However, the symbols they use no longer bear any resemblance to real ducks, which makes this level of representation the most removed from the children's actual experience.

Enactive representation occurs in its most rudimentary form within the first year of life. Infants think in terms of actions and about objects by acting on them. Gradually, these enactive episodes become more elaborate, blossoming into pretend play in toddlerhood. Iconic representation first appears at about 18 months, with symbolic representation following soon after. As one form of representation emerges, children do not discard earlier forms. Rather, they build on and combine the different modes to enhance their conceptualizations and understandings.

The importance of these different modes of representation provides a rationale for including materials and experiences related to all three in early childhood classrooms. Children do not outgrow their need for pretend play, art, or construction materials when moving into the elementary grades. Nor is toddlerhood too early to encourage children to experiment with drawing or writing surfaces and related tools and implements. This continuum also suggests that the developmentally appropriate early childhood curriculum gives children ample opportunity to explore concepts through enactive representation prior to introducing children to the more abstract iconic and symbolic representations related to those concepts.

Exploratory to Goal Directed

Exploration　There are many different notions of how children move along the continuum from randomly experimenting with objects and relationships to purposefully applying the knowledge and skills they gain. However, even theories that represent otherwise incompatible interpretations begin at the exploration phase. That is, children experiment and "play around" with objects and materials prior to using them in prescribed ways. Exploration is a time of self-discovery that occurs through the spontaneous manipulation of objects and informal social interactions with peers and adults. Knowledge grows as these interactions are mentally organized (Bergen, 1988a). This is why children who had never seen a lotto game would have difficulty starting to play it right away. They need time to handle the pieces, look at the different pictures on the cards and boards, and experiment with making some matches. Prior to ever seeing that particular game, youngsters would need many previous chances to explore the whole notion of game playing, working with others in a group, and so forth. Were they to plunge into the game without that exploratory experience, chances are they would explore anyway, thereby missing some of the directions or not paying attention to the course of the action. The adult, trying to keep the children on task, would be fighting children's natural tendencies to explore. Neither adult nor children would benefit from the experience. For the adult, playing lotto might turn into a discipline-focused confrontation; for the children, the cognitive aspects of the game would not necessarily register.

The early childhood years mark a time when much of children's attention and energy is focused on exploring the world around them. As Hymes (1980) says, children are the aliens to the planet; they are the new beings for whom experiences are fresh and unfamiliar. We "old-timers" sometimes forget how novel it all is for children and how much there is to discover. Also, all the discovering is not over by ages 4 or 5 or 7 or 8. The exploration phase is the threshold from which children gradually acquire knowledge and skills, practice their newfound understandings and behaviors, and eventually generalize what they have discovered across a variety of situations. It is the foundation of all understanding.

Acquisition   Once children have thoroughly explored a phenomenon, they display signs of being ready to move to the acquisition phase of learning. Children signal this when they ask, "How do you play this game?" "What comes next?" or "Why is the grass green?" Using a variety of indirect and direct instructional strategies, teachers respond to children's cues. In doing so, they help children refine their understanding, guide their attention, and make connections (Bredekamp, 1991; Deiner, 1993). This form of inquiry is usually more goal oriented for both teachers and children than is characteristic of pure exploration. However, it is neither rigid nor unidirectional in nature. Children still have a lot of latitude in how they proceed and in the paths they take.

Practice   Acquisition of new knowledge and skills is followed by a time during which children concentrate on practicing what they have learned. They use the new behavior or knowledge repeatedly and in a variety of circumstances. This is exemplified by the child who, having learned to play lotto, wants to play again and again, enjoying rather than tiring of the repetitions. Children who have just learned to wash the dishes beg to do them, at least for a while, and youngsters who have learned to dribble a basketball try it out in the hall, on the playground, in the gym, and on the sidewalk. In every case, the child's practice is self-motivated and self-initiated. It represents the tangible way in which children gain mastery. Teachers facilitate children's practice when they allow them time to play out the same scenarios over and over again and when they follow children's lead in repeating activities more than once as well as varying the practice conditions.

Generalization   Eventually, children have enough grounding to apply their newfound knowledge or skills to novel situations. When this happens, they enter the generalization phase of learning, which is the most advanced and goal-directed phase along the learning continuum. Within this phase children apply what they have learned in many ways and adjust their thinking to fit new circumstances or demands. They also formulate novel hypotheses, which may prompt them to initiate new explorations, thereby beginning the cycle again (Bredekamp, 1991). It is worth noting that the goal orientation so prominent in the general-

ization phase remains internally inspired. Therefore, the role of the teacher becomes that of creating vehicles for children to make applications to real-world situations and providing meaningful situations children can use for learning.

Children proceed from exploratory to goal-directed activity within all realms of learning: aesthetic, affective, cognitive, language, physical, and social. Where they are in the process depends on their backlog of experiences and understandings as well as the learning opportunities available to them. Therefore, each child's progress along the continuum will differ for various threads within each realm as well as from realm to realm. In other words, children are not in any one phase of learning for everything simultaneously. Instead, youngsters may just be starting to explore some concepts or skills while acquiring, practicing, or generalizing others.

To accommodate such differences within and among children, teachers have to provide them with broad-based, open-ended activities. From these, children extrapolate experiences that correspond to the phase of learning most relevant to them. Thus, several children working with puzzles may use them for different purposes—exploration, practice, and so forth. Repeating activities is also a good idea because children need many opportunities to progress along the learning continuum. Furthermore, teachers must support children in whatever phase of learning they are in for a given activity using different instructional strategies as necessary (e.g., providing many varied materials for exploration; offering feedback, information, or asking questions as appropriate; giving children chances to practice what they have learned under many different conditions; and encouraging children to apply what they have learned to new situations). Such adaptations are more easily made within individualized and small-group instructional formats than whole-group ones.

Inaccurate to More Accurate

Children develop hypotheses about the world in which they live according to internal processes of acquiring, structuring, and restructuring knowledge. Subsequently, young children's natural thinking and reasoning processes are filled with trial and error and incorrect conclusions. All of these come about as a result of children's continuous efforts to order the world into understandable patterns (McKee, 1991). These so-called mistakes are central to children's mental development. They serve as the means by which children refine their thinking and enlarge it. As children experience the mental conflict that arises through events that challenge their deductions, they resolve the dilemma through further mental activity and so gradually develop more accurate thinking.

Because of this principle, educators must be cautious about focusing on children producing "right" answers. A child who answers "correctly" may be responding from rote memorization or inaccurate conclusions rather than accurate reasoning processes. For this reason, it is better to emphasize how children derive answers. Activities that involve children developing predictions, evaluating their experiences, problem solving, and figuring out what they know as well as how they know should be featured throughout the day.

Impulsive to Controlled

Young children are active, noisy beings who come about these characteristics naturally. It is hard for them to control their impulses to touch, make sounds, move, or go after what they want. Waiting and holding back are acquired skills that develop in tandem with children's cognitive, physical, emotional, and social concepts and behaviors. Their acquisition is supported when teachers and administrators create classroom environments in which children have opportunities to move about freely, express themselves openly, learn alternate strategies for achieving their goals, and practice ways of delaying gratification that are in keeping with their comprehension and abilities. Forcing children into a passive, inactive

state is unnatural and interferes with all other aspects of their development and learning.

Implications of Developmental Direction

1. Practitioners use the principle of developmental direction as a guide for designing activities to support children's progress from less mature/complex levels of knowledge and skill to more sophisticated ones.
2. Early childhood educators assume that within each activity, individual children will be in different places along the continuums associated with developmental direction. Their plans reflect this understanding.
3. Practitioners use the principle of developmental direction as a guide for simplifying and extending activities and routines in accordance with children's needs and interests.

SUMMARY

In this chapter, we outlined fundamental principles of childhood development and learning as well as the overarching principle of developmental direction. Corresponding implications for program design and classroom practice were identified for each of these. As readers explore the ramifications of these concepts in the chapters that follow, the ideas expressed here will be revisited again and again. There is no element of early childhood education they do not touch. Activities and routines, materials, the physical environment, classroom management, methods of parental involvement, and assessment procedures are all influenced by these principles. With this understanding, it is time to turn our attention to setting the stage for children's learning.

 Applying What You Read in This Chapter

1. **Discuss**
   a. Based on your reading and your experiences with young children, discuss each of the questions that open this chapter.
   b. Select two principles of development and learning you believe are most important for people untrained in early childhood education to know about. Explain your choices and what you would emphasize about each.

   c. Assume you have been asked to orient two new staff members who have worked with children before but not with ones between 3 and 8 years of age. For a preschool program, presume the person has worked with high schoolers; for a school-age program, assume the person has experience with 2-year-olds only. Describe the most important things you would want the new staff members to know about the age groups with whom they will work.

d. Based on your own experiences growing up, provide examples related to three of the principles of development and learning described in this chapter.

2. **Observe**

a. Observe two children of approximately the same age who are involved in the same activity. Note similarities in their behavior as well as differences.

b. Observe a teacher carrying out an activity with one or more children. Identify which of the following continuums related to developmental direction were evident throughout the time you observed:

   Simple to complex.
   Known to unknown.
   Self to other.
   Whole to part.
   Concrete to abstract.
   Enactive to symbolic.
   Exploratory to goal directed.
   Inaccurate to more accurate.
   Impulsive to self-controlled.

   Provide examples to illustrate your observations.

3. **Carry out an activity**

a. First, choose one of the following early childhood activities:

   Child learning to button her coat.
   Child learning to tell a familiar story from beginning to end.
   Child stacking nesting cups in order.
   Child learning to wait her turn at the snack table.
   Child learning to wash his hands properly.

   Next, select one of the principles of developmental direction outlined in this chapter. Then explain how you would use that principle to support children's forward progress in the activity you chose.

b. Select a trade book aimed at parents describing some aspect of child development. Describe to what extent the book you chose supports or fails to support the principles of development and learning you read about in this chapter.

c. Create a bumper sticker that captures the essence of one of the principles of development or learning described in Chapter 2.

d. Review written information describing an early childhood program in your community. Based on the program's written philosophy and program description, discuss to what extent the program is congruent or incongruent with the principles described in Chapter 2.

4. **Create something for your portfolio**

a. Select a fundamental belief you have about child development and learning. Think both about children in general and specifically about the ages of the children in a program where you are working, volunteering, or doing a practicum. Describe how that belief would impact the following program dimensions: the children's program, staff, materials, physical space, budget, and family involvement. Identify practices that would be incompatible with the principle you have chosen.

5. **Add to your journal**

a. What is the most significant thing you have learned about child development and learning based on your readings and experience with children?

b. Reflect on the extent to which the content of this chapter corresponds to what you have observed in the field. What is your reaction to any discrepancies you perceive?

c. In what ways have you utilized child development and learning principles in your work with children? What goals do you have for yourself in this regard?

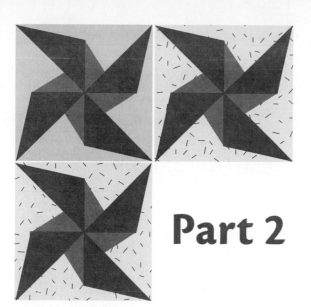

Part 2

Setting the Stage for Learning

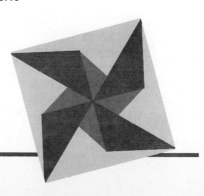

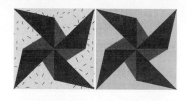

Chapter 3

Planning and Implementing Effective Small-Group Activities

You may wonder:

Why do teachers write lesson plans? Why are plans necessary?

Is formal planning as important for children in childcare settings or nursery schools as it is for children enrolled in elementary programs?

As a teacher in my own classroom, will I have to write the same kind of plans as I'm writing now?

As an early childhood professional, what kinds of teaching strategies should I use?

How can I implement a single plan that accommodates developmental differences among children?

In this introduction to planning and implementing effective small-group activities, we present information to help you answer these questions.

Estaban Ramirez is student teaching in the kindergarten of an employer-sponsored childcare center. His roommates are amazed at the time and care he puts into writing lesson plans. After all, the children are only 5 and 6 years old. His friends cannot understand how planning for children that age could be so involved.

Sometimes people are surprised at how much planning it takes to ensure a smoothly running early childhood classroom. They may erroneously assume that children's participation is mostly spontaneous, requiring little more from adults than simply putting out materials for children to use. However, the difference be-

tween providing children with truly educational experiences and merely keeping them busy or entertained is *planning* (Anziano, Billman, Kostelnik, & Soundy, 1995). In fact, planning is a key element of *high-quality* early childhood programs, and the ability to plan developmentally appropriate activities distinguishes *effective* practices from ineffective ones (Bredekamp & Copple, 1997; Doherty-Derkowski, 1995).

WHY PLAN?

Thorough planning provides the foundation for effective teaching. Early childhood professionals plan ahead to create positive environments for teaching and learning (Freiberg & Driscoll, 1996). Although the design of teachers' plans varies from program to program, the aims of planning are universal. Planning helps teachers do the following:

❑ Organize their thoughts and actions.
❑ Think creatively about what they want to do.
❑ Gather needed equipment and materials in advance.
❑ Map out ways to address immediate instructional objectives and long-term educational aims.
❑ Address the needs of the "whole child."
❑ Tailor programs to accommodate the needs of specific children.
❑ Address differences among learners.
❑ Communicate to others what they are doing.
❑ Identify a standard by which learning and teaching can be accurately and appropriately evaluated.

Appropriate planning leads to purposeful and comprehensive instruction. This conveys a sense of direction and order that children perceive and appreciate (Doyle, 1986). Implementing carefully sequenced plans gives teachers valuable information about children, materials, teaching methods, and outcomes. As a result, teachers are better able to chart the progress of individual students and the group as a whole, noting where advances are being made and where change might be necessary (Dodge, 1995). In this way, early childhood professionals use their plans as a basis for assessing children's development and learning as well as their own teaching.

Lack of planning, on the other hand, results in chaos. Children may wander about aimlessly or engage in inappropriate behavior for lack of something better to do. Also, valuable instruction time is lost when teachers are scrambling at the last minute to get their lessons together or gather needed materials. Other negative consequences of inadequate planning include meeting the needs of some youngsters but not all and creating superficial, irrelevant activities that fail to stimulate children's learning. In every instance, poor planning yields poor-quality programs for children. To avoid these negative results, early childhood practitioners must acquire effective planning skills.

CHARACTERISTICS OF EFFECTIVE PLANNING

Effective early childhood planning takes into account individuals and groups of children. It addresses immediate objectives and long-term goals as well as what is currently going on in the classroom and what might be needed in the future. Such planning reflects the teacher's knowledge and understanding of how young children develop and learn and the context in which children's learning takes place. A strong grasp of relevant subject matter is also necessary (Bredekamp & Copple, 1997; Saracho, 1993). Additionally, whether designed for a single activity or for the program as a whole, good planning is flexible enough to accommodate children's changing needs and to take advantage of teachable moments as they arise.

TEACHERS AS PLANNERS

The act of planning involves purpose, organization, foresight, preparation, and deliberate decision making. Most importantly, early childhood educators keep in mind the children for whom their plans are being developed: their needs, interests, and strengths (Deiner, 1993). Effective planners also take into account the materials at their disposal, the physical space in which the plan will be carried out, and the context of classroom, family, and community. Thus, teachers engaged in developmentally appropriate practices recognize the ecological nature of planning. They understand that although a plan may be technically correct, if it is created without considering specific children and context, it could be inappropriate. Janet Fowler learned this lesson her first day on the job.

Janet arrived at the Willow Street Cooperative Preschool to begin work as the new head teacher. Among the activities she planned for the day was marble painting at the art table during free-choice time. She wanted to provide an open-ended art activity the children would enjoy. She also thought it would be nice for them to create decorations for the room. Janet reasoned this would be a good way for the children to make the classroom their own as well as have fun.

Getting to the classroom early, Janet set up the materials: four metal pie pans, marbles, circles of paper cut to fit the bottom of the pans, baby food jars half filled with thick poster paint, plastic spoons for retrieving the marbles from the jars, and smocks. She posted a sign on which were drawn four figures, illustrating that four children at a time could participate in the activity. She covered the table with newspaper to protect it and positioned a drying rack nearby where children could hang their fin-ished paintings. Looking over the area, she felt satisfied that everything was ready and went to the door to greet the children and parent volunteer as they came into the classroom.

The children were intrigued by the materials at the art table. However, before Janet could get everyone to put on a smock, Carl poured some of the paint onto the news-paper, treating it like finger paint. As he tried to push his sleeves out of the way, paint ran down his elbows and onto his shirt. LaTanya tried to roll her marble in a pan with no paper but a lot of paint. As she moved the marble in the pan, paint sloshed over the sides. Soon six or seven children were crowded around the table trying to get to the materials. Voices rose as children became upset over not getting a turn or stepping in spilled paint. While Janet struggled to help the children, she wondered how the activity had so quickly gotten out of hand. This was not what had happened when she tried the same ac-tivity last spring with the 4-year-olds in the Head Start center where she had worked.

What Janet did not realize was that the children at the Willow Street Cooperative Preschool had never tried marble painting before. Moreover, none of the children had access to similar paints at home. Because poster paints were only rarely used at the school in the past, even returning children had little background with the medium. Additionally, the youngsters had no prior experience with the use of signs to indicate how many children could participate in an area at a time. Although such symbols are generally a good structuring tool, children do not automatically know what they mean. Finally, Janet forgot that children who are in a classroom from fall to spring know much more about classroom routines and expectations than do youngsters coming together for the first time. Her plan for marble painting, which worked well with one group of chil-dren, was ineffective with this group at this time. Al-though Janet had a good plan, which included a goal and careful preparation, she forgot to consider the con-textual nature of planning. To avoid such mistakes, ef-fective planners assume each of the following roles as they plan: diagnostician, designer, organizer, and evalu-ator (Brewer, 1998; Hildebrand, 1997b; Saracho, 1993).

Teachers as Diagnosticians   The first phase of plan-ning involves thinking about the children in relation

to what is being taught. This phase enables the teacher to make an appropriate match between instruction and the knowledge, skills, and understandings children bring to the activity. In their diagnostic role, teachers ask themselves questions such as the following:

What experiences have the children had?

What are the children interested in knowing or finding out?

What abilities and skills do the children possess?

What do families hope their children will learn?

What goal does the program/school district have for the children?

What are my short-term goals for the children?

What are my long-term goals for individual chil-dren and the entire group?

What is the correct level of challenge for this child/these children in relation to this activity?

Practitioners find out the answers to these ques-tions by observing children carefully, talking with chil-dren, and keeping records of children's interactions with materials, peers, and adults. Asking families to supply relevant information is another strategy you can use in the diagnostic phase of planning. Informal assessments throughout the day's activities are the pri-mary source for such information at both the prepri-mary and primary levels. More formal strategies such as designing specific activities to garner information about children's ideas and skills and asking for periodic work samples are also useful.

Teachers as Designers   After making an initial diag-nosis of children's needs and capabilities, teachers con-sider how to frame their instruction within the guide-lines of developmentally appropriate practice. This means thinking about ways to apply the principles of child development and learning described in Chapter 2 of this textbook. The overarching principle of devel-opmental direction is a further consideration. Sam-ple questions related to the designer role include the following:

How does what I know about child development and learning relate to this plan?

How does what I know about developmental di-rection relate to this plan? For instance, how might children proceed from simple to complex within this plan? Or, how might children proceed from concrete to abstract within this plan?

How can I start with the children's knowledge of this and relate it to what I want to teach?

Teachers as Organizers   Using the information of the previous planning phases, teachers next plan to organize the instruction. Organizing involves analyzing resources, considering long-term goals, determining short-range objectives, identifying potential materials, and matching goals/objectives with strategies. Typical questions teachers ask as organizers are these:

What is the purpose of this plan?

What abilities, skills, and understandings must children possess to successfully participate?

What processes will help children achieve identified goals?

What is the sequence in which learning might logically take place?

What materials are necessary to carry out the plan?

When and where will the plan be implemented?

How can I make the best use of the materials and resources available?

How will I know that the children are learning?

How will I measure their learning and document their progress?

Teachers as Evaluators   A significant role for every teacher is that of evaluator. In the planning process, this dimension requires teachers to think about the match between what they plan and what actually occurs. Teachers plan in advance evaluation questions to answer when the activity is over. Answers to these questions help teachers analyze the current state of affairs and plan for the future. Typical questions considered within the evaluator role include these:

How closely did the plan match what happened?

Did the plan meet the children's instructional needs?

Who benefited/did not benefit from participating in the plan and why?

What are ways to extend this plan in the future?

How should the plan be changed and why?

What unanticipated events occurred that should be considered in future planning?

Teachers as Writers   Working your way through the dimensions of planning just described is best done in writing (Hildebrand, 1997b). Written plans provide a tangible record of the teacher's thinking and a tool for communicating with others. Past plans are more easily retrieved in written form, serving as a valuable resource for future planning. They also document instruction for personal and accountability purposes. Most significantly, writing plans down can actually aid in thinking through your ideas from start to finish (Bodrova & Leong, 1996). Written forms provide a methodical guide for answering all the relevant questions teachers must pose as diagnosticians, designers, organizers, and evaluators. Not only does writing ensure that each dimension is addressed, but repeatedly going through the step-by-step process of written planning creates habits that gradually become internalized. In fact, some people claim that the main value of writing plans is not the final product achieved but the thinking process that produces them (Shoemaker, 1995, 55).

Novices and seasoned practitioners alike "benefit from thinking through their plans in written form. Both must know *why* they are doing *what* they are doing and *how* specifically they will accomplish their aims" (Eliason & Jenkins, 1994). However, the amount of detail that goes into written plans varies with the writer's experience. In general, inexperienced planners profit from writing their ideas in great detail. This makes it easier to check for accuracy and completeness. As teachers gain practice writing and thinking about planning, the need for extensive written detail gradually decreases. Over time, teachers become better able to think comprehensively while writing only what is necessary for *someone else* (e.g., a parent volunteer, assistants in the program, or the substitute teacher) to follow their plan successfully. In this way, learning to plan proceeds from the concrete act of representing all your thinking to the more abstract form of conveying only its essence. Planning also shifts from focusing mostly on enhancing your own comprehension to helping other people understand what you intend.

In this text we present detailed activity plans first to help you think through all the necessary steps involved in effective planning. Later, we present an abbreviated form that many experienced teachers use in their day-to-day work with children. Regardless of whether you are a new or an experienced planner, you must think about certain things in order to create developmentally appropriate plans for children. These considerations are basic to all planning.

PLANNING BASICS

Teachers plan activities for solitary children, for small groups of children, and for the entire class to participate in at one time. All of these activity types can be thought about in similar ways with minor variations. In this chapter we focus on activity plans in which five or six children participate at a time. Such experiences are often featured during small-group times or free-choice periods in early childhood classrooms. These kinds of activities form the building blocks for teachers' planning on a daily, weekly, and yearly basis (Deiner, 1993). In the chapter that follows, we discuss how to plan and implement activities in which the entire class participates at once. All of the elements that should be incorporated in a typical activity plan are outlined in Figure 3.1. A sample plan follows in Figure 3.2.

FIGURE 3.1
Activity Plan Format

Domain   One of the six curricular domains identified in this text: aesthetic, affective, cognitive, language, social, and physical.

Activity Name   The title of the activity.

Intermediate Objective   Intermediate objectives are listed in each of the chapters describing the curriculum. These identify desirable behaviors relevant to children's development and learning within the domain.

Content   The content that will be addressed in the activity. This content identifies the terms/vocabulary, facts, and principles relevant to the lesson.

Assumptions   The prerequisite knowledge and abilities the planner assumes children are bringing to the activity. The knowledge and skills children need to participate in the activity.

Immediate Objectives   A list of specific instructional objectives leading to the intermediate objective and tailored to meet the needs of the children involved.

Materials   A list of all necessary props or equipment.

Procedures   A step-by-step description of how to implement the activity. Procedures may include multiple teaching strategies.

Simplification   Ideas for reducing the complexity or abstractness of the activity.

Extension   Ideas for making the activity more challenging as children demonstrate the desire and ability to expand their knowledge and skills.

Hints for Success   Ways to structure the environment to increase safety and children's independence with the materials and to make it easier for the adult to set up or manage the activity.

Evaluation   Ways to assess children's learning and the teaching methods used.

FIGURE 3.2
Sample Activity Plan

Domain Language   **Activity Name** Turnip Story Sequence

Intermediate Objective: Children will listen to a story, and then discuss the story sequence (Language Domain, Intermediate Objective 9).

Content
1. Sequence refers to the order in which events occur.
2. A story describes a series of events that progresses from beginning to end.
3. Changing the sequence of events in a story may change the story's meaning.

Assumptions
1. The children can see the flannel board and flannel figures clearly.
.. The children have sufficient receptive listening skills to attend to the story.
3. The children have heard the story of the Big, Big Turnip before.

Immediate Objectives
The child will be able to do these things:
1. Listen to the story one time through.
2. Name the characters in the story as the teacher points to them following his or her enactment of the story.
3. Assist the teacher in retelling the story in the correct sequence.

Materials: Flannel figures corresponding to the characters in the story "The Big, Big Turnip," a flannel board

Procedures

Objective 1: The child will **listen** to the story one time through.

Invite children to listen to the story "The Big, Big Turnip." Tell the story with enthusiasm and expression, placing the flannel board pieces on the board at appropriate points. Emphasize the names of the characters and the sequence in which they appear by repeating them each time a new character is introduced. Leave the characters on the board when the story is over.

Objective 2: The child will **name** the characters in the story as the teacher points to them following his or her enactment of the story.

Encourage the children to name the characters in order. Point to each one in line, beginning with the farmer. Ask the children to say the character's name when you point to it.

Objective 3: The child will **assist the teacher** in retelling the story in the correct sequence.

Hide the characters behind the flannel board. Ask the children to help tell the story by telling you which character to put on the board next.

Repeat this part of the activity more than once. Vary the procedure by giving each child a character that he or she is to put on the board when it is time for that character to appear in the story.

Simplification: Put the flannel board pieces at the bottom of the board facing the children. Raise them to the top of the board in sequence as you tell the story.

(continued on the next page)

FIGURE 3.2
(continued)

> **Extension:** Tell the story making mistakes in the sequence. Ask the children to help by correcting mistakes they hear. Ask children to talk about how the meaning of the story changed when the sequence varied. Another option is to encourage children to tell the story on their own.
>
> **Hints for Success:** Begin placing the flannel board pieces far enough to the right-hand side of the board so there is adequate room for all the characters to fit in a straight line across it.
>
> Make the materials available the rest of the day and the next several days so children can use the figures to tell stories on their own.
>
> **Evaluation:** Using a performance checklist, identify which of the three objectives outlined in this activity plan individual children met. Based on your observations of children's participation, describe how that information will influence your future instruction related to story sequence.

CREATING DEVELOPMENTALLY APPROPRIATE PLANS

All of the component parts of the activity plans just described are critical to the planning process. Considered individually, each makes an important contribution to the writer's understanding of how to translate goals for children into developmentally appropriate learning experiences (Dodge, 1995). Taken altogether, they address the diagnostic, design, organization, and evaluation roles of the effective planner. Let us recap what must be considered for each element.

Domain

The Children's Comprehensive Curriculum is divided into six domains representing the various aspects of whole-child learning described in Chapter 2 of this volume. Although curriculum integration is our ultimate aim, we have discovered that planners are most effective when they concentrate on one domain at a time until they are thoroughly familiar with the curriculum and are skilled in writing plans (Kostelnik, 1997a). With this in mind, your first task is to choose a domain within which to write your plan: aesthetics, affective, cognitive, language, physical, or social.

Activity Name

The name you select for your activity should be brief and descriptive. Cute titles that are hard to decipher are not as useful as functional names that clarify the main focus of your plan.

Intermediate Objective

Select an intermediate objective on which to concentrate within the domain you have selected. These are listed in the curriculum chapters of this textbook. This objective answers the question, "What is the purpose of this plan?"

Content

This segment of the plan identifies what you will teach. It should be developed based on your diagnosis of what the children already know and what would be useful and worthwhile for them to learn. Content addresses terms, facts, and principles relevant to the domain and the intermediate objective you have chosen. Terms are the vocabulary that describe activity-related objects and events (e.g., a *lamb* is a baby sheep, or *piglet* is the name given to a baby pig). Something known to exist or to have happened is a *fact* (e.g., sheep give birth to lambs; pigs give birth to piglets). Principles refer to combinations of facts and the relationships among them (e.g., animals give birth only to their own kind).

Accuracy is critical. Research your terms, facts, and principles and be able to explain in your own words what the lesson is about. Write down these ideas so both you or anyone else who is carrying out the plan will have a clear understanding of its content.

Assumptions

The assumptions represent the abilities, skills, and understandings children must possess to successfully participate in what is planned. There are two ways to develop an appropriate set of assumptions. One is to first determine what children already know and can do. Do this by observing and diagnosing their level of development prior to initiating your activity plan. (Suggestions for how to gather such information are offered in Chapter 16.) Next, organize your plan to build on these assumptions. For example, if you are aware that children already know how to blow bubbles without sucking in the water, your plan could expand on this ability. However, if you know that the children have not yet mastered blowing out, your plan may focus on teaching them this skill. Another approach to developing assumptions is to think of an activity that addresses the intermediate objective you have chosen. Next, consider what children will have to know or be able to do to participate. Observe children to determine if your assumptions are realistic. For instance, you may wish to carry out the story sequence activity described in Figure 3.2. That activity in its entirety takes about 20 minutes. Assuming that 3-year-olds can sit through such a long story and then participate in a follow-up discussion is not in keeping with what we know about the attention span and motor development of children this age. Recognizing this, you will choose a briefer story or eliminate one or two of the objectives. Shortening the activity increases the likelihood that children will enjoy their participation as well as benefit from it.

Immediate Objectives

Immediate objectives represent the step-by-step progression a child could go through to pursue a certain intermediate objective. This segment of the plan out-

lines the order in which children's learning might logically take place. Consequently, the intermediate objective and the immediate objectives are closely related. To create such a sequence, you will find the principle of developmental direction particularly useful. That principle gives you a tool for thinking about how to break down the broadly stated intermediate objective into a graduated series of more specifically defined aims. For instance, the intermediate objective of having children organize objects and events via classification can be broken down into several substeps. Possibilities include the following: exploring the objects, grouping them by at least one similar property, describing how they are alike, and regrouping them in a new way. These substeps progress from simple to more complex, from concrete to more abstract, and from exploratory to more goal directed and can be applied to any set of objects—leaves, shells, rocks, toy vehicles, keys, or buttons.

When formulating immediate objectives, think in terms of behavior (Charlesworth & Lind, 1995; Schmoker, 1996). That is, identify specific child actions that will signify that an objective has been achieved.

What objectives do you think the teacher has for the children in this activity?

With this in mind, immediate objectives are characterized by action words that you can observe as they occur, such as name, point, show, tell, describe, make, find, circle, select, compare, sort, measure, count, observe, predict, estimate, and evaluate. The immediate objectives for a leaf-sorting activity might be as follows. The child will (1) explore the various properties of the leaves (size, color, shape, edge, flexibility, and so on); (2) group the leaves according to one common property of her own choosing; (3) tell what property he used to group the leaves; and (4) regroup the objects, changing from one property to another of her own choosing. When objectives are stated in behavioral terms, you are able to determine the extent to which children successfully engage in the activity. If the objectives are all achieved, the children are ready for more challenging experiences. However, if children do not achieve some objectives, repeat the activity another time, create an alternate plan, or try a different mode of presentation. Breaking the objectives into even smaller steps may also be appropriate (Lay-Dopyera & Dopyera, 1993).

Because children develop and learn at varying rates, groups of children commonly perform at differing levels of the immediate objectives sequence. Some youngsters will spend a great deal of time exploring the leaves; others may be interested in grouping the leaves almost immediately; still others may be ready to move beyond single-property classification to grouping the leaves according to multiple criteria. Your job will be to follow the children's lead and challenge them with the next step of the sequence as appropriate. However, not every child will go through the entire sequence you plan in a single day. It might take some children all year or even longer to achieve the most advanced objectives. This is why you should repeat activities several times during the year and why developmentally appropriate activity plans include no less than three immediate objectives. In this way, the sequence of immediate objectives you create supplies a direction for learning and teaching in the classroom. They do not constitute performance criteria that all children must achieve simultaneously.

Materials

Determining what resources are needed to carry out a plan is an organizational function. This section requires a complete list of the materials you need to execute your plan. Effective planners consider everything necessary for the set-up, implementation, and clean-up phases of the activity. Enough detail should be provided that someone else would know what was needed even in your absence. Also, if you are doing something you have never tried before, it is recommended that you experiment with the materials yourself prior to using them with children. For instance, Mr. Buthelezi discovered that to make a "tornado in a bottle," he needed stronger tape than he had initially planned to use. During a test run, he found that the connection between the two inverted soft-drink bottles leaked after the liquid in the bottles was swirled several times. Duct tape held better than the masking tape he had originally selected. Trying the materials in advance avoided a classroom mess and made it more likely that children could concentrate on the experiment rather than on leaky bottles.

Procedures

Planning the procedure requires both design and organizational skills. The primary focus of your planning is to select the processes you will use to facilitate children's achievement of the immediate objectives. To determine these, you will have to apply knowledge of child development and learning as well as an understanding of effective instructional techniques. More about how to do this is described in the section of this chapter entitled "Common Teaching Strategies." For now, it is most important to understand that procedures are designed to support the intermediate and immediate objectives associated with your activity plan. For every objective, corresponding processes are selected. This congruence between objectives and procedures is illustrated in Figure 3.2. The easiest way to accomplish congruence is to plan procedures in a stepwise fashion that matches the immediate objectives. For instance, if the activity involves children sorting leaves, the writer must plan to make a variety of leaves available for children to explore, provide opportunities for children to examine the leaves, include a process by which children will be encouraged to group the leaves, and make sure a process is planned to facilitate children's talking about their groupings. You cannot assume that such procedures happen automatically. Instead, planners must decide what strategies will enable children to move in the desired direction while still remaining open to child-initiated interests and learning. To achieve this, most plans encompass a whole array of strategies rather than relying on just one.

Another important sign of good planning is the extent to which the planner anticipates the conditions necessary for children to pursue particular objectives. In other words, if an objective is for children to explore the leaves, having a time and place to do so must be planned. Rushing children into the sorting process or placing the activity in a spot where children do not have enough room to examine them undermines exploration. If another objective involves children describing the rationale behind particular groupings, the teacher should plan to listen to hear if children discuss these criteria on their own or be prepared to ask them to tell why they grouped the leaves in a certain way. Ensuring the presence of such conditions throughout the procedures section of your plan is necessary to support children's progress through the stated objectives.

Simplifications

Simplifications represent ways to modify the activity for children who are not achieving the objectives you have identified. Sometimes the simplifications address inaccurate assumptions you have made. For instance, in the previous example on marble painting, Janet Fowler assumed that children at the Willow Street Cooperative Preschool were familiar with marble painting. Upon discovering that her assumption was incorrect, she should have revised the activity to make it less complex. Because the children had not had access to poster paint in the past, she could have provided paint and brushes at the easel so that children could get used to the paint without the added complication of manipulating several objectives at once. Once children were more experienced painters, she could have introduced the marbles and pie tins, knowing that the children would be more successful. At other times, simplifications serve as a further breakdown of a particular task. To simplify a task means to make it simpler, more known, more focused on self, more focused on the whole rather than the parts, more concrete, more enactive, or more exploratory. Thus, a child who is trying to button her coat with minimal success may do better if you start the button for her and then have her pull it through the hole. Similarly, a child who is struggling with a 15-piece puzzle may do better with a puzzle having fewer pieces or pieces that are more distinct from one another. Simi-

larly, a youngster who is having difficulty solving a mathematical word problem (symbolic representation) could benefit from drawing it on paper (iconic representation) or even representing it using objects (enactive representation).

Extensions

Children who achieve all the objectives you have identified benefit from trying more advanced steps. The extension ideas you create provide such challenges. To extend an activity means to make it more complex, more unknown, more focused on others than on self, more focused on its component parts, more abstract, more symbolic, more goal directed, more accurate, and more independent. For instance, children who can group objects according to single properties could be invited to classify them using multiple properties such as size and shape at the same time. Children who can think of one way to share an item could be challenged to think of alternate ways as well. Youngsters who can write certain words with adult assistance could be helped to develop strategies for remembering how to write those words on their own or use those known words to create a story. All of these strategies move children beyond their current level of functioning to more advanced levels of performance in accordance with their needs and abilities.

Hints for Success

This section of the activity plan includes the advance preparation and structuring techniques you will use to make the activity safe, functional, and more independent for children. For instance, in the leaf-sorting activity cited earlier, it would be important to provide children with leaves they could explore safely without fear of poisoning or other harmful outcomes. If you are having children wash doll babies in the water table, you will plan to supply plenty of smocks and make sure the table is on a nonslippery surface so children are protected if water splashes over the edge. If you are using a tape recorder, you will plan to locate the activity near a working outlet or have a backup set of batteries so the machine is in working order the whole time it is needed. If you are bringing worms for children to explore, moistening the soil periodically is important for keeping the worms alive. If you are telling the children a story using props, you may plan to keep the props hidden until you are ready to reveal them as a way to stimulate the children's attention. Parboiling vegetables will make them easier for children to cut and enable youngsters to do most of the chopping with minimal adult assistance. If you are teaching place value using beans for grouping, you may plan for each child to have separate cups in which to count the beans. The cups could be used with place value mats with the labeled headings 100s, 10s, and 1s. The cups and mats would make it easier for children to keep track of their beans without spilling them or having the "one-hundreds" group run into the "tens" group and so on. Reminding yourself of these precautions in writing makes it more likely that both you and the children will experience success once the activity is underway.

Evaluation

The evaluation portion of each activity plan represents both an ending and a beginning relative to the plan-

ning process. Closure comes about by gathering information to use in reflecting on what happened within the activity. Such information can assist you in assessing the accuracy of your assumptions, the content of the lesson, the effectiveness of your teaching methods, and child outcomes. These data help you to gauge your own learning as well as the children's. However, appropriate evaluation does not simply describe the past. Instead, it also provides ideas for the future. What did you find out that will be useful to consider next time? How will you use what you have learned? How might you change the direction of your planning? Answers to these questions will inform your plans for days and weeks to come.

To guide your thinking, it is useful to pose specific evaluation questions and to answer them in writing. Typical evaluation questions are depicted in Figure 3.3. Some of these are answered by the planners themselves, some are completed by other members of the teaching

FIGURE 3.3
Typical Evaluation Questions
Regarding Children's Learning
and Teaching Effectiveness

Children's Participation
1. Who participated in this activity?
2. To what extent was the activity of interest to the children? How do you know?
3. How did you get the children involved in the activity?
4. How accurate were your assumptions?

What Children Learned
1. Which children achieved which objectives?
2. Did children appear to understand the content of the lesson? How do you know?
3. What did children say or do in the activity to demonstrate that they were learning?
4. What indicated that the activity was developmentally appropriate for children in the group?

Teaching Effectiveness
1. How did advance preparation (or lack of it) contribute to the success (or lack of success) of the activity?
2. How did the materials meet the needs of the children who participated?
3. Was the activity carried out as planned? What changes were made and why? Did the changes enhance or detract from the activity?
4. If you were to use this activity again, what would you repeat and what would you change? Why?
5. What activities might be implemented to strengthen children's comprehension?
6. What did you learn from this activity?

team, and some may be addressed by the children. In this way, evaluation becomes a dynamic, communal part of early childhood education. Most planners select three or four self-evaluation or activity-evaluation questions to answer for each plan. By varying the questions from day to day and from one plan to the next, it is possible to gain a lot of information in a short time. Such information might be gathered through observations, anecdotal records, performance checklists, rating scales, samples of children's work, participation charts, and children's assessments of their work or progress. More about the specific strategies to gather evaluative data is described in Chapter 16.

DEVELOPMENTALLY APPROPRIATE TEACHING STRATEGIES

Children learn in many different ways, so the strategies that best support their learning vary too. These variations are important to consider when you are planning activities. Let us look at three examples of different approaches to enhancing children's learning.

A teacher plans for 3-year-olds to match plastic jars to their lids. To support the children's learning, the teacher will provide them with a collection of containers and lids that vary in size, color, and shape. Because the children are familiar with the materials, the teacher plans for them to carry out the activity with minimal adult direction. However, she also plans to stop by the area periodically to describe the size, shape, and color of the lids as she talks to the children about their experiences.

The kindergartners at Fairview School have been placing planks to form inclined planes in the block area for several days. They have enjoyed racing their toy cars down the ramps to see how far they will go. Capitalizing on their interests, the teacher plans an activity in which children will observe, predict, and discover ways to make the cars go farther by varying the angles of the ramps. The teacher also plans for the children to analyze and interpret the results of their experiments. In order to help the children engage in these scientific processes, the teacher plans what she will do and say to gain the children's attention, help them recall their past observations of the cars going down the ramps, make predictions of what they think will happen when the angle of the ramp is changed, and then evaluate their predictions. The procedure she plans combines questioning, in-

forming, listening, paraphrasing, and recording the children's ideas.

Today, Mr. Rosenshine wants to teach the children in his second-grade class new motions to a familiar song. He plans to demonstrate the song first, then have the children imitate his movements several times, then have them catch him making mistakes, and finally do the song independently without watching him model the actions. He assumes it will take several repetitions before the children are able to sing the words and do the motions simultaneously on their own.

In each of the preceding activities, teachers carefully considered the teaching strategies they would use to facilitate children's learning. Their planned procedures ranged from providing opportunities for exploration to verbally underscoring children's discoveries to developing step-by-step methods aimed at guiding children through set processes. Although these strategies varied in type, degree of formality, complexity, and directiveness, they shared the common characteristic of having been selected in concert with teachers' goals for children. As such, they were designed to support the learning objectives associated with each plan.

WHAT TEACHING STRATEGIES ARE BEST?

At one time, early childhood educators wondered whether direct instructional methods such as explaining and demonstrating were best for teaching children or if indirect teaching techniques such as inviting and paraphrasing were more effective (Evans, 1975). Over the past decade, we have come to realize that both direct and indirect instruction can be more or less appropriate depending on the goals of the activity and the needs of individual children. For instance, indirect strategies that enhance children's exploratory behavior are well suited to children discovering the properties of modeling dough, different ways they can move their bodies, or the operation of levers. However, such approaches are less well suited to children learning the names of the stars, the specific procedures involved in a tornado drill, or the precise rules for a particular game. Likewise, demonstrations (a form of direct instruction) may help children learn the motions to a song but inhibit children from creating their own motions to the words. Which strategies teachers choose depends on what they want children to learn. This leads teachers in the designing and planning phases of instruction to ask, "Which strategies are most suitable for meeting the goals and objectives of this lesson?" (Pica, 1995). When there is a good match between goals, objectives, and teaching strategies, children benefit. Creating such a match requires planners to become familiar with a wide array of potential teaching strategies and methods for incorporating those strategies into their activity plans.

COMMON TEACHING STRATEGIES

There are so many teaching strategies planners might consider using that it would be impossible to outline all of them here. However, what follows is a representative sample of common instructional methods used by early childhood professionals. The first three strategies—ensuring sensory involvement, preparing environmental cues, and task analysis—are preparatory methods that shape your plans before they are ever carried out. The other dozen strategies that follow those are ones you think about in advance but actually implement only after children are on the scene. All of them are used alone or in combination to enhance children's learning in a variety of activities.

Ensuring Sensory Involvement

This strategy involves making sure there are ways for children to be actively engaged in the instruction, using as many senses as possible. All learning begins with perception: seeing, hearing, touching, tasting, and smelling. Children learn best using all their senses (Bredekamp & Copple, 1997; Hendrick, 1997). Because there is widespread agreement about the importance of hands-on learning, you might assume that every activity for young children would naturally include a high level of sensory involvement by children. However, anyone who has ever seen children sit through a 15-minute talk on the color green, watched children listen to a CD for the sound of an instrument they have never seen or heard in person, or listened to children read a story about pomegranates (a fruit with which many have had no experience) knows that appropriate sensory involvement is not guaranteed without careful planning. The most effective means of sensory engagement involving the most senses is firsthand experience. This means planners must consider ways to give children direct contact with real objects, people, places, and events (Vance, 1973). If you are teaching children about the color green, provide objects of many shades of green for children to see and handle. If you are

First-hand experiences are best!

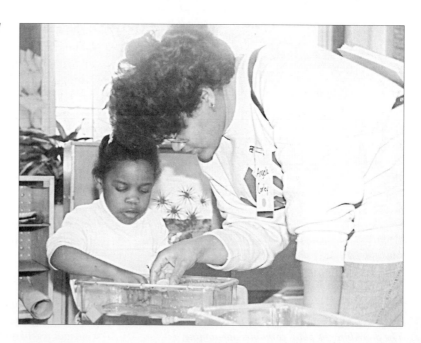

teaching children to listen for the sound of an oboe, first show them an oboe and let them touch the instrument. Have someone play the instrument while children watch. If you are teaching about pomegranates, show children real pomegranates and give them opportunities to examine them through taste, touch, and smell. If no firsthand experience is possible, seriously reconsider whether the activity is actually age appropriate. The younger the children, the less valid it is to rely on secondhand rather than firsthand involvement. As children mature and express curiosity about people, objects, and events somewhat removed from their immediate experience, continue to plan activities that provide the maximum sensory involvement, keeping the following guidelines in mind:

❏ Firsthand experiences are best.
❏ Firsthand experiences should precede representational or more abstract ones (e.g., show real fruit prior to pictures of fruit).
❏ Models are more concrete than pictures; pictures are more concrete than words.
❏ Plan activities so that sensory involvement occurs earlier in the procedure rather than later.

Preparing Environmental Cues

Children can learn a great deal from observing cues in the environment (Hendrick, 1997; Hildebrand, 1997a). Environmental cues signal the children about expectations for tasks or learning areas that may not be verbally specified. Four chairs around the snack table provide evidence that four children may participate at one time. A sign on the cracker basket with a hand showing three fingers or the numeral 3 indicates that each child may take three crackers. Children can learn to turn on and shut down the computer by referring to a pictograph outlining the appropriate steps. If six children are participating in an art activity in which only two pairs of scissors are available, an unspoken message is that children must share the scissors if everyone is to have the chance to use them. These nonverbal signals support objectives related to independence, cooperation, and self-regulation.

Task Analysis

Task analysis involves breaking tasks into their component parts so they are easier for children to master.

This is an essential early childhood planning strategy (Cummings, 1986; Essa, 1996). For instance, it is unrealistic to expect 4-year-old children to learn how to set a table all at once. Instead, teachers begin to plan by analyzing the knowledge, skills, and procedures necessary to achieve the goal of setting the table. Next, they arrange these smaller increments into a logical sequence, planning to introduce new steps as children master previous ones. This process is depicted in Figure 3.4. What should be covered early and what comes later becomes clear in this analysis. The result of using a task-analysis approach is purposeful instruction through which children expand their repertoire of skills, experiencing success all along the way. The combination of intermediate objective, immediate objectives, simplifications, and extensions required in the activity plans you are learning to write comes about through task analysis. The principle of developmental

FIGURE 3.4
Sample Steps in Setting a Table

1. What is the goal?
   Set the table.

2. What will the finished arrangement look like?

3. What are the skills or steps involved?
   a. Get out plates.
   b. Put a plate at each person's place.
   c. Fold napkin.
   d. Place napkin to left of each plate.

4. What do children need to know?
   a. Where to find plates.
   b. How to fold napkin.
   c. Where utensils are positioned.

5. What part will I teach first?

direction, described in Chapter 2, provides one set of criteria for figuring out logical sequences around which to create your plans. Other sequences are presented in the curriculum portions of this text.

Scaffolding

Scaffolding is the process of providing and then gradually removing external support for children's learning. During the scaffolding process, the original task is not changed, but how the child participates in the task is made easier with assistance. As children take more responsibility for performing an objective, assistance is gradually withdrawn (Bodrova & Leong, 1996). For example, Mr. Kaye has planned a counting activity. Children select a bag of "treasures" and count the number of objects inside. As Mr. Kaye works with the children, he notices that Cathleen knows the names of the numbers but counts some objects more than once and others not at all. He recognizes this as a situation in which scaffolding could be used to enhance Cathleen's ability to count accurately. In this case, the teacher might take Cathleen's hand, pointing with her to each object and counting them one at a time, orally. With repetition, Mr. Kaye will stop counting aloud but continue to help Cathleen point to the objects. Eventually, Cathleen will be able to count each object, one at a time, without Mr. Kaye's physical or verbal assistance. The scaffolding process began with the teacher providing maximum assistance and taking primary responsibility for pursuing the objective (counting). Gradually, however, this responsibility shifted to Cathleen until she was able to achieve the objective unassisted. The same principles are at work when teachers plan activities to teach children how to decide who goes first in a board game (Berk & Winsler, 1995; Fox, 1993). At first, the adult may serve as an actual member of the group, providing direct support as the children work through this social dilemma. However, over time, the teacher will take a more passive role providing fewer cues, enabling children to lead one another to mutual resolution. Eventually, children will be able to carry out this cooperative task with minimal adult presence.

Obviously, children's capacity to achieve higher levels of functioning will be influenced by their development and past experiences. Earlier in this text we discussed the idea that children learn best when they have opportunities to engage in activities that are slightly beyond their current level of mastery. Scaffolding provides a means for helping individual children move from a level of assisted performance to independent functioning. In other words, children benefit when they have chances to stretch their cognitive, language, social, and physical skills in joint activity with "experts" who can help them perform at levels higher than they could achieve completely on their own (Davidson, 1996). Such experts may be adults or peers. The scaffolding techniques may be verbal or physical and may or may not include props.

Effective planners think about their activity plans in terms of potential scaffolding opportunities. They consider who could serve as the experts and ways in which the activity could promote joint interactions. In addition, they think of types of supports (physical or verbal) that could be put in place as well as how to gradually withdraw those supports in accordance with children's needs.

Guided Practice

Four-year-old Tony heads for the puzzle area every day. At the beginning of the year, he mostly enjoyed knob puzzles that had a few distinct pieces. Since then he has moved on to interlocking puzzles that vary in color and shape. Most recently, he has become intrigued with the new floor puzzle of a bus. He has tried that puzzle each day, sometimes on his own, sometimes with other children, and sometimes with the teacher's help. Tony's teacher supports his learning by providing time, space, and materials for him to practice his puzzle-making skills. When she plans for the puzzle area, she considers ways to maintain the children's interest and provide them with appropriate challenges. Each week, she holds over a few favorites from the week before and then adds new puzzles for novelty. She also includes different types of puzzles and ones of varying degrees of difficulty. Tony's teacher is planning using the strategy of guided practice.

A basic premise of early childhood education is that children learn through repetition (Bredekamp & Copple, 1997). Real learning does not occur in a single episode. Children need many opportunities to engage concepts, explore ideas, and try out skills to gain mastery. In other words, children need a chance to practice what they are learning and to generalize what they have learned to new situations (Harmin, 1994). That practice is most beneficial when the conditions under which it takes place vary slightly from one time to the next. Such practice episodes may occur within a day or over several weeks time. Thus, Tony increases his puzzle-making skills by working on some of the same, as well as a few new puzzles over time. An-Sook learns to hop by hopping on one foot and then the other; hopping sideways and backward; hopping inside and outside; hopping on even surfaces and uneven ones; and hopping alone and with friends. The first graders in Mrs. Rohde's room become more proficient at forming their letters by writing in the pretend grocery, making signs to post around the room, writing in their journals, making lists, and writing notes to themselves to help them remember "important stuff." Deliberately setting the stage for these kinds of practice opportunities is essential to effective planning.

Invitations

Verbal invitations encourage children to participate in activities by creating openings for them to explore materials or to interact with you or other children. Samples include the following: "Come and see what we're doing here," "Here's a place for you right next to LaKesha," and "Check out the new materials in the reading center. I saw a book I'm sure you'll enjoy." It is a good idea to plan a few invitations in advance so you have a better idea of how to motivate children to try various activities.

Behavior Reflections

Sometimes called information talk or descriptive feedback, behavior reflections are verbal descriptions of children's actions (Kostelnik et al., 1998; Sharp, 1987). They are nonjudgmental statements made to children regarding some aspect of their actions.

Situation: Outdoors, a child is sorting real leaves into small piles.

Adult: You found some red and brown leaves. (Or either of the following: You have several different leaves in your piles; You're putting together the leaves that are alike.)

Situation: Two children are matching lids to jars.

Adult: You two are working together. (Or: Each of you has found a lid to match a jar; Mareesa, your lid is square. Kyoko, your lid is round. You both found different-shaped lids.)

Behavior reflections help draw children's attention to certain aspects of an experience they may only faintly perceive and expose them to vocabulary that describes their experience (Lay-Dopyera & Dopyera, 1993). They also summarize children's actions in a way that is informative without being intrusive. For instance, children acting on materials might hear their teacher say, "Your fingers are moving gently over the water making small ripples" or "When you turned the puzzle piece around, it fit." Summarizations like these do not interrupt children's actions. Youngsters do not have to stop what they are doing to attend to the lesson. However, they do prompt children to focus specifically on their actions, which in turn helps them to solidify and internalize those actions. Behavior reflections may also induce children to explore additional ways of moving their fingers over the water or turning other pieces in the puzzle to make them fit (Trepanier-Street, 1991, 195). Thus, behavior reflections increase children's self-awareness and understanding.

Paraphrase Reflections

Similar in form to behavior reflections, paraphrase reflections are restatements in your own words of something the child has said. These nonevaluative comments are sometimes referred to as verbal expansions or active listening (Hildebrand, 1997a; Sharp, 1987). Using words slightly different from those spoken by the child, paraphrase reflections broaden children's vocabulary and grammatical structures. At times they also prompt children to expand on what they are saying. This helps them to refine and clarify key concepts and messages. When children respond to your reflections, you also gain valuable insights into their thinking. Such insights will influence how you proceed with the activity as well as help shape the direction of future planning. Finally, because paraphrase reflections allow children to take the lead in adult–child conversations, children interpret their use as a signal of adult interest and caring (Kostelnik et al., 1998). Such feelings enhance the learning climate in early childhood classrooms.

Situation:	Outdoors, a child is sorting real leaves into two piles. He says, "These leaves are pointy. These leaves are round."
Adult:	You found two different kinds of leaves. (Or: You noticed the edges of the leaves made them look different from one another. You're sorting the leaves according to their shape.)
Child:	These (pointing to three leaves on the side) have holes.
Adult:	You made a special pile just for leaves with holes. You have three piles all together.

Modeling

Children learn many things by imitating others (Bandura, 1989; Pica, 1995). Watching a friend play a game, seeing the teacher use a sculpting tool in a certain way, listening to a peer "think aloud" about how to solve a math problem, or observing how one person greets another are all lessons from which children may profit. Even though much of what children imitate is unplanned, teachers can enhance the effectiveness of classroom activities when they deliberately use modeling to help children learn new or appropriate behaviors (Lay-Dopyera & Dopyera, 1993). For example, when Ms. Pritchard holds a snake gently, she is modeling a positive attitude toward snakes she hopes the children will emulate. Likewise, when Mrs. Levine visits the pretend restaurant, she models being a customer by sitting down and saying things to the children like, "Hmm, now what will I have? Do you have a menu? Oh, that sounds good. I'd like a salad and a milkshake. How much will that cost?" Her modeling provides children with examples of how a customer might behave. When Mr. Petricic models looking up information he does not know, he is conveying to children ways of using reference materials to answer questions. Models such as these have the greatest impact when their behavior is obvious to the children. This means children are best able to imitate a model with whom they can interact or whose behavior is pointed out to them (Kostelnik et al., 1998). Self-descriptions such as "I'm not sure how many stomachs a cow has. I'll have to look that up" are useful signals of the modeling that is about to take place. Similarly, peer models are highlighted when teachers say things like, " Look, John has discovered a new way to use the paint" or "Natalie found another way to add three columns of numbers."

Effective Praise

Planners often assume that praise automatically promotes children's positive behaviors and encourages them to persist at tasks. Unfortunately, some praise actually has the potential to lower children's self-

The teacher uses effective praise when she says, "You found a way to surprise the reader at the end!"

TABLE 3.1
A Comparison of Ineffective and Effective Praise

Ineffective Praise	Effective Praise
Good job. Nicely done.	You spent a lot of time on this story. You looked up some important information that made the setting more exciting.
You are a great writer.	You found a way to surprise the reader at the end.
Look at Rodney. Everyone should try to write as neatly as he does.	You used two words in this story you never wrote before.
You were lucky to come up with such a good idea.	The time you spent editing paid off. You were able to come up with just the right words to finish your story.
Mary, good job. Carl, good job.	Mary, you used a lot of animal sounds in your story. Carl, you added a joke to your story to make it funny.

confidence and inhibit their achievement (Kamii, 1984; Miller, 1995). Thus, there is a difference between ineffective and effective praise. Ineffective praise is general, repetitive, and not really genuine. It evaluates children, compares them to one another in unfavorable ways, links their success to luck, and tends to interrupt their work and concentration. Effective praise, on the other hand, is specific, acknowledges children's actions, and compares their progress to their past performance. It links their success to effort and ability, is individualized to fit the child and the situation, and is nonintrusive (Kostelnik et al., 1998). The differences between ineffective praise and effective praise are illustrated in Table 3.1.

Telling/Explaining/Informing

During their field trip to the animal barns, Jonathan points to a llama and asks the man who is leading the tour, "What's that?" The man answers, "That's called a llama. You say it, llama." Jonathan repeats the new word, "llama." The children are full of questions: "Where do llamas come from?" "Why do they have such heavy coats?" "Do big llamas have baby llamas?" "How big is the biggest llama in the world?" The tour guide answers each question simply and directly. Simultaneously, he draws the children's attention to the sights, sounds, and smells associated with the llamas. Anyone who wishes may touch the animal's coat, look into the llama's

feed trough, and handle some of the feed pellets. When Jonathan sees his mom at the end of the day, the first thing he says is, "Guess what we saw today? A llama! And they get real big and people use their hair to make hats." Obviously, Jonathan is pleased with his newly acquired knowledge.

On their field trip to the barn, children discovered that the llama's coat was thick by looking at and touching it. However, they could not discover the name of the animal in the same way—they had to be told it was a llama. Information such as the names for things, historical facts, and customary behaviors are learned through social transmission. That is, people tell you either directly through verbal communication or indirectly through books, television, or computer technology. In any case, important information can be conveyed to children through telling and explaining.

Effective explanations build on children's first-hand experiences and take place within a context that is meaningful to them. Such is the case when the teacher plans to teach a new game by referring to situations and skills already familiar to the children.

Remember how you always take turns outside riding the bikes? You can play this game (pick-up sticks) by taking turns, too. First, Peter, let John pick up all the sticks he can without moving any of the others. And then, John, you let Peter do it next. (Lay-Dopyera & Dopyera, 1993, 242)

In this way, relevant information can be incorporated into the ongoing conversations you have with children each day.

The children note the interesting shape of the leaves on a large pin oak tree in the playyard. Their teacher says, "You noticed that tree has pointy leaves. It's called an oak tree. Look and see if all the leaves on that tree are the same shape. What do you see?" The teacher pauses to give the children a chance to look and answer. In response to Jeremy's discovery of an acorn, she says, "Oh, Jeremy, you found an acorn. Acorns are the seeds out of which oak trees grow. Look on the ground to see if you can find some more." The teacher might also plan a follow-up activity in which the children examine the acorns, splitting them open and finding out the names of the seed parts inside.

In early childhood programs, much information is introduced on a just-in-time basis. That is, as children demonstrate a need to know something, the appropriate information is offered. For instance, children in the pretend grocery store get into a squabble over the cash register. Five children want to "work" in the store, but there is only one register. The teacher observes to see if the children can resolve the difficulty themselves; however, they seem stumped. The only job they know about is the cashier's job. The teacher decides that the time is ripe to offer some useful information. She enters the store saying, "Hello, I'm the district manager. Have you done an inventory yet? One of the jobs for people who work at the grocery is to count all the items on the shelves. Another job is to make sure each item has a price tag. Who will make the price tags for our store?" Armed with this new information, the children's play resumes, with the children having a broader idea of the possible roles they might play.

At other times, adults determine in advance that they want to teach children certain information. Such decisions may be based on interests previously expressed by children, or they may be dictated by social expectations such as how to wash one's hands properly or behave during a fire drill. In any case, teachers plan activities to teach children specific vocabulary, facts, or routines. Teachers convey such information through telling, explaining coupled with modeling, and some form of hands-on involvement by the children.

In all of these examples, telling, explaining, and informing in early childhood education involves more than merely reciting facts. Such information is tied to children's experiences and requires involvement by them that goes beyond simply listening. Effective planners look at each activity plan in terms of what explanations or information may be necessary to support children's learning. They also make sure they have sufficient background to answer children's questions and provide accurate explanations as necessary.

Do-It Signals

Simple directions to children such as "look here," "tell me what you see," "show me how you like to dance," "put together the leaves that are alike," "find a key that doesn't fit," or "guess how many are in the jar" are called do-it signals. Beginning with a verb, do-it signals are short statements that prompt children to engage in some action. In other words, they tell children to do something. When children follow the do-it direction, their actions demonstrate to the teacher what children do and do not understand. For instance, if, as part of a lesson aimed at examining the parts of fruits, the teacher gives a do-it signal to the child to show her the rind and the child hands her a seed, the child's action tells the teacher the child may not know the difference. The teacher would respond with additional experiences and information as appropriate.

Do-it signals should not be phrased as questions such as "Can you count to five for me?" or "Who can count to five for me?" Queries like these fail to lead children into action. The appropriate do-it signal would be to say, "Count to five for me." These kinds of positive statements give children a clearer idea of what to do.

Challenges

"Show me how tall you can be." "Find a way to make a tower using five different block shapes." "Figure out two different ways to make this wooden board sink." Challenges are open-ended variations of do-it signals. Challenges motivate children to create their own solutions to teacher-suggested tasks (Pica, 1995). In this way, challenges provide shared opportunities for children and adults to control activity outcomes. Adults shape the initial direction of the activity, and children determine its application.

A variation on the basic challenge occurs when adults challenge children to think about something in a new or different way. For example, Elliot has divided a set of keys into three groups. One group includes all the round gold keys, another group has all the angular gold keys, and a third group includes all the silver keys. Having observed Elliot at work, the teacher approaches with a round copper-colored key and says, "I just found this key. Show me where it belongs with the keys that you've sorted." Elliot is now faced with the challenge of reconsidering his groupings to accommodate a new element that does not exactly fit. The children are faced with a similar challenge when they declare that only men can be firefighters. A few days later, the teacher invites a female firefighter to visit the class and talk about her work. Again the children are challenged to reconsider their thinking in light of new evidence that does not match their previous conceptions.

Effective planners carefully observe and listen to children as they participate in activities. Based on the information they glean directly from children, teachers plan challenges to stretch children's thinking beyond their current perceptions. As part of the challenge, teachers talk with children, encouraging them to put their thinking into words. Throughout this process, teachers are careful not to expect children to accomplish every challenge in a single activity or to change their thinking simply because they are faced with conflicting information.

Questions

Questions are basic instructional tools common to every early childhood classroom. However, the kinds of questions adults ask dictate the quality of the answers they receive (Trepanier-Street, 1991). Effective questions are purposeful (tied directly to the objectives you are trying to teach), thought provoking (going beyond the obvious to stimulate higher levels of thinking), clear (understandable), and brief (to the point). Questions that meet these standards are the most likely to gain children's attention and help them learn (Cliatt & Shaw, 1992). When questions are used simply to pass the time or when they are too many in number or become intrusive, children stop paying attention, and the quality of their responses decreases (Kostelnik et al., 1998). Also, questions should never be used to demonstrate children's lack of knowledge and understanding when no previous experience or instruction has been provided. This is a negative form of pretesting, as when Ms. Johnson shows a picture of an aardvark to a group of 4-year-olds and asks, "What is the name of this animal?" When adults ask questions they have no reason to believe children can answer, children respond with silence or mistakes. In both cases, youngsters get the message that they should know the answer and that their failure to respond correctly is a fault. Using poor-quality questions like these is something professionals must avoid.

Many taxonomies describe possible questions to ask children. Although they differ in terminology, questions that go beyond simple yes/no and one-word answers are generally the most desirable. Additionally, using a variety of questions is preferable to relying on only one kind (Cassidy, 1989; Charlesworth & Lind, 1995; Kilmer & Hoffman, 1995). Based on the criteria just outlined, we offer in Table 3.2 several categories of questions for teachers to incorporate in their plans. Besides considering the range of questions you plan to pose to children, there are a few other things to think about as well (Cliatt & Shaw, 1992; Kilmer & Hofman, 1995; Taylor, 1993).

Limit amount	❏ Ask only one question at a time. Plan your questions carefully.
Provide time	❏ Give children enough time to respond to your questions . Wait several seconds for children to answer. Do not appear impatient or undermine their thinking by answering your own questions.
Use do-it signals	❏ Phrase some of your questions as do-it signals to add variety. "Tell me what happened when we put the snowball in the hot water."
Ask all	❏ Phrase questions to the entire group of children, not only to individuals. "Let's all think of the ways these two piles of leaves are alike. Jake, you begin."
Listen and reflect	❏ Listen carefully to children's responses. Acknowledge their remarks using behavior and paraphrase reflections. Focus on the process of their thinking, not merely the correctness of their response.
Redirect	❏ If a child's answer seems wrong or off track, follow up by saying something like, "What made you think . . . ?" or "Tell us more about. . . ." Children sometimes make connections that are less obvious to grown-ups.

TABLE 3.2
Types of Questions and Examples

You Plan to Enhance Children's Ability to	Sample Questions
Observe	What do you see/hear/smell/taste/feel?
Reconstruct previous experiences	What do you remember about the people at the pizza parlor? What happened the last time we put the rock in the sunshine?
Relate cause and effect	What can you do to make it happen? What happens when/if you do ____? When does it happen?
Predict	What do you think will happen next?
Evaluate	What happened? You thought ____ would happen? How did that compare to what actually happened? Which poem is your favorite? Why? How will you know the art area is clean enough? What will help you decide?
Generalize	Now that you saw what we found when we cut open the lemon, what do you think we will find when we cut open this orange?
Compare	How are they alike/different? Which things go together?
Reason	How did you decide those went together?
Discriminate among objects and events	Which one doesn't belong? Which one is not an oak tree?
Solve problems	What can we do to find out how many marbles are in the jar?
Quantify	How many? How long? How far?
Imagine something	What would it be like if people had long tails?
Propose alternatives	What is another way you could group these objects?
Utilize factual knowledge	Where do you suppose we could find a worm at this time of year?
Infer	What else can you think of that works like this? Why do you think it happened? How do your observations compare with other children's?
Become aware of their thinking processes	How did you know. . .? What made you decide . . .?
Apply	How can you use what you learned?
Make decisions	What do you think we should do now that we know ____?
Communicate	How can you show, remember, share with others what you did/learned?

Address
misconceptions

❑ If the child's answer to a question is indicative of a true misconception, handle the situation matter-of-factly. Paraphrase the child's idea and then offer more accurate information. "You thought the this was an apple because it is red. This is a tomato. Tomatoes are sometimes red, too."

Silence

A group of six children is in the block area. They have used almost every block for an elaborate building that stretches from one side of the rug to the other. They are laughing and talking to one another, sharing materials, and taking on the roles of construction workers. Mr. Moon observes silently from nearby, noting that Teisha has become part of the group. This is the first time she has moved into a learning center involving more than one or two children. He writes a quick anecdotal record to remind himself of this milestone. Mr. Moon also notices the children are sustaining the activity well. He does not interrupt but remains nearby to provide support if needed.

The children and their teacher are investigating a large horseshoe crab shell one of the children brought back from a week at the beach. The teacher has just said, "Tell me what you notice about this big shell." She remains silent for several seconds to give the children a chance to answer.

Coral and Aiysha are engaged in a story-mapping activity in which they are figuring out the distinguishing characteristics of each character. They are deeply absorbed in their discussion. Their teacher listens attentively for a few moments and then moves to another group of children. The children continue their analysis.

In each of these situations, teachers used silence to support children's learning. Remaining quiet can be an effective teaching strategy, especially when it is coupled with attentive observation of children and the context in which they are functioning (Freiberg & Driscoll, 1996; Kostelnik et al., 1998). Too much adult talk, inappropriate adult talk, or adult talk at the wrong time detracts from a positive learning environment. For instance, it has been well documented that many teachers are too quick to respond to their own questions or too swift to move from one child to the next when a child fails to respond immediately to a question or do-it signal (Rowe, 1974). Children need at least 3 to 5 seconds to process what has been said and to formulate a response. Getting into the habit of giving children a few seconds of "wait time" is an effective use of silence. Likewise, children perceive the learning environment as more supportive when teachers refrain from inserting themselves into the center of every interaction and when they avoid interrupting children who are deeply engaged in communicating with one another. In these cases, children interpret the adult's silence as a sign of warmth and respect.

COMBINING STRATEGIES TO PROMOTE LEARNING IN DIFFERENT WAYS

Although children's sensory involvement is integral to every lesson, the other teaching strategies just described can be combined in different ways to create ac-

tivities that vary in function and form. The most significant variation among activities is the extent to which either children or adults determine processes and outcomes. For some activities, how and what is learned is mostly determined by the children; in other activities, children and teachers share responsibility for how the activity transpires and what ends are achieved; still other activities place primary control for what happens with the adult. Due to what we know about how young children learn best, child-directed experiences and shared activities are much more prevalent in high-quality early childhood programs than are adult-controlled activities. However, all three variations can be used appropriately at one time or another to support children's learning. With these ideas in mind, we describe seven generic activity types that form the basis for planning and teaching in early childhood education today: (1) exploratory activities, (2) guided discovery, (3) problem solving, (4) discussions, (5) cooperative learning, (6) demonstrations, and (7) direct instruction activities. These were selected because they represent common approaches to teaching in the early years. They are appropriate for use with the entire range of children from 3 through 8 years because they span child-centered and shared and adult-controlled methods and because they are adaptable to every domain of the curriculum. These seven activity types do not cover all the possibilities, but they represent the foundations upon which most other activity variations build. More specific techniques commonly associated with particular domains, such as story mapping or conflict mediation, are addressed in the domain-related chapters to which they apply.

Exploratory Activities

Much of what young children learn comes about through naturalistic explorations of the environment. Through self-initiated examinations of people, places, objects, and events, children construct their own knowledge rather than having information imposed on them. Exploratory activities enable children to carry out firsthand investigations proceeding at their own pace and making most of the decisions about what is done and how and when it is done (Taylor, 1993). Because there are no prescribed answers, children discover things for themselves, taking the activity in whatever direction suits their interests.

Even though children assume primary responsibility for the direction of exploratory activities, teachers do more than make available materials for children to use. They consider what broad experiences they want children to have and the best ways to support children's involvement in those experiences. For instance, Ms. Habibi encourages children's exploration of sand by putting damp sand in the sand table one day, and dry sand on another. She provides a variety of props such as sifters, measuring cups, sieves, containers, shovels, slotted spoons, and nonslotted utensils and gives children plenty of time to engage in the activity. She also invites children to the area, occasionally commenting on what they are doing and saying as a way to acknowledge individuals and support children's involvement.

To enhance children's learning to the fullest, exploratory activities require careful planning. Teachers rely heavily on the strategies of sensory involvement and environmental cues to stimulate children's interest and enable them to participate freely and safely. Adults use behavior and paraphrase reflections to acknowledge children's actions and discoveries. However, because they have no predetermined agenda for what they want the children to learn, teachers avoid potentially leading strategies such as do-it signals or questions that guide children's thinking in particular directions.

Guided Discovery

Teachers plan guided-discovery experiences by focusing on the learning process itself, not on children generating particular solutions. Their aim is for youngsters to make connections and build concepts through interactions with people and objects. The role of children in guided-discovery activities is to construct knowledge for themselves: making choices and decisions, experimenting and experiencing, raising questions, and finding their own answers (Klein, 1990). The role of the adult is to serve as a resource: emphasizing how to find answers, providing information and tools as necessary, and supporting children's progress through domain-related processes (Bredekamp & Copple, 1997). Both children and adults influence the direction of guided-discovery activities. Adults provide the broad parameters in which learning takes place; children determine the essence of what is learned.

Guided-discovery activities build on exploration, incorporating the additional teaching strategies of modeling, effective praise, telling and explaining, do-it signals, challenges, and questions. This means that when the sand table is being used for guided discovery, the activity looks different from when the sand is being used for an exploratory activity. For instance, Ms. Jamison plans a guided-discovery activity in which she wants children to think about the idea that volume, shape, and color are distinct properties of objects. She sets out several one-cup measures of different colors and shapes and dampens the sand. As children pack the sand and mold it using the measuring cups, the teacher comments on the size and shape of the cups and the sand structures they are building. She also asks questions such as "Which measuring cup holds the most? How could you find out? What is the same about these measuring cups? What is different? How do you know? You discovered that the blue cup and the red one hold the same amount of sand. Look at this yellow cup. Will it hold more or less sand than those cups?" Such verbalizations are interspersed with periods of attentive adult silence to allow children plenty of opportunities to talk about their ideas and what interests them about the materials and each other. Using this combination of strategies, Ms. Jamison gently guides children's thinking along certain lines but allows children to come to their own conclusions based on the evidence of their experience. Sometimes the children's conclusions are not scientifically correct. When this happens, Ms. Jamison offers a challenge to stimulate children to think about the objects in new ways. However, because this is a guided-discovery activity, she ultimately accepts the children's ideas no matter what they are (Cliatt & Shaw, 1992). She does not tell children they are wrong or make them parrot "correct" answers. Instead, she uses what she finds out about children's thought processes to plan guided-practice experiences through which children gradually construct more accurate concepts for themselves. The activity described in Figure 3.2 is a guided discovery example.

Problem Solving

Problem-solving activities are variations of guided-discovery experiences. Children plan, predict, make decisions, observe the results of their actions, and form conclusions while adults serve as facilitators (Harlan, 1988; Hendrick, 1997). Young children are intrigued by movement problems (How many different ways can you move from point A to point B?), discussion problems (What would happen if . . . ?), strategy problems (What strategies do you need to play a board game?), and skill problems (How many different ways can a set of objects be grouped?). Sometimes these problems arise out of naturally occurring events, and sometimes they are planned by adults. The best problems for children to think about engage them in various ways, allow them to gather information concretely, and have more than one possible solution. The more immediate, observable, and obvious the problem, the easier it is for children to evaluate their actions and come to their own conclusions (Goffin & Tull, 1985). All good problems prompt children to analyze, synthesize, and evaluate events, information, and ideas, thereby encouraging children to make new mental connections and construct fresh ideas (Freiberg & Driscoll, 1996).

The problem-solving process is similar for every curricular domain. A typical sequence of steps is one associated with scientific problem solving:

1. Becoming aware of a problem (noticing, observing, and identifying).
2. Hypothesizing or proposing an explanation (thinking of possible reasons why things happen, gathering information, making intelligent guesses based on experience, and predicting).
3. Experimenting (testing ideas).
4. Drawing conclusions (observing results, making generalizations, determining if alternative hypotheses are needed, and reflecting on the results of their actions).
5. Communicating results (talking about what happened, recording what happened, and making plans for further experimentation with a new hypothesis).

Mrs. Radechek is using scientific problem solving when she supplies materials at the water table for children to use in a "sink and float" experiment. Having encouraged children to explore similar materials in the water table on many previous occasions, she prepares to guide them in discovering which properties of objects seem to have a bearing on whether they sink or float. Mrs. Radechek thinks carefully about the materials she will provide as well as what she will say and do to help children proceed through the steps of the scientific process. Her ultimate aim is for children to generate their own ideas about the following:

❏ What they see (John says, "The bottle cap floats. The plastic boat floats. The rock is on the bottom.").

❏ Why things happen (John says, "The blue stuff stays on top. The brown thing sank.").
❏ What will happen when another object is placed in the water (John predicts, "The 'brown' popsicle stick will sink.").
❏ The outcomes of their predictions (John says, "It floated.").
❏ Alternative hypotheses (John says, "Maybe being long is what makes things float.").

Although John generated a hypothesis that was incorrect (e.g., color is related to floating and sinking), his investigations eventually led him to reject color as a significant property and switch to something else. By observing, hypothesizing, experimenting, and drawing conclusions many times and with many variations, John will gradually construct more accurate concepts. In this problem-solving activity, John acted on objects in purposeful ways, applied his own notions of how the world works, and reflected on his experiences with the help of his teacher. Mrs. Radechek's role included supporting John's investigation ("Tell me what you see. You noticed the bottle cap is blue and the boat is blue. You've decided being blue is what makes things float.") as well as asking questions and offering challenges as appropriate ("What do you think will happen when you put the popsicle stick in the water?"). The process of problem solving was the ultimate goal, not the physics of water displacement (floating). By observing and listening carefully, the teacher gleaned valuable information to use for future planning. This sink-and-float activity was one in which adult and child shared control and from which both learned.

The steps characteristic of social inquiry are similar to those associated with the scientific method:

1. Becoming aware of a problem (noticing, observing, and identifying).
2. Gathering information (thinking of possible reasons why things happen, gathering information, and making intelligent guesses based on experience).
3. Designing a plan or solution.
4. Trying out a plan or solution
5. Drawing conclusions (observing results, making generalizations, and determining if alternative plans are needed).
6. Communicating results.

Children might engage in social inquiry as they generate ideas for rules in the block area, determine how to resolve a conflict between the boys and the girls on the playground, choose a name for the class iguana, or develop an equitable plan for using the computer. The Appendix provides a sample problem-solving plan.

Discussions

There is much to talk about in early childhood classrooms:

❏ What is happening in the program? Who will water the plants? What are ways cooperative reading partners can help each other when someone is absent? Why are some people upset with what is going on in the block area? Where should we hang the graphs we made? When will be the best time to celebrate Flopsy Bunny's birthday? How does it feel when someone makes a mistake and other people laugh?

❏ What is happening to children away from the program? Jessica has a new baby at her house. Tanya's grandma is visiting. Rudy's dog died. Carlos went to the Panther's game over the weekend. Roger got scared when he heard people yelling and banging outside his window. Selma will be moving with her family soon. Kyle is up to the third level on Donkey Kong Two.

❏ What is happening in the community and world at large? Children notice many things: There was a big storm last night. A new shopping center is being built. The Pirates won the game yesterday. Peo-

ple will be voting next week. Children wonder many things: Can women be firefighters or just men? Why do some trees lose their leaves and other trees do not? How much does it cost to fly to Florida? How high is the sky? What happened to all the dinosaurs? What does it mean to vote?

Discussion implies reciprocal interactions among teachers and children; adults talk to children, children talk to adults, and children talk to one another. Using invitations, reflections, questions, and statements, teachers guide the conversation but encourage children to express themselves and communicate their ideas aloud. Throughout the discussion, teachers talk, but children talk as much as, if not more than, the adults (Cliatt & Shaw, 1992). Sometimes a record is made of the discussion, as when a group makes a list of classroom rules, generates ideas for names for the guinea pig, or lists suggestions for a new ending to a familiar story. Sometimes no tangible record is made. In both cases, responsibility for discussion is a shared endeavor, in which children and adults influence processes and outcomes together.

Cooperative Learning

Early childhood educators have long stressed the value of children working cooperatively with one another. Until recently, benefits were mostly described in terms

These children are listening carefully to one another's ideas as they participate in a cooperative learning activity.

of children's positive feelings of competence and self-worth as well as enhanced social skills (Crary, 1984; Spivack & Shure, 1974). Today cooperative learning is recognized as having benefits beyond the affective and social realms. In fact, cooperative learning arrangements have been successfully utilized in all areas of the curriculum, increasing children's time on task, promoting tolerance among children, and broadening children's repertoire of learning strategies (Lay-Dopyera & Dopyera, 1993). "Cooperative groups also foster active learning, allowing children many chances to speak, to take initiative, to make choices, and generally develop good lifelong learning habits" (Harmin, 1994, 95).

Cooperative learning is defined as "students working together in groups small enough that everyone can participate in a collective task that has been clearly defined, without constant, direct supervision by the teacher" (Cohen, 1994, 3). Such learning involves shared responsibility among teachers and children to accomplish educational objectives. Teachers set the stage and lend intermittent support to groups of children working together. Children carry out tasks, serving as colleagues and mentors to one another. Creating a group mural, collaborating on selecting a name for their cooperative group, writing a class dictionary, solving math story problems, reading in pairs, creating a three-dimensional representation of their community, investigating how frogs live, and combining talents to create a meal are examples of cooperative projects teachers have planned for and with children ages 4 through 8.

True cooperative learning is characterized by the following expectations (Johnson & Johnson, 1991):

❏ All members of a cooperative group are responsible for their own learning and the learning of their group members.
❏ Children contribute to one another's learning by helping, supporting, encouraging, critiquing, motivating, and praising each other's work.
❏ Each individual is accountable for the group effort. Activities are structured so each person shares responsibility for the achievement of the objectives. Feedback is provided to individuals and the group as a whole.
❏ Children must have opportunities to reflect on their group work.

Obviously, children as young as three as well as older children who have had no previous experience with cooperative learning are not equipped to function in a cooperative group independently. In addition, you cannot simply put children in groups and expect that they will know how to cooperate. Teachers must deliberately plan ways for children to learn how to work together to achieve mutual goals regardless of age (Harmin, 1994; Kostelnik et al., 1998; Marcus & McDonald, 1990). At first, teachers plan to be centrally involved in helping children acquire the skills necessary to communicate, solve problems, and resolve conflicts. Research shows that class time devoted to group dynamics, team building, interpersonal and small-group skills is time well spent (Cohen, 1994). Activities can be specially designed to promote cooperative behaviors in any area of the classroom as well as in learning centers created for this purpose. More information about these strategies is offered in Chapter 5, Chapter 10, and Chapter 13. As children become more independent in their skills, they are better able to carry out cooperative activities such as playing a game with minimum adult support. Eventually, planning shifts to the children monitoring themselves and working in cooperative groups to address objectives in any curricular domain.

Younger children tend to work best in small groups, including temporary groups (e.g., children move in and out of the art area during free-choice time, contributing to a group collage) and ones in which group membership remains stable for several days or weeks. Older children in grades one and two benefit from working in pairs. Periodic experimentation with slightly larger groups is also appropriate. However, groups of more than three or four are best avoided because they tend to result in passive participation (Harmin, 1994). Groups may be formed through teacher assignment or self-selection. Depending on the children and the circumstances, students' progression from assisted learning to independent functioning may take several weeks or all year. Preschoolers and inexperienced older children will likely advance from constant supervision to some independence; experienced children in first and second grade will be able to work for longer periods on their own.

Even though cooperative learning calls for children to rely on peers rather than adults, teachers are not uninvolved. They provide clear direction to groups getting underway. Once children begin working, practitioners continually move from group to group. They lend support, observe and assess children's progress, and determine how to use what they find in future plans. Consequently, cooperative learning incorporates on-the- spot strategies such as reflecting children's naturally occurring cooperative behaviors and giving children "just in time" information. It also utilizes planned techniques such as task analysis, scaffolding, guided practice, modeling, effective praise, telling and informing, do-it signals, challenges, and questions. These may be combined in guided discovery, problem solving, discussion, or direct-teaching activities aimed at helping children develop greater collaborative skills.

Demonstrations

Generally, demonstrations involve one person showing others how something works or how a task is to be carried out. When people demonstrate something, the direction of the activity is completely up to them. Teachers use demonstrations to illustrate instructions, offer children a preview of something they will do later, or open a lesson in a dramatic way (Cliatt & Shaw, 1992). Demonstrations combine do-it signals and modeling and generally consist of three steps: (1) gaining children's attention, (2) showing children something, and (3) prompting children to respond to what they saw in words or actions. For instance, teachers at the Tree Top Child Development Center open each day with a greeting time, during which they demonstrate one of the materials that will be available to children in the room throughout the free-choice portion of the day. Typical items are games (e.g., lotto, dominos), experiments (e.g., dissolving substances in water), or novel materials the children have not used before. Today the children will have a chance to scrape vegetables to make "Stone Soup." Their teacher plans to demonstrate the safe way to scrape the potatoes and other items that will go into the soup. She hides some vegetables and a scraper in a paper bag and places it behind her chair. Following one or two opening songs, she pulls out the bag. Giving the children a few introductory hints, she encourages them to guess what they think might be inside (gaining the children's attention). After some guesses are made, she reveals the vegetables and the scraper and proceeds to show the children how to scrape away from their bodies and over a plastic bowl (showing the children something). Finally, she has the

children make the appropriate scraping motion, as they pretend to scrape a favorite vegetable (children respond). The demonstration ends. The teacher assumes the children will need additional support as they attempt to scrape vegetables for real. However, she is satisfied that she has introduced the safe way to handle the scrapers in a manner children understood and enjoyed.

Demonstrations may constitute an entire activity as illustrated by the vegetable scraper demonstration. Alternately, demonstrations are sometimes only a small part of a larger interaction. For instance, a teacher or peer might demonstrate the proper amount of food to feed the guinea pig, how to reboot the computer, or how to capture air in a jar by putting the jar straight into the water upside down. Even in these brief situations, the same instructional process is followed: gain attention, model, and prompt children to respond in some way. The children's response may be verbal or involve an action of some type such as shaking out the approximate amount of food, telling the first step in rebooting the computer, or trying to capture air in their own jars. When demonstrations of any kind are planned for young children, it is best to keep them short and to ensure sensory involvement early in the procedure. A demonstration sample plan is presented in the Appendix.

Direct Instruction

Children who participate in direct-instruction activities learn information or actions created by others but do not construct that knowledge for themselves. For instance, a child who wants to ride a bike must master the appropriate hand signals in order to ride on the street. Such signals have been socially agreed upon and handed down from one generation to the next. It is not safe for children to rely on personally constructed signalling systems because such systems are not meaningful to others on the road. In early childhood classrooms, direct instruction is used to teach children terms, strategies, precise factual information, and routines (Freiberg & Driscoll, 1996; Lay-Dopyera & Dopyera, 1993). Although more indirect methods can also be used for these same aims, the advantages of direct instruction are that it uses time efficiently, produces immediate results, teaches children to follow directions, and lends itself to on-the-spot evaluation (Pica, 1995).

Sam Borzage is using direct-instruction techniques when he points to one of three kiwis from among the many fruits the children are examining and says, "This is a kiwi. You say it, kiwi." The children repeat the word *kiwi,* and Sam uses effective praise to acknowledge their response. After a few more repetitions of the word *kiwi,* Sam points to a red apple and says enthusiastically, "Is this a kiwi?" The children say in chorus, "No!" Sam smiles and says, "You knew this wasn't a kiwi. Let me see if I can fool you." Sam points to an orange and whispers, "Is this a kiwi?" The youngsters laugh and say, "No!" Sam laughs, too. He points to a kiwi and says in a squeaky voice, "Is this a kiwi?" The youngsters loudly say, "Yes!" Sam says, "Good. You knew that was a kiwi." He points to a lime, which is green like the kiwi. "Is this a kiwi?" he queries. The children are not so sure. Sam says matter-of-factly, "This is not a kiwi." He points to the kiwi, "*This* is a kiwi." After several instances of discriminating kiwis from other fruits, Sam says, "Show me a kiwi." Most of the children are able to point to a kiwi from among the fruits on the table. The lesson has taken only a few minutes, and Sam is pleased to hear the children using the word *kiwi* in their conversations with one another. He then shifts the activity into an exploratory mode by cutting open some of the fruit and encouraging children to investigate them as they choose.

The children in Selena Domingo's class are also receiving direct instruction when she uses a similar instructional sequence to address the appropriate use of capital letters at the beginning of sentences. First, she incorporates the instruction into a dictated story experience. Later, children will have practice using capital letters in sentences they write in their journal and in the science logs they are keeping in their cooperative groups.

Direct instruction is more than simply telling or showing children something. It encompasses task analysis, modeling, effective praise, informing and explaining, do-it signals, and challenges. Teachers either ignore inappropriate responses or provide corrective feedback as necessary. This emphasis on working toward a correct response is a significant distinction between direct instruction and exploration or guided-discovery activities. In direct instruction, the role of the adult is to combine a variety of teaching strategies so that children are right most of the time and to lead children through the required steps in such a way that youngsters learn correct responses relatively quickly. As

Sam illustrated in the kiwi activity, teachers vary their voices, their facial expressions, and the pace of the activity as part of direct instruction. They also use gestures, intentional mistakes, surprises, pauses, and enthusiasm to stimulate children's interest and to draw their attention to essential elements of the lesson (Lay-Dopyera & Dopyera, 1993). Key elements of a typical direct instruction sequence are outlined in Table 3.3.

During direct-instruction activities, adults make most of the decisions regarding what, how, and when students will implement certain tasks (Gallahue, 1993a). This level of control requires teachers to plan such lessons very carefully and to use the method sparingly. Short lessons are best. Also, something taught via direct instruction (e.g., learning a polite way to answer the telephone) is best supplemented by child-centered instruction in which there is shared responsibility for the activity (e.g., using the phone in the pretend play area, incorporating answering the telephone in role-play or puppet-play activities). In this way, direct instruction can be combined with other activity types to provide children with a well-rounded set of experiences. In fact, there is strong evidence that direct instruction makes a positive difference when it is used in combination with child-centered and shared activities as part of whole language teaching, mathematics education, social skills development, and in physical education (Baroody, 1993; Delpit, 1991; McGinnis & Goldstein, 1990; Spear-Swerling & Sternberg, 1994). Conversely, classrooms in which direct instruction is totally ignored yield less positive learning outcomes for children (McIntryre & Pressley, 1996).

Direct Instruction as Part of a Larger Learning Experience   One way to ensure that direct instruction is used appropriately and effectively with young children is to consider its place in supporting the principle of exploratory to goal-directed learning. As you will remember from Chapter 2, children move along a continuum from randomly experimenting with objects and relationships to purposefully applying the knowledge and skills they gain. This developmental sequence consists of exploration, acquisition, practice, and generalization. Direct instruction is most supportive of the acquisition phase of learning. Keeping that in mind, planners must remember that exploration always precedes any prescribed use of materials or actions. Children need lots of time to explore before moving on to

TABLE 3.3
Direct Instruction Steps With Accompanying Verbal Cues

Sequence of Steps	Sample Verbal Cues
The attention step	Look up here. I have something to tell you. Find a spot where you can see the pictures. Listen to this.
The show or tell step	Here is a _____. This is how to _____. This is what to do first.
The discriminate step (using several examples and nonexamples)	Which is the _____? Show me something that is not _____.
The apply step	Make a _____. Tell how to _____. Show how to _____. Give me an example of _____. What will happen if _____?

acquisition. For instance, children who have had few chances to examine flowers in real life will have difficulty learning facts about them. Exploration can take place on previous occasions as well as immediately prior to encountering factual information. The decision to move into acquisition is often signalled by the children (e.g., "Teacher, what's this?" or "How does the water get in the leaves?"). When children start to ask questions about an experience or when they are able to describe or show some basic understanding of a phenomenon, they are ready to acquire new knowledge and skills. In the acquire phase, teachers or peers provide instruction, and children do things to demonstrate understanding. After a small amount of instruction has been offered, children need to practice what they have learned prior to moving on to something else. For this reason, teachers use guided practice within the same activity or in other activities to reinforce the original experience. Eventually, children will generalize or apply what they have learned in one situation to a circumstance new to them. Often, children's generalization activities occur spontaneously (e.g., children generalize what they have learned about flowers in the garden to blossoms they see growing on trees). At other times, practitioners set up subsequent experiences that make such generalizations more likely to happen. The relationship among exploratory to goal-directed learning, teacher's strategies, and children's responses is outlined in Table 3.4.

Planning for Differences Among Children as Part of Direct Instruction   For every activity, there are differences among children as to which phase of the learning continuum is occupying their attention. For instance, when learning about ladybugs, one child might be involved in exploration because he has had no previous encounters with ladybugs. Another child, who has seen or had a ladybug land on her hand in the past, may be ready to learn some facts about these insects. This child is at the acquire phase of learning. Yet another child, who knows many things about ladybugs, may want to practice identifying and temporarily catching the insects outdoors. There may also be children who know so much about ladybugs that they focus on using what they know to help them better understand other flying insects. These youngsters are at the generalization phase of learning about ladybugs. To meet the needs of all the children, teacher's direct instruction plans address all four phases. Effective planners, however, recognize that individual children will not progress from exploration to generalization in one lesson. Instead, the teacher's written plan will be used again and again throughout the year. An example of a complete direct instruction activity plan is presented in the Appendix.

TABLE 3.4
The Relationship Between Exploratory to Goal-Directed Phases of Learning,
Sample Teaching Strategies, and Children's Behavior

Learning Phase	Teaching Strategy (procedures)	Child's Response (objectives)
Explore	Invite, offer, provide, encourage, reflect, imitate, use silence	Observe, touch, smell, taste, hear, examine, talk about, ask questions
Acquire	Elaborate, reflect, model, demonstrate, ask questions, tell/explain/inform, do-it signals, effective praise, correct, or ignore inaccurate responses	Carry out an action
Practice	Invite, offer, provide, encourage, reflect, vary, simplify, or expand	Repeat previous action with variations
Generalize	Reflect, ask child to describe his or her thinking	Transfer knowledge from one situation to another

MAKING AND IMPLEMENTING PLANS

Now that you are familiar with all the parts of a plan, sample teaching strategies, and typical activity types, you are ready to create and carry out your own plans. As you do so, keep the following guidelines in mind:

❏ Choose a curricular domain within which to plan your activity. Practice writing plans in each of the six domains: aesthetic, affective, cognitive, language, physical, and social.

❏ Do *not* confine your planning only to those domains with which you are most comfortable.

❏ Select an intermediate objective that supports the domain you have chosen. Refer to the list of intermediate objectives presented for each curricular domain. Choose one that fits the learning needs of the children for whom you are planning. Remember that the most basic intermediate objectives are listed first, followed by more advanced objectives. Use the initial intermediate objectives when planning for preschoolers or inexperienced first and second graders. Choose intermediate objectives further down the list as children gain experience and demonstrate mastery.

❏ Do *not* write any part of the activity before you have chosen the intermediate objective.

❏ Brainstorm activity ideas that could support the intermediate objective you have selected. Choose one to develop into an activity plan. Make sure the ac-

tivity is appropriate and of potential interest to children. Consider both developmental and contextual factors in making a final choice. Over time, make sure to plan activities that encompass all seven types described in this chapter.

❏ Do *not* select activities just because you have a particular prop or saw a great idea in an activity book. Remember to tailor your plans to meet the specific needs of the children with whom you are working.

❏ Write your plan. At first write down as much detail as possible. After you gain experience, use a shorter format but still think through your plans, referring to all the parts outlined in this chapter. Use the writing process to help you think comprehensively and creatively about the activities you plan.

❏ Do *not* assume you will be able to remember everything without writing it down.

❏ Verify each element of your plan for accuracy. Make sure that the individual segments of your plan comply with the definitions presented in Figure 3.1. Also refer to the Appendix for sample plans. These definitions should help you develop appropriate activity names, assumptions, objectives, material lists, procedures, hints for success, simplifications, extensions, and evaluation items.

❏ Do *not* suppose that effective planning happens quickly or easily. It will take time to perfect your planning skills.

❏ Complete your plan. Include all the elements listed in Figures 3.1 and 3.2.

❏ Do *not* skip or combine parts of the activity plan.

❏ Check that all the elements of your plan are congruent. The activity name, assumptions, content, objectives, procedures, simplifications, extensions, and evaluation should all relate to the intermediate objective. For instance, if the intermediate objective focuses on story sequence as illustrated in Figure 3.2, the objectives should be about story sequence, not about choosing favorite illustrations or describing the difference between fiction and fact. In a congruent plan the procedures will be closely linked to the objectives. When the objective states that "children will listen to the story one time through," the procedure must be planned to include reading the story aloud. Likewise, the content of the activity should revolve around story sequence, not information about how turnips grow in the ground. If growing turnips is what you really want children to know about, the intermediate objective would be "Children will learn facts about the natural world," and the rest of the plan would support that aim. If story sequence is the focus of the activity, the simplifications and extensions should build on this idea or break it down into smaller steps for children to manage. Extensions that have children drawing pictures of turnips or mashing them with a hand masher do not support children's development of the story sequence concept. Paying attention to congruence lends substance to your plans.

❏ Do *not* assume congruence happens simply because materials remain constant. To create the necessary curricular match throughout the entire activity, keep the intermediate objective in mind at all times. Make all parts of the plan relate to it.

❏ Prepare to carry out your plan. Gather materials in advance. Think about who will implement the activity and when, where, and how to do it. Experiment with unfamiliar activities and rehearse procedures you have not tried before. Anticipate how children might respond, and consider ways of supporting them under those circumstances.

❏ Do *not* wait until the last minute to collect what you need or to think about how you will prepare, supervise, and clean up the activity.

❏ Implement your plan. Try to follow the plan as written, adapting as necessary. Make note of children's participation, achievement of objectives, and the effectiveness/lack of effectiveness of the teaching methods you chose.

❏ *Do not* abandon your plan in the excitement of carrying it out. Neither should you rigidly follow a plan merely because that is what is written if children's behavior indicates some changes are necessary. Strike a balance between implementing plans as anticipated and remaining flexible enough to respond to children's cues.

❏ Reflect on the children's learning experiences as well as your own. Keep written records of what was accomplished. Make notes about what to change next time and how to build on the children's interests and accomplishments. Use this information to create new activity plans and to make records of children's progress.

❏ Do *not* fail to follow through on what children learn as a result of the activity. For instance, if several children meet all the objectives of the story sequence plan, prepare to move into the extensions another time soon. Avoid thinking you will remember what you observed. With so much happening every day, it is easy to forget important details. Write anecdotes, keep work samples, and answer the evaluation questions in writing to provide a resource for future planning.

SUMMARY

Planning is a key ingredient in creating developmentally appropriate programs for young children. Early childhood professionals plan for organizational, educational, and accountability purposes. Effective planning requires teachers to consider many things simultaneously. These factors include individual children and groups of children as well as past, present, and future needs and expectations. Within the planning role, teachers first think about the children in relation to what is being taught. This initial diagnostic step enables teachers to make an appropriate match between instruction and the knowledge, skills, and understandings children bring to the classroom. Following their diagnosis, early childhood professionals design, organize, and evaluate their plans. All of these functions are best expressed in writing. Novice planners write in much detail. More experienced planners keep in mind all the same elements of planning they wrote as beginners but record only the essence of their thinking.

A typical written activity plan includes the following components:

1. The curricular domain in which the activity is planned.
2. A name for the activity.
3. An intermediate objective from within the chosen domain.
4. Content covering relevant terms, facts, and principles.
5. Assumptions about what children already know and can do as well as what abilities they need to participate in the activity.
6. At least three immediate objectives, focusing on child performance.
7. All necessary materials.
8. Sample procedures.
9. Ideas for how to simplify the activity.
10. Ideas for ways to extend the activity.
11. Hints for success.
12. Three or four evaluation questions.

Children learn in many different ways. The teaching strategies that support their learning vary accordingly. Some strategies are more appropriate in certain situations than are others. Which strategies professionals use depends on what they want children to learn. Thus, establishing congruence between the goals and objectives of the activity and the selected strategies outlined in the procedure portion of the plan is essential. Four common teaching strategies are ensuring children's sensory involvement, task analysis, scaffolding, and guided practice. These strategies influence activity design and ways in which tasks are presented to children. Invitations, behavior and paraphrase reflections, modeling, effective praise, telling/explaining/informing, do-it signals, challenges, and questions are all verbal strategies that support children's learning more or less directively. Silence can also be an effective teaching strategy when it is used to deliberately facilitate children's peer interactions and self-discoveries.

All the teaching strategies described in this chapter can be combined in different ways to create activities that vary in function and form. Another dimension along which activities contrast has to do with who controls processes and outcomes—children or adults. Some activities are primarily child controlled, others involve shared responsibility between children and adults, and some activities are directed primarily by adults. The first two kinds of activities are the most prevalent in high-quality early childhood programs. However, all three have an appropriate place in the overall delivery of effective early childhood education. With this understanding in mind, seven generic activity types that form the basis for planning were presented in a sequence that proceeded from an entirely child-centered orientation to more adult-directed forms. The seven types included exploratory activities, guided discovery, problem solving, discussions, cooperative learning, demonstrations, and direct instruction. Definitions and examples of each activity type are provided in this chapter. A step-by-step description of the do's and don'ts involved in making plans is also provided. Sample plans are presented in the Appendix.

Applying What You Read in This Chapter

1. **Discuss**
   a. Based on your reading and your experiences with young children, discuss each of the questions that open this chapter.
   b. Imagine you are going to interact with children using art materials. The things available include modeling dough, various utensils such as forks, spatulas, cookie cutters, and rolling pins. Discuss what you would do to promote children's learning in an exploratory activity. Discuss how your strategies might change if you switched to a problem-solving mode. What kinds of problems might children pursue with the dough?
   c. Refer to the sample teaching strategies outlined in this chapter and select a strategy you already feel comfortable using with children. Select a second strategy you will have to work on either to become more familiar with it or more adept at using it. Explain your choices.
   d. You observe a classroom in which the children are to learn about the relative size of objects by circling the biggest items in rows depicted on a

ditto sheet. How does this correspond to your ideas about how children learn best? What other, if any, teaching strategies and types might you suggest to support children's learning?

2. **Observe**
   a. Observe the exploratory play of a younger child (below 5 years of age) and an older child (6, 7, or 8 years of age) in an open-ended activity such as sand play, block play, or water play. Describe similarities and differences between the two children in terms of what they say and do in their explorations.
   b. Watch a seasoned practitioner interact with children in an activity for at least 15 minutes. Refer to the teaching strategies outlined in this chapter and identify no fewer than three different strategies used by the adult. Describe what the adult said and did that fit the definitions offered. Conclude this observation by identifying the generic activity type you believe you saw. Explain your answer.

3. **Carry out an activity**
   a. Refer to the Story Sequence Activity outlined in Figure 3.2. Review the procedures portion of the plan. Talk about which of the sample teaching strategies outlined in this chapter are represented

in the procedures. Based on your understanding of the generic activity types described in this chapter, assign this plan to one of those categories. Explain your answer.

4. **Create something for your portfolio**
   a. Develop a statement of no more than one page, describing your beliefs about planning and ways you intend to engage in effective planning as you work with children.
   b. Select a written plan you have actually implemented with children. Evaluate the effectiveness of your teaching. Finally, write a synopsis of how you might teach the lesson again with the same group of children.

5. **Add to your journal**
   a. What is the most significant thing you have learned about planning and teaching based on your readings and experience with children?
   b. Reflect on the extent to which the content of this chapter corresponds to what you have observed in the field. What is your reaction to any discrepancies you perceive?
   c. What goals do you have for yourself related to planning and teaching activities for young children? How do you intend to pursue those goals?

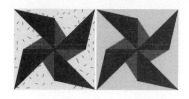

Chapter 4

Planning and Implementing Effective Whole-Group Activities

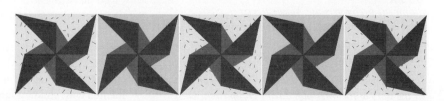

You may wonder:

With so much emphasis on individual learning, when is it appropriate to teach all the children the same thing at the same time?

What makes a good group time for preschoolers? for school-age children?

What teaching strategies help children benefit the most from whole-group instruction?

What do I need to know to manage a successful field trip?

Whom should I invite as a classroom visitor?

I n this introduction to planning and implementing whole-group instruction for young children, we present information to help you answer these questions.

Every day the 3-year-olds come together at about ten in the morning for a 10-minute circle time. Today, the teacher starts off singing, "There was a farmer had a dog, and Bingo was his name-o." The children clap as they join in singing the familiar song.

A firefighter has come to show the children the special equipment firefighters use. Youngsters sit in a circle, trying on hats and boots as the firefighter explains their use. Many are especially intrigued by the oxygen tanks and masks she shows them.

The kindergartners in Mrs. Howe's class are helping her tell the story of the three pigs during group time. Each time Mrs. Howe says the word pig, *that is their signal to snort. The snorting has led to lots of giggles as children hasten to come in on cue.*

The second graders in Mr. LaPierre's class gather on the rug for a short class meeting on measuring. The teacher invites them to watch as Louie shows how he solved the problem of measuring the size of the class guinea pig.

All of the children and adults just described are engaged in whole-group instruction. These are times during the day when all or most of the children gather in one place to share the same learning experience simultaneously. Nearly every early childhood classroom includes periods of whole-group activity, which are commonly referred to as group times and are implemented with children ranging from 3 to 8 years of age. Half-day programs usually have one or two group times in their schedule; full-day programs may have as many as three or four. The curricular focus of a particular group time might be aesthetic, affective, cognitive, language, physical, or social. Consequently, group times incorporate a wide range of activities (Brewer, 1998; Graves et al., 1996; Jackman, 1997). On any given day, the whole class may come together to do the following:

❏ Sing, dance, and experience music.
❏ Act out stories or hear them aloud.
❏ Play games.
❏ Participate in movement activities.
❏ Get instructions.
❏ Interact with a resource person.
❏ Learn about what is coming next.
❏ Discuss a problem in the room.
❏ Observe a demonstration.
❏ Plan for the session.
❏ Report on work or show others what they have accomplished.
❏ Reflect on the day.

Naturally, adults select only one or two of these activities per group time. Thus, although some group-time routines are the same from day to day, others are varied to maintain children's interest and address different aspects of the curriculum.

Carried out appropriately, group times benefit everyone involved. Most importantly, they foster cohesive group feelings. Group times are ideal for conveying important information everyone needs—a visitor is coming, the guinea pig died, these are the activities from which to choose today, or this is where we are going on the field trip. No one is left out, and everyone hears the same thing at the same time, which facilitates communication among group members. In addition, looking around the circle, children see the faces and hear the ideas of all the children in the class, not just a few as is the case in small-group activities. The joyous experience of singing together or dictating a story to which everyone contributes prompts satisfaction and pleasure in one another's company. Children who share their work, talk about their day, or otherwise engage in group discussions construct shared meanings and explore together the give and take of group membership. All these experiences foster a sense of community.

On the other hand, when whole-group instruction is carried out *inappropriately,* it is an unpleasant experi-

ence dominated by children's lack of attention, distracting behaviors, adult reprimands, and frustration for all (McAfee, 1985). Under these circumstances, teachers report that group time is the most challenging and difficult time of the day, both for them and for the children (Educational Productions, 1988). The difference between positive whole-group experiences and negative ones is careful planning and advance preparation.

PLANNING EFFECTIVE GROUP TIMES

All group times have four parts: (1) the *opening,* when children are gathering and starting to become engaged in the group, (2) the *body,* when the teacher and children are focusing on the main purpose of the group time, (3) the *closing,* when the teacher summarizes the activity and guides children into the next portion of the day, and (4) the *transitions,* the times between each activity included in the group time. All of these segments must be considered both separately and in relation to one another to provide a comprehensive whole-group experience.

The Opening

The primary purpose of the opening is to signal the beginning of group time and capture children's interest. This portion usually consists of two or three short activities (e.g., an action rhyme, followed by a "stretching" poem, followed by a quiet song aimed at bringing the children's energy level down and focusing their attention on the *body* of the group). Experienced group leaders plan to be at the large-group area to greet children as they arrive. They do not expect children to sit on the rug waiting while the adult engages in last-minute cleanup or searches for needed items. As soon as two or three children are ready, the leader begins rather than waiting until the very last child appears. Finger plays, songs, and humorous poetry attract children to the circle and are easy for children to enter at any point. Turn-taking songs and discussions are left for the *body* because children find it harder to join them midway. Youngsters who are still cleaning up or finishing an activity elsewhere soon recognize the opening activities as a signal that whole-group instruction is about to start. Effective planners think of ways to securely gain children's involvement before moving on to the body of the group time. For instance, they plan to sing a song a few times—not just once—with variations (e.g., singing the "eensie weensey spider" using normal pitch; singing it again as a tiny spider with a high-pitched voice; and singing it one last time as a huge spider with a deep-pitched voice). Another strategy is to move fluidly from one song or finger play to another, being careful not to interrupt the flow of the opening by talking in between. Thus, the group leader might start by chanting "five little hot dogs frying in a pan" (Figure 4.1) and use that finger play as a way to shift into a song involving hand motions, such as "My Finger is Starting to Wiggle" (Figure 4.2). Likewise, in a first- or second-grade group, the teacher might move from a familiar action rhyme such as "three short-necked buzzards" (Figure 4.3) to introducing a factual lesson on

FIGURE 4.1
Five Little Hot Dogs

Five little hot dogs frying in a pan (Hold right
   hand up showing five fingers),
the grease got hot (Hold left hand palm side
   up, rub with right palm in circular motion),
and one (Hold up one finger) went bam!
   (clap hard)
(Repeat words counting down four, three, two, and one)

No little hot dogs frying in a pan (Hold right hand
   up showing closed fist),
The grease got hot, and the pan went BAM!
   (End with BIG CLAP!)

FIGURE 4.2
My Finger is Starting to Wiggle
(tune: The Bear Went Over the Mountain)

My finger is starting to wiggle, my finger is
   starting to wiggle,
my finger is starting to wiggle, wiggle all
   around.

My foot is starting to wiggle, my foot is starting to wiggle,
my foot is starting to wiggle, wiggle all
   around.
(Repeat with different body parts and corresponding
   motions)

FIGURE 4.3
Three Short-Necked Buzzards
(This rhyme is said while standing.)

Three short-necked buzzards (Hold up three fingers, raise shoulders, scrunch neck, resume natural
   posture),
three short-necked buzzards (Repeat motions
   described in preceding line),
three short-necked buzzards (Repeat motions
   just described),
sitting on a dead tree (Hold arms out in an
   uneven position like the branches of a tree, stand on
   one foot).
(Repeat words and motions for two, one, and no short-
   necked buzzards)

identifying birds by their beaks and claws. The sequence of activities and the transition from one to another is planned in advance.

The Body

When most of the children are participating, the leader moves into the main purpose of the activity. Children participate most successfully when they understand what is going to happen each step of the way (Hendrick, 1996). The group leader introduces the body of the group by telling the children about the activity and then inviting their participation through strategies such as asking an open-ended question or posing a problem. Props are used to stimulate children's curiosity and interest. For instance, in introducing a guided-discovery activity about animals hatched from eggs, the first-grade teacher shows the children a real egg and says, "Look at what I have. See this egg? Today you will hear a story all about eggs. While I'm reading the story, listen for the names of animals hatched from eggs. Afterward, we'll talk about them." The teacher gives clear, specific directions to the children and uses effective praise to acknowledge appropriate behavior. Teaching strategies such as inviting, reflecting, modeling, telling, explaining, do-it signals, challenges, and questions can help support children's learning. Using an expressive face, voice, and gestures as well as props, demonstrations, pictures, humor, and mime are other ways to keep children involved and attentive.

The Closing

The closing signals the end of the group experience and serves as a transition to the next part of the day. Group leaders use this time to summarize key ideas and direct individual children into other learning activities. They never simply send children away from the group; instead, the leaders direct them toward a different activity. In some cases, early childhood professionals explain what is available and ask the children to choose one of them. An alternative is for group leaders to lightly tap the children one at a time (or use some other signal) to release them from the group. In other classrooms, teachers say something like "All the people wearing red can get up and put on their coats to go outside. Now the people wearing blue can start getting dressed." This staggers the children's exit from the area, enabling them to more easily shift from whole-group instruction to the next scheduled activity (Machado, 1995).

Group-Time Transitions

Group time is really a series of short activities connected by transitions, which are the glue that fuse the individual group-time elements into a cohesive whole. For example, a traditional group time might include the following events: introductory song, movement rhyme, short story told with props, stretching rhyme, another song, and exit from group. How well the group flows from beginning to end has a lot to do with how smooth and interesting the transitions are. It is at transition points that either children become intrigued by what is coming next or their attention begins to wander. Consider the difference between the following transitions to the song "Old McDonald":

Group Leader 1:   "Okay, everybody! Let's sing Old McDonald. Ready? Come on, let's get ready. Okay? One, two, three, Old McDonald had a farm, ee ii ee ii oo"

Group Leader 2:   (said with great enthusiasm) "There was so much block building going on today! I noticed a lot of you were making pens for the animals. I said to myself, '"It looks just like Old McDonald's farm.'" *Adult begins singing,* "Old McDonald had a farm, ee ii ee ii oo"

The first example was not very interesting and did nothing to engage the children's attention. The adult's words sounded like directions, not an invitation to get involved. Group Leader 2 capitalized on the children's earlier activity to stimulate their interest and lead them into singing the song. Linking the song to the children themselves and using an expressive voice were two strategies the second adult used to make the transition to music. The leader's words served as a bridge from the finger play she had just finished to a new activity—the song "Old McDonald."

In another situation, Gene Casqueiro, kindergarten teacher, uses the element of surprise to capture children's attention during the opening to a group time focused on storytelling (Educational Productions, 1988).

As children come to the group-time area, Gene sits on a chair facing them, holding a small carton of milk and a four-ounce paper cup in his hands. The children are intrigued.

Taking a dark gray tray lined with waxed paper from under his chair, the adult balances it on his knees. All the while, he talks softly to the children, describing his actions as he carries them out and explaining that he will be reading a story in just a minute. He goes on to say that his throat is dry, and he wants to take a little drink so he can read more comfortably.

When children make comments such as "My throat is dry, too," the teacher uses paraphrase reflections to incorporate their remarks into the interaction. "You're thirsty. After group time you can get something to drink at the snack table."

Gene pours a little milk into the paper cup. Taking a sip, he places the cup on the tray and says, "That's better. Now, where is my book. Oh, there it is." He continues to talk, maintaining eye contact with the children the whole time.

Picking up a paperback copy of the book he will read, he says, "One thing you have to be careful of is that you don't end up . . . oh no . . . it spilled. (He gently knocks over the cup on the tray.) Oh well, you know what they say, you can't cry (he pauses dramatically) . . . over spilt milk." Some children say the last words with him in chorus.

The teacher holds the tray where the children can see the milk make little pools of various shapes on the waxed

During group time, children gain a sense of community in the classroom.

paper. After a moment or two, Gene puts the tray on a nearby shelf. Showing the children the cover of the book he says, "Today the story happens to be, "It Looked Like Spilt Milk." And I just happened to spill my milk. What a coincidence." The children laugh.

Gene continues, "Well, let's see what this story is all about." Opening the book, he begins to read. The children listen with rapt attention.

This teacher combined words, gestures, and props to capture the children's interest and lead up to the title of the book. That opening was a lot more fun and did more to help children become engaged than simply saying, "Here's today's book. It's called, "It Looked Like Spilt Milk."

Transitions need not be elaborate. However, they should be thought out in advance. The aim is to have the opening, body, and closing flow smoothly, one after the other in a way that makes sense to children and helps them focus on what the leader is trying to convey. Thus, transitions require the same careful planning that goes into selecting the music, stories, demonstrations, and games that make up each portion of group time.

WRITING GROUP-TIME PLANS

Just as with all other forms of planning, whole-group experiences require a written plan. Written plans help ensure that group time has an educational focus each day and prompts teachers to use a variety of teaching strategies as well as activity types (McAffee, 1985). Many of the elements of the activity plan format outlined earlier in this volume still apply when writing plans for group times. However, the format has been adjusted to take into account planning decisions unique to whole-group instruction, such as the sequence of each lesson (opening, body, and closing) and the transition out of group time to the next event in the day. When practitioners are first learning to plan group times, they benefit from writing out all the parts of the plan. Later, a more abbreviated form can be used. A sample plan appropriate for whole-group instruction of all types is presented in Figure 4.4.

GROUP-TIME PREPARATIONS AND STRATEGIES

Location

Early childhood professionals locate the whole-group instruction area away from attractive items such as dress-up clothes and open shelves or temporarily cover those items to minimize distractions. Arranging for comfortable seating where children can easily see the group leader and sit close enough together to hear one another's voices is another consideration (Lay-Dopyera & Dopyera, 1993). Some teachers prefer having children sit in a circle, others have children sit in a clustered group, and still others prefer having children sit in a horseshoe-shaped configuration, with the adult facing the group at the open end. Sometimes the shape is

FIGURE 4.4
Sample Group-Time Plan

Date: Monday, March 17, 2000   **Activity Name:** Whole-Group Storytelling

Age of Children: 5 to 7 years

Intermediate Objective(s): Children will take on roles and act out their interpretations of those roles to tell a familiar story.

Content

1. Stories are sometimes told by one person; sometimes by groups of people.
2. The people or animals portrayed in a story are called the story characters.
3. Storytellers combine words, sounds, facial expressions, gestures, and other body motions to communicate the story.

Assumptions

1. Children are familiar with the story of the Billy Goats Gruff.
2. Children understand the meaning of the words "let's pretend."

Materials: None

Opening

1. Songs: "Hello Everybody" (incorporate children's names into song) and "I Had a Cat and the Cat Pleased Me"
2. Transition to body by talking about animals in song; lead into animals in story.

Body

3. Introduce whole-group storytelling: "Earlier this morning you heard me tell the story of the Three Billy Goats Gruff. Now, I will tell the story, and we will all act it out together."
4. Set the scene. Briefly review major events in the story and the characters. Explain that each child can be any character he or she wishes or decide to be several in turn (first the "littlest" billy goat, then the middle-size billy goat, and so on). Explain that you will be the storyteller and perhaps take on a role or two as well.
5. Begin the story ("Once upon a time . . ."), and continue the story, moving from event to event until the conclusion.
6. Announce "The End."'
7. Transition into the closing by having children clap for themselves.

Closing

8. Review with children the ways they acted like the billy goats and the troll.
9. Acknowledge children's participation using effective praise: "That was fun. You pretended so well. Some children pretended to be the biggest billy goat, some children pretended to be all three billy goats, and some children pretended to be the troll. We will play that story again soon. You can even play it yourselves when we go outside."

Transition to Next Portion of the Day

10. Dismiss by shoe color or type to go outdoors.

Hints for Success: Help children get into their roles. Offer cues such as "Now it's time for the littlest billy goat to go over the bridge. Look like a billy goat. Let's see you start across the bridge."

(continued on the next page)

FIGURE 4.4
(continued)

Carry out the activity only after the children are thoroughly familiar with the story.

The first few times, keep the story enactment short (about 5 to 7 minutes). As children gain experience, assist them in thinking of details to add, thereby extending the time of participation.

Evaluation Questions:

1. In what ways did children enact their roles?
2. How did the children differ in their interpretation of the three goats?
3. How adequate were the initial directions in helping children to interpret the story successfully? What changes might be necessary in explaining or supporting this activity another time?

---

marked with tape on the floor in a continuous line or as a series of *x*s. This gives children a specific spot on which to sit. In every case, it is critical to make sure everyone has enough room to see, hear, and move comfortably. Children who are crammed together pay more attention to protecting personal space or touching their neighbor than focusing on the whole-group activity.

Focus

The foundation for planning a good group time is knowing *what* you want children to learn, and then selecting activities to support that aim. *Having no learning objectives* leads to confusion, superficial treatment of content, and a haphazard approach to skill development. Trying to address *too many objectives* in one experience yields the same outcomes. Experienced group leaders choose one or two intermediate objectives around which to plan. In order to enhance children's understanding and provide some depth of experience, teachers relate one activity to the next. They also vary the curricular focus featured in the body of the group time from day to day. This keeps group times fresh and enables teachers to address different learning objectives over time. Thus, Monday's group time may be dominated by language-related activities, and Tuesday's group time may highlight social learning. On Wednesday, the main focus may shift to the physical domain.

Pace and Variety

Experienced professionals change the pace and variety of each whole-group activity. Quiet segments are followed by more active times; listening is interspersed with doing; teacher-directed activities are counterbalanced by child-initiated and shared types of activities. Activities demanding high concentration or effort by children, such as learning a new song or watching a demonstration, are addressed early in the body of the circle time when children are still fresh (Hendrick, 1996). As the group time winds down, children sing familiar songs and engage in relaxing activities such as stretching or listening to soothing music before starting something new.

Materials

Group times are kept interesting with the use of a variety of props (Stephens, 1996). These may include books, flannel boards, puppets, musical instruments, audiotapes or CDs, sections of videotape, nature items, real objects, pictures, charts, posters, and story books large enough for children to see. Group leaders are better able to attend to the children when they have selected their materials in advance and are thoroughly familiar with the stories, songs, poems, or instructions they intend to convey. They do not simply pull a book from the shelf at the last minute, nor do they begin a demonstration they have not thought through. Materials are carefully selected, keeping in mind the objectives of the circle time as well as ongoing emphases such as appreciation of diversity. Ms. Richards illustrates this blend of foci when she carries out a demonstration of household utensils using spatulas, tortilla turners, and chopsticks. This array of real materials is useful in addressing the intermediate objective of increasing children's awareness of tools and their function. They also support Ms. Richards's desire for multicultural inclusion. She stores all the necessary items close at hand but out of sight of the children until she needs them. To remind herself of the exact sequence of the activities she planned for group time, Ms. Richards posts a large agenda near the whole-group area, which she glances at from time to time to remind herself of what comes next. Other teachers have found it helpful to post the words to new songs or poems at eye level near the group area for their own reference and the children's.

Advanced Preparation

To increase their confidence and to avoid potential problems, group leaders practice new stories or songs before trying them out with the children. Before the children arrive on the rug, the leaders figure out the best place to position the puppet stage so everyone can see. They arrange the flannel board pieces in the correct order to avoid fumbling with them during the story. They make sure in advance that there are enough jingle bells for every child to have one. They rehearse the words they will use for the transition from one group activity to another. Strategies such as these make it more likely that group time will proceed smoothly and enjoyably for everyone.

Active Involvement

Remembering to give children firsthand experiences is as critical for group time as it is for all other learning activities. Thus, high-interest activities and ones in which children can become actively engaged are desirable for children of all ages. Additionally, whole-group instruction is appropriate only when all the children in the group are able to participate in the learning. If the activity is relevant for just certain members of the class, it is better offered during small-group or learning-center-based activity times.

Group-Time Teaching Methods

All of the teaching strategies described in Chapter 3 are applicable to whole-group instruction (ensuring sensory involvement, preparing environmental cues, task analysis, scaffolding, guided practice, invitations, behavior and paraphrase reflections, effective praise, telling/explaining/informing, do-it signals, challenges,

questions, and silence). So are all the activity types described in that chapter including exploration, guided discovery, problem solving, discussion, cooperative learning, and direct instruction activities. Here are some additional strategies group leaders use regularly (Dodge, 1995; Stephens, 1996; Torgeson, 1996). Effective group leaders often do the following:

❏ Make whole-group experiences a predictable part of the daily schedule (e.g., group time always follows cleanup or usually occurs first thing in the morning or is the last thing in the afternoon).

❏ Seat themselves where they can see *all* the children.

❏ Continually scan the group to determine children's level of interest and involvement.

❏ Make sure all the children can see them (e.g., they do not have children sit in their laps or directly at their sides where children cannot see the leader's face; some sit on a *low* chair just a little above the group or on the floor at the front of a horseshoe shape to make it easier for children to focus on what the leader is doing).

❏ Create an atmosphere to support group-time activities (e.g., use audiotaped sounds of a meadow to introduce an insect activity, dim the lights to tell a nighttime story).

❏ Use facial expressions, gestures, and variations in their voices to maintain children's attention.

❏ Involve children in setting guidelines for appropriate group-time behavior.

❏ Clarify the expectations for children's group-time behavior.

❏ Pass out materials for children to handle when they need them, not before, and collect them before going on to the next activity.

❏ Allow children to influence the group-time agenda by giving them choices (e.g., children decide what motions to make or choose between two stories to hear or two games to play).

❏ Change, shorten, or eliminate whole-group activities that are not working.

❏ Extend or repeat activities that children really enjoy.

❏ Practice, practice, practice. Experience brings effectiveness.

Preparing Other Adults to Support Group-Time Learning

Some teachers have sole responsibility for an entire group of youngsters, whereas others work in a team with staff or volunteers. When multiple people are present during group time, it is best for children if everyone is familiar with its procedures. Although there is no one right way to do things, adults should have a mutual understanding of their roles and responsibilities during the activity. Typical expectations include the following: (a) adults are expected to sit among the children, not next to each other or off to the side, (b) adults should sing along and do the motions, and (c) adults should help children focus on the leader or wait their turn to talk. Taking time to define everyone's level of participation, identifying strategies for helping children become engaged, and figuring out ways to support children who are easily distracted is important in the preparation phase of planning. Likewise, all adults should understand to what extent children are expected to come to the circle-time activity and what to do if children refuse to participate. The best way to come to these mutual understandings is to discuss them ahead of time and to communicate group-time expectations to both adults and children.

VARIATIONS ON STANDARD GROUP TIMES

The standard group time carried out in most early childhood programs combines a variety of activities such as songs, stories, and movement as well as typical routines like a job chart or weather wheel. In addition, early childhood professionals sometimes incorporate specialty groups into the daily schedule. These are periods of whole-group instruction whose purpose is more specific than the general group times described so far. They are called by certain names such as greeting time, planning time, music time, or author's circle. Early childhood professionals may regularly use one or more of these specialized group times once or twice during the week. Some common variations are described as follows:

Greeting Times

Hello everybody, yes indeed,
hello everybody, yes indeed,
hello everybody, yes indeed,
sing children, sing!

Hello to Marsha, yes indeed,
hello to LaToya, yes indeed,
hello to Samson, yes indeed,
sing, children, sing.

Greeting times begin the session, welcoming children and helping them make the transition from home to the early childhood program (Graves et al., 1996). Children have an opportunity to say hello to one another and share news of the day before dispersing into more individualized activities. Greeting times may also be used to introduce children to activities and materials available during the day. Sometimes this introduction involves simply telling children what their choices are, and sometimes it includes demonstrations of materials children will have a chance to use later in learning centers, individually, or in small groups. Other typical greeting-time activities include daily routines such as reporting on the weather or children volunteering to do certain classroom jobs like watering the plants or carrying around the cleanup sign. Greeting times are generally *brief* and often are followed by free-choice or learning center time. A second, more traditional, group time usually follows later in the session.

Planning Times

Some children start their day making a plan for how they will spend some of their time in the classroom (Clayton, 1989). Although this may take place individually, often children plan or at least announce their plans during a short group time. The purpose of planning time is to encourage children to make decisions and set goals. Plans may be verbal or written, using pictures or words. A sample "picture-plan" is presented in Figure 4.5. After children become familiar with the activities that are available during the day, they identify two or three things to do and (sometimes) the order in which they will do them. At times, children make these decisions on their own. In other circumstances, children collaborate with peers or adults in making their choices. Some plans include "have to" activities (ones the teacher has said must be completed) as well as "choice" activities from which children may freely select. As the day progresses, children periodically refer to their plans to determine how well they are following them. Some programs end with a whole-group closing time during which children

FIGURE 4.5
Planning/Reporting

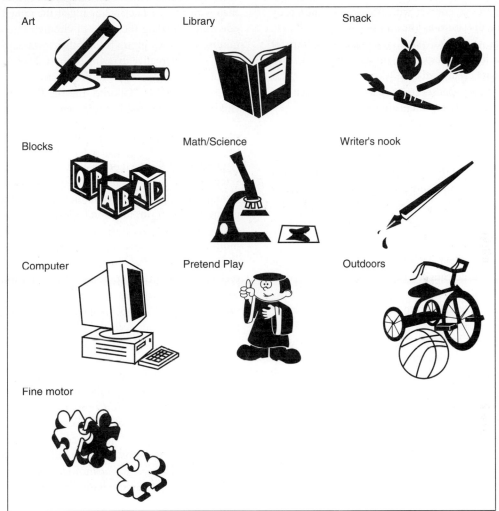

describe the extent to which they followed plans made earlier in the day. In other places, this reflection on the day is carried out one-to-one with an adult or in small-group time.

Storytelling Groups

"Once upon a time. . . ." Few children can resist the enjoyment promised by those words. Everybody likes a good story! Storytelling without a book, telling stories using flannel boards, puppets, or props, and enacting stories through dramatic movement are all activities well suited to whole-group instruction. Effective storytellers use various techniques to capture children's interest and hold it from the beginning of the story to the end (Kostelnik et al., 1991; Machado, 1995). They do the following:

- ❏ Choose stories related to the children's interests.
- ❏ Tell both familiar stories and new ones.
- ❏ Know their story well (this often includes practicing the story beforehand).

❏ Begin the story in a dramatic voice to get children's attention.

❏ Maintain eye contact with individual children by continually scanning the group.

❏ Change the speed, pitch, volume, and rhythm of their voice to correspond to the meaning of the story.

❏ Articulate each word clearly.

❏ Use dramatic pauses to build suspense or facilitate transitions between events in the story.

❏ Change their voice for each character in the story.

❏ Provide an opportunity for children to participate in the story by making sounds or appropriate gestures or having them say repeated phrases in chorus (such as "I'll huff and I'll puff and I'll blow your house down.").

Music Groups

In many programs music time is an essential feature of the daily schedule. Singing, experimenting with rhythm and beat, and moving to music are typical activities during these specialty group activities (Lay-Dopyera & Dopyera, 1993). See Chapter 8 for guidelines related to several different kinds of music activities. In every case, music times emphasize mutual enjoyment and interactive learning.

Read-Aloud Times

During these group times, adults read to children. The aim is to provide adult reading models and to share literature with youngsters in the group. Teachers may also address such literacy goals as oral language, print concepts, and story sense. Picture books with large, colorful illustrations, "Big Books," and chapter books make suitable reading materials depending on the age of the children and their interests. During read-aloud times, children tend not to sit in a circle but rather cluster around the adult, who often sits in a chair so children can more easily see and hear. When illustrations are shown, the adult turns the pages from the bottom so children have a clear view of the pictures. Holding the book up high enough for everyone to see is another essential strategy. Books with complex illustrations or small ones are better read to children individually than in a large group. In many programs, read-aloud time is a daily activity.

In addition to whole-group approaches to reading aloud, young children need opportunities for close personal interactions around books (Davidson, 1996). These are often better afforded in groups of four or five than with the whole class looking at the same book at one time. Dividing the circle of children into smaller groups, with each group having their own copy of the book, is an alternative to trying to show 20 children the pictures in a single book. Another alternative is reading a familiar story like "Clifford, the Big Red Dog" with children reading along in their own paperback copies.

Friendship Circles

A group-time format aimed at helping children develop effective social skills is the friendship circle. Although there are many variations on this specialty-group time, all forms focus on children learning to talk with one another in constructive ways as well as promoting children's development of social networks (Schmidt et al., 1992; Sharpe, 1997). Time is set aside each day for children to practice scripts they will use to talk about their feelings and resolve conflicts. This is sometimes called "I care" language—telling the other person (a) how they feel, (b) what the person did to prompt those feelings, and (c) what they want (e.g., "Jane, I *feel* upset *when you* forget to tell me it's my turn at the computer and *I want* a turn," or "Casey, I *feel* happy *when you* remember to tell me it's my turn at the computer and *I want* a turn."). Children discuss hypothetical, but typical, classroom situations. They also determine a variety of ways such problems might be solved—taking turns, listening, talking it over, getting help, sharing, or acknowledging a mistake. Friendship circles may stand on their own or serve as a foundation for class meetings.

Class Meetings

Class meetings deal with life in the classroom and are a form of children's self-government (Gartrell, 1994; Musson, 1994). They are usually aimed at topics and issues that directly affect the group as a whole such as how to manage the use of the new computers, what to do about children teasing each other, or deciding on a name for the class iguana. These are primarily discussion activities in which both adults and children become actively involved. During these times, children explore problems, suggest solutions, and develop plans (Musson, 1994). Just as with any group time, class meetings have a clear purpose and are guided by rules everyone knows (i.e., one person talks at a time, children listen respectfully, participants have a choice to speak or not, etc.). The evidence indicates that children as young as three can successfully participate in short meetings involving the whole group (Greenberg, 1992; Hendrick, 1997). There is further evidence that such meetings create a sense of community among children, leading to increased cooperation and ownership of classroom decision making (Castle & Rogers, 1994). As children gain maturity and experience, class meetings may be scheduled regularly to ensure smooth classroom functioning and provide opportunities for children to practice skills associated with democratic living (Glasser, 1985). Reaching consensus, learning to compromise, and making decisions by voting are typical skills that children gain through participation in class meetings.

Brainstorming Groups

K = What do we *K*now?

W = What do we *W*ant to know?

H = *H*ow do we want to find out?

L = What did we *L*earn?

H = *H*ow did we learn?

The KWHLH formula describes the content of specialty-group times that early childhood professionals use to increase children's understanding and involvement in their own learning. Such instruction times are usually tied to some theme or project the children are studying. At an initial whole-group gathering, children brainstorm a list of what they know about a particular topic (Kohn, 1993). The adult does not comment on the accuracy of what children think they know. As a result, this first list often combines faulty with accurate information. Next, the children create a list of what they want to find out and a third list of the means they may use to get answers to their questions. The information on these three lists influences both the teacher's planning and that of the children. Once the theme or project is under way, the children add to the lists or revise them as appropriate. To conclude the unit, the group comes together to discuss what they learned and the strategies that led to their increased knowledge. This becomes an additional brainstorming session in which children have an opportunity to consider a wide-ranging array of possibil-

ities. Comparing their original ideas with what was really true or the processes actually used to find out are additional ways children analyze their learning strategies and the outcomes of their involvement with the topic. An example of a set of KWHLH lists related to spiders that was generated by children in a multiage class (kindergarten through second grade) is presented in Figure 4.6.

FIGURE 4.6
KWHLH Lists About Spiders

What do we *know* about spiders?
Spiders are insects.
Spiders make webs.
Spiders live in an ant hole.
Spiders eat bugs.
Spiders lay eggs.
Spiders have goop around their eggs.
Spiders crawl on you.
Spiders go in tunnels and make spider webs.
Spiders are black.
Spiders bite you.
Spiders have eight legs.
Spiders are sometimes found in basements.

What do we *want* to know about spiders?
What do spiders do all day?
Why do they make webs?
What are baby spiders called?

How do we want to find out about spiders?
We can look in books.
We can watch spiders outside.
We can look for other places that spiders might live.
We can talk to people who know a lot about spiders.
We can watch a show about spiders.

What did we *learn* about spiders?
~~Spiders are insects~~. Spiders are arachnids.
Spiders make webs. Most spiders spin webs. Webs help spiders catch insects to eat. Webs help to keep the spider safe. Some spiders are "wandering" spiders. They don't make webs.
Spiders live in an ant hole. We found spiders at school, at home, and outside.
Spiders eat bugs.
Spiders lay eggs.
Spiders have goop around their eggs. This is called the egg sac. It is made of spider silk.

(continued on the next page)

FIGURE 4.6
(continued)

Spiders crawl on you.
Spiders go in tunnels and make spider webs.
Spiders are black. They can also be brown,
  white, and purple.
Spiders bite you. Most spiders are not poison-
  ous. Don't touch a spider unless you know it's
  not harmful.
Spiders have eight legs.
Spiders are sometimes found in basements.
Baby spiders are called spiderlings.
Spiders live about one year.
Spiders help people by eating insects that are
  harmful to plants.
People make up stories about pretend spiders
  like "Anansi."

How did we learn about spiders?

We talked to Mr. Boyle (farmer) and Ms. Kumar
  (librarian).
We made a spider web from string.
We found spider webs outside and at school.
We looked in books. We visited the library.
We made our own book about spiders.
We played a spider game.
We made "toothpick" spiders.
We watched two spiders.

Minilessons

There are occasions when early childhood professionals wish to convey specific information to the group as a whole. Providing instructions for how to carry out a fire drill, demonstrating place value, or teaching children map-reading strategies are examples. The best minilessons are short and to the point. They also incorporate all the characteristics of active learning associated with developmentally appropriate practice—they are not simply lectures. This kind of whole-group instruction usually precedes small-group or individualized learning experiences that build on what was presented to the entire class. For instance, Felicitas Moreno wants to teach the first graders in her class some of the same writing processes professional writers use—gathering ideas before writing, writing more than one draft, revising what they have written, and editing their work for capitalization, punctuation, and spelling with the help of older peers or adults (Graves, 1983; McGee & Richgels, 1990). With this in mind, she

conducts a *writer's workshop* for a few minutes each morning. Each writer's workshop is really a minilesson on a single topic such as how to brainstorm ideas for something to write about or how to put ideas in order from beginning to end. Sometimes Ms. Moreno demonstrates how to do something; sometimes the children work as a group to help one another. These minilessons are followed by a 15-minute writing period during which children work individually or in pairs.

Author's Chair

This specialty-group time gives children an opportunity to read something they have written (such as journals or self-designed books) to the group as a whole (McGee & Richgels, 1990.) Usually two or three children who have indicated they are ready to share their writing get a chance to read each day. Listeners ask questions following the reading (for instance, "What is going to happen next?" Or "How did you decide on the name of the story?"). They also provide feedback (such as "You thought up a really good title. It told exactly what the story was going to be about." Or "The joke you added on the last page was a fun way to end the story." Or "Those facts about toads were cool."). Such comments

This young writer proudly shares her work from the author's chair.

may be offered by children or adults. Author's circles highlight children's efforts to communicate their thoughts through writing and give group members a chance to celebrate one another's accomplishments.

Reporting Times

Reporting times provide organized opportunities for children to describe something they have done or to show their work to peers. For instance, the 4-year-olds in Mrs. Reed's class have come back from a field trip to a bakery. Each child has a chance to describe one thing he or she saw. All the items are compiled on a master list that is then posted in the room. In John Kamwi's first-grade class, the children meet three times a week in the late afternoon to report on something they have learned related to the theme. Usually four or five children get a chance to report each day. Their reports may be completely verbal or involve showing the others things they have made or classroom materials (such as books or artifacts) related to what they are talking about. Reporting times provide closure to the day's activities and foster a sense of group involvement in each person's efforts.

COMMON QUESTIONS PRACTITIONERS ASK ABOUT WHOLE-GROUP INSTRUCTION

1. **Should all children be required to participate in group time?** Early childhood professionals are divided in how they respond to this query. Some teachers believe that the goals of group time are so critical that every child should participate to the best of his or her ability. This means having each child come to the group and remain there. Other practitioners assume that, if group time is interesting enough, most children will want to join the group anyway but believe that they should not be required to do so. Youngsters who do not wish to participate may engage in quiet activities away from the group as long as they do not disturb others. Such expectations often vary according to the age and developmental abilities of the children. Consequently, younger, less experienced children may have more flexibility about participation than older, more experienced youngsters. Whichever approach you choose, it is important to be clear and consistent in your expectations so children know what is appropriate and what behaviors demonstrate compliance.

2. **What are some strategies for facilitating conversations among a large group of children?** Many group-time activities involve engaging children in conversation. However, some adults are so nervous that the discussion might get away from them that they hesitate to carry out this form of whole-group instruction. Instead, they rigidly enforce a rule of "no talking." Other group leaders attempt discussions only to have them end in chaos or with little being accomplished. Both problems can be avoided by helping children learn skills associated with the art of conversation (Freiberg & Driscoll, 1996). The place to *begin* is *in small groups* of two or three children with an adult. Even grown-ups find it difficult to converse in groups of 20 people at a time! Conversations can take place at various times of the day, formally or informally, indoors or outside. Prompting discussions with *open-ended questions, reminding children about verbal turn taking, paraphrasing one child to another,* and *helping them relate their response to the idea expressed by their peer* are all ways to enhance children's conversational abilities.

Introduce whole-group discussions by *incorporating children's spontaneous remarks* into the normal flow of the group-time activities. Eventually move to purposeful group conversations. *Use the strategies described in Chapter 3 related to guided participation, problem solving, and discussion activities.* If several children want to speak at once, *create a conversation lineup:* "First we'll listen to LaVelle, then Duane, then Grace." Periodically, *remind children* of the central question they are answering, and *recap what has been said* so far. Avoid setting up situations in which children must answer in ways that are absolutely right or wrong. Conversations are not verbal tests. If a child says something that is obviously incorrect, do not say, "Wrong!" but do not ignore the remark completely. Otherwise, you may perpetuate the acquisition of erroneous information. Instead, *find something correct* in the response, then *add a strategy or information* to make it more accurate. For example, the children were talking about fish. One child pronounced that little fish eat big ones. The teacher replied, "You know that fish sometimes eat each other. I'm not sure who eats whom. Let's spend some time this afternoon finding out if little fish eat big fish or if big fish eat the little ones. During our reporting group, we can tell people what we discovered." Another strategy is to *ask for group responses as well as individual replies* to questions you pose. Mr.

Gogglin does this as part of an estimating activity when he says, "Earlier today some people thought there might be 100 marbles in this jar. Who here estimates that the number of marbles in this jar is 100?" On a large easel pad nearby, he records the names of children who say they agree or make some physical sign of agreement. Next he asks, "Who estimates that there are fewer marbles than that?" Children respond, and he records their names. Returning to a one-person-at-a-time procedure, Mr. Gogglin says, "Stephen, you said you thought there were fewer marbles. Tell us how you decided that."

Finally, keep initial group discussions short. *Gradually increase* their *length* and complexity as children become more comfortable and adept.

3. **What should the group leader do when children interrupt a story or presentation?** The best way to avoid interruptions is to make sure children are comfortable and in a good position to see before you begin. This avoids complaints of "Teacher, I can't see." Or "Teacher, she's squishing me." Another strategy is to tell children before you begin that they will have a chance to talk when you are finished. However, children who make a connection between what you are doing and their own lives may find it too difficult to wait. There are generally two options when this happens: Incorporate their remarks into the ongoing presentation, or remind them to save their comments for the end. Sometimes it is possible to combine the two. For example, a teacher is reading the book *Green Eggs and Ham* by Dr. Seuss. Jeremy interrupts excitedly, "I had eggs for breakfast. Mine were scrambled." Immediately, the other children chime in with comments about eggs and breakfast. The teacher treats their remarks as signs of interest and says, "It sounds like you know a lot about eggs and breakfast. Let's hear what Sam did about those green eggs he had, and we'll talk about your eggs when the story is over." She continues reading. This kind of gentle redirection is more helpful and less disruptive then a long discourse on how impolite it is to interrupt. If the children continued, she might momentarily close the book and say something like "You have lots to say. This story is most fun when you can hear the rhythm of the words. If you keep interrupting, the rhythm will be spoiled. Wait until the story is over; then we will have a good long talk." After the story is over, she waits a moment to savor the mood and then expresses her appreciation to the children for waiting. Turning her attention to Jeremy she says, "Now Jeremy, tell me about those eggs you had for breakfast."

4. **What can be done to support easily distractible children?** If the group as a whole is having a hard time paying attention, it may be a sign that group time has gone on too long or that the content is not relevant or engaging. In these situations, it is best to revise your group-time plans on the spot and rethink them for the future. On the other hand, if there are one or two children who consistently find it difficult to remain focused, more targeted techniques are advisable. These are designed to help children be more successful and get the most out of whole-group experiences.

❑ Tell children who have difficulty settling down in group what will be happening during group time before they enter it. For instance, during cleanup time each day, the teacher tells Carlita the topic or main activity that will be featured at circle time. This helps Carlita make the mental transition from cleanup to group more comfortably.

❑ Have easily distractible children sit near an adult who can cue them as necessary (e.g., "Look up at the book" or "See the shell she is holding" or "Listen for what comes next."). If no other adults are available, the child could sit within arm's length of the leader (not on the leader's lap) to see and hear more clearly, without being the center of attention.

❑ Over time, use a scaffolding strategy to help the child function more independently within the group. For instance, the child may begin the year sitting on an adult's lap. Gradually supports would be withdrawn by having the child sit next to the adult, then sit one or two people away from adult, and finally sit wherever in the circle he or she chooses.

❑ Give the child something for which to watch or listen (e.g., "This is a song about an animal. When I've sung it through, tell me what animal it was about.") This strategy could be implemented privately or with the group as a whole.

❑ Give the child something to do in the group—turn the pages or pass out the rhythm instruments.

❑ Have the child start off participating in the group and then allow him or her to leave the group time midway and work quietly nearby. Gradually increase the amount of time the child stays with the group.

❑ Break the larger group into smaller groups, so that easily distractible children have more opportunities for personal attention, less waiting, and fewer competing stimuli with which to cope.

5. **What should the group leader do when children become unhappy or angry during group time?** Clarissa is not pleased with the choice of rhythm instruments that are left when it is her turn to select one. Luellen cries when she does not get her favorite colored ribbon for creative movement. Jeremiah becomes angry when he does not get to sit next to a special friend in the circle. In each of these situations, the group leader is faced with having to tend to the needs of an individual child while trying to keep the activities going for the group as a whole. There are several strategies group leaders can use in such circumstances.

❑ *Minimize potential problems over materials.* Make sure there are enough so that even the last child has at least two or three items from which to select. Although the child may still not get his or her favorite, making a choice is a more palatable option to children than settling for the one that is left. Also, if children are using rhythm instruments or some other items, have them trade midway through the activity. Announce that this will happen before you pass out the materials so children will know they will have more than one opportunity to select the object of their choice.

❑ *Acknowledge children's emotions with a simple non-evaluative statement.* "You really wanted the pink ribbon." "You were hoping to sit next to Carlos at group." When adults underscore children's emotions verbally, they exhibit sensitivity and caring in a way children can understand. This acknowledgement makes children feel heard and accepted (Kostelnik et al., 1998). Although such statements do not necessarily resolve the dilemma, they serve as a foundation for eventual problem solving. They also provide some comfort to children for whom no other satisfactory solution is possible at the time.

❑ *Problem solve whenever possible.* Give children information that may help them deal with their feelings (e.g., "In a few minutes we will be trading ribbons. You will have another chance to get a pink one."). When problems arise among children who have adequate conversational abilities, invite the child or others in the group to help figure out a solution for now or the next time (e.g., Jeremiah really wants to sit next to Carlos, but so do Ralph and Lauren. What can people do when more than one person wants to sit in the same place?"). This kind of problem solving could go on with the group as a whole or be carried out between the concerned parties quietly a little away from the group area. Depending on the flexibility of your agenda, such conversations could occur during group time or afterward.

❑ *If other adults are available, solicit their help rather than trying to deal with each problem yourself.* Signal the other adult nonverbally or use words, "Mrs. Johnson, please help Jeremiah find a spot to sit." Or "It looks like Luellen is sad. Please see what comfort you can give her."

❑ *When necessary, state clear, matter-of-fact limits.* Sometimes there is no easy solution to a child's dilemma. Under these circumstances children may behave inappropriately, grabbing an item from another child or refusing to sit down. If that happens, acknowledge the child's concern, then give the child a positive direction about what to do next ("Jeremiah, you really wanted to sit next to Carlos. There are no places left next to him. I'm worried the other children can't see the book when you stand in front of them. Find another spot to sit.").

6. **What about show-and-tell?** Show-and-tell is a routine whole-group experience in many early childhood classrooms. However, the practice gets mixed reviews from teachers and parents (Hendrick, 1996; Spangler, 1997). Some see show-and-tell as a means for children to develop both listening and speaking skills. Some like the idea that children have a chance to become the center of attention in an approved way. On the other hand, some people express concern that children may become bored sitting for long periods of time or feel coerced into speaking before the group. Still others worry that children develop competitive feelings in the process or feel left out if they think they have nothing worthwhile to share. Each teacher must decide what to do about show-and-tell. If teachers choose to carry out this experience, they should have a clear curricular goal in mind and then select strategies to match that goal. For example, if the goal relates to listening and speaking, teachers must remember that children

initially practice these skills best in small groups. Thus, having one day when children share items from home in groups of three or four is a more appropriate strategy than having several children try to show-and-tell about their items in front of the entire class each day. To minimize the idea that show-and-tell is really a time to show-off, ask children to bring in items that fit particular criteria. For instance, "bring in something blue or something that begins with the letter *k,* or something you found in your front yard." Also, make sure that children who have no items to share or who forget can find something to talk about using materials available in the program. Before show-and-tell gets under way, establish some simple rules to govern how items will be supervised. Some early childhood educators require that items remain put away until the appointed time. Some ask children to designate in advance whether the item is something they can only look at or actually touch. Such precautions do a lot to avoid tears and conflicts. Finally, be prepared to ask children one or two open-ended questions regarding the items they brought. It often helps to tell children in advance what these questions will be. Many young children have a hard time answering on the spot. They do better with some time to think about what they might say.

ADAPTING WHOLE-GROUP INSTRUCTION TO CHILDREN OF DIFFERENT AGES AND ABILITIES

Although the guidelines for whole-group instruction are the same for all children, some accommodations based on age and ability are necessary to enhance children's enjoyment and learning.

Younger, less experienced children enjoy group times that share these characteristics:

Are short in duration (10 to 15 minutes in length).

Are high on participation.

Are low on talk.

Include short songs and stories.

Begin with a familiar activity each time (e.g., a song the children know well or a favorite finger play).

Older, more experienced children enjoy group times that are structured as follows:

Are longer in duration (20 to 30 minutes).

Are high in participation.

Include discussion.

Include songs with several verses and more complex stories.

Involve both familiar and novel activities.

Include an element of surprise.

Focus on factual information as well as problem solving.

Teachers working with children in mixed-age groups must consider all the children in the group rather than simply teaching "to the middle." This could involve starting out with a whole group, implementing a short agenda, then dividing children into smaller groups to better accommodate their varying abilities and interests. Another strategy is to carry out an action-oriented body of the group with everyone and then invite children who want to stay for a longer story or conversation to do so while dismissing the others to carry out quiet activities elsewhere in the room.

Sample group-time plans for younger preschoolers and a mixed-age group of children 6 through 8 years of age are presented in Figure 4.7. Review the sample group times presented in Figure 4.7. Decide how the two group times are similar and different. Look for evidence of how each group time was tailored to meet the needs of younger or older children.

PITFALLS TO AVOID IN PLANNING GROUP TIMES

As described earlier, whole-group instruction has many potential benefits for children. Unfortunately, these benefits are not always realized. Many of the problems associated with whole-group instruction could be averted by better planning. Here are a few common mistakes people make and ways to avoid them.

Lack of Adequate Preparation

Early childhood professionals are busy people. There are so many things to do in a day that actually planning whole-group instruction may seem impossible or unnecessary. Some practitioners assume that changing the songs and the book featured at group time each day is enough variety. Others may gather the children and do whatever comes to mind until the whole-group portion of the daily schedule is over. Still others have a general idea of what they want to accomplish but

---

3-Year-Olds

Date: Monday, August 15, 2000   **Activity Name:** Rhythm Stick Fun

Age of Children: 3 years

Intermediate Objective(s): Children will explore the use of a musical instrument (rhythm sticks)

Content

1. Rhythm sticks are usually played by making a sound on the beat of the music.
2. Beat is the recurring pulse heard or sensed through the music.
3. There is more than one way to play rhythm sticks.
4. Playing rhythm sticks involves knowing when and when not to make sounds.

Assumptions

1. Children are familiar with coming to group time.
2. Children have not used rhythm sticks before.
3. Children will feel the beat in the song.

Materials: Rhythm sticks, enough for two per child and adult.

Opening

1. Song, "Everybody, sit down, sit down, sit down, everybody, sit down, sit down here" (tune: "Everybody do this"). Clap on the beat as you sing.
2. Transition to body—continue song, making motions in time with the beat. "Everybody, clap your hands, clap your hands, clap your hands, everybody, clap your hands, just like me. Everybody, tap your feet . . . everybody, shake your head . . ."

Body

3. Say: "We just sang a song using our hands and feet to make special sounds with the song. We'll sing that song again using musical instruments called rhythm sticks. Watch me as I show you how to use the rhythm sticks."

   Do: Take two of the rhythm sticks and demonstrate to the class how they work. Tap them together quietly, then louder; tap them quickly, then slowly; rub them together in a circular motion to make a gentle swishing sound. Tell the children what you are doing as you make the various sounds.

4. Say: "Before I pass out the sticks, I want to show you a signal that I will use when everyone's sticks must be quiet. When I hold the ends of my rhythm sticks on my shoulders like this, it means be quiet. When I play my sticks, that means it's time for you to play."

   Now it's time to pass out the sticks. As you get your sticks, place them on your shoulder like this in the 'be quiet' position."

   Do: Ask the adults to pass out the rhythm sticks, and remind the children to hold the sticks against their shoulders. Model this behavior as the children receive their sticks.

(continued on the next page)

FIGURE 4.7
(continued)

5. Say: "Now that everyone has their rhythm sticks, let's practice how to use them. Take your sticks and tap them together like this. Try tapping them fast like this. Now slowly. Tap them loud. Now softly. Rub your sticks together like this to make another kind of soft sound. You're doing a great job! Now let's sing a song while we play our instruments."

Now sing, "Everybody, tap your sticks, tap your sticks, tap your sticks, everybody, tap your sticks, just like this." Keep singing the song, each time changing the method of tapping the sticks as practiced earlier. Match the way you sing the words with the way you play the sticks. For example, as you are tapping quietly, sing in a very quiet voice.

Closing

6. Say: "We have had a great time playing the rhythm sticks. That was fun. It's time now to pass your rhythm sticks to an adult."

Transition to Next Portion of the Day

7. Say: "Let's get in our jack-in-the-boxes."

Do: Model huddling low to the floor on hands and knees, face in arms resting on the floor.

Say: "Jack in the box, you sit so still. Won't you come out? Yes, I will."

Do: On the last words, pop up on knees, hands outstretched above head. Repeat once more.

Say: "This time stay in your jack-in-the-box until I tap you. Then you may get up and find a place to play."

Do: Tap each child one at a time until all have been released from the group.

Hints for Success: To facilitate the process of passing out the rhythm sticks, place several pairs in paper bags so each supporting adult will have one bag of rhythm sticks to pass out when you say it is time to do so.

Evaluation Questions

1. To what extent were children able to use the rhythm sticks as modeled?
2. Did anyone have difficulty finding the beat? If so, what scaffolding strategy might you use to help him or her next time?
3. What future activities will you create based on the children's experience in this activity?

Primary School Mixed-Age Group

Date: Monday, April 15, 2000   **Activity Name:** Global Fun

Age of Children: 6, 7, and 8 years

Intermediate Objective(s): Children will gain knowledge related to social studies (maps and globes)

Content

❏ A globe is a sphere on which is drawn a map of the earth.
❏ The brown and green shapes on the globe represent land.
❏ The blue shapes on the globe represent water.
❏ The earth's surface contains more water than land.

FIGURE 4.7
(continued)

Assumptions

❏ Children are familiar with two-dimensional maps.
❏ Children know how to play simple games with rules.
❏ Children understand how "tallies" work.

Materials: Books in book basket, calendar materials, poem chart with acetate cover, large flat map of the United States, "Waldo" character, state coloring chart, crayons, box with individual cards giving information about each of the 50 states, three plastic globes (about the size of a basketball), very small stickers (enough for each child to have one).

Transition into Opening

❏ **Books:** As children come into the room the first thing each day, they are greeted by teacher and then choose books from a book basket on the group-time rug. Children read individually or with other children.

After 15 minutes the "book leader" collects the books and puts them in the basket while children sing the "bookworm" song.

Opening

❏ **Songs/chants:** One or two class favorites.
❏ **Calendar:** Calendar helper locates yesterday, today, and tomorrow on calendar. Child adds a popsicle stick to the "ones" box to represent the number of days the children have been in school this year and writes the corresponding numeral.
❏ **Poem of the week:** (Poem about traveling) One child points to the words on the poetry chart as the group recites it together. The teacher calls on children to circle and read the words with *th, sh,* or *ch* digraphs.

Transition to Body

❏ **Movement activity:** Short stretching exercise that refers to geographic features (climb up the mountain, swim through the sea, etc.)

Body

❏ **State review:** Teacher says, "It's Cara's turn to choose a new state. She will move Waldo to a new state on the map of the United States." Cara chooses any state. Teacher asks her why she chose that state, asks the group if they know anything about the state or anyone who lives there, or if anyone has traveled there. Cara locates the state she chose on the coloring map and colors it in any color. Adult pulls the corresponding state card out of the state box and gives children some information about the state. Cara uses the pointer and points to each state previously chosen as children recite the names of the states.
❏ **Land or water game:** Adult divides children into three groups. Each group gets a globe.

Adult explains that this is a globe and that globes are a type of map. Adult uses guided-discovery strategies as children examine globes.

What do you notice about this object?
What do you think the colors mean?
(Adult provides information as necessary.)
What do you think you see more of—land or water?

(continued on next page)

FIGURE 4.7
(continued)

Adult collects globes, puts two aside, and explains: "We're going to play a game to help us locate land and water on the globe. Raise the hand that you write with in the air. Now point to the ceiling with your pointer finger, and I am going to come around and put a sticker on your fingernail. Here are the rules to the game. When you have the globe, decide who you will roll it to, then call out their name. Be sure to roll the globe." Adult demonstrates. "When you catch the globe, look at your sticker finger and decide if it has landed on land or water." Adult writes the words *water* and *land* on the board or on chart paper. "If your finger touches land, I will put a tally mark under that word. If your finger touches water, I will put a tally mark under that word. Which do you predict will have more tally marks, land or water? Why?

Group plays game until everyone has had a chance to catch the globe and identify land or water. At the game's end, adult and children count the tally marks and talk about the results.

Closing

❏ Adult lets children know globes will be available if they would like to play the land and water game during free-choice time. Suggests the children could see if they get the same basic results each time.

Transition to Next Portion of the Day

❏ Adult briefly describes choices available during free-choice time. Adult asks who would like to start on their journals (and so forth) and then dismisses children in small numbers as they indicate their choices.

Hints for Success

❏ Encourage children to roll the globe rather than throwing or bouncing it so it is easier to catch and remains in the circle.

Evaluation Questions

❏ To what extent were children able to identify land and water?
❏ How accurate were children's observations?
❏ What unexpected outcomes may have occurred during this group time?
❏ What future activities will you create based on the children's experience in this activity?

Source: For three-year olds: Grace Spalding, Child Development Laboratories, Department of Family and Child Ecology, Michigan State University, East Lansing, Michigan. For primary school mixed-age group: Deborah Sharpe, Wilkshire Early Childhood Center, Haslett Public Schools, Haslett, Michigan.

continually interrupt themselves or halt the group because they do not have everything they need immediately at hand. When this happens, children become restless and inattentive. Control problems proliferate under these circumstances, and children leave group time having gained little of educational value (McAffee, 1985). The antidote for the problem is to plan ahead for whole-group instruction. Joanne Hendrick, a long-time early childhood teacher/director and professor emerita at the University of Oklahoma says, "Providing educationally worthwhile group times takes self-discipline and energy combined with sincere convictions . . . self-discipline to sit down and plan such experiences in advance, energy to carry out plans once they have been made, and conviction that group time is valuable enough to make careful planning a consistent

FIGURE 4.8
Abbreviated Group-Time Agenda

Activity Name: Whole-Group Storytelling

Intermediate Objective(s): Children will take on roles and act out their interpretations of those roles to tell a familiar story.

Opening: Songs, "Hello, Everybody" and "I Had a Cat and the Cat Pleased Me"
Transition to body—talk about animals in song, lead into animals in story.

Body: Introduce whole-group storytelling.
Begin the story of the Billy Goats Gruff; continue by encouraging children to act out various roles.
Announce "The End."

Closing: Review with children the ways they acted like the billy goats and the troll.
Acknowledge children's participation.

Transition to Next Portion of the Day: Dismiss by shoe color or type to go outdoors.

part of the program . . . not just once in a while, but daily" (Hendrick, 1997, 387). At first, it will be necessary to write out a whole-group plan for each group time. Once the decision-making steps involved are internalized, written plans become more brief, often encompassing only the educational objective and the highlighted feature activity for each whole-group segment of the day. An abbreviated group time agenda for the Billy Goats Gruff group time featured earlier in this chapter is presented in Figure 4.8.

Relying on Whole-Group Instruction to Meet Objectives Better Addressed in Smaller Groups

Sometimes practitioners plan activities using a whole-group format when children would benefit more from working on the task with fewer peers. For instance, attending to others and waiting your turn to speak are important receptive listening skills. Children learn these behaviors like they learn everything else—a little at a time and gradually. Being expected to wait long enough for 10 or 20 other youngsters to say an idea, have their turn to touch the turtle, or come to the front of the group, one at a time, is inappropriate for most youngsters 3 to 8 years of age. Although children need practice improving their turn-taking skills, task analysis would suggest that the wait time has to be reduced.

One way to accomplish this is to divide the total number of children into smaller groups for discussions and other turn-taking activities. Such divisions could happen during scheduled group times by dividing preschoolers into smaller groups according to the number of adults available. First- and second-grade children could be divided into self-directed groups of four or five children each. Children complete a task and then reconvene as a whole. For example, the teacher has a variety of shells for children to examine. Rather than passing the shells around the entire circle one at a time, she has the children form four smaller groups within the large group area. Each group gets four or five shells to look at, making it possible for youngsters to handle and examine the shells without much waiting. After several minutes, all twenty children come together again to talk about what they observed.

Another strategy is to reserve activities that require much waiting for periods in the day other than group time. This does not mean that children should never have to wait as part of whole-group instruction. However, those periods should be brief.

Selecting Inappropriate Materials

Picture books with illustrations that are too small, too pale, or too busy for children to see clearly; songs that have too many verses; flannel board pieces that do not stick; incomplete items; and things that malfunction are examples of inappropriate group-time materials. It is also important to remember that representational materials are more difficult for children to learn from than real objects. Whenever possible, group leaders choose the real things over a replica, a replica over a picture, and a picture over words alone. Whole-group activities that rely heavily on talk with few other sensory prompts are reconsidered in light of what planners know about the children, children's experience, and the context of the learning environment. Likewise, items that support the theme but undermine other curricular goals are avoided or revised to make them more appropriate. This was the case for Marlene Grubbs, who wanted to teach children about settings in which community workers functioned. Searching through the program's picture file, she found a set of community helper pictures that were large, colorful, and supportive of her main idea. Unfortunately, they depicted only male workers and did not represent the full range of possibilities for boys and girls that Marlene wanted to portray. Rather than being satisfied with the pictures as they were, Marlene sought additional images that included women as well. This kind of attention to detail helped Marlene ensure that her group-time materials were appropriate both in terms of her short-range objectives (supporting the theme) and her long-range goals (promoting respect for both genders).

Incorporating Too Many Routinized Activities Into Whole-Group Instruction

In some classrooms, daily activities like the calendar, completing a weather chart, assigning classroom jobs, show-and-tell, and taking roll all take place during whole-group instruction. Furthermore, it is not unusual for many of these routines to be combined in the same time period. This makes group times longer and shortens the time available for other whole-group activities. Consequently, children's enthusiasm for group time may be dulled, children wait long periods, and their exposure to the real core of group-time activities comes when they are no longer fresh and interested. There are several ways to avoid these negative outcomes. One is to eliminate some routines altogether. Some early childhood professionals strongly believe activities like the calendar and show-and-tell are developmentally inappropriate due to their abstract nature

and the use of procedures that may create competition or unfavorable comparisons among children (Brewer, 1998; Katz, 1996). However, many practitioners believe that certain classroom rituals add to the predictability of the day and that children benefit from making choices or participating in discussions relative to such matters. No matter what routines you decide are appropriate for the children in your class, always remember to consider each one in terms of what children are learning and whether whole-group instruction is the best mode for approaching that learning. For instance, attendance could be completed as children arrive, and completing the weather chart could be a learning center activity instead of a mandatory whole-group endeavor each day. Similarly, show-and-tell could shift from being a whole-group activity to one carried out in small groups. Additionally, because many programs have more than one group time a day, essential routines can be divided among them. This frees up time for children and teachers to engage in other, more varied whole-group activities.

Waiting Too Long to Engage Children in Active Learning

Young children are naturally impulsive. They find waiting difficult. Active bodies and active minds make it hard for them to sit still or concentrate on something happening 3 feet away rather than something closer like the movement of a peer or an ant crossing the floor right in front of them. It is asking a lot to have children listen quietly to a group leader who is several persons away from them and to sit for many minutes without moving. Thus, a long-winded opening that consists of 15 minutes of telling and explaining before getting to something more engaging in the body of the group time is too long for most children ages 3 to 8 years of age. Likewise, asking 3- and 4-year-olds to sit through the calendar, four songs, and a story before dancing with scarves is pushing the limits of their abilities. Even youngsters in the first and second grade find it demanding to sit so long with no other form of engagement. Group time is not a synonym for "sit time," nor does whole-group instruction have to be passive. Planning appropriate group times means getting children actively involved early in the procedure and often. Such engagement can take many forms. For example, children who are singing a song can do the motions, clap or

The best group times include periods of active movement.

slap their thighs in time to the music, change positions (stand up, sway, crouch, put their hands over their head, and so forth), listen for certain words or phrases in the song, vary the volume and pitch of their voices, vary the speed of the words, and engage in call and response. Children listening to a story can become more active participants by responding with a motion to various instructions within the story, saying a repeated line in chorus, miming some of the characters' actions, or filling in a word or line as relevant.

A guided-discovery activity could include items for children to handle as well as questions to answer as they go along rather than having all the talk at the end of the procedure. During a demonstration children might watch for certain things to happen or signal the leader in a special way when they note a process is beginning or ending. Youngsters could also talk the leader through a demonstrated procedure, catch the leader making "mistakes," or imitate actions through pantomime or using objects.

Group Times Going on Too Long

Early childhood professionals have different beliefs regarding the suitability of large-group time for preschoolers. Some counsel against using whole-group instruction with children 3 and 4 years of age at all

(Brewer, 1998). Others caution that such times should begin for only a few minutes a day, lengthening gradually as children become more experienced (Hendrick, 1996). As children in kindergarten and first and second grade develop group-time skills, their overall ability to enjoy and benefit from whole-group activities as long as 20 to 30 minutes increases. However, this remains true only so long as the other criteria defining appropriate group times, such as active involvement and purposeful activity, are maintained. No matter what age the children are, it is always better to bring group time to an end before children lose interest (Jackman, 1997). Thus, group time follows the theatrical adage, "Always leave them wanting more." Remember, too, that activities carried out in group time should be repeated or supplemented beyond the whole-group instruction period. For instance, a flannel board story featured during group time could be made available in the library corner for children to use to reenact the story, the materials to conduct an experiment demonstrated at group time could be offered to smaller groups of children later in the day, and the book written, published, and read by a first or second grade "author" can be displayed for children to reread on their own.

All of the whole-group instruction activities described so far occur daily or at least weekly. Other whole-group gatherings are less frequent but no less important—field trips and classroom visits by members of the community.

FIELD TRIPS AND VISITORS

A walk around the block, a trip to the grocery store, or an excursion to the local arboretum all provide active, concrete opportunities for children to learn about people, places, and things outside the immediate realm of the classroom. Excursions into the community broaden children's understanding of the world in which they live and offer ways to diversify the curriculum through firsthand experience (Anziano et al., 1995). Such trips may be as simple as visiting the mailbox on the corner or as elaborate as a day at the museum. They may take only 20 minutes to complete or occupy most of the session. They may sometimes require transportation. No matter what the circumstances, all field trips require careful planning, implementation, and follow-up.

Planning a Field Trip

Planning a successful field trip requires generating thoughtful answers to the following questions.

1. *What is the purpose of the trip?* Because their function is to help children make sense of the world, field trips, like all other educational activities, must have a definite purpose clearly tied to the curriculum (Eliason & Jenkins, 1994). The best way to ensure that this happens is to plan around one or two objectives within any of the curricular domains described in this book. For example, a trip to a garden could focus on plant identification (cognitive domain), or it could emphasize children's using all their senses to experience the wonder and beauty of the garden (aesthetic domain). Although one focus does not entirely preclude the other, the activities you carry out at the garden will differ depending on the goal you choose. For instance, to foster plant identification skills, Eileen Verstoefel organized a plant scavenger hunt to stimulate children's interest in recognizing certain plants. Each small group of children had a plant book and notepad to use in recording their observations. Adult comments at the garden centered around labeling the plants and promoting children's observations aimed at differentiating one plant from another. The strategies associated with an aesthetic goal would not be exactly the same. For instance, to encourage children to use their senses, the

teacher might have them sit in a circle, close their eyes, listen quietly, and then describe the sounds they hear. Youngsters would be urged to smell the plants and touch them gently. Arranging with garden personnel to allow children to taste some edible plants would also contribute to children's aesthetic awareness. The names of the plants would not be emphasized nearly so much as the sensory impressions children were having. In each case, children would learn from their garden experience, but the primary result of that learning would have been shaped by the purpose of the trip.

2. *What is your destination?* There are many wonderful places for children to visit in their communities. Refer to Table 4.1 for a partial listing of these. However, not every site is appropriate for every group of children. For instance, a place that is fascinating to 8-year-olds (like the local television station they watch every day) could be incredibly boring and incomprehensible to 3-year-olds. Likewise, visiting a greenhouse could be quite interesting if the plants are low enough for children to see easily but very frustrating and ineffective if the plants are on high shelves far above the children's eye level. Thus, after you have chosen a potential site based on what you want the children to learn, it is important to visit the site in advance to determine its actual suitability.

During this preliminary visit, do the following:

❏ *Consider to what extent the site allows children to act like children.* This includes (a) moving about freely, (b) making some noise, and (c) participating in a hands-on activity rather than remaining passive observers (Hendrick, 1996). The more closely the site meets these conditions, the more successful the trip will be.

❏ *Determine how well the site will support your educational goals.* Preview what children will actually see, hear, and do. If on-site personnel are to be involved, talk with them in advance, discussing the developmental needs of the children involved, the amount of time available, and the size of the group. Talk about your goals and find out how well site-based resource people can help you achieve them. Keep the children's interests and abilities in mind at all times. Remember that a field trip that worked well with a previous group of children may or may not be suitable for the current group with whom you are working. Also, people and places change. This

TABLE 4.1
Potential Field Trip Sites

Orchard	Dentist's or Doctor's Office	Bakery
Greenhouse	Veterinarian's Office	Retail Store
Garden	Artist's Studio	Restaurant
Natural Wooded Area	Television or Radio Studio	Museum
Park	Newspaper Office	Garage
Butterfly House	Construction Site	Car Wash
Fish Hatchery	Fire Station	Bus Ride
Stream or Pond	Post Office	Library
Farm	Train, Truck, or Air Terminal	Grocery or Market
Nature Center	Boat Dock/Marina	Pet Store
Planetarium	Home for the Elderly	Water Treatment Plant
Aviary	Hair Styling Shop	Recycling Center
Aquarium	Weather Station	Theater
Meadow/Plain	Lumber Yard	Laundromat
Bridge	Gymnasium	Stadium
City Fountain	Ice Rink/Roller Rink	Teacher's Home

makes a preliminary visit desirable even if you have been to a location before.

❑ *Determine how long the trip will take.* Inexperienced and younger children as well as ones enrolled in half-day programs should spend no more than 20 minutes walking or riding (one way) to the site. Older, more experienced youngsters enrolled in full-day programs can tolerate up to one hour of riding time in one direction without ill effect (Eliason & Jenkins, 1994; Michigan Family Independence Agency, 1996). No matter how attractive the final destination is, if children have been walking or riding too long to get there, they will neither enjoy nor benefit from the experience. It is better to make long-distance trips when children are beyond the early childhood years.

❑ *Consider how to meet children's biological needs during the trip.* These include using the toilet, having access to food and water, and resting periodically. If it is not possible to meet these needs, choose another place to visit.

❑ *Check the site for handicapper accessibility.* Will everyone have easy access to all areas of the site in which the group will be participating? It is not acceptable to exclude any member of your party due to inaccessibility. In addition, think through how children, family members, or staff members with special needs will benefit from traveling to this site. For instance, a children's play that makes no accommo-

dation for people with severe hearing loss will not be the best choice if you have a child with this condition in your group.

❑ *Check for potential safety hazards,* both at the site and getting there and back. Every effort must be made to ensure the safety of all participants. Any place in which safety is questionable is inappropriate.

❑ *Determine logistical details specific to the site.* These might include determining a potential meeting place outside or inside the facility, a suggested sequence through the facility, where to take shelter in case it rains or is too hot, special events that may occur during your time at the site (e.g., feeding times at the zoo), and what to be sure to see or avoid.

Once the site has been selected and finalized, early childhood professionals continue planning by answering the next seven questions.

3. *When will the trip take place?* The time and date of the trip will be influenced by site availability, access to transportation (if necessary), obtainable adult support, and the time of day when children are most alert and comfortable. Another factor to consider is whether the trip will serve as an introduction upon which future classroom experiences will build or function as a capstone experience aimed at helping children synthesize what they have learned. Once these questions have been answered, plan accordingly.

4. *How will children get to the site?* Whether you have planned a walking field trip or one requiring transportation, it is essential to think through the route you will take and anticipate any problems that might arise on the way.

For a *walking field trip,* walk the route yourself, remaining alert to potential dangers such as construction or fast moving traffic. Plan how you want the children to walk: single file, as partners, holding hands, or paired with an adult. Prepare to take along a lightweight STOP sign for an adult to hold up in case you reach a difficult corner without crossing assistance. Assign one adult to be responsible for handling the sign whenever you need it (Rohde, 1996). Be realistic about how far your class can walk in comfort. If necessary, plan to walk in only one direction. For example, children may walk to the post office several blocks away and then return by van to the center or school.

For *field trips requiring transportation,* the program may provide drivers as well as buses or vans. In many programs, this must be arranged several weeks in advance, and permission must be obtained from appropriate program supervisors. Other programs rely on parent volunteers to drive. When soliciting adult drivers from children's families, advance notice is necessary to make sure enough vehicles and seat belts are available. In addition, it is important to make sure every driver has a legal driver's license and appropriate insurance. Soliciting backup drivers in case someone cannot make it at the last minute is a good idea as well. If going by car, each vehicle should have these items:

a. A map showing the route between the program and the field trip site.

b. The phone numbers of the early childhood program and the site you will be visiting.

c. A list of all persons riding in the vehicle.

d. A seat belt for each person.

e. A field trip first-aid kit (bandages, soap, moist towelettes, paper cups, a fresh container of potable water).

f. An emergency card for each child riding in the vehicle, listing a place to reach the parent and emergency medical information (these are required by law for all children enrolled in most state-licensed preschool programs and are a good idea for elementary children, too).

g. Sample songs to sing or information for adults to share with children on the way to the site or coming back to the program.

h. A schedule of the day, specified times for gathering, such as snack and lunch times, a designated time for leaving, and procedures in case someone gets lost or becomes ill.

Prepare all of these items in advance and have them on hand the day of the trip.

5. *What kind of supervision will be necessary?* Adult supervision involves keeping children safe as well as drawing their attention to relevant features of the trip, extending concepts, and answering questions. Plan supervision based on the number of children going as well as logistical considerations such as having to cross busy streets or going to a crowded location in which it may be difficult for any one adult to keep track of more than two or three children at once. If possible, it is helpful if the group leader is not responsible for a particular group of children. This allows him or her to keep a global view of the group as a whole, to more easily address unexpected problems that may arise, and to interact with resource people at the site as necessary. For children ages 3 to 5, a ratio of one adult to every three or four children is desirable; for youngsters 6 to 8, there should be one adult to every five or six children (Eliason & Jenkins, 1994; MSU Child Development Laboratories, 1997). Regardless of how small the group might be, there should always be at least two adults. If you are going by car, van, or bus, plan to have two adults in each vehicle, one to drive and one to supervise the children. In addition, have at least one adult available to stay at the center or school if a child does not have permission to go on the trip or if a child refuses to participate. If there are not enough adults to carry out the trip safely and enjoyably, the trip should be postponed to a time when adequate supervision is available.

6. *How will permission be obtained for children to participate?* In most states permission must be granted by parents or guardians before children can take part in any excursion away from the center or school. Some programs ask families to sign a blanket form once a year allowing children to take part in program-sponsored field trips; others require separate permission slips for each trip. A sample consent form is pre-

FIGURE 4.9
Field Trip Announcement/
Consent Form

Part 1: Introduction: Where (name and location of site), when (day and date), and why (purpose of trip) you are going.

Part 2: Permission for child to participate: (Child's name) has my permission to participate in the field trip described above. I understand that transportation will be provided by (private automobile/program vehicles) and that the group will be leaving (name of program) at approximately (insert time) and returning at approximately (insert time).

_____
(parent/guardian signature/date)

Part 3: Opportunity to decline participation: I prefer that my child not participate in the field trip described above and will make alternate arrangements for her/his care on that day.

(*Or, depending on program policy*)

I prefer that my child not participate in the field trip described above and expect that he or she will remain at the program site that day.

_____
(parent/guardian signature/date)

Part 4: Request for drivers: I would be willing to drive. My vehicle is in safe operating condition, is insured, and I have a valid driver's license. My vehicle has _____ seat belts in addition to one for the driver.

This permission form was created by Donna Howe, specialist, Department of Family and Child Ecology, Michigan State University

sented in Figure 4.9. Even when parents provide blanket permission, they must be notified before each field trip and told when and where the children will be going. *No* child may go on a field trip without written permission from his or her parent/guardian. Follow-up phone calls or written reminders are sometimes necessary to acquire all appropriate permissions.

7. *In what ways might parents or other family members be involved in the field trip?* Field trips provide great opportunities to include parents and other family members in children's educational experiences. Inviting parents to come along on a trip to the farm, to the river to feed the ducks, or to the bicycle shop promotes home-school interaction and contributes to a sense of community among children and adults. Moreover, family members can provide supervision or transportation to make certain trips possible. Another option is to visit a parent's place of work and have him or her

serve as tour guide. In any case, if you plan to have parents participate, they must be given ample notice of when and where the trip will take place, its purpose, and what their role will be. Written notification is a must. When these are supplemented by personal invitations, parents know they are truly welcome. Only after you have answered all of these questions satisfactorily are you ready to actually carry out the field trip you have planned.

8. *How will the lesson continue after the field trip is over?* For children to get the most out of a field trip, it is important that they have opportunities to tell what they have learned and to build on their experience after they return to the center or school. Plan how this will happen in advance. Do not leave such learning to chance.

9. *What is your backup plan?* Anticipate what might go wrong and have an alternate strategy in mind for these dilemmas. What will you do if a driver calls in

sick, how will you handle it if someone gets lost en route, what will you do if a parent says his or her child cannot participate at the last minute? The time to figure out what to do in such circumstances is beforehand, not afterward. Brainstorm with colleagues about potential problems and their solutions. In addition, sometimes things happen that prompt cancellation of the trip altogether—a site might unexpectedly close, or it may rain on field trip day. Thus, every field trip plan should include what you will do if the original activity falls through or does not take the full amount of time you allotted. This means you should have rainy-day alternatives to outdoor excursions or some activities to get out if the trip is shorter than planned and children get back to the building 45 minutes earlier than expected. Some teachers have a repertoire of stories, songs, and games they keep in mind for just these kinds of occasions. Others keep a backup box in which they have materials for activities they can access in a hurry if conditions warrant. One kindergarten teacher's backup box contained the following items from which she could select one or more as the situation required: (1) an audiotape the children particularly enjoyed and colored streamers, (2) directions on index cards for some lively cooperative games that were easy for an adult to get started, (3) an electric popcorn popper, oil, raw popcorn, napkins, and (4) a stack of felt caps the teacher could use to act out the story "Caps for Sale." If she used an activity, she would replace the materials with something else for another time. In this way the backup box was kept "fresh" and interesting.

FIELD TRIP DAY

Children learn best and support personnel are most helpful when they have an idea of what will happen before, during, and after a field trip. Thus, the first step in field-trip implementation is preparing children and adults for what to expect.

Preparing the Children

At the Hilltop Nursery School, children have been involved in a variety of activities over several days focused on vehicles and vehicle repair. Today, Ms. Oblicki uses a whole-group information time to prepare children for a trip to a local garage. She explains that during this trip they will have a chance to see mechanics working on ve-

hicles using a variety of tools and machines. The teacher describes how the children will be divided into small groups with each group assigned to a particular adult. The children are cautioned to remain with their group at all times. Ms. Oblicki explains what will happen once they arrive at the garage and the rules everyone must follow around the tools and vehicles. Next, she invites the children to talk about what they think they will see. She makes a list of their ideas and encourages them to look for these things when they get to their destination. The teacher says they will refer to this list when the group returns from their outing.

The children at the Walnut Acres after-school program will walk several blocks to see different kinds of buildings along the route. This is a path the children have traveled many times before but with different purposes in mind. Prior to assembling the children, the teacher follows the route, taking pictures of distinctive buildings along the way. Back at the program, he puts the pictures on a bulletin board and invites the children to look at them throughout the week, explaining that these are sites they will see during their walk. The morning of the outing, the children select partners. They are reminded that they will be walking side by side, not running. Next, the teacher challenges the children to look along the way for the places they saw in the pictures. Each pair of children is given one building to find. He mentions that when they get back, they will have a chance to talk about "their buildings." They may even try to arrange the pictures in the order in which they appeared during the walk.

In each teacher's preparation of the children for the field trip, she or he included the following information: a reason for the trip, group assignments, what to expect, what to look for, safety precautions, and necessary limits. Such information helps children behave in constructive, safe ways and get the most out of their field-trip experience. Final details include making sure the children have had a chance to use the toilet and minimizing the amount of wait time required for them to stand in line or sit all bundled up in a vehicle before the trip begins. Providing the children with colorful tags to wear on which the program name and phone number are prominently displayed is a safety precaution many programs take. These provide valuable information in case a child becomes separated from the group but do not reveal the child's name to strangers.

Preparing the Adults

Just as children benefit from knowing about things in advance, so do adults. Adults accompanying children on a field trip need to hear everything involved in the children's preparation as well as guidelines regarding their supervisory responsibilities (Hildebrand, 1997b). Adults feel more comfortable when they have been informed of the rules and any special considerations such as how to interact with a child who moves only with the aid of a walker or strategies to help an easily frustrated child feel more relaxed during the trip. Volunteers and support staff will be better able to support the field-trip focus if you make clear what it is and provide a few ideas for things they might do or say in keeping with that focus. Provide such guidelines in writing as well as orally. Ask volunteers to arrive a few minutes early so there is enough time to orient them to the trip and allow them to ask questions as necessary.

At the Field Trip Site

Four phrases characterize what should happen while any field trip is in progress: count, teach, remain flexible, enjoy!

Count Know exactly how many youngsters are in the group. Count the children frequently throughout the time you are away. *Never* leave the field trip site itself or any stop along the way without making certain every child is present.

Teach Remember that field trips are firsthand experiences aimed at enhancing children's understanding of the world around them. They are not simply diversions, nor are they rigidly structured one-way presentations of information. Teaching strategies associated with guided instruction and problem-solving activities are well suited to these experiences. Brief instances of direct instruction may also be appropriate. With these strategies in mind, follow through on the curricular focus you planned for the trip. Draw children's attention to relevant cues in the environment, and respond to children's remarks with that focus in mind. If you have prepared the adults adequately, they should support the educational aims of the trip. If you notice that some folks seem to have completely forgotten its purpose, offer gentle reminders or model a few sample things to say or do.

Remain Flexible Take advantage of spontaneous events from which children might benefit. For instance, the children were visiting the Sun Rise Restaurant to see noodles being made by hand. The purpose for the field trip was for children to develop an awareness of and respect for the traditions and culture of others. While they were there, several children noticed the restaurant owner's many songbirds kept in large bamboo cages in the garden. They were intrigued. Did people eat the birds, they wondered? Why were there so many birds? Did the birds have names? It was clear that the birds had captured the children's interest. Rather than ignoring the children's queries, the field trip leader asked the owner if he would talk about the birds and if the children could see them. What followed was a delightful exchange between owner and children in which children learned about a Hong Kong custom the owner was proud to share. Noodle making was no longer a central focus as youngsters admired the birds and interacted with them in the garden. Although the original activity was revised, the goal of the trip was fulfilled. The teacher's flexibility enabled the children to follow through on their interests while simultaneously engaging in an activity that supported the trip's purpose.

Enjoy If you have planned well, the actual implementation of the field trip should proceed relatively smoothly. You should not be so frazzled with last-minute adjustments and details that there is no time to appreciate the site you have visited or interact with the children during the time there. Appropriate planning and preparation will make field trip day more relaxed and enjoyable.

FOLLOWING THE FIELD TRIP

Activities

A field trip does not end when children return to the early childhood program. Youngsters need opportunities to reflect on what they saw, heard, and experienced. Field trip plans should include one or more follow-up activities in which children

❏ Participate in group discussions.
❏ Look at pictures or make an album of pictures taken on the trip.
❏ Draw pictures or make a collage related to the trip.
❏ Dictate stories about what they experienced.

Following a field trip to an animal hospital, these boys recreate what they saw back in the classroom.

❑ Write in their journals or create a group newsletter to send home to family members, outlining the key things they learned.
❑ Reconstruct the field-trip experience in pretend play or with blocks.
❑ Role play in relation to the trip.
❑ Use items collected during the trip to create something back at the center or school (e.g., children make soup from vegetables purchased at the grocery, or they make a classroom reference book from the leaves they gathered on a nature walk).
❑ Visit the site again, with a new goal in mind (e.g., children make repeated visits to a pond during the year, attending to different details each time).

Thank-You Note

Every field trip should end with the children drawing pictures or writing letters thanking volunteers who provided supervision on the trip or people who guided their visit at the field-trip site (Hildebrand, 1997b). These tokens of appreciation can be individually cre-

ated or generated by the group as a whole. Not only do thank-you activities provide a sense of closure to the trip, but they also demonstrate the role of courtesy in community living.

Evaluation

As soon after the field trip as possible, the experience should be evaluated (Taylor, 1995). What did the children gain from the trip? How well was the educational purpose of the trip fulfilled? To what extent did the trip proceed as expected? What were some things you did not anticipate? What were the strengths of the trip? How could the trip have been improved? Would you recommend going back to the same place another time? Why or why not? What follow-up activities would best support the children's learning? What are some things family members might like to know about the children's experience? Questions such as these could be answered by the children and/or the adults. The answers should be incorporated in future planning.

FIELD TRIP EXAMPLE

Early in the fall, teachers at the El Shabaz Child Development Center decided to capitalize on the children's enjoyment of by taking them to see oranges growing in a grove. Following preliminary visits to two different sites, they selected Bird's Orange Grove as a field-trip destination. A summary of what they thought about in planning, carrying out, and following-up on the field trip is presented in Figure 4.10.

FIELD TRIP ALTERNATIVES

Field trips are wonderful learning opportunities for children and adults, but sometimes they are not the best option for a particular group of children at a particular time. For instance, early in the year, when children are not used to program routines or are just beginning to develop trusting relationships with program adults, field trips may cause unnecessary disruptions in the day's routine. On other occasions, the field trip site may be too far away, too costly, or too difficult to reach to make the journey worthwhile. One option is to make on-site excursions in the building or on program grounds to get children used to functioning in a whole group away from the classroom. A visit to the office, the boiler room, the kitchen, the marshy area outside, or a

FIGURE 4.10
A Field Trip to the Orange Grove

I. Planning and Preparation

A. Planning

1. Purpose: For children to learn how oranges grow
2. Destination: Bird's Orange Grove
3. When: Friday, September 20, 9 A.M.
4. Travel: Fifteen minutes by car one way, volunteer drivers needed. At least 23 seat belts necessary for children and staff; adult volunteers would add to this total.
5. Supervision: One adult for every four children; at least two adults needed beyond current staff
6. Permission: All families notified beforehand of location, time, and goal of trip. Written permission obtained from all parents/guardians for children to participate.
7. Family Involvement: Weekly newsletter used to invite adult family members to drive and to request family apple recipes.

B. Preparing the Children

1. One week before: Trip culminated the week's activities about oranges: Children tasted oranges, made orange juice, saw pictures of oranges growing, and pretended to sell oranges in a make-believe fruit stand; books were available about oranges and how they grow.
2. Day before: Talked with children about what they thought they would see at the orange grove. Asked them to generate a list of questions they wanted answered on the visit. Talked about strategies such as asking and observing to get answers.
3. Field trip day: Told children purpose of trip, reminded them of questions generated day before, divided them into groups of four children per adult (this was accomplished using color-coded tags), reminded children of appropriate behavior in cars and on the trip.

C. Preparing the Adults

1. One week before: Arranged transportation including backup drivers, collected and prepared necessary materials (map, lists of children, field trip first-aid kits, snack items). Made sure there was one driver and one adult rider per vehicle.
2. Day before: Confirmed drivers and volunteers one last time.
3. Field trip day: Prepared adults with specific guidelines and relevant information. Described purpose, key vocabulary, and things to look for or point out to children at the orchard. Talked about what to do if a group became separated from the others, where the bathrooms were, and how to support James (a child with Down's syndrome). Emphasized that adults were to keep track of the four children assigned to them.

II. At the Orange Grove

A. Used questions generated by the children as a basis for what to look for and ask about at the grove.
B. Made sure each child had a chance to see the grove, the orange press, and the fruit market.

(continued on the next page)

FIGURE 4.10
(continued)

    C. Took photographs of the experience.
    D. Purchased some oranges to take back to the program.
    E. Counted frequently: made sure children stayed with the group.

III. After the Trip
    A. Thanked all adult participants for their help.
    B. Carried out follow-up discussions and activities with the children. (That day the children participated in a group time during which they talked about answers to the questions they had generated earlier. The following Monday they wrote a thank-you note to the grove owner and tasted oranges purchased at the grove. On Tuesday, the children looked at pictures taken during the trip and wrote an experience story about the grove. They also added items to pretend play based on what they saw during their outing and created a classroom recipe book using orange recipes provided by their families.)
    C. Evaluated trip in terms of goals and educational value for children.
    D. Evaluated adult support during trip.

IV. Backup Plan
    A. In case of heavy rain, the trip would have been canceled until the following Tuesday. Children would have participated in regularly scheduled activities in the classroom. Most of these were carryovers from the previous day; one or two were originally scheduled for the following Tuesday. Group time would include the song "There was a Tree" and the flannel board story, "The Life of an Orange Tree" made up by the teacher.

---

hunt for insects on program property all provide excellent opportunities for expanding children's learning beyond classroom boundaries. Another option is inviting someone from the community to make a program visit.

Classroom Visitors

Persons from the community who have specific knowledge or skills can extend children's knowledge and motivate their interests by visiting the classroom (Spodek, Saracho, & Davis, 1991). How to plan, implement, and follow up on effective classroom visits parallels most of the steps involved in planning field trips.

Purpose The first thing to do when thinking about inviting anyone to be a classroom visitor is to ask why the visitor will be coming. How will he or she contribute to the children's understandings? The way you answer these questions defines the purpose of the visit. Being clear about purpose makes it easier to determine whom to invite, as well as how and when the visit will take place. A clear purpose also makes it more likely that children and visitor will enjoy and profit from their time together.

Selecting a Visitor Parents, family members, and community resource people all have the potential to be interesting classroom visitors. Readers are referred to Table 4.2 for a list of possibilities. After you have read these suggestions, think about potential visitors who might be available in your community. The person you choose should be someone who has something to show the children (e.g., demonstrate the art of pantomime, show children his or her stamp collection, or show children how to brush and comb a dog) or has something the children can do (e.g., examine seeds, participate in a story, try on scuba gear, make tortillas). Visitors should avoid lecturing. Instead, hands-on learning and active participation remain central features of the best presentations. If visitors are not sure how to accomplish this, talk over potential strategies as you prepare him or her for the visit.

TABLE 4.2
Potential Visitors

Parents of the Children	Storyteller	Pet Owner
Grandparents	Theater People	Mime
Humane Society Spokesperson	Collector of Any Kind	Puppeteer
Artist	Health Professional	Dancer
Musician	Insect Specialist	Author/Writer
Athlete with Equipment	Rock Specialist	Weather Reporter
Firefighter	Carpenter	Person Who Uses American
Police Officer	Plumber	Sign Language
Leader Dog Trainer	Scientist	Program Personnel
Beekeeper	Kite Flyer	(custodian, bus driver,
Flower Arranger	Person Who Works with	secretary, etc.)
Chef/Cook	Plants	Animal Visitors

Preparing the Visitor   Someone who is an expert in baking bread, identifying insects, or plumbing will still need help working with the children. This is true even if he or she has visited other programs before. Every group of children is unique. Prepare your visitor in advance by talking about the developmental characteristics of the children in your group, their need for simple explanations, and the desirability of some form of active participation. Make clear the educational aim of the visit. Confirm when the person will come, how long he or she should plan to stay, and the format in which the visit will take place. For instance, a visitor may address the whole group the entire time or introduce a concept at group time and then remain with the children as they work in small groups later in the session. The visit may be indoors or outdoors.

Preparing the Children   The children should be forewarned that a visitor is coming and know the purpose of his or her visit. They can generate questions in advance and be primed for what to look for when they know that a parent is coming to group time to show how she bathes and dresses her baby or that a musician will be demonstrating the sounds different instruments make. Simple guidelines for how children are to behave during the visit should also be previewed before the visitor arrives.

Preparing the Adults   Adult preparation includes the why, how, where, and when of the visit as well as specific suggestions for the adult supervisory role. For instance, a visitor may need help with equipment, keeping children away from certain items, or making sure that all the children can see at all times. Encourage adults to actively support children's participation rather than remaining passively on the sidelines or becoming so engrossed in the demonstration themselves that they fail to help children in need. Talk about what to do if a child becomes too uncomfortable to participate or if children are disruptive. Going over these details in advance helps adults know what to do and makes it easier for them to provide effective support during the visit.

Backup Plans   It is just as important to have a backup plan for a visitor as it is for a field trip. Things do happen that might cause a visitor to be late or miss a scheduled visit. Plan in advance what you will do if this happens.

Participation   The watchwords *teach, remain flexible,* and *enjoy* are as true for visitors as they are for other whole-group activities. Having a visitor does not mean time off for other adults in the room. Although a resource person may have center stage for a while, early childhood professionals continue to have responsibilities for ensuring the educational value of the experience for the children and recognizing teachable moments. The better planned the activity, the more enjoyable it will be to all concerned.

Postvisit Procedures   Having a resource person visit should not be an isolated event. Plan for follow-up activities as well as an opportunity for children to communicate their thanks after the visitor has gone. Every visit should be evaluated, too. What did children gain from the visit? How well was the educational purpose of the visit fulfilled? To what extent did the visit proceed as expected? What unexpected things occurred? How might you improve a future visit based on what you learned from this one? Would you recommend having the same visitor another time? Why or why not? What would families like to know about this visit?

SUMMARY

Most early childhood classrooms include some whole-group instruction each day. The most common whole-group experiences are group times. Group times can be used to enhance learning across the curriculum and to develop a sense of community within the classroom. The extent to which such benefits happen is directly influenced by the quality of the planning and preparation that go into them. The format for writing group-time plans maintains some of the same planning elements described for other kinds of activity plans. One difference is that the procedures section outlines the opening, the body, and the closing of the activity. Another difference is that a specific strategy is identified for helping children move from group time to the next

portion of the day. Group times may be traditional in form or serve specialty functions in early childhood classrooms. Typically both types of group times are used sometime during the day. Pitfalls to avoid in planning or implementing group-time activities include the following: failing to prepare adequately, using whole-group instruction when an individual or small-group experience would facilitate children's learning better, poor selection of materials, making too many routinized activities part of group time, waiting too long to engage children in active learning, and failing to end whole-group instruction soon enough. The bad news is that these mistakes can negate the positive benefits children could potentially derive from group-time learning experiences. The good news is that such problems are avoidable through appropriate planning, preparation, practice, and experience.

Field trips and classroom visitors are other potential whole-group activities. The success of these depends on how well thought out they are and how carefully children, adults, and resource people are prepared and supported throughout the experience. Follow-up activities and backup plans are additional factors group leaders must consider in taking a field trip or inviting someone to visit the classroom.

✖ Applying What You Read in This Chapter

1. **Discuss**
   a. Based on your reading and experiences with young children, discuss each of the questions that open this chapter.
   b. Discuss three different ways you could create a group time around the story "The Little Red Hen."
   c. Review the group times outlined for 3-year-olds and primary school mixed-age students in Figure 4.7. Find the common elements in those group times. Then describe how they have been tailored to meet the needs of children of differing ages.
   d. Imagine that a person from the Humane Society has brought a very friendly dog to your classroom to use in talking about animal care. One of the children is extremely frightened. How will you handle the situation?

   e. You have scheduled a visitor to demonstrate pretzel making to the children. Fifteen minutes before she is supposed to arrive, you learn the visitor will be 45 minutes late. What will you do?

2. **Observe**
   a. Watch a group time in an early childhood program. Based on your observations, identify the purpose of the group time and create an agenda that corresponds to what you saw. Critique the effectiveness of what you observed.
   b. Observe a group of children being prepared to go on a field trip. What strategies were used to help children anticipate what was going to happen? What instructions did they receive? Critique the effectiveness of what you observed.
   c. Observe a classroom visitor interact with the children. What do you believe was the main purpose

of the visit? Describe how well you believe that purpose was achieved.

3. **Carry out an activity**

   a. Plan a group time for a specific group of children. Create a detailed written plan for what you will do. If possible, carry out the group time and evaluate the results in writing. Another option is to ask a friend to observe you and provide feedback.

   b. Plan a field trip or visitor for the children with whom you are working. Use the corresponding steps in this chapter to guide your planning. Carry out the activity and evaluate the results.

4. **Create something for your portfolio**

   a. Describe a group time you planned and carried out with children. Identify the learning objectives for children and evaluate the results.

   b. Videotape a group time you implemented with children. Make this tape no more than 10 to 15 minutes long. On an index card, identify relevant learning objectives for children.

   c. On one page, describe a field trip or visitor you arranged for the children. Describe what you learned from this experience.

5. **Add to your journal**

   a. What is the most significant thing you have learned about whole-group planning and implementation based on your readings and experience with children?

   b. Reflect on the extent to which the information in this chapter corresponds to what you have observed in the field. What is your reaction to any discrepancies you perceive?

   c. What goals do you have for yourself related to whole-group instruction for young children? How do you intend to pursue those goals?

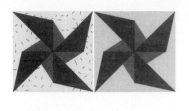

Chapter 5

Organizing Space, Materials, Time, and Children's Groups

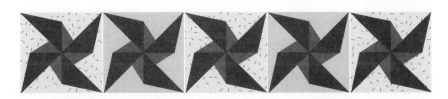

You may wonder:

What is the first task when entering an early childhood setting
   as a professional?

How do I arrange the classroom?

What materials will I need?

How do I decide on the order of the day? when to do what?

How can I provide for activity learning?

Which combinations of children should be gathered together
   for instruction?

In this chapter we present information related to these questions.

Surveying the rich array of materials available, a kindergarten child sighed contentedly and said, "I must be special. Look at the party they made for me," as she entered her sunny, comfortable classroom for the first time.

Entering the subterranean classroom of his childcare program, a 4-year-old child pronounced the gloomy setting as a "dooky place" (Greenman, 1988) in spite of the fact that his teacher had made efforts to humanize the setting.

Even the youngest children are aware of and responsive to the symbols of their physical environment. They pay attention to aesthetics, function, and the social and learning opportunities there. Even preschoolers have opinions on what would make their childcare center

more appealing as became very clear when some of them were asked to complete the following sentence:

"I wish my classroom had . . . "

❑ *a fountain that squirted orange soda.*
❑ *a pig. I can't have one at home.*
❑ *more boys. There's too many girls here.*
❑ *blue walls.*
❑ *painting every day.*
❑ *lots more books. (Kostelnik, 1997a)*

Primary-grade children also want classrooms that stimulate, provide a variety of choices, and offer both social and solitary opportunities. Professionals who organize the environment with the needs and desires of children in mind provide these opportunities and support the children's learning at the same time.

ORGANIZING THE PHYSICAL ENVIRONMENT

Safety

Teachers are responsible for overseeing the building, room, and playground safety and training children to use materials and equipment safely. The children's safety is always the top priority. Three- to five-year-olds need much more careful supervision for all safety practices than children aged 6 to 8 because they are less likely to have learned safe practices well. However, all children during the early childhood period should be monitored by adults, as they have yet to learn what is safe and what is dangerous. Children should never be left unsupervised outdoors, even on newly constructed, safer playgrounds. One-half to two-thirds of all accidents for 3- to 5-year-olds happen outdoors (Taylor & Morris, 1996). Supervision of children under 8 years of age is always a significant factor as are the design and maintenance of the building and playground. Supervision can be simplified by adjusting the physical environment itself to minimize potential hazards. Consider the following guidelines:

Indoors

1. Cover electrical outlets except when in use.
2. Use extension cords only when necessary, and be certain that they are of adequate size. Never string them together for long distances or across pathways.
3. Remain with any electrical appliance or heat source if children are present.
4. Remove (and repair if possible) any materials or pieces of equipment that appear unsafe, including those on the playground.
5. When you must attend to other things, place tools on high shelves or move tables near equipment that may be unsafe when an adult is not present. For example, prevent 4-year-old children from touching a cooling iron after a project in which crayon shreds were melted between sheets of wax paper by putting the iron in an inaccessible spot.
6. Place all chemicals (plant fertilizer, cleaning compounds, medicines, etc.) out of reach of children.
7. Scan the environment regularly for safety hazards such as water or sand on pathways, clutter near exits, and improper use of equipment.

8. Include teaching children the safe use of materials as a normal part of instruction.
9. Teach children to recognize the common symbols indicating a dangerous situation or object, such as the symbols for poison or stop.
10. Maintain first-aid kits including plastic gloves and toxic-waste disposal bags to handle small injuries. Use universal precautions when exposed to blood indoors and out (American Public Health Association & American Academy of Pediatrics, 1992).

Outdoors

1. Bring children to play on playgrounds designed for their age group. A playground for children 3–5 is different from one designed for children 6–12.
2. Scan the playground for materials that do not belong there (glass, refuse) and remove it. Scan the playground periodically during the growing season for poisonous plants such as poison ivy and have it removed if found. Many decorative, common plants have poisonous parts, and vegetation should be checked locally for safety.
3. Periodically check wood equipment for splinters; sand and treat at least annually.
4. Wet down metal slides during the summer so the surface is cool enough to slide, and check that metal is not dangerously cold during the winter.
5. Report maintenance needs and follow up on them to ensure completion of the work.
6. Check the force absorbent material under climbers, slides, swings, and other equipment. At the time of installation, these materials to ameliorate falls are level. As children play, they dig holes through use. Fill these holes so that cement and metal support structures are covered.
7. Common hazards are entrapment of the head or other body parts, falls from heights, equipment that can pinch or crush fingers, protrusions, sharp areas, and slippery surfaces (Frost, 1992). Report maintenance needs to the appropriate administrators.
8. Maintain pathways so that they are not slippery. Sweep off sand on sidewalks during the summer. Apply sand and/or salt to icy spots during winter.
9. Store children's play materials after use, and keep pathways free from hazards.

10. Scan the area for objects that might trip children. Remove objects in pathways. Contain loose parts in areas where children expect to find them and out of the normal running areas.
11. Teach children to use play equipment safely.

Comfort

Teachers are responsible for ensuring that children can use work and play places easily and comfortably enough to engage in meaningful activities. Children work best when the temperature is comfortable, the air is fresh, and light is adequate. Most practitioners are accustomed to adjusting these dimensions regularly; however, if the building does not have windows that open and close, a round cushion fan is useful even in winter to move air. Lighting in most schools is usually full intensity, with on and off switches. A dimmer switch is inexpensive and can be installed with any lighting system. Children tend to be quieter and more socially interactive in less than full-intensity light, but they need the latter for close work.

Children are also most comfortable when the size of the furniture is correct for their heights. As public schools move into serving children under 5 years of age, they will have to purchase chairs and tables that are adjusted for the height of younger children.

The weather and climatic conditions vary considerably so that comfort outdoors may be supported by shade trees, wind barriers, or covered play areas for rainy or snowy conditions. During hot weather, a nearby water source is especially useful.

Space

Teachers are responsible for planning the effective use of classroom space. Facilities are not within the control of classroom personnel, but the use of space within the room can be modified to support curricular goals. Ideally the floor space will be at least 35 square feet per child, not counting closets or immovable storage, hallways, and so on, although some experts recommend up to 100 square feet per child for indoor space (Spodek et al., 1991). Outdoor space should be two to three times that for the number of children playing at one time. With greater densities (more children or less space), teachers can expect more disruptive behavior

(Polloway, 1974). The probability of children physically bumping into each other increases at the same time that space to spread out is reduced. Sometimes facilities that might at first glance appear very limited can be adapted. For example, in high-ceiling classrooms, a loft can be placed with stairs to increase the total space available. Activity centers that are fairly stable, such as the listening center, could be placed on the top level, with another center, such as pretend play, underneath, which would make better use of the vertical space.

The organization of physical space is an effective predictor of program quality as it affects what children can do, determines the ease with which they are able to carry out their plans, and affects the ways in which they use materials (Kritchevsky & Prescott, 1977; Schickedanz, York, et al., 1990). Vertical space provided by walls, the backs of storage units, bulletin boards, and even windows may be used to support children's learning (Readdick & Bartlett, 1994). For example, an interactive word/picture activity could be secured to a window shade mounted on the wall and returned to the roll position when not in use. When materials are accessible and children have been taught how to use and take care of them, the children are able to use them to investigate, express their ideas, experiment, and construct representations. At the same time, independence and a sense of competence are valued outcomes. On the other hand, when resources are not available, children must wait for adults to make all of the plans and decisions before engaging in learning activities; dependence of action and thought may be undesired consequences of such a physical organization of space.

When teachers arrange space in the classroom, they must consider how that arrangement will influence children's behavior. Children need private space where they can work independently or gain control of their own thoughts and feelings. A study carrel, secluded chair, or pile of pillows can meet this need. The coat storage area, cubby, or children's school bags are other private places that children might store their work and private possessions. Landscaped areas where children can sit near bushes, under trees, or well away from equipment provide for private spaces outdoors.

A small group space for two to six children encourages them to interact quietly with one another, talking at conversational levels. They are likely to exhibit cooperative and helping behaviors when they are in close personal space (2 feet) and when the task set for the group is noncompetitive. Small group spaces should vary in size, with secluded spaces for a pair of children as well as for four to six children. Often a small table with the appropriate number of chairs may meet this need. When areas are designed for small groups rather than only for individuals or large groups, behaviors such as wandering, running, fighting over materials, repeating the same activity over and over again, crawling under tables, and consistently depending on adults for the things children need can be minimized (Dodge, 1989).

Often the selection of outdoor play equipment determines the configuration of individual and small-group spaces. Swings are for one person at a time. Usually climbers are for three to five children at a time, depending upon the size and the complexity of the climbing structure. Mobile equipment such as tricycles and climbing apparatus such as ladders and crates may involve two or more children, depending on how the items are used.

The third kind of space is for a large group in which children listen to stories, sing, engage in games or other movement activities, and share whole-group instruction. Although it is possible to carry out some common activities while children are seated at desks or tables, it is often preferable to have a separate area where children can sit on the floor. They are closer together, can see pictures or demonstrations better, and often feel more like a cohesive group.

Most outdoor large-group areas are very large indeed, spaced so that children may engage in ball games and other whole-group activities designed for enhancing motor development. Ideally, there would be a second large outdoor space where children could gather comfortably in the shade for demonstrations and instruction.

To structure all three types of space, separate them by clear, physical boundaries. Imaginary boundaries, such as a pretend line between two children sitting side by side at a table, are not effective. Children naturally expect to interact with neighbors. They can determine the appropriate number of participants for a specific space by the number of chairs or the amount of floor space within the boundaries. Teachers have also effectively used signs indicating the number of children for a given area. Storage units, pathways, equipment, low

dividers, and even the arrangement of materials on a table can delineate boundaries. As one second-grade teacher indicated, "I painted an old bathtub red, filled it with pillows, and placed it near the window. When a child wishes to be alone, he or she gets a book and sits in the tub. The other children do not bother him or her and neither do I. When ready, the child returns to the ongoing activity." Another second-grade teacher put an area rug in the classroom because "whenever we are working together on the rug, children know that they must work quietly and that cooperation is expected."

Fences, paved surfaces, curbs, sandpits, grass, and other structural features usually establish the boundaries in outdoor areas. Adults may add movable features such as tents, blankets, or temporary orange cones to mark other areas for specific planned events.

Pathways between activity areas that allow children to move readily from one activity to another without interfering with ongoing learning of other children must be planned so that the flow of children in the classroom or outdoors is smooth and efficient.

Sound

Sound control is an ongoing challenge in programs that encourage independent work, cooperative work, and center work. Hard surfaces in the classroom are easy to keep clean but tend to increase noise, and softer surfaces that absorb noise give a warmer, more resilient surface to touch but are more difficult to maintain. Hard-surface floors are best where there are messy activities or children are likely to track in dirt from outdoors. Carpeted floors are best in areas in which children will be sitting and playing actively. Many facilities have sound control in the ceilings, and a few have installed sound-absorbent units on cement walls to reduce noise.

Although teachers cannot control most of the surfaces built into the facility, they can and should give some thought to noise control. A generally noisy environment from which children cannot get relief is not conducive to overall cognitive development or academic achievement (Moore, 1987). Teachers have little control over external noise but may adjust the classroom environment to modify the amount of noise and plan for quiet and active participation of children. With soft, sound absorbing materials in the classroom, normal noise is diminished. For example, large pillows placed on a small carpet instead of chairs, can be used in the independent reading area so that children can read aloud without disturbing others nearby. Draperies, carpet, pillows, stuffed animals, and upholstered furniture are all sound absorbent. Rooms with large expanses of bulletin boards are quieter than those with plain hard-wall surfaces.

A second strategy to control sound environmentally is to increase the secluded spaces for one or two children and decrease the number of spaces for six or more children. This can be done by using furniture or mobile screens for barriers between activity areas or decreasing the floor area of some of the centers.

Noisy activities should be arranged close to each other and away from the quieter activities. For example, block play and pretend play tend to be noisier. These should be in an area of the room away from the book corner or listening center.

Some children are noisier in highly complex environments. If a particular center seems to be noisy, unproductive, congested, or disruptive, carefully observe what is going on. Sometimes the activity needs to be redesigned or reorganized, separated into two activities, or possibly eliminated. Sometimes simply adjusting the amount of table or floor space will correct the difficulty.

One of the big advantages to outdoor learning is that children may be as quiet or as noisy as they like. Often activities that generate a lot of purposeful noise such as exploring musical instruments are better offered in the outdoor setting where others are much less likely to be disturbed. However, even outdoors, children must be considerate of other children in classrooms nearby if windows are open for air circulation. If this should be the case, the really noisy activities should be moved far enough away from the building to minimize disturbing others rather than eliminating fruitful learning opportunities.

Child Size

Furnishings, tools, and equipment should be appropriate for the size of the children using them. This means that tables and chairs selected for 5- and 6-year-olds are usually too large for 3- and 4-year-olds. Children experience serious discomfort if their feet do not touch the floor while seated and conversely if their knees bump into the table when the furnishings are too short for a particularly tall young child. Small scissors are easier to manage than adult-size scissors. Outdoor climbers have rungs closer together for 3- to 5-year-olds than would be appropriately challenging for their larger and older counterparts. The rates at which preschool children enter into complex play also appears to be related to the size of the space and the child-sized structures and equipment in the space (Tegano, 1996).

Mobility

Teachers are responsible for planning programs that actively involve children and allow them to move from place to place in an orderly manner during the session. Pathways should be wide enough for children to walk on without bumping into other children or interfering with the work and play of others. Avoid long empty spaces as they invite running or hurrying. Instead, break up the space by carefully arranging the centers. When children must move around a diagonally placed table or walk around a pair of easels, they slow down. Some teachers use the center of the room as open space, with learning areas arranged on large tables or clusters of small tables placed so that traffic must move around them.

Attractiveness

An attractive environment is one that appeals to the senses. Texture, color, pattern, design, scent, and sound all contribute to the sense of beauty and place. An attractive environment communicates to everyone but especially to the children and adults who work and play there.

Meaning emerges as emotions are associated with a place. People shape an environment, yet they are also shaped by it (Greenman, 1995). An attractive learning environment is child centered, serene, exciting, inviting children to engage, and providing privacy for reflection.

Teachers are responsible for providing children with a clean and orderly environment. When teachers demonstrate their own respect for cleanliness and attractiveness, children are more likely to imitate this desirable behavior. Organize the classroom so that it is uncluttered, clean, and visually appealing. An orderly environment is more interesting, and children can see the materials that are intended to attract their attention. Adults who sit down on the floor and look around have a keener perspective of the room from the child's point of view. Sometimes a room that appears attractive at an adult level may give a different impression when seen from the child's height.

Teachers help children care for their learning and living environment. As a part of the learning responsibility, children should be encouraged to put materials back where they belong. This is also an opportunity for children to learn classifying, matching, and reading skills if the storage areas are adequately labeled. Keeping working surfaces clean is also a reasonable expectation of children. Before children leave a messy area, encourage them to wipe the surfaces and clean up for the next child's use. Pictographs or written instructions for cleaning and storage also contribute to children's emerging literacy skills because the information is practical, useful, and meaningful to them. Teachers also may encourage older children in making choices about the room, selecting and constructing bulletin boards, decorating selected spaces, and contributing to the physical space in such a way that it reflects the group of children working and playing there.

Ultimately, adults must arrange the physical environment to contribute to the ongoing instructional program. Materials, bulletin boards, and pictures should be rotated to reflect various topical themes. Bright touches attract children to centers where the teacher intends them to become engaged. Both elements added to attract children and the substance of the learning centers should be changed regularly and reflect the changing needs and interests of the children. Overall, simplicity is the key to the entire physical setting. Remove extraneous materials. Each object visible in the room should have a purpose and meaning for the children. When you ask yourself, "Is this contributing to the goal I had in mind?" or "What am I trying to accomplish with this?" you should have a clear, immediate answer. Avoid leaving children's work displayed longer than one week; take it down and display other, newer work.

The elements of the physical environment fit together in a comprehensible way and are designed to make life in that place a rich experience. The effective use of light and art from around the world, children's art displays, plants, and animals add to the beauty and livability of the classroom. A classroom that is more homelike and less institutional helps children feel secure and ready to learn (Silvern, 1988).

The natural environment is unparalleled in opportunities to enhance children's experiences of beauty, interesting scents, and wildlife in all forms. Tiny gardens or clustered plantings, vegetation permitted to grow on fencing, scented herbs and shrubs, and flowers in a playground stimulate the senses and the curiosity of young children. If these are combined with birdbaths and feeders, the attractiveness and opportunities for children to learn about the natural environment will be enhanced. Children also have a role to play in maintaining the outdoor play-learning environment by watering plants, filling feeders and baths, and participating in picking up paper and other bits of materials that blow in (Frost, Talbot, & Monroe, 1990).

Storage

Teachers are responsible for the selection, storage, and display of materials. Objects should be stored near the area of use. Ideally, materials will be in open shelving if children are to have ready access to them and in closed cupboards or on high shelves if the teacher needs to maintain control of the materials. For example, pencils, paper, scissors, and paste are frequently used and should be readily accessible each day near the tables at which they are used. On the other hand, fingerpaint or a microscope might be put away and retrieved as needed. Materials that are small and have many pieces such as counters, small plastic building blocks, or fabric scraps should be stored in plastic containers. Usually the cardboard boxes in which the materials are sold do not hold up well in long-term use. Transparent plastic boxes are a good alternative. Teachers should also consider safety in storage, especially when stacking containers or placing heavy items on high shelves.

Easily accessible storage for outdoor learning materials is as essential as for indoor materials. Wheeled toys, tools, containers, sleds, and other materials essential for the optimal use of outdoor learning should be securely stored in a large outdoor shed or a closet opening to the outdoor areas. Teachers and children alike will find such storage convenient but will use the contents more frequently than if they must carry mobile equipment some distance.

Safety, comfort, space, noise control, mobility, attractiveness, and storage are elements that must be considered in any arrangement of the learning envi-

Children have ready access to materials that are stored near the area where they will use them.

ronment. One of the most effective ways to organize for developmentally appropriate programs is to plan for *learning centers.* A learning center or activity area, as it is sometimes called, is a space within the setting, prepared with a careful selection of materials, that is structured to promote specific goals.

WHY USE LEARNING CENTERS?

Mrs. Lakashul visited a kindergarten group near her home the spring before her own child would be entering. Coming in mid-morning, she saw small groups of children busily engaged in a variety of activities. Occasionally one child would leave an area and begin another activity elsewhere. Conversations and the clink of materials could be heard, though the room was not really noisy.

The teacher stayed with a small group of children for several minutes until she finished showing them how to use the materials and then moved on to another group. Children's writing samples and labeled drawings were on the wall. Children were intensely engaged and obviously enjoying the activity. At the end of the session, Mrs. Lakashul said, "Children love it here, don't they? How do you ever manage to have so many children so busy at the same time?"

"Oh, children enjoy learning centers. I plan activities for each area, and children accomplish their goals at their own pace," replied Ms. Green.

Learning centers in early childhood settings have proven to be an apt and responsive vehicle for meeting the needs of young children. Centers are carefully designed areas that contain planned learning activities and materials drawn from the program's basic skills curriculum and from the themes being taught (Day, 1988a, 91). Because they offer choices to children, the difficulties usually connected to developmental and experiential differences are minimized. Centers enable youngsters to take charge of their own work.

Centers allow active and purposeful construction of the learning environment by adults in order to promote the development of essential skills and abilities in children. When well constructed and carefully thought out, learning centers resemble an effective blend between a workshop and library setting.

Because children are free to move about the room, centers allow for different attention spans and need for movement, as well as the wide range of developmental differences usually found in young children. Used in collaboration with thematic planning, they provide a setting for children to explore concepts in an in-depth and integrated manner. When adults use guided-discovery approaches and children are encouraged to experiment, divergent as well as convergent thought is promoted (Clayton, 1989). Cooperative learning, which teaches both leadership and following skills to children, is easily implemented in a center-based classroom.

Benefits to teachers are as numerous. Their responsibilities in the early childhood context to prepare and monitor the environment, evaluate both children and programming in the setting, and bring about responsive and needed changes to support optimal development in the children (McKee, 1990a) are made easier through the use of learning centers. Very simply, they are free to be up and about the room and involved in spontaneously evaluating the children's use of materials and learning experiences. Teachers introduce new materials and centers and then move among the children providing support and instruction. Teachers can watch to see which kinds of activities actively engage individual children and which promote only cursory interest. They can note where children are able to integrate and transfer concepts developed in one area to their work and play in other areas with different materials.

Because children in learning centers are active and busy, the teacher is also able to use brief periods of the time to work with selected individuals or small groups of children on various aspects of knowledge and skill building. Evaluation of children's progress, which should take place in the natural setting by the teacher, is more easily accomplished.

The many advantages resulting from implementing a center approach may not be readily apparent to parents, board members, or administrators, who may need reassurance and information about what children are actually doing and learning. Strategies to share information about the learning taking place include a listing of developing concepts and skills posted in a particular center area, guided tours conducted by trained parents or older students, newsletters, or letters sent directly to parents and other interested persons.

CHARACTERISTICS OF EFFECTIVE EARLY CHILDHOOD LEARNING CENTERS

Establishing learning centers in the early childhood classroom is not a guarantee, of course, that optimal knowledge and skill building will take place. Much thought has to go into the use of the physical space available; number and kinds of centers; materials, supplies, and resources; quality of thematic units; interest levels, talents, and abilities of the children; and the overseeing of activity, evaluation, and feedback to children by knowledgeable and capable adults. Children must be equipped with the "necessary skills and prerequisite knowledge for effective use of the centers," including the purposes of the centers, ways to exercise self-discipline, and strategies for self-appraisal related to what they are learning from participating in center activity (Day,

1988b, 75). In general, however, well-constructed centers are built with attention to the following:

1. They are organized and implemented on the basis of knowledge the teacher has about the children and their abilities. For every activity and experience that occurs in a classroom, teachers must ask themselves the following questions:

❑ How does this activity center contribute to long-range outcome goals?
❑ What domain-related objectives are the basis for this activity/experience? What do I hope the children will gain from this?
❑ How does this activity build on past knowledge of most of the children?
❑ Is this the best possible way to present such an idea/concept?
❑ Is this the best possible use of the children's time?
❑ Are the activities, experiences, and materials well matched to the developmental levels and interests of the children?
❑ How will I evaluate the effectiveness of this activity/experience?

2. Activities presented within the centers are flexible and adaptable rather than rigid and static (Ministry of Education, Victoria, Province of British Columbia, 1988). Although you may have in mind a particular outcome following children's use of materials in a center, you will want to be alert for paths children wish to take in their own exploration and use of the materials. Children often have good ideas about creative and divergent ways to use available materials! In a well-designed learning center, children can work on domain-related goals established by the teacher while still fulfilling their own needs in that or another domain. This can be accomplished by using basic open-ended materials stored and available in each area in addition to newly introduced materials.

3. The array of learning centers provided to children in a day—and over time—are well diversified and provide for a balance of cognitive, affective, and psychomotor development (Clayton, 1989; Cummings, 1990a). Activities represent a cross-section of domains. The centers should be balanced to provide a comprehensive curriculum and adjusted for the age of the children. In addition, the amount of space needed by a specific center might also be adjusted as children

develop, with a language arts center for 3-year-olds being enlarged and enhanced for separate reading, writing, and listening centers for the 5- or 6-year-old.

4. Children understand how to use the learning centers properly (McKee, 1990a). Center-based activity can be much more successful when teachers take time to introduce children to new activities and materials before children encounter them. Some teachers prefer to give children "previews of coming attractions" by letting them know just before they prepare to leave what to expect the next day. Others plan an opening or greeting time in their schedules. Talk about what children will find in the room that may be new or unusual, any safety information they need to have in working with certain materials, and any limits on numbers of children who can be involved on a particular day. This is also a time when demonstrations of the use of particular materials or work with unfamiliar equipment can take place. With guidance, children may generate the rules of behavior in each center so that mutual expectations are clear and respect for other people and materials is fostered.

After children have had opportunities to explore the materials, teachers may wish to assign certain tasks to be completed with the materials. For example, as part of a thematic unit on clothing, one teacher set up a center as a "shoe shop." One of the tasks the children had was to weigh one of their own shoes with nonstandard weights, record the number on a paper shoe the teacher had provided, and place their work in a shoe box positioned in the area. The teacher demonstrated the activity from start to finish by weighing one of her own shoes and having the children count the numbers of weights used. She then recorded the number on one of the paper shoes and placed it in the designated shoe box. The teacher reminded the children that, in this particular activity, it would be important to keep the container of nonstandard weights in the shoe-shop area and limit use of them on that particular day to the children who were involved in weighing, although children might be interested in using the weights to weigh other objects in the shoe-shop area. Besides serving the purpose of knowledge and skill building about use of the materials, such introductions also activate children's curiosity and encourage them to visit a particular center.

In addition to these kinds of introductions, the focus of a learning center may be made evident to children by the placement of materials within it. For instance, after children have had previous experience with rubbings of objects, the teacher may highlight a leaf-rubbing activity by putting all the relevant materials in the middle of the art table. This would draw children's attention to the leaves, crayons, and paper, which would make the activity appear inviting. Yet children could still have access to other art supplies stored on shelves nearby. Written directions in the form of pictographs or words (see Figure 5.1) as well as periodic participation by the teacher are other ways the goals and procedures of an activity can be made clear to children.

5. The same learning center, at different times, can be used to address different objectives. Materials are not bound to any one domain. Depending on how teachers structure a learning center and how they set goals, the same materials (e.g., art materials, blocks) could be used to address the cognitive domain one day, the language domain on another, and the social domain on yet another.

6. Teachers use learning-center time as a period to interact spontaneously with children rather than time to grade students' work or prepare other materials and activities. They are available to children and able to take advantage of appropriate opportunities to enhance, extend, and evaluate cognitive, social, affective, and physical learning experiences and developmental outcomes. They are able to hold brief conferences with children about processes and products as children act on the materials in the room. Teachers who choose to be active with the children during this time are also able to ward off potential difficulties as children work and play together in the context.

Keep these questions in mind as you read the following section.

❏ Have you wondered how to construct the centers you have seen in classrooms or on film?
❏ Do you know where to put various types of centers in the space available?
❏ Could you organize a learning center if you had the equipment, furnishings, and materials?

EXAMPLES OF CENTERS

The kinds of centers found in any early childhood setting vary dramatically in terms of number, materials

FIGURE 5.1
Painting at the Easel Pictograph

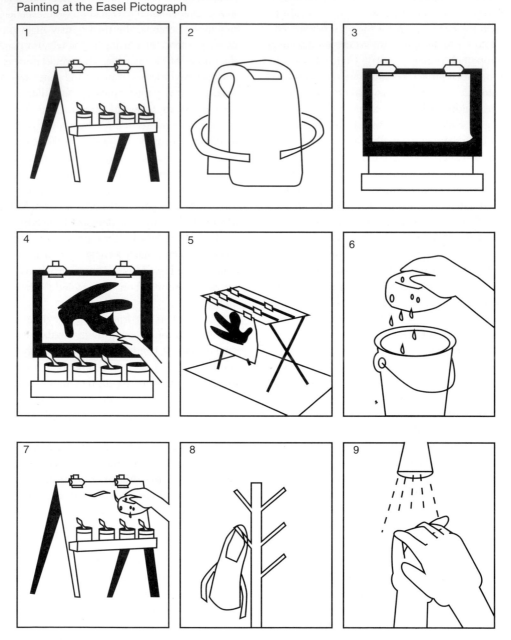

Source: Drawing by Barbara Rohde. Used with permission.

and equipment available, and creative ideas generated by both teachers and children. Included here are descriptions of centers often found in many early childhood settings, that is, "core" centers (McKee, 1990b) and also several examples of special-interest centers.

Most of the core centers may be used outdoors as well as indoors if the climate and weather permit. In addition, there are a few specialized outdoor centers.

Core centers may change slightly in the materials that are added or subtracted but not in their particular focus. Included here may be a language arts center, creative arts and construction center (two- and three-dimensional art/modeling), science/exploration/collections center, math/manipulative materials and table games, a dramatic play area, blocks, gross motor, music, and wheeled toys, and a large-group area. Some of these centers may be broken down further into sub-center areas. For example, a book corner and listening center may be established separately from a writing center, although some content areas such as these naturally lend themselves to integration so that children will have easier access to equipment and materials needed to carry out their ideas.

Special-interest centers may be set up for shorter periods of time (one day to a few weeks), based on the interests of the children and teacher. For example, large-motor-skill equipment such as a climber or balance beam may be added, particularly when weather or space would limit outdoor use of such equipment. Music, woodworking, cooking centers, and special collections of one kind or another are introduced, removed, and then reintroduced periodically. Such centers may require the use of additional adults to monitor and/or support children's use of materials or space. Teachers who work on a day-to-day basis with the help of a full-time aide or parent volunteers often elect to add one or more of these centers to their repertoire of core centers, making them available to children on a more consistent basis.

Following are descriptions of some core centers that are often included in early childhood learning environments, preschool through second grade, and the benefits derived from them.

Language Arts Center

The most important rationale for providing language experiences to children via a center-based approach is that it supports children's emerging language skills and abilities. A special part of the classroom becomes an arena for children's active discovery of language through quality, age-appropriate experiences in listening, reading, writing, drawing, and story reenactment. Children are able to collaborate and compare their products, both with one another and against the rich and diverse literature sources introduced into the environment.

Some teachers interact personally with each child on a daily basis in this center through the use of brief "mailbox" messages. Students eagerly look forward to checking each day to see what special messages the teacher has left and frequently respond by writing one to the teacher. At first, it may be only a word or their name and a picture. Eventually, as children's skills grow, the messages do, also (Routman, 1987). Children also begin to write notes to one another and answer messages received. Mailbox "messaging" in the language arts center is a highly motivating activity; children enjoy the surprise element of finding and leaving messages and are writing for real purposes. This is a powerful factor in their wanting to develop literacy skills.

Story reenactment may be a part of the language arts center for younger children but is frequently an independent center for children in kindergarten and primary grades. A well-read book and props related to the story that define the characters and the action are essential for the children to enact the story successfully. Sometimes stories are retold using puppets, flannel boards, or other similar strategies.

Listening centers with story tapes and books may be either a periodic addition for younger children or a regular part of the kindergarten and primary classrooms. Overall, the general guidelines for organizing a language arts center are presented in Figure 5.2.

Creative Arts and Construction Center

Young children are naturally drawn to creative arts and construction materials with which they can produce two- and three-dimensional products representing their perceptions, feelings, and ideas about their world. You can often hear children egocentrically expressing those thoughts aloud as they tactilely manipulate a variety of textures, patterns, shapes, and products in this area. Here children's cognitive perceptions are revealed as they move developmentally from simple to more complex views of their world. Cows can be any color, not just brown or black and white; the sky is something over their heads, not coming down in a distance to meet a horizon; adults tower over children, and suns are reserved only for happy, warm pictures, not for every picture. In construction activity, children develop increasingly sophisticated skills in manipulating materials, arranging and rearranging them to represent aspects of their world. The role of the teacher is to demonstrate the skills children need to use materials, stimulate thinking, and encourage children's explorations (see Chapter 8).

FIGURE 5.2
Guidelines for Setting Up a
Language Arts Center

1. Place the language arts area in a quiet portion of the room away from traffic. An electrical outlet is desirable and necessary for listening to recorded literature.
2. Provide materials for all areas of language development: listening, speaking, reading, and writing.
3. Display an assortment of writing materials such as small note pads, receipt tapes, post-it notes, and various sizes of writing implements so children may choose.
4. Display the front covers of books rather than the spine.
5. A child-sized table and chair are necessary for writing.
6. A sheet-covered mattress and/or large pillows make a comfortable spot for book reading and viewing.
7. Display the alphabet and written messages within the children's view when seated in the area. Do not expect them to be able to use such displays on top of chalk boards.
8. Provide books that remain in the area so that children may read them again and again.
9. Add and remove books related to themes.

There should be explicit valuing and reinforcement of children's personal expression and private interpretations. Some guidelines for organizing the space and materials are in Figure 5.3.

Science/Exploration/Collections Center

Basically, children who are engaged in sciencing are given a chance to observe and manipulate a variety of constructed and natural objects in ways that help them to recognize similarities, differences, and relationships among the objects and phenomena. They sniff, look at, listen to, feel, pinch, and if possible taste a variety of materials in order to develop and extend their ability to make careful and accurate observations.

Encouraging children's investigation of natural and constructed phenomena in their world is the primary focus of this center. Teachers guide children toward an understanding of scientific processes as they have them scan, explore, discover, attend, observe, sort, classify, vary conditions, compare, predict, describe, label, and evaluate outcomes. In addition to learning the scientific method, children come also to value the role their own sensory perceptions, imaginations, and intuition play in understanding these phenomena.

To prepare the science/exploration/collections center adequately, teachers must become efficient in gathering, taking inventory, and replacing science resources, protecting children's safety, organizing interesting indoor and outdoor experiences, arranging the environment, and making themselves available to children for spontaneous discussions. They also need to be alert to the quality of science experiences they are providing and ensure that these contribute to conceptual growth rather than fostering magical thinking.

Although young scientists benefit most from exploring and working with real materials, many good videotapes are now available and can be stocked near a VCR and monitor for the children's independent use. Exciting full-color, realistic photographs can be gathered and selectively displayed in the center. Teachers who want to attract children, rather than dust, to a science center will work hard at setting up attractive, attention-getting displays, using novelty, humor, simplicity, and suspense to draw children (Holt, 1988). Even though many sciencing materials will be offered selectively to children, basic supplies should be consistently available on low shelves or in drawers marked with pictures and labels of contents. Use the guidelines in Figure 5.4.

FIGURE 5.3
Guidelines for Setting Up a
Creative Arts and Construction
Center

1. Place the art materials center near a water source.
2. Arrange storage and furnishings to provide easy entry into the area; ensure that traffic does not flow through it. A corner is desirable.
3. Store papers, scissors, adhesives, markers, crayons, and other art materials in an easily accessible unit.
4. Provide a rack or table where wet products may dry.
5. Provide a space where children's work may be displayed and/or a system where work is sent home regularly.
6. Provide materials for maintaining the area, such as sponges and paper towels, where children may get them; provide paint smocks to cover clothing.
7. Easels may be arranged so that children work alone or side by side. Usually a large table and chairs are also in this area.
8. Demonstrate the use and care of materials as they are introduced to children.
9. Label shelves and containers and use pictographs or written instructions to enable children to act autonomously.
10. Display art books and publications about the use of media so that they are easily visible.

FIGURE 5.4
Guidelines for Setting Up a
Science/Exploration/Collections
Center

1. The science center location often depends upon the nature of the science content. Growing plants require either sunlight or a grow light. Studies of water volume and pressure require a water source. Collections may be placed anywhere.
2. Demonstate the use, care, and storage of the tools.
3. Provide a simple pictograph or written or oral directions.
4. Cameras, writing or drawing paper, and pencils are necessary for recording observations.
5. Place reference books in the center with sections marked that are relevant to the theme. If these materials are available, young children will examine documents intended for adults.

Manipulative Materials/Table Games Center

For children to acquire mathematical concepts, attach language and symbols to these concepts, and grow in their ability to learn new concepts, they need a great deal of hands-on experience with diverse logicomathematical materials. The activities and gaming experiences children encounter in a math/manipulative materials/table games center guide them toward increasingly complex organization of motor behavior, perceptual development, and mathematical concepts.

The teacher's role is to provide stimulating materials and structure sequential experiences that will move the children from a concrete, intuitive level of thinking to higher, reflective, and autonomous thought (Cruikshank, Fitzgerald, & Jensen, 1980). Although children will eventually not be so reliant on concrete materials, they are extremely important beginning tools to facilitate conceptualization. In the beginnings of concept development, abstract symbolization interferes with children's understanding. No matter how carefully adults design or simplify the presentation of

FIGURE 5.5

Guidelines for Setting Up a Manipulative Materials/Table Games Center

1. Place a large table with chairs adjacent to open shelves in any convenient location.
2. Provide ample materials at varying levels of difficulty on the shelves well spaced for younger children. Cluster similar toys together. Materials for all aspects of mathematics and quantitative thinking should be available.
3. Provide clear plastic containers labeled with words or pictures for cleanup.
4. Introduce new games, materials, and tasks; demonstrate the use and care of the materials.
5. Provide a balance of open-ended materials (pegs, Legos, sewing cards), self-correcting materials (wooden cylinders, puzzles, nesting boxes), collectibles (bottle caps, buttons, sea shells, baby-food jar tops), and games (lotto, concentration, and cards).
6. Provide writing materials for older children to record their work, or place the center near the writing center.
7. Refrain from storing all manipulatives on the display shelves. Rotate items from the storage area to the display area regularly.
8. To keep interest high, rotate materials between mornings and afternoons for children in full-day programs.
9. Display written directions or pictographs to indicate what to do or how to do an activity. Also, display written materials such as directions for games or the use of manipulatives and related books so that children can see them.

abstract symbols to young children, they inevitably understand only what they can concretely discern from direct sensory experience. The numeral *III* or *3* does not have meaning in and of itself until the child has counted out three objects several times and then associated the numeral with the quantity of three. The most viable arena in which to give children time for such exploration and application of logicomathematical materials and games is in a center that highlights activity revolving around patterning, sorting, classifying, varying, comparing, graphing, and connecting numbers and symbols. The objectives and activities outlined in the mathematics section of Chapter 10 can be carried out most successfully through organized center activity. In addition, this center might focus on fine motor skills, problem solving activities, or enhancement of memory skills. To organize this center, refer to the guidelines in Figure 5.5.

Blocks Center

Many skills and abilities are fostered in the blocks center because this relatively open-ended material is readily adapted to all developmental domains. Besides fine and gross motor coordination that develop from children's bending, lifting, stacking, balancing, pushing, pulling, and reaching, there is also increased understanding of directionality, manual dexterity, eye-hand coordination, configuration, problem solving, socialization, and conceptualization of patterns, symmetry, and balance (McKee, 1990b). When literacy enhanced, the block center may provide actual reading and writing experiences (Stroud, 1995). Photographs and sketches of block structures allow this construction form to be saved over time and are an excellent starting place for either taking dictation about the children's work or their writing about their building (Stritzel, 1995).

Unit blocks and large hollow blocks are critical to an effective block center. They may be supplemented with theme-related materials such as trucks and trains or with other dramatic play props such as hats or hoses. Children frequently make signs to communicate the meaning of their structures. Suggestions for the organization of the block space are shown in Figure 5.6 (Dodge & Colker, 1996; Clayton, 1989).

FIGURE 5.6
Guidelines for Setting Up a
Blocks Center

1. Place the block area in a large space that may be used at other times for whole-group instruction.
2. Arrange storage units to enclose three sides of the area. This diminishes the flow of traffic through the area.
3. Locate the area in the noisy part of the room (normal block play is not quiet).
4. Provide a firm, unpatterned floor covering in the block area. This may be either an area rug or a carpet. A firm, flat surface is desirable to minimize balance problems with blocks.
5. Label the storage areas with silhouettes of the blocks that should go on each shelf.
6. Provide bins for the storage of other props to support block play on nearby shelves and change them regularly to create interest and stimulate desired play. They should be visible but not mixed with the blocks.
7. Establish rules for treating the blocks with care. Children should take only the blocks they plan to use. The blocks should remain clean and unmarked.
8. For older children, provide materials for making signs and floor tape to mark areas for individual play. Usually younger children spread out more while they work together, whereas older ones may do a complex group project in smaller spaces.
9. Post a sign indicating the number of children that may use the area. Using words or a pictograph, place a reminder of the rules for safe group play with blocks where children may see it.
10. Place books, magazines, adding machine tape, architectural blueprints, and other literacy items related to buildings, architecture, and theme-related construction in the area.
11. If the area is also used for large-group instruction, attach fabric (use velcro fasteners) over the blocks displayed on shelves. This allows the area to be closed and creates a visual boundary, enabling children to focus on the activities in whole-group experiences.

Pretend-Play Center

In the pretend-play center, children interact with one another to reenact their own life experiences and play any number of imagined roles. Here they have a chance to be in charge! They can pretend to be an authority figure (doctor, teacher, big brother, police officer, mother, or father), someone who does dangerous, risky things (soldier, boxer, or race car driver), or even someone who does bad things (robber or monster). They can experiment with cause and effect with only pretend consequences. Because peers are relative equals, they can debate and hope to win their share of victories. They can integrate and extend their understanding about what happens in particular settings (pizza place, beauty shop, or post office) and build varying perspectives about social, family, and gender roles. In addition to benefits already cited, children gain in self-expression, vocabulary development, sense of belonging and cooperating, and various modes of social exchanges that require the development of physical, logicomathematical, and social knowledge.

The ages and developmental levels of the children being served and individual needs and interests are important considerations in promoting certain activities and experiences in the pretend-play center. For example, younger children may have a real need to use the center for housekeeping. They will want relevant props, such as dolls, doll furniture, and dress-up clothes.

Most older children will also enjoy using house-keeping materials occasionally. However, they may be more interested in using the center when it is equipped to simulate other contexts they are coming to know about in their ever-widening world: stores, a space command center, TV station, auto repair clinic, restaurant, formal school setting, post office, or hospital. This will be especially true in encouraging boys to use the center. Also, the activities and experiences will be played out in very different ways by younger and older children. Care should be taken so that the diversity and scope of the roles children have available are not restrictive as may happen in a series of theme-related, pretend-play sets (Petrakos & Howe, 1996). As children mature, their play may become more realistic. Instead of merely playing at pizza making, they will want to make the real thing and "sell" it to classmates who come in, sit down, order, eat, and pay before leaving.

Should space and other resources be available, two pretend-play centers are desirable. The interaction between a theme-related center and a house center often brings together boys and girls who do not usually choose to work or play together. Opportunities for creativity, social interaction, and understanding complex relationships (such as that between work and family) are often fostered.

Older primary-aged children often use props of pretend play to stage plays and spend time and energy in planning and producing these events. The suggestions in Figure 5.7 will assist you in setting up a pretend-play center.

Cooperative Project Learning Center

The cooperative project area is an area in which children work together toward a common goal. The activities offered there involve tasks too big or too complex for any one child to complete alone. Thus, the emphasis is on collaborating, generating ideas, developing

FIGURE 5.7
Guidelines for Setting Up a
Pretend-Play Center

1. Place the pretend-play center in the noisy portion of the room. Having it adjacent to the block area would encourage extension of the play using another material.
2. Create boundaries with furniture or other equipment.
3. Enclose the center so that children may easily determine when they are in or out of the center. Avoid lining up the equipment against a wall. A wall may be one boundary, and the equipment placed to form a corner or opposite wall.
4. Store the props so that children may see them easily, and label the storage areas so that children may take care of the materials.
5. Place cookbooks, home repair books, clothing patterns, newspapers, or other documents typically found in households in the home-making area.
6. Change the center regularly. Add new props and remove some on a once or twice a week basis. Younger children may need the same set-up for a longer time than older children.
7. If only one center is available for older children, change it biweekly or monthly to coordinate with other learning events.
8. Include appropriate books, photos with labels, and other publications for the theme such as catalogs on camping gear for a camp theme.
9. Store prop boxes for theme-related pretend play in a closet or on a high shelf. Do not allow clutter to accumulate in the pretend-play center.

plans, giving suggestions, listening to one another's opinions, negotiating, and evaluating the participants' work. Some teachers plan a cooperative project each week; others offer one per month and then let it continue at a pace determined by the children's interests. The physical setting of the cooperative learning center may be in any area of the room. Necessarily children must have the following:

❏ Adequate space for the children engaged in the project.
❏ Storage for the project and related materials from one day to the next.
❏ Specific tools and materials necessary to complete the project.

For instance, in a classroom in which dinosaurs constituted the theme, the kindergarten children created a "Boxosaurus."

Day 1: The children planned how to make a large dinosaur out of boxes (a Boxosaurus). They generated ideas regarding the parts of the dinosaur that should be made, tools and materials needed, and who would help with each stage of production: assembly, painting, and decorating. The teacher wrote out their plan for all to see.

Day 2: The children gathered materials and began the assembly stage of production.

Day 3: The painting phase of the project was introduced.

Day 4: The children added various decorations to the Boxosaurus.

Day 5: The children measured all the parts of the Boxosaurus and recorded the vital statistics on a graph.

Day 6: The children evaluated their work. They responded to such questions as these: Could the job have been done as well by one person? How satisfied were the children with the results? How might the children change their plan in the future? What kinds of decisions were necessary throughout the project, and how did they turn out?

Other projects children have carried out include making a meal over a period of several days and then eating it on the last day, creating a replica of their town using small boxes and other "beautiful junk," scripting and producing a class dramatization, and building a museum through which they eventually conducted tours for another class.

There are no particular guidelines for cooperative projects as they often require specialized use of another center or an extension of a center or are organized around several centers existing in the classroom. However, provision for protecting the project during the period of days or weeks that it is in use may require floor space away from traffic areas.

Large-Group Center

Perhaps this center is one that most develops a spirit of unity within the classroom. Here children come together with the teacher as a group for a number of purposes: singing, listening to a story, discussing what is to occur or what has happened during the day, writing a group letter to someone, participating in a choral reading or musical activity, attending to entertainment or information from visitors, engaging in finger plays, or reenacting a story. It is a place where a lot of enjoyable experiences happen and safe learning occurs: It is not even noticable when a child does not know every word in the song or in the story being read. And because lots of stories, songs, poems, and rhymes are shared over and over, eventually children do know every word and are proud of it! To develop a space for whole-group instruction, use the suggestions in Figure 5.8.

Sand and Water Centers

Sand and water have been used for many years in early childhood programs because the materials are so versatile. Children have complete control of the materials and, when accessories are carefully selected, learn about the flow of fluids, volume, skills in measuring, comparing, observing, and evaluating. Children develop eye-hand coordination in pouring, measuring, scrubbing, grasping, and squeezing activities and strengthen small muscles in digging, ladling, carrying, and controlling the materials. Usually children share the area, engaging in conversation and cooperatively using materials. The process is very soothing and relaxing as well. This is often an area where children with special needs prosper, as most are eager to participate and successful in doing so. Ideal for children of age 3 to 5 for exploration and sensory experiences, the sand and water centers are exceptionally useful in teaching principles of numeric operations when standard

FIGURE 5.8
Guide for Setting Up a Large-Group Center

1. Provide sufficient space to seat children and adults comfortably. This is usually on the floor, so a rug or carpet is desirable.
2. Locate it near an electrical outlet so audiovisual equipment may be used.
3. Close open cupboards, or cover other materials to diminish distractions.
4. For young children, floor tape making seating spots may be useful.
5. Arrange a focal point where the teacher and specialized materials are located. Big books, music players or instruments, or easels for experience stories are typical. Bulletin boards with songs and poetry posted on them are helpful in this area.

measures are used and concepts such as conservation of volume when containers of various shapes but the same volume are provided. Additionally, children's social and language skills may be promoted as well as supporting other concepts when properly facilitated (Crosser, 1994). Often sand and water centers are provided both indoors and outdoors. (See Figure 5.9.)

Outdoor Nature Center

Plants and small animals such as insects, reptiles, birds, and mice may live in an undisturbed section of the playground. Usually at the back of the school property,

the land may remain uncultivated, unplanted, and unmowed so that the natural wild flora and fauna may grow. Not much land is required to provide a place where children might discover worms, insects, and butterflies. Children are fascinated by the natural environment, and much is to be learned from it (Rivkin, 1995). Many cognitive and aesthetic activities may be developed to use in this naturalized setting (Cohen, 1994; Wilson, 1995). The Cooperative Extension Service in each region of the United States has written materials related to naturalized gardens and can identify poisonous plants. The guidelines in Figure 5.10 are very general.

FIGURE 5.9
Guidelines for Setting Up a Sand and Water Center

1. Place a covered sand/water table near the source of water on a hard surface flooring. If hard surface is not available, place it on a large heavy plastic sheet in a carpeted room. Big pans can be used and hung on the walls when not in use if covered tables are not available.
2. A 5–10-gallon plastic covered pail is useful for storing the sand when water is in the table.
3. Store accessories near the area and select them carefully to meet the learning goals. Avoid using the same ones all the time.
4. Provide a child-sized broom and a sponge mop in the area so children can clean up after themselves and plastic smocks so children do not get wet.
5. If space and resources allow, sand and water tableware are desirable.
6. Use pictographs, photos, or display books with drawings related to the concepts you want the children to explore.

FIGURE 5.10
Guidelines for Setting Up an
Outdoor Nature Center

1. Select an area of the outdoors away from traffic. This is usually in the back of the school yard or lot.
2. If the area is covered with gravel or hard-packed or otherwise inhospitable soil, cultivate the earth and add compost. Worms, dry leaves, and other vegetable materials may be added to the area.
3. If the area is big enough, transplant shrubs and other plants native to the region that attract butterflies and other insects.
4. Wait. Over time this area will become an interesting place for children to explore and participate in guided-learning experiences related to the natural environment.
5. Hang and maintain bird feeders.

Commercial Playground Centers

Many playgrounds have commercially constructed climbing units and other equipment to encourage physical and pretend play that meets established safety guidelines for playgrounds. In traditional playgrounds such equipment is free standing, and in contemporary playgrounds pieces are combined in more architecturally pleasing configurations, although there is no great difference in children's use of equipment (Dempsey & Frost, 1993). Children's play outdoors differs from that indoors. Outdoor play is more social for both boys and girls than indoor play; it tends to support gross motor skill development, and, for boys, it may be a primary environment for the development of language (Dempsey & Frost, 1993). Interestingly, children of working parents appear to excel in many developmental areas during outdoor rather than indoor play, perhaps because of more experience (Dempsey & Frost, 1993). Professional staff may have input when playground equipment is purchased but are always responsible for supervising children in the safe use of equipment (Frost, 1992). Figure 5.11 provides guidelines for using playground equipment as a learning center (Frost, 1991; Zeece & Graul, 1993).

Other Centers

Depending on climate and season, the scope and variety of learning centers outdoors may complement or duplicate learning centers indoors. In addition, numerous other centers are common either indoors or out, such as those for woodworking, music, mathema-

tics, computers, construction, and sensory exploration and those related to specific themes such as grocery stores or spaceships. Other resources are available to describe the construction of such centers (Ard & Pitts, 1990; Dodge & Colker, 1996; Isbell, 1995; Pattillo & Vaughan, 1996; Rivkin, 1995).

DEALING WITH IMPLEMENTATION ISSUES

Parents, teachers, and administrators often have a number of questions about classrooms that include large segments of time devoted to center activity:

"How can you tell what they're learning?"

"How do you know what children are participating in since they're all over the room?"

"What if a child never visits the language arts center and spends all her time playing with blocks?"

"Will he ever learn to read?"

"Can I still use reading groups?"

"There are so many materials needed. Where can I get them all?"

"I'm uncomfortable not having any structured time. Do I have to use centers all day long?"

Getting Started

Construction of learning centers depends on the philosophy of the professional staff; resources such as numbers of staff available, funding, materials, and space;

FIGURE 5.11
Guidelines for Supervising Outdoor Play Equipment/ Playground

1. Know first aid and have appropriate materials on hand to clean and care for minor injuries. Know the procedure to implement in case of serious injury.

2. Examine the playground with other staff members, and establish written guidelines on how children are to use equipment.

3. Avoid allowing too many children on the same piece of equipment at the same time. Encourage turn taking, and direct children's attention to other activities.

4. Demonstrate to children and other adults how to use equipment. For example, children should use three-point climbing on structures. This means that only one foot or hand should move at time, and the other three extremities should be in contact with the equipment.

5. Avoid lifting young children up to trees, slides, or climbers. If they cannot get up there by themselves, then they are probably unsafe being there. Children who are not "pushed" by adults or teased into it by other children tend to remain on equipment for which their skills are best suited.

6. Constantly observe play patterns to note possible hazards, and suggest appropriate equipment or usage changes.

7. Construct and maintain a schedule for using the playground with other class groups. Avoid overcrowding.

8. Prepare written accident reports with special attention to surface conditions, type and extent of the injury, age of the child, and a summary of how the accident happened. Note weather conditions. Periodically review these looking for patterns of injuries and needs for supervisory changes.

and any constraints such as a program's established curricular and evaluation requirements. Preplanning involves deciding on room arrangement, organization of materials, number of centers to be used, time to be allotted to center participation, and introduction of the process to children. The "comfort level" of each teacher involved needs to be addressed as well. Teachers beginning to use centers for the first time should set up the number and kinds of centers they feel they can manage, keep in order those that need the least direction and contact from the teacher, utilize materials familiar to the children, and have a clear and direct purpose. When the physical environment is carefully planned, when there is a consistency in routines, when expectations and limits are clearly understood, when there are choices regarding use of toys and learning materials, and when children have been taught appropriate inter-

action strategies, centers are fun, safe, and stimulating (Ford, 1993). Later, teachers can add or expand already established centers to be more responsive to the interests and needs of the children and an expanded curricular framework.

Structuring Self-Sustaining Centers

Although the presence of aides and volunteers in an early childhood classroom certainly can enhance learning center activity potential, additional adult support is not always possible, particularly in the primary grades. Many classroom teachers find themselves the only adult overseeing everything that goes on in the classroom. When this is the case, teachers must become skillful in setting up centers that are self-sustaining and need less direct guidance. The following guidelines

Some centers should be self-sustaining, requiring only initial guidance from the teacher.

are for enhancing learning center activity that requires initial guidance only or allows completely independent action on the part of the children.

1. Introduce the activity during large group, explaining its purpose and demonstrating actual use of materials. Give children the opportunity to ask questions. Children are told where and for how long materials will be available and given necessary reminders about using them cooperatively with others, such as keeping resources only in the learning center so that others can find them.

2. Introduce new centers and more complex activities only after general center activity has begun. Work closely with an initial, smaller group of children who can then assist other children subsequently wanting to participate. Polaroid pictures of children going through each of the steps in an activity can be taken, with sequential steps numbered and labeled. This contributes not only to children's autonomy in the classroom but also to their understanding of the sequential nature of product development.

3. Use a variety of direction-giving strategies, such as pictographs for very young children and written instructions or oral instructions on the tape recorder for older children.

4. Structure activities in which children can complete a project independently. One teacher had planned to make fruit salad with her preschoolers and considered eliminating the activity altogether when she learned that a parent volunteer was ill and would not be coming in

to help. Instead, she slightly altered her original plans. She brought in only soft fruit, put it all in the water table, and provided plastic knives. She put footprints on the floor around the sides of the water table to indicate how many children were allowed to participate at any given time and explained these guidelines to the children in large group before learning center activities were made available. Thus, she was able to move ahead with the activity, which went very well with only periodic guidance on her part.

Deciding How Many Centers to Make Available

How many centers to operate at any particular time will depend on physical space and the teacher's wish to limit or expand learning options for children. In general, at least $1^1/_2$ center activity "slots" should be made available per child; for example, 20 children would require at least 30 activity spaces.

Monitoring Children's Use of Centers

When moving to a center-based approach, good record keeping and evaluation will be important if the teacher is to have a clear idea of the accomplishments of each child. Useful evaluation can take place through observation when children have complete freedom of choice, which is most often the case with very young children. Participation by older children may include teacher-assigned tasks to complete or choices from a few options so that specific processes or skills can be observed and documented.

Several approaches have been useful to professionals using centers. The first is to keep careful records of the activities available to children on a daily basis. The teacher first must have a clear idea of the overall goals and program objectives. Once these have been clearly developed and listed, activities planned to support them are briefly described and dated. Some teachers leave space for comments on the success of the activity. This becomes a record of program presentations, but it does not provide information about individual involvement and performance.

Two approaches that can determine which activities children are selecting work fairly well. Participation charts can be developed that provide a systematic basis for recording such information. A list of children's names going down a page and a list of centers going across the page form a checklist that can be used quickly several times a week at different times during center activity to give a reasonable sample of children's involvement (see Chapter 16 for a more explicit example of this). Another strategy is to provide a set of "tickets" for each child with his or her name written on them. These tickets are then deposited in a box or envelope in each of the centers as children enter the activity. The teacher determines the number of tickets that each child has available on a given day. The number of tickets is related to the amount of time for choice of activities and the time teachers think children will need in particular activities. This approach was highly successful for a group of children who had difficulty making choices and sticking to the choices they made. The teacher then recorded which children had been in which centers after they went home by checking them off as she picked up the tickets.

This approach is sometimes modified for older children by having two colors of tickets. One color represents the center or centers where the teacher expects all the children to participate during the day or week, and the other color may be used anywhere. The centers are clearly labeled with the color of tickets that may be used there. The teacher distributes a few of the color-coded tickets each day, and children are asked to use them only in specific centers. Although children may choose the teacher-indicated center at other times, they must choose it at least once during the period indicated by the teacher. In one first-grade classroom in Fort Wayne, Indiana, the first thing children do when they arrive each morning is to check the "learning center guide" written on the blackboard. This guide lets them know what centers will be available during the day. It also identifies the centers in which each child must participate, which vary from child to child. A sample of the learning-center guide is provided in Table 5.1.

Children are free to choose any of the available centers. However, they must be sure to visit and complete the task in the center under which their names appear. When they have completed an activity that was listed as a "have to," the children cross out their names on the board. In another class with a similar schedule, children keep track of their have-to centers on a form that includes the week's activities (see Figures 5.12 and 5.13). These are then kept by each child in a folder from which he or she will select portfolio materials at the end of the week. The teacher determines "have-to" centers based on children's interests and learning needs. She changes the children's names daily so that youngsters have different have-to assignments each day.

Another technique used by some first-grade teachers who wanted to be sure language arts were highlighted was to have all of the alternative centers relate to reading skills during a 60- to 80-minute period of the day. Children were given pictographs (strips of paper with drawings in 1-inch segments) representing specific activities. The children colored in their pictographs as they completed each task. Less advanced children had shorter pictographs with three or four designated centers, and more advanced students had up to 10 segments. Teachers also placed a check mark on the pictograph for some children, which indicated they needed to check with the teacher before coloring in the segment. Children later recorded their progress on a master pictograph of all children in the class.

TABLE 5.1
"Have-To" Centers

Painting	Listening	Computer	Reading	Games	Math	Journals	Cooperative Project
Tara	Megan	David	Leroy	Anne	Jerry	Carol	Beth
Lisa	Tom N.	Barry	Leslie	Sam	Ian	Cal	Sarah
Viola	Mark	Tom W.	Mara	Andy	Tara	Leroy	Ian
	Barry	Sarah	Cal	Carol	Beth	Sam	Lisa
	Jerry	Beth	Anne	Tom N.	Barry	Leslie	David
	Lisa		Megan	Viola	Andy	Mara	
			Mark			Sarah	

FIGURE 5.12

Sample Activity Report

Activity Report	Week of
ART TABLE	PRETEND PLAY
BLOCKS/CONSTRUCTION	PUZZLES
BOOKS	SNACK
COMPUTER	WOODWORKING
EASEL	WRITING
MATH	

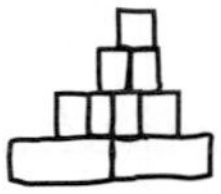

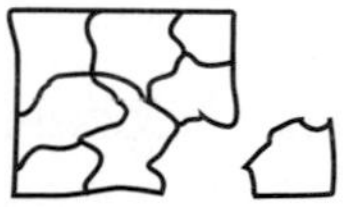

This is how I felt about the day:	Terrible	Sad	O.K.	Good	Terrific!
Monday	1	2	3	4	5
Tuesday	1	2	3	4	5
Wednesday	1	2	3	4	5
Thursday	1	2	3	4	5
Friday	1	2	3	4	5

Source: From Donna Howe, Child Development Laboratories, Department of Family and Child Ecology, College of Human Ecology, Michigan State University. Adapted with permission.

FIGURE 5.13
Sample Evaluation Form

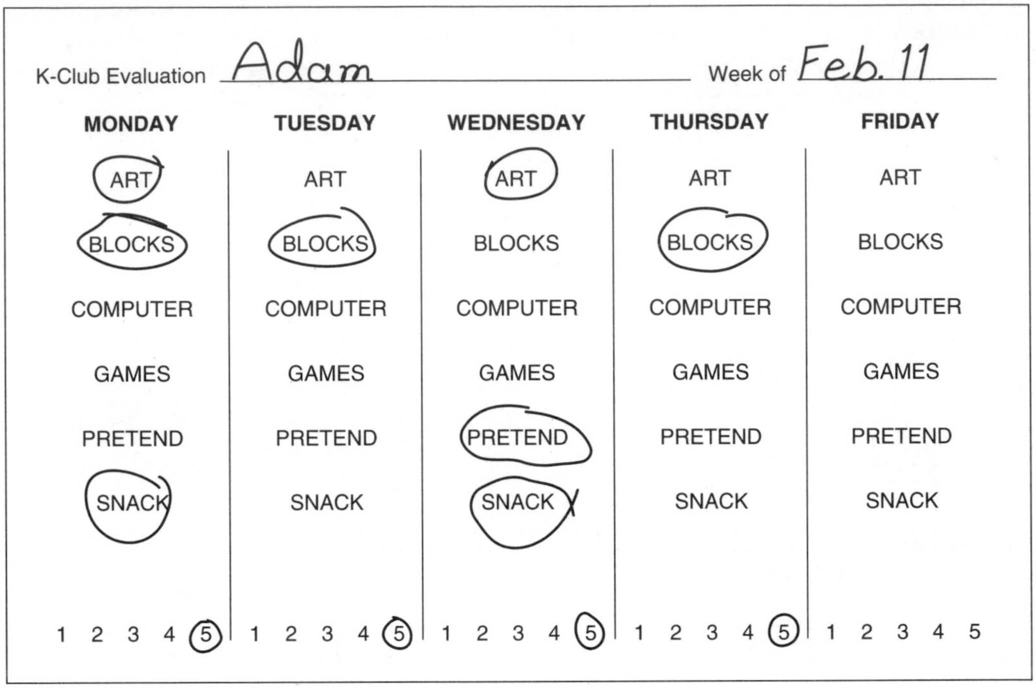

K-Club Evaluation Adam Week of Feb. 11

MONDAY	TUESDAY	WEDNESDAY	THURSDAY	FRIDAY
ART	ART	ART	ART	ART
BLOCKS	BLOCKS	BLOCKS	BLOCKS	BLOCKS
COMPUTER	COMPUTER	COMPUTER	COMPUTER	COMPUTER
GAMES	GAMES	GAMES	GAMES	GAMES
PRETEND	PRETEND	PRETEND	PRETEND	PRETEND
SNACK	SNACK	SNACK	SNACK	SNACK
1 2 3 4 5	1 2 3 4 5	1 2 3 4 5	1 2 3 4 5	1 2 3 4 5

Source: From Donna Howe, Child Development Laboratories, Department of Family and Child Ecology, College of Human Ecology, Michigan State University. Adapted with permission.

Evaluating Skill Development

To check on children's development of basic skills, some teachers select small groups of children and provide key activities that are instructional and provide information on child performance. These small-group activities are in operation during center activity, and the group of children selected will vary, depending on the teacher's objective and the children's need for information. For example, one teacher noticed that four children were having difficulty leaving spaces between words in their journal writing. During center activity, she asked the four of them to come together to discuss the need for a strategy to help them remember and asked them what could be done. It was interesting that the children offered different solutions. One suggested putting periods between each word to indicate a space. Another thought that hyphens would be helpful until she remembered simply to leave a space. The important thing here is that the children were involved in solving the problem rather than relying on the teacher to do so or being told the "correct" way to improve their writing. It did not take long for the four children to begin leaving spaces between their words, and the temporary aids they had devised—periods and hyphens—soon disappeared.

Although teachers could include traditional reading groups during learning center activities, the technique of selective small-group structuring is more effective than the traditional maintenance of static groups (e.g., established reading groups such as the Bluebirds, Cardinals, and Orioles). Small groups of children are brought together for specific purposes and problem solving. These groups are as variable as the problems children are likely to encounter while growing in their conceptualization and competence in working with objects and people. Children are less apt to see themselves as "slow" or "only average" across an entire subject such as reading or math, as can happen when placement is based on ability grouping or tracking. Instead, they have opportunities to participate in diverse kinds of meetings with other children who are simply working on similar aspects of problem solving.

Teacher-made checklists are helpful in looking at individual and general class progress in any domain of interest. For example, a preschool teacher wanting to document evidence of social interaction listed each of the children's names across the top of an observation form and variables down the left-hand side such as "developing friendship skills," "initiating play/work with others," "cooperating with others," "helpful to others," and so forth. A clipboard containing the developed checklist was kept readily available over the next week, and when certain behaviors were observed, they were dated and documented. A second-grade teacher interested in whether children were picking up phonics skills made a listing of those he had been introducing in large and small groups through a variety of literature experiences. From this, he developed a checklist with spaces to record when a child had been introduced to the particular skill, when the child had participated in activities that supported development of the skills, and when the child demonstrated mastery of the skill. Additional strategies for assessing children's learning are discussed in Chapter 16.

Up to this point learning centers have been discussed one at a time. However, as a functional matter, centers must be combined into one cohesive whole and carefully placed into a classroom.

Organizing Physical Space in the Classroom

Few classrooms are ideal. Consider the organization of the space in these classrooms. The preschool classroom (Figure 5.14) is long and rectangular but has a sizable segment of space cut out of the middle that diminishes visual supervision from some segments of the classroom. The kindergarten classroom (Figure 5.15) has the advantage of a large adjacent storage area, but again the classroom has numerous corners. In both instances the teachers have carefully selected the size of the centers located in hard-to-see spots and the nature of the activities going on in them when setting up the classroom. The first-grade classroom (Figure 5.16) has a more traditional shape and has been arranged to accommodate center-based instruction for most of the

day. Whole-group instruction occurs in the block area with the children sitting on the floor. Subject matter labels are used to denote the activities that are usually located in the various areas of the room, but these are not rigid. For example, social studies activities are often located at the center labeled "Spelling," and many science activities are moved to the art table when more space is needed or when more children are at work in the center. A summary of things to look for are suggested in Figure 5.17 (Dodge, 1988; Gullo, 1994).

Organizing Outdoor Environments

The principles of using the indoor environment to influence development apply also to outdoor environments. The three playgrounds in Figures 5.18–5.20 illustrate playgrounds that support the full age group of several learning centers. Note that many features such as play structures, water sources, hard surfaces, trees, fences, hills, and plantings are fixed.

Playground 1 (Figure 5.18) nearest the school, is for the youngest children. Sand is used under the climbing structure to absorb the force of falls but is also available in the curbed sand box nearby. The climbing/slide structure is bounded by a hard surface used for wheeled toys. Designed for children under the age of 5, the structure has short risers, a stair, an arched climbing structure, or a chain climber to various heights of the structure for a variety of challenges for younger children. Both a single-person slide and a lower two-person slide provide differences in comfort in high places. A tire swing structure is adjacent to the climbing apparatus and is large enough for three small children. A pretend play house at the far end of the yard features a doorway, windows, shelves, and seats. The floor is of a force-absorbent material that absorbs heat and light, making it snow and ice free earlier than the turf or sand-covered areas. A picnic table shaded by a large tree is convenient for snacks or table activities. Between Playgrounds 1 and 2 and opening into both is a sizable shed for storing snowshovels, sand and water toys, wheeled vehicles, water tables, tables, chairs, and other occasionally used equipment.

Playground 2 (Figure 5.19) features a turf-covered hill encircled by a track with a canvas-covered tunnel for wheeled toys. Running and small-group games are supported by an open grassy lawn. The drinking fountain near the storage shed is accessible from all three

FIGURE 5.14
Preschool Classroom

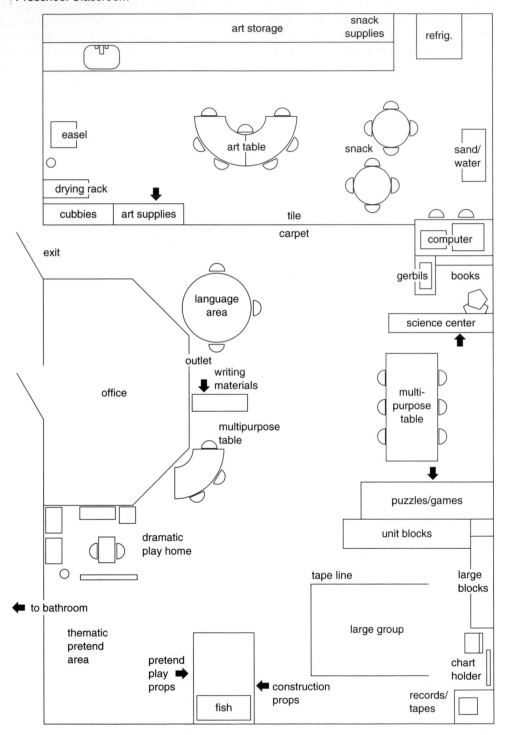

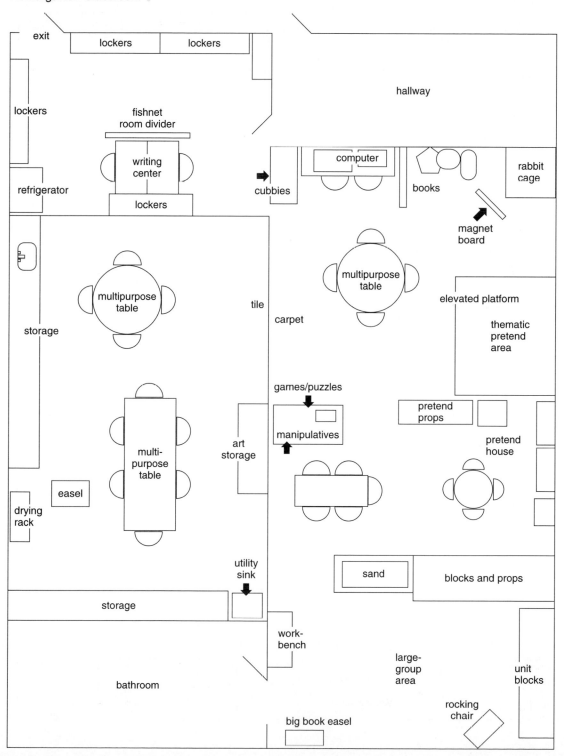

FIGURE 5.15
Kindergarten Classroom

FIGURE 5.16
First-Grade Classroom

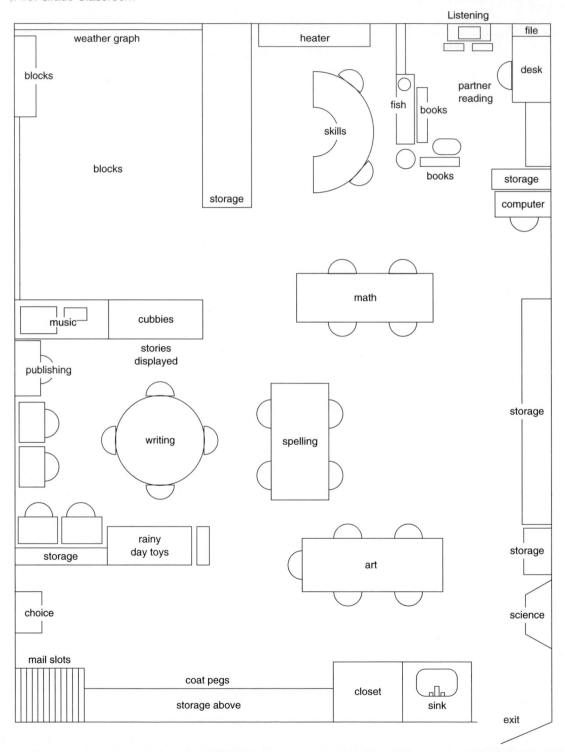

FIGURE 5.17
Questions to Ask to Assess the
Physical Arrangement of the
Room

1. Can children move from one part of the room to another without interfering with other children?
2. Are the boundaries between learning centers clear?
3. Are areas arranged to encourage active child choice?
4. Are pathways arranged so that children do not interrupt each other?
5. Is storage nearby and labeled so children can put things away?
6. Are centers placed so that quiet areas are separate from more active, noisy areas?
7. Are there places where children may work alone? with a small group? with a large group?
8. Are temporary centers adjacent to core centers to which they are related?
9. Can adults see the children all the time?
10. Is the group big enough for adults and children to gather with comfort?
11. Has the classroom been checked for safety with special attention to electrical outlets, extension cords, sources of heat, and potential for falls?
12. Are furnishings child sized?
13. Do the decorations reflect the specific backgrounds, experiences, and identities of the children?
14. Is the environment filled with words, books, and symbols?
15. Is there a convenient place for children to keep their personal things?
16. Are adult areas separated from child areas?

gated playgrounds. Nearby is a basketlike hoop where balls shoot out in three different directions. Tucked into corners are herb gardens where children are encouraged to touch, smell, and taste these pungent plants. A variety of insects and worms are usually seen here. Birds are encouraged through the selection of flowering, seed-bearing trees and shrubs along the drive and by bird feeders in Playground 1; the hilltop has shade trees suitable for climbing. Bushes at the one end and corner of this playground provide spaces for children to play hide and seek, make "camps," and engage in a variety of pretend play experiences. Teachers have noticed that children act as if they cannot be seen even during the winter when there are no leaves. Storage for tricycles, sleds, shovels, and other items is available in a locked shed adjacent to the tent-shaped rope climber. Close to the walk are two other pieces of equipment, one in which children may lift themselves up and is similar to parallel bars and another with a

roller where youngsters may climb up and run in place. Children play under hoses during the heat of summer that are strung across Playground 1 to the open grassy area. A gated, hard surface walk connects the parking lot and the walkway to the building along which children draw with chalk or play hopscotch. Children of any age are safe in this more naturalized setting.

Playground 3 (Figure 5.20) is bounded by a fence and a hedge of bushes that protect it visually from the street and parking lot as well as serving as a windbreak on two sides. Trees line the adjacent drive and the gated fence into Playground 2. This entire playground is sand covered for safety. The large complex play structure can easily accommodate a classroom of older preschool or primary children, 5- to 8-year-olds. The structure has a tall straight slide, a covered twisty one, an enclosed straight one, and a lower slide with rollers rather than a smooth surface. The risers are higher than on Playground 1, and the play areas

FIGURE 5.18
Playground 1

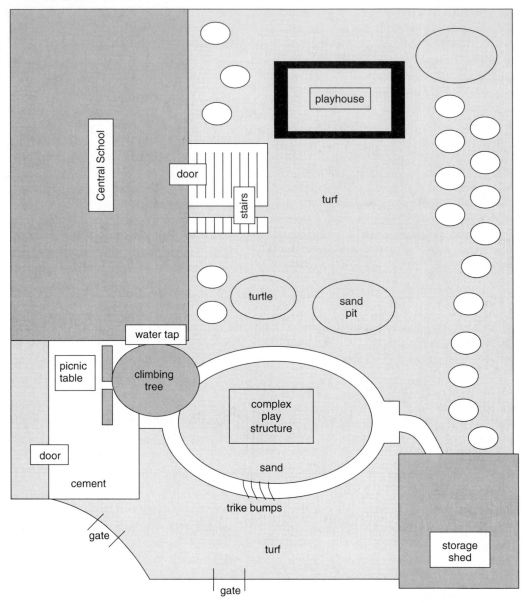

FIGURE 5.19
Playground 2

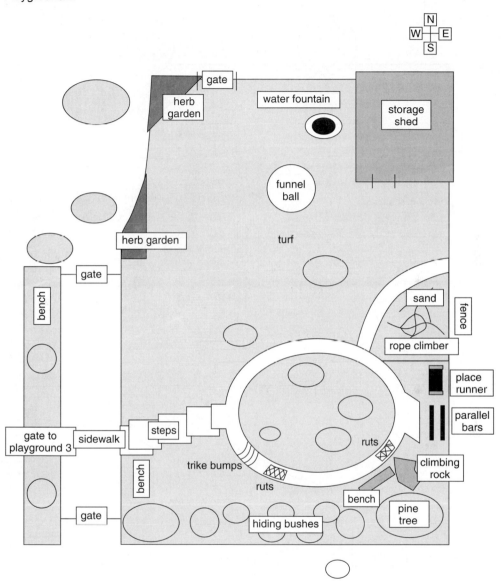

are connected with a hanging bridge in one place and a chain walk in another. Children have many access points and a variety of climbing challenges available on this very large structure. A tire swing that holds two to three children is adjacent.

Along one edge of Playground 3 a vcgctablc garden is established and nurtured. Vines such as cucumber and pole beans grace the fencing during late summer. Hardy plants such as radishes, peppers, bush beans, carrots, and onions grow here. Selection of plants is based on the edibility of stem, blossom, leaf, and root as well as hardiness. Most of the produce is fed to the assorted classroom animals, although children also engage in tasting.

On all playgrounds, many centers are fixed. Teachers add wheeled vehicles or jump ropes to be

FIGURE 5.20
Playground 3

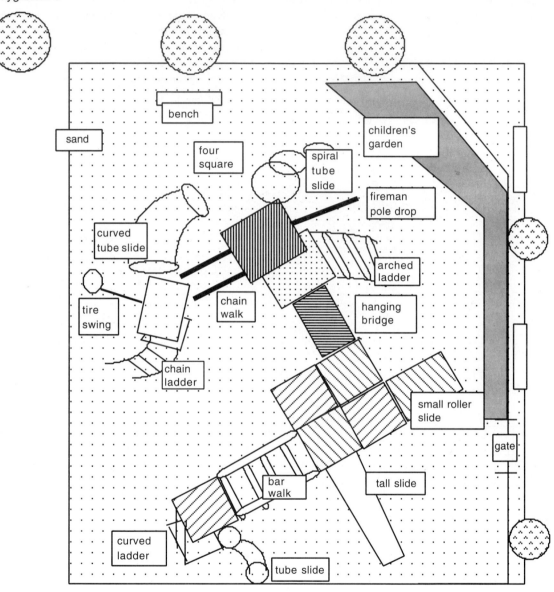

used on the hard surfaces, select digging equipment, or introduce balls and striking implements (ground hockey sticks, or bats) to promote specific motor skills. In addition, the storage sheds opening onto Playgrounds 1 and 2 hold tables, chairs, fence-hung easels, and other equipment for the expansion of the variety of centers.

Some desirable features such as a roofed outdoor play area, a large yard for game play, and a more easily accessed water supply are not available. Playgrounds, perhaps more than any other feature of the learning environment, must be designed and organized to accommodate the climate and terrain of the school or center. Changing major equipment is both expensive and somewhat difficult and requires careful planning. However, adjusting the environment outdoors for small changes works as well as indoor adjustments.

ADJUSTING THE PHYSICAL ENVIRONMENT

When the physical environment is managed so that children are receiving clear cues as to their expected behavior with materials or in a specific place, the teacher is providing an indirect approach to guidance (Kostelnik, et al., 1998; Eliason & Jenkins, 1994; Hildebrand, 1995). The goals of this strategy are to

- ❑ Stimulate learning possibilities.
- ❑ Protect children.
- ❑ Protect equipment.
- ❑ Maintain a peaceful learning environment. (Crosser, 1994, 186)

Children respond in predictable ways to changes in the environment. There are three fundamental ways for adjusting the environment: The teacher adds something to or removes something from the environment or alters something to make it safer and easier to use correctly.

Adding to the Environment

To improve children's abilities to maintain a clean and orderly classroom, several things might be done. Putting a colored cube in a plastic bag outside the bin where the inch cubes should be stored helps children locate the bin easily. Adding drawings for children 3 to 5 years of age and labels to shelves for the 6- to 8-year-olds works well. Adding a cloth covering to the front of the block shelf forms an effective barrier so that children are not distracted when that center is not open.

To make a learning center more successful, the teacher might add a sorting tray or muffin tin to a classification task or provide a hula hoop for a youngster trying to count out 10 sets of seven different objects on the floor. Such structuring increases orderliness as well as the probability of success for the child. A simple thing like giving children inexpensive meat trays or paper plates to place colored cubes in while they are constructing a pattern enables them to use the same bin of materials without inadvertently taking someone else's selection.

If the teacher wants children to record their findings in an activity in which objects are weighed, then pencils and paper (or graph paper) should be added to the learning center. Adding reference books to various learning centers in the room supports the goal of children learning to figure out information for themselves. For example, one teacher placed a telephone book in the housekeeping pretend-play area and a children's encyclopedia with the section on hamsters marked and displayed near the hamster cage. Children are basically curious and will use these reference materials, given appropriate support and instruction. One group of first-grade youngsters learned the principle of alphabetical order when a homemade telephone listing of children in the school, paper, and pencils were placed as props in a housekeeping center with only occasional assistance in locating desired numbers.

Guidance by manipulating the physical environment is the least intrusive and sometimes the most effective approach to an orderly classroom. In one classroom where the teacher was continuously admonishing a group of 6-year-olds to play cooperatively with the blocks, she introduced a sign that said "6 Children." Once children's attention was focused on the sign, they agreed to monitor the overcrowding in the center themselves. In a second-grade classroom where children were having difficulty with story reenactment when the teacher was not in the center, the teacher added a few distinctive props and a name tag for each character. These materials were sufficient to help the children keep track of the story line and the identity of each of the story characters.

Removing Something From the Environment

Occasionally, simply removing chairs from an area is sufficient to let children know that fewer than the usual number of children can work in that center at the same time. In a Head Start classroom, the teacher removed 10 pairs of scissors from the basket because she was unable to assist more than six inexperienced children at the same time. When several youngsters persistently became unruly as they drove their large wheeled trucks through a kindergarten classroom, the teacher simply placed the trucks in storage at the end of the day for the time being. In a suburban school, a first-grade teacher removed toys children had brought from home that youngsters had added to centers because they distracted the children from their work. When materials distract children from engaging in profitable experiences, when they pose hazards, or when teachers need to streamline centers to provide cues for children's appropriate behavior, adults should remove or reduce them so that appropriate behavior is most likely to occur.

Altering the Environment

Indirect child guidance through managing the physical environment sometimes takes more ingenuity. A first-grade teacher substituted an electric pencil sharpener for the traditional variety so that children would not grind their pencils to nubs, and she would not have to remind them repeatedly. A kindergarten teacher provided a simple wooden boot jack so that children would no longer use the edge of their lockers to pull off their boots. A teacher of 4-year-olds used a baby cupboard safety device to ensure that the cabinet where plant fertilizers were kept remained closed. One third-grade teacher obtained one taller table and higher chair for a youngster who was exceptionally tall and appeared to fidget uncomfortably in the furnishings that were suitable for his classmates. Sometimes these adjustments are even simpler: adding detergent to drippy paint, placing floor tape on the floor to designate an area for primary children to build with blocks, adding flour to the playdough third graders are making but did not measure correctly.

Teachers must also accommodate children with special needs. Children in wheelchairs or walkers need wider pathways than do children who walk unaided. Some of them may need trays attached to their chairs to work, while others can work successfully at a table with a cutout portion. Teachers who have vision-impaired children must examine the environment very carefully so that pathways are kept clear and the arrangements of the room remain stable over time. Children with hearing aids often experience excessive background noise, so teachers may need to adjust the location of centers or the amount of soft things in the environment. Children who are emotionally vulnerable may profit from having a private place where they may go when under stress. Teachers can also assist more able children to become aware of potential hazards to the less able and make the appropriate accommodations.

Teachers must observe their children carefully in the environments they have created and adjust the physical environment first if children are failing to engage in productive activities as desired. Play and work can be facilitated in this way without complete reliance on admonitions and verbal directions, which if overused can be wearing on children and adults alike. When these strategies are used consistently between the ages of 3 and 5, older children learn to apply them to new situations as they emerge.

Center-based learning occurs best in a well-ordered environment where ample storage is available for each core center, where children learn to put away materials and use them safely and appropriately, and where the environment is clean, pleasant, and designed for action. All of this is feasible by providing the appropriate furnishings, equipment, and materials and by teaching children how to use and care for them.

SELECTING MATERIALS FOR EACH CURRICULAR DOMAIN

Because hands-on learning is a fundamental premise of Developmentally Appropriate Practice, a variety of materials is necessary to provide a balanced program. Many programs have found that, because most of them add equipment and materials a little at a time, it takes from three to five years to supply classrooms adequately. Some primary-school programs have redirected workbook money into materials purchase. This is more efficient use of resources as materials last longer. With continuous use, all materials should be added to or replaced as they become lost or broken. In addition, nearly all classrooms have insufficient storage space for these materials, so mobile storage, additional shelving high in the room for long-term storage, and plastic containers, bins, or baskets to contain multi-piece manipulatives should be obtained early in the acquisition plan.

Programs for 3- to 5-year-olds often begin with appropriate equipment but must plan for replacement and expansion of choices. Childcare centers have the particularly challenging task of providing interesting materials for the morning and different but appropriate materials for the late afternoon so that children's interest is maintained while their learning progresses. Fortunately, many excellent alternatives are available that address similar competencies. For example, the seriation tasks of stacking containers can be met with stacking circular cups, hexagon cups, octagon cups, kitty in the keg, square boxes, and Russian nesting dolls. For the preschool child, the perceptually new material is treated as a different task, and children approach and use such playthings with interest and enjoyment.

GENERAL GUIDELINES TO THE SELECTION AND USE OF MATERIALS

Provide materials that are developmentally and age appropriate (Bredekamp & Copple, 1997). Young children require materials that support hands-on experiences. Indeed, if children are unable to have some form of hands-on experience, then, most likely, the topic is being introduced prematurely. For example, children learn about plants by growing them. They learn about culture by sharing family traditions within the class. They learn about geography by finding something in the classroom using a map. They learn about reading and writing by participating in functional written communications. The greater the number of manipulative materials and firsthand experiences with real things, the better. In Chapters 1, 3, and 4, you reviewed principles of development and how to apply these concepts to adult-planned activities. When a book such as this one is directed to programs serving a wide range of ages—3 to 8 years—the specific selections are important at each age level. For example, simple balance scales are adequate for 4-year-olds to understand the concepts *heavy* and *light,* but a more accurate scale with weights or a calibrated spring scale is more appropriate for 7- or 8-

year-olds who must learn to add and subtract accurately using them. Both scales provide direct experience with the concepts of mass, volume, and weight. Regardless of the age of the children, teachers have common goals:

❏ Stimulate learning possibilities.
❏ Protect children.
❏ Protect equipment.
❏ Maintain a peaceful learning environment. (Crosser, 1992, 26)

To implement these goals, some general guides have been developed.

Provide for Firsthand Experiences with Real Things Individual children vary greatly in their abilities to handle abstract concepts. All programs should have opportunities for them to begin instruction using concrete materials first and later reconstruct their experiences using increasingly abstract materials. Children gain exposure to more abstract experiences as they mature and are more capable of understanding symbolic representations. Many children prematurely learn to comply with requests by adults to use more abstract materials. They go through the activity but do not emerge with increased understanding or comprehension. Children construct their own concepts as a result of guided use of real things. Generally, selecting materials or designing activities that are either too easy or too difficult results in wasted time and misused materials. In either case, children are not profitably involved in learning. The presentation in Table 5.2 illustrates concrete materials, bridging materials, and more abstract

TABLE 5.2
Examples of Materials Varying From Concrete to Abstract

Concrete	Increasingly Abstract	Abstract
Bulb planted in soil for observation	Photographs of bulb growth	Discussion or graph of plant growth
Parquetry blocks and corresponding colored pattern cards outlining each shape	Parquetry blocks and black-and-white pattern cards outlining each shape	Parquetry blocks and pattern cards outlining a general shape rather than individual shapes
Unit blocks	Graph paper	Numerals
Field trip	Film or pictures	Letters or words
Cooking activity	Pretend play kitchen	Picture book recipe

materials. Three- to five-year-old and younger children need the predominance of the concrete materials, whereas seven- and eight-year-olds may use a mixture of concrete and a few more abstract materials as a basis for learning. All children throughout schooling profit from hands-on learning regardless of age.

Provide Materials That Are Complete, Safe, and Usable Puzzles with missing pieces, dull scissors, unstable climbing equipment, and broken tools or equipment should be repaired or replaced. Materials that do not work do not contribute to the learning experience but rather engender frustration and distress. For instance, if a set of materials is constructed by the teacher, the items should be sturdy and usable so that many children can interact with them. Laminating railroad board items rather than making them from construction paper, which tears easily, is initially more expensive, but the material lasts throughout the activity and often may be used in subsequent years.

Provide Literacy-Related Materials in All Centers Children of all ages will use functional literacy materials consistently if they are available: Cookbooks and paper to make grocery lists for the housekeeping center; drawing paper and pens to record plant growth; and markers and music score paper when children are trying out instruments. Books may go anywhere (Goldhaber, 1997). When resources are available, children try to use them, asking questions and seeking information, thus the teachable moment is generated from the skillful use of materials.

Provide Materials That Represent the Diversity of the United States and Most Particularly the Diversity of the Local Community Music, art, games, play materials, and photos are available that do the following:

❏ Depict men and women in a variety of work roles as well as the traditional ones.
❏ Illustrate families of various compositions and ages.
❏ Show workers in agriculture, business, education, health, and service occupations.
❏ Portray all races and religions of the world respectfully.
❏ Represent the variety of lifestyles and family incomes honorably.

When positive images and experiences are included in the day-to-day classroom practices, teachers can help enrich children's understandings of diverse populations (Henniger, 1995).

Demonstrate the Proper Use of Materials and Equipment Teachers sometimes assume that children ought to know how to use materials properly. Because the children who come into the learning environment are diverse in their experiences and family resources, such assumptions are not practical. A simple direct demonstration of materials and equipment at the time of first use increases the probability of safety as well as conserving the materials. For example, the 5-year-old who may know how to use cellophane tape may not understand the use and function of paste and may have never seen glue. Rarely do young children know how to conserve these products appropriately. In addition, the appropriate use of a material such as blocks changes as children learn and mature. Three-year-olds need much space as they generate horizontal structures such as roads or sprawling buildings that are simple enclosures. Seven-year-olds may build very successfully in smaller spaces about 3 feet square. Children of all ages need stimulation for their ideas and direction in appropriate behavior while using the center independently or with other children.

Purchase Sturdy, High-Quality Equipment A set of hardwood blocks is expensive as an initial purchase, but because they are almost indestructible, they can be used for 40 years or more. Housekeeping furnishings made of hardwood and carefully crafted last over a decade, in contrast to products designed for home use, which last 3 or 4 years. High-quality materials are also necessary for effective instruction. For example, a toy xylophone in comparison to a quality instrument is lacking in tone and often off pitch. Administrators and teachers who make long-range plans and purchase high-quality equipment find that durability offsets the initial cost.

Demonstrate the Proper Care and Storage of Materials and Supervise Children as They Take On Organizational Tasks Show children how to wash brushes, wipe tables, roll dough into balls and place it into containers, sort small items into appropriate storage containers, dust if necessary, and wash and wax blocks occasionally. Label shelves or containers with words, symbols, or pictures depending on the age of the children so children may put things away. Storage, of course, should be near the place of use and accessible to children. Housekeeping work is worthy of respect, and children can be taught pride in the care and maintenance of their work spaces. Caring for work spaces also accurately reflects the behavior of adults in their work environments.

Give Reasons for the Standards You Set for Children's Use of Materials   In one first-grade classroom, the teacher indicated, "If I see someone being careless with materials once, I demonstrate again and remind them what they are supposed to be doing. I explain that everyone wants a turn to use the materials, and if they are destroyed, no one else can use them. The children in my group know that continued misuse of materials leads to the lost privilege of using them" (Whiren, 1990). Giving children reasons for the standards helps them understand the principles involved. Individual and group responsibility are also learned as children develop a work ethic and standards for appropriate group behavior.

Using the Same Materials for Many Purposes

Some materials (blocks, sand, water, clay, and computers with appropriate software) are extremely flexible in their use. The same items may be used to meet goals across the curriculum. In the developmentally appropriate classroom, children are often free to use such materials to meet their own needs, which may be related to any domain. On other occasions, the teacher guides children's use of materials to address particular curricular goals. For example, collage materials, which have traditionally been associated with aesthetics, can be adapted for use in other domains as well because the material is content free. This is illustrated in the sample activities cited in Figure 5.21.

Each of the activities in Figure 5.21 is designed for center use in which children may choose to engage in the activity. Naturally, when the collage materials are being used for one domain, other activities with other materials are planned for the remaining ones. Notice that the difference in domains is apparent in the strategies and guidance provided by the teacher. This demonstrates the potential for adults to consider materials flexibly and broadly.

ORGANIZING TIME INTO A SCHEDULE

Grandmother Herb came to visit Nathan's nursery school. Happy and eager for her to see his school, he entered the

play yard where he was greeted by a teacher and moved quickly to the climbing equipment. He climbed, slid, rode tricycles, walked a balance beam, and dug in the sand during this outdoor period. When the teachers began to sing a song, he moved quickly to the stairway where the group gathered before entering the building.

Taking off his own wraps, he walked into the room and sat in a large area where others were gathering and looking at picture books. Soon Ms. Eppinger led the children in a finger play, read a short story, and told the children what was in store for the day. Dismissing the youngsters in small groups, the teacher moved through the centers to see that all of the children were immersed in their chosen task.

Grandmother Herb watched as Nathan moved independently from one area of the room to another during the center time. She sat next to him while he was working with the dough; another child came by with a sign that announced that the children had 5 minutes left. Nathan explained that it was time to put away the materials as he continued to roll out the dough and cut it. When his grandmother asked if there was anything she should do, this group of 3-year-olds explained exactly what to do and how as they put the dough in a covered container, carried their tools to the sink, wiped off the table, and moved to the large-group area.

Grandmother was astonished that children who had just turned three could move through the day with such ease, take care of themselves and their materials, and be so independent.

How does a child know what to do and when to do it? What made the movements from one place to the next smooth? Are there principles of planning the day's schedule that can be applied to any group of children? You will understand the answers to these and other questions as you peruse the following sections.

The ultimate goal in preparing a schedule for the day is to provide a social context in which children feel comfortable and secure. Such a schedule would allow time for children to begin a task, engage in it, and complete it without hurry or interruption. Routines represented by the schedule are predictable so that children feel continuity from one day to the next and from one week to the next. In developing the fundamental plan or routines of the day, teachers must consider the pace at which children work, the variety that children need in mode of instruction and in the

FIGURE 5.21
Collage Materials in Several Domains

Affective

Activity: 1-2-3-4-5 Collage
Purpose: To work through a task from beginning to completion
Procedure: Select several items for a collage. Make your collage, show it to a friend, and talk about it. Put your extra materials away, and announce "the end."

Aesthetic

Activity: Color Collage
Purpose: To contribute to the aesthetic environment of the school
Procedure: Make a collage in colors you like best. When you are finished, hang up your work for everyone to see and enjoy.

Physical

Activity: Snip or Tear Collage
Purpose: To practice fine motor skills
Procedure: Choose some large paper. Either cut or tear it into little pieces to make your collage.

Language

Activity: Texture Collage
Purpose: To increase children's descriptive vocabulary
Procedure: Choose some materials from the box that feel different. Create a collage of many varied textures. Tell someone else as many words as you can think of to describe the textures.

Social

Activity: Buddy-up Collage
Purpose: To practice negotiation skills
Procedure: Each of you will receive a bag containing different collage materials. If you need or want something from someone else's bag, find a way to ask, trade, or share to get what you want.

Cognitive

Activity: Number Collage
Purpose: To practice number skills
Procedure: There are four pans of materials for you to choose from. Select four items from each pan and glue them onto your paper. You will then have four sets of four.

groupings of children that work together, and the overall balance of the program.

Routines

Routines are patterns of behavior that, once learned, are incorporated automatically into the daily life of children and adults. Age of children, length of day, and type of program determine the selection of the routine events. In Figure 5.22 some sample routines are defined. In the section that follows, the fitting together of the routines into a daily schedule for different program types and age groups is illustrated.

In this classroom, regular instructional time outdoors is an important part of the daily schedule.

Pace

The pace or speed of daily activities is often determined by the overall schedule of events. Teachers must decide who is to set the pace. When adults set the pace, children change activities when told to do so. Some children may be finished well ahead of schedule, and others may be just beginning an activity. Adults generally set the times in the schedule when children must be in a specific place at a specific time. Therefore, times for recess, lunch, special teachers, and special events must be established by adults.

There are other times when it is appropriate for children to set their own pace. For example, when some tasks are required and others are optional within a long time segment, children may set their own speed of moving through the planned experiences. One child may complete only the assigned tasks, another child may complete one or two additional activities without feeling any pressure or need to hurry, and a third child may not be able to complete the assigned tasks on a specific day and may need more than one day to accomplish the educational goals successfully. Children vary considerably in the pace of learning, task completion, their need for repetition, and the attention and intensity they bring to each learning experience. Such individual differences in style or pace can best be managed by encouraging self-regulation. Teachers, of course, have the responsibility to guide and encourage children who appear to be disengaged, distracted, or otherwise uninvolved in the program.

Usually 3- to 5-year-olds thrive in an open setting where most of their program day has child-paced activities. Many youngsters of this age are just beginning to attain the self-control necessary to pursue a task in depth. Older children respond well to a balanced program of child- and adult-directed activities.

Variety

Provide learning experiences in a variety of group compositions. The size of the group of children engaging in a learning experience affects the nature of children's and adults' interpersonal interaction as well as the methods of instruction. Whole-group instruction is planned and directed by the teacher toward all children. Listening to music, reading aloud to children, and making plans for the day are generally done with the whole class. The small-group period is often a time when children are working toward very specific skills. Usually the groups are pulled together based either on the observed needs of the children or a balance between more and less skillful children. Teachers may have each group rotate the tasks daily or work on the same skill using different materials during the week. Once the children have been shown how to do the task

FIGURE 5.22
Typical Routines in Early Childhood Programs

Arrival: Children enter the program from family automobiles, neighborhood streets, or buses. They remove and store outer clothing and move into the classroom.

Morning exercises: Attendance, discussion of weather, identifying the date on a calendar, assigning daily tasks like watering plants, collecting milk or lunch money.

Greeting time: Teachers greet children individually or in a group, introduce the centers available, give assignments, or otherwise convey the plan of the day to the children.

Center time/Free choice/Free play: Children engage in activities designed by the teacher. Often the activities represent all domains of learning.

Limited free choice: A restricted array of choices. This may be used in childcare programs during the long arrival time. Sometimes, particularly with primary grades, a particular domain has many activities from which children choose, such as language arts.

Five-minute warning: This may be verbal or a nonverbal signal given near the end of center time so that children know that projects will soon be put away.

Cleanup: Children put away materials, wipe tables, and attend to room maintenance tasks.

Group time: A planned agenda of whole-group instruction. For younger children, thematic instruction music, a literature experience, or a group motor experience are typical. Any subject matter may be presented to older youngsters.

Transitions: The movement between major time segments when all of the children are changing activities. They occur between all major routine segments.

Toileting: This routine is determined mostly by the location of plumbing and the age of the children. It always includes getting children to and from the toilet, assisting with clothing if necessary, using the toilet, and hand washing. It may include toilet learning and diapering for younger or special needs children.

Meals: Breakfast, snacks, and lunch may be served in either family-style or cafeteria settings. Some children also carry lunches. Hand washing, moving to the lunch area, eating, and cleanup are included.

Naps: Setting up cots, getting comforters such as favored toys, blankets, sheets, and getting children settled in a quiet darkened area for rest is typical. Some children need to be patted, listen to music, or engage in other forms of comforting to fall asleep.

Journals: Children communicate graphically, initially through drawing, then a combination of words and drawings, and eventually through written communications.

Drop everything and read (D.E.A.R.): Adults and children engage in individual silent reading.

and all groups are started, then the teacher may focus on one or more groups for more intensive instruction. The teacher must monitor the ongoing work of all the groups when this strategy is being used. During free-choice time, both the task and the group of children are selected by the child. Individual activities may be initiated by either the child or the adult but are carried out by one child working alone. Developmentally appropriate classrooms have daily opportunities for children to work alone, with small groups, and with the whole group.

Variety may also be achieved by changing the purpose, size, composition, and duration of the group. The purpose that a group of children may have for working in a small group may vary, with some groups working together to clean an area of the room, another group working on a common mural, and a third group meeting with the teacher for reading instruction. Children work in pairs, groups of three or four, or casual groupings at centers where the group size varies as children move in and out of the specific center.

The actual composition of groups may be determined by the teacher, common interests of the children, friendships, or chance. Knowing that some children share a common interest, such as baseball, may provide the perfect vehicle for learning about players, reading scores, or figuring averages. Other small groups may be based on a common skill they have or need to practice. Of course, teachers are very familiar with friendship groups as they form and re-form throughout the year. Chance groupings are usually the outgrowth of other factors such as the speed with which children finish a task. Another format is small coaching groups of children in which their abilities are deliberately mixed so that the more capable may assist their peers in learning. Each type has specific strengths that allow it to contribute to the total program. For example, friendship groupings take advantage of the children's knowledge of each other. Little time is lost in negotiating for leadership or learning to share ideas. Usually friendship groups already have mechanisms for establishing leadership. In addition, children are more likely to continue the learning activity beyond the classroom. The formation and utilization of all these groups vary throughout the year as the needs of the class change.

Variety of activities and materials used within the program is also important in maintaining interest and enthusiasm in the program. For example, in childcare settings, table toys used during the morning may be put away during nap time, and toys designed to meet similar needs put out for children to use after naps are more likely to be used than if the same materials were in place all day.

Balance

A balance between self-selected activities and small-group, teacher-led activities must also be maintained (Hendrick, 1997). Children have opportunities to make decisions and develop their unique interests and competencies when they are allowed choices within the curriculum. If all of the alternatives are well planned, wholesome choices consistent with the overall curricular goals, teachers can feel confident that children are learning from materials and each other when the teacher is otherwise engaged.

The schedule must also take into account the balance between physically active and passive tasks. Usually children function best when vigorous and quiet activities are alternated. For example, outdoor play or gym should follow or precede periods of whole-group instruction. Most young children cannot be physically passive in prolonged time periods. Movement that is embedded with a longer time period, such as moving to another center, or substantial handling of materials allows for moderate physical involvement.

Children also need balance in the amount of time indoors and outdoors. Frequently recess is not seen as an integral part of the educational program, but children are learning all the time, not just when they are indoors. Because more and more children are engaged in programs from 9 to 11 hours a day, some provision for outdoor play must be made to promote health and fitness. Therefore, teachers should provide opportunities to learn desired habits and skills outdoors. For example, teachers may take children outside as a component of instruction related to the natural environment. In addition, outdoor play equipment and space should be evaluated for its safety and educational value. If teacher aides or parent volunteers supervise children during periods outdoors, they must become involved in the strategies being used in other parts of the program to promote the children's social and physical development.

A group of kindergarten, first-, and second-grade teachers representing a variety of communities identified the following characteristics of a balanced schedule (Kostelnik, 1990):

❏ Short and long time segments.
❏ Active and quiet periods.
❏ Self- and teacher-directed activities.

Within time periods, children should have opportunities to explore, acquire skills and information, and practice emerging competencies. Variety in the focus of activity is important as well. Children need chances to focus on materials, interact with their peers, and engage in teacher-child interactions. A rule of thumb is that one-third of the time children should engage in large-group activities, one-third of the time they should engage in small-group experiences, and one-third of the time they should spend in individual activities (Katz, 1987). Considering how difficult it is even for adults to sit still, this is probably a reasonable guideline for structuring time allotments in any learning environment if good learning involvement and outcomes are desired. Balance of time indoors and on the playground is another component needing attention, as many primary programs have diminished the outdoor experience as they focus on the basics. When children have less than 30 minutes to play outdoors, they are unable to attain the higher levels of social and cognitive play (Dempsey & Frost, 1993). The balance of these many dimensions varies across age levels as well as throughout the school year.

A common error beginning teachers make is to divide the program into too many time segments requiring whole-group transitions in their attempt to provide for routines, appropriate pace, variety, and balance. Whole-group transitions are time consuming and stressful for most adults and children. Individual transitions, as is common during center time, are easy and barely noticeable. Experienced primary and kindergarten teachers usually structure at least 45 to 60 minutes for centers if possible. Breaking this up into more than one period such as two 25-minute segments is problematic; it tends to fracture children's concentration and ability to sustain involvement. In programs lasting 9 to 12 hours, two or three long center times interspersed with shorter small- or large-group activities work well. Weather permitting, one of these center times occurs out of doors.

Adapting the Schedule

Schedules will vary depending upon the specific characteristics of the individuals within the group. Some children have less self-control and fewer skills in regulating their own behavior than others. Groups of children are thus likely to vary considerably in their ability to engage in a responsive learning environment. Therefore, even within programs, schedules are likely to vary from room to room. Also, the time allotments within the daily schedule will change over the course of the year. The amount of time outdoors is related to climate and weather. Variations are appropriate by season and from one climate to another. Schedules also change as children mature. As children grow in their capacity to do independent work and as the level of their involvement in learning center activities increases, greater amounts of time should be devoted to tasks that require these capacities.

Integration

In a developmentally appropriate classroom, the teacher attempts to integrate topics in science, health, social studies, and other important segments of information by providing reading experiences from information books, setting up centers with related activities, and developing full units of study that incorporate all of the developmental domains on specific topics such as trees, families, or dental health. Therefore, separate segments of time with those labels generally do not appear in the daily schedule.

How to Prepare a Schedule

1. Prepare a form that designates space in 15-minute intervals beginning a half hour before the start of the session and ending a half hour after the session and divided by the days of the week.

2. Block in time segments that are established for your group at the building level (may include meals, time on the playground, and access to library or other specialty teachers).

3. Place whole-group instruction in time segments so that this approach may be used for group planning, giving directions on the use of centers, or shared experiences with music, literature, and games. A short whole-group activity before center time is very useful to help children focus on alternatives and remind them of their learning goals and responsibilities.

Whole-group activities should not exceed 15 minutes of sedentary time or 20 minutes of active time for 3-year-olds. Whole-group, teacher-directed instruction for 7-year-olds should not exceed 20 to 30 minutes. When an activity alternates between hands-on activity and teacher direction, it may be longer and still successful.

4. Schedule center time so that children have a minimum of one hour to engage in self-directed learning. Three- and four-year-olds may need less time at the beginning of the year, and eight-year-olds may be profitably engaged for two hours or more. Some teachers have independent work by pairs of children at one time of the day and more openly flowing small groups in centers at another time. The opportunity for self-pacing among children is important here.

5. Indicate where teacher-directed, small-group instruction will occur. If this is embedded into the center time, carefully consider how to bring children into the small group and supervise the centers. Several sets of small groups working cooperatively on projects may also be planned. Teacher-directed small groups usually last 10 to 15 minutes for the youngest children and 15 to 20 minutes for older children.

6. Minimize transitions of the whole group. Confusion, noise, and interpersonal conflicts are not uncommon when all children are moving at the same time. With fewer of these transitions, there are many fewer instances of disruption.

7. On all occasions children must know which activity occurs next, where to go, and what to do. Schedules should be discussed with the children and clear communication signals given. Signal five minutes before center or independent work is to be set aside so that children have an opportunity to bring their work to a close.

8. Clearly indicate times of cleaning up, putting on and taking off outdoor clothing, doing classroom chores and maintenance tasks, collecting lunch money, taking attendance, and tending to other responsibilities that the teacher and children share. Although these activities are seldom seen as part of the curriculum, many of them can become important opportunities for children to develop in the affective and social domains.

9. Allow for flexibility. If children are to respect their work and the learning of others, they must have an opportunity to complete their tasks. Some small groups will become so interested in their learning activity that they will pursue it much longer if allowed to

do so. In general, child-generated learning about topics that truly interest the children lasts much longer than the guides suggested here. Teacher-controlled learning in which children have less interest may be much shorter in duration.

10. Prepare children for changes in routines. The daily schedule is a source of predictability and security for children. If the schedule must be altered to respond to the children's needs, follow these steps:

❑ Identify the goal to be met by the change in the schedule.

❑ Consider more than one alternative change. Can the change be accommodated without altering the whole schedule? Can an addition be made within free-choice or center time and not change the duration or sequence of events?

❑ Discuss the changes with the children. Usually telling them briefly the day before and reminding them early on the day of the change are sufficient. Write the change on a poster or the chalkboard for older children, posting the new schedule. An alternative would be to write the current schedule on sentence strips and then rearrange them with the children.

❑ If new or more independent behavior will be required of the children, discuss this with them. Changes in schedule are opportunities for addressing affective and social learning goals.

❑ Allow time for children to accommodate to the alterations. Three- and four-year-olds usually take three weeks to be comfortable with a new schedule; six- and seven-year-olds may adapt in half that time.

If possible, plan major schedule changes after holidays or school vacations. Every time children are out of school longer than the weekend, they are experiencing a schedule change. Three- and four-year-olds may repeat their separation behaviors; five- and six-year-olds will take several days to readapt to school. If teachers modify their schedules when children must go through an adjustment period anyway, the number of adjustment times is reduced.

11. Schedule a closing with the children at the end of each day. A variety of strategies for this are in Chapter 4. Regardless of how the closing exercise is handled, children find a routine pattern at the end of the day a satisfying finish.

SAMPLE SCHEDULES

Preprimary Schedule

Presented next are two schedules that are fairly typical for children of 3 to 4 years (Figures 5.23 and 5.24). Most noticeable are the long time segments within the schedule. Many activities would occur within each of the long time sequences, some of which are self-selected and others teacher initiated or directed. All choices are planned according to the curricular goals in this book.

Several sample schedules are provided, each coming from a different program. Note that some variations occur. These plans were in use at varying times of the year and in rural, suburban, and urban schools. The teachers using them necessarily adapted their program to fit the needs of the children, the school schedule, and the curriculum of the program.

The full-day schedule does not have a sharp time for beginning and ending because children arrive according to parental work schedules and leave gradually. Toileting is normally by demand, with adult reminders as scheduled for both groups to avoid accidents. Also, meals are handled both as a part of center time and as a whole-group experience. During the winter months, many programs adjust their schedules so that outdoor play is at the beginning and end of the day to avoid the time-consuming process of helping children with snowsuits and boots more than one time.

Kindergarten Schedule

Each schedule here was designed in response to the children's behavioral skills and needs (Figures 5.25–

5.28). The literacy skill development and mathematical thinking activities are incorporated in the open-choice time. All centers have materials for recording by drawing, writing, graphing, or using other materials to represent an idea, such as a hardboard thermometer whose given temperature could be adjusted via string. Schedule C is from an all-day, alternate-day program. In this case, "all day" means a morning session and an afternoon session with lunch between and is not as long as the full-day childcare schedule. Schedule D is from a classroom in which children had very limited entry skills. The children are experiencing center-based instruction for the first time and beginning to develop skills for participating in a group.

First-Grade Schedule

Considerable variation in schedules is common. The one given here incorporates a number of special, once-a-week activities common for all first-grade classrooms in the district (Figure 5.29). It uses a materials-based math program and the whole-language approach (Sharpe, 1990). A clear attempt to minimize whole-group transitions has been made.

The last schedule in Figure 5.30 demonstrates the combination of group reading instruction and center-based instruction. Centers are set up by goal area such as math or social studies or by activities, yet children also have opportunities for teacher-directed instruction in language. Other activities are used instead of workbooks.

FIGURE 5.23
Half-Day Program for Three- to Five-Year-Olds

Minutes	Activity
5–10	Arrival, individual greeting
45–60	Indoor free choice
10	Cleanup, toileting
10–15	Snack
15–20	Group time
30–45	Outdoor play/Indoor gross motor play
5–10	Review of day/ Dismissal

FIGURE 5.24
Full-Day Program for Three- and
Four-Year-Olds

Minutes	Activity
60	Arrival and limited choice
15	Greeting time; morning exercises
15	Toileting/Hand washing
30–45	Breakfast/Snack
45–60	Free choice: centers
10–15	Cleanup
15–20	Group time
10–20	Transition outdoors, getting wraps
35–45	Outdoor free choice
10	Cleanup outdoors
10–20	Transition indoors/Undressing
10–15	Toileting/Washing hands/Quiet music and looking at picture books
45	Lunch
15	Toileting; getting settled on cots
15	Quiet transition: story record, teacher reading or telling a story, quiet music
45–60	Naps: provisions made for children who wake early or cannot sleep
30	Wake up time, fold and put away blankets, put on shoes, toileting
45	Indoor free play; open snack as a center
10–15	Cleanup
15–20	Small group instruction
10–20	Transition outdoors/Getting dressed
60	Outdoor free play: Dismissal occurs gradually as parents arrive to get children

FIGURE 5.25
Kindergarten Schedule A:
Program Without Whole-Group
Instruction

Minutes	Activity
10–15	Arrival/Morning exercises
60–80	Centers
10	Cleanup
10–15	Small-group time
10	Snack
30	Outdoor play/Gym or special instruction
5–10	Closing exercises/Dismissal

FIGURE 5.26
Kindergarten Schedule B:
Program With Whole-Group
Instruction

Minutes	Activity
5–10	Arrival
60–80	Centers
10	Cleanup
20–25	Whole-group instruction
10	Toileting/Transition outdoors
15–30	Outdoors or gym
5–10	Attendance, closing exercises/Dismissal

FIGURE 5.27
Kindergarten Schedule C:
Double Session or "Full Day"

Minutes	Activity
20	Limited choice, lunch count, attendance
15	Morning exercises, planning the day
150	Center time
10	Cleanup
25	Group time
10	Toileting/Transition to lunch
40	Lunch
30	Toileting/Quiet individual activities, films
25	Materials-based math experiences
30	Gym
15	Sharing/Evaluation/Closing
20	Outdoor play dismissal

FIGURE 5.28
Kindergarten Schedule D:
Inexperienced Children in a
Group Setting

Minutes	Activity
15	Morning exercises; whole-group greeting
30–45	Limited choice: multiple centers in one domain
5–10	Cleanup and preparation to go outdoors
15–25	Outdoor play/Transition indoors
20–30	Group time: theme related, music, alphabet
45–60	Free choice of centers in all domains
5–10	Cleanup
10–15	Individual evaluation/Dismissal

FIGURE 5.29

First-Grade Schedule With
Whole-Group Language
Instruction and Hands-On
Mathematics, Some Traditional
Content Separations

Minutes	Activity
25	Arrival, morning exercises, collecting folders on Monday, journals
25	Whole group: discussion, songs, movement, thematic instruction, common writing experiences, explanation of small-group activities and demonstrations if appropriate. Directions written on board.
65	Small groups of children rotating among reading group with the teacher, reading and writing with a "study buddy," center choice as available in other domains
15–20	Transition, toileting, recess
20	Snack and story from a chapter book read by the teacher
MWF 20	Spelling: rules, finger spelling, and individual chalkboard practice
TTh 20	Gym
20	Sharing, readers' chair, author's circle. Each day one child writes clues for a guessing game and places it in a mystery box.
70	Lunch, outdoor play
M 40	Whole-group mathematics
TWTH 15	Drop Everything and Read (D.E.A.R.)
TW 25	Process writing. Children engage in creative writing, have a peer conference before signing up for a teacher conference, editing, and publishing
TH 25	Library
MTWF 45	Centers: some new each week, some "must do," teacher circulates.
TH 45	Music with speclalty teacher
15	Recess
M 30	Music
T	Projects related to themes or to health, social studies, or science
W	Math activities
TH	Math and spelling review
F	Science or social studies
5–10	Cleanup and dismissal

FIGURE 5.30
Sample Schedule for Full-Day Kindergarten and First Grade

9:05–9:15	Daily business: attendance, pledge
9:15–9:30	Large group: explain schedule for morning and directions on how to do independent work
9:30–10:00	Small group: focus on any content or skill that the teacher deems appropriate
10:00–10:30	Large group: motor skills in the gym
10:30–11:45	Children are divided into groups of 4–7

Language Art Centers

Start:	9:35	10:35	11:00	11:25	
Group:	1	2	3	4	Creative writing
	2	3	4	1	Listening
	3	4	1	2	Reading
	4	1	2	3	Independent work

11:45–12:40	Recess and lunch
12:40–12:45	Attendance; go over schedule for afternoon
12:45–1:05	Large group: calendar (skills: counting, days of week, months, time, etc.), story time
1:05–1:45	Math Their Way: individual or small-group instruction with activities
1:45–2:00	Music (large group): always involves movement

Free-choice learning centers or separate time periods, depending on the project, from 2:00–3:20

2:00–2:20	Science or social studies: varies in form depending on the project
2:20–2:45	"Author's chair": children share their stories in large group
2:45–3:20	Free-choice activity: often based on some type of theme
3:20–3:30	Cleanup and dismissal

Second-Grade Schedule

Many similar activities occur as they did in the first grade (Figure 5.31). This teacher has more regularity in schedule across the week than did the first-grade teacher. She also reports that throughout the year, she operates on longer time segments than is represented in this schedule, which was used in the autumn (MacLean, 1990). A sample direction/record sheet is presented in Figure 5.32 that illustrates some of the activities children do on their own.

ORGANIZING THE CHILDREN

Harry is an outgoing youngster who has just turned 6. Only yesterday, he wanted to count the days left in the school year by 13s. Most of the children in his class are just learning to count to 100 by ones, but Harry has little difficulty with skip counting. He also enjoys simple math operations and is usually accurate in deriving the answers.

Miriam, also age 6, is very quiet. Though it is close to the end of the year, she has made little progress in working out the simplest number combinations. Her counting has improved, but she still finds it confusing to go beyond 20.

Dustin, who is 6 years old as well, is cheerful and friendly. He can sing a counting song, though he has difficulty counting groups greater than five. Born with Down's Syndrome, Dustin has just achieved independence in using the toilet and can take care of his personal needs. His vocabulary is functional, and he is making slow but steady progress in a variety of domains.

Do these children belong in the same classroom or in different classrooms? Should children who are similar be grouped together? The classroom teacher generally does not make this decision. Instead, this is a function of the program as a whole although classroom teachers often have a voice in organizational strategies.

At one time, rural schools in North America served children between 3 and 4 to 16 years of age with

FIGURE 5.31

Second-Grade Schedule With a Variation of Traditional Reading Groups

Minutes	Activity
25	Opening exercises, Wonderfully Exciting Books, an at-home reading program
20	Big books: whole-group reading activity, teacher modeling
4–5	Aerobics for children
30	Reading groups: • Read with the teacher • Read silently or with a partner • Variety of language arts activities; children read literature increasing in length and difficulty • Teacher use of observational assessment including videotapes and audiotapes
30	Centers (health, social studies, science, etc.); children participate in planning some of the centers
15	Recess
15	Media/Story time: theme-related films, choral reading, chapter books, filmstrips variety of presentation is a goal
30	Reading groups: • Read with the teacher • Read silently or with a partner • Variety of language arts activities; children read literature increasing in length and difficulty • Teacher use of observational assessment including videotapes and audiotapes
10	Whole-group demonstration of math materials and center work
20	Chapter books: teacher reads aloud
10	D.E.A.R.
30	Reading groups: • Read with the teacher • Read silently or with a partner • Variety of language arts activities; children read literature increasing in length and difficulty • Teacher use of observational assessment including videotapes and audiotapes
15	Journals
45	Gym with a specialty teacher
30	Centers
10	Closing exercises: author's chair, sharing, music, daily evaluation
	Dismissal

FIGURE 5.32
Center Selections from a "Penguin" Unit Over a Week

Centers

_____ Name

_____ Scale—measure 56 each of 2 things.

* _____ Water table–measure and compare foam to measuring bird seed to water.

_____ Find these places on the pull-down world map *and* globe:

Antarctica   New Zealand   Australia   South Africa
Falkland Islands   Galapagos Islands

_____ Tell the 4 directions on a compass and where the needle points.

_____ Measure the height of the penguins on the penguin cards and arrange little to big.

* _____ Read "Penguins" quietly to yourself.

_____ Basic "Bear Facts": M _____ T _____ W _____ Th _____ F _____

_____ Fill in the overlapping shapes.

* _____ Put a note on your TV at home to watch the "Trans-Antarctica Expedition" Dec. 17 (Sunday) on ABC.

* _____ Write the names of *all* Mr. Popper's penguins.

_____ Make a "Super Dad Penguin Poem" poster.

_____ Walk like a penguin (*carefully!*) across room.

* _____ Tell Fred why penguins like to "toboggan."

* _____ Compare how you stay warm in cold weather to the way penguins do.

* _____ Write real facts from "Mr. Popper's Penguins."

* _____ "Mr. Popper's Penguins" activities 1 _____ 2 _____ 3 _____ 4 _____ 5 _____
6 _____ Penguin Book _____ Popper's Worksheet _____

_____ Color the "Follow the Directions" paper.

_____ Read and color "The Anxious Snowman."

_____ Spelling M _____ T _____ W _____ Th _____ F _____

Sunday   Monday   Tuesday   Wednesday   month
Thursday   Friday   Saturday   week   year

* means *write about it.*

one teacher, all in the one-room school house. From the turn of the century to the 1950s, a general move put children of like ages into groups as graded classrooms. This process enabled states to set goals to be achieved in a systematic manner during the schooling process. During the same period, an increasing proportion of the population attended high schools. States established ages for mandatory education and for programs for which school funding would be available, usually beginning at age 5 or 6. This means that any child may enter the public school and has a right to an education regardless of ability, race, ethnicity, religion, or sex. This right was confirmed for special needs children in 1975 (PL94–142). Access to educational services for younger children with special needs was ensured in 1987 (PL–99–457). Given that all children have a right to an education, how this educational experience should be organized has long been discussed.

Homogeneous Groups

When children are organized so that they are as similar as possible, the grouping is called a *homogeneous* group. Over many years, adults have grouped children using easily distinguishable criteria including age, sex, religion, race, and ability. In turn, each of these arbitrary means for grouping youngsters has been criticized as being biased. Two arbitrary classifications—ability and/or age—are still used in some programs. Ability tracking by IQ or level of demonstrated skill in a prescribed area of the curriculum, generally reading or math, has been common practice since the early 1900s. The foundation for grouping like children together is sometimes based on the maturationist view that certain children are simply too immature to do the work expected within a particular classroom or grade. Within this mode of thinking, children considered too young are frequently placed in an alternative program such as developmental kindergarten or transitional first grade, placed in groups that move at a slower pace, or delayed in proceeding through the system. In the latter instance, children are asked to wait at home another year. This is essentially denying access to the educational experience to a subgroup of the population. A second rationale for grouping children judged to be very similar is that instruction will be much more efficient when children who are alike are together. A third rationale is not related to children's learning. It would place children in groups to meet the record-keeping functions necessary for funding sources. (Programs that have chosen not to do this have been able to work out the administrative difficulties and place children in more diverse groups.) Unfortunately, ability grouping frequently has the side effect of decreasing other aspects of diversity in the classroom with children of color, males, and those coming from poorer families more frequently tracked into lower achieving groups (Dawson, 1987; Soderman & Phillips, 1986). One variation of ability grouping popular in some communities is to provide separate classrooms for the gifted and talented children. Rarely are children of unusual musical or artistic talent selected if their reading and math scores are more typical of their peers. Because inclusion of most special needs children in regular programs has been supported by law, fewer completely segregated programs for such youngsters are maintained.

Long-term ability grouping fails to improve children's academic achievement and simultaneously damages many children's self-concepts. For instance, higher-achieving children do not do better when together, and lower-achieving children do much worse in homogeneous classrooms, partly due to unequal treatment (Glickman, 1991; Johnson & Winogard, 1985). Only age grouping with all other arbitrary means of separating children appears to have widespread support.

Heterogeneous Groups

When children are organized so that there are no arbitrary criteria for putting children together, they are in a *heterogeneous* group. Groupings in which children are mixed in terms of ability, cultural differences, gender, race, and socioeconomic background offer many benefits. Children representing diversity in rates of learning, styles, abilities, and talents work comfortably together in a developmentally appropriate program and their achievement is enhanced (Barbour, 1990). When the classroom is heterogeneous, the adult groups children for specific episodes of learning, with the composition of each group depending upon the objective and domain of learning. In this way, grouping at the classroom level may achieve the efficiency many adults find helpful while keeping the total group diverse. Some teachers have found cross-age tutoring to be beneficial to all the children as older elementary children tutor primary children for rather short periods during a week, while at the same time increasing the age diversity of the programs (Schneider & Barone, 1997).

Another way in which groups with even greater heterogeneity is achieved is by family grouping in which children up to two years apart in age are in classrooms together. Katz and her colleagues report the following advantages of mixed-age grouping (Katz, Evangelou, & Hartman, 1990):

> Mixed-age groupings resemble the neighborhood and family groupings of the past in which the socialization of children by other children occurs normally. With many children spending increasing amounts of time in formal programs, these mixed-age groupings give them natural opportunities to interact with others in the early childhood period.

> Older children in mixed-age groups have opportunities to learn leadership skills and prosocial behaviors in interactions with younger children not possible with age-mates. Younger children have older ones to imitate and are able to learn new, mature social-play skills.

Children's cognitive skills may be enhanced as they work on problems with others whose knowledge or abilities are similar but not identical. Opportunities for "cognitive conflict" that challenge but do not exceed children's capacities stimulate the thinking of all the participants.

Mixed-age groupings serve to relax the rigid, lock-step curriculum with narrowly defined age-graded expectations, which are inappropriate for many children.

The positive outcomes listed here hold true for children and programs throughout the preprimary and primary years. However, there is strong evidence that the impact of heterogeneous groupings of children 6 years old and younger is especially beneficial (Katz et al., 1990)

Child-Generated Groups

Children work well together for reasons of their own. Sometimes children choose to work with their particular friends or with people who share a common interest, and sometimes they seek out other children because of their particular knowledge and skills. Children learn from each other and are comfortable both in showing others how to do something as well as being the one shown. Leadership often flows from one child to another. A child with moderate academic competencies may have outstanding social skills and emerge as the leader in contexts where social problem solving is needed.

Center-based learning provides many opportunities for children to work together in groupings of their own choosing. Within the schedules supplied, there are also opportunities for the professional to draw those children together who share a common instructional need. Center learning also provides opportunities for children to learn from each other rather than solely from the adults.

SUMMARY

The organizational responsibilities of the teacher using developmentally appropriate practices are considerable. Classrooms must be arranged to facilitate quiet movement and help children maintain a focus on their work. Learning centers are carefully designed to meet a variety of goals indoors and out. Equipment and materials must be chosen to meet the specific goals of the curriculum. Time is organized into the schedule of the day, which is generally divided into long time blocks with children moving among carefully selected centers for at least part of every day. Children are grouped heterogeneously as classrooms with small, focused instructional groupings to meet the specific educational needs of the children. The purpose of all organizational work is to prepare the physical, cognitive, aesthetic, and social environment so that there are opportunities for learning and growth-producing interaction among the people in that context. Fortunately, once the basic plans are made and implemented, teachers can concentrate on fine tuning them to suit particular children and meet individual needs.

✖ Applying What You Read in This Chapter

1. **Discuss**
   a. What are the advantages and disadvantages of learning centers as an important part of the early childhood classroom?
   b. Imagine that you are in an established program. Discuss the advantages and disadvantages of having cross-age grouping in all classrooms rather than graded classrooms.
   c. Refer to the section on scheduling children's days. Discuss the principles you can derive for organizing the schedule and that can be applied to any group.

   d. How will literacy be properly supported if children participate in center time during the primary grades? Explain how this will be done.
   e. Describe the teacher's role in keeping children safe and healthy via the physical environment.

2. **Observe**
   a. Observe children in a classroom for at least a half day and record the schedule they are currently using. Note the number of full-group transitions and describe the behavior of the children. Also note individual transitions as a child completes one task and goes to another during center time.

b. Scan a playground in a city park or school yard. Identify features that provide safe activity and features that might pose a hazard. List what should be done to eliminate hazards.

c. Observe empty classrooms at more than one location. Sketch sample layouts of furnishings and materials and describe how you think the experiences in the various classrooms would differ for the children therein. Discuss your observations with others.

3. **Carry out an activity**

a. While you are participating as a volunteer or student in a setting, alter the structure of materials or furnishings in some way to influence the behavior of the children. Review this chapter to help you decide what you might do.

b. Carry out the classroom surveillance as suggested in Figure 5.17.

c. Use a floor plan provided in this text or in the classroom where you have had experience. Re-

arrange the furnishings and explain how this rearrangement would affect the children's behavior. Now try rearranging furnishings to achieve one of the following potential goals:

❑ More cooperative behavior.
❑ More helping and sharing.
❑ A quieter environment.
❑ More creativity.

4. **Create something for your portfolio**

a. Develop at least one pictograph to use with young children for a basic routine that you would expect them to implement independently after some initial guidance.

5. **Add to your journal**

a. Reflect on the experience you have had in organizing for learning and compare it to what you have read in this chapter.

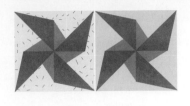

Chapter 6

Promoting Self-Discipline in Children

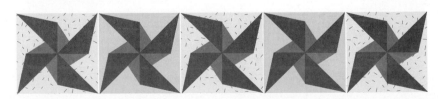

You may wonder:

How do children learn which behaviors are acceptable in early childhood settings and which are not?

Why do children seem to listen better to some teachers than to others?

How can I justify taking the time to teach children about self-discipline when there are so many other areas of the curriculum I have to cover?

What strategies are most effective in teaching children how to get along in the classroom?

What happens if my guidance strategies are different from ones children experience at home?

In this chapter on promoting self-discipline in children, we present information to help you answer these questions.

The following incidents occur in a kindergarten during the course of one session:

Jeremiah runs across the room to get something out of his backpack.

| Teacher 1 thinks: | *He knows better than that!* |
| Teacher 2 thinks: | *Jeremiah's excited about whatever he's got in there. He could use a reminder to walk inside.* |

Samatha interrupts the story "Caps for Sale" saying, "I like the checked cap best." Other children declare their favorites as well. Soon everyone is talking at once.

| Teacher 1 says: | *I'll never get this story done if you keep interrupting. Shh.* |
| Teacher 2 says: | *You're excited to tell me which cap you like best. It's hard to hear with* |

everyone talking at once. Speak one at a time. Samatha, what color did you say you liked best?

Leonard continues painting during cleanup time.

| Teacher 1 thinks: | *Leonard is so uncooperative. Why can't he listen to directions?* |
| Teacher 2 thinks: | *Leonard needs some physical assistance to stop what he's doing and make the transition to cleanup.* |

Two children get into a fierce shoving match over who will be the line leader on the way to the gym.

| Teacher 1 thinks: | *This is unacceptable behavior. I'd better get over there. No gym time today.* |
| Teacher 2 thinks: | *This is unacceptable behavior. I'd better get over there. They need some help using words to settle this argument.* |

Both of these teachers are tired at the end of a busy day with children. Both find the children's behavior demanding and anticipate having to put a great deal of energy into socializing children to act properly in their classrooms. However, Teacher 1 assumes the children are deliberately disobedient. She foresees having to spend her time "keeping on top of" the children, making sure they behave, and views incidents of misbehavior as interruptions. Teacher 2, on the other hand, assumes the children are just learning how to conduct themselves in group settings and will make mistakes in the process. She anticipates having to spend her time teaching children the skills they will need to get along in the classroom and to be successful learners. She views incidents of misbehavior as teachable moments.

These teachers illustrate differing attitudes about children's classroom behavior and the teacher's role in maintaining classroom discipline. Teacher 2 exemplifies attitudes and roles compatible with developmentally appropriate practices. Teacher 1 does not.

WHAT CHILDREN NEED TO KNOW

For children to become truly engaged in the learning process, they must have a sense of how to behave in their center, school, or family childcare home. Here is a list of some of the fundamental skills they need to thrive in group environments (Damon, 1988a, 1995). Children are most successful when they know how to express their needs and wants constructively, respond with compassion to the needs of others, act with civility, take care of materials, act safely, constructively engage in learning activities, attend to instruction, distinguish acceptable from unacceptable classroom behavior, help, and cooperate. These are not things children automatically know how to do. Consequently, early childhood professionals do not expect children to come to their programs already understanding what constitutes appropriate classroom behavior, nor do they simply demand that children act in certain ways (Gartrell, 1997; Glasser, 1990; Read, Gardner, & Mahler, 1993). Instead, adults teach children what is expected and how to conduct themselves appropriately. These educational aims require the same kind of planning and teaching that other aspects of the curriculum demand. Just as teachers provide opportunities for chil-

dren to learn about science, math, and literacy, so, too, do they provide opportunities for children to learn how to interact with others and manage their behavior independently and in groups. When children make mistakes or demonstrate ignorance, early childhood professionals do more than simply correct children. They teach children appropriate alternative strategies they can eventually apply on their own. Thus, in developmentally appropriate classrooms, professionals focus their efforts on helping children develop self-discipline (Bredekamp & Copple, 1997).

WHAT IS SELF-DISCIPLINE?

The after-school kids bound off the buses. They jostle, bump into each other, head for the hall, drop their backpacks, hurry into the lavatories, race to the snack bar. Some head for the gym to hear the rules for a kickball game—eight-year-old Matt is among them. He listens attentive and eager, for about five minutes. Then he begins to squirm, look around, and elbow the children next to him. . . . Jeremy, the teacher's aide, steps quietly in behind Matt. 'Remember, Matt, be calm. You know how to wait,' he whispers. Matt says to himself, 'I can wait, I can wait.' He gets himself under control and waits for the game to begin. (Steiner & Whelan, 1995)

In this example, Matt, with the help of a supportive adult, managed to control his natural impulses to move about. He also resisted the temptation to continue poking at his peers. These are signs that he is developing skills associated with self-discipline. "Self-discipline is the voluntary, internal regulation of behavior" (Marion, 1995, p. 26). It involves acting in socially acceptable ways based on reasoning, concern for others, and an understanding of acceptable and unacceptable behavior. Self-disciplined people do not need others to make them do the right thing or to forbid them from engaging in antisocial conduct. Neither are they dependent on external rewards or punishments to guide their actions. Instead, they consider other people's needs and feelings while simultaneously adapting their actions to fit the rules of the society in which they live. Self-disciplined children *control negative impulses, resist temptation*, and *delay gratification* independent of supervision. They also *initiate positive social interactions* and *undertake constructive social plans* without having to be told (Bukatko & Daehler, 1995; Knopczyk and Rodes,

TABLE 6.1

Components of Self-Discipline as Exhibited by Young Children

Behavior	Examples
Initiating positive social acts	Shannon comforts Latosha, who is sad about a ruined project. Jason shares his glue with a newcomer to the art center.
Making and carrying out social plans	Vinny wants a turn with the magnifying glass. He figures out a strategy for getting one, such as trading, and then tries bargaining with another child.
	Ashley recognizes that Marcus is having difficulty carrying several balls out to the playground. She helps him by holding the door open.
Resisting temptation	Jerome walks all the way over to the trash bin to deposit his gum wrapper, although he is tempted simply to drop the crumpled paper on the playground.
Inhibiting negative impulses	Anthony suppresses the urge to strike out in anger when someone accidentally trips him. Hessa refrains from laughing aloud when Anthony falls down.
Delaying gratification	Rachel waits for Marla to finish telling her story before blurting out her own exciting news.
	Steven postpones taking another fruit kabob until everyone else gets one.

1996; Mischel, 1978). Refer to Table 6.1 for examples of what these behaviors look like in children's lives.

HOW SELF-DISCIPLINE EVOLVES

Self-discipline evolves gradually in an "outside" to "inside" developmental process (Marion, 1995). That is, children proceed from relying on others to control their behavior for them to eventually achieving greater self-regulation. This gradual shift in control from others to self is a significant developmental task that begins in infancy and continues throughout the teenage years.

The Earliest Days—No Regulation

Infants have no sense of right or wrong. They also have no skills to regulate their behavior in accordance with other people's needs or expectations. This means they lack self-discipline of any kind. Gradually, through experience and maturation, toddlers and young preschoolers become capable of responding to external controls applied by parents and teachers as a means for

behaving in certain ways. This form of regulation is called adherence.

Adherence (External Regulation)

Children motivated by adherence rely on adults to control their actions for them. The most basic form of external control involves physical assistance. Here are some examples:

The teacher escorts Jamie to a chair at the science table. Jamie takes a seat.

The parent volunteer holds Melanie on her lap during group time to help her focus on the story. Melanie attends to the story.

The playground supervisor physically separates two children who are fighting on the playground. The children stop pushing one another.

The after-school aide puts her hand over Michael's to keep him from waving the saw around at the workbench. Michael keeps the saw low.

Gradually, children also learn to respond to verbal cues as a means for knowing what to do and what not to do. For instance:

> The teacher reminds Diego to wash his hands before sitting down for lunch. Diego washes his hands.
>
> Sandra's dad talks her through the steps involved in feeding the iguana. Sandra feeds the iguana correctly.
>
> The teacher's aide provides Joshua with a script of what to say during an argument with Michael. Joshua tells Michael, "I wasn't done yet."

In each of these situations, adults provided controls children were not able to exercise on their own.

Another form of adherence occurs when children act in certain ways either to gain rewards or avoid negative consequences (Bukatko & Daehler, 1995; Kostelnik et al., 1998). You can see adherence in operation when a child who has been scolded for dumping all the puzzles on the floor eventually refrains from dumping them again to avoid additional corrections. Likewise, children's desire to receive the praise of an adult or approval from a peer may prompt them to use the paints properly or share a toy with another child. In each case, rewards and negative consequences have contributed to children's early differentiations of acceptable and unacceptable actions. Relying on these kinds of external controls is a step beyond having no control at all. It is also a necessary first phase in moving from lack of self-discipline to internal methods of regulation. However, adherence has drawbacks that make it an undesirable end in and of itself.

Consider the following situation. The children are lining up at the door to go outside. Mr. Martin, their teacher, has promised a smiley face sticker to every child who gets in line with no cutting ahead. Adrian, who is near the end of the line, wants to be first but quietly stands in place because she wants the sticker. Her behavior is regulated by the promise of the reward, not by concern for the rights of her classmates. Under these circumstances, Adrian will probably follow the teacher's directions but only when the teacher is present. Because she has no internal basis for following the rule, she may resort to pushing or cutting in front of others if she thinks the teacher is not looking.

Adrian illustrates the basic problem with adherence. Children who are dependent on external controls must be monitored constantly. They behave appropriately only in situations in which physical or verbal assistance is readily available and ones in which the threat of punishment or the promise of a reward is obvious. When such controls are missing, the possibility of misbehavior is high. Having no other means for understanding right and wrong, they lack the self-direction necessary to act appropriately on their own.

Identification (Shared Regulation)

A more advanced degree of self-regulation occurs when children follow a rule in imitation of someone they admire. Children's positive actions become their way of emulating the conduct and values of the important people in their lives (Berk, 1997; Hoffman, 1970). This phenomenon is sometimes called identification. Because children tend to identify with the nurturant, powerful figures in their lives, teachers are often the focus of their admiration. This is especially true when children and teachers enjoy positive relations with one another.

Children who rely on identification adopt another person's code of conduct to guide their actions but still have little understanding of the real reasons that underlie those behaviors. For instance, influenced by identification, Jacob may wait his turn in line because a teacher he especially likes advocates such conduct. However, he does not grasp the concept of fairness that waiting represents. In addition, identification requires children to second-guess how another person might behave under certain conditions. If Jacob comes across a situation to which he has never seen the teacher respond, he may be at a loss for what to do himself.

Identification represents shared behavior regulation. Children remain dependent on an outside source to help them control their actions but are beginning to use internal thought processes as well. They do not need constant monitoring. Yet, they still have no way to figure out what to do in unfamiliar circumstances. Consequently, even though identification is a more advanced form of self-regulation than adherence, it still does not represent the highest form of self-discipline.

Internalization (Self-Regulation)

When children construct a personal sense of right and wrong and act in ways consistent with what they believe to be right, we say they have internalized that behavior (Hoffman, 1970; Shaffer, 1995). In other words, children act in certain ways because they feel it is the right thing to do, not to gain a reward or the approval of others (Kohn, 1996). Children in this phase of behavior regulation feel concern and a sense of responsibility for the welfare and rights of others as well as for themselves. They also comprehend moral concepts such as justice, truth, and honor (Shapiro, 1997). For these reasons, internalization represents the ultimate form of self-discipline.

Sophie demonstrates internalization when she waits her turn in line even though she is tempted to push ahead. The reasoning that guides her behavior is that cutting in front of others would interfere with their rights. This violates her sense of honor, prompting Sophie to remain where she is in the line.

Children who have internalized certain standards of behavior understand the reasons behind acceptable and unacceptable actions. This gives them a reference for figuring out how to behave appropriately in all kinds of situations, even unfamiliar ones. These understandings eliminate the need for constant supervision. Children can be depended upon to regulate their own behavior. Moreover, internalized behaviors are long lasting. Children who internalize notions of fair play or honesty will abide by those ideals long after their contacts with certain adults are over and in spite of the temptation or opportunity to act otherwise (Kostelnik et al., 1998; Newman & Newman, 1997).

ARE YOUNG CHILDREN CAPABLE OF INTERNALIZATION?

No, but foundations are established early

There is strong evidence that children between the ages of 3 and 8 years old are incapable of regulating their behavior according to internalized standards (Walker, 1989; Walker, DeVries, & Trevarthan, 1989). They are more likely to rely on adherence and identification instead. However, during early childhood, children develop skills and understandings that contribute to internalization later in life. With appropriate adult support, children can begin to distinguish appropriate actions from inappropriate ones and develop a sense of why this is so. They can also become more aware of other's feelings, the impact their actions have on people and things, and alternate strategies for achieving their aims. Children who do not learn these things in early childhood have a harder time achieving internalization later on (Berk, 1997; Magid & McKelvey, 1987). This makes the time between 3 and 8 years an optimal period in which children develop the fundamental skills and concepts necessary for selfdiscipline to develop.

Rates of development vary interpersonally and intrapersonally

Research supports the notion of a developmental progression in the evolution of self-discipline, but it also indicates that children achieve such conduct at rates and in degrees that vary from child to child (Bukatko & Daehler, 1995). For instance, Noel may require several experiences to learn to raise her hand before speaking at circle time. LaRene may grasp this notion much sooner. Furthermore, the same child may at different times be motivated to follow certain rules for different reasons. These reasons are often bound by circumstance (Burton, 1963, 1984). That is, Juanita may keep out of the mud to avoid a reprimand. She may adopt a similar attitude toward cheating as that held by an admired teacher. And when she accidently receives too many milk tokens, she may return some because it would not feel right to keep them. Such variations in self-regulation are typical throughout life.

DEGREES OF SELF-DISCIPLINE EXHIBITED BY YOUNG CHILDREN OVER TIME

Early childhood professionals expect to see variations in the degree to which individual children and a group of children as a whole demonstrate self-discipline. At first, many youngsters will be dependent on external controls. Uncertain about program rules, they will rely on constant adult reminders and monitoring to achieve compliance. Some children will soon figure out which behaviors are rewarded and which are not and use that knowledge to guide their actions. Others will take longer to recognize and use this kind of information. Gradually, as early childhood professionals build relationships with the children, many children will begin to identify with the adults' standards of behavior. When this happens, children will try to follow teachers' codes of conduct and behave in ways aimed at pleasing them. After many months, as children come to understand the rationale for certain teacher expectations, a few may demonstrate internalization of common rules, such as walking indoors or handling the gerbil gently.

With each new teacher and each change of setting, the process begins anew. However, as children work their way through a program, their reliance on external controls will likely lessen, especially for rules that are upheld from one classroom to the next.

There is no way to predict how many youngsters will eventually achieve the highest form of self-discipline. Early on, children's degrees of self-discipline will vary widely. Some will need constant monitoring, and others will rely on identification as a basis for regulating their actions. Others will have developed internal mechanisms for controlling their behavior. These differences are a normal result of children's development and experience.

DEVELOPMENTAL INFLUENCES ON SELF-DISCIPLINE

Children's capacity for self-discipline increases with maturity. Although 4- and 5-year-olds are generally able to regulate themselves in some situations, they are not capable of the same degree of self-control as children who are 8 and 9 years of age. Several developmental factors contribute to these age differences, including ones related to children's emotional, cognitive, and language development and memory skills. In each of these 2 areas, children's increasing understanding and skills emerge according to the principles of developmental direction: simple to complex, concrete to abstract, and inaccurate to more accurate.

Emotional Development

Emotions provide children with strong, internal signals regarding the appropriateness or inappropriateness of their behavior. As children learn to pay attention to these signals, their self-control increases. Two of the most important emotion-based regulators are guilt and empathy (Eisenberg, 1986; Erikson, 1963; Hoffman, 1990). Guilt warns children that current, past, or planned actions are inappropriate. It serves as a brake, causing children to reconsider or stop their actions. Empathy (understanding others' feelings and reacting with complimentary affect) conveys the opposite message. It prompts children to engage in positive actions in response to other people's emotions. Children as young as 2 are capable of both guilt and empathy (Emde et al., 1991; Goleman, 1995). However, what induces these emotions in preschoolers is different from what prompts them in second and third graders.

Empathy Empathy is what sometimes prompts children to comfort a victim, offer to share, or be willing to take turns. Empathy is the driving force behind Alice's response to Lucinda, a 4-year-old who was crying after her mother left. Alice, her classmate, rubbed Lucinda's back gently and said, "That's okay. I'll be your mommy 'til your mommy comes back." Alice recognized Lucinda's distress, empathized with her predicament, and offered a plan to help. All of these are behaviors related to self-discipline (Zavitkovsky, 1986).

At first, infants and toddlers tend to duplicate the overt signals of distress they witness in others. That is why a 2-year-old might cry upon seeing or hearing another child's sobs. By the time they are 3, children recognize that another person's distress calls for relevant action on their part, such as soothing a peer who has fallen down. However, their responses tend to be limited to only one or two strategies. As children progress through the later preschool and early elementary years, they become more adept at responding in a variety of ways to offer encouragement, comfort, and support (Miller, 1995).

Guilt Initially, children experience guilt only when they violate a known rule or fail to meet the expectations of the important adults in their lives. For instance,

Children need adult support as they develop the emotional and cognitive skills necessary to follow rules on their own.

4-year-old Carl slaps Selma in a struggle over the cookie cutters. Selma begins to cry. Triumphant over having gained a desired possession, Carl is unmoved by Selma's distress. He experiences no guilt until the teacher reminds him that the rule is "Hitting is not allowed." Once he becomes aware of the contradiction between his behavior and the rule, Carl may feel guilty about breaking it and disappointing the teacher. On the other hand, were he 7 or 8, Carl might empathize with Selma's unhappy response and feel remorse and guilt at being the source of it (Hoffman, 1967; Williams & Bybee, 1994). This combination of both empathy and guilt could even prompt him to do something to make up for his earlier actions. Violation of a formal rule would not figure as prominently in his feelings as it had during the preschool years. Instead, Carl would be more focused on the internal distress his actions had caused another person and, as a consequence, himself. Eventually, during middle childhood, children feel guilt and empathy even when they are not the cause but perceive that they could have done something to prevent a problem (Kostelnik et al., 1998). Hence, a 10-year-old seeing an argument between Carl and Selma might intercede out of empathy toward two persons in distress and to avoid feeling guilty

over not helping. In this way, children gradually respond to guilt and empathy as a way to support their personal notions of right and wrong. This gradual shift from external prompts to internal ones contributes to the inner control children need to achieve self-discipline. Although it has its beginnings early in life, such complex and "other-oriented" motivation does not fully emerge until adolescence.

What this means for early childhood educators is that they will witness some occasions when children offer help or comfort to their peers and others when the same children seem oblivious to people's reactions or concerns. In either case, children's emotional development is enhanced when adults point out how their actions affect those around them ("You shared the playdough with Sheree. She looks happy" or "When you pushed Mark, he got angry."). Likewise, children follow rules better when they are taught how those rules protect people's feelings ("Those are William's cars. He doesn't like it when you grab. Ask him to share."). Finally, when children demonstrate that they have responded out of empathy or guilt, their efforts need to be recognized and reinforced ("You're trying to help Sandra feel better. That's a kind thing to do" or "You didn't mean to step on Leon's fingers.").

Cognitive Development

Children's notions of what constitutes "good" and "bad" behavior changes with age (Kohlberg, 1964; Piaget, 1965; Tisak & Block, 1990). Whether they judge that an action is right or wrong is influenced by their powers of reason and the extent to which they comprehend the perspective of another person. How well they conduct themselves from one situation to another is further affected by the cognitive processes of centration, irreversibility, and the extent to which children are able to associate one behavior with another.

Children's Reasoning About Right and Wrong

Four- to six-year-olds make judgments about right and wrong based mainly on whether behaviors are immediately rewarded or punished. Children interpret actions that result in social rewards (i.e., a smile, positive words, getting what they want) as good and those that incur social costs (i.e., a frown, negative words, having their goals blocked) as negative. For instance, children conclude that taking turns is good because teachers praise them or that pushing and shoving over who goes first is bad because adults correct them. The link between goodness/rewards and badness/punishments remains constant even if the behavior is viewed differently by society. For this reason, young children who observe a classmate gain attention by clowning around may interpret silliness as "good" because it is reinforced. They might also conclude that comforting a classmate is "bad" if the victim rejects their efforts or other children make fun of their attempts.

Another way children of this age decide that actions are bad is if they result in physical harm to people or property or if they violate people's rights (Tisak & Block, 1990). Those that do, such as hitting, breaking, or calling names, are readily identified by children as unacceptable. Behaviors that disrupt the social order of the group, such as not putting toys away, and those that violate interpersonal trust, like telling a secret, are not interpreted as inappropriate by children until middle childhood.

Because the moral reasoning of younger children is still immature, they need a lot of support in knowing what is expected and why. Adults who state their expectations clearly and offer reasons for those expectations help children progress toward self-discipline. The reasons that will make the most sense to children between ages 3 and 8 years are ones that focus on harmful effects to people ("Tell him you're angry; don't hit. Hitting hurts."), property ("Wear a smock so you don't get paint on your clothes."), and human rights ("It's important that everyone get a turn.").

Children's Perspective-Taking Abilities

To interact effectively with others and make accurate judgments about what actions would be right or wrong in particular situations, children must understand what other people think, feel, or know (Kostelnik et al., 1998). This understanding is called perspective taking. Because this skill is just emerging in young children, youngsters 8 years of age and younger often have difficulty putting themselves in another person's shoes. That dilemma is a result of being unable, rather than unwilling, to comprehend or predict other people's thoughts (Waite-Stupiansky, 1997). Thus, children have trouble recognizing other people's viewpoints, especially when those views conflict with their own. They erroneously assume that everyone interprets each situation just like they do. Not until such differences are brought to children's attention do they begin to recognize that their perspective is not shared. At this age children benefit from hearing that there is more than one way to view a situation. This information could be supplied as relevant situations arise ("You want a turn on the tricycle. Harry wants a turn, too" or "You're having fun painting. I'm worried that the paint is getting on your sleeves.") or through planned activities, such as reading a story in which different characters see the same situation differently.

Sometime between their sixth and eighth year, children start realizing that their interpretation of a situation and that of another person might not match (Bukatko & Daehler, 1995; Selman, 1976). Still, they do not always know what the differences are, or they may conclude that variations are a result of the other person's having access to incorrect or incomplete information. As a result, second and third graders often go to great lengths trying to convince others that their view is the logical one. This trait sometimes makes them appear argumentative or lacking in sensitivity. On these occasions, adults must remind themselves that such behaviors are an outgrowth of children's immature reasoning, not tactics aimed at deliberately frustrating them (Kostelnik & Stein, 1990). When this happens, children need adults to listen carefully, without interruption, and then acknowledge their perspective.

Children also need to hear the facts of the situation repeated, more than once, and in varying ways.

The Impact of Centration   Throughout the early childhood period, children tend to focus their attention on a single aspect of a situation, neglecting other important features that might help them approach the situation more accurately or effectively (Peterson & Felton-Collins, 1991). This phenomenon, known as centration, results in children having a limited rather than comprehensive perception of social events. For instance, centration causes children to overlook important details regarding their actions as well as the behavior of others. This is exemplified when Rayanne focuses so intently on using the glitter paint for her project that she does not realize that other children are waiting for some or that she is using it all. Centration also prompts children to focus on only one way to achieve their aims. Caleb demonstrates centrated thinking when he says "please" over and over again to get a chance to play with another child's toy from home, even though he is refused several times. Even when youngsters recognize that their actions are inappropriate, they may be unable to generate suitable alternate behaviors without adult support. The younger the child, the more this is so. The ability to see an event from more than one angle and to consider several different ways to respond happens only gradually over the course of many years. This ability is enhanced when early childhood professionals point out options to children and help youngsters brainstorm suitable alternatives in problem situations.

The Effects of Irreversible Thinking   Young children's behavior is further influenced by the irreversible nature of their thinking. Evidence suggests that it is difficult for them to mentally reverse a physical action they are in the process of carrying out (Flavell, 1977; Waite-Stupiansky, 1997). As a result, children are not adept at contemplating opposite actions, and they have difficulty interrupting ongoing behaviors. This in turn influences their ability to regulate personal actions and respond to adult directions that are stated in negative terms. For instance, when Kyley pushes on the door of the toy stove to open it, the words "Don't push" called out by the parent volunteer hold little meaning for her. She is unable mentally to transpose the physical act of pushing into its opposite action of

pulling or stopping. Neither can she interrupt her pushing simply by thinking about what to do. She needs assistance to reverse her behavior. Such assistance could be a verbal direction from the adult to *pull* on the door or adult modeling of the desired behavior. With maturation, children improve in their ability to mentally reverse physical actions, but the influence of irreversible thinking remains evident throughout the preschool and early elementary years. Because irreversibility is such a powerful force in children's thinking, adults must remember to state directions and expectations in positive terms. Modeling the desired conduct also helps children understand what the adult wants him or her to do or stop doing.

Associating Behaviors in Meaningful Ways   Younger children tend to view social behaviors as self-contained events. It is hard for them to see how a current action (e.g., calling a peer names) relates to what has gone on before or what might happen in the future (e.g., child will avoid the name-caller from then on). They also have difficulty comprehending how one action (e.g., hitting) is very much like another one (e.g., kicking). This is especially true when associating those behaviors requires abstract thinking (e.g., the notion of hurting someone). Adults who offer children reasons for what is and what is not acceptable help children recognize these connections (e.g., "I can't let you hit; hitting hurts" and "It's not okay to kick. Kicking hurts."). With maturity and experience, 7- and 8-year-olds become more proficient at making such generalizations on their own. Also, they become better able mentally to categorize like behaviors and comprehend the similarities among potential outcomes (i.e., hitting, kicking, pinching, biting are all potentially hurtful behaviors, which makes them unacceptable). However, these understandings are still forming even during the adolescent years, and it is not until then that children can be expected to make accurate connections entirely on their own.

Recognizing Changes in What Is Acceptable Behavior at Different Ages   It is worth noting that as children's thinking becomes more complex, they must continually readjust their notions of desirable and undesirable categories of behavior. For instance, throughout the preschool years children learn to seek help from adults when they see trouble and work cooperatively to get things done. Many preschoolers learn these lessons well. But, as they move into first and second grade, such formerly desirable behaviors take on negative connotations. Labeled tattling and cheating by adults, such actions are often discouraged. At first, these new interpretations are confusing to children, causing them either to persist in relying on old concepts or to become immobilized by uncertainty. Through trial and error, they eventually incorporate new definitions into their thinking and act accordingly. This reprocessing of information occurs repeatedly throughout the grade school years. It is enhanced when adults provide concrete rationales to children for classroom expectations and when teachers exercise patience as children work toward more comprehensive, sophisticated understandings.

Language Development

As children acquire greater and more complex language skills, their capacity for self-control also increases. This is because language contributes to their understanding of why rules are made and gives them more tools for attaining their goals in socially acceptable ways.

Interpersonal Speech   Children as young as 3 and 4 years of age come to the early childhood program with command of a well-developed receptive vocabulary and the ability to express their basic needs (Berk, 1997). Yet, they are not always successful at telling others what they want or responding to verbal directions. As a result, it is not unusual for young children to resort to physical actions in these circumstances. They may grab, dash away, refuse to answer, push, or strike out rather than use words to express themselves. At such times, these children need teacher assistance in figuring out what to say ("You seem upset. Say to Martha, 'I'm using this now'" or "You don't want Jonathan to chase you. Say, 'Stop.'"). As the elementary years progress, children become more proficient in both receiving and giving verbal messages (Maccoby, 1984; Marion, 1995). They find words a more satisfactory and precise way to communicate. However, second and third graders often still need support in figuring out the best words to use in emotionally charged circumstances or situations that are new to them.

Private Speech   In addition to the words they direct toward others, young children use private speech (self-talk) as a means to exercise self-control (Berk & Winsler, 1995; Vygotsky, 1978; Wertsch, 1985). That is, they reduce frustration, postpone rewards, or remind themselves of what to do by talking aloud to themselves. We hear this when a preschooler says to herself, "blue shoes, blue shoes" as a reminder of what she is looking for and when a second grader outlines his approach to an assignment in a mumbled tone as a way to help himself plan. The self-talk Matt employed to help himself wait through the directions to the kickball game (described earlier) provides another good example of children's use of private speech to gain control of their actions. Consequently, when adults hear children talking to themselves, they should allow them to continue rather than asking them to hush. Offering children sample self-talk scripts is another way adults can help children move toward greater self-regulation.

Memory Skills

Closely related to language are skills associated with memory. As children grow older, their memory does not necessarily increase—they just become better able to use stored data as a resource for determining future behavior (Maccoby, 1984). Preschool children and children in the lower elementary grades are still very dependent on having others show or tell them how to behave in new situations. In addition, they periodically "forget" expectations from one day to the next or from one setting to another. In order to be successful, they need frequent reminders about rules and procedures and clear explanations about what to expect when routines change or new activities are introduced. As children reach second and third grade, they will be better able to remember appropriate ways to act without continual adult support (Kostelnik et al., 1998). At this age, children benefit when adults talk with them about strategies they can use to remember what is acceptable and what is not.

HOW EXPERIENCE INFLUENCES SELF-DISCIPLINE

As you can see, development plays a vital role in how well children eventually regulate their own behavior. Children's day-to-day experiences with peers and adults are other factors that influence the degree to which children achieve self-discipline (Reynolds, 1996). The most frequent modes of experience include modeling, attribution, instruction, and consequences (Bandura, 1989; Eaton, 1997; Moore, 1986).

Modeling

One way children learn what is expected of them is by imitating the actions of powerful adults with whom they have strong, affectionate associations (Bandura, 1989; Moore, 1986). Early childhood professionals serve as such models who, through their behavior, demonstrate compliance or lack of compliance with certain standards of conduct. Young children learn potent lessons regarding desirable attitudes and behaviors as well as how to enact them when they observe their teachers treat others with kindness, tell the truth, use reasoning as a way to solve problems, or assist someone in need. Alternately, because youngsters also follow negative models, they sometimes imitate the aggressive or thoughtless acts they observe in those around them.

Attribution

Attribution is a verbal strategy adults use to influence children's images of themselves and therefore their behavior (Grusec & Mills, 1982; Moore, 1986). Teachers use attributions unconsciously or deliberately to direct children's attention to positive traits (brave, smart, or kind) or negative ones (stupid, lazy, or good-for-nothing). For instance, teachers may characterize children as "patient" or "good at waiting." When this occurs, children gradually become even more patient and better able to delay gratification. On the other hand, when adults tell children they are naughty or irresponsible, children not only incorporate these negative labels into their self-image but also adapt in greater measure the corresponding behaviors to support them (Dreikurs & Soltz, 1964; Kostelnik et al., 1998). Attribution induces children to think of themselves in the terms described and behave in corresponding ways to live up to the adult's image of them.

Instruction

Instruction may be carried out indirectly, in response to an ongoing interaction, or in planned lessons.

Indirect Instruction   Indirect instruction involves all the behind-the-scenes work and planning that ultimately influence the behavior of young children (Hildebrand, 1997a). These teaching methods tend to be aimed not at any one child but at creating a classroom atmosphere in which self-control is enhanced. We have already focused in this text on positive methods of indi-

rect instruction. For instance, the use of environmental cues, as described in Chapters 3 and 4, signal children about the expectations for tasks or learning areas that may not be verbally specified. Similarly, the strategies you read about in Chapter 5 were designed to help children manage their own behavior and get along with peers. How adults organize space, equipment, materials, and the schedule of the day affects the degree to which children develop the skills they need to be self-regulating. Warning children of transitions in advance, for example, makes it easier for them to anticipate a change in routine and adjust their behavior accordingly. Simply expecting children to shift quickly one from one activity to the next without warning fails to supply the tools children need to regulate their behavior well.

On-the-Spot-Coaching   In contrast to the indirect methods just described, on-the-spot coaching involves physical or verbal intervention aimed at influencing the behavior of particular children at a particular time. What is right, what is wrong, which behaviors are expected, which are restricted, how behavior standards are to be met, and how children's behavior appears to others are directly conveyed to children in words and actions. This assistance is provided as relevant situations arise, allowing early childhood professionals to take advantage of teachable moments throughout the day. In doing so, they not only remind children of appropriate behavioral standards, they also supply children with information they can use to regulate their own future behavior. This instruction takes place within a relevant context and in a way that is supportive, not punitive. Thus, early childhood professionals teach children self-control directly using verbal strategies such as informing, suggesting, advising, explaining, reasoning, encouraging, and clarifying (Maccoby, 1984; Weinstein & Mignano, 1997). Typical remarks include "Cover your mouth when you cough," "Maybe you could take turns," "Tell him you're angry—don't hit," "Mr. Ramirez really appreciated when you helped him carry those boxes," or "When you didn't say 'Hi' back, she thought you didn't like her." Physical assistance, demonstrations, redirection, distraction, substitution, removal, and physical restraint are additional techniques associated with direct instruction (Eaton, 1997; Gartrell, 1997; Wolfgang, 1996).

Planned Lessons   On-the-spot coaching occurs at various times throughout the day as children's behavior warrants it. Planned lessons, on the other hand, are thought out by the teacher in advance and may constitute part or all of an activity. Such lessons may be carried out at any time of the day, using one or more of the teaching strategies described in Chapter 3. The following activities illustrate this kind of instruction.

Mr. Wilson wants children to learn the words please *and* thank you. *He plans to teach his class the following rhyme, "Two little magic words open any door with ease. One little word is 'thanks.' The other little word is 'please.'" He carries out this minilesson during the circle time at the end of the day.*

In Ms. Carson's multiage primary class the children are planning and carrying out a group project—building a rocket out of an old refrigerator box. Their teacher gathers materials in advance and prepares a large open space in which they can work. She also leads the children in a discussion of the steps they think they might use to implement their project from start to finish. As the children proceed, Ms. Carson helps them refer to their plan to see how well they are following it.

Consequences

Other instructional tools early childhood professionals use are consequences. These come in two varieties—positive and negative—and are aimed at rewarding desirable behaviors or penalizing negative ones. For example, practitioners reward children for following rules using praise ("You remembered your pictures from home; now you're ready for today's work on animals") and tangible rewards ("Here's a star sticker for remembering to return your library book" or "You did such a good job cleaning up, you can have 10 more minutes of recess."). Such strategies are aimed at increasing the likelihood that children will repeat their positive acts in the future and are examples of positive-consequences (Wolfgang, 1996).

Teachers use negative consequences to reduce the probability that undesirable behaviors will be repeated (Dinkmeyer & McKay, 1988; Vasta et al., 1995). The way in which negative consequences are enacted influences how effective they are in promoting self-discipline. Negative consequences that are harsh, unreasonable, and shameful cause children to feel demeaned or fearful. Neither of these reactions leads to guilt or empathy,

necessary emotions for the emergence of self-discipline. On the other hand, some negative consequences are constructive actions that help children learn alternative ways to achieve their aims through the process of being corrected. They enable children to approximate desirable conduct and remind them of the impact their actions have on themselves and others (Eaton, 1997). Corrective action taken in this manner provides children with valuable information they can use to guide their actions on their own in the future.

HOW ADULT DISCIPLINE STYLES INFLUENCE CHILDREN'S SELF-DISCIPLINE

Instruction, modeling, attribution, and consequences are practices all early childhood professionals use in one way or another. Such strategies can be combined differently, resulting in distinct adult-discipline styles. These variations in style have been the subject of research for more than 25 years. Although we still have much to learn, we can safely say that most adults approach child guidance in one of three ways: from a permissive standpoint, an authoritarian point of view, or an authoritative perspective (Baumrind, 1967, 1973, 1995). Each of these discipline styles is characterized by certain adult attitudes and strategies related to the social dimensions of control, communication, maturity demands, and nurturance.

1. *Control* is the way and extent to which parents and teachers enforce compliance with their expectations.
2. *Communication* involves how much information adults provide children throughout the guidance process.
3. *Maturity* demands describe the level at which adults set their expectations for children's behavior and compliance.
4. *Nurturance* refers to how much caring and concern are expressed toward children.

Differences among the permissive, authoritarian, and authoritative styles result from varying combinations of these four dimensions (Bukatko & Daehler, 1995; Marion, 1995; Vasta et al., 1995).

> Permissive adults are low in control, make few maturity demands, and engage in minimal communication with children. They usually rank high in nurturance but in some cases may be low within this dimension as well.

FIGURE 6.1

Differences in Attitudes and Practices Among the Permissive, Authoritarian, and Authoritative Discipline Styles

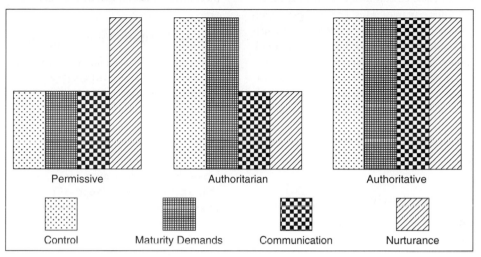

Adults employing an authoritarian style are high in control and maturity demands and low in communication and nurturance.

Early childhood professionals who are high in all four dimensions demonstrate an authoritative style (see Figure 6.1).

Few people personify a "pure" style regardless of which one they adopt. In fact, from time to time, adults may demonstrate behaviors characteristic of all three. However, it is also common for adults to gravitate more toward one style than the others. Recognizing the characteristics of each and their impact on children helps us to understand the relationship between adult behavior and child-outcomes. Knowing this, early childhood professionals can make deliberate choices regarding their approach to child guidance. Such information also helps us to better appreciate the goals parents have for their children's behavior and the strategies they use to achieve their aims.

The Permissive Teaching Style

Permissive teachers treat children with warmth and affection. However, they pay little attention to shaping children's present or future behavior. Some teachers do this because they believe that having positive relationships with children is enough to get youngsters to behave in socially acceptable ways. Others believe that

behavior controls stifle children's development. Still others drift into this approach simply because they do not know how to get children to "listen." Whatever the reason, permissive adults provide very little instruction to children about what is acceptable behavior and what is not. They do not talk with children about how their behavior affects others or help children recognize other people's needs. Because they have low expectations for children's conduct, they give children minimal responsibility and ignore most negative behaviors. If a child engages in some gross misconduct, permissive adults use love withdrawal as their primary means of discipline ("I don't like children who hit.") (Baumrind, 1978; Shaffer, 1995). This temporarily denies children the one social support permissive adults are usually willing to provide—nurturance.

Unfortunately, children subjected to a permissive approach show few signs of self-discipline. In fact, they exhibit the lowest levels of independence and internal control of all the approaches to child guidance that we will examine (Baumrind, 1967; Berk, 1997). This happens for several reasons. To begin with, because the impact of their behavior on others is not explained, children fail to develop feelings of guilt or empathy, necessary ingredients for self-regulation. The fact that youngsters receive very few cues about which behaviors are socially acceptable and which are not also means children do not develop the backlog of experience they need to make appropriate decisions in the future. To make matters worse, peers and adults tend to view their unrestricted conduct as immature, inconsiderate, and unacceptable. This negative perception contributes to children's feelings of anxiety and low self-esteem. As a result, children who interact mainly with permissive adults tend to be withdrawn, unproductive, and dissatisfied with their lives. By adolescence, the permis-sive style is correlated with delinquent behavior and poor academic performance (Patterson & Stouthamer-Loeber, 1984; Pulkkinen, 1982). These unfortunate outcomes are similar to those associated with the style that is its direct opposite, the authoritarian style.

The Authoritarian Teaching Style

Unlike permissive educators, authoritarian teachers have high standards for children's behavior and exert strong control over children's actions. To achieve those standards and control, they act as strict taskmasters who value children's unquestioning obedience above all else. Theirs is the philosophy of "I say and you obey" and "Do it because I said so!" Failure to meet their expectations is dealt with swiftly and forcefully, most often through shaming techniques or physical punishment. In either case, their chief aim is to show children who is boss as opposed to helping children consider how their behavior affects others or how to figure out what better strategies to use in the future. Not too surprisingly, authoritarian adults have cold, distant relationships with young children. Youngsters view them as harsh disciplinarians who focus more on finding mistakes than on recognizing their efforts to behave appropriately (Shaffer, 1996).

The coercive discipline strategies characteristic of the authoritarian style cause children to maintain an external orientation to behavior regulation. In the short term, youngsters act in required ways out of fear or unreasoned obedience, not out of empathy or concern for others (Newman & Newman, 1997). This impedes their ability to develop the reasoning and caring necessary for self-discipline. In the long run, children whose primary experiences are with authoritarian adults tend to become unfriendly, suspicious, resentful, and unhappy in the classroom. They are often underachievers and exhibit increased incidents of misconduct as well as extreme antisocial behaviors (Baumrind, 1983, 1995; Maccoby & Martin, 1983). These outcomes add up to

a dismal prognosis for children who are the product of this style. A more positive outcome results from the authoritative approach we consider next.

The Authoritative Teaching Style

Authoritative teachers combine the positive dimensions of permissiveness (nurturance) and authoritarianism (maturity demands and control) while avoiding the negative ones (Bukatko & Daehler, 1995). In addition, they rely on some strategies permissive and authoritarian adults fail to use altogether, such as clear communication and other-oriented reasoning. Early childhood professionals who adopt an authoritative style encourage children to assume appropriate responsibility and get what they need in socially acceptable ways. When children attempt a new skill, adults acknowledge their accomplishments; when children face challenges, teachers help them develop new approaches. These methods contribute to children's feelings of competence and worth. Simultaneously, authoritative teachers establish high standards for children's behavior and are quick to take action to teach them how to strive toward those standards. Explanations, demonstrations, suggestions, and reasoning are the primary instructional strategies they use (Hendrick, 1996; LeFrancois, 1992). When children behave inappropriately, authoritative adults take advantage of the opportunity to discuss guilt, empathy, and the perspectives of others. They also provide on-the-spot coaching to help children recognize acceptable and unacceptable behaviors as well as potential alternatives. This nonpunitive form of child guidance is sometimes called inductive discipline because adults induce children to regulate their own behavior based on the impact their actions will have on themselves and others (Kostelnik et al., 1998).

The authoritative approach to child guidance is the style most strongly related to the development of self-discipline (Franz et al., 1991; Vasta et al., 1995). Children know what is expected of them. They also develop the skills necessary to behave in accordance with that knowledge. Such youngsters tend to be sensitive to the needs of others, happy, and cooperative. They are well equipped to resist temptation, delay gratification, and control their negative impulses. They are also better able to initiate and maintain constructive social plans on their own (Baumrind, 1983, 1995). Consequently, their behavior is the most internalized of the three patterns described in this text. For all these reasons, children benefit when early childhood professionals adopt an authoritative approach to child guidance.

Adopting an Authoritative Approach to Child Guidance

Because authoritative teaching represents the most effective way to promote self-discipline in children, it is strongly aligned with developmentally appropriate practice. Permissive strategies and authoritarian methods are categorized as inappropriate (Bredekamp & Copple, 1997). People used to believe that teachers were authoritarian, permissive, or authoritative as a direct result of their personality or their temperament. It was further assumed that not much could be done to change a person's natural style (Lewin, Lippitt, & White, 1939). We now know that, although early childhood educators do have personality traits and abilities that seem more in keeping with one style or another, through training and practice any early childhood professional can learn to be more authoritative (Kostelnik et al., 1998; Peters & Kostelnik, 1981). The following strategies in combination exemplify an au-

thoritative approach. They are listed sequentially so that preventative strategies precede remedial ones.

❏ **Authoritative teachers build positive relationships with children** (Gartrell, 1997; Kontos & Wilcox-Herzog, 1997). Children's social learning is facilitated when they view the adults with whom they interact as sources of comfort and encouragement (Garbarino, 1995). Creating emotionally supportive relationships with children, therefore, is the cornerstone on which authoritative teaching rests. In the classrooms of authoritative teachers, children are treated with warmth, caring, empathy, and respect. Adults interact with each child each day in ways children interpret as supportive, attentive, and enjoyable. Teachers enhance their relationships with children when they do the following things:

Greet children by name.

Get down to the children's eye level when talking with them.

Smile at children often.

Listen carefully to what children have to say.

Speak politely to children.

Invite children to talk or interact with them.

Authoritative teaching begins with positive teacher/child relationships.

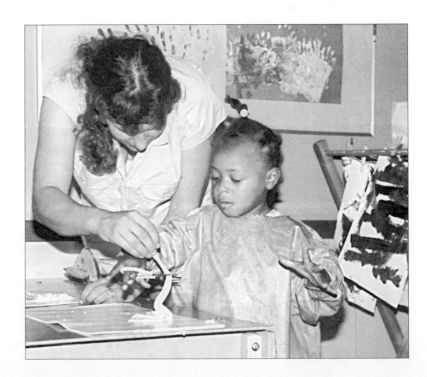

Comfort children who are unhappy or afraid.

Laugh with children at their jokes.

Talk with children about their (the children's) feelings.

Assist children in finding constructive ways to express their emotions to others.

Authoritative teachers never coerce, shame, taunt, or physically hurt children for any reason.

❏ **Authoritative teachers model behaviors they hope children will imitate** (Bandura, 1989; Reynolds, 1996). Setting a good example is an effective way to teach children right from wrong because it proves to them that certain behaviors are really desirable. But simply observing appropriate actions does not necessarily teach children how to enact them themselves. To move to that level of learning, children's attention must be drawn to the specifics of the model's behavior. Teachers provide such guidance when they point out the model's actions and talk children through what they are seeing. This helps youngsters identify critical facets of an interaction they might otherwise miss. Therefore, if a teacher wants children to copy his gentle handling of the class gerbil, it would be useful to say, "Watch how I pick up the gerbil. First, I'll put both hands under her tummy so I don't drop her. See how I'm holding my fingers? This way I don't squeeze her too hard." Showing children the procedure without direct explanation or hoping that they will figure it out themselves simply by watching is less likely to result in accurate imitation. Moreover, modeling is most potent when the teacher behaves in ways consistent with his or her words. Mrs. Lopez, who emphasizes the value of polite behaviors and remembers to say "please," "thank you," and "excuse me" when talking to the children, illustrates such congruence. She is more likely to achieve compliance with her expectations than will Mrs. Kelly, who preaches good manners but frequently interrupts children or orders them to do things without the customary social graces.

❏ **Authoritative teachers use positive attribution to support children's favorable self-perceptions** (Moore, 1986; Wittmer & Honig, 1994). Teachers help children become tidier, less impulsive, more generous, or more cooperative by referring to them in these terms and espousing their belief that the child in question can act in these ways. For instance, when the

children are standing at the door, Mrs. Martine notices their efforts to wait and makes remarks such as "Corey, you're waiting very patiently," "Janice, you really know how to wait—you're standing with your arms down and your feet still," and "Keiko, you're showing a lot of patience standing there." Children hear remarks such as these frequently. The teacher does not wait for full compliance but recognizes approximations toward the desired end. In this way, children gradually perceive themselves as capable of exercising patience and become more patient over time. Likewise, before starting a small-group activity, Mr. Noor prefaces his directions by stating, "This project is going to require a lot of cooperation, and I know you can do it." In both examples, teachers have deliberately used positive attribution to promote children's positive self-image and increase their repertoire of socially acceptable behaviors.

❏ **Authoritative teachers emphasize cooperation rather than competition to promote empathy among children and increase children's social skills.** They encourage all children to do their best but never at one another's expense (Marion, 1995). Thus, they *avoid* pitting one child or group of children against another (e.g., "Let's see who will get the most problems right, the boys or the girls.") and *refrain* from using competition to motivate children to get things done (e.g., "Let's see who can put the most blocks away" or "Whoever gets the most problems right can pick the game for recess."). Similarly, they do not *reinforce* one child at the expense of another (e.g., "Cathleen, your paper is so very neat, I wish the rest of the class would try hard like you."). Such competitive strategies cause children to conclude there can be only one winner and that helping or cooperating with others will sabotage their chances to come out on top. To counteract self-centered thinking, teachers focus on individual progress and group accomplishments instead (e.g., "You got more problems right today than you did yesterday" or "Let's see how quickly we can all put the blocks away."). Remarks like these clear the way for students to come to one another's aid and work together as appropriate. In addition, group rewards encourage children to work as a team to accomplish common aims. Putting up a star for each book read by the class or each act of kindness shown is one way to help children keep track of their progress as a whole and direct their attention to the positive outcomes an entire group can achieve.

❏ **Authoritative teachers help children learn prosocial skills as a way to promote empathy and social competence** (Honig & Wittmer, 1996). Teachers plan activities such as inviting children to create a mural cooperatively or assigning "buddies" to help one another with a project as a way to accomplish this aim. They read books that focus on helpful or cooperative behaviors and lead class discussions about these concepts. They also demonstrate kindness through skits and role-playing activities. Readers may refer to Chapter 13, for examples of this type of instruction. Teachers also carry out on-the-spot instruction to help children learn the basics of kindness—what it looks like and how it feels. Inviting children to comfort an injured classmate or giving children information about how their teasing hurt another child's feelings are typical situations in which such on-the-spot teaching could happen.

❏ **Authoritative teachers help children learn to negotiate as a way to achieve their aims nonaggressively** (Miller, 1994; Weinstein & Mignano, 1997). Teachers do this in three ways. One is to create natural opportunities for children to practice negotiation skills. For instance, rather than putting the same color of paint on two easels to avoid arguments, the teacher makes available different colors at each. He or she then urges the children to find ways to share their resources. Children are allowed to work things out for themselves with on-the-spot coaching provided by peers or the adult.

A second approach is for teachers to use puppets, flannel board stories, story books, or skits to illustrate relevant negotiation skills such as sharing, taking turns, and bargaining (Crary, 1996). Children have chances to see both appropriate and inappropriate skill use, evaluate the tactics chosen, and generate ideas for alternate resolutions.

A third strategy is to turn children's everyday arguments into opportunities for them to learn conflict resolution techniques in real-life situations. This method is particularly important because even youngsters who can rationally discuss the value of negotiation within the context of a planned activity may forget and resort to aggressive strategies in the heat of actual confrontations. At times like these, children benefit from having a mediator assist them through the steps necessary for reconciliation to occur. Mediators are often adults, but they may also be other children in the program

(DeVogue, 1996; Stein & Kostelnik, 1984). Readers may refer to Chapter 13 for a step-by-step model of conflict mediation and how to teach children effective mediation skills.

❏ **Authoritative teachers encourage children to participate in the rule-making process** (Bickart, Dodge, & Jablon, 1997; Weinstein & Mignano, 1997). Early childhood professionals hold class meetings and open-ended discussions in which they invite children to help create the broad rules by which everyone in the class will live. Such a discussion might begin with the teacher asking, "How can we make our classroom a safe, comfortable, and happy place to learn?" Children's ideas are written on a chart and then posted for all to see. Sample rules might be the following: Be helpful to others. Solve problems with words. Treat others the way you wish to be treated. Respect people's property. Act in ways that are safe. Similar discussions are carried on throughout the year so that youngsters may consider the value of their rules over time and revise them as necessary. In this way children and teachers share responsibility for typical classroom rules and for making sure they are followed.

Even very young children can help create mean-ingful rules for the classroom.

❏ **Authoritative teachers intervene and redirect children's behavior when their actions could hurt someone, damage property, or interfere with the rights of others** (Bredekamp & Copple, 1997). When authoritative teachers see a potential problem brewing, they ask themselves the following questions: (a) Is the child's behavior potentially or currently unsafe for the child or others? (b) Does the child's behavior threaten to damage property? (c) Does the child's behavior interfere with the rights of others? If the answer to any of these questions is yes, the teacher intervenes by setting a limit on the child's behavior. This involves explaining why the behavior is unacceptable and redirecting the child to engage in a more appropriate action. This alternate behavior becomes a rule for the situation at hand (Kostelnik et al., 1998). For instance, Mr. Woodson observes that Mallory is squeezing the guinea pig until it squeals. Knowing that the animal is frightened, he intervenes. Placing his hand lightly on Mallory's, he says, "You're having fun with the guinea pig. He sounds like you might be squeezing too hard. That hurts. Hold him gently like this." If Mallory cannot loosen her grip, Mr. Woodson will physically assist her in holding the animal more appropriately or put the frightened creature back in its cage for a while. Although individual teachers vary in their interpretation of what makes a situation potentially dangerous or threatening, considering these three questions is a consistent, dependable means for deciding when to set limits on children's behavior.

❏ **Authoritative teachers address problem behaviors that are important enough to deal with each time they occur and ignore those that are not** (Bredekamp & Copple, 1997). Authoritative teachers set only limits that are *important* enough to enforce *each time* the problem behavior arises (Gootman, 1988). They realize that not every minor infraction requires intervention. For instance, when Ms. Williams sees a child deliberately ruin another child's artwork, she intervenes immediately, reminding children of the rule about respecting people's property. Also, she continues to enforce the rule, day after day, no matter how tired or otherwise occupied she might be. On the other hand, although she sometimes finds it irritating for children to smack their lips loudly while they eat, there are many days when she does not want to be bothered with restricting that behavior. Because "on again, off again" limits do not provide the consistent enforcement children need to learn them, Ms. Williams tolerates this minor annoyance in order to address more important issues for the time being. Later, if she determines that children's lip smacking truly interferes with their ability to eat safely, she would then make "quiet lips" a limit and enforce it each day. Thus, the criterion of *importance* helps authoritative teachers order their priorities and focus on only a few guidelines for behavior at a time. This makes it more likely that children will be able to follow them successfully.

❏ **Authoritative teachers state their expectations in reasonable, definable, and positive ways** (Clarizio, 1980; Kostelnik et al., 1998). *Reasonable* means children can actually do the required behavior; that is, youngsters have both the knowledge and ability to meet the expectation. For instance, if children are expected to work on their journals independently, the teacher must first determine if they already possess the necessary skills—knowledge of where the journals are kept, previous practice with paper and writing tools, the ability to distinguish their property from that of others, and the skills to write in a focused way for a period of time. If children lack know-how about any of these things, the teacher might revise the rule to match their abilities or spend time teaching them the required actions.

Definable expectations are ones in which both the adult and child have the same understanding of the expectation. Effective statements identify the exact behaviors the adult wants the child to perform. Specific expectations such as "Walk, don't run" or "Knock over only your own blocks" are easier for children to follow than are vague statements such as "Act nice" or "Behave yourself."

Finally, children are more successful at meeting expectations that tell them what to do instead of what not to do. "Put your hands in your pockets" is less difficult for children to respond to than "Don't fidget" or "No pushing." Likewise, "Sing softly; don't shout" is more apt to lead to compliance than the statement "Don't shout" all by itself. Therefore, how expectations are stated has much to do with how well children can follow them. Teachers who state *positive* rules are more likely to help children move toward internalization than those who do not.

❏ **Authoritative teachers offer children reasons explaining that certain behaviors are acceptable or unacceptable** (Brody & Shaffer, 1982; Faber & Mazlish, 1995). Reasons help expectations and limits make sense. And the reasons that make the most sense to children between the ages of 3 and 8 are ones that are specific, that help them associate one behavior with another, and that match their developmental understandings. Mr. Ramirez is addressing these three criteria when he tells Dana, who is shouting across the room to a friend, "Walk over and tell her what you found so other people can concentrate on their work." In this way, he has linked the desired action to the rights of others in the class. In other situations, he might refer to safety issues or the protection of property because these are the reasons children this age find most credible. It would be too general and therefore inappropriate to simply forbid Dana to talk "because I said so" or "because that's the rule in our room." Reasons are essential to the critical thinking necessary for self-discipline to develop. Therefore, authoritative teachers provide reasons every single time they make a rule or intervene to correct a child's mistaken behavior (e.g., "I'm worried you'll fall if you run. Please walk" or "There are only enough cupcakes for everyone to have one. Put one back.").

❏ **Authoritative teachers often remind children of the rules** (Bickart, Dodge, & Jablon, 1997). They know children may forget what constitutes appropriate behavior from one day to the next or from one situation to another. They also realize that although children may understand that certain behaviors such as running in the classroom are not allowed, youngsters may not be capable of substituting a more acceptable action without coaching. Teachers' reminders take two forms. First, they talk with children about desirable behaviors at times when infractions are not an issue. Such discussions allow children to calmly explore the value and reasons for certain expectations without the added pressure of conflict between their needs or desires and those of others. Second, early childhood professionals remind children of the rules at the very moment those rules are needed. For example, teachers say, "Remember to walk in the classroom" when children are caught running. They avoid accusatory statements such as "How many times have I told you about running inside?" or "You know better than to run inside." These latter phrases fail to teach children the appropriate alternate behavior and do not help them remember what to do the next time. The former reminder serves as a minilesson from which children can extract meaningful information for the future.

❏ **Authoritative teachers use substitution to channel children's inappropriate behaviors in more positive directions** (Bredekamp & Copple, 1997). If a child is making jokes during the Author's Chair group time, the early childhood professional substitutes another time of the day for this behavior ("You may tell jokes *after* group is over, not now."). If a child is pounding on a fragile toy, the adult substitutes pounding at the workbench. If a child is washing the table with dirty water, the adult gets the child to substitute clean water instead. When several children are talking and therefore blocking the entrance to the classroom, the adult asks them to move to a better spot. In each case, the children's actions were rechanneled by substituting a more appropriate time, object, or place for an unacceptable one.

❏ **Authoritative teachers use positive consequences to maintain children's desirable behaviors** (Wolfgang, 1996). They recognize the effort it takes for children to display positive behaviors or compliance, and they take the time to acknowledge those productive outcomes. One way they do this is by using effective praise (Goode & Brophy, 1984; Hitz & Driscoll, 1988). As you remember from Chapter 3, this means giving children specific feedback about the appropriate behaviors they display and why such actions are desirable. Thus, Ms. Tanimoto reinforces Bert's efforts to remember to raise his hand by saying, "Bert, you remembered to raise your hand. That shows you have something to tell us." She does not simply say, "Good job, Bert." The former comment highlights Bert's appropriate behavior in a way that makes sense to him and acknowledges that he has followed a classroom rule. Conversely, the perfunctory "Good job" gives Bert little information and may lose its meaning over time.

Sometimes positive consequences are implemented in the form of earned privileges. For instance, if the rule is "Push the keys on the computer one at a time," children might be told that when they demonstrate this skill that they can use the computer on their own. By granting increased independence, the teacher rewards children for carrying out the desired action.

❏ **Authoritative teachers stop children's unsafe behavior first and then work on resolving the problem that prompted it** (Reynolds, 1996; Wolfgang, 1996). When children's actions are potentially harmful to themselves or others, teachers step in immediately to halt the dangerous actions. At times that requires physical intervention such as positioning themselves between two angry children or using mild physical restraint. Once the dangerous situation has been neutralized and children can focus on what is being said, the adult begins to help children work through the difficulty. This may be accomplished through holding a conversation, redirecting, offering children choices, removing the child from the situation for a brief time, or modifying the environment in some way to make it easier for children to meet their needs and get along.

❏ **Authoritative teachers use logical consequences to help children learn acceptable conduct from the experience of being corrected** (Eaton, 1997). *Logical consequences* teach children alternate behaviors to replace the inappropriate strategies they may be using to satisfy their needs and desires. As these substitute means are strengthened through practice and positive consequences, children gradually incorporate them into their behavioral repertoire, which makes it easier for them to act appropriately in the future.

Logical consequences make an obvious connection between the child's behavior and the resulting intervention (Gootman, 1988; Wolfgang, 1996). Consequences of this type help children either rehearse the desired behavior or, in some way, restore a problem situation to a more positive state. For example, if the rule is "Walk, don't run" and Louise runs down the hall, a logical consequence would be to have her retrace her steps and walk. The act of walking actually approximates the rule and allows Louise to enact it physically. This provides her with a better reminder of it than simply scolding her. Children who practice rules in this way increase their chances for future compliance.

At times, such approximations are not feasible, and so restitution is an alternate choice. For instance, if Julie draws on the classroom wall, it would be logical to insist that she wash off the marks. This action returns the wall to a more acceptable state and shows Julie that the unacceptable act of defacing the classroom will not be tolerated. This type of teacher intervention is a better solution than simply forbidding her to participate in a favorite activity or making her sit away from the group for awhile. Although the latter acts demonstrate adult displeasure, they do not teach Julie responsibility toward school property. Used too often, such unrelated consequences keep children at the adherence level of compliance rather than providing them with the tools needed for internalization.

❏ **Authoritative teachers warn children of the logical consequences for breaking rules before applying them.** This is accomplished through an either-or statement that repeats the rule and describes to the child what will happen if the rule is broken (Kostelnik et al., 1998). For example, if the rule is "Push your sleeves up before you paint," the warning could be "Either push your sleeves up yourself, or I will help you." If the rule is "Wait your turn in line," the warning might be "Either wait your turn, or go back to the end of the line." In both cases, the warning gives children the opportunity and incentive to change their behavior themselves. It also serves as a signal that if they do not comply of their own accord, the adult will take steps to ensure their compliance. Maintaining a calm demeanor is essential so that the warning becomes a plain statement of fact rather than a threat. Its purpose is to provide maximum guidance to children before adult enforcement.

❏ **Authoritative teachers follow through on their warnings when children fail to comply.** Following through is essential because it helps children make a connection between the broken rule and a more desirable, alternate behavior. Because logical consequences are educational in nature, following through gives children valuable information about how to redirect their behavior (Newman & Newman, 1997). It also shows them that adults mean what they say, which makes the classroom a more predictable place in which to learn.

The follow-through procedure consists of first acknowledging the child's desire within the situation. This is a nonevaluative summary of the event from the child's point of view. The next step is to repeat the warning briefly and then declare that the consequence will take place. A sample script follows: "Ralph, you're eager to get a drink. Remember I said either wait your turn or go to the end of the line. Now go to the end of the line." The teacher waits a moment to see if Ralph can do it himself. If not, the teacher might have to escort Ralph to the designated spot as a way to maintain enforcement.

Following through in this way must be *consistent*. Every time the rule is broken, the consequence must be enforced. Rules enforced erratically, varying from situation to situation or from child to child, are ones that children ignore. Authoritative teachers thus insist on only a few rules as a way to maintain consistency.

Rule enforcement must be *immediate*. Once the teacher gives the warning and a short time for the child to comply, he or she must follow through if compliance does not occur. Long delays between when the child breaks the rule and when the follow-through takes place diminish the educational impact of the consequence.

When warnings are consistently followed by enactment of logical consequences, teachers' actions become predictable to children. Youngsters learn that if they do not comply at the warning stage, a follow-through will take place. This encourages them to respond to the warning without having to experience a consequence directly. Behavior change at this point shows some self-regulation by children, although at the adherence level. Gradually, children learn to use rules and their accompanying reasons as a behavior guide. In this way, they begin to exercise greater control over their conduct while teachers exert less. Thus, children gradually make the transition from external to internal behavior controls.

❏ **Authoritative teachers collaborate with parents to promote children's self-discipline** (Gartrell, 1997; Kostelnik et al., 1998). Children benefit when all the significant adults in their lives communicate and work together toward mutual goals. With this aim in mind, teachers talk with parents about parent's expectations for their children and the guidance strategies they use at home. In turn, they acquaint families with expectations held for children in the early childhood setting, answering parental questions honestly and openly. In addition, early childhood staff discuss with parents mutual ways to help children achieve self-control. These conversations are held in a spirit of shared learning and support.

RELATIONSHIP BETWEEN AUTHORITATIVE TEACHING AND DEVELOPMENTALLY APPROPRIATE PRACTICE

Although the strategies associated with authoritative teaching are strongly associated with developmentally appropriate practice, they are not sufficient by themselves to equal it. As with all other aspects of early childhood education, early childhood professionals must ask themselves if their expectations and methods for maintaining them with children are age appropriate, individually appropriate, and socially and culturally appropriate. With these queries in mind, let us consider the following expectation typical in many early childhood classrooms,

At grouptime, children must raise their hands to speak.

Question: Is this expectation age appropriate?

Answer: This is not an age-appropriate expectation for 3-year-olds, who are just learning to converse in groups. Based on what we know about young children's need for sensory involvement and movement, grouptime activities should not be dominated by verbal turn taking and waiting. A better strategy would be to practice such skills in small groups of two or three children at a time. In either case, hand-raising is not a particularly useful way to help young children learn to talk together.

Children 7 and 8 years of age will be better equipped to respond to this rule. They have both the verbal and physical skills necessary to wait and to signal with a raised hand their desire to talk.

Question: Is this expectation individually appropriate?

Answer: This might be an appropriate expectation for Dan, who has had many opportunities to participate in circle-time conversations and who is feeling relaxed and comfortable in the group. It may be less appropriate for Duwana, who is new to the classroom and is feeling apprehensive about participating in the group conversation.

Question: Is this expectation socially and culturally appropriate?

Answer: This may fit the cultural experience of some children. However, it may be less relevant to children whose family and community experiences include a strong emphasis on group response and spontaneous affirmations of things that are being said. Program setting and activity type are other sociocultural factors to consider. Raising one's hand to speak might make sense as part of a demonstration, but it may be irrelevant if brainstorming was the group activity underway.

This example illustrates the complexity of guiding children's behavior. There are no "one size fits all" answers. Instead, early childhood professionals continually make judgments about the standards they set and the strategies they use. Adults gear their guidance strategies to match and respect children's current capabilities, simultaneously recognizing that what may work best for one group of children may not be suitable for a second group and that what is effective for one child may not be best for another (Bredekamp &

Copple, 1997). This element of judgment combined with the strategies characteristic of authoritative teaching are the most effective way to promote self-discipline in children.

AUTHORITATIVE TEACHING AND THE IMPORTANCE OF TEAMWORK AMONG STAFF

All the authoritative teaching strategies outlined here can be adopted by individual teachers with positive results (Gordon & Browne, 1996; Peters & Kostelnik, 1981). Those who use such techniques report greater self-satisfaction and confidence in their disciplinary actions, increased harmony in the classroom, and more frequent incidents of positive behaviors among children (Kontos & Wilcox-Herzog, 1997; Richberg, 1991). These productive outcomes are enhanced even further when authoritative methods are used throughout an entire classroom or program. That is, self-discipline among children is even more likely to develop and flourish when all personnel in the early childhood setting (full-time, part-time, paid, and volunteer) collectively and consciously set out to adopt an authoritative style (Gartrell, 1997; Hyman & D'Alessandro, 1984). The following section is an abbreviated summary of how one program went about accomplishing this aim.

Planning and Organizing a Programwide Guidance Policy

Teachers and administrators as well as parents whose children were enrolled at Adams Elementary expressed concern over worsening behavior problems at the school. They noted that incidents of students fighting, disruptive behavior, and children defying teachers seemed on the rise. Such difficulties were especially prevalent in the halls and on the playground. Moreover, they were not confined to any particular classroom or grade level but seemed to pervade the whole school. Problems were just as likely to occur in the preschool class or the kindergarten as they were in the fifth grade. Both adults and children lamented the unhappy atmosphere that resulted.

The Process

February—Defining the Problem   Following a series of informal discussions, the issue of poor discipline was brought up at an after-school staff meeting. The staff agreed that something had to be done to improve the learning environment at Adams School. Individual teachers volunteered to solicit disciplinary procedures from other area schools for the Adams staff to review.

March—Defining the Problem   At an after-school meeting, the Adams staff read through materials gathered from other schools. After much discussion, they agreed that a buildingwide disciplinary policy was desirable. However, they were not comfortable with the penalty-oriented procedures that characterized most of the materials they had read. The principal was asked to contact a child development expert at a nearby university to help the staff examine the issues and provide suggestions about what to do next.

April—Defining the Problem   At a breakfast meeting with the university consultant, the principal and several staff members discussed various discipline-related concerns. At its conclusion, they agreed that solving the disciplinary problems at Adams School would be the focus of staff training for the entire next school year. A later analysis of that discussion revealed the following problems:

❏ School rules were vague ("Share your smile" and "Respect others.") or negative ("Don't run in school.").

❏ Rule enforcement lacked immediacy. Staff were hesitant to correct other teachers' children; playground and lunchroom infractions were referred by monitors to classroom teachers to deal with long after they occurred.

❏ Rule enforcement was inconsistent from adult to adult, child to child, and situation to situation. Staff varied in the rules they enforced, the kinds of consequences they used, the times when consequences were applied, and the events that prompted a trip to the office. They also differed in their ideas of what should happen "at the office" and if and when children should be suspended from school.

❏ Little time was spent teaching children the rules. It was assumed that students should know what to do and why.

❏ Children spent a lot of time in situations with adults with whom they had no close ties (on the bus, in the lunchroom, and on the playground). The primary adult role during these times was to watch for infractions.

May–June—Preparation The principal, the university consultant, three teachers representing the staff, and three parent volunteers met and developed a training proposal. It was submitted to the total staff and approved with suggested revisions. It was agreed that the focus of the plan would be on a comprehensive approach to positive guidance rather than simply on penalties for infractions.

July–August—Preparation The training proposal was next submitted to the district office as a professional development project. Funds were granted to pay for two half-days of in-service training, refreshments for eight working sessions, written materials for each participant, and the cost of the consultant. School staff agreed to devote six after-school staff meetings to the project. A parent volunteer from each classroom was invited to participate in these sessions.

October—Training and Planning Session 1 entailed a group discussion of self-discipline and principles of authoritative rule making. Session 2 was a group discussion of appropriate consequences.

November—Training and Planning Session 3 involved a group discussion of how to promote children's prosocial behavior.

January—Training and Planning Teachers began practicing some of the skills they had learned in sessions 1, 2, and 3. Teachers conducted discussions with children about rights and rules and recorded their ideas. Specialists, lunchroom aides, playground volunteers, and bus drivers also visited classrooms to discuss rules beyond the classroom. The children and staff generated 280 rules. These were turned over to the consultant who eliminated duplicates and grouped the remaining rules into categories for staff review. At a Parent Teacher Organization (PTO) meeting, parents were invited to make suggestions about children's school conduct and their own role in a schoolwide guidance plan.

February—Training and Planning Session 4 was a half-day in-service program devoted to having the staff and parent representatives further consolidate the rules and link them to authoritative principles. The result was the 12 rules that appear in Figure 6.2.

March—Training and Planning Session 5 was another half-day in-service meeting devoted to developing logical consequences to support each rule and determining appropriate unrelated consequences. Teachers engaged in mutual problem solving regarding their use of the authoritative skills they had been practicing since January.

April—Training and Planning Session 6 was a workshop for volunteers and bus drivers to review the guidance plan and to practice authoritative strategies. Session 7 was a workshop for teachers and administrators to review the guidance plan and practice authoritative strategies.

May—Training and Planning An open meeting was held with parents to elicit reactions, review the guidance plan, and demonstrate authoritative strategies.

June—Training and Planning Session 8 involved an after-school meeting to revise the written plan in accordance with feedback received from all groups concerned. It was agreed that future rule changes must be discussed and approved by the staff, parents, and children. Procedural changes would require adult approval only.

July and August—Training and Planning Volunteers from the committee met to clarify details of the guidance plan and develop a fall orientation for children, parents, and staff. The plan was sent to all families and staff with a cover letter prior to the first day of school.

September—Implementation A day-two assembly for parents and children was held in a spirit of celebration and community fellowship. The Adams School Guidance Plan was introduced by the principal and the guidance counselor, and everyone had an opportunity to ask questions and make statements about the plan. The next day, classroom orientations were conducted, emphasizing the children's contributions. Later in the month, lunchroom, playground, and schoolbus orientations were also carried out classroom by classroom. The guidance counselor assumed responsibility for these orientations in conjunction with the relevant supervising adults. These support personnel also spent time in classrooms getting to know the children.

FIGURE 6.2
The Adams School Guidance Plan

Preamble

The ultimate aim of the Adams School Guidance Plan is to create a happy, predictable learning environment in which both children and adults flourish. School staff, volunteers, children, and parents all contributed to this document. It was created with the following beliefs in mind:

❑ People learn best in an environment in which they are safe and treated with kindness and respect.

❑ Everyone at Adams School has certain rights. These rights form the basis for school rules.

❑ Rules are guides for behavior. They tell people what to do versus what not to do.

❑ People learn best when they know what the rules are and why those rules exist.

❑ When people behave in ways consistent with school expectations, their efforts should be acknowledged.

❑ When people's behaviors are inconsistent with school rules, consequences aimed at teaching more appropriate behaviors should be used. The first consequences of choice are logical ones, that is, consequences directly related to the broken rule. If such consequences are used to no avail, appropriate unrelated consequences (involving loss of certain school privileges) will be carried out.

Rights and Rules at Adams School

People have the right to play and work in a clean school.

Rule 1: Keep the school building clean.
Examples of this rule as suggested by the children:
　　a. Pick up all litter and gum and dispose of it in trash containers.
　　b. Preserve hall and room bulletin boards.
Rule 2: Keep the classrooms clean.
Examples of this rule as suggested by the children:
　　a. Clean up your own mess.
　　b. Return materials to their proper place.
Rule 3: Keep the bathrooms clean.
Examples of this rule as suggested by the children:
　　a. Put litter and paper towels in trash containers only, not in sinks or toilets.
　　b. Flush toilets after using.
Rule 4: Keep the lunchroom clean.
Examples of this rule as suggested by the children:
　　a. Keep food on trays, in lunchboxes, or in your mouth.
　　b. No putting food on people.

People have the right to feel and be safe at school and on school grounds.

Rule 5: Play safely outdoors.
Examples of this rule as suggested by the children:
　　a. Stay on the playground.
　　b. Don't push people off equipment.

FIGURE 6.2
(continued)

Rule 6: Behave safely inside the school building.
Examples of this rule as suggested by the children:

    a. Walk in school.
    b. Leave things that might hurt or frighten yourself or others at home, including hardballs, wooden or steel bats, any kinds of guns or knives.

Rule 7: Behave safely on the way to and from school.
Examples of this rule as suggested by the children:

    a. Stay seated on the bus.
    b. Obey safety monitors at the crossings.

People have the right to feel good about how they are treated at school.

Rule 8: Respect the personal property of others.
Examples of this rule as suggested by the children:

    a. Touch other people's personal property only with their permission.
    b. Stay out of other people's desks, backpacks, cubbies, and lunch space.

Rule 9: Treat people with respect.
Examples of this rule as suggested by the children:

    a. Stop (e.g., chasing or teasing) when children say "stop."
    b. Do not peek at others in the bathroom.
    c. Wait your turn.

Rule 10: Be kind to others.
Examples of this rule as suggested by the children:

    a. Be patient with others.
    b. Offer encouraging words rather than laughing at the mistakes of others.
    c. Offer put-ups, not put-downs.

Rule 11: Be helpful to others.
Examples of this rule as suggested by the children:

    a. Speak quietly while inside.
    b. Offer to help one another by carrying things, picking up something dropped and giving it back, or opening doors.
    c. Offer to share materials, give information, and provide assistance.
    d. Help children in conflict. If children are arguing without striking one another, stand by to offer ideas, if asked, but do not interfere. If children are arguing and physically hurting one another, tell an adult.

Rule 12: Use nonhurtful ways to express yourself and to get what you want.
Examples of this rule as suggested by the children:

    a. Speak politely to others (no teasing, bugging, swearing, putting down, or name calling).
    b. Resolve conflicts in a peaceful manner by discussing, persuading, negotiating, or compromising.

Implementation

All adults working with children at Adams School will proceed through the following steps in teaching and enforcing school rules.

Step 1: If a child's behavior violates a school rule, the child will be reminded of the rule and the reason behind it in a serious, firm tone. If the child complies, he or she will be praised. If the behavior continues, the adult will proceed to Step 2.

(continued on the next page)

FIGURE 6.2

(continued)

Step 2: The adult will issue a verbal warning to the child. The warning will include a repetition of the rule and identification of what logical consequence will occur if the child continues the unacceptable behavior. The warning will be stated matter-of-factly.

Step 3: The child will be given a few moments to comply. If this happens, the child will be praised. If compliance is not forthcoming, the adult will proceed to Step 4.

Step 4: The adult will follow through with the stated consequence.

If the rule violation involves the destruction of property, a logical consequence would be to have the child repair, replace, or clean up the damaged item or area.

If the rule violation involves unsafe use of objects or equipment or dangerous actions within the school building or on the playground, a logical consequence would be to have the child rehearse the appropriate alternate behavior with adult assistance if necessary.

If the rule violation involves dangerous or unkind acts toward peers (verbal and/or physical abuse), the logical consequences in the case of physical injury would be for the perpetrator to assist with first aid needs and accompany the victim to the nurse if necessary. In the case of emotional injury, the students involved will be expected to work toward reaching a mutually agreeable solution through dialogue. This may be supported through the efforts of an adult or peer mediator.

Step 5: If children fail to comply with the preceding consequences, they will be reminded that further noncompliance will result in the unrelated consequence of losing recess privileges.

Step 6: The child will be given a few moments to carry out the logical consequence. If the child complies, the episode is over, and the child may resume his or her normal activities.

If the child continues the problem behavior or refuses to carry out the logical consequence, he or she will be told to report to the planning room either immediately (if the incident occurs during the noon hour or recess) or at the soonest recess time. He or she will be given a paper identifying which rule was broken to give to the adult in charge. (The planning room will be supervised by different staff members on a rotating basis.)

❏ First visit within a week—The child remains in the planning room for the rest of the noon hour or recess (maximum of 15 minutes). The child works with the planning room supervisor to develop a prevention plan for avoiding this problem behavior in the future. Library books are available for children to read for the rest of the time. The behavior report and a copy of the child's prevention plan are sent to the child's teacher and to the principal.

❏ Second visit within a week (for the same infraction)—The child remains in the planning room for the rest of the noon hour or recess. Revisions are made to the prevention plan as needed. The behavior report and prevention plan are sent to the child's teacher, the principal, and the child's parents for a signature. Recess privileges will not be reinstated until the signed form is returned.

❏ Third visit within a week (for the same infraction)—The child will call his or her parent or write/dictate a letter explaining the problem. The principal or designate will cover for teachers who are supervising children throughout this phase. The parent will be informed that the next infraction for the week will result in a school conference between the family and school personnel. A signed form must be returned to the school in which the parent acknowledges receipt of this information.

FIGURE 6.2
(continued)

❏ Fourth visit within a week (for the same broken rule)—Parents will confer with student and school personnel before recess privileges are reinstated.

❏ Fifth visit within a week (for the same broken rule)—A 1-day in-school suspension will be invoked.

Students begin with a clean slate the first school day of each week.

October—Implementation   A newsletter was sent home from school to parents describing initial results of the plan. A PTO meeting was held highlighting the plan and giving parents opportunities to brainstorm related problem-solving strategies for use at home.

November—Implementation   Meetings were held with all paid and volunteer school personnel to discuss successes, concerns, and possible revisions.

January—Implementation   The guidance counselor began to train fourth and fifth graders who had volunteered to be playground mediators.

February—Implementation   Peer mediation on the playground began. Adult playground monitors participated in a workshop on cooperative games (at their own request) to gain strategies for promoting prosocial behavior on the playground.

March and April—Implementation   Meetings were held with parents, children, staff, and volunteers to discuss successes, concerns, and possible revisions.

May—Implementation   Plans were made for maintaining the Adams School Guidance Plan the next year.

The Results

After a year of implementation, initial results of the Adams School Guidance Plan as described in Figure 6.2 were positive. Surveys and interviews with teachers, administrators, volunteers, children, and parents indicated a widely held perception among all groups that the school atmosphere had greatly improved. On-site observations clearly showed that the adults' emphasis was on teaching children the rules and acknowledging children's positive behaviors rather than

simply penalizing inappropriate actions. Most infractions were dealt with on the spot. During the first three months of school, the planning room was used almost every week. However, no child moved beyond a second visit within a given week. By January, the planning room received less use. This trend continued throughout the rest of the year, with entire weeks of disuse occurring by May (Preston, 1991; Richberg, 1991). Six years later, the plan remains in effect, even though the program has experienced a change in principal and some teachers. The results remain positive, with both adults and children reporting a true sense of community at the school (C. Preston, Personal Communication, 1997). Adults and children have identified the following strengths as contributing to the plan's success:

❏ The plan was based on a team effort that included everyone who might potentially be affected by it.

❏ The plan set forth only a few broad rules that children, parents, and staff helped to define.

❏ It emphasized teaching alternative behaviors to replace inappropriate ones.

❏ It established a link between beliefs (rights) and actions (rules).

❏ It provided a consistent guide for appropriate school behavior known to everyone, adults and children alike.

❏ The plan included opportunities for home and school input over time.

❏ The plan included opportunities for staff, children, and parents to discuss ideas and work together to find solutions.

❏ The plan endowed all participants with a sense of competence, accomplishment, and hope.

The Adams School Guidance Plan is simply an example of one program's approach to adopting authoritative strategies aimed at enhancing children's development of self-discipline. The product it created was uniquely suited to its own circumstances and would not exactly match those of another program. However, the process the school went through is illustrative of what any program might do in creating its own programwide guidance plan.

QUESTIONS ADULTS ASK ABOUT PROMOTING SELF-DISCIPLINE IN CHILDREN

Teaching children self-discipline is a challenging task. This subject prompts many questions from teachers, administrators, and parents regarding philosophy and implementation. The following are some of the most common issues they think about.

Don't Authoritative Strategies Take Up a Lot of Time?

What If I Am the Only Teacher in the Room?

The guidance strategies early childhood professionals use when children are young influence the attitudes and dispositions they will carry with them into later life (Glasser, 1990; Katz & Chard, 1989). Likewise, the strategies they use early in the year affect how well children behave as the year goes on. If self-discipline is our ultimate aim, then we must consciously use the authoritative strategies that fit that goal, right from the start. Initially, such strategies will be more time consuming than authoritarian or permissive techniques. However, as the weeks and months go by, children will gradually grow in their ability to monitor their own behavior. As children's skills increase, not only will they refrain from inappropriate actions, but they will also initiate greater numbers of positive ones as well. When these conditions prevail, time spent on corrective action becomes less and less, making the initial investment of teacher time well worth the effort.

Practitioners who have sole responsibility for a group of children may wonder how they can afford to focus on one or two children in the midst of the group with no one else to supervise the remaining children. On these occasions, it helps to remember that when adults acknowledge children's positive behavior, set limits, or enforce consequences, these interactions serve as teachable moments both for the children whose behavior is their focus and for other children nearby. Thus, there is a ripple effect that comes from adopting an authoritative style. This results in a classroom environment in which adult actions are predictable, rational, and nonpunitive. All of these conditions promote self-discipline. The creation of such an environment is important for teams of adults and for adults who are on their own. As children gain the skills they need to monitor their own behavior, they become partners in the learning process. The need for an adult to provide continual on-the-spot supervision diminishes. Children take on this responsibility themselves. In the long run this saves time and makes it easier to manage the classroom.

Why Can't I Just Tell Children "No"? I've Heard of a Discipline Approach That Simply Informs Children of the Rules and Then Places a Checkmark for Each Violation by Their Names on the Board. It Sounds Like a Time Saver. What's Wrong With It?

When children misbehave, adults sometimes find it quicker and easier simply to say "Stop" or "We don't do that here." Occasionally these shortcuts have the desired effect: Children quit what they are doing. Unfortunately, such success is usually short lived, and children repeat the same infractions later on. Moreover, youngsters tend to comply only under direct supervision. The moment the adult's back is turned or the child is in a new circumstance, the problem behavior resumes. Such lapses occur because admonitions alone do not lead to children's internalization of the rules but to adherence instead (Palardy, 1995). The same is true for any disciplinary procedure that emphasizes rewards and consequences to the exclusion of reasoning, rehearsal, restitution, and cooperation. The former methods promote children's reliance on external controls; the latter enhance self-discipline.

Shouldn't Children Already Know How to Behave by the Time They Get to Kindergarten and First and Second Grade?

Children do not enter kindergarten and first and second grade having mastered the social realm. Even youngsters who have had the benefit of previous nursery school or childcare experience find that the expectations from teachers and peers in elementary school are more structured or elaborate than those they have encountered in the past. The first three years of elementary education mark a transitional period during which children must redefine themselves within the context of an institution more formal than the family, neighborhood, or child-care center (Alexander & Entwistle, 1988; Bickart, Dodge, & Jablon, 1997). Throughout this time children are determining the boundaries of the student role and ways to function successfully within it. As a result, children in the early grades continually experiment with assorted social strategies, discovering what works and what does not and what is allowed and what is not.

Not only does this kind of learning take time, but it cannot be hurried. Children are not simply memorizing school rules—they are having to construct an understanding of what each rule means as well as apply that conception to their own behavior. Consequently, knowing the rules and being able to follow them independently are two important but very different tasks, with the latter being much more challenging than the first. It is unrealistic for school personnel or parents to expect children to have achieved self-discipline before they enter school or soon thereafter. It takes years, not days or weeks, for such mastery to develop. For these reasons, child guidance deserves special consideration in the early elementary curriculum. Adults cannot simply demand that children engage in socially acceptable behaviors; instead, they must focus on teaching children how to do so.

How Can We Achieve Consistency Among All the Adults in Our Program?

The essential element in achieving long-term consistency is communication. Communication is enhanced when the following things occur:

❏ Guidance policies are written down and known to all.

❏ Orientations are conducted for new staff members and families.

❏ Periodic staff meetings are held in which practitioners brainstorm solutions to typical behavior problems, discuss ways to promote positive child behaviors, and reach a consensus about how certain rules will be interpreted and enforced.

❏ Program policies are reviewed and revised annually or as needed.

Communication is also essential day to day. This is especially true when some children push the limits with one adult, only to move on to someone else when a follow-through is in the offing. That is, the same child may engage in a series of inappropriate actions without experiencing any real consequences. Adults minimize such problems when they advise one another of the warnings they have given certain children. This is best done within the child's hearing so that he or she becomes aware that a particular rule is still in effect regardless of location. For instance, if Leona has been warned that pushing again on the playground will result in her having to sit on the side for 5 minutes, other staff members should be alerted that this is the case. Anyone seeing her push once more can enforce the consequence regardless of whether it takes place near the swings or on the slide. Such communication creates a consistent environment in which Leona will soon learn that pushing is truly unacceptable.

How Can We Promote Consistency Between the Way Guidance Is Handled in the Program and How It Is Addressed at Home?

The key to achieving some measure of consistency between home and program is to establish open channels of communication in which all parties feel valued and respected. The first step is for each group to share basic information. Parents need to know how children will be socialized in the early childhood setting and the rationale for particular goals and strategies. It is also necessary for them to receive accurate information about their own role in the process. Practitioners in turn need to know about parents' aspirations for their children and measures they use at home to promote these aims. This kind of information could be exchanged during a home visit, at a program orientation, or through written materials.

Consistency is further enhanced when parents, teachers, and administrators get together to explore values and philosophies. Workshops, parent-teacher conferences, and informal discussions at the classroom or program level are effective ways for school staff and parents to share ideas and problem-solving techniques related to child socialization (Bickart, Dodge, & Jablon, 1997; National Association of Elementary School Principals, 1990). These times are most productive when the emphasis is on mutual understanding and collaboration.

What Can Be Done When Conflicts Exist Between the Teacher's and Parents' Approaches to Discipline?

Many times the influential people in children's lives have different ideas about how children should behave. Consequently, they may advocate conflicting codes of conduct. For instance, in the interest of group harmony, program personnel may require children to respond to bullying from peers by using nonviolent strategies. Family members, more focused on children's self-defense skills, may encourage them to "fight it out" when threatened. Both ideas—harmonious living and personal safety—have merit, but they are different and seem to call for incompatible responses from children. This puts children in a dilemma: To obey one set of expectations, they have to violate another.

Whenever contradictory situations such as these arise, there are three ways they might be handled. The first is for teachers and parents to discuss their differences honestly and directly, searching for common ground. In the preceding situation, it is likely that both teachers and parents want children to be safe. They agree on the goal, but their means for achieving it differ. If they recognize their mutual aim, they will have a compatible base from which to explore potential resolutions to the child's predicament.

On other occasions, conflicts arise from differences in style. Teachers sometimes believe they have little in common with parents who hold nonauthoritative attitudes toward discipline. Likewise, parents who espouse more authoritarian or permissive philosophies may question the authoritative techniques used in the program. Under these circumstances, the most effective approach is to emphasize the similarities between philosophies rather than concentrating on the discrepancies (Bollin, 1989). Authoritarian and authoritative styles both advocate firm control and high standards; laissez-faire and authoritative styles promote warm, accepting relationships between children and adults. Discussing authoritative strategies in terms of how they support these overarching principles provides some common ground between philosophies.

For instance, parents with more authoritarian attitudes may believe that offering children choices is unnecessary or undesirable because youngsters should simply do as they are told. To help such parents feel more comfortable with choices for children, the teacher could point out that the adult first establishes boundaries on the child's behavior (such as getting dressed now) and then offers the child a choice (what color shirt to wear). This explanation combines an authoritative value (helping children achieve independence) with an authoritarian one (achieving compliance) and builds a bridge between the two.

A third strategy for reducing children's confusion over contradictory home-program expectations is to help children realize that adults have differing reactions to their behavior. This enables teachers to stress that certain standards may be situation-specific: "You're upset. At home you don't have to pick up. That may be, but it bothers me when the puzzles are all over the floor. Pieces could be lost. Here at the center everybody is expected to help. Find a puzzle to put away."

On those rare occasions when no mutually satisfactory resolution seems possible, it is best to acknowledge that differences exist and make clear to parents how and why authoritative strategies will be used at school. Children benefit from exposure to authoritative models, even when other adults in their lives are more authoritarian or permissive. Teachers and administrators who reason with children provide alternate models of interaction and problem solving for children to evaluate and try out themselves.

What About Sending Rule Violators to the Administrator's Office?

The old standby of sending children to see the principal or director when they are disruptive actually undermines the classroom teacher's authority and makes subsequent confrontations between adult and child more likely. Although teachers may wish to impress on children the seriousness of their misdeeds by banishing them from the classroom, the message actually conveyed is "I give up" or "I don't know how to handle your behavior." A better alternative is to use logical consequences consistently within the classroom each time children act in unacceptable ways. This familiarizes them with appropriate alternate behaviors and shows them that early childhood professionals mean what they say. Early on, teachers may have to sacrifice instructional time with the group in order to follow through on stated consequences with an individual child. The story may be set aside for the day or the math activity shortened. However, these immediate liabilities will be offset in the future because fewer such incidents will occur (Kostelnik et al., 1998). Children will come to recognize the predictability of the adult's response and discover that corrective action is always taken without the adult losing patience or giving in. Trips to the office will happen rarely and only in the most serious circumstances. When they do, it will be in the company of the teacher, who with the principal or director will participate in a team-oriented approach to problem solving with the child.

The Authoritative Style Doesn't Include Physical Punishment. Doesn't That Lead to Undisciplined Classrooms and Chaotic Programs?

Shouldn't Programs Hang On to Corporal Punishment as a Last Resort for Use With Children With Whom Nothing Else Works?

The answer to these questions is an unequivocal NO! Professionals who use or wish they could use spanking in early childhood settings assume that physical punishment improves children's behavior and contributes to a more effective learning environment. Nothing could be further from the truth.

There is no research evidence that corporal punishment in early childhood programs yields any positive outcomes. On the contrary, studies by such groups as the National Education Association (NEA), the Association for Childhood Education International (ACEI), and the National Parent Teacher Association (NPTA) have shown that rather than curbing disciplinary problems, corporal punishment makes them worse. For instance, children subjected to corporal punishment in centers and schools become more aggressive, destructive, and coercive over time (Hyman, 1990). Incidents of vandalism, attacks against program personnel, and more disruptive child behavior in the classroom, halls, and lunchrooms and on the playground have also been reported (Ball, 1989). Possible explanations for such trends include the obvious fact that no matter how it is structured, the adult administering the paddling is modeling aggressive behavior as an acceptable way of controlling the actions of other people. Because corporal punishment focuses on teaching through fear and pain it has many negative outcomes:

❏ Physical punishment keeps children at adherence and gives them no tools with which to build self-discipline.

❏ Children whose behavior is aggressive do not learn alternatives to such strategies when subjected to methods so closely mirroring their own. The lesson they learn is that might makes right.

❏ Children can become so used to physical pain that it is no longer a deterrent. In fact, children subjected to frequent paddlings sometimes interpret such punishment as a badge of honor and a way to gain status with peers. This is particularly true as children become older. As a result, children's unacceptable behavior continues.

❏ The use of physical punishment often serves as the stimulus for vengeful counterattacks by children in the future. These may be directed at either adults or peers.

Findings such as these indicate that corporal punishment benefits neither children nor the practitioners who carry it out (NAEYC, 1993; Vasta et al., 1995). Many nonviolent alternatives exist, and there are numerous schools and centers that effectively use the authoritative strategies described in this chapter. Such programs operate in urban, rural, and suburban communities; high-crime and low-crime areas; and wealthy and poor neighborhoods. Although each of these programs has its own approach to positive discipline, there are certain beliefs and practices they share in common (Coletta, 1994; Gootman, 1988; Hyman & D'Allasandro, 1984). Several of these were evident in the Adams School Guidance Plan described earlier in this chapter.

❏ Educators assume that teachers, children, administrators, and parents have the capacity to solve problems and make decisions.

❏ Time is allocated for program staff, children, and parents to plan and organize the alternative discipline system.

❏ The system that is ultimately devised is consistent throughout the school. Everyone is involved in a unified approach.

❏ All rules are based on the principles of safety and protection of property and rights. Those listed are kept at a minimum and are stated clearly and positively.

❏ Rules are enforced firmly, fairly, and matter-of-factly.

❏ The consequences for breaking the rules are logical and realistic.

❑ All staff and volunteers are trained in authoritative strategies.
❑ Parents are welcome in the program and encouraged to become involved in program activities.
❑ Methods for examining children's extreme behaviors are established, and appropriate referrals are available to children, parents, and staff.

From this discussion one can conclude that corporal punishment has no place in developmentally appropriate early childhood programs. Spanking hurts children, and it negates the development of self-discipline. As early childhood professionals, we are ethically responsibile for using discipline strategies that demonstrate respect and compassion toward children while also setting limits on inappropriate behavior. The authoritative strategies presented throughout this chapter represent a wide array of methods you can use in an effective approach to child guidance.

SUMMARY

Young children are not born knowing the rules of society or the settings in which they participate. How to achieve their goals in socially acceptable ways, get along with others, and adjust their personal behavior within the bounds of societal expectations are things children *have to learn how to do.* This learning begins at birth and continues throughout the school years. Parents, teachers, other significant adults in children's lives, and peers all contribute to the lessons children experience during this time. Initially, young children depend on others to direct their behavior for them. However, in time, they learn to respond to rewards and punishments or the moral codes of admired adults as clues for how to behave. These guides are useful and necessary but do not represent the most self-disciplined form of social behavior; that occurs only if children treat certain standards of conduct as logical extensions of their beliefs and personal values. Whenever children think about their behavior in that way, they are said to have reached internalization. Internalization equals self-discipline. Self-disciplined children do not simply comply with adult standards minus adult supervision. They grow into ethical, compassionate people who do what they think is right in order to support their internally constructed perceptions of right and wrong.

The extent to which children exhibit self-discipline is affected by developmental factors such as emotional maturity, cognition, language, and memory. Another major influence is children's daily experiences with people. Throughout the early childhood period, parents and teachers in particular have a tremendous impact on what social behaviors children adopt. These grownups use a variety of socialization strategies such as modeling, attribution, instruction, and consequences to help children learn acceptable codes of behavior. However, not all adults use or combine these strategies in the same way. Three of the most common variations—permissive, authoritarian, and authoritative—have been the subject of much research. All three styles have some positive attributes. But the permissive and authoritarian styles yield negative results that undermine self-regulation and positive social adjustment in children. The authoritative style has been most strongly linked to the development of self-discipline. Consequently, much of this chapter has been devoted to describing techniques associated with authoritative teaching. Such strategies can be applied in a single classroom or on a programwide basis.

That content is the subject of Part 3 of this text, which begins with Chapter 8.

✖ Applying What You Read in This Chapter

1. **Discuss**
   a. Based on your reading and experiences with young children, discuss each of the questions that open this chapter.
   b. Based on the ideas and strategies outlined in this chapter, discuss what you might do in the following situations:
      ❑ Jennifer and Marlene each want to use a rolling pin at the dough table. There is only one rolling pin available.
      ❑ The pretend play area is set up for four children. You notice seven children playing there.
      ❑ A parent calls to report that children are rowdy at the bus stop each day. She is worried that some of the younger children will get hurt as a result of the older children's chasing and shoving.
      ❑ Sharon slams her book on the table. "I can't read this. I'll never read this. It's too hard," she screams.

2. **Observe**

a. Observe a group of children in a classroom or outdoors. What are some of the positive behaviors you notice among the children? What are some of the problems they encounter in getting along? How do the children respond to one another in these situations? What implications do your observations have for your approach to child guidance?

b. Observe a classroom of teachers and children. What are some of the strategies adults use to guide children's behavior? Do these strategies support or detract from the long-range goal of helping children achieve self-discipline?

3. **Carry out an activity**

a. Read an article on child guidance. Summarize the primary points the author makes. Describe to what extent the article supports or challenges what you have read in this chapter.

b. Interview two early childhood educators who work with children of different ages. Ask them to describe the most common discipline problems they face. How do they solve those problems when they arise?

c. Attend a community presentation or workshop related to child guidance. What was the presenter's main message? What kinds of questions did people in the audience have about the topic? What is your reaction to what you heard?

4. **Create something for your portfolio**

a. Describe a situation in which you guided a child's behavior. What was the child doing? What did you do? How effective was your approach? What might you do if the same situation were to come up again?

b. Ask a supervisor to identify three strengths you demonstrate using an authoritative style with children. Also ask him or her to identify something you could be working on in the future. Develop a plan to maintain your strengths and improve in the area identified.

5. **Add to your journal**

a. What is the most significant thing you have learned about promoting self-discipline in children based on your readings and experience with children?

b. Describe what you would have to do to become more authoritative in your approach to child guidance.

c. Make a list of the most pressing questions you have about promoting children's development of self-discipline. Describe how you will obtain answers to your questions.

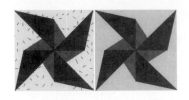

Chapter 7

Strengthening Developmentally Appropriate Programs Through Family Involvement

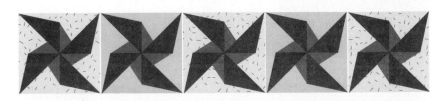

You may wonder:

What does family involvement really mean?

Why are people so interested in getting parents or other significant family members involved in early childhood programs? Would it not be easier if parents parented and teachers taught?

Why is it that some parents get so caught up in their children's education and other parents do not?

How should I respond to family members who seem unable or unwilling to become involved in the early childhood program?

What are some effective strategies for working with family members as partners in children's education?

In this chapter on building family partnerships in early childhood education, we present information to help you answer these questions.

A tear trickled down Tish Kelley's cheek. The mother of a 3-year-old, she thought that on the first day of preschool, her daughter would cling to her at least a little. But Joelle Kelley entered the classroom happily, eager to play with the toys and the other children. "Bye, mom, you can go now." Tish sighed, "Only 3 years old and already she doesn't need me."

In talking with the teacher at their spring conference, Jorge's grandmother mentions that 4-year-old Jorge seems uninterested in the phonics flashcards she has purchased. "He just doesn't care about learning to read," she laments.

During a home visit with the kindergarten teacher, Patrick's father explains that Patrick has been diagnosed as showing signs of Attention Deficit Disorder. He stresses that Patrick is a loving child who needs plenty of affection, simple directions, and clear boundaries.

At a school-sponsored curriculum night, Kathy Hale, a parent of a first grader, mentions that she is a weaver. She says, "My daughter loves to watch the loom in action. Would you like me to come in some time and show the children how to weave?"

Mrs. Salari wonders whether or not her 8-year-old son is showing signs of a learning disability. Her best friend says yes, her mother-in-law says no, and now she is asking your opinion as an early childhood professional.

Imagine you are the teacher in each of these circumstances. Take a moment to consider the family members you have just met. They are all different. Yet, they are also alike in many ways.

❏ Each of them is a significant person in the life of a young child.
❏ Each has an emotional investment in that child.
❏ All have ideas and opinions about raising and educating young children.
❏ Each family member has the potential to become more actively involved in the early childhood program in which his or her child participates.

What you do and say in situations like the ones just described will influence the degree to which families feel welcome in your classroom and to what extent they become active in their children's education. For this reason, it is important that you think carefully about your relationships with children's families and how you might encourage them to become involved in the early childhood program.

THE CHANGING NATURE OF FAMILY INVOLVEMENT IN EARLY CHILDHOOD EDUCATION

The notion of involving parents or other significant family members in children's early education is not new. For years, connecting home and school has been a fundamental aim of parent cooperative nursery schools, Head Start, and other early intervention programs. Those efforts have had such promising outcomes that now, when we talk about creating or maintaining developmentally appropriate education programs, we always include family involvement as an essential component (Bredekamp & Copple, 1997; Larson & Haupt, 1997). In fact, the National Association of State Boards of Education (NASBE, 1988) recommends that all education programs serving children ages 3 through 8 do the following things:

❏ Promote an environment in which family members are valued as primary influences in their children's lives and as essential partners in the education of their children.
❏ Recognize that the self-esteem of parents/significant family members is integral to the development of the child and should be enhanced by the family's positive interaction with the program.

❏ Include family members in decision making about their own child and the overall early childhood program.
❏ Assure opportunities and access for family members to observe and volunteer in the classroom.
❏ Promote an exchange of information and ideas between family members and teachers which will benefit the child.
❏ Provide a gradual and supportive transition process from home to school for those young children entering school for the first time. (p. 19)

The nature of family involvement described here contradicts long-standing stereotypes. First, it goes beyond focusing solely on parents to include *any* person who has primary responsibility for making decisions about the well-being of each child. In some families this includes grandparents or another elder in the family or even older siblings (Chang, Salazar, & DeLeong, 1994). The traditional role of family members attending the once-a-year "family night at the center" or simply providing refreshments for school parties has also been expanded. Opportunities for family inclusion in the life of the center or school are numerous and varied. Finally, the role of the early childhood program now encompasses more than the mere sponsorship of a fall open house or a periodic rounding up of experts to speak to family members about current issues in education. That old vision relegated family involvement to a few obligatory events dominated by one-way communication from the program to home. It assumed that educators knew best and family members knew little, and it assigned early childhood professionals leadership positions, with family members serving as followers. Today there is a clear emphasis on two-way communication and on families and professionals working together to enhance children's learning (Briggs, Jalongo, & Brown, 1997).

As you can see, the concept of family involvement within a developmentally appropriate framework is much more comprehensive, interactive, and collaborative than the stereotypic model people used to have in mind. Within this newer interpretation, involving family members in children's education is a continuous process that incorporates parents and other extended family members in various phases of the total educational program, including planning, implementation, and assessment (Bredekamp & Copple, 1997; Seefeldt, 1985). Family members and early childhood

TABLE 7.1
Five Major Types of Family Involvement

Type 1: Child Rearing	Type 2: Communicating	Type 3: Volunteering	Type 4: Learning at Home	Type 5: Representing Other Families
The program helps family members create supportive learning environments at home. Parents acquire the parenting and child-rearing skills needed to prepare children for school, supervise them, teach, and guide children at each level.	The program reaches family members through effective communications. Family members receive and respond to communications from the center or school regarding educational programs and children's progress.	The program recruits and organizes family help. Family members become directly involved on site—they assist teachers, administrators, and children in classrooms or other areas of the program. Family members also come to the school or center to support student performances or other events and attend workshops or other programs for their own education or training.	The program provides family members with ideas for helping children at home. Family members respond to child-initiated requests for help as well as ideas or instructions from teachers. Parents monitor or assist their children at home in learning activities that are coordinated with children's experiences at the school or center.	The program recruits and trains family members. Family members take decision-making roles on advisory councils or on other committees or groups at the program, district, or state level. Family members may become involved in community activities or independent advocacy groups that monitor the program and work for educational improvement.

Source: Adapted from Five Types of Parent Involvement: Linking Practices and Outcomes by J.L. Epstein, in *School and Family Partnerships: Preparing Educators and Improving Schools* (1998). Boulder, CO: Westview Press.

professionals form an alliance in which they develop a common understanding of what children are like—how they develop, how they behave, the challenges they face, and how they can be helped to meet these challenges. The adults also come to a shared conception of what good education is—what it looks like, how it operates, what it strives to achieve, what it requires, and what it precludes (Hymes, 1974). When such alliances occur, family members and teachers actually learn together, mutually supporting one another in their efforts to make life more meaningful for the children and themselves (Goldberg, 1997; Swick & Duff, 1978). In this way professionals and families become partners in the education process.

The coalition between family members and teachers can take place in several different ways and with varying degrees of participation by both groups. Joyce Epstein, a leading researcher on the subject, has identified five categories of family partnering that range from lesser to greater ties between children's homes and early education programs (see Table 7.1).

The desirability of all five types of family involvement is currently so well accepted that the federal government now mandates inclusion of parents and other significant family members as participants, advisors, and knowledgeable consumers of services in all phases of Project Head Start, the education of children with disabilities (Public Laws 94–142 and 99–457), and in federally administered childcare. State governments have followed suit as exemplified by the California School Improvement Plan and the Michigan Standards of Quality for Preschool Programs for Four-Year-Olds. As a result, in early childhood programs all across the United States, family members today are involved in children's education at all levels—from tutors at home to classroom participants, from volunteers to paid employees, from advisors to program decision makers. Those involved include first-time parents, teenage parents, older parents, single parents, dual-career parents, stepparents, parents of children with disabilities, grandparents, foster parents, aunts, uncles, and sometimes older brothers and sisters (Chang, Salazar, & DeLeong, 1994; Powell, 1989). Moreover, although originally targeted at programs for very young children, family participation efforts have reached beyond these, into elementary, middle, and high schools (Galen, 1991; Weinstein & Mignano, 1997). All of this has come about because we have discovered that children, parents, and programs benefit greatly when family members take an active part in young children's educational experiences.

HOW CHILDREN BENEFIT FROM FAMILY INVOLVEMENT

It is not possible to "grow" people unless you nurture their roots.—Martin Luther King, Jr. (1984)

Most of what each child learns has its roots in the home. There children first develop emotions and values, and there they learn to walk, talk, and make sense of their everyday surroundings. Parents teach not only directly but also indirectly by approving or disapproving and supporting or negating what children learn elsewhere (Bobbitt & Paolucci, 1986). Including parents and grandparents in early childhood programs, therefore, provides continuity between home and school and enhances children's learning in both environments. For instance, family participation has been linked to greater awareness and responsiveness in children, more complex child language skills, greater problem-solving abilities in children, increased academic performance, and significant gains in cognitive as well as physical skill development (Henderson & Berla, 1994; Larsen & Haupt, 1997).

HOW FAMILY MEMBERS BENEFIT

The two women met by chance at the grocery store—one a former "co-op" mom; the other, the cooperative nursery school teacher. "You'd never recognize Damon. He's 5 foot 6 and still growing," gushed the mom. Parent and teacher talked for several minutes about Damon's current

accomplishments at the middle school. The teacher was pleased. She remembered a time when this mother found her son's challenging behavior almost too much to bear. As they were about to part, the mother caught the teacher by the hand and whispered, "I never thanked you, you know. You were a life saver. You really helped me to appreciate my son. I've never forgotten it."

Although every family is not affected as dramatically as this mother was, the results of parents' involvement in their children's education are often very encouraging. Parents who become involved in their children's education are known to gain greater understanding of their children's development and needs, exhibit greater acceptance of children's individual differences, find more enjoyment in their children, and develop more flexible child-rearing attitudes (Brewer, 1998; Meier, 1978). Increased feelings of competence and self-worth have also been reported (Powell, 1989). Although there are no studies that focus exclusively on how extended family members benefit, we can assume that many of the advantages for parents are true for other family participants as well.

PROGRAM BENEFITS

The Community Calendar
Local Items of Interest:

This week the children and teachers in Mrs. Waters' room will be conducting child-led family conferences. The purpose of these conferences is for children, families, and teachers to work together to review each child's progress and plan future goals.

Families and staff at the Glencairn Elementary School planned, raised funds, and helped build a new playground for the children during the past year. Called the "Field of Dreams," this playground is a real dream come true.

Family and community members provided 1,600 volunteer hours for the Reading First program at Allen Street School.

Today's "KIDS at the Capitol" rally was held to draw legislative attention to children's issues in our state. Among the participants were parents and grandparents from our local Maple Hill Head Start Center as well as other early childhood programs statewide.

Obviously, children and families benefit when families are closely involved in the life of the center or school. The same is true for early childhood programs overall. For instance, active participation by family members has been found to provide them with more accurate and timely information regarding program aims and strategies. Closer contact between home and school gives both family members and teachers a more complete picture of children's abilities and improves their consistency in working toward desired goals (Umansky, 1983). This in turn seems to promote family identification with the program, which heightens family members' satisfaction and increases children's success (Bronfenbrenner, 1977; Revicki, 1982). Additionally, as parents and other family members become more influential in program decision making and increasingly active in school or center activities, they are more likely to communicate to children the importance of the programs in which both they and the children are involved (U.S. Department of Education, 1986).

Involved family members also serve as additional human resources to early childhood programs, extending the reach of the program, making it possible for children to receive more individual attention, and making available additional knowledge and skills to teachers and administrators (Berger, 1995; Institute for Responsive Education, 1990). Finally, we know that highly involved parents and grandparents are more likely to support program policies, offer financial assistance, and rally community efforts to promote or maintain the early childhood programs with which they are affiliated.

BARRIERS TO FAMILY INVOLVEMENT

With all the benefits that come from family involvement, it seems that both teachers and families would be eager to engage in the process. Yet, frequently families and professionals have certain misperceptions about one another that hinder the development of effective home-school relations. For instance, the two groups sometimes feel that they are working at cross purposes (see Table 7.2) (Gonzalez-Mena & Widmeyer, 1997).

With so many demands on their attention and so many hopes wrapped up in the children, families and professionals often find it difficult to understand one another's point of view. They may interpret different ways of doing things as wrong or as subtle criticisms of their own approaches or as deliberate attempts to undermine their goals. None of these perceptions foster feelings of trust and cooperation.

Another dilemma occurs when family members and teachers both feel unwelcome (the family member in the program or the teacher in the home) or ill suited

TABLE 7.2
Mutual Misperceptions of Teachers and Families

Teachers Wonder Why Family Members	Families Wonder Why Teachers
Tend to linger after saying good-bye to their child. (Don't families know this makes the separation process harder?)	Are in such a rush to get them out of the room. (Don't teachers know this makes the separation process harder?)
Push for academics too soon. (Don't families know how children learn?)	Don't make the program more like "real" school. (Don't teachers know I want my child to learn?)
Get upset when their child gets dirty. (Can't families see this is a sign of learning?)	Don't keep their children cleaner. (Can't teachers see this is a sign of learning?)
Don't do a better job teaching children to behave. (They can't control him at home but want us to control him at the program.)	Don't do a better job teaching children to behave. (They can't control him at the program but want us to control him at home.)
Always criticize them. (Can't families see we're doing our best?)	Always criticize us. (Can't teachers see we're doing our best?)

Family members need to feel welcome in the program to become involved in children's learning.

to function in a collegial capacity (the parent as teacher or the teacher as peer). The teacher may be viewed as less helpful and less interested in the family than he or she really is, and teachers are likely to underestimate family members' strong desire to be included in their children's education (Weinstein & Mignano, 1997). For example, researchers affiliated with the Carnegie Foundation for the Advancement of Teaching (CFAT) report that of the 21,000 teachers they contacted, 90 percent considered the level of parental involvement in their classrooms inadequate (CFAT, 1988). Yet, less than half the teachers responding to a subsequent survey made family involvement a high priority in their classrooms. They believed that such efforts would prove fruitless (Brandt & Epstein, 1989; Walde & Baker, 1990). Convinced that today's parents (especially from low-income, single-parent, and dual-career families) would be unwilling or unable to participate in program-related activities, many teachers chose not to involve them at all. However, the results of several family questionnaires throughout the past decade run counter to this perception. Large numbers

of parents (as many as 90 percent) report caring a great deal about their children's performance in school and being interested in learning effective ways to support children's learning on the home front (Epstein, 1986; Snow, 1982). Approximately 20 percent of the parents surveyed were already successfully involved. Another 70 percent wanted to become more active in their child's schooling but did not know how to go about it (Brandt & Epstein, 1989). In particular, inner-city parents, single parents who work outside the home, and parents of children beyond the preschool years report the fewest opportunities for contact with teachers and other program personnel (Berger, 1995).

This huge discrepancy between family members' stated desires and the degree to which they actually participate stems from several sources. Some family members believe that because they lack professional teaching skills, they are unsuitable partners in the educational process (Froyen, 1993). Others hold back because they are unsure of what to do—how to offer support at home or what strategies to use. Still others feel rebuffed because, at their child's school or center, family involvement is confined to menial tasks or is so ill timed (last-minute, inconvenient hours) or so poorly conceived (disorganized, irrelevant, and uninteresting) that only a few family members have the means or desire to come forward. In other cases, family members answer requests for volunteering but receive no follow-up contact or acknowledgment of their interest. Also, it is not uncommon for family members to be treated as intruders at school. Rebuffed, ignored, or patronized, many family members conclude they have little to contribute (Greenberg, 1989; Rosenthal & Sawyers, 1996).

These obstacles to family involvement are intensified among low-income families, many of whom have a history of unfavorable school experiences dating from their own childhood. They may relive those unhappy times when their offspring enter programs outside the home. Moreover, because it is not unusual for program personnel to focus on what they perceive to be low-income or minority family deficits, family members' initial negative perceptions are often reinforced. Matters become worse over time because low-income families are usually contacted by teachers or administrators only when their children are having problems (Institute for Responsive Education, 1990). These kinds of encounters contribute to families' feelings of shame, anger, distrust, or hopelessness, all of which detract from their motivation to become involved in the formal education process.

A readjustment of attitudes in programs and at home as well as more concerted efforts to emphasize the partnership aspects of family involvement are needed if these obstacles to family involvement are to be overcome. Evidence currently indicates that the early years are an optimal period for this to happen (Briggs, Jalongo, & Brown, 1997).

CHARACTERISTICS OF EFFECTIVE FAMILY INVOLVEMENT

As educators have become increasingly aware of the benefits of family involvement and the obstacles that sometimes hinder its development, their attention has shifted from answering the query "Why?" to exploring the question "How?" Consequently, much of the research of the past decade has focused on discovering those variables that characterize effective family involvement efforts. From these studies, four key elements have been

identified: collaboration, variety, intensity, and individuation. A brief overview of each of these follows.

Collaboration

Parents and teachers are more similar than different—they have many goals in common and a need to share information. (Brewer, 1998, p. 163)

Collaborative relations between early childhood personnel and families yield fruitful results for adults as well as for children. Such relations are most apt to develop when families and teachers recognize each other's importance in the life of the child. Because neither school nor family has the resources to take on the entire job of educating the young, it is not in their best interests to attempt to duplicate one another's efforts. Rather, children's education is enhanced when home and school see themselves as distinct entities, performing complementary, interconnected functions (Griffore & Bubolz, 1986). One interpretation of how family members and teachers might function in a mutually supportive relationship is offered in Table 7.3.

TABLE 7.3
The Home-School Alliance

10 Things Family Members Wish Teachers Would Do	10 Things Teachers Wish Family Members Would Do
Help build children's self-esteem.	Provide the resources at home for reading and learning.
Get to know each child.	
Communicate often and openly with families.	Set a good example.
Give family members direction for how to work with children at home.	Encourage children to try to do their best in school.
Maintain high academic and behavioral standards.	Emphasize academics.
Welcome and encourage family involvement.	Support the program's rules and goals.
Be active in and support family council or PTA activities and/or projects.	Call teachers more often and earlier if there is a problem.
Provide enrichment activities.	Take responsibility as parents.
Expect and encourage respect for other children, classroom visitors, and yourself.	View drinking alcoholic beverages by underage youth and excessive partying as a serious matter, not a joke.
Remember that family members are allies and want to help.	Be aware of what is going on in the early childhood program and become more involved in program activities.

Source: From PTA Today, November 1984. Complete article available from the National PTA, 700 N. Rush St., Chicago, IL 60611-2571. © 1988 National PTA School Is What WE Make It! planning kit. Adapted with permission.

Collaboration is enhanced when there are open channels of communication between professionals and families and when they work together to enhance children's learning (Brewer, 1998; Epstein, 1998). Thus, family involvement represents a balance of power between families and teachers—a partnership. In this partnership each member is valued and recognized as a "child expert." Families know their own child better than anyone else does. Teachers know many different children and also have specialized knowledge of child development, program content, and educational strategies. When family members and teachers combine their areas of expertise, collaboration becomes a reality.

Variety

Lisa Digby is the room mother for her son's second-grade classroom. She belongs to the PTO and the library committee. Whenever a job needs doing at school, Mrs. Digby can be counted on to help.

Carole Wilson has been to school once, the day she enrolled her daughter for kindergarten. She works an 8-hour shift at a shirt factory and has a part-time job at Red's, a local convenience store. She has little time to spend at school volunteering.

If you were to talk to these mothers, you would find that both are keenly interested in their child's early education, and both want to be included in some way. However, what works for one will not necessarily suit the other.

Family members differ in the extent to which they are willing or able to take part in educational programs and in how they wish to be included. Consequently, effective family involvement encompasses a variety of means for family members to participate and does not require all parents to be involved in the same ways, at the same time, or to the same degree (Epstein, 1998). Variety can be considered in terms of the kinds of contacts that occur between home and program, the format they take, who initiates them, for what purpose exchanges are made, where they occur, how frequently they take place, the resources required for participation, and the level of response necessary for success to be achieved. These variations are outlined in Figure 7.1.

The more variety, the better. This is true both within a single home-program interchange and across the whole array of contacts that transpire throughout the child's life at the center or school. When a broad mixture of family involvement opportunities is created, programs demonstrate their interest in and acceptance of many different kinds of families. Also, families receive visible proof that they may contribute according to their own preferences, talents, resources, and degree of comfort with the interface between home and early childhood program (Berger, 1995).

Intensity

> *The more we get together, together, together,*
> *The more we get together, the happier we'll be.*

This familiar children's song makes an important point that can be applied to family involvement. The greater the number of contacts between families and the early childhood program and the more frequently they occur, the more likely it is that parent participation outcomes will be positive (Lazar, 1981; Powell, 1989). This suggests that a certain duration of contact is necessary to promote the development of trusting relationships between parents and practitioners. Also, when opportunities for involvement are numerous, families can more easily find entrees to programs that better suit their needs and interests. In addition, it has been found that family members generally do not feel a part of their child's education unless the school or center places particular emphasis on involving them (Gotts & Purnell, 1986). Frequent, varied contact over time conveys the message that parents are valued by the program and that their inclusion is not simply tolerated but actually welcomed and expected.

Individuation

> *Every shoe fits not every foot.*—Anonymous

Educational programs are most likely to elicit a positive response from families when opportunities for participation are tailored to meet families' particular needs and perceptions (Eastman, 1988; Epstein, 1998). There is no one formula for family involvement and no single program that can be generalized successfully to every population. Instead, the best outcomes emerge when there is a match between what early childhood programs set out to do and what families want, when there is congruence between the strategies implemented and those to which family members feel receptive, and when program designers take into account

Kind of Contact
Predetermined agenda – – – informal structure

Scheduled – – – spontaneous
Face-to-face – – – indirect

Format
Written – – – verbal
Goal directed – – – open ended
Presentation or discussion – – – hands-on experience
Large group – – – small group – – – individual

Purpose
Provide input – – – elicit input – – – collaborate
Build – – – establish – – – maintain – – – change relationships,
    goals, strategies

Initiator
Child – – – family member – – – program personnel

Location
Home – – – program – – – community

Frequency
One-time event – – – several times – – – continuous

Role of Parent
Receiver of information – – – program supporter – – – audience –
– – home tutor – – – classroom participant – – – colearner – – –
decision maker – – – advocate

Resources Required
Time and energy (ranges from little to much) – – – skills (ranges
from few to many, general to specialized)

It is possible to combine variables within each characteristic as
well as create combinations among them.

family constraints such as childcare and transportation needs, employment obligations, and economic or physical stress, such as fatigue from coping (Powell, 1989; Shoemaker, 1995). Once this process is under way, the chances for collaboration improve; as collaboration becomes greater, so do opportunities for individuation.

As you might assume, families are more likely to become partners in their children's education when practitioners take into account collaboration, variety, intensity, and individuation. Because those dimensions of family involvement are so important, they provide the backdrop for the rest of this chapter. In the pages that follow, you will read about specific strategies for creating partnerships with families around children's early education.

EFFECTIVE FAMILY INVOLVEMENT TECHNIQUES

All of the strategies suggested here could be used in individual classrooms or generalized to whole programs. We have listed about 50 different ideas to give you a wide array of options to consider. *However, no single person or program would institute every strategy.* A more likely approach would be to adapt one or two ideas from each of several categories to create a comprehensive family involvement plan. Such plans would be individualized to meet the needs of the children, families, and staff members within your program. Regardless of how simple or elaborate a family involvement plan might be, the goal is always the same—to reach out to families and help them feel included and an integral part of their child's education (Kendall, 1996). The first step is always the same, too—to establish positive relationships with families.

Establishing Relationships With Families

It's important to me that families know as much as they can about me so that they can feel comfortable leaving their child with me. It's not easy leaving your child with a stranger.—Texia Thorne, teacher

I think they're terrific. The teachers seem to care not only for my children, but they care about me. When I come in looking tired, they ask me, "How are you doing? What can I do to help you? How are you feeling?—Debbie King, Kristine's mom

No matter what your position in an early childhood program—practitioner-in-training, teacher, or administrator—you can begin to establish positive relationships with the families of the children in your group. Follow these simple guidelines to forge closer ties with the most significant people in children's lives.

Show that you truly care about each child. An old Danish proverb states, "Who takes the child by the hand takes the mother by the heart." Keep this message constantly in mind and recognize that, first and foremost, families want early childhood professionals to pay attention to their children and treat them as special (Reisman, 1996). Show families you care by treating each child as an important, valued human being. Demonstrate this in your words and deeds each day. Recognize, also, that a loving education includes making sure that children go outdoors with all the clothing their family sent that day, that children's noses get wiped, that children's tear-stained faces get washed, and that notes from home are read and answered. Oversights of these "details" speak volumes to families and may give the unintended impression that you are too busy or uninterested to care.

Make personal contact with families. There is no substitute for face-to-face communication between people. If you are fortunate enough to work in an early childhood program in which families come into the building to drop off or retrieve their children, take advantage of these times to greet family members, inquire about their day, and have a friendly word. This means making yourself available at these times rather than rushing about making last-minute preparations or focusing solely on getting the children into their coats to go home. If you do not see families on a regular basis, take advantage of the times when you do. Mingle with family members at program events rather than chatting with your colleagues. Put yourself in the role of host, greeting family members and seeing that they have things to do or people with whom to talk.

Treat parents and other significant family members as individuals. Communicate with them on a one-to-one basis, not only in groups. Periodically, provide time for family members to talk with you privately. Interact with them as people in their own right, not simply as Felicia's mom or Pedro's dad.

Show genuine interest in family members by listening carefully and responding. A real barrier to family involvement occurs when family members form the impression that early childhood personnel are too busy or too distant to give much thought to what family members are thinking or feeling. Dispel this notion by doing the following things:

❏ *Provide openings for family members to share their concerns or inquire about their child's program experience.* "What changes have you seen in Jack recently?" "What are Anne's favorite play activities at home?" "Do you have anything you're wondering about regarding Suman's development?"

❏ *Listen attentively when family members talk to you.* Maintain appropriate eye contact and provide other nonverbal cues such as nodding or matching the person's mood with congruent affect to show you are grasping their message. (For instance, if a family member is telling you something humorous, respond with smiles. If the tenor is serious, respond in kind.)

❏ *Ask questions relevant to family comments.*

❏ *Invite family members to elaborate on what they are saying.* "Tell me more about that" or "Then what happened?" Such comments help family members to feel heard and valued.

❏ *Remain silent long enough for family members to gather their thoughts.* Once you have asked a question or made a remark in response to something a family member has said, pause. Avoid rushing on with additional talk simply because you are unsure of what to do next.

❏ *Respond to family member's queries honestly and directly.* If you do not know the answer to something, say so. Promise to find out. Then do it.

Be courteous to family members. Treat family members with consideration and respect. Pay attention to nonverbal behaviors (e.g., facial expressions, posture, and gestures) and words. Implement the following strategies daily:

❏ *Greet family members when you see them.* Address them by their proper names, using Mr., Ms., Mrs., or Dr. Pronounce family names correctly.

❏ *Avoid using professional jargon unnecessarily.* Using terminology people do not understand implies an unequal relationship and sometimes makes families feel unwelcome or uncomfortable talking with you. Use familiar words to explain what you mean (for instance, talk about "children working together" instead of "cooperative learning," "pretend play" instead of "imitation and symbolic play," "acknowledging the child's point of view" instead of "reflective listening," and so on).

❏ *Avoid addressing notices and newsletters home with the words "Dear Parents."* This implies that all children in the program are living in two-parent families. A more inclusive salutation would be "Dear Family Members."

❏ *Arrange to have relevant program materials translated in the home languages of the families in your classroom.* Provide a translator (perhaps a family member from another family) to facilitate conversations between you and new families whose home language you do not speak. Learn a few words in each family's home language. If family members feel embarrassed about their English skills, it is sometimes helpful to share how frustrated you "feel at not being able to communicate in the parents' language. This helps to break down any tinge of superior/inferior perceptions from the relationship, and keeps both of you on the same level as human beings" (Lee, 1997, p. 58).

Honor family confidentiality. Mrs. LaRosa's husband left her this morning. Shannon O'Malley is thinking about going back to school. Vincent Kaminski has been

diagnosed with a serious illness. LaKeesha Marcus was fired today. All of these family concerns may have been shared with you by family members who trust you to keep them to yourself. Maintain that trust. Remember that personal information should never be shared with anyone not directly involved in the problem, including coworkers, members of other families, or outside friends (Lane & Signer, 1990). Not only is violating this trust unethical, but it could also ruin your relationship with the family and that family member's relationship with the program forever.

Focus on family strengths. Early childhood professionals enhance the possibilities for relationship building when they look for family strengths rather than focusing solely on what appear to be family faults (Hohman & Weikart, 1995; Rosenthal & Sawyers, 1996). You can achieve this in several ways:

❏ *Concentrate on what family members can do, not only on what they have difficulty accomplishing.* Make a deliberate effort to identify at least one strength for each family in your class. Find ways to build on these strengths during the year.

❏ *Catch yourself using judgmental labels in reference to families.* When this happens, try to think of them in alternate ways. For instance, initially you might think, Sarah comes from a "broken" home. Leon is a "fatherless" child. Shift to a more positive perspective. Sarah comes from a family in which her grandmother is tremendously supportive. Leon's mom works hard to keep her family together. You need not totally ignore family problems or concerns, but you should avoid "labeling" families and thinking of them in a deficit mode.

❏ *Listen respectfully when children share information about their family with you.* Be careful to avoid making judgmental comments such as "How awful" or "I wouldn't boast about that." Instead, reflect children's feelings about what they have shared (e.g., "You sound excited" or "That worried you.").

❏ *Make sure classroom materials reflect the culture groups and family compositions of the families in your group.* This is a very visible sign that you value each child's family.

❏ *Try to look at situations from the family's point of view.* For instance, a parent who is having a difficult time separating from his child at nursery school is not simply being uncooperative. Rather, he may be feeling guilty about leaving the child or worried that the child is not getting the attention he would receive at home. Likewise, a parent who fails to respond to a call from the program may be overwhelmed by work demands, not simply uninterested in her child. Trying to see things from each family's perspective will help you to appreciate family circumstances and find alternate, more effective means of communicating.

❏ *Provide positive feedback to families about their children's progress and their own childrearing successes.* Offer information to family members illustrating children's increasing abilities. For instance, knowing that Ruby's mother was concerned about Ruby's skills in relating to other children, the teacher sent home the following note. "Today, Ruby offered her turn at the computer to a child who was anxious to get involved before time ran out. She did this all on her own. I thought you'd enjoy hearing about her growing awareness of the needs of others." Comments or brief notes about things both you and the family are working on together go a long way toward helping families feel like partners in the education process.

Share control with families. If family members are to become truly involved, we must be willing to include them as partners in the education process (Hohman & Weikart, 1995). There are several ways in which you can communicate this desire to families.

❏ *Take your cues from family members.* If they indicate a desire to communicate in certain ways, follow through. If the message seems to be, "I'm not ready," avoid pushing too hard. Wait a while and then try again. Interact with families in ways that seem to feel most comfortable to them. Some family members will appreciate a phone call, others would prefer you communicate in writing, and still others would like an in-person conference. Try to accommodate these preferences as best you can.

❏ *Learn from family members.* Watch how a mother interacts with her child: What words does she use, and what nonverbal behaviors do you see that seem to be effective? Imitate these in your own behavior with the child. Ask family members about their children. How do they help the child make transitions at home? What are the child's special interests? This kind of information could be a tremendous

help in facilitating your communication with each child and says to families that you value their knowledge and skills.

❏ *Collaborate with family members on decisions regarding their child's education experience.* Deciding together on certain goals for children and strategies for achieving those goals is an important component of shared control. So is including family members in finding solutions to problems. Do not simply announce to parents what you are going to do to address certain issues in the classroom. Instead, if you see that a problem is developing in which help from home would be useful (e.g., Samantha is having a hard time separating from her mother; Doug is not paying attention to directions in class; Marcel is getting into fights with children on the playground), initiate a dialogue with the appropriate family members and invite them to work with you in finding a solution (Gonzalez-Mena & Widmeyer, 1997). When you engage in these practices, shared control clearly translates into shared decision making.

Make frequent attempts to include families in children's early education. Begin by planning several simple contacts throughout the year rather than depending on one elaborate event. Offer some one-time involvement opportunities (such as an orientation or a hands-on workshop) as well as a few that encourage sustained participation over time (such as a weekly newsletter, inviting family members to volunteer in the classroom each month, or asking for periodic help with materials at home).

Offer many different ways for families to become involved in their children's education. Remember to diversify the kind of contacts you make, the format they take, their purpose, and location. Also, vary what role family members assume as well as the time, energy, and physical resources required to participate. Make sure to create involvement opportunities related to all five types of family involvement. Examples of a variety of practices to support each type are presented in Table 7.4.

Tailor the involvement strategies you select to meet the needs of the families with whom you are working now. Avoid relying on the same approaches time after time without considering how family needs might differ from one year to the next. For instance, last year a Saturday morning pancake breakfast was just the thing to

TABLE 7.4

Examples of Practices to Promote the Five Types of Family Involvement

Type 1: Child Rearing	Type 2: Communicating	Type 3: Volunteering	Type 4: Learning at Home	Type 5: Representing Other Families
Provide suggestions for home conditions that support children's learning.	Conduct conferences with every family at least once a year, with follow-up as needed.	Develop a school or center volunteer program whose focus is on supporting early learning activities.	Provide information to families on concept and skill development in young children.	Encourage family participation and leadership on center or school advisory councils or committees such as curriculum or playground improvement.
Provide workshops, videotapes, computerized phone messages on child-rearing and school center issues.	Make available translators for families who speak languages other than your own.	Create a family club for school volunteers.	Provide calendars that describe simple daily or weekly learning activities that families can try at home with their children.	Support family members as they become involved in independent advocacy groups
	Send home anecdotes regarding children's progress and participation in program activities for parents to review and comment on.	Conduct an annual survey to identify all available talents, times, and interests of family volunteers.	Make available a toy-lending library for family use that includes a variety of appropriate educational materials.	
	Provide opportunities for families to communicate information, knowledge, needs, and opinions to people in the program.	Invite family members to participate in the classroom on a one-time or ongoing basis.	Conduct workshops in which family members learn how to teach specific early learning skills via home activities.	
	Create opportunities for informal conversations between family members and program personnel: coffee klatches, once-a-month breakfasts or lunches with the children at the center, forums, open houses, interactive workshops, and program-initiated outings are typical social events that can bring the people from home and program closer together.			
	Make available a family library containing books about children's development and learning. Include books that contain games, activity ideas, and toys to make from simple household materials.			

Source: Adapted from the Five Types of Parent Involvement: Linking Practices and Outcomes by J.L. Epstein, in *School and Family Partnerships: Preparing Educators and Improving Schools* (1998). Boulder, CO: Westview Press. Adapted with permission.

stimulate family interest and enjoyment of the program. This year, however, the children have been creating a classroom museum. A visit by family members to take a tour of the project might be a better match between the children's interests and their desire to include their families in their investigations. Likewise, you may have found that in the past, evening family/teacher forums have been successful for attracting family input into the program. However, due to changes in families' life circumstances, evening sessions may be more of a burden than they used to be. If that is the case, try something else. In addition to avoiding habitual approaches, be cautious of commercially prepared parent involvement programs. These do not always match the interests and requirements of a particular group of families. If your school or center has adapted such a program, review it carefully. Carry out only those segments that are suitable for your group.

Gathering Information From Families

Vivian Paley, a former kindergarten teacher and noted author, tells the story of a father who came to school to share with the children memories of his childhood. Inviting family members to tell family stories was one way she found to gather family information that was comfortable for adults and valuable for children (Paley, 1995, p. 46).

> "I was born in a small village near Calcutta in India," Vijay's father tells the class. "We had a sliver of a stream that ran along between our village and the forest. From the moment our summer holidays began, all the children played in the stream. We built dams out of stones to make the water tumble faster and we sailed pieces of wood, pretending they were ships on the ocean. One day my cousin Kishore screamed that he saw a bear in the woods and we all ran home. Then he said it was a joke and we were all angry with him. However, we didn't want to waste time being angry because soon it would be time to return to school. And, so, every day, if our mothers wanted to find us, they knew we would be playing in the stream."
>
> We stare at Mr. Shah as we had never seen him before. Then we look at Vijay, our shy Vijay, and he is grinning. "There!" his smile seems to be saying. "Now you see how much there is to know about me."

Gathering information from families could happen informally (e.g., chatting with families at drop-off and pick-up time or making conversation at program events) as well as in more formal ways. A few basic strategies are outlined next.

Use enrollment or intake information as a way to learn more about the families of the children in your classroom. When families first enroll their children in an early childhood program, they are often asked to supply information about their child in writing on an enrollment form or verbally through an initial intake interview. Typical questions families might be asked are presented in Figure 7.2.

Throughout the program year, invite family members to share anecdotes and information about their child. These might be used as the basis for classroom activities and to increase your knowledge of the child and his or her family. Word such requests as invitations to share information, not as commands to meet your expectations. Figures 7.3 and 7.4 offer two examples.

Ask for input from family members about their learning goals for their children. Talk with parents/ grandparents about children's activities at home as well as what skills or behaviors they would like to see further developed. Give them a short list of program-related goals for children such as those depicted in Figure 7.5. Ask them to rank these goals in relation to their own child and according to their own perceptions of which are least important and which are most important. Collect the information and use it in designing activities for the classroom. Refer to family members' lists periodically, and use them as the basis for some of your communications with families throughout the year.

Find out about family interests and discover ways in which family members might like to become involved in the early childhood program. Recently, a mother asked if she could visit her child's kindergarten for the morning. The teacher, very pleased, said yes and assigned the parent to the art table. Several weeks later, by happenstance, the teacher found out the mother was an accomplished cabinet maker. Although the mother had enjoyed the art area, the teacher regretted having missed an opportunity to have her help children with some real woodworking skills. This oversight was not a major problem; however, it points out the importance of knowing each family member's talents and interests and making plans with those interests in mind. Some teachers use a family interest form like the one shown

FIGURE 7.2

Family Information of Interest to Educators

Source: Adapted from *Parents as Partners in Education* by E.H. Berger. (1995). New York: Macmillan; *The Anti-Bias Curriculum: Tools for Empowering Children* by L. Derman-Sparks and the ABC Task Force, 1989, Washington DC: National Education of Young Children; *Roots and Wings: Affirming Culture in Early Childhood Settings* by S. York. (1991). St. Paul, MN: Toys n' Things Press; and Michigan State University Child Development Laboratories enrollment forms.

Family Structure

❑ How many children are in your family?
❑ Who lives in your household?
❑ Who else takes care of your child during the day or on weekends?
❑ How are decisions made in your family?

Child Rearing

❑ What words does your child use for urination? Bowel movement? Private body parts?
❑ Describe your child's eating schedule.
❑ What foods does your child like or dislike? Are there any foods to which your child is allergic?
❑ Describe your child's sleeping schedule.
❑ How do you put your child to sleep?
❑ How does your child react when he or she is angry or unhappy? Excited or confused?
❑ How does your child relax or comfort himself or herself?
❑ What are your child's favorite activities?
❑ How do you handle the following situations?

Toilet training
Sharing
Messy play (paints, sand, water)
Sex roles
Racial concerns

❑ Who does your child play with at home?
❑ What rules do you have for your child at home?
❑ What do you do to teach your child to behave?
❑ What are your child's responsibilities at home?
❑ Are there other things you think we should know about your child?

Family Culture

❑ What is your ethnic or cultural background?
❑ What languages are spoken in your home?
❑ What traditions, objects, or foods symbolize your family?

in Figure 7.6 to form a sense of how to tailor family involvement opportunities to best suit individual families. Such a form could be presented and explained during a family gathering, program orientation, or home visit. This is also a good tool for family "mentors" to use and talk about with new families.

Seek out cultural information. Read about the cultural heritage of the families you serve and then check with them to see if what you learned through reading accurately reflects their practices and beliefs (Mangione, Lally, & Signer, 1993). Carol Brunson Phillips, national coordinator of the Child Development Associate Credential, offers this advice for early childhood professionals who are working with children from cultures other than their own. Early childhood professionals "have a responsibility to get their hands on some good literature about the cultural groups with whom they are working, and begin to take that information

FIGURE 7.3
Request for Information About Child: Example 1

Dear Families:

Soon we will begin a unit on how people are born and grow. We need some pictures and information about your child as a baby. Please fill out this form and use this plastic bag to send in one or two baby pictures of your child or your child's "baby book" if you have one. We will be sure to keep things clean and safe and will return them by the end of next week.

Our Child as an infant

Our child, _____, was _____, inches long at birth and weighed _____ pounds. Our child liked to eat _____ when he/she was a baby. He/she didn't like _____.His/her first word was _____. His/her hair was _____. (Please share any information that would tell us about the child as a baby such as habits, sleeping patterns, favorite toys, etc.)

Source: Adapted from *Teaching Young Children Using Themes*, M.J. Kostelnik (Ed,), 1991, Glenview, IL: Good Year Books.

FIGURE 7.4
Request for Information About Child: Example 2

The Family Name Game

Purpose:	To record some of your family names and expressions for things to help your child discover your family's unique language.
You'll need:	Pen or pencil
Time:	Varies
How to do it:	Write the names or expressions your family has used or uses now for these categories. *Warning:*You may need extra sheets of paper. One family who did this activity came up with over 40 names they call their cat.

People (nicknames)	Pets (nicknames)	Places (rooms, community places)
_____	_____	_____
_____	_____	_____
_____	_____	_____

Food (meals, snacks, dishes)	Activities/Actions (eating, working, playing)	Things (tools, toys, clothes)
_____	_____	_____
_____	_____	_____
_____	_____	_____

Other Situations/Occasions

_____	_____	_____
_____	_____	_____
_____	_____	_____

What else?
1. Write a family dictionary for your family's unique language.
2. Make a list of expressions you associate with particular family members.

Source: Adapted from the 4-H Folkpatterns Project, Cooperative Extension Service, Michigan State University, East Lansing.

FIGURE 7.5
Personalized Goals for Children

Below are listed 21 goals early childhood teachers commonly have for the children in their class. All of them are important. However, some goals will probably seem more relevant for your child than others. This year we would like to use information you provide to personalize your child's experience in our program. For this reason we would like you to prioritize these goals in the following way:

1. Read the entire list of goals.
2. Cross out any goal to which you are opposed altogether.
3. Add any goal you particularly value that is not included on the list.
4. Select the *three* goals you consider *most* important and assign them a value of 7.
5. Assign a value of 6 to the *three* goals you consider next in importance.
6. Continue this process by assigning a value of 5 to three goals, a value of 4 to three goals, a value of 3 to three goals, a value of 2 to three goals, and a value of 1 to the remaining goals you consider least important for your child.

Please note: Teachers work on all of the listed goals sometime during the year. The information you provide helps them know which areas to emphasize when working with your child.

Child's name: _____ Child's age: _____

_____ A. Develop an appreciation of art, music, movement, drama, and poetry
_____ B. Learn to make choices and decisions
_____ C. Learn to get along with other children
_____ D. Become more aware of personal feelings and the feelings of others
_____ E. Learn to appreciate people of varying races and cultures
_____ F. Learn how to work independently
_____ G. Learn how to persist at a task
_____ H. Develop effective problem-solving skills
_____ I. Learn scientific or historical facts
_____ J. Increase his or her vocabulary
_____ K. Develop good listening skills
_____ L. Develop confidence in using his or her body
_____ M. Develop a positive attitude toward school/center
_____ N. Learn appropriate manners
_____ O. Learn how to express himself or herself using words rather than physical force
_____ P. Make a successful separation from home to school/center
_____ Q. Develop basic perceptual skills such as recognizing patterns or sequences in objects and events
_____ R. Develop basic prereading skills such as grouping objects and events
_____ S. Develop basic premath skills such as arranging objects in order, grouping objects into sets, recognizing the concept of "oneness"
_____ T. Learn the alphabet
_____ U. Learn how to dress him- or herself
_____ V. Learn how to count
_____ W. Other _____

Source: Adapted from materials developed by the Child Development Laboratories, Family and Child Ecology Department, College of Human Ecology, Michigan State University, East Lansing.

FIGURE 7.6
Family Interest Survey

FAMILY INTEREST SURVEY

Your Name _____

Child's Name _____

We are delighted that you and your child are enrolled at Central School this year. We look forward to working with you. As you know, we encourage family members to be involved in our program as much as possible. To give us an idea of ways you would like to become a partner in the education process, please check your areas of interest below. Thank you. We look forward to partnering with you.

Potential Family Interests

_____ Working with my child at home.
_____ Sending in materials from home.
_____ Translating materials for families in the program.
_____ Reviewing materials for the program.
_____ Building or making materials for the program.
_____ Helping with the family toy-lending library.
_____ Helping to find potential field trip sites or community visitors.
_____ Helping with community trips.
_____ Working with the teaching team to develop ideas for the classroom.
_____ Planning special events in the community.
_____ Planning special events at the center.
_____ Attending events for parents.
_____ Serving as a family "mentor."
_____ Attending a family-to-family support group.
_____ Serving on the parent advisory council.

---

and present it to families. A very honest, open, basic approach would be to say to parents, 'I read this about the culture group that you belong to. Is it true? Does your family believe this? Is this information in any way helpful to me in my effort to provide a culturally relevant experience for your child?'" (p. 12).

Ask for evaluative feedback from families throughout the year. Let families know their opinions count by providing numerous opportunities for them to provide feedback about their child's experiences in the early childhood program as well as their own. Suggestion boxes near the program entrance, short questionnaires sent home that can be returned anonymously in a postage-paid envelope, written or verbal evaluations administered at the end of workshops or other school events, and telephone surveys conducted by staff or parents are some methods that prompt family input.

Another effective strategy is to hold family-teacher forums once or twice a year at school. These regularly scheduled, informal gatherings give family members and teachers a chance to evaluate the program together. Loosely structured around a broad topic, such as children's personal safety issues or promoting children's problem-solving skills, they provide for mutual exploration of educational ideas and strategies. Moreover, family members may ask questions and make suggestions for changes or additions to early childhood programs in an atmosphere where such communication is clearly welcome.

As a follow-up to these evaluation efforts, let family members know you intend to act on some of their suggestions. Later, inform them (through a program newsletter and/or at a group meeting) of change that have resulted from family input.

Keeping Families Informed

Is my child happy? Is my child learning?

What does my child do all day?

How are you addressing reading in the classroom?

I don't understand my child's new report card. Where are the letter grades we used to get in school?

These are typical questions family members have about early childhood education in general and their child's current setting in particular. Anticipating such questions and communicating relevant information to families is an important part of being an early childhood professional. How you respond to unanticipated queries or demands for information will also be important.

Develop written materials for your classroom in which you make clear your desire to include families in their children's early education. Identify benefits to children, families, and the program as a whole when families become involved in the program in some way. Provide specific guidelines for the form family involvement could take and how home-school contacts might evolve. For example, let families know they are wel-come to visit the classroom or that there will be jobs they can do at home if they choose. Send these materials home to families and go over them on a home visit or during a program orientation at the school or center.

Acquaint family members with your educational philosophy, the content of the curriculum, program goals, and the expectations you have for children in your classroom. Integrate this content into a beginning-of-the-year family orientation as well as in any written materials (e.g., handbook, program brochure, written bulletins, or videotape of program activities) sent home describing the curriculum. Discuss child development and program goals for children, offering examples of related classroom activities family members might see or hear about. Use hands-on activities to help family members better understand the materials in the classroom and their relationship to children's learning.

Familiarize families with a typical day for children in the program. Family members feel more comfortable with the program if they can envision how their child spends his or her time there. Acquainting families with school or center routines can be accomplished in several ways. At the very least, families should receive a

Provide family members the information they need to become partners in the education process.

copy of your daily schedule that outlines the timing of classroom events and explains the general purpose of each segment. Some teachers also utilize a slide or video presentation, held early in the year, that illustrates how children in their class move through the day. Motivated to attend by seeing pictures of their own child, parents leave having learned more about the early childhood program and its philosophy. A similar outcome occurs when programs put on a "miniday" in the evening or on the weekend, when parents proceed through an abbreviated but total schedule in the company of their child. Children are proud to lead their mom, dad, or grandparent through the routine, and family members gain insights into their child's classroom participation.

Periodically write one- or two-line notes regarding children's positive program experiences. Send these "happy notes" home with the child to demonstrate your interest in both the child and the parent (Berger, 1995). A child's first journey to the top of the climber, an enthusiastic creative writing experience, or the child's pride in knowing many new facts about insects are all good occasions for a short handwritten note from you. If you write one note every other day, the families in a class of 30 children could receive three or four such contacts in a year. Once or twice, include an instant snapshot of the child happily engaged in a classroom activity as a keepsake for families of the child's early school experience.

Create a weekly or monthly newsletter to inform families of the program and children's experiences away from home. This simple form of communication can familiarize families with what is happening in the classroom, give family members ideas for things to talk about with their youngsters at home, and stimulate family members to engage in home-based learning with their children.

Newsletters produced at the preschool level are usually written by the teacher. Those designed for the early elementary grades may include contributions from the children (Berger, 1995). In either case, make newsletters short and visually interesting by using subheadings and graphics. Avoid overcrowding. Divide the content into sections in which items are highlighted by outlining, indenting, bolding, capitalizing, or changing typeface.

The content of the newsletter may include one or more of the following items:

❑ A review of the children's experiences at the center or school since the last newsletter.

❑ A description of activities children will take part in throughout the next several days or weeks.

❑ Specific, practical examples of how family members could address or reinforce children's learning at home.

❑ A brief discussion of the theme (if you engage in theme teaching) and what facets of it children will be exploring.

❑ Relevant classroom, family, or community news.

❑ Invitations to family members to participate in the classroom, donate materials, or suggest upcoming classroom events.

Stay in touch with family members who seem unresponsive. Avoid stereotyping family members as uncaring or impossible to work with. Remain pleasant when you see them. Periodically send notes home letting families know about their children's positive participation in program-based activities. Continue to offer simple, easy-to-do suggestions for home-based participation. Keep the input from the program as positive as possible, and make few demands. You might not see immediate results; however, you could be contributing to a more favorable impression of the educational process for that family member. This in turn could serve as the foundation for greater participation later in the child's education.

Establishing Two-Way Communication Between Families and the Program

Everyone wants to feel that he or she has something to offer. The most depressing feeling in the world is the feeling of having nothing to offer—nothing that's acceptable.—Fred Rogers (1997)

Both teachers and families have valuable things to offer one another: insights, information, ideas, and support. The back-and-forth flow of communication helps each of them develop a more complete picture of the child and their own role in that child's early education. Thus, the concept of two-way communication between home and formal group setting is a critical element of developmentally appropriate practice. Here are some ways to begin establishing reciprocal relations with families.

Vary the communication strategies you use rather than relying on a single method. Make sure to exchange

TABLE 7.5
Home-Program Communication

Ways to Convey General Program Information	Ways to Convey Specific Information About Individual Children
A program handbook	Enrollment forms
A videotape of program activities	Telephone calls
Orientation meetings	Home visits
Home visits	Greeting and pickup routines
Newsletters	"Happy notes"
Bulletin boards	Photos of children engaged in activities
Program visits/observations by family members	Family-teacher notebooks kept for individual children
Educational programs for families	Regular and special conferences
Social events for families	
Articles sent home to families	
Family-teacher forums	

information with families regarding the program in general and their own children in particular. Both kinds of communication are necessary if family members and practitioners are to know and understand one another (Bundy, 1991; Brewer, 1998). Table 7.5 provides a summary of communication strategies by type (general vs. specific).

Take advantage of arrival and departure routines as a time to establish two-way communication with families. As one childcare provider stated, "It's great to have family conferences, but those happen only once in a while. Most of my communicating with parents goes on in the five minutes I see them at 8:00 A.M. or the 5 minutes at 5:30 P.M. That's when I develop rapport with them, get in tidbits about child development in, and try to problem-solve because parents are always in a hurry. Yet those five minutes add up. Before you know it we've been having weeks of mini-contacts, day after day, and we have come to know a lot about one another and about the child as well" (Sciarra & Dorsey, 1990, 360).

Establish telephone hours during which you and family members may call each other. Set aside one or two hours each week for this purpose, varying and dividing the time between two or more days. In a note home to families, notify them of your availability as well as the telephone number where you can be reached (at home or at the program). Also ask family members to indicate which time might be the most convenient for a call from you.

Early in the year, establish a positive basis for communication by calling each family very briefly to introduce yourself and share a short happy anecdote about the child. This practice does much to dispel the dread some family members have that a call from a teacher always means trouble. It also makes it easier for parents to contact you as needs arise. Make it a goal to touch base in this way with each child's family two or three times a year.

Create a notebook for an individual child through which family members and staff communicate as it is sent back and forth between the child's home and the program. This notebook can serve as an alternative to the "happy notes" described earlier. Write brief anecdotes to the parent regarding the child's school experience. Encourage family members to write about home events (e.g., visitors, changes in routine, illness, disruptions, accomplishments, and interests) that might influence the child's performance in the program. A line or two conveyed once or twice a week between the home and school settings can do much to expand family members' and the teacher's knowledge about the child and each other. This strategy is particularly effective when children participate in multiple educational settings outside the home, such as after-school childcare or a special education program. Passing the notebook among all these settings increases communication and makes it more likely that the child will receive a better coordinated program. Sample entries are provided in Figure 7.7 for Sarah, a 5-year-old child

FIGURE 7.7

An Example of Family-Teacher Communication Using Notebook Entries

Jan. 8, 1998

Sarah had a wonderful Christmas vacation. We spent the last week in Miami—temps 80–84 degrees, sunny, swimming every day. She is *not* eager to be back, I'm afraid. We tried to tell her that kids who live in Florida have to go to school and don't get to swim all day and go out every night to dinner with Grandma & Grandpa. She's not convinced.

Mrs. G. (Mom)

1-8-98

Hi. Welcome back. Sarah is "stacking" in her wheelchair—is there a change in seating? Just curious. She ate a good lunch.

Leslie (special ed. teacher)

1-8-98

I hate to be out of it—please define *stacking*. Sarah spent today at a tea party with Michelle and Kelly and Lara. They discussed vacations, served "milkshakes" and muffins. Ryan asked Sarah several times to come and see his block structure. She finally agreed.

Dana (childcare teacher)

1-9-98

Dana, "stacking" is a postural problem where the head is tilted back and her shoulders flopped forward. Sarah will sit up if we say "Can you pick your shoulders up better?" or anything similar, and she's very proud that she's able to do so.

Leslie

1-12-98

Sarah is bringing dinosaur stickers for sharing—the other kids can have one to take home.

Mrs. G.

1-12-98

Stickers were a hit! Sarah would like to also share with her Adams School friends. Sarah enjoyed reaching for and grasping scarves in the gym. She chose pink ones (we didn't have purple). She elected to "supervise" the art area where Michelle and Kyle asked her for choices for the Boxosaurus decorations.

Dana

1-13-98

Sarah was very rigid in PT today. She relaxed during "rolling inside the barrel"—her favorite activity—but tightened up when she attempted any play activities or position changes. I asked her if she was upset, "no", unhappy, "no," So I'm not sure what the problem was.

Leslie

1-14-98

Sarah was able to say "yes" or "no" (with her eyes) to answer "Mother, may I?" She seemed to like this. We measured things in the room, including her chair, with cubes at small group.

Dana

with cerebral palsy who attends a special education class in the morning and an after-school childcare program in the afternoon.

Carry out home visits as a way to get to know children and family members in surroundings familiar to them. Although time consuming, such contacts are a powerful means to demonstrate interest in the child and his or her family as well as your willingness to move out of the formal educational setting into a setting in which parents are in charge (Weinstein & Mignano, 1997). Visiting children at home also enables you to meet other family members or persons living there and observe the child in context.

Home visits also benefit family members by giving them a chance to talk to the teacher privately and exclusively. Parents or other important adults in the child's life may feel more comfortable voicing certain concerns in the confines of their home than they would at school. When these visits are conducted early in the child's participation in the program, children have the advantage of meeting their teacher in the setting in which they are most confident. When they arrive at the center or school, the teacher is already familiar to them.

Despite all of these potentially favorable outcomes, some family members are uneasy with home visits. They may be ashamed of where they live, fear their child will misbehave, or suspect that the teacher is merely prying into their private affairs. To avoid aggravating such negative perceptions, give families the option of holding the visit at another place (e.g., coffee shop, playground, church, or community center) or postpone your visit until you have established a relationship in other ways and the family is more receptive to your coming (Berger, 1995).

Teachers, too, may have qualms about going to children's homes. They may feel unsafe in certain neighborhoods or believe that the hours invested will prove too great. Additionally, some programs discourage home visits because of liability concerns or unavailable compensation. Yet, home visit programs can and do occur in many early childhood programs. Once confined mostly to preschool settings, some schools now schedule K-2 home visits during "record days" for the district or when the upper grades are having conference days. For instance, K-2 teachers at the Mary Harrison school in Toledo, Oregon, requested a small re-

muneration per family for home visits equal to that allowed for middle and high school teacher participation in extracurricular activities. Altogether, they visited 97 percent of the families enrolled at home or in other public locations in the evenings and on Saturdays. Both teachers and parents were enthusiastic about the visits and agreed to continue the practice in coming years. Parents felt genuine interest from teachers, and teachers found the insights and relationship enhancement that occurred well worth their time and energy (Cummings, 1991b). Suggestions for conducting successful home visits are offered in Figure 7.8.

Structure family conferences to emphasize collaboration between family members and teachers. Consider the following points as you plan each conference (Berger, 1995; Gonzalez-Mena & Widmeyer, 1997).

❏ Create a cordial written invitation in which family members have options for scheduling times and you express a real desire to meet them.

❏ Provide family members with sample questions they might ask of you as well as examples of questions you might ask them (see Figure 7.9). When providing these, assure parents that they are just samples and do not preclude any other inquiries parents may have.

❏ Confirm each appointment with a brief personal call to clarify family members' questions or a short note to let them know you are looking forward to meeting with them.

❏ Allow enough time for each conference to ensure a genuine exchange of ideas and information.

❏ Secure a private, comfortable place in which to conduct the conference.

❏ Greet family members and thank them for coming. Take time to engage in welcoming social rituals such as offering a cup of tea or chatting for a few moments about the weather or inquiring about an extended family member before beginning the more factual content of the conference.

❏ Begin on a positive note by conveying a pleasant anecdote about the child.

❏ Briefly outline the major areas you hope to cover. Ask family members if they have additional items they would like to add. Mention that the purpose of this conference is to exchange ideas. Urge family members to ask questions or interject their own comments as you go along.

FIGURE 7.8
Home Visit Hints

Before contacting families, determine the purpose of your visit. Some teachers choose to focus primarily on meeting and working with the child; others prefer to make the adult family member their major focus. Still others decide to split their attention somewhat evenly between the two.

Create a format for your time in the home that supports your purpose in going there. A sample agenda for the third option cited above might be as follows:

1. Arrive.
2. Greet family member and child.
3. Chat with family member a few moments. Give him or her program forms to fill out and a short description of how children spend the day at the center or school. Usually these are written materials, but some programs offer information on audiocassette for parents who cannot read.
4. Explain that next you'd like to get acquainted with the child and that you'll have a chance to talk to the family member in about 15 minutes.
5. Play and talk with the child while family member is writing, reading, or listening. Use modeling dough you have brought with you as a play material.
6. Give the child markers and paper brought with you and ask him or her to draw a picture that you can take back to school to hang up in the room.
7. While the child draws, talk with family member(s) about concerns, interests, and questions.
8. Close by taking a photograph of the child and family member(s) to put in the child's cubby or in a school album.

Supplies needed:

Map with directions to child's residence
Markers
Paper
Modeling dough
Camera
Film
Audiocassette tape player

Inform families of your intention to carry out home visits in a letter. Explain the purpose of the visit, how long it will last (not more than an hour), and potential dates from which they might choose for one to take place.

Follow up on the letter with a phone call a few days later to arrange a mutually convenient time for your visit and to obtain directions.

Carry out each home visit at the appointed time.

Follow the visit with a short note of thanks to the family for allowing you to come, and include a positive comment regarding the time you spent together.

❏ Throughout the conference, refer to the goals the family members signified as most important on the personalized goal sheet (refer to Figure 7.5) they filled out at the beginning of the year. Provide evidence of the child's progress in these areas. Add other goals you may also be focusing on.

FIGURE 7.9
Potential Family Conference Questions

Sample Teacher Questions

1. How does your child seem to feel about school?
2. Which activities or parts of the day does your child talk about at home?
3. Which children does your child talk about at home?
4. How does your child spend his or her free time?
5. Is there anything that your child dreads?
6. What are your child's interests and favorite activities outside of school?

Sample Family Questions

1. How has my child adjusted to school routines?
2. How well does my child get along with other children? Who seems to be his or her best friends?
3. How does my child react to discipline? What methods do you use to promote self-discipline and cooperation?
4. Are there any skills you are working on at school that I/we might support at home?
5. Are there any areas in which my child needs special help?
6. Does my child display any special interests or talents at school that we might support at home?
7. Does my child seem to be self-confident, happy, and secure? If not, what do you think the home or program can do to increase his or her feelings of self-worth?

❏ Keep the conference as conversational as possible, eliciting comments from family members as you go along.

❏ Answer family members' questions directly, honestly, and tactfully. Avoid using jargon and judgmental terms to describe the child. Deal in specifics rather than generalities, and base your discussion on objective observations and concrete examples of work.

❏ End on a positive note.

❏ Collaborate on future goals and strategies.

❏ Clarify and summarize the discussion.

❏ Make plans to continue talking in the future.

Readers may refer to Chapter 16, for information on child-led conferences. That conference style provides another way to increase the collaboration between home and the early childhood program.

Collaborate with families to support linguistically diverse children at home and in the program. Ask family members to teach you some words and phrases that could be useful in interacting with the child. In-vite family members to the program to tell stories, sing songs in their home language, and share other oral traditions typical of their family. Encourage families to bring music, objects, or foods into the classroom to share and talk about. Ask them to provide storybooks, newspapers, and magazines that feature their home language in print for use in the classroom. When working with older children, provide ways in which family members can use their primary language to help their children with program-related assignments or activities at home. Create a home library that includes a variety of print materials written in families' home languages for children to borrow. Make clear the importance of the child's home language to the child and therefore to you. Stress that although children will be learning English in the formal group setting, such learning does not require children to abandon or reject the language of the home (Kostelnik, Stein, Whiren, & Soderman, 1998).

Make contact with noncustodial parents. Provide opportunities for them to participate in home visits, open houses, and other school activities whenever possible. Mail newsletters to those who live elsewhere.

Work with family members to support the development and learning of children with special needs. All family members have the potential to learn and grow with their children. Families of children with disabilities are—more than most families—forced to confront similarities and differences and to reexamine their assumptions and values. It is crucial that you support such families as they become contributing members of the educational team (Deiner, 1993). To do this, use the techniques you have learned so far as well as additional strategies described here.

❏ *Gather and share information regarding all aspects of the child's development and learning.* Children with disabilities are whole beings. They cannot be summed up by a single label such as "hearing impaired" or "language delayed." When you talk to families, avoid focusing only on the child's disability. Talk about the whole child.

❏ *Treat families with respect, not pity.* Families are families first and the family of a child with a disability second (Deiner, 1993). They will have many of the same strengths, needs, concerns, hopes, and dreams expressed by other families in your class. Keep these in mind as you communicate with them.

❏ *Listen empathically as families express their feelings about their child.* Family members have many reactions to their child's disability. Some deny the reality of the situation. Others feel angry, helpless, or depressed. Others are proud of their child and his or her accomplishments. In every case, the best approach is to listen without giving a lot of advice or telling families how to feel. Paraphrase reflections (described in Chapter 3) are an excellent tool that show your interest and efforts to understand.

❏ *Expect families to vary in their expectations for their child.* Some may believe the child has enough problems already. Such families often have low expectations for children's performance in the early childhood program. Other families view a disability as something to be overcome. They may expect their child to excel beyond normal development and learning for any child that age. Many families will be somewhere in between those extremes (Deiner, 1993). Respond with sensitivity to these variations. There is no one "right" attitude. Accept families as they are and help them as you would any other family in determining reasonable expectations for their children.

❏ *Learn about the child's disability.* You do not need to be an expert on every form of disability, but you do need to know how to obtain relevant information. Families themselves can be an excellent resource. Ask family members to tell you about their children and how they work with them at home. Read articles and books about various disabling conditions. Find out where in your community there are human resources to support children and families in education settings if a child has a disability.

❏ *Work cooperatively with other professionals involved in the child's life.* Often children with disabilities take part in a wide array of services involving professionals from varying agencies and backgrounds. You will be one member of this team. You may participate in a formal planning process with other team members and the family. However, there may be many times when coordination becomes difficult or communication breaks down. Make an effort to communicate with the other helping professionals in children's lives. The travelling notebook described in Figure 7.7 was one example of how to do this.

Integrating Families Into the Program

Hanging at the top of the stairs at the Cesar Chavez School is a large quilt containing more than 100 fabric squares—each one different. Some are colored with fabric crayons, others are stitched and sewn, and still others have been embroidered or quilted. This quilt came about through a cooperative effort of families, staff, and children. Each family and staff member received a plain cloth square on which they could sew, cut and paste, or draw a picture or some other symbol that captured their feelings about Cesar Chavez School. Families could work on the squares at home or at workshops in which family members along with children were given materials and guidance in how to create a square of their own choosing. Emphasis was placed on participation by many people rather than achieving a perfect final product. As a result, even children and adults who believed they lacked arts and crafts talent were enticed into the project. The quilt took several months to complete. Today it hangs as a warm and loving tribute to the community spirit of Cesar Chavez School. It is also visible proof that families, children, and staff are partners in the educational process.

The quilt at Cesar Chavez School is a good example of how one early childhood setting integrated families into the ongoing life of the program. The Schoolwide Guidance Policy developed by families and staff at the Adams School, described in Chapter 6, is another example of how family members and early childhood professionals combined their efforts to achieve positive outcomes for children. Here are additional strategies you can use.

Institute an open-door policy in which family members are welcome to come to the classroom/program unannounced. Invite family members to watch or participate in some aspect of the children's day. Provide simple guidelines so that family guests will know what to expect from you and the children while they are on site. For instance, let them know if there is a place from which they can observe unobtrusively. Make clear the times when you are available to chat and times when your attention must be focused on the children. Offer suggestions of typical times during the day when parents might drop in for a short while to interact with the children without arranging in advance to do so. Snack time, the story time before recess or nap, and outdoor times are periods of the day when parent visitors might easily be accommodated.

Invite family members to visit the classroom for particular occasions. These times might be incorporated into a whole-group social affair such as a family-child breakfast or a Sunday afternoon open house. Family members might also be invited to share in a certain classroom activity such as making applesauce or planting seeds. Consider asking individual parents to become involved in a specific project (e.g., making bread, supervising the children's creation of a "Boxosaurus," or listening to children read). Likewise, suggest that family members share their interests or experience with children via free-choice activities or at a circle time. In every case, let families know they are welcome and that their presence will enrich the program. Issue your invitations long enough in advance for family members to arrange time to be there. Follow up each visit by asking family members to fill out a reaction sheet. Provide a simple form on which they can briefly record their impressions, suggestions, and questions. This evaluation lets families know that their opinions are valued. It also tells them they can influence their child's educational experience through direct contact with the children and feedback to the teacher.

Children enjoy having their parents serve as "teachers" in the classroom.

Encourage family members to participate in the classroom as volunteer teachers for part or all of a day. Issue an invitation in which you describe the volunteer role. Make it clear that family members, by virtue of their life experiences, have the skills necessary to do the job. Follow up by speaking to individual family members about how they might become involved. Support your volunteers using the suggestions outlined in Figure 7.10.

Involve family members in making classroom collections/materials either for their own use or for children to use at school. Ask parents/grandparents to donate a song, story, or recipe that is a favorite in their family. Collect these from family members individually (in writing or in person), or plan a program event in which such items are shared. A potluck dinner or family songfest in which children also participate may pave the way for beginning such a collection. Likewise, stories can be obtained by inviting family members one at a time to spend a portion of their day in the classroom telling their child's favorite bedtime story. During the telling, the teacher can note the book used or tape-record the parent's rendition and later transcribe it and add it to a class anthology. An evening story hour in which children come dressed for bed, are served a light snack, and hear three or four short selections by family

FIGURE 7.10

Guidelines for Working With Family Members as Teachers in the Classroom

---

❏ *Establish clear guidelines for family volunteers reagarding their responsibilities in the classroom.* Offer specific suggestions to what volunteers are to do and a rationale for delegated responsibilities. An activity card with this information could be prepared and then handed to a different parent day after day. Read the card aloud, or prepare an illustrated chart if the parent is an uncertain reader. An example of such a card is offered below.

> Welcome! Today please:
> 1. greet children and help them find name tags. Goal: to make them feel welcome and learn how their name looks.
> 2. supervise matching game. Goal: for children to notice similarities and differences.
> 3. join the children at lunch. Encourage them to pour and serve themselves. Goal: to model trying new foods (Payne, 1991).

❏ *Take time to demonstrate some of the activities family members are to supervise that day.*

❏ *Help family members feel welcome in the classroom.* Introduce them to the children, and provide youngsters with name tags so that parents can interact with them more comfortably.

❏ *Inform family members that when they volunteer in the classroom, all children in the group will view them as a teacher.* Remind the child that Mom, Dad, or Grandma will be helping many children and will have special responsibilities throughout the day. This helps clarify the adult's role for both Mom, Dad, or Grandma and for the the child (Payne, 1991).

❏ *Talk with family members about how to handle some potentially disruptive situations in the classroom.* Also discuss what to do if their own child is involved. When this latter issue is ignored until it happens, some family members may fail to act or may overreact out of embarrrassment. Neither response is conducive to the family members feeling comfortable at school.

❏ *Give family volunteers in the classroom meaningful tasks to carry out,* helping children in the pretend area, engaging children in conversation, assisting children at the snack table. Avoid requesting them only to do "busy work" like washing the easel and brushes or cutting straws for a future fine motor activity. If family members are to become partners in the educational process, they must be given real responsibilities from which they can derive genuine satisfaction.

❏ *Notice family members successes in the classroom and comment on their helpfulness and effectiveness.* Describe their work in terms of better class functioning and individual child learning. This will underscore their value to the educational process.

---

members and teachers has also proven popular in some programs (Zimmer, 1990). In each case, collections such as these are tangible evidence of parents' contributions to the program. They can be assembled over time with minimum hardship to either families or staff. Moreover, they signal to family members that their cultural traditions are valued by the program and worth sharing with others.

Create home-based alternatives to on-site volunteering. For instance, ask family members to volunteer to prepare materials at home, make arrangements for field trips and resource people, coordinate parent discussion groups, find resource materials at the library, compare prices of certain types of materials or equipment at local stores, or react to activity plans that will eventually be used in the classroom.

Provide home-based learning activities for family members and children to do together. This strategy is appropriate for all families but most especially for ones whose time is limited because of employment and family constraints. In fact, the evidence suggests that for these families, home-based learning is the single most effective means of parent involvement (Epstein, 1984).

To achieve positive outcomes, however, families require clear expectations and guidelines for what to do. With this in mind, let parents know early in the program that home-based activities are essential to helping children learn. Ask them to carry out activities at home for which you provide specific, yet brief, written or audiotaped directions. Provide these on a regular (e.g., weekly) basis. For each activity, invite family members also to tell you how easy it was to do and how much they and their children enjoyed it. Offer feedback to families about how their assistance at home is affecting their child's learning.

Invite interested family members to participate in policy-making decisions. For instance, ask family members to help create program-playground rules, develop snack guidelines, or generate ideas for specific classroom practices. Collaborating with parents in evaluating classroom materials as well as commercially available equipment or programs are other appropriate ways of giving family members decision-making powers in early childhood education. If your program has a governing body such as a family council or governing board, encourage families in your group to consider participating as attendees and as decision makers.

Show genuine pleasure in every family members' attempts, no matter how large or small, to support the children's education. Continually let families know how much you appreciate the time and effort they put into their child's education, not just because their help allows you to do a better job but also because the children benefit so greatly. Extend your personal thank-you often. In addition, acknowledge family contributions in classroom newsletters or community newspapers. Families also may be officially recognized at program events or with tangible tokens of appreciation such as certificates, plaques, or thank-you notes from the children.

Providing Family Education

At a recent get-together for the families in her room, Consuelo Montoya invited the participants to give her ideas about topics they'd like to explore in the coming months. Families came up with five ideas. Next, Consuelo put up a sign at the entrance to her room asking family members to put a mark by the idea they most wanted to have a chance to talk about. Families who couldn't come in person were invited to telephone their preferences. Here are the results:

Consuelo Montoya's Classroom—Family Topics Wish List

> *Sibling Rivalry = /////////////*
> *Healthy Snacks Kids Will Eat = /////*
> *Celebrating Family Traditions = ////////*
> *How to Help Children Make Friends = ////////////////*
> *Taming the TV Monster ////////*

Based on these outcomes, Consuelo plans to organize a workshop soon on "How to Help Children Make Friends." She and another teacher will gather ideas and information for families and then share it during a family education evening at the center. A workshop on Sibling Rivalry could come next. For that workshop, Consuelo is thinking of inviting family members to talk about what they do at home when the bickering starts.

This was an example of one teacher's approach to developing family education opportunities for families of children enrolled in her classroom. There are many ways to carry out this important facet of family involvement. Here are some guidelines for how to begin.

Conduct a simple needs assessment of family member concerns and interests related to childrearing and other family issues. This process could be carried out for your classroom alone, among several classes, or on a programwide basis.

There are several different ways to proceed. One is to invite family members to a brainstorming session in which mutual concerns are generated. Another approach is to conduct a brief written or telephone survey in which family members identify those issues that are most important to them. A third technique is to provide family members with a broad range of potential issues that could be addressed and then ask them to prioritize those issues according to their own needs. Use the summary of the results to provide direction for future parent education efforts.

Identify the most pressing needs for the group, and make sure to deal with them early. A word of caution is advisable here: Avoid simply going with the notion of majority rule. Instead, look at the concerns in terms of various demographic subgroupings such as low-income families or single-parent households. Try to determine which concerns are shared by everyone in the group and which may be specific to certain families. For example, workshops on "sibling rivalry" and "children and television" would be of interest to a broad range of families in your class, whereas blended families might find these topics pertinent: "Living with other people's children" or "Dealing with step-parent stereotypes." Addressing both general and specific concerns in your plan will give it the widest possible appeal and will be more sensitive to all families served by the program.

Invite family members to educational workshops that involve both them and the child. Consider using a format in which children receive childcare half of the time while their family members discuss program-related information with other family members and staff. The second half of the session could be devoted to parents and children working together, practicing skills, or creating make-it/take-it items for use at home. A sample agenda for one such workshop is offered in Figure 7.11.

Carry out periodic child-study sessions with family members. Together, observe or discuss children's physical, social, or cognitive skills, and then brainstorm activity ideas for school, center, or home. Next, engage in mutual problem solving related to children's learning and development.

Help family members anticipate typical developmental changes throughout the early childhood period. Knowing what to expect in advance empowers family members to respond appropriately when such changes occur and makes them more confident teachers of

FIGURE 7.11
Saturday Morning Family-Child Motor Skills Workshop

9:00–9:15	*Arrival*	Children are taken to supervised childcare rooms.
9:15–10:15	*Discussion*	Ms. Iamfit talks with family members about the development of motor skills such as throwing, catching, and skipping.
10:15–10:30		Family members pick up preschool-aged children from childcare rooms, receive nametags, and go to first activity station.
10:30–11:30	*Activity stations*	Family members rotate from station to station every ten minutes, approximately six families per station.
		1. Make it/take it: Family members and children choose to make one or more gross motor items for use at home—nylon paddles, milk jug scoops, newspaper balls; also provided are instructions and activity ideas for jump ropes, suspended balls, streamers, and pillow balls. 2. Throw/catch 3. Striking 4. Gallop/skip 5. Balance 6. Nutritional Awareness and Snack
11:30–11:40	*Closing*	All participants gather in the rainy day room for a large-group song with movement.

This workshop will be repeated next Friday from 6:30 to 9:00 P.M.

their own children. A note home to families, a brief discussion in the classroom newsletter, a small-group discussion, or an organized workshop on a related topic are a few ways to get this kind of information home. Chatting informally with family members individually and frequently is another valuable way to convey developmental information to parents. These personal contacts are especially useful because teachers can provide appropriate information and answer questions with a specific child in mind.

Provide general information about child development and learning to family members in take-home form. Books, pamphlets, cassettes, and videotapes can be made available through a parent lending library. In a box easily accessible to parents, file articles culled from magazines, newsletters, and early childhood journals such as *Young Children, Day Care and Early Education,* and *Childhood Education* (Bundy, 1991). Provide more than one copy of each article so that you can recommend relevant readings and parents can take them home with no obligation to return them. Periodically send home a note, highlighting new material available for parents to borrow or keep. Organize family discussions around one or more of these or give family members a check-off sheet on which they can indicate whether they would like a particular article sent home with their child.

Facilitating Family-to-Family Support

A group of parents was seated at a picnic table for the Sugar Hill Child Development Center end-of-year potluck. Eventually the conversation got around to what they liked best about the program. In addition to the satisfaction many derived from watching their children develop and learn in a happy, safe, and stimulating program, the thing they most appreciated was having a chance to talk with other family members who were coping with some of the same child-rearing challenges.

"I just want to talk with a grown-up sometimes. Not about the office or my work, but about how they get their kid to take vitamins or what if she doesn't want to kiss grandma."

"I've been here four years, and my two best friends are moms I met at school work parties."

"It's easy to feel like you're the only one whose child is or isn't doing something. (Remember Tim and the shoes?)

But here there are other parents I can talk to . . . Makes you feel less alone."

These families have voiced one of the most significant benefits of family involvement, the opportunity to get to know and interact with other family members responsible for raising a child. Such positive outcomes are more likely to happen when early childhood programs take deliberate steps to help families make these contacts.

Arrange opportunities for family members to talk with one another informally. Plan some casual get-togethers whose primary aim is to give family members an opportunity to build their social networks and communicate with their peers. Make sure to include an unstructured break to facilitate family-to-family conversation during more formally scheduled events. There is strong evidence that these informal exchanges are every bit as valuable to family members as the regularly scheduled program (Powell, 1989). In fact, for single parents, strengthening informal social networks may be the most effective means of eliciting their involvement in their children's education (Cochran & Henderson, 1986). The same is true for families whose home language is not English. Linking parents who speak the same language and encouraging informal support networks helps create a sense of belonging that families appreciate (Lee, 1997).

Work with other teachers, parents, and administrators to organize a family-to-family mentoring program. Pairing new families with family members already familiar with program philosophy and practices helps ease the entree of the newcomers and gives established families a responsible, important means of involvement. Give the mentors guidelines for how to fulfill their role. Some of their duties might include the following:

❏ Calling new family members to welcome them and answer their initial questions.

❏ Arranging to meet new families prior to their involvement in the program to provide a tour of the facility.

❏ Inviting new families to accompany them to open houses or orientation sessions held early in the year.

❏ Translating relevant program materials or serving as translators during family conferences or other program-related gatherings.

❏ Checking in periodically to answer questions and provide information as needed.

Talk to your program administrator about creating peer support groups for teen parents, single parents, working parents, families of children with disabilities, and non-custodial parents. Suggest that your program promote these kinds of get-togethers by providing the location for group meetings and childcare during that time. If such groups are already part of your program, make sure individual parents in your class know about them.

Suggest that a place in the school or center be set aside as a family lounge. This room would encourage informal contacts among family members and between family members and the staff. It could also serve as a headquarters for program-related family projects. A living-room type of atmosphere seems welcoming to family members, as does a pot of coffee and a family reference library. Family members also appreciate a large bulletin board on which are posted announcements, community news, and parent requests for childcare, toys, clothing, or transportation. Updating information often, removing out-of-date material, keeping the board neat and organized, and placing it in a prominent spot prompts family members to check it frequently.

SUMMARY

Practitioners and family members who work together create a strong foundation for developmentally appro-priate programs for young children. This chapter has described the aims and benefits of family involvement in early childhood education. The principles of collab-oration, variety, intensity, and individuation provide a framework for thinking about successful approaches to including families. Based on these principles, a variety of strategies for increasing family involvement have been suggested. The guidelines we selected highlight the broad repertoire of skills you will need to work more effectively with families. However, *you will not use all of these strategies in any single year.* Although many questions remain as to how to reach and involve *all* families, there is no doubt that the inclusion of the child's family will continue to remain a high priority among educators of young children. Our job as early childhood professionals is to keep investigating alter-native methods of family involvement and welcome family members as full-fledged partners in the educa-tion process.

This chapter is the last in Part 2. You now have a wide array of tools to design a developmentally appro-priate curriculum for young children including small- and whole-group planning and implementation skills, organizing and time-management skills, guidance strategies, and techniques for including family mem-bers in children's early education. Part 3, which comes next, focuses on the curriculum.

✖ Applying What You Read in This Chapter

1. **Discuss**
   a. Based on your reading and your experiences with families, discuss each of the questions that open this chapter.
   b. The early childhood program in which you are working will be having a family event to wel-come new families at the beginning of the pro-gram year. Based on what you have read in this chapter, how would you make sure the event was sensitive to the needs of a diverse array of fami-lies?
   c. Assume you that you are a teacher of 4-year-olds. Leon's grandmother will be volunteering in your classroom today. What will you do to en-sure that the experience is a positive one for Leon, his grandmother, and yourself?

   d. Describe how you would apply the principles of age appropriateness, individual appropriateness, and sociocultural appropriateness to the concept of family involvement.
   e. Discuss the pros and cons of home visits. How could you overcome the drawbacks to this family involvement strategy?

2. **Observe**
   a. Observe a program in which family members volunteer in the classroom. What does the head teacher do to make the experience a success for families, children, and staff?
   b. Arrange to accompany an early childhood pro-fessional on a home visit. What is the purpose of the visit from the practitioner's perspective? De-scribe what the practitioner does to address that

purpose. Explain how the family responded and whether the original purpose was achieved. Were any additional outcomes accomplished? What were they?

c. Observe a family involvement event at an early childhood program. Describe the purpose of the event, how families came to know about it, and the support strategies designed to facilitate family involvement. Use Figure 7.1 to guide your description. Describe what occurred during the event and family reactions to it.

3. **Carry out an activity**

a. Think about an early childhood setting in which you are or have been involved. Create a comprehensive family involvement plan for that program by choosing one or two strategies from at least three different categories listed in this chapter. Provide reasons for your choices.

b. Interview an early childhood educator about his or her work with families. Ask the practitioner to describe some of the things he or she does to help families feel welcome and involved in their child's education.

c. Identify the cultural background of a family or families in your program that varies from your own. Find a community event/resource through which you might learn more about that culture group. Participate and describe what you discovered about the culture and about yourself.

d. Plan a family involvement event. (You do not necessarily have to carry it out at this time.) Define its purpose, the necessary preparation, and a means of evaluating its effectiveness.

4. **Create something for your portfolio**

a. Take pictures and record families' reactions to a family involvement activity you planned.

b. Create a family newsletter for a specific group of children. Provide a written rationale for why you developed your newsletter as you did.

5. **Add to your journal**

a. What is the most significant thing you have learned about family involvement based on your readings and experience with children and families?

b. Make a list of the most pressing concerns you have about family involvement. Describe what you will do to address your concerns.

c. Describe a positive interaction you had with a family. What made it work? Describe a less successful interaction. What went awry, and how might you avoid a poor outcome in the future?

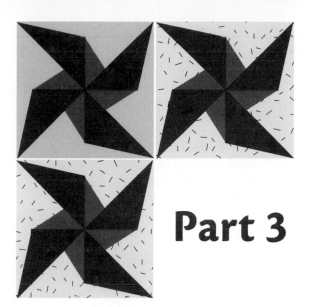

Part 3

The Curriculum

As a prospective parent is being shown around the center, she asks the director, "What kind of curriculum do you follow?"

The first-, second-, and third-grade teachers have been called together to reexamine the social studies curriculum for the lower elementary grades. There is much talk about how that curriculum should look in comparison to the one adopted by the upper elementary committee.

Mrs. Cohen, a new kindergarten teacher, asks whether she will be expected to teach children to "write on the lines." She is told, "Oh, no. We dropped that from the curriculum two years ago"

The program staff has spent an exciting day learning about children's self-esteem. The question they want answered is, How can we best address self-esteem within our curriculum?

As part of the accreditation process for their school, the early childhood coordinator is asked to submit a copy of the curriculum for review.

Curriculum is something everyone connected with education talks about, yet it can mean different things to different people. When some individuals discuss curriculum, they are simply referring to the goals and objectives of the program. Others have in mind a written plan for student learning or a syllabus that lists topics of study and how they will be taught (Brewer, 1998). Still others equate curriculum with certain materials or types of activities commonly associated with a particular center or school. The form the curriculum takes can also vary from detailed written descriptions to sets of beliefs and experiences that can be grasped only by observing the program in action (Schwartz & Robison, 1982). Because there are so many interpretations of curriculum, we will clarify how that term relates to the curriculum detailed in the next six chapters.

THE CURRICULUM DEFINED

Curriculum is all of the organized educational experiences provided for children by the early childhood program. These experiences can take place inside the classroom or beyond, involving educators, family members, and other people in the community. In its written form, curriculum includes stated goals and objectives, strategies and activities aimed at supporting all aspects of children's development and learning, and methods of assessing children's progress and program effectiveness.

Formulated within a framework of developmental appropriateness, the curriculum described in the chapters that follow represents one interpretation of how to educate children from 3 through 8 years of age. Hereafter, it will be referred to as the Children's Comprehensive Curriculum. The Children's Comprehensive Curriculum has a twofold purpose: (a) to help children develop the knowledge, skills, attitudes, and dispositions essential to becoming happy, contributing members of society and (b) to give educators the tools necessary to facilitate such learning. Developed in its original form by faculty in the Department of Family and Child Ecology at Michigan State University, the Children's Comprehensive Curriculum has been implemented and evaluated in the Child Development Laboratories on campus for the past ten years. Variations of it have been adopted by nursery schoo,l childcare, Head Start, Chapter I, and preprimary special education programs throughout Michigan. Numerous school districts have also used the curriculum as the basis for redesigning their goals, objectives, and methods for kindergarten through the fifth grade. The version offered in this book represents an amalgamation of these adaptations.

The Children's Comprehensive Curriculum

The Children's Comprehensive Curriculum is divided into six domains: aesthetic, affective, cognitive, language, physical, and social. Considered individually, the six domains represent major facets of child development.

Although we realize that no one aspect of development can be isolated from the rest, we have found that purposeful planning for each domain results in a more comprehensive approach to instruction. Thus, taken altogether, the entire array represents a "whole child" approach to teaching. It unites an understanding of what is (e.g., how children develop and learn) with value statements of what ought to be (e.g., goals and objectives for children's development and learning now and in the future) and with methods for achieving these aims (e.g., teaching strategies and activities). A brief overview of each domain within the Children's Comprehensive Curriculum is presented in Table 1.

TABLE 1
Curricular Domains Within the Children's
Comprehensive Curriculum

Domain	Developmental Focus
Aesthetic	Appreciation of the arts and enjoyment of sensory experiences
Affective	Trust, autonomy, initiative, industry, self-awareness, self-esteem
Cognitive	Perception, physical knowledge, logical-mathematical knowledge, social-conventional knowledge, scientific understanding, critical thinking skills
Language	Receptive language, listening skills, expressive language, reading, and writing
Physical	Fine and gross motor skills, body awareness, physical health
Social	Social skills and socialization

Why Emphasize Developmental Domains Over Subjects?

Practitioners more accustomed to the traditional subject-matter designations of art, math, science, reading, social studies, physical education, and the like may question the child-oriented categories of developmental domains. They may wonder whether the material included within the following chapters will meet their needs and to what extent domains relate to their work with children.

Although it is true that standard curriculum divisions are comfortable because they are familiar, subject matter alone is not a sufficient source of curriculum (Spodek, 1973). Too often it leads to fragmented, isolated skill development or the exclusion of other kinds of knowledge and skills essential to children's ultimate success in society. Consequently, a subject-matter orientation is not comprehensive enough to suit our purposes. We prefer to emphasize a broader range of perceptions, dispositions, knowledge, and skills. For instance, art and music are covered under aesthetics but so too are dance and other sensory experiences. The af-

fective domain addresses learning processes related to self-awareness and self-esteem and also the development of independence and a sense of industry. Science and math are components of the cognitive domain but do not constitute the whole of it. This domain also includes problem solving, critical thinking, and perception. Reading is found within the language domain, and so are listening, speaking, and writing. The physical domain encompasses gross and fine motor skills, health, and body image. Incorporated within the social domain are social studies content along with processes and skills fundamental to children's increased social competence.

As children participate in the six developmental domains, they experience a comprehensive educational curriculum that goes beyond the subject-oriented programs characteristic of many primary schools. The domain-focused curriculum also transcends the traditional materials-based programs associated with numerous preprimary settings.

Why Emphasize Developmental Domains Over Materials?

Several philosophers throughout the history of early childhood education have advocated the inclusion of certain materials to enhance particular learning goals for children. Froebel's gifts; Montessori's pink tower; and Hartley, Frank, and Goldenson's emphasis on blocks, water, and clay are typical examples. In each case the role of the teacher was closely tied to facilitating children's use of these items. However, in the 1940s and 1950s, many teachers began to take a more passive role, treating the curriculum as inherent in the materials. That notion stemmed from maturational and psychoanalytic perspectives that assumed development merely unfolded in a benign environment or children needed certain materials to use in cathartic ways (Hartley, Frank, & Goldenson, 1952; Read, 1966). That point of view has given way to the more interactive approach designated in Chapters 1 and 2.

The idea that materials do the teaching is still prevalent today, however. Many practitioners assume that if they have the right equipment, the instructional aspects of the program will take care of themselves (Kostelnik, 1990). When teachers assume this posture, goals for children's learning are often unspecified or ambiguous, and teachers may neglect to challenge children sufficiently. Instead, their main focus becomes one of monitoring children for appropriate material use. Although having carefully selected materials and equipment is a necessary ingredient of quality children's programs, it is not a sufficient foundation for the early childhood curriculum (Bredekamp & Copple, 1997). Materials supplement the curriculum; they do not equal it. Moreover, the same material can be used to support learning across domains. This broader view distinguishes a domain-focused curriculum from a materials-based approach.

THE STRUCTURE OF CHAPTERS 8 THROUGH 13

Each of the next six chapters focuses on a single curricular domain. All of them include these segments:

I. Introduction—This part of the chapter describes the importance of the domain to children and its relevance to early childhood education.

II. Issues—A brief discussion of current educational issues related to the domain and how they might be addressed in early childhood programs is offered next.

III. Goals and Objectives—For each domain an ultimate goal and a list of intermediate objectives are presented. The ultimate goal is a global statement about the idealized long-range educational purpose of the domain. Ultimate goals are lifelong in intent, spanning the entire period of an individual's educational experience. They are equally applicable to children in preprimary programs, elementary school, and middle or high school and beyond. Knowing the ultimate goal for each domain helps educators keep sight of "the big picture," giving them a focus that goes beyond any one particular skill or bit of knowledge. Ultimate goals are guideposts educators can use to gauge how well their instructional practices support long-term aims as well as immediate outcomes.

Each ultimate goal is further broken down into several intermediate objectives. Intermediate objectives identify distinctive categories of behavior relative to children's development and learning within the domain. They help educators recognize domain-related skill patterns and concepts and outline the content and processes around

which practitioners should plan classroom instruction. In this guide these are listed in sequence from most fundamental to most complex. Consequently, the intermediate objectives can be used as a guide for sequencing learning experiences for each domain. Their purpose is to give teachers needed direction in planning while simultaneously allowing them the autonomy to decide how best to address each objective in light of children's interests and capabilities. Thus, teachers can use the intermediate objectives as a source of activity ideas. Such activities could include classroom routines, children's explorations of objects and concepts using classroom materials, and teacher-initiated lessons. A diagram depicting the relationship between the ultimate goal, the intermediate objectives, and activities for a sample domain is offered in Table 2.

Once teachers have settled on activities that address the intermediate objectives they have chosen, it is possible for them to identify more specific instructional objectives (e.g., behavioral objectives) suited to the learning needs of children in their class. We believe these latter objectives are best created by individuals who actually know the children. For that reason, we have not attempted to identify those in this guide.

IV. Teaching Strategies—This segment offers practical, pervasive strategies teachers can use to address the domain in their classrooms. The suggested techniques have been developed by practitioners in the field and represent concrete ways to operationalize the goals and objectives cited in the preceding section.

V. Activity Suggestions—Each of the curriculum-focused chapters ends with a selection of sample activities that support the domain. All activities include the following components:

A. Activity name.

B. Intermediate objective to which the activity relates.

C. Recommended materials.

D. General procedure for carrying out the activity with children 5 to 6 years of age.

E. Suggestions for simplifying the activity for children 3 to 4 years of age.

F. Suggestions for extending the activity for children 7 to 8 years of age.

TABLE 2

The Relationship Between the Ultimate Goal, Selected Intermediate Objectives, and Sample Activities for the Physical Domain

Ultimate Goal	Intermediate Objectives	Sample Activities
	Children will	
	1. develop awareness of the location of their body parts.	a. sing and act out the "Head Shoulders, Knees, and Toes" song.
		b. make body tracings, labeling external body parts.
		c. play the "Hokey Pokey" game, emphasizing left and right.
		d. make body tracings, labeling internal body parts.
For children to achieve physical competence and develop knowledge, attitudes, skills, and behaviors related to a healthy lifestyle	2. engage in activities that require balance.	a. walk the balance beam.
		b. play the "statue" game.
		c. use stilts.
		d. ride a two-wheel bike.
	3. practice fine motor skills.	a. move small objects with kitchen tongs.
		b. string beads.
		c. make letters in sand on trays.
		d. cut out snowflakes.
	4. learn health and safety procedures.	a. brush their teeth each day.
		b. sing "This is the way we wash our face" to the tune of "Here we go 'round the mulberry bush."
		c. play the "red light, green light" game.
		d. read a story about "good touch and bad touch."

These activity suggestions are illustrative, not exhaustive, examples of the types of activities and lessons teachers can plan for use inside and outside the classroom. However, we have strived to present a broad array of activities that cover the range of intermediate objectives within the domain.

RECONCILING THE USE OF DOMAINS WITH OTHER CURRICULAR APPROACHES

Some practitioners work in programs in which the curricular focus is established on a programwide or even statewide basis. Teachers faced with having to reconcile a more traditional subject-based or materials-based curriculum with domains have two options. First, they can advocate for a domain-focused orientation within their organization. Second, they can look for ways to integrate their current curricular approach with the one suggested here. Most often that involves subsuming subjects or materials under the broader construct of domains. For instance, some school districts have adopted the six curricular domains along with the ultimate goals and intermediate objectives for each one. Next, committees have examined current subject-related instructional objectives (often found in a district-adopted curriculum guide) to determine their appropriateness and the extent to which they support a particular domain. Based on the committees' recommendations, suitable revisions in objectives, classroom practices, and assessment tools are enacted. Individual practitioners can pursue a similar path, clustering subjects under domains and then evaluating their instructional practices in terms of the ultimate goals for each one.

Likewise, practitioners used to thinking of curriculum as materials have begun by taking equipment standard to their program and generating ideas for using that material to support intermediate objectives within various domains. Blocks, for instance, can be used to address objectives in any one of the six curricular domains. This same process can be repeated with other objects such as art materials, puzzles, small manipulative items, sand, and water. An example of this method of integration was provided in Chapter 5.

In conclusion, as more and more programs consider adopting policies and procedures to support developmentally appropriate practice, the notion of curricular domains will become increasingly common. There are already numerous programs in which such designations are being used (Battle Creek Public Schools, 1990; Carman-Ainsworth Community Schools, 1986; Forest Hills Public Schools, 1988; Michigan Department of Education, 1985; Midland Public Schools, 1991; Ministry of Education, Province of British Columbia, 1989; Traverse City Public Schools, 1987). One purpose of this text is to help educators better understand this approach to curriculum planning and implementation. The best way to get started is to examine what each domain entails, beginning with the aesthetic domain.

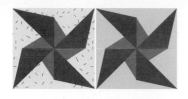

Chapter 8

The Aesthetic Domain

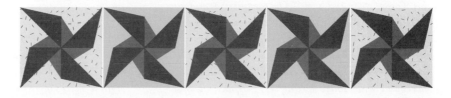

You may wonder:

What is meant by the word *aesthetic*?

What are the arts?

Why is aesthetic education important for children's learning?

What can I do to enhance aesthetic development?

I n this chapter about stimulating children's aesthetic interests and participation, we present information to help you answer these questions.

The teacher carefully uncovers a large print of the painting, An Afternoon at La Grande Jatte, by George Seurat. "Tell me what you see in this painting." The group of 5-year-olds seated on the floor kneel up to look more closely. Albert announces, "This is good work. I like it." Gillian says, "It's a happy earth." Bowa agrees, "I like this. Lots of color and a cat." The teacher nods and asks, "Where is this place?" Paul points to the corner, "I see boats." Caitlin notices, "There's a lady trying to catch a fish." Kimberly leans in and says, "I see a monkey and a dog. I think it's South America or Africa." Their teacher smiles and says, "You're looking very carefully; I wonder what you think the artist was trying to tell us in this

painting." Jill shouts, "It's about a wedding, there's the wedding girl."

Four-year-old Melanie looks from rock to rock on the tray, searching for her favorite. She notices that they are different colors, some are smooth, and some sparkle when water is poured over them. Picking one up she announces, "Here it is. This is my best." The teaching assistant, Mr. Rey, says, "You chose rock number 14, Melanie. Tell me what you like about that rock, and I'll write it on our chart."

Dora stands in front of her second-grade teacher, as Mrs. Openheimer strums chords softly on the guitar. As the child listens and watches intently, her head and shoulders begin to sway slowly from side to side. She moves slowly to the music, focusing on the gentle rhythm.

Amber's class is dramatizing the story of "The Three Billy Goats Gruff." She decides to be one of the goats going across the bridge. She practices using her best billy goat voice to say "It is I, Middle Billy Goat Gruff."

The first graders have been working in small groups for 15 minutes. Jeff's group is responsible for making various trees for the class mural. The boys are busy discussing what trees look like, cutting, arranging, and gluing paper shapes they have produced. Jeff decides his tree needs more leaves; he searches through the scrap box for the colors he wants. "Mine will be very leafy," he says with pride.

Each of the youngsters just described is involved in an aesthetic activity appropriate for early childhood educational settings. Activities such as these "provide necessary opportunities for children to develop creativity and perceptual awareness, and also significant possibilities for children to experience success in ways that might not otherwise be available to them" (Dixon & Chalmers, 1990).

AESTHETICS DEFINED

The word *aesthetics* comes from a Greek word, *aisthetickos,* which refers to the ability to perceive through the senses. Aesthetics has evolved into a branch of philosophy and curriculum that deals with artistic sensibilities and focuses on determining what is beautiful and good, as well as on appreciation (Jalongo & Stamp, 1997). Aesthetics is defined by the Consortium of National Arts Education Associations (1994) as "a branch of philosophy that focuses on the nature of beauty, the nature and value of art, and the inquiry process and human responses associated with these topics." In simple terms, aesthetics is a person's capacity to perceive, be sensitive to, and respond to human creations in the arts and beauty in the environment.

WHAT ARE THE ARTS?

The arts are defined as both the work and the process of producing the work. In the broadest sense the arts refer to all of the creative forms produced throughout human history: visual arts, performing arts, useable arts, and literary arts. Visual arts include painting, drawing, sculpture, print making, woodcarving, mosaics, collage, architectural design, and others. Performing arts include singing, dancing, playing instruments, dramatics, story-

telling, creative movement, puppetry, and others. Useable arts (crafts) include weaving, ceramics, pottery, knitting, basketry, jewelry making, furniture making, and countless others. Literary arts include writing original stories, poetry, plays, commercials, jokes, skits, and so on.

SCOPE OF THIS CHAPTER

Aesthetic learning encompasses a broad spectrum of experiences related to many different art forms and appreciation of the beauty in the natural world. Throughout this chapter, the arts refer to all of the various forms including music, dance, drama, and visual arts. Although this chapter provides a variety of examples, other activities involving the natural world, performing arts, storytelling, poetry, movement, dance, and drama can be found in other chapters throughout the book. For example, nature activities are found in the chapter on cognition; storytelling activities are located in chapters dealing with pretend play and language; movement and dance activities are also found in the chapter devoted to the physical domain. For our purposes, literary arts are included in the language domain chapter. In addition, teachers can transform many activities into aesthetic experiences by selecting an aesthetic goal (such as to *gain pleasure from a variety of sensory experiences* or to *contribute to the aesthetic environment of the school)* and focusing on this purpose in carrying out the lesson.

AESTHETIC EDUCATION FOR YOUNG CHILDREN

Aesthetic education in early childhood is a deliberate effort by teachers to provide experiences in the arts, nurture awareness of the arts, foster appreciation of various arts, and develop skills in evaluating art forms (Jalongo and Stamp, 1997). Aesthetic experiences may be either responsive or productive; see Figure 8.1. Figure 8.2 presents the components of aesthetic development.

Responsive aesthetic experiences involve the learner in appreciation of beauty in nature, appreciation of the arts, and formation of judgments and preferences in those areas. In the activities just described, the 5-year-olds (through appreciation of visual art), Melanie (through appreciation of beauty in nature and preference formation), and Dora (through appreciation of performing art) are involved in responsive aesthetic learning.

FIGURE 8.1
Aesthetic Development Model

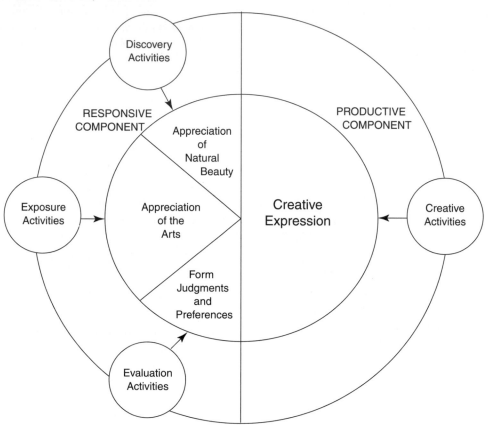

Discovery activities encourage children to respond to natural beauty. Students explore details of natural objects using all their senses. Teachers may use outdoor settings, inspiring children to watch, listen, smell, or touch while emphasizing respect and appreciation.

Exposure activities broaden students' experience with the arts. They provide opportunities for children as observers and consumers to hear a variety of music, watch dance performances, view the visual arts in its many forms, or experience live theater as an audience.

Evaluation activities encourage children to discuss and evaluate a variety of visual art, music, dance, and drama forms. Students select criteria for evaluation and express preferences based on those criteria.

Productive aesthetic experiences engage the learner with active materials, props, instruments, and tools useful for making their own art, music, drama, or dance. Therefore, *creative activities* stimulate creative thinking and provide opportunities for self-expression through the arts. Painting a self-portrait, gluing felt into a pleasing design, or experimenting with movement to music are examples of creative activities. At the beginning of this chapter, both Amber (through drama) and Jeff (through visual art) were engaged in creative activities. Following is an example of how a teacher used three different aesthetic experiences to enhance learning.

Mrs. Gonzalez's first graders are studying about air. This week their focus is things that move in air. Their teacher explains that some art can move in air. She hangs several examples of mobiles (a seashell mobile, a wooden bird mobile from Mexico, and a baby's nursery mobile made of stuffed cloth shapes) in the classroom. The children examine the mobiles and talk about their individual experiences with mobiles. They notice the shapes, colors, and effects of air movement, an "exposure activity."

FIGURE 8.2
Aesthetic Development Components

RESPONSIVE EXPERIENCES		
Discovery Activities		Goal – Appreciation of Natural Beauty
	Examples	• observing beautiful fish • exploring interesting rocks • watching clouds • discovering beauty in spiderwebs • smelling flowers
Exposure Activities		Goal - Appreciation of the Arts
	Examples	• looking at details in paintings • exploring sculptures • watching dancing • listening to music • attending a play
Evaluation Activities		Goal – Forming Judgments and Preferences
	Examples	• comparing several baskets • selecting their best collage for a portfolio • choosing a favorite song • telling what they like about the dance
PRODUCTIVE EXPERIENCES		
Creative Activities		Goal – Creative Expression
	Examples	• playing an instrument • dancing • fingerpainting • singing a song • making a wire sculpture • playing a role in a drama

The next day, Mrs. Gonzalez shows the class a picture of a famous mobile entitled Lobster Trap and Fish Tail *by Alexander Calder (Abrams, 1985). She asks them to imagine how it was made and to tell what they like about it, an "evaluation activity."*

Finally, she displays a collection of materials and discusses ways students could use them at the art center to make their own mobiles. She provides scissors, a variety of paper, hole punches, markers, thin wooden dowels, and string. By now students have many different ideas for their own mobiles; some ask for assistance in attaching and suspending the shapes, but most work independently *at this "creative activity." As the students finish, they hang their unique mobiles throughout the classroom.*

IMPORTANCE OF AESTHETIC LEARNING

There are many reasons to engage children in aesthetic activities. Experiences in this domain stimulate youngsters to respect themselves as achievers, communicate their ideas and feelings, discover their own point of view, appreciate different viewpoints and cultures, create change in their environment, and make aesthetic discoveries and judgments (Cohen & Gainer, 1995).

Creative expression is a part of aesthetic learning that is vital to education. "Art is increasingly accepted as a basic form of understanding. It seems only reasonable, then, to say that one of the principle functions of schooling should be the provision of instruction in aesthetic knowing" (Smith, 1992).

In recent years, aesthetic learning has been valued as a tool for meeting other significant educational needs. As stated at the Mid-Atlantic Regional Forum on National Educational Goals (May 1991), the arts play a vital role in establishing a bond between the generations that technology sometimes drives apart. This important link is "the glue that holds [the generations] together and contributes to a shared affective experience" for people of all ages.

Engaging a class of youngsters in the visual arts, music, dance, and dramatics can bring prosocial qualities to the climate of the group. The class that sings together, creates puppets together, plays instruments together, and dances together is more likely to behave cooperatively in other circumstances. Activities such as these can build group cohesion and social solidarity.

In addition, learning in other domains is greatly enhanced through aesthetic experiences. Respected developmental psychologist Howard Gardner, through his work on multiple intelligences, supports the notion that many children learn best in ways other than the verbal, mathematical, or logical approach (Gardner, 1990). Those youngsters make connections to learning more readily through kinesthetic, tactile, auditory, interpersonal, and spatial means available through the arts. When the arts, creativity, and aesthetics are not part of the curriculum, teaching and learning become monotonous, spiritless, and routine. It makes sense that aesthetics should be a part of every child's education.

RELATIONSHIP BETWEEN AESTHETIC LEARNING AND KNOWING

Connections between the arts and thinking are well established. Aesthetic learning involves processing information, creativity, communication, and cognitive knowing. One has only to look at the communication of thoughts present in the work by young children involved with the Reggio Emilia approach to see how important this connection is (Edwards, Gandini, & Forman, 1993). Creativity, defined as re-

forming individual parts to make a new whole (synthesis), is found at the top of Benjamin Bloom's taxonomy of thinking (Bloom, 1984) and described as the most complex level of thinking. It requires students to create a thought, an idea, or a product that is novel or original (Winebrenner, 1992). The relationships between thinking and feeling and between mind and body are critical to unleashing creativity (Goleman, Kaufman, & Ray, 1992). For young children, creative thinking is directly linked to activities such as dramatics and dramatic play and is a critical component of cognitive development (Yawkey, 1983). According to Victor Lowenfeld, the development of artistic ability and creative thinking should be considered one and the same (Lowenfeld & Brittain, 1965).

Howard Gardner's work helps us expand our view of nonverbal forms of knowledge to include musical, bodily-kinesthetic, spacial, and visual (Wright, 1997). Aesthetic activities provide ways to explore these forms of knowing and play a tremendous role in developing perception.

When children engage in aesthetic experiences, they encounter four subgroups of knowledge: physical, logical-mathematical, representational, and social-conventional. Children also have chances to consider how and why they think as they do. This additional type of knowledge is described as metacognition. Each of these is discussed further in Chapter 10. For now, we will explore how aesthetics fosters all types of learning.

Physical Knowledge in Aesthetic Learning

Construction of aesthetic physical knowledge involves discovery of the physical characteristics of materials in art, music, dance, and drama. For example, by using musical instruments students learn about the variety of sounds they make, how they produce sounds, and what they can do musically. Through experimenting with movement children become aware of body positions, gestures, the feel of movement, control of their limbs, and physical characteristics of dance. Through hands-on experiences with clay, for example, children learn what that medium feels like, what it will do when combined with water, how the clay can be transformed with fingers and tools, and the limitations of clay (it dries hard if not kept moist).

Logical-Mathematical Knowledge in Aesthetic Learning

Through both productive and responsive experiences, children mentally construct or recognize relationships of size, shape, area, placement, distance, timing, loudness, and other aspects of art, music, dance, or drama. These are examples of logical-mathematical knowledge. Therefore, when a kindergartner adds blue scribbles above her self-portrait, she uses logical-mathematical knowledge to express her relationship to the sky. Playing instruments or singing involve use of rhythm, beat, long and short tones, loud and quiet sounds, and so on—all mathematically based. Similarly, when a child engages in tap dance, he practices slower and faster taps and higher and lower movements and attempts to match his motions to the movements of his teacher. All of these involve logical-mathematical knowledge.

As teachers use the vocabulary of the arts, they give children richer language to use for describing, comparing, evaluating, and expressing preferences in the arts. Here are some commonly used terms:

Visual Art Terms

line   A mark that continues a dot made by a tool on a surface (e.g., long, thick, fat, light, bold, curvey, or vertical).

color   A characteristic or visual sensation of light (e.g., primary, warm, intense, light, bright).

shape   Form; the outside edge of an object or enclosed space (e.g., curved, open, closed, abstract).

texture   The surface quality or how an object feels (e.g., rough, smooth, hard, soft, coarse, fine).

design   Composition; the overall combined elements (e.g., harmonious, busy, quiet, dramatic).

balance   Forms appear to be in proportion to each other (e.g., equal, symmetrical, formal).

pattern   A recurring sequence of elements (lines, colors, or shapes) (e.g., regular, complex, simple, common, unusual).

space   How the artist uses surface area (e.g., positive, negative, full, empty).

The following are some musical terms children benefit from knowing:

Musical Terms

beat   The steady pulse of music (e.g., fast, slow, regular, obvious).

dynamics   Gradations of volume in a musical piece (e.g., louder, quieter, softer).

harmony   Combinations of tones sounded simultaneously.

melody   The tune, or how pitches move up and down in music.

pitch   Highness or lowness of musical sounds.

rhythm   Groupings of long and short musical sounds (e.g., simple, complex, syncopated).

tempo   Relative rate of speed of the musical piece; fast, slow, moderate.

timbre   Quality of tones distinguishing one instrument from another.

Representational Knowledge in Aesthetic Learning

Producing original visual art, music, drama, or dance requires that one think of an experience, idea, or feeling and then express it by manipulating the elements of the medium. These are highly symbolic activities that involve the learner in focused representational thought. Being able to imagine something not present and then finding ways to express that thinking concretely to others is a major cognitive accomplishment (Seefeldt, 1995a).

Social-Conventional Knowledge in Aesthetic Learning

Through social-conventional knowledge in the arts, we teach understanding and respect for cultural traditions, history, and heritage. Experiences with music, the visual arts, dance, and dramatics serve as powerful symbols of cultural identity (Dowling & Harwood, 1986) for children. An important role of aesthetic learning is to lay the groundwork for strong links to achievements of the past.

Social-conventional knowledge is part of aesthetic experiences when the learner acquires concepts and understandings related to the arts in society. For example, the names and characteristics of cultural dances (such as ballet, polka, hula, waltz, tango, or square dance) are passed from generation to generation as social-conventional knowledge. Moreover, when teachers describe techniques in the visual arts using terms such as portrait, landscape, still-life, print, watercolor, sand painting, mosaic, applique, or collage, they utilize social-conventional knowledge. In the art of drama there are conventions such as monologue, dialogue, skit, rehearsal, and many dramatic techniques to learn. When children learn acceptable respectful audience behavior for musical performances or observer behavior when they visit an art museum or gallery, they are learning social-conventional knowledge.

Metacognition in Aesthetic Learning

A simple way to define metacognition is thinking about thinking. Teachers help children think about their own thought processes by asking carefully chosen questions at the appropriate time. In aesthetic learning, metacognitive processing is valuable for organizing thinking, making decisions about a sequence of steps, and helping students to develop greater insight into their self-expressive work. When a teacher responds to a child's unique idea by asking, "How did you figure that out?" he encourages the student to consider the process she used to arrive at her solution. Other questions that stimulate similar thinking are "How did you know?" "What clues are you using to help find your answer?" "What steps did you use to make your (creation)?" or "What made you choose that instead of this?"

THE AESTHETIC DOMAIN AND DEVELOPMENT

Young children are naturally curious; because of this, the aesthetic domain is particularly relevant to them. Youngsters enjoy exploring nature, are motivated to create art and music, delight in the movement of dance, and spend hours in meaningful dramatic play. Aesthetic milestones in the development of aesthetic preferences, musical interests, vocal music, instrumental music, creative movement, visual representations, and drama are presented here.

DEVELOPMENT OF AESTHETIC PREFERENCES

Children's early aesthetic responses begin with sensory exploration of objects and sounds. A child may demonstrate preferences for a particular texture or smell, such as the soft edge on a blanket or a particular beloved toy. By the time children are 5 years old, research shows that their preferences for certain kinds of music begin to surface (Peery & Peery, 1986). Many children as early as 3 or 4 years old begin to make choices from their environment, gathering and exploring collections of particular objects such as stones, shells, or buttons. At a later stage, these collections become more sophisticated and must be acquired by very deliberate searches. For some children, the treasured objects may be bottle caps, coins, or baseball cards. Other children are fascinated by special dolls, models of horses, and so on. In addition, children are likely to enjoy spontaneous conversations about these special objects and demonstrate beginning levels of adult aesthetic evaluative behaviors—describing, analyzing, interpreting, and judging—but often need help organizing their comments and applying criteria.

At first the process of manipulation is much more important to them than the product created. A youngster's early art, music, dance, or drama is made without regard to the effect of their work on others. Later, a greater attempt to communicate ideas and meaning becomes important to children, and they begin to evaluate their work according to emerging aesthetic standards, based on their own developing taste and combined with messages they receive from their environment (Feeney & Moravick, 1987).

DEVELOPMENT OF MUSICAL INTEREST

Studies give educators an idea of how musical interests develop in children (McDonald & Simons, 1989). In infancy the appeal is usually the quality of sound. Babies often show interest when adults sing to them, in the sound of bells and soft music. As children grow and are exposed to various musical experiences, their interests broaden to include the element of melody; they learn to prefer what they become familiar with, particularly enjoying songs with repetition, in which the same melody is heard again and again, such as Did You Feed My Cow? (Jenkins, 1991). Later, children take a keener interest in pitch—recognizing when sounds go up or down and discriminating changes in sounds. Studies have also shown that young children have difficulty attending to more than one musical dimension (such as pitch, volume, duration, rhythm, beat, or tempo) simultaneously, and, when asked to make decisions about what they hear, do not respond with any degree of accuracy. By 5 or 6 years of age, many children demonstrate understanding of sound contrasts such as high/low, loud/soft, and up/down. Six-year-olds are able to identify pairs of chords as the same or different (McDonald & Simons, 1989). Though it is understood by educators that, within any group of children of a given age, a wide range of musical abilities will be found, it is also clear that musical interest and appreciation can be enhanced through a variety of regular musical experiences.

DEVELOPMENT OF VOCAL MUSIC (SINGING) BEHAVIORS

Infants explore musical sounds through vocal play and experimentation. A 2-year-old may produce "phrase-songs," which consist of rhythmic repetition of a word or phrase with pitch inflection, close to that of speech. Much of their singing is self-generated and spontaneous, occurring as they explore sounds or play with language. By 3 years of age many youngsters, if encouraged to express themselves musically, begin to impose structure on their improvisations by repeating selected patterns. Young children's pitch range of their spontaneous singing can be quite extensive. However, when learning songs by imitation, a more limited range (usually from D to A above middle C) seems to be most comfortable. Many 3-year-olds are able to sing whole songs and develop a large repertoire (McDonald, 1993). As their vocal control is gained, boys and girls expand their range of useable pitches and produce melodies more accurately. Later, they are able to fit together diverse rhythm patterns and appear to sense the function of form. By 5 years of age, many children can utilize a steady accurate beat, melody, and rhythm repetitions in their singing (McDonald & Simons, 1989). The process of learning to sing in tune depends upon opportunities, encouragement, and positive feedback so they know they are matching pitches. Children in the early primary grades can learn songs that are reasonably complex. Songs with greater demands on memory and sequencing skills, such as "High Hopes" (Arnold, 1995) or "Swinging on a Star" (Bartels, 1990), are not beyond most children 6–8 years old.

DEVELOPMENT OF MUSICAL INSTRUMENT INTEREST

Early in life, infants begin to intentionally make sounds by kicking or hitting objects. Their fascination with making sounds expands as they become more mobile.

Young children do not initially use rhythm or melody instruments to produce tunes but rather to experience sound. By 3, children are creating patterns by repetitions, and by 5 years of age they can make a steady beat (Moog, 1976). Four- to six-year-olds are ready for more group experiences involving exploration of rhythm and melody instruments. Soon after they become interested in the "right way" to play simple instruments. By 6 years of age, many children begin to imitate conventional music patterns and unfortunately lose some creative spontaneity. Youngsters at this stage benefit from plenty of opportunities to freely explore instruments, with encouragement to improvise melodies and create their own expressive music (Moorhead & Pond, 1978).

DEVELOPMENT OF CREATIVE MOVEMENT AND DANCE

From the earliest days of life, babies respond to music through body movement. Even newborns become more active when lively music is played and calmer when slower, quieter music is played (Wilcox, 1994). Infants sway and bounce, and by 18 months, they include clapping, tapping, and spinning in larger spaces. Two-year-olds tend to respond actively to rhythmic music, but each at his or her own tempo. By 3 years, they have gained greater coordination in movement; they enjoy moving and dancing creatively with others and participating in singing games that involve movement From 4 to 6 years, children increase in clapping and marching responses to a steady beat and enjoy participating in action songs such as "Shake My Sillies Out" (Raffi, 1987), "Here We Go Looby Lou," or "Old Brass Wagon" (Axton, 1995). They are becoming more skilled at synchronizing movement with the rhythmic beat of music. By 6–8 years old children have mastered basic movements and can match those movements to music. They can also invent their own movements to a piece of music and are more capable of following more complicated instructions in simple folk dances (Jalongo & Stamp, 1997).

DEVELOPMENT OF CREATIVE VISUAL ART EXPRESSION

Children's visual art representations change and develop new characteristics as they mature and have more experiences. Studies have shown that this occurs in all cultures. Children go through a similar pattern of artistic growth everywhere in the world, but individual children go through the sequences at different rates and have unique outcomes (Koster, 1997). Toddlers take pleasure in the physical movement of a crayon, pencil, or marker and gradually notice the resulting marks they make on paper. The way those uncontrolled marks change was the subject of an enormous research project by Rhonda Kellogg from the 1950s through the 1970s. She collected and studied over one million examples of children's drawings from all over the world. Her unparalleled work analyzed the patterns in children's drawings and showed that marks made by youngsters the world over were similar. She

identified and categorized 20 different kinds of basic scribbles, studied various placement patterns, and investigated ways young children combined shapes (Kellogg, 1969, 1979). Viktor Lowenfeld and W. Brittain's classic work in the early 1960s described developmental stages of drawings from toddler to adolescent and are summarized in Figure 8.3.

Children's drawings gradually change from random scribbling to controlled scribbles when children reach 4 years of age. Between 4 and 7 years, youngsters develop a set of visual symbols of their own invention to represent familiar concepts that they apply to various media. They learn that their creations communicate messages to other people and begin to

FIGURE 8.3
Stages of Creative Representation

Age Range	Stage	Description
2–4	1. Scribble (Early)	Disordered scribbles—purely kinesthetic; establishing motor coordination.
	Scribble (Middle)	Controlled scribbles—child notices connection between motions and resulting marks; variety of motions increases; color useful to distinguish marks from background.
	Scribble (Late)	Naming scribbles—child's thinking changes from kinesthetic responding to mental pictures; connects marks to world around him/her; color begins to have some meaning to child.
4–7	2. Representational Preschematic (Early)	Preschematic (Early)Controls scribbling motions to produce simple symbols that relate to his/her visual world (circle, vertical and horizontal lines); symbols change often; objects randomly placed; color choice relate to emotional reactions; produces a person symbol.
	Preschematic (Late)	Gains greater control that allows for experimentation with variety of symbols; exaggeration of certain symbols indicate importance; color continues as emotional reaction choice.
7–9	3. Schematic	Arrives at highly individualized visual symbols (schema) that satisfy him/her and are used repeatedly; schemas represent child's active knowledge of objects; schemas change only when meaningful experiences influence their thinking; spacial relationships not random; baseline used, inside-outside shown simultaneously; colors represent perception of reality.

The Scribble Stage

value the product. By the time children reach age 8, their drawings have become more complex, often involving multiple views and details. They are interested in many forms of artistic expression and, with encouragement, continue to refine their visual perceptions as they mature.

Descriptions of artistic stages are useful as guides to expectations at various ages and stages of development. However, many children reach these milestones much more quickly (Thompson, 1995). Variations in development and children's previous experiences with the visual arts make a difference in artistic progress.

DEVELOPMENT OF ENACTMENT OR DRAMATIC BEHAVIORS

Infants enjoy beginning enactments in such games as "This Little Piggy" or "Peek-a-Boo." By one year of age, most children can enact simple gestures meaning eat or sleep or pretending to touch a forbidden object. By 2, children are attempting to enact simple finger plays such as "Eensy, Weensy Spider" and using real-life objects to take on familiar caregiving roles such as

feeding or rocking the baby. Children from 3–5 become capable of deferred imitation, that is, they imitate movements of objects they have experienced in the past, even when the model is not present (Inhelder & Piaget, 1964). Pretend play and imaginative role-playing greatly increase during this period. Children 6–8 years old demonstrate continued interest in fantasy, but there is an emerging emphasis on nonfiction accounts of experiences in their play. As children learn to read and write, they may write and perform their own creative dramas, if encouraged. They also seek more elaborate props and begin to participate in more formal types of drama. Development affects the kinds of aesthetic activities children are likely to engage in. Figure 8.4 (adapted from Jalongo & Stamp, 1997) provides a sampling of activities.

AESTHETIC LEARNING AND THE ROLE OF THE TEACHER

The way teachers relate to aesthetics and the arts can greatly affect children's aesthetic development. When teachers nurture the arts in their classrooms, build on children's interests and abilities, encourage individual expression, and praise children's work, an enthusiasm for learning grows (Colbert, 1997). "One has only to

The Preschematic Stage

FIGURE 8.4

Examples of Aesthetic Activities for Growing Children

Aesthetic Component	1–3-Year-Olds Activities	3–5-Year-Olds Activities	6–8-Year-Olds Activities
Responsive: Aesthetic Preferences	Exploring natural objects, music, and child-appropriate art objects (wooden toys, dolls, bells).	Exploring and collecting objects. Describing what they like about valued objects and own work.	Exploring, collecting, describing, analyzing, interpreting and evaluating objects, their own work and work of others.
Responsive: Musical Interests	Lullaby. Musical toys. Songs with repetitions and simple melody ("Ring around the Rosie").	Repetitive and cumulative songs. Tunes with more complex melody. Guided listening to range of music.	Wide variety of songs, kinds of music, relating music to various moods and settings. Interest in musical notation.
Productive: Vocal Music	Songs with simple tunes that repeat. Songs that use child's name.	Improvising. Singing while swinging. Songs with repetitions. Substituting words ("Mary Wore a Red Dress").	Singing more complex songs ("Swinging on a Star'). Silly songs. Rounds ("Make New Friends"). Beginning to use musical notation.
Productive: Musical Instruments	Manipulating objects with sounds (e.g. bells, xylophone, tambourines, triangle).	Simple instruments and music with definite rhythm. Cooperative instruments. Improvisation.	Imitation of established melodies and rhythms. Some improvisation and using instruments to accompany own song.
Productive: Creative Movement and Dance	Spontaneous movement to music using legs and arms.	Singing and dancing games ("Farmer in Dell"). Action songs ("Bingo," "Head Shoulders"). Using props (scarf, hoop).	Improvisations. Simple folk dances. Beginning interest in organized dance instruction (tap, ballet).
Productive: Creative Visual Art Expression	Multisensory experiences with age-appropriate art materials (crayons, paint, markers, playdough).	Drawing with variety of tools. Constructing with blocks, paper, clay. Collage, murals, mobiles, painting in various ways. Simple print-making.	Drawing. Combining drawing with writing. Crafts, woodworking, pottery, building, weaving, puppets. Imitating styles of artists (pointillism).
Productive: Story Enactment and Creative Drama	Imitation. Action stories and songs, finger plays. Stories with simple plot and familiar experiences. Roles suggested by objects (purse, shoes).	Creative dramatics with props (store, restaurant). Enacting longer finger plays ("In a Cabin in the Woods"), songs ("The Green Grass Grew"). Puppets for story enactment.	Creating pretend scenarios using dolls, small animals, or action figures. Putting on shows for an audience using elements of drama (character, motivation, conflict, costume, performance). Plays with a script. Reader's theater.

The Schematic Stage

look at the environment and the children's art work from Reggio Emilia to see that moving art to the center of the curriculum has a strong impact on children's self-expression and learning" (Spaggiari, 1987). Teachers can positively influence the extent to which students value the arts and provide a rich background of experiences that free them to become creative producers and tasteful consumers of the arts as adults.

How does the teacher do this? Teachers who are the most effective in providing high-quality arts experiences for young children know how to share their enthusiasm for the arts and aesthetics, continue to be avid learners in the arts, focus on developing children's creativity, and strive to become more creative themselves (Jalongo & Stamp, 1997).

TEACHING STRATEGIES FOR QUALITY AESTHETIC EXPERIENCES

1. *Model aesthetic awareness and enthusiasm.* Respond to the aesthetic qualities of the world around you. Point out the beauty you see in the sky, trees,

clouds, rocks, and other natural objects. Talk about discoveries you have made and the enthusiasm you have about works of art or music you enjoy. Demonstrate a positive attitude about opportunities to be involved in the arts both in and out of this setting. Be a role model for how to be engaged in the arts. For example, tell children ways you are a participant or observer (saw a theater performance, listened to music, played an instrument, or attended a recital). Emphasize the enjoyment you and your family or friends derive from this kind of activity. Arrange for an artist, a musician, or a dancer to visit your class to show what they do. Take the class to visit an artist in his studio. If this is not possible, visit the local high school drama team as they rehearse for a performance or the band as they prepare for a concert.

2. *Prepare an aesthetics-friendly classroom environment.* Use the physical environment of the classroom as examples of aesthetic experiences. Mount and display children's art work at their eye level. Occasionally play music during activities for pure enjoyment. Encourage children to sing during various times of the

day for pleasure, such as arrival or departure times. Remove clutter and use shelf tops as places for displaying plants, sculpture, and items of natural beauty such as shells, flower arrangements, or beautiful rocks. Display reproductions of the work of famous artists in classroom as decorations or use them in art appreciation activities.

3. *Organize an art center or "creation station" with appropriate materials.* Maintain supplies in labeled containers, allowing easy access to basic materials, and store the more specialized ones for occasional use.

A Caution About Art Materials. Many early childhood educators favor the use of a great variety of materials and constantly search for new and different ones to introduce to youngsters. These same teachers are reluctant to repeat an art activity or even to offer the same materials two days in a row, perhaps for fear children will get bored. Dr. Carol Seefeldt, professor of early childhood and child development at the University of Maryland, warns that "children continually faced with new media are never able to gain control over, or develop skill in the use of any one medium. Unless children have the opportunity to gain experience with basic medium over time, they will find it difficult to achieve the skills required to use that medium as a means of artistic expression" (Seefeldt, 1987).

Young children should have many chances to use *basic art materials* to develop this sense of mastery. Teachers should make basic materials (such as those in Table 8.1) available many days in a row and repeat activities several times. For example, painting at the easel should be a nearly daily offering. Fingerpainting should be offered several times a month. Drawing with crayons, pencil, or markers on plain paper should be encouraged as often as possible.

4. *Select appropriate music-supporting materials.* Young children need a rich musical environment in which to grow (MENC, 1994). When children have many opportunities to explore and create with basic rhythm instruments, experiment with a variety of pitched instruments, and listen to many different kinds of music, their enjoyment and participation with musical experiences are greatly enhanced. The music materials in Table 8.2 are recommended for early childhood programs:

5. *Provide a variety of creative movement props.* Movement is an important musical response because it is nonverbal and allows the observer to better understand what aspects of the music the child is sensing (Bredekamp & Rosegrant, 1995). These props can motivate creative movement exploration for youngsters: plastic hoops, scarves in a variety of colors, streamers or

Children enjoy creating a variety of musical sounds.

TABLE 8.1
Art Materials and Tools

Basic Art Materials for Young Children	**Inappropriate Art Materials**
❑ tempera paints—red, yellow, blue, white, black	❑ oil-based paints
❑ watercolor paints (paint boxes with refillable colors or larger paintcakes)	❑ inks that are not water-soluble
❑ fingerpaint and fingerpaint paper	❑ leaded paints of any kind
❑ manila paper—two sizes	❑ turpentine, paint thinners
❑ newsprint paper—variety of sizes	❑ asbestos products
❑ construction paper—variety of colors and white; variety of sizes	❑ chemically treated wood
❑ crayons (fat and thin in a variety of colors)	❑ products that are toxic or create toxic fumes
❑ pencils—various sizes	❑ permanent markers
❑ nonpermanent markers in varied sizes and colors	**Occasional Art Materials**
❑ art chalk (softer than writing chalk)	❑ variety papers: tissue paper, wax, inexpensive white drawing paper, crepe paper, foil, cellophane, etc.
❑ white nontoxic glue	❑ wood glue
❑ white paste	❑ glue sticks
❑ supply of old newspapers	❑ pipe cleaners
❑ modeling dough (homemade is best)	❑ plastic or paper straws
❑ collage materials (recycled)	❑ yarn of various colors
Basic Art Tools	❑ string
❑ paint brushes—various sizes, shapes	❑ cardboard of various thicknesses
❑ tape (magic, masking, and plastic)	❑ potter's (ceramic, drying) clay
❑ scissors	❑ liquid starch
❑ staplers	❑ wood scraps
❑ paper fasteners	❑ glitter
❑ hole punches	❑ clean old socks
❑ recycled plastic containers of various sizes	❑ small cardboard boxes
❑ tongue depressors (craft sticks)	❑ clean styrofoam trays
❑ rulers	❑ colored sand
❑ 2–4 rollers (brayers)	❑ natural materials—leaves, stones, shells, acorns, gourds, etc.

flags (crepe paper attached to short, safe handles such as wide popsicle sticks), rhythm sticks, tambourine, paper towel rolls, pom poms, and batons.

6. *Provide props for dramatics.* Table 8.3 presents suggestions to stimulate creative dramatics.

7. *Value all aspects of the creative expression process.* No matter what stage of development the child is in, teachers should recognize and value that level. Individual developmental differences are expected in any group of children. The way teachers and other support adults respond to the child's aesthetic products (for example, the drawing, the dance, the song, or the dramatic production) will have lasting effects on the individual. Adult responses to children's attempts at creative expression either help establish an environment of acceptance and encouragement or make it clear to children that their own ideas will not be tolerated. In general, teachers should use praise judiciously. Be flexible and prepared for unique actions and products (such as the child who chooses only one color of paint when a range of colors is offered, or the student who uses the props for Three Billy Goats Gruff to create his own story about Mars). Engage in dialogue about the child's work, showing interest and responding to problems. Use guidance; facilitate by using stimulating questions (such as, "Do your people from Mars have names?" or "How will they solve their problem of no food on Mars?"). Show children you value their efforts and experimentation.

TABLE 8.2
Music Materials and Tools

Basic Rhythm Instruments

- ❏ drums
- ❏ rhythm sticks (wooden or plastic dowels, broom handles, or paper towel rolls)
- ❏ maracas
- ❏ triangles
- ❏ jingle bells
- ❏ sand blocks
- ❏ tambourine
- ❏ clappers

Basic Pitched-Instruments

- ❏ xylophones
- ❏ tone bells
- ❏ simple wooden or plastic recorders
- ❏ kazoos

Other Musical Materials

- ❏ record player with a variety of records
- ❏ tape recorder with speakers and a collection of taped music
- ❏ CD player with a collection of music CDs
- ❏ simple cassette tape recorder that can be used by children
- ❏ chord instruments (such as guitar, autoharp, piano, keyboard) add interest and variety to children's singing, but are not necessary for musical success in the classroom.

TABLE 8.3
Drama Materials and Props

Props That Suggest Roles

- ❏ firehats and short hoses, paper towel rolls, maps, boots, badges
- ❏ cash register, play money, empty food containers
- ❏ menus, plastic dishes, apron, play money, trays
- ❏ steering wheel, earphones, board with knobs and dials

Props Related to Stories

- ❏ "The Three Little Pigs": pile of sticks tied together, cardboard bricks, ears, pot
- ❏ "Billy Goats Gruff": a table (bridge), a Troll mask, paper horns
- ❏ "Caps for Sale": paper plate caps in various colors, monkey tails, chairs for tree limbs

Simple Costumes and Props That Stimulate Imagination

- ❏ magic wand, top hat, cloak, crown, microphone, animal noses

Miscellaneous Props

- ❏ masks
- ❏ stuffed animals
- ❏ hand and finger puppets

Let children know you like it when they use their own ideas in aesthetic activities, especially if they are different from others' or your own. Use words such as "Your picture doesn't have to look like Matthew's. I like it when everyone's looks different; everyone has his own different ideas, and that's good."

8. *Teach children to respect and care for materials.* Teachers should demonstrate how to clean and store materials properly. For example, rhythm instruments should be carefully placed into storage containers at the end of the activity. Paint brushes should be washed carefully and layed flat or handle-down to air dry. Watercolor paint boxes should be rinsed with clean water and left open to dry. Replacing caps on markers will preserve their moisture for longer use. Paper scraps large enough to be used another day should be kept in a scrap collection box and recycled.

9. *Motivate creativity through a variety of strategies.* Teachers should help children choose interesting subjects, expand their range of responses to their world, be more creative, and stimulate more imaginative responses through direct and indirect motivational strategies such as these:

a. *Provide direct hands-on time with materials* guided by your words. As children explore the objects, dis-

cuss the sensory aspects associated with the experience (e.g., how it feels, what sounds can be made with it, how it smells, what different textures can be noticed, which colors can they see, etc.).

b. *Show examples of quality art and beautiful craftsmanship* such as baskets, carvings, musical instruments or quilts, and real paintings occasionally instead of reproductions, so children actually see and feel how paint was applied or threads were worked into the design.

c. *Demonstrate new techniques.* Using the same materials that children will use, show ways to manipulate the tools and substances to achieve particular effects.

d. *Use motivational dialogue.* Following demonstrations, engage children in "motivational dialogue" (Herberholz & Hanson, 1995; Lowenfeld & Brittain, 1965) in which children suggest ideas that might work with that technique or material. For example, "Since you know a good way to fasten pieces together, what can we make with our clay today? Who has an idea?" or "Now that you know how to use the tape player, what songs will you record onto your tape?" Write their ideas on a large list.

e. *Role-play ideas.* One of the best ways young children learn about something is to experience the

Interactive demonstrations help children explore new techniques.

concept with their whole body. Children's art work increases in creativity and detail following role-playing experiences. For example, teachers can suggest children move like tall trees blowing in the wind, be a wave crashing to the shore, or crouch like tiny mice in the grass. Afterward, children apply those ideas to making pictures or creating a drama or a dance.

f. *Show and discuss pictures of real objects.* This kind of motivation can help children notice more, enhance the appeal of expressing their own perceptions, and break down stereotype ideas they may have developed through other experiences. For example, shown a picture of a thunderstorm, children use the rhythm instruments to create their own storm with great gusto; shown several pictures of homes (a log cabin, an apartment house, a two-bedroom ranch, and an igloo) and after a short discussion of homes, children create more interesting cardboard box homes with greater insights.

g. *Encourage imagining.* Suggest that children close their eyes and imagine something very different from their immediate surroundings; for example, ask them what they might see, hear, and smell if they were standing at the seashore or walking deep in the forest. For older children, suggest they change their perspective such as imagining what they could see looking down from a very tall tree flying over the rooftops or what it would be like being an ant and looking up from an ant hill. Have them describe what they are picturing in their minds and encourage them to listen to each other's ideas. Then offer materials to make what they imagined.

h. *Use nonverbal reinforcement.* Rather than verbal praise directed at the work itself, occasionally respond positively to children's efforts, enthusiasm, and concentration using smiles, pats on the back, or thumbs-up gestures as children work. This technique can be very reinforcing.

i. *Connect creative experiences to a concept they are learning.* Mrs. Martin is teaching about opposites (e.g., high-low, fast-slow, and big-little). After brainstorming examples of opposites and making a list with the students, she challenges them to use their clay to express and illustrate two opposite words. Later, students find their two words in the dictionary and make signs to display next to their creations on the windowsill.

10. *Explore the materials before asking children to use them.* Try to spend a few minutes with new aesthetic materials before the children do in order to become familiar with what they can do and to recognize any problems children may encounter. For example, if the paint is too runny, additional thick paint or detergent should be added beforehand to avoid drips and disappointed artists. If the autoharp is out of tune, take time to tune it to make the sounds more pleasant and appealing.

11. *Avoid making a product when demonstrating a technique.* Introduce the class to any new technique or material that may need explanation. For example, show children how to hold down the buttons on the autoharp to create different chords while strumming lightly across the strings; show various ways to apply glue to styrofoam where it is most needed and appropriate amounts to use. Focus on the technique instead of the subject matter in a demonstration. When demonstrating art materials, avoid making a recognizable picture. The reason for this is simple: whatever the teacher makes will establish an extremely strong model, and children will want to copy it. Children will believe that this is the product the teacher wants and abandon their own ideas. Even very creative individuals have a difficult time thinking beyond what their teacher shows them as the "correct way." For example, in a demonstration of the techniques of crayon resist, the teacher stresses pressing hard on the crayons. She uses crayons to make uninteresting lines and shapes that could be anything instead of making flowers with the crayons. The demonstration is followed by asking children to tell what kind of picture they will make. This strategy gets children thinking and engages their own creativity.

A different way to focus on the technique, not the subject matter, is to make an imaginary picture during the demonstration; that is, present the steps of the process using gestures using the tools without really making anything and without showing a finished product. Children are more likely to use their own ideas when this strategy is utilized.

12. *Involve children in music experiences daily.* All children sing; "they begin as soon as they gain sufficient control over their voice to talk. It is one unmistakable universal that there is no human culture in which people do not sing" (Dowling & Harwood, 1986). Even teachers with little musical training or those who feel less than adequate singing can share the

joy of music with youngsters. At various times throughout the day such as transitions, clean up, opening of group meetings, or at the end of the day, teachers should sing songs with the class, play a recorded piece of music as background, or encourage children to clap along as they tap rhythms with a tambourine.

13. *Provide a large uncluttered space for creative movement.* Young children need plenty of space in which to move and many opportunities to practice moving without bumping into others. Push furniture and equipment aside to accommodate the greatest amount of freedom and safety during creative movement activities.

14. *Begin each creative movement experience with a similar routine warm-up and end with a similar cooldown.* A familiar opening and closing will help youngsters know what is expected of them, assist them in getting ready to move, build on what they already know, and feel successful before and after they learn new concepts.

15. *Accept children's own ideas for creative movement.* Avoid overdirecting; remember that creative movement is self-expression; expect students to individually respond to suggestions from you or to the music. Encourage children to look at each other's creative responses occasionally. Allow individuals to volunteer to share their movement ideas, but avoid requiring them to perform.

16. *Utilize the principle of developmental direction in aesthetic teaching.* In Chapter 2 you learned about the principle of developmental direction and the fact that children moved through a cycle of learning beginning with *exploration,* moving through *acquisition,* through *practice,* toward *generalization.* Teachers who are cognizant of this cycle of learning

❏ Plan activities that help children become more aware through *exploration* of materials.
❏ Provide opportunities for children to *ask questions* and *seek information* from a variety of sources.
❏ Plan activities that allow children to *practice* using new information.
❏ Plan activities that help children *generalize* and *apply* the knowledge they have acquired.

By planning aesthetic experiences that are both responsive and productive, teachers stimulate learning at all levels of this cycle of learning. In this domain children become aware of aesthetics through discovery and exposure activities. Through exposure and creative ac-

tivities with unfamiliar materials, children explore new ideas related to the arts. Evaluation activities give children experience with asking questions and evaluating processes and products in the arts. Finally, creative activities with familiar materials give students time and opportunities to practice, generalize, and apply what they have learned to new situations.

17. *Discover and use picture book illustrations as works of art.* Every year new and wonderful children's books are published that contain perfect examples of visual artistic expression. Teachers should share with their students at least one beautiful book each day. Help children discover the joy of art available to hold in one's hand, explore and recognize techniques, and open doors to insights. Before (or after) reading the story each day, take time to introduce each picture as a painting, discussing the visual qualities. What child has ever read Maurice Sendak's *Where the Wild Things Are* (Sendak, 1963), Lois Ehlert's *Eating the Alphabet Fruits and Vegetables from A to Z* (Ehlert, 1989), or Rylant's *The Relatives Came* (Rylant, 1985) without pausing to look at the incredible pictures? Teachers should treat books as priceless gifts with each illustration a gem to be treasured. This demonstration of appreciation can influence children to develop a lifelong interest in collecting good art and owning beautiful books (Szekely, 1990).

Other activities using book illustrations for a variety of purposes are these:

❏ Find a selected artistic style, such as Eric Carle's painted papers, in a collection of books.
❏ Compare artistic interpretations of a familiar subject (e.g., grandmothers) in picture books such as *Charlie and Grandma* by Sally Ward (1986), *Gifts* by Jo Ellen Bogart (1994), *My Grammy* by Marsha Kibbey (1988), and *Bigmama's* by Donald Crews (1991).
❏ Study and imitate an illustrator's use of materials (technique) such as collage in any book by Ezra Jack Keats, use of colored clays in *Gifts* by Jo Ellen Bogart, or mixed media technique in pictures by Leo Lionni.

18. *Use different kinds of questions to help children describe, analyze, interpret, and judge works in the arts.* Questions can extend children's ability to respond to the arts. Using various kinds of questions in discussions regarding the arts, elicit a variety of kinds of thinking from children:

a. *Cognitive memory questions* motivate thinking about facts (e.g., "What do you see [or hear]? What are some words to describe this?").

b. *Convergent questions,* or closed questions, have expected answers (e.g., "What is the largest thing in this painting? What was the slowest part of that song?").

c. *Divergent questions,* or open-ended questions, have many possible answers (e.g., "Why do you like dancing?").

d. *Evaluative questions* ask for children's values (e.g., "What part of that dance did you like the best? Which shell is your favorite? Why?") (Tauton, 1983).

19. *Avoid reinforcing only a realistic approach.* Children recognize when teachers truly value individual differences. Teachers who reward (verbally or nonverbally) only art work that contains naturalistic symbols of real objects and ignore more abstract and less pictorial works severely limit young children's creative expression of thoughts, feelings, and events. Young children often experiment with materials without intending to relate their finished product to reality or even to their inner thoughts. They may be fascinated by the way the colors change when they touch each other or how the sand sticks to the glue and not to the paper. Adults who insist they "see something" in children's pictures impose the value of realism that can force children into this narrow mode of expression and the frustration of such limits. If teachers focus instead on the artistic elements of the work (such as color used, lines, arrangement of shapes, etc.) or the effort expended by the artist, students see that they are free to utilize whatever means of expression they want, without worrying their work will be devalued.

20. *Involve all of the children in the arts.* The arts provide opportunities for success for all of the students, regardless of their abilities or handicapping conditions. Activities with various visual art media and music should be adapted to allow as much participation as possible according to the individual needs of the children. Creative dramatics and creative movement should be approached in an open-ended manner to provide success on many different levels for all children, including students with special needs.

APPROACHES TO TEACHING THE ARTS

As you learned in Chapter 3, there are different approaches to teaching anything. Some are more teacher controlled, some more child controlled, and others share the control between teacher and children (see Figure 8.5). Just as these approaches can be applied to teaching in general, they also apply to teaching in the arts.

The various approaches can be thought of as a continuum from closed to open approaches. The more aspects of the activity the teacher chooses and controls, the more teacher controlled it is. The fewer aspects of the activity the teacher chooses, the more the student selects for him- or herself, and the more child controlled is the experience. Figure 8.5 shows this continuum of teaching approaches and how it relates to the arts. Notice the variety of dimensions of the art activity that can be more or less controlled by the teacher. *Materials* are what are used for the activity (e.g., paint, wood, glue, salt, etc.). *Techniques* are how the materials are manipulated and the tools used (e.g., gluing sand on paper, cutting cloth strips, shaping paper mache). *Subject* is the topic or theme of the activity (e.g., birds, the ocean, germs) *Product* is what the finished work will look or sound like (e.g., a map, a list, a picture, an ornament).

Consider examples of the three teaching approaches on the continuum. For our purposes, the example will relate to visual art. However, teaching any of the arts (music, creative movement, drama, or dance) could apply. Assume that Teacher A plans a fingerpainting activity that is completely *teacher-controlled.* She chooses fingerpaint paper, cuts it to 8″ × 11″ and selects blue fingerpaint (the materials). She describes (the technique) applying the blue paint with a spoon and using their fingers to spread it on the paper. She tells them they will all be making pictures of the sky today (subject) and that their sky paintings (product) will be hung on the wall when they are dry. As children take turns, she reminds them of the way they are to work, pointing out that they should stop "messing around" with the paint and make their sky pictures. All the children produce similar blue paintings, which pleases the teacher because she plans to glue one die-cut bird to each painting to go along with their theme. After their paintings dry, several children have a hard time identifying their pictures. Some children toss theirs into the trash. Children reacted negatively to the art experience because there were no choices, opportunities to be creative, or motivation to express any part of themselves.

FIGURE 8.5
Continuum of Teaching Approaches

Teacher Controlled ———— Shared Control ————— Child Controlled	
Teacher chooses all materials	Child chooses all materials
Teacher chooses techniques	Child chooses techniques
Teacher chooses subject	Child chooses subject
Teacher plans the product	Child chooses the product
No input from child	All input from child
High teacher intervention	Low teacher intervention

Teacher B's approach to the art activity is completely *child controlled.* Children are free to work with any materials they want, using whatever techniques they devise. They may select any subject and produce any product they wish. The teacher does not enter the art area, assuming this would interfere with children's creativity. Today during choice time a few children enter the area, look around, and then leave. One child spends her whole choice time in the art area, using markers, scissors, yarn, and glue to make a picture for her mom. Teacher B notices that not many children use the art area, and she wonders why. Most of the children did not take advantage of the freedom to choose in the art area because they were not motivated to experience the art materials; they missed an opportunity to use art as a means to express their ideas.

Teacher C's approach to teaching the activity is *shared control.* She plans some aspects of the activity but leaves many aspects open for children to choose. She arranges newspaper on one end of the art table and lays smocks on two chairs. She places two open containers of fingerpaint, one red and one blue, on the newspaper, with a plastic spoon in each. She wets a clean sponge and puts it on a dish near the paint. She also lays a pencil and one piece of fingerpaint paper in front of each chair. As children come in, she gathers them together and demonstrates how to use the materials if they choose to fingerpaint today. As she moves the paint on her paper, she asks them to tell her what she could paint. She listens to their ideas and makes observations such as "You're thinking about making hand prints with the paint" and "Danny, you want to make your dog with the paint." She purposely

does not make a recognizable picture but instead focuses on a variety of ways to move her fingers. She asks probing questions such as "What if I used both colors of paint?" While she demonstrates washing her hands, she suggests they begin a waiting list because only two children can fingerpaint at a time. During the morning, she checks in to see how the painting is going. She comments on how well the children are taking turns and remembering to wear smocks. She points out that Michelle found her own way to use her fingers in the paint. Most of the children participate, and each of their paintings is unique. Several children use the other end of the table to make their own creations using other basic materials they took from labeled containers on the art shelf. When paintings are dry, the children easily find their own and are able to tell something about theirs because the experience was meaningful to them. This leads to a writing activity later in the week. Teacher C has facilitated the activity through the physical set-up, demonstration, discussion, and offer of choices. Her teaching approach provides a balance of independence and sensitive intervention without monopolizing the activity. She has motivated children to think and problem-solve, taught them about procedure, sharing, and cooperation, and provided new insight into themselves as artists.

CURRENT EDUCATIONAL ISSUES

Teachers and administrators are faced with many issues that affect their thinking, planning, and implementation of educational programs for young children.

Some of the current issues dealing with aesthetic development are discussed next.

Teaching the Arts Without Special Training

I have to teach art and music in my classroom, but I don't have the training. Isn't it best to leave those things to the specialists?

Classroom teachers need not be artists or musicians to teach children to appreciate the arts and be aware of beauty in their natural surroundings. Any personally productive experiences that teachers have had, whether writing a paper in college, decorating a home, or planning a vegetable garden, can help them identify with the act of creating. "Every teacher does not have to be practiced in all media in order to think creatively. It is rather the intense experience accompanying any creative occupation that is important for keeping alive the teacher's appreciation and understanding of creative experiences of their students" (Lowenfeld & Brittain, 1965). Teachers who believe the arts and a love of natural beauty are important and who openly demonstrate these attitudes and encourage children to involve themselves in creative endeavors do much to influence children's positive attitudes and aesthetic development regardless of the teacher's specialized background or training.

Schools with music, art, dance, or drama specialists available to primary teachers are privileged to be able to take advantage of their expertise. Unfortunately, even districts with such resource people cannot meet the needs of individual elementary classrooms for frequent, meaningful, integrated aesthetic experiences for young children.

Teachers are wise to utilize specialists when possible, to observe strategies of motivation and responding to children's work, and to ask for advice concerning materials and techniques unfamiliar to them. However, teachers should avoid relying on specialists to provide the bulk of aesthetic experiences. Instead, weekly planning should include aesthetic experiences designed for their particular group of youngsters, based on knowledge of individual and group needs and on that unique understanding of the children only classroom teachers can achieve. Children should have frequent opportunities for singing, making music, dancing, and drama with their classroom teacher, in both planned and spontaneous activities throughout each week.

Teacher-Designed Models As Art

I have a number of art projects I do. The parents love it when the kids bring home their paper turkey all decorated the way I teach them. What's the harm?

Teachers sometimes fall into the trap of presenting art materials with a particular end-product in mind, one designed either by the teacher or by a commercial publisher, and believe they are encouraging aesthetic growth. Nothing could be farther from the truth. Listen as well-meaning Ms. Jones introduces the activity. "Today we're all going to make turkeys just like this one (holds up a completed brown paper tracing of a hand, with four fingers colored as feathers, and a head indicated with an eye colored on the thumb). First you trace your hand on the paper I gave you, and then take your red crayon and. . . ." When children are expected to follow step-by-step directions, severely limited to the teacher's idea and choice of materials and techniques, the child is forced to produce something that most likely holds no meaning for him or her and frequently causes feelings of frustration when they observe their finished product does not meet the standard set by the teacher's model.

The good intentions of Ms. Jones for a fun activity result in children with negative attitudes about art, convinced they can never be any good at it. Moreover, activities such as this are very destructive to whatever creative thinking children may bring to the activity because all of the finished work is intended to look alike, and children are not reinforced for imaginative approaches to the task set down by the teacher.

Now consider how this activity could be presented in a way that encourages more creative thinking and results: "Does anyone know the name of this bird?" (Mr. Tiel holds up a large photograph of a real turkey.) "What do you notice about it? How many legs does it have? Look carefully at the neck; notice that reddish-orange piece of skin . . ." and so on. "Has anyone ever seen a turkey? Where do you think you'd find a turkey? Where else? What would that look like? OK, you had really good ideas. Today you may go to the art center and make your own kind of turkey if you want, any way you want. Remember, everyone's will be different because we all have our own ideas. There are some materials on the shelf nearby" (he points to baskets and small trays holding a variety of paper, crayons, scissors, glue sticks, markers, yarn, real feathers, pipe cleaners, and scrap paper pieces) "to use. If you want to use something that's not on the shelf, just ask me. I'll come by and see how you're doing in a while. Your turkey could be big or little, fat or thin, whatever you want. Now, who will be the first four at the center?" Children who are interested and motivated readily move to the art table. Those who wish to make something different are also encouraged to take a turn. Finished works are hung or put aside to dry. The children produce a flock of unique creations that are personally satisfying. Children look at each other's work, notice new things, and learn from each other. Mr. Tiel has used the photograph as the only model for children and facilitated their learning instead of limiting it to a stereotype.

Using Coloring Books and Coloring Pages

My Art 100 professor says coloring books are not good for kids; well, I used them when I was growing up, and I loved them. What's the problem?

Most children experience coloring books and coloring dittos sometime during their childhood. Many find them fun, and the activity provides practice with fine motor control. There is even an element of creativity involved when children make choices about which colors to use to fill in the spaces. However, a steady diet of fill-in-the-adult-drawn-pictures can lead children to mistrust their own ability to draw. Children who use coloring books frequently demonstrate less confidence in their ability to make their own pictures. It appears that well-meaning coloring activities tend to establish a powerful adult model for drawings that children know they will never be able to match. Some youngsters say "I can't draw" and believe it. Coloring books may appear harmless, but because studies show that human creativity peaks around age $4^1/2$, they seem particularly destructive to young children reaching the height of their creative lives. Teachers and parents can take advantage of children's enthusiasm for "coloring" by handing them a drawing pad instead of a coloring book and encouraging them to make their own wonderful pictures with those lovely crayons.

Responding to Children's Art

I don't know what to say to children when they show me their art. I don't want to say the wrong thing.

Traditionally, adults respond in various ways to children's art work and each approach can affect the child artist in different ways. Dr. Robert Schirrmacher (1993) analyzed the impact of six kinds of adult responses: complimentary, judgmental, valuing, questioning, probing, and correcting. Figure 8.6 presents a short summary of the impact of each adult approach to a young student's art.

Responding Effectively to Children's Aesthetic Products

Frequently adults think children need a verbal response to their work when a nonverbal signal such as a thumbs up, smile, or nod would be sufficient. When a verbal response is needed, teachers should shift from looking for representation (adult realism) to a more effective approach, such as focusing on one or more of the elements of visual arts: line, color, form, texture, composition, balance, pattern, or contrast. These kinds of comments encourage aesthetic awareness and may establish the beginning of dialogue if the child is comfortable discussing his or her work further (Schirrmacher, 1986). Probing responses that are used occasionally encourage children to talk about their work from their own perspective. Listen to what the child says and respond in terms of that, remaining nonjudgmental but interested. Older children frequently use more realism in their art work, and their pictures contain obvious recognizable symbols; it is still advisable for teachers to remain as objective as possible in their responses. Comments can indicate understanding of meaning but do not establish a preference for realism over nonrepresentational art. Teachers can bring closure to their comments by indicating progress the child is making, effort put in, or simply acknowledging their feelings. Figure 8.7 presents several examples.

Competition

"The prettiest paintings will be hung in the hallway for parents to see." "Hold up your constructions, and we'll see which one is the best." "Our daughter suddenly stopped singing after her experience in the vocal contest in elementary school."

Young children who are given opportunities for free creative expression in art and music are confused by

FIGURE 8.6
Impact of Various Responses to Children's Art

Response	Example	Impact on Child
Complimentary	"Very nice."	Cuts off discussion.
Judgmental	"Great work, Joey."	Empty comment with overuse. Child thinks anything he or she does is terrific, no matter how little effort.
Valuing	"I like that a lot."	Puts emphasis on the product, not the process. Too often rewards what is recognizable by adults; ignores personal expression that is not.
Questioning	"What is it?"	Insists it be something; disregards abstract expression. Disappoints the artist who thinks it is obvious.
Probing	"Tell me all about it."	Encourages child to discuss; avoids passing judgment on child's work. Assumes child will enjoy/learn from verbalizing ideas.
Correcting	"Very good, but the grass should be green."	Assumes child must copy reality. Can discourage creative expression.

FIGURE 8.7
Effective Responses to Children's Art

Response	Examples	Impact on Child
1. Acknowledge effort.	1. "You worked a long time on that."	1. My hard work is noticed.
2. Recognize one of the aesthetic elements.	2. "You used lots of different shapes. The bright yellow areas look even brighter next to the dark gray ones."	2. Yes, I did. I never noticed that before.
3. Indicate understanding.	3. "I noticed your tree has lots of fruit. The people are standing in the rain in your picture."	3. Good, they know what I mean.
4. Acknowledge child's feelings.	4. "You're pretty proud of your collage. You're disappointed in your painting."	4. I don't have to feel the same about all of my art.
5. Ask for information.	5. "Show me a part that you like." "Tell me something about your picture."	5. I can say things about my art that only I know.
6. Broaden child's self-concept.	6. "You really like animals."	6. Yes, I guess I do.
7. Indicate progress.	7. "This is the third drawing you've made about our field trip."	7. I've accomplished a lot.

practices that include competition. Children's musical and artistic expression are highly individual with no two children entirely alike; indeed, an important goal of aesthetic development is to bring out this uniqueness—to show it is valuable and to encourage every child's involvement, assuming a broad range of talent, experience, and insights. To young children, there is no right or wrong way to create, so to say there is a "best" product is meaningless to them. Imposing arbitrary adult standards of artistic excellence on their work is inappropriate and unacceptable for young children. "Particularly in the early years, children should be free from competitive and other imposed adult standards that can limit self-expression" (Dixon & Chalmers, 1990). Teachers should be careful to encourage free creative expression and to avoid using words that communicate competition or instill fear of failure such as "good," "bad," "best," "worst," "right," "wrong," "cheat," and "mistake." Likewise, all children should be encouraged to sing, dance, and participate in musical production without regard to performance criteria. If music is seen as sharing and communicating rather than performance, children are freer to explore their creative capacities.

Regular classroom or hall art displays are usually held for the children's sake and are a good way of showing what has been accomplished. Displaying children's art tells students that the teacher values their efforts, thinks the works of art are important, and likes them as individuals. Therefore, it is important to show some of every student's work whenever possible; unfortunately, when space is limited, not all work can be exhibited, and teachers are forced to make selections. In this event, teachers could ask children to help choose what will be displayed and make selections based on what the child feels he/she would like to have exhibited, having children take turns being the exhibitors. Using this strategy changes the focus to the child choosing what they feel best about instead of the teacher imposing selection criteria from an adult point of view. It also involves them in an evaluation process that is personally meaningful.

Although pattern work and copying can meet other educational goals (see chapters regarding cognitive and physical development), no work should be displayed as art that does not express the child's own experience. Therefore, teacher-designed patterns (such as the hand-tracing turkey described earlier) where

each student's product is nearly identical to the next do not reflect individual expression and should not be reinforced as successful artistic works.

Young children need not see their work displayed for long periods of time. Many youngsters quickly lose the intimate relationship to their own work when it is displayed too long; often very young children want to take things home as soon as possible. Teachers who change class displays frequently make more opportunities for children's work to be recognized and lend variety to the aesthetic environment of the school.

Another way teachers show they value creative aesthetic expression is by placing samples of each student's art work in individual portfolios, kept as a record of progress over a period of time (e.g., two months), and then sent home or given to parents at an evaluation conference. Children should be involved in the choosing process, teaching them to make selections for their portfolio from their own work. Such artifacts are extremely valuable in demonstrating the student's growth over time. In addition, musical accomplishments can be recorded on audio cassette tapes. Children should be encouraged to record themselves singing songs, telling stories, playing musical instruments, and creating rhythms; they are more likely to do this if there is no pressure to be perfect. By preserving these creative endeavors, children may replay their own tape for themselves or for friends, and recordings can be available for conferences with parents.

Impact of Funding Cuts in the Arts

My district is cutting back on money for art and music. I'm concerned about how this will affect the children.

When districts integrate the arts extensively into the curriculum, making the visual arts, music, dance, and drama part of the fabric of daily classroom experiences, they take advantage of the powerful positive influence that aesthetic growth can have on children's lives and community attitudes, judgments, and values. However, some districts experiencing financial problems see the arts as expendable. Schools that have their funds for the arts cut frequently respond by narrowing the range of aesthetic opportunities for youngsters to a few public "end product" goals such as an annual art display, a single dramatic production, or a concert. Although these activities are valuable, educators are beginning to recognize the loss of the arts in the daily curriculum as a mistake. This limited approach to aesthetic learning cannot accommodate the broad range of individual interests and learning styles of all of the children. As a result, many young children only rarely participate in creative tasks, and some are not involved at all. Cutting of school funds for the arts can produce these results:

1. Fewer opportunities for creative experiences.
2. A narrower range of chances for success for students.
3. Decreased motivation among students.
4. Limited recognition of talents.
5. Less valuing and appreciation of cultural heritage.
6. Less incentive to imagine, problem-solve, and make decisions.
7. Class groups lose cohesive bond.
8. A widening gap between children and older generations.
9. Aesthetic tastes more strongly influenced by mass media.
10. Children seek satisfying experiences elsewhere (streets, drugs, etc.).

In recent years, aesthetic learning has been valued as a tool for meeting other significant educational needs. As stated at the Mid-Atlantic Regional Forum on National Educational Goals (May 1991), the arts play a vital role in establishing a bond between the generations that technology sometimes drives apart. This important link is "the glue that holds [the generations] together and contributes to a shared affective experience" for people of all ages. Knowing the consequences of such cuts in the arts, teachers should do all they can to urge administrators and community leaders to speak out for maintaining strong programs that place high value on regular aesthetic experiences for children.

NATIONAL GOALS

Aesthetic Goals and Objectives

Incorporating the 1994 National Standards for Arts Education and 1993 Music Education Standards.

Ultimate Goal   For children to become aware of, appreciate, and participate in creative processes that integrate feelings, thoughts, perceptions, and actions within the arts and other sensory experiences and to achieve pleasurable, personally meaningful ends.

Intermediate Objectives   As children progress toward the ultimate goal, they will demonstrate the following competencies:

1. Gain pleasure from natural beauty and other sensory experiences with no other goal in mind.
2. Become familiar with various forms of the arts (visual art, music, dance, drama).
3. Become familiar with various styles within a particular art form (e.g., in dance: ballet, tap, folk, and square).
4. Use various materials, tools, techniques, and processes in the arts.
5. Recognize and respond to basic elements of visual art (line, color, shape or form, texture, composition, balance, pattern, space).
6. Recognize and respond to basic elements of music (beat, pitch, melody, rhythm, harmony, dynamics, tempo, timbre, texture, form).
7. Recognize, reflect on, and discuss aesthetic experiences.
8. Work collaboratively with others to create art, music, dance, or drama.
9. Appreciate the arts as means of nonverbal communication.
10. Recognize their own strengths as creative and performing artists.
11. Engage in art and music criticism (describe, analyze, interpret, and judge).
12. Contribute to the aesthetic environment of the early childhood program.
13. Develop a concept of the arts as a lifelong pursuit.
14. Begin to understand and appreciate the arts in relation to history and cultures, their own and others.
15. Recognize and respond to connections between the arts and other disciplines.

ACTIVITY SUGGESTIONS

✎ **Class Visit to an Art Museum**

Objective 2   For children to become familiar with various forms of the arts (visual art, music, dance, drama).

Procedure   Take the class to an art gallery. Visit ahead of time, taking note of what pieces might interest the group. Purchase postcard prints of some of the art works. Distribute these to small-group leaders, along with suggestions for things to point out. Encourage the groups to move slowly through the exhibits, looking for the art works depicted on the postcards. Move among the small groups, asking questions to motivate children to notice variety in use of materials, subject matter, and kinds of art (paintings, drawings, sculpture, carved designs, etc.) represented.

To simplify Go for a very short time. Arrange for very small groups or pairs of children assigned to each adult. Prepare adults to look at things in general, stopping to analyze those pieces children show interest in.

To extend Plan a longer visit, prepare children ahead for some particular art works they will see. Analyze these carefully as they discover them. Plan follow-up activities of drawing or painting something they remember.

✎ **Listen to This!**

Objective 3 For children to become familiar with various styles within a particular art form.

Procedure Arrange a tape recorder or record player and a collection of musical pieces in a quiet corner of the room. Encourage children to take turns listening to the music selections alone or with a friend. To focus attention on appreciation of a range of music, select pieces that vary greatly in style, such as folk, rock, classical piano, catchy tunes from commercials, TV theme songs, marching band music, part of a symphony, chamber music, and jazz. If making your own tape, organize the selections with blank spaces between them, so children can easily distinguish beginnings and endings.

To simplify Limit the number of music styles to two or three.

To extend Ask children to bring in samples of various music they enjoy at home. Encourage parents to contribute to a collection of samples, especially requesting music from various cultures.

✎ **Balancing Act**

Objective 5 For children to recognize and respond to basic elements of visual arts (balance).

Procedure Introduce the idea of balance (and unbalance) by showing a balance scale. Using identical objects or a variety of objects, ask children to tell whether it is unbalanced or balanced. Show other examples of the concepts using groups of children, groups of ob-

jects, and groups of pictures of objects. Show children several reproductions of famous paintings; have them point out the objects and tell if they think the picture is balanced or not and why.

To simplify Leave the scale out for experimentation for several days with three-dimensional objects. Then apply the concept to the pictures.

To extend Providing construction paper (suggest they cut or tear shapes) and paste, have children make a picture or design and tell if it is balanced or unbalanced and why.

✎ **Pitch Play**

Objective 6 For children to recognize and respond to basic elements of music (pitch).

Procedure Teach children how to have musical "conversations" that involve matching pitches with one person leading, and the other responding, like an echo. Demonstrate with another adult or a competent child. Suggest the child listen to what you sing, and then repeat your words using the same sounds and matching pitches. For example, the leader sings: "Hel-lo" using two pitches, one for each syllable. Response: "Hel-lo." Practice this using various words until it is easier.

Next, have the child lead, and you reply with different words but matched pitches. The leader sings: "Hel-lo." Response: "Hi there."

Finally, switch roles again and have the student make up his or her own response to your lead, still matching your pitches.

To simplify Start simple, using one-pitch conversations.

To extend Use two sets of pitched instruments such as bells or xylophones, using the same procedure. One leads, and the other echoes. Be sure to start with two pitches that are very different (high-low) and gradually utilize ones that are more difficult to distinguish (high-middle) or (middle-low).

✎ **Oh Up! Oh Down!**

Objective 4 For children to use various materials, tools, techniques, and processes in the arts.

Procedure After reading or hearing a story they particularly enjoyed, suggest the group stand up and form a circle or stand facing each other. Tell children they are going to use their bodies to become people, animals, or objects in the story. Teach them signals to begin and end their dramatic interpretations: "Oh-up" means to stand up and begin, "Oh-down" means to stop and crouch down. Have everyone go down into a crouch, and then say, "When we come up, we're all going to be (e.g., the papa bear tasting his porridge). Oh-up! . . . (do it with them) . . . Oh-down!" Verbally reinforce creative ideas children use. Repeat the procedure using other ideas. Encourage children to participate, but do not force them. If some children insist on watching, select a place nearby where they may easily join in if they change their mind.

To simplify Select ideas that are obvious and easy to visualize (e.g., "Be the baby bear crying over his broken chair" or "Be Goldilocks going to sleep in the bed."). Do this for a short time and end before the children get tired.

To extend After the obvious ones, select ideas that are more subtle (e.g., "Be the chair that breaks when Goldilocks sits down" or "Be the door that opens when she knocks.") Let children take turns being the leader, suggesting ideas. Or use this as a warm-up exercise to actually acting out the whole story as a class.

✎ Let's Stick Together

Objective 4 For children to use various materials, tools, techniques, and processes in the arts.

Procedure Potter's clay offers opportunities for three-dimensional sculpture and ceramic design. However, occasionally in the drying process, attached pieces fall off. Discuss this with the children, and demonstrate a technique that attaches clay pieces together, so this will not happen. Prepare two pieces of clay to attach. Using a tool that makes shallow cuts (such as a table knife, fork, or wooden ceramic tool), score cross-hatching lines into the surfaces to be joined. Then apply plain water with a finger to wet both scored surfaces and produce a slippery film (called "slip"). Press the pieces together and blend the clay to completely cover the line of attachment. Give children clay, tools, and water and suggest they practice attaching pieces together.

To simplify Younger children can attach small pieces to larger flat pieces using this technique.

To extend Invite children to think of things that have parts (e.g., animals have legs, head, and tails) to attach. Brainstorm ideas. Encourage them to work on their own creations, using the technique demonstrated.

✎ Art Talk

Objective 7 For children to recognize, reflect on, and discuss aesthetic experiences.

Procedure Plan an aesthetic experience for the class such as experimenting with watercolor paints on wet paper or listening to the music of "Fantasia" on tape. Afterward, gather children together to discuss what they remember, know, think, and value about the experience. Ask various questions such as "What did you see or hear? What do you remember about that?" (cognitive memory) "What colors of paint were we using today?" (convergent) "What shapes did you notice? What words can we use to describe different parts of this music?" (divergent) "How did you like this? What was the best part? Why do you say that?" (evaluative).

To simplify Ask only one or two questions. Keep the discussion short but listen to everyone's reply.

To extend Follow up the discussion by having children write or dictate their feelings about the experience.

✎ Group Paintings

Objective 8 For children to work collaboratively with others to create art, music, dance, or drama.

Procedure Organize a floor or table area large enough for several groups of children to paint together; lay newspaper to protect the surface. Gather materials for each group: a large piece of newsprint or butcher paper and 4–6 colors of poster paint in a muffin tin or cans. Show children the materials. Explain that they will be working together in small groups, with each group making one painting. Suggest they think of topics for their paintings (such as a baseball game, winter, imaginary insects, the city, the forest, or germs). Begin to generate ideas for paintings that stimulate imagination and appeal to their interests. Make a list of ideas children suggest. If needed, narrow the list to match the number of groups. Then have children select a group (four or five) based on their interest in a particular subject. Encourage children to share their materials, cooperate with each other, and sign their work.

To Simplify　Limit the number of children in the small groups to two or three; have one group paint at a time; place one brush in each color of paint.

To Extend　Have each small group plan their painting together before they actually begin. Provide pencils and erasers for sketching their plan. Encourage groups to decide in advance what part of the painting each person will paint. When paintings are dry, ask each group to tell about their work.

✎ What Does It Mean?

Objective 9　For children to appreciate the arts as means of nonverbal communication.

Procedure　Point to a written sign or message in your classroom. Read it aloud and ask what the message tells us. Discuss the fact that some art, music, and dance communicate ideas to an audience without using words. Show children a print of a painting that has an appropriate and understandable message, such as Degas's *Dancers With Fans* (Abrams, 1985), depicting ballet dancers on a stage, or Homer's *Snap the Whip* (Abrams, 1985), showing young boys playing in a school yard. Do *not* tell children the title. Ask the children to look carefully, notice details about the picture, and tell what they think the artist was communicating. Let students know there are no right answers, that anyone's ideas can be valid, and that sometimes the same work has many messages. Accept all ideas. Later, tell children about how each piece of art has a title, which helps us understand the message of the picture. Give the title of the picture and listen to children's comments.

Follow this by providing familiar drawing materials (crayons or markers and paper) and suggest children make a picture with a message. Display the pictures and give students time to look at and speculate about what message each might be communicating. Ask the artists to tell about what their message is and to give their work a title. Display titles with their pictures.

To simplify　Relate the concept of artistic nonverbal messages to other nonverbal messages like gestures, facial expressions and body language. Stay with the obvious messages, and use examples that communicate more obviously.

To extend　Show an example of a painting in which the message is less obvious, more abstract, and nonrepresentational such as Mondrian's *Broadway Boogie Woogie* (Abrams, 1985), a composition of geometric shapes, or Miro's *Hirondelle/Armour* (Abrams, 1985), a colorful work with lively shapes open to many interpretations. Encourage children to offer opinions about what the artist is communicating.

✎ Name That Tune

Objective 6　For children to recognize and respond to basic elements of music (melody).

Procedure　Teach and practice singing a number of simple children's songs with the children such as "Itsy Bitsy Spider," "She'll Be Comin' Round the Mountain," "Mary Had a Little Lamb," "Yankee Doodle," "Old McDonald Had a Farm," and so on. After the tunes have become very familiar to the children, explain that you are going to play a game with the class. Hum without using the words (or use a kazoo to create the melodies), asking children to listen and name each song.

To simplify　Use very short simple songs that children know well.

To extend　Teach the class some new songs and try this exercise. Try it again the following day, without singing them with words first.

✎ Artists in Our Town

Objective 14　For children to begin to understand and appreciate the arts in relation to history and children's cultures, their own and others.

Procedure　Invite a visual artist, musician, dancer, or actor (one of the parents or a community person) to visit the class; ask the artist to bring samples of their work, completed and in progress, and the tools they use. Ask your guest to demonstrate their art and discuss how he or she became interested in it. Encourage children to ask questions and respond to the guest.

To simplify　Keep the presentation short (10 to 15 minutes). Arrange the artist and his or her tools in an area of the classroom where children can talk with him or her during a free-choice time.

To extend　Send a note home to parents requesting they help their child find someone they know (in their family or neighborhood) who is an artist, musician, dancer, or actor. Explain that your objective is to help children understand more about art in the culture. Ask them to help their child talk to that person and ask some questions such as What kind of artist are you? How did you get interested in that art form? How old were you when you started that art? Provide time for children to report to the class about the artist they found.

✎ Feel The Beat

Objective 6   For children to recognize and respond to basic elements of music (beat and tempo).

Procedure   Play a number of recorded instrumental selections with an obvious beat (a steady pulse) and a variety of tempos (relative speed of the beat). An audiotape demonstrating different kinds of music can be made with pauses between short musical segments. Play the tape and respond with your hands to the beat (clap hands, slap thighs). Have the children begin in a sitting position and say, "Listen to the music. Feel the beat. Clap on the beat with me" (do not expect young children to match the beat exactly). Next, suggest children move their hands a different way to the beat (punch the air, point a finger, wave, etc.). Next, suggest the children move more of their body to the beat (nod their head, shrug their shoulders, sway their hips, step in place, walk to the beat).

To simplify   For those children who do not feel the beat, help them by placing their hands over yours as you clap. Then switch, having your hands cover theirs. Try using a verbal cue on the beat to help children become more aware. Say "beat . . . beat . . . beat . . . beat . . . beat" or "clap . . . clap . . . clap . . . clap." Younger

children are better able to keep time with a moderate tempo than with a slower tempo.

To extend   Offer children simple rhythm instruments to tap the beat of the music such as rhythm sticks or empty paper towel tubes. Demonstrate tapping on the floor, softly on a shoe, or on the thigh. Explain the terms *beat* and *tempo;* play a game in which children take turns demonstrating a fast tempo, a slow tempo, and a medium tempo by hitting a tambourine as everyone else moves in time to that beat.

✎ My Own Song

Objective 10   For children to recognize their own strengths as creative and performing artists.

Procedure   Model and encourage children to select familiar tunes and sing their own words to them. For example, to the tune of "Frère Jacques" or "Are You Sleeping" sing, "Going home now, going home now, going home, going home, going going home, going going home, going home, going home."

To simplify   Suggest that children sing their own name using the melody of a very familiar simple song, such as "Mary, Mary, Mary, Mary, Mary, Mary, Mary, Mary . . ."

To extend   Encourage children to use more extensive personal descriptions with the melody. Frère Jacques can sound like, "My name's Sandy, my name's Sandy, how are you, how are you, I live in a white house with a dog named Patches, I like school, I like school."

✖ Applying What You Read in This Chapter

1. **Discuss**
   a. Think about how you feel about using coloring books and coloring pages with young children. Discuss your thinking with a partner, giving a rational argument for your stance.
   b. Obtain an example of children's art. Consider several ways you, as their teacher, could respond appropriately to the child's work. Tell how each response may affect the child.
   c. Talk about and list as many ways you can think of that teachers can use music in the classroom.
2. **Observe**
   a. Locate a program or school that has an arts specialist (art, music, dance, creative movement, or

drama) working with the children. Arrange to observe as the specialist works with a group. Take notes on the strategies, techniques, and content of the lesson, and discuss your observations.
3. **Carry out an activity**
   a. Plan a music activity using musical instruments to teach two of the following musical concepts (beat, rhythm, tempo, pitch). Carry out the activity with a group of children. Evaluate your results.
   b. Select a familiar story for children to enact. Make a collection of props that will stimulate the children to act it out. Plan how you will introduce the story and props to the children and

how you will motivate them to participate in the activity.

4. **For your portfolio**
   a. Review the three teaching approaches described in this chapter. Think about which approach you will use primarily with the arts and why. Create a statement describing your choice and tell how it fits with your philosophy of education.

5. **Personal reflection**
   a. Consider your own background in the arts. What formal and informal experiences did you have as a child? Were they positive or negative? Think about your current participation in the arts. What experiences influenced this current participation? Consider how this affects your disposition toward teaching the arts.

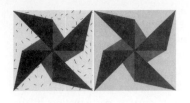

Chapter 9

The Affective Domain

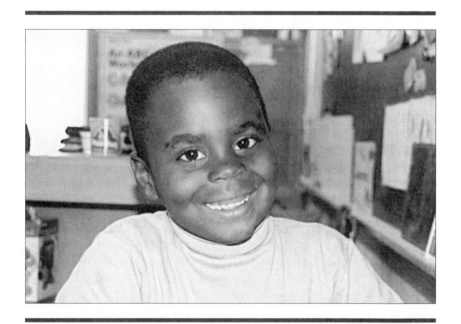

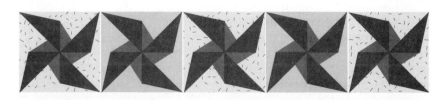

You may wonder:

How do children develop self-awareness and a secure sense of self?

How do variations in children's personality development influence their self-esteem?

What is interpersonal intelligence? How does it relate to an individual's sense of self? Is it different from or synonymous with emotional intelligence?

How can I help children who are not coping well with stress to develop affective strengths?

How involved should I be in children's affective development? What place should affective development have in the overall curriculum?

How will I know if my efforts to support children's affective development are successful?

In this chapter on the affective domain, we present information to help you answer these questions.

> When we were one or two years old, we had what we might visualize as a 360 degree personality. Energy radiated out from all parts of our body and our psyche. A child running is a living globe of energy. We had a ball of energy, all right, but one day we noticed that [others] didn't like certain parts of that ball. . . . Behind us we have an invisible bag, and the part of us [others] didn't like . . . we put in the bag. . . . But why would we give away, or put into the bag, so much of ourselves? Why would we do it so young? And if we have put away so much of our anger, spontaneities, hungers, enthusiasms, our rowdy and unattractive parts, then how can we live? What holds us together? (Bly, 1988, 17–24)

Learning appropriate ways to express every aspect of their personality is one of the toughest jobs young children have. They struggle daily with refining self-help and social skills, mastering unfamiliar tasks, and coping with their own emotions and tensions. Although to some extent adults also deal with these same challenges, most do so from a broader base of experiences and with a great many more resources than are available to children.

Most of the emotional repertoire adults need in order to contend with everyday life challenges—self-awareness, self-esteem, self-respect, belief in themselves and in their future, and feelings of competency—is forged in childhood. In early childhood settings in which professionals take an active role in supporting children's affective development, numerous examples can be found: a teacher comforting a preschooler who is distressed that his mother has left; a teacher conducting a group discussion with the class about a beloved guinea pig who has died; a teacher offering genuine praise to a child who has worked carefully through a challenging math story problem; and a teacher helping a child develop a script to enter a play group of peers.

An adolescent's or adult's mental health, relationships, ability to deal with disappointments, and general perceptions of the world will depend on how well the different aspects of intrapersonal strength were nurtured in the early years. In early childhood classrooms, this will take more than attention to establishing a warm and supportive classroom environment. In addition, professionals must build components into the curriculum that promote growth in self-awareness, personal decision making, managing intense feelings and emotions, and handling stress. Children must also be given guidance in taking others' feelings and concerns into account, communicating with others, developing personal insight and assertiveness, self-acceptance, and personal responsibility taking (Goleman, 1995). It is on these premises that the ideas for helping children form strong intrapersonal and interpersonal structures are set forth in this chapter.

EMOTIONAL DEVELOPMENT FROM A PSYCHOSOCIAL PERSPECTIVE

Newborns have no sense of self as apart from their immediate caregiver. However, by the time they are a year and a half in age, they clearly are beginning to understand the differences between themselves and others.

We see this in their frequent use of the word "mine," their delight in identifying themselves in pictures and mirrors, and increasingly correct use of pronouns when referring to others. During the preschool years, children move to physical attributes to describe their uniqueness ("I'm a boy. I'm three. I live in a blue house!"). Somewhat later, they begin to make comparisons between themselves and others ("I can run faster than my little brother!"), and by early elementary school, they are defining themselves in terms of psychological traits ("I turn my work in on time.") and internal states and beliefs ("I hate it when I can't stay up to watch TV!") (Kostelnik et al., 1998).

Fully in tandem with growing self-awareness is the child's emotional development. Erik Erikson (1963) saw human development as the result of an individual's progressive resolution of conflicts between his or her own needs and social demands. As was pointed out in Chapter 1, Erikson theorized that development continues over the entire life cycle of an individual rather than being primarily set in infancy or early childhood (see Table 9.1). However, the ability to deal with later-stage problems was viewed as dependent on how well an individual dealt with and resolved crises in earlier stages.

Setting the stage for later trust or mistrust in social interaction is the primary caregivers' handling of a child in the first year of life. During this critical first stage, children learn that adults caring for them can be counted on to behave either affectionately and predictably most of the time or insensitively and neglectfully in response to their distress and needs.

As children move into the second and third year of life, the trust or mistrust they have developed

TABLE 9.1
Erik Erikson's Psychosocial Theory of Personality Development

Stage	Approximate Age	Conflict Resolution Area
1	Infancy	Trust vs. mistrust
2	About 1–3 years of age	Autonomy vs. doubt
3	About 4–5 years of age	Initiative vs. guilt
4	About 6–11 years of age	Industry vs. inferiority
5	Adolescence	Identity vs. role confusion
6	Young adulthood	Intimacy vs. isolation
7	Middle age	Generativity vs. self-absorption
8	Old age	Integrity vs. despair

impacts on achievement of subsequent developmental tasks. It is then that children begin to exercise increasing autonomy as physical, cognitive, and social abilities also develop. For those children experiencing day-to-day encouragement for active exploration in a safe, encouraging high-quality environment, increased confidence and competence are likely to be the outcome.

On the other hand, children who live in chaotic environments with overly critical and controlling adults are more likely to develop a sense of shame and doubt about themselves and their capabilities for dealing with an enlarging life space. Predictably, these children move less competently into the third stage outlined by Erikson—initiative versus guilt. During this period, 4- and 5-year-olds develop a sense of how others value their efforts to explore ideas, carry out plans, gain information, and master new skills. Children who develop a strong sense of initiative gain pleasure from increased competence. They seek ways to use their energy in appropriate and constructive ways and enjoy cooperating with others in activities that involve the use of real tools (woodworking materials, computers, and tape recorders, magnifying glasses, magnets, and kitchen utensils) in their building of skills.

Conversely, children who have experienced less nurturing care in early stages of development are less likely to initiate activity on their own or be successful in ventures to do so. There may be problems related to task completion, and these children often demonstrate less ability in problem solving or decision making. They may hang back in play or act so aggressively that they fail to make meaningful friendships. For example, a 4-year-old boy who had grown bored watching his mother try on eyeglass frames in an optometrist's office began teasing a little girl standing by her mother, who was also trying on frames. Despite the fact that his behavior became highly inappropriate and annoying to others, his mother ignored what he was doing. At one point, the small girl said to him, "You're bad!" Surprisingly, the tone of her voice brought an abrupt stop to his teasing. He looked confused for a minute and then went to his mother to report the affront.

"She said I'm bad," he complained.

"Well, you *are* bad," said his mother, not even looking at him.

The long-term effect of such labeling on the child's self-image is predictable, unfortunately, particularly when there is little or no effort to provide him with more appropriate behavior skills.

Middle childhood (approximately 6–12 years of age) is a period of industry versus inferiority when children come to feel they are able, competent persons or largely incapable of mastering the skills that others value. Adults in formal learning situations as well as those interacting with children in extracurricular experiences have numerous opportunities to foster industriousness. This happens when professionals recognize and genuinely praise successes, encourage children to explore skill building in a variety of areas, help children set realistic goals, and set up tasks so that children can work step-by-step toward mastery and success (Kostelnik et al., 1998).

From the preschool years until preadolescence, children struggle with developing responsibility and living up to the reasonable expectations of those they come into contact with. They learn that doing so requires effort on their part and that making poor choices about following through on such tasks as homework and household chores results in the disappointment and/or disdain of others.

To the extent that children feel free to assert themselves in everyday interactions with peers, teachers, parents, and others and are also reinforced for efforts at skill building and successful accomplishments, they will develop an industrious approach to learning. When their efforts have been discouraged, ignored, or short-circuited by others, a sense of inferiority and low self-esteem results, which causes them to veer away from challenges and responsibilities or to behave in a hostile and socially inappropriate manner. These behaviors, while frustrating to professionals working with these children, are simply natural defensive mechanisms in youngsters who have experienced significant contact with others who are insensitive to and unsupportive of their developmental needs. Although most educators empathically recognize the stimulus for such behavior, the conduct of poorly nurtured children is often disruptive and time-consuming, impacting negatively on both their progress and that of other children. Professionals frequently find themselves with some ambivalence toward these children who are so difficult to manage on a day-to-day basis.

Of the eight stages of development delineated by Erikson, young children have already experienced two or three by the time they enter the primary grades. Although children bring with them very different background experiences, strengths, and needs, it is likely that the school experience will also have much to do with the child's success in confronting conflicts experienced while in stages 3, 4, and 5. Children in the primary grades want to be competent and recognized by others as competent. Educators can take advantage of this "optimal period" and natural motivation of children to guide them toward more fully integrated intrapersonal and interpersonal strengths. This calls for including in the early childhood program an adequate focus on the development of self-awareness, cooperative relationships, mutual respect, and a climate of fairness, caring, and participation. Also, truly effective schools must work closely with families and the community before children ever enter the formal system. Those linkages with families must then be maintained and strengthened as children move through the developmental tasks of early childhood and into adolescence and young adulthood.

EMOTIONAL DEVELOPMENT FROM A COGNITIVE PERSPECTIVE

In terms of developing and understanding their own emotions, children progress through a predictable sequence that is highly dependent on their emerging cognitive capabilities and language development. Included in the process is neurological growth that supports higher levels of thinking, the development of a fundamental knowledge base for the organizing and connecting of incoming information, and social experiences that help to mediate temperament and form the child's affective dispositions, overall character, and emotional intelligence.

Neurobiological Beginnings of Emotional Development

Brain constructs that govern the emotions are among the first circuits constructed following the birth of a child. Initial feelings of distress and comfort experienced by young infants are eventually transformed into more complex feelings of joy and sadness, envy, empathy for others, pride, and shame (Nash, 1997, 53).

Environmental trauma following birth, such as abuse and high levels of stress, is thought to have a debilitating effect on brain development and organization, particularly with respect to emotional responses. According to Dr. Bruce Perry, Baylor College of Medicine, Dr. Linda Mayes of the Yale Child Study Center, and neuroscientist Dr. Megan Gunnar of the University of Minnesota:

> If the brain's organization reflects its experience, and the experience of the traumatized child is fear and stress, then the neurochemical responses to fear and stress become the most powerful architects of the brain, actually changing the structure of the brain.
>
> Trauma elevates stress hormones, such as cortisol, that wash over the tender brain like acid. As a result, regions in the cortex of the limbic system (responsible for emotions, including attachment) are 20 to 30 percent smaller in abused children than in normal kids; these regions also have fewer synapses.
>
> In adults who were abused as children, the memory-making hippocampus is smaller than in nonabused adults. This effect, too, is believed to be the result of the toxic effects of cortisol.
>
> High cortisol levels during the vulnerable years of zero to 3 increase activity in the brain structure involved in vigilance and arousal. As a result, the brain is wired to be on hair-trigger alert. Regions that were activated by the original trauma are immediately reactivated whenever the child dreams of, thinks about or is reminded of the trauma. Thus, children with the higher cortisol levels score lowest on inhibitory control and have problems in attention regulation and self-control. (Begley, 1997b, 31–32)

The implications related to neurobiological findings about emotional beginnings correlate well with Erikson's perspectives. Young children obviously require positive nurturing right from the beginning in order to develop emotional strength, and they need continued support on a day-to-day basis as they progress through adolescence. Although good or poor beginnings do not predict with absolute certainty a child's psychological makeup, it is becoming clearer that high-quality early contexts yield far less vulnerability. Brazelton (1992, 13) describes the potential consequences:

> A child who cannot focus his attention, who is suspicious rather than trusting, sad or angry rather than optimistic, destructive rather than respectful and one who is overcome with anxiety, preoccupied with frightening fantasy and feels generally unhappy about himself—such a child has little opportunity at all, let alone equal opportunity, to claim the possibilities of the world as his own.

Developing a Fundamental Knowledge Base for Affective Development

As in every other domain, children are active in constructing a knowledge base they will use in every internal and external operation related to their emerging emotional structures. With respect to *physical knowledge,* they become increasingly aware of their tendencies to react and behave under certain conditions and gain awareness about their own dispositions, capabilities, and abilities. Their *logical-mathematical knowledge* is enhanced as they develop the logical organization to deal with incoming affective information (How am I like others? How am I different than others?) and also recognize and contrast the distinct and recurrent patterns in their own behavior and that of others. *Representational knowledge* increases as they learn new ways to express their inner emotional thoughts and feelings through increased verbalization as language develops, through the refined use of body language, and also through written expression as literacy skills emerge. In the *social-conventional* arena, they are intensely interested in learning more about how others view them, what the rules are for socially acceptable ways of behaving, and more about gender, ethnicity, and interpersonal applications.

Children exercise their increasingly sophisticated *metacognitive abilities* by putting their sensory channel modalities to work to investigate emotional cause and effect. As they do so, they grow in their conscious conceptualization of their own emotional strength and limitations (self-awareness, self-esteem, self-concept), develop greater instincts about themselves and others, and acquire strategies to affect their own emotions and those of others. In the earlier example of the 4-year-old who had been told by his mother, "You are bad!" that experience and many others add daily to his emotional knowledge base. Physically, he sees himself as able to get away with pretty outrageous behavior and still be ignored by his parent. Logically, he comes to know that he is perceived in the situation as "bad" rather than "good," and he chooses to represent that "badness" by continuing to tease his peer, despite the negative feedback given to him by everyone else in the context. All of this and the labels that are pinned on—bad boy—are part of his growing social conventional knowledge about himself. Metacognitively, he is learning that his behavior can cause irritation to others

(a confusing mix of positive and negative emotion) but also be an attention-getting mechanism (a highly positive emotion), something that he craves and can actively elicit without undue consequence in the form of punishment. Conversely, a child who receives authentic messages that he or she is fun, capable, or intelligent can be seen to represent those concepts in play and other interpersonal behaviors.

Theoretical Constructs of Intrapersonal and Emotional Intelligence

Howard Gardner (1983, 1993a) has indicated that the two forms of personal intelligence that are included in his concept of multiple intelligences—interpersonal intelligence (see Chapter 10) and intrapersonal intelligence—are not well understood but "immensely important" in understanding others and ourselves. Intrapersonal intelligence constitutes the internal aspects of the self, "the feeling life, one's range of emotions, the capacity to effect discriminations among these emotions and eventually to label them and to draw upon them as a means of understanding and guiding one's own behavior. A person with good intrapersonal intelligence has a viable and effective model of himself or herself" (1993, 24–25). In underscoring the neurobiological basis for variation in brain organization and development, Gardner cites the child with autism as an example where intrapersonal intelligence is impaired, often with complementary greater development in another area.

Daniel Goleman (1995, 41), author of *Emotional Intelligence,* writes that Gardner tends to emphasize *thoughts* about feelings in his theory, rather than emotions themselves. When questioned about this, Gardner told Goleman that intrapersonal intelligence was "emotionally tuning into yourself. It's the visceral-feeling signals you get that are essential for interpersonal intelligence." Rather than seeing the visceral feelings as necessary to develop interpersonal intelligence, Goleman and others (Salovey & Mayer, 1990; Sternberg, 1985, 1988, 1997) view such feelings as "personal" or emotional intelligence and view the understanding and management of these emotions as crucial to every choice children make in the "rough-and-tumble" of life. In addition, children's success and relationships with others require building on their own self-awareness by actively marshalling their emotions to accomplish a goal (e.g., paying attention, delaying gratification, stifling impulsiveness), recognizing and reacting to others' needs (empathy and altruism, being attuned to subtle and overt signals from others), and social competence (interpersonal intelligence).

The hundreds of emotions that children experience everyday are triggered by both large and small events, their interactions with others, and demands that are placed on them. At first, very young children think of their emotions as simply happy, mad, sad, and afraid. These core emotions form the foundations from which all other emotions emerge. This is a gradual process occurring during the first five years of life.

Children younger than five years of age generally are not aware that people can experience more than one emotion at a time. For example, if they experience a parent expressing anger toward them, they believe the parent is *completely* angry and, therefore, not holding other emotions at the same time such as love, fear, sadness, or disappointment.

Five- and six-year-olds, on the other hand, develop the recognition that people can feel more than one emotion at a time but still believe that contrasting emotions such as feeling angry and loving, smart and stupid, or happy and sad about the same *event* are not possible. For example, on learning that the family would be moving to another state, 6-year-old Kevin expressed his profound sadness about leaving his friends, his favorite tree swing in his back yard, and his school. As well as acknowledging his feelings, his first-grade teacher discussed with him some possibilities he had not considered about the town that he was moving to and that it would be fun to send E-mail back and forth to one another. She underscored the fact that changes we encounter can cause both unhappy and happy feelings and that she understood his feelings right now were mostly sad ones. She encouraged him to tell her about the fun things he was going to find when he wrote to her.

It is not until middle elementary school that children begin to understand that such events as their parents' divorce or moving to another town can cause both positive and negative emotions and that people can hold contrasting feelings simultaneously about other persons, objects, or situations. Even with this understanding, however, there may be considerable confusion and a sense of anxiety over not having a clear-cut response (Kostelnik et al., 1998).

Children younger than 10 years of age, however, generally do not associate the source of their emotions with what happens in their own minds. Rather, there is a more simplistic and direct linking of their emotional state to their physical state of being. If they miss a parent or are hungry, tired, or injured, they perceive emotions such as sadness, irritability, anger, or fearfulness as directly resulting from the situation itself rather than from what they *think* about the situation or how they interpret it. They are also unaware that a person can feel certain emotions internally and mask them externally. Thus, they may not be alert for subtle cues in others' responses to them when their social behavior is inappropriate or "thoughtless."

Here it should be noted that early psychosocial development also includes the construction of one's ethnic profile. This is fluid and shifts subtly, depending on the context in which children find themselves, but identity is strongly influenced by their social experiences (McLeod, 1997). First graders, for example, who are involved with reading materials will naturally look for pictures of families like *their* families. When African American, Native American, Latino, or Asian children fail to see people like themselves, there is no "confirmation of legitimate existence"; thus, the child receives a strong message that his or her ethnic category does not warrant endorsement. There may arise in these learners a reluctance to pursue tasks in an environment that fails to include people like themselves (Boyer, 1990, 39).

As primary children move toward the period of concrete operations (Piaget, 1952, 1954), developing more sophisticated intellectual capacity, they are better equipped to evaluate their own social skills and status in light of others' behavior and expectations. In developing a consolidated sense of themselves, children watch others' compliance and transgressions and the consequential approval or disapproval of that behavior. They listen to evaluations of their own and others' actions and begin to formulate a rudimentary understanding of the desires, beliefs, and emotions of others.

VARIATIONS IN PERSONALITY DEVELOPMENT

Even when teachers and parents are fairly sensitive about factors influencing the self-esteem of growing children, negative interaction styles can develop when children are perceived to be difficult and consistently hard to manage. Children exhibit very different personality attributes that may, in fact, be inherited characteristics. Included are such traits as these:

❏ Activity level—motor activity and inactivity
❏ Rhythmicity—predictability in bodily function
❏ Approach/withdrawal—child's' initial responses to new object, people, foods, etc.
❏ Adaptability—response to change
❏ Intensity of reaction—energy level in response to stimuli and impulse control
❏ Responsiveness threshold—level of stimulation necessary to evoke a response
❏ Attention span and persistence—time spent in pursuit of activity
❏ Distractibility—vulnerability to interference when pursuing activity

In a series of longitudinal studies to look at individual temperament in young children based on these traits (Thomas & Chess, 1977, 1980, 1984; Thomas, Chess, Birch, Hartzig, & Korn, 1963; McDevitt & Carey, 1978), researchers have documented three basic types: easy (40 percent of those children studied); difficult (10 percent); and slow to warm up (about 15 percent). About 35 percent of children studied could not be classified into one of these categories. It is, of course, the "difficult" and "slow-to-warm-up" children who react more negatively to change or seem to march to a slightly different drummer than most children. These are the children who often keep teachers awake at night thinking about more effective ways to deal with them. Goleman (1995) reminds us that, fortunately, temperament is not necessarily destiny and that what makes a difference are the emotional experiences the child will have while growing up.

Often when adults look on these differences in personality as stubbornness on the part of the child, a power struggle can be set into motion. Altering a difficult child's behavior and still having both adult and child maintain a healthy sense of autonomy and power can be a very fragile undertaking. It calls for respecting such differences as legitimate but helping the child to see and appreciate how some changes might be personally advantageous, for example, in getting along better with others and forming friendships. Jerome Kagan (1998, pp. 55–56) warns practitioners not to get too caught up in the "new romance with biology" by awarding temperament *too* strong a voice in responding to children. What is critical to remember, he notes, is that no human psychological profile is a product of genetic influences or environmental influences alone. Instead, it is a fabric consisting of both kinds of threads. Inherited characteristics are always modified by the child's experiences with others.

Adults wishing or attempting to modify children's interactive styles will need to examine what part their own personality is playing in the situation. It may be that the child's behavior is perfectly appropriate but simply irritating because of personality differences between child and adult. Legitimately, this may call for compromise. For example, perhaps the slow-to-warm-up child might not balk at schedule changes so much if the teacher took more care in warning the child ahead of time about them. It may be that the more active child is unable to sit still in large-group presentations but that large-group sessions are also longer than necessary because they are a favorite part of the adult's teaching day. Shortening them somewhat, at least for a period of time, and having the child adapt to increasingly longer sessions may be a workable compromise.

SELF-ESTEEM IN THE EARLY LEARNING ENVIRONMENT

In a first-grade classroom, an educational consultant recently observed a group of children who had viewed a tape on space rockets and then had been invited by their teacher to draw a picture of a rocket. The teacher reminded the children to put their name on their pictures and also to date them so that the work could be entered into their writing portfolios. As the consultant drew near to watch Michael, who was drawing an especially creative rocket, he glanced up at her and then quickly covered the poorly scrawled name he had written in the upper left corner. When the adult smiled and complimented him on his beautiful rocket, he smiled back but kept his printing covered, covertly watching until she moved on and only then withdrawing his hand. Six-year-old Michael had already learned to be ashamed of his efforts to print.

In another classroom, a troubled child told his teacher, "I'm no good!" She responded emphatically, "No, no, no—you *are* good. We aren't going to talk like that. I don't want to hear anyone in this room putting himself down!" The child, who for some time had been experiencing alcoholic and abusive parents arguing and moving toward divorce, had trusted the teacher enough to bring his pain openly to her. He was being truthful about his feelings about himself. No matter how undeserved, he felt worthless. Wanting to help him think better of himself, the teacher had unwittingly (and unfortunately) denied both his emotions and his pain.

Each day of a child's life is filled with events and successful and unsuccessful interactions with others. One infant's cries are responded to promptly with nurturing warmth and concern: another is left for long periods without adult attention or contact. One 2-year-old's parent views his child's frequent "no" as an expression of her growing autonomy; another's parent sees it as the beginning of a power struggle and something that must be curbed. Five-year-old Brian's reluctance to join in with other children is seen by his teacher as a need to build social strategies; to his father, it is a source of irritation and "sissiness." The second graders in Mrs. Milan's class learn mostly in silence when she is not speaking and by responding to her directions; those in the second-grade classroom down the hall are encouraged to be independent and self-reliant and to rely on their own thinking as much as possible (Gestwicki, 1995b). Cumulatively, these become the "potent and orderly forces" that result in the child building an internal picture of him- or herself—as worthy, capable, lovable, and significant, or useless, inept, unlovable, and discounted (Elkins, 1979; Rogers, 1961).

Though an individual's "self" or concept of self, like everything else in an organism, develops and changes over the life span, there is evidence that global self-concept (i.e., all the beliefs a person has about him- or herself) is structured fairly early in life and appears to be well developed by the time a child is 8 or 9 years old. Components of the self—perceptions about how competent one is intellectually, physically, emotionally, and so forth—are known as *self-esteem*. These perceptions are affected by how valued, lovable, and worthwhile a person feels in any particular situation. The resulting feelings of self-worth are reflected in a child's overt behavior in the classroom, in the peer group, and on the playground. Clues and patterns that suggest whether a child is experiencing low self-esteem can be found in the child's negative self-statement ("I'm rotten at this!" "I can never get anything right"); elaborate defenses to protect fragile egos; problematic behavior (unrealistic fear, unjustified anger, continued lying, conceit, overconcern with past or future); avoid-

ance of play, projects, or working with others; or lack of interest in appearance, cleanliness, and care of possessions (Mental Health Association, 1982)

Because young children are still malleable, those who come with positive self-perceptions and those who come to school with somewhat damaged selves because of unsupportive situations will each continue to modify this most basic building block of emotional life. Professionals must be careful to be positive and confirming for *all* children, not just those who are having emotional difficulties. Children who arrive at the school door with apparently high self-esteem may run into difficulty when academic tasks become overly challenging or ethnic and racial biases are at work among children, despite the teacher's best effort to rid the classroom of them. In such cases, teachers must be active in insulating children from a negative view of themselves and provide strategies for coping. Poorly nurtured children also need a great deal of support from a patient, caring, and knowledgeable teacher so they can move in a more positive direction. This will call for a professional using constructive disciplinary strategies on a consistent basis in tandem with genuine reinforcement every time these children choose prosocial behavior. It calls for focusing daily attention on each of them, providing opportunities for them to work out their feelings through play, and teaching them to practice positive self-talk in difficult situations ("This is hard, but if I keep trying, I'll learn how to do it"). Positive behavioral changes can be facilitated by offering encouraging statements that verbalize positive aspects of a tough situation without denying children's feelings (Kostelnik et al., 1998). For example, the teacher who responded to the child who said "I'm no good" by saying "No, no, no—you *are* good" might have said instead, "It sounds as if you're having a rough morning. In spite of that, you've managed to complete all of that project. Let's look at what you still have left to do."

Ultimately, children's self-understanding is the result of the diverse and cumulative experiences with significant others in their world, both adults and peers. Urie Bronfenbrenner, professor of human development at Cornell University, maintains that not only do children need nurturing adults in their world who "are crazy about them"; there must also be times when those same adults are cool and capable of delivering authentic, corrective feedback to a child who has stepped outside of appropriate behavior boundaries. Curry and

Johnson (1990) suggest that children "develop senses of resilience, power, competence, trust, and optimism from repeated experiences in which they transform negative states into positive ones" (p. 155). They add that children may be at risk when they experience persistently positive as well as persistently negative self-feelings, with the former resulting in narcissistic self-absorption and an inability to deal adequately with social challenges.

Because primary children are both "nicer and meaner than their preschool counterparts" (Curry & Johnson, 1990, 82–83), they have no qualms about rejecting children who are self-absorbed, uncoopera-tive, disruptive, and inappropriately hostile.. Unless there is intervention in such cases to provide and rein-force more appropriate skills and behaviors, such chil-dren come to accept the negative identity ascribed to them by others. Later, they often tend to isolate them-selves from others or gang up with other aggressive and hostile children who have also experienced rejec-tion. Clearly, the fostering of effective social skills needed to work and play well with others is worth spending time on in the classroom. The constructed early childhood learning ethos that promotes in young children shared ownership, a sense of community, and responsible participation in turn motivates further pos-itive development of cooperation, control, connected-ness, and mastery.

CHILDREN'S STRESS REACTIONS IN RESPONSE TO OVERWHELMING EMOTIONAL DEMAND

All of the aspects of affective development discussed (i.e., emotional development, self-esteem, and person-ality), in combination with the quality of care giving the child experiences, result in a child's ability to cope with perceived demands in the environment.

Children can experience overwhelming demand from any number of sources today. These range from individual stressors (disabling conditions, inadequate or imbalanced diet, difficult personality) and intrafamilial stressors (birth of a sibling, death of a loved one or pet, a parent getting a more important job, moving to a new house, marital transition of parents, poverty, abuse, and/or neglect) to those outside the family. Extrafa-milial sources include unsatisfactory childcare, poor match between developmental levels and classroom ex-

pectations in the school setting, lack of appreciation of cultural differences, negative peer relationships in the neighborhood, birthday parties or sleepovers at some-one else's home, and unsafe factors in the community. Other potential challenges may include the fast-paced society children live in, the push to grow up and be in-dependent of adult support, high-fat diets, a lack of ex-ercise to release tension, too many extracurricular activ-ities, and heavy exposure to television.

When the child's developed resources are unequal to the demands experienced, behavioral disorders and increased psychological vulnerability will result. We see this in the growing numbers of children being tagged with the label Attention Deficit Hyperactivity Disorder (ADHD), mental and conduct disorders, school failure, psychosomatic illness, and early involvement in criminal behavior, drugs, sexual activity, and alcohol.

Those who are most effective in coping with *normal* stressors (getting up and dressed in time for the school bus, being disappointed once in a while, being left out of a play opportunity) learn how to cope with bigger issues. Also, children who can find or generate more alternatives to cope usually do much better and build confidence in managing stressful situations.

Stress can overwhelm children as well as adults.

Children cope with these stressors with the same sorts of strategies that many adults use. Children also employ defense mechanisms that include denial, regression, withdrawal, and impulsive acting out. These behaviors in children are clear-cut signs that they need additional or different skills in perceiving or dealing adequately with a situation.

How can we determine whether a child is emotionally healthy? Hendrick (1996, 118–119) suggests that teachers consider the following questions about a child who seems troubled, noting that if the majority of them can be answered affirmatively, the chance is good that the child is functioning in a healthy manner:

Is the child working on emotional tasks that are appropriate for his or her age?

Is the child learning to separate from his or her family without undue stress and able to form an attachment with at least one other adult in the setting?

Is the child learning to conform to routines without undue fuss?

Is the child able to become deeply involved in play?

Does the child have the ability to settle down and concentrate?

Does the child usually interact with others in an appropriate and nonaggressive way?

Does the child have access to the full range of feelings, and is he or she learning to deal with them in an age-appropriate way?

When stressful situations go on for long periods of time and the child is unable to experience relief, other symptoms may appear such as increased irritability, depression, anxiety, sleep disturbances, somatic problems, or a dramatic increase or decrease in appetite. Highly stressed children *look* stressed. Significant and long-standing tension may manifest itself in the quality of speech, as dark circles under the eyes, in the child's posture, and occasionally in compulsive behaviors.

Without additional help, children who are unable to cope effectively will hardly be able to benefit from what is going on in the classroom academically and socially. Nor do children necessarily benefit from the teacher offering quick fixes, dictating "appropriate" responses, or pushing them to talk when they are not ready to do so. Chandler (1985) has outlined the following questions that may be useful when adults must design some plan for intervention:

1. Is it possible to reduce stress through environmental manipulation?
2. Is it possible to reduce stress through changing the attitude and behavior of significant adults?
3. Is it possible to modify the child's extreme behavior so that it more closely approximates normal coping responses?
4. Is it possible to reduce stress by helping the child adopt a more realistic perception of himself and his life situation? (p. 184)

Helping the child to replace ineffective strategies will again call for a patient and carefully planned approach from the teacher that utilizes many of the guidelines suggested in this chapter. When additional focused attention and support are not helpful, other professionals may need to be drawn in to help the child modify emotional upset and responses.

CURRENT EDUCATIONAL ISSUES

Although everyone agrees that good emotional health is necessary for effective functioning and a positive quality of life, not everyone agrees that educational professionals should be actively involved in guiding the development of young children in this arena. Several issues form the basis of that opposition.

Inclusion of Affective Education in the Curriculum

The first is the belief that academic achievement should be the primary and only concern in an educational context and that affective development should be left as the legitimate province of the family. This sort of attitude goes against a philosophical concern for the overall development of young children. An important principle of developmentally appropriate practice is that the needs of the whole child must be addressed. Because the four major realms of development—physical, social, emotional, and intellectual—are highly interdependent, failing to provide spontaneous or planned experiences in the affective arena geared toward the development of positive affect would be obviously self-defeating (Currie, 1988).

In addition, children are moving out of the family's care and into the extrafamilial arena earlier and earlier, with professionals in childcare centers and educational settings assuming increasing responsibility for nurturing children as well as educating and keeping them safe. Moreover, increasing numbers of children come to the school setting with poorly formed attachments and in need of both emotional resources and a warm, trusting relationship with an adult to correct the direction of their affective development. A study by Erickson, Sroufe, and Egeland (1985) indicates that 4- and 5-year-old children who had formed weak affective ties predictably demonstrated poor school performance. They were less independent and more noncompliant, had poorer social interactional skills, and lacked confidence and assertiveness. Such children are more at risk for hostility, negative self-esteem, negative self-adequacy, emotional instability, emotional unresponsiveness, and a negative world view (Currie, 1988). Richard Weissbourd, author of *The Vulnerable Child* (1996), has identified school conditions necessary for children to find a capacity for work, love, and play. They need protection from destruction and prejudice, a continuous relationship with a consistently attentive and caring adult, opportunities in school and in the community for real achievement, and strong friendships with adults and other children (Scherer, 1997).

Professional Competence

A second issue raised by those opposing teacher involvement with affective education is related to the perceived lack of training by professionals to be competent, sensitive, and effective in this area. It may be true that in the past and in particular institutions of higher learning, much of teacher training was focused on academic content and methods, with only cursory attention to the affective and social. More attention was given to structuring consequences for negative behavior than on developing children's self-esteem or establishing a positive classroom climate to nurture emotional development. As a result, many beginning teachers found themselves ill equipped to deal with children's affective and social problems and bought heavily into artificial methods for keeping children "under control."

Currently, in high-quality programs of study, preservice teachers are now equipped with training in un-

derstanding developmental sequences and the need to work with all children in a sensitive and supportive way. They also learn strategies for intervention when children lack emotional stability and social skills and are made aware of the need to design an atmosphere of trust and experiences for children that will actively enhance positive development. Similarly, effective public school systems are providing in-service aid to teachers to help children develop more positive self-esteem, find appropriate outlets for strong feelings, deal with natural and acquired fears, and learn conflict management. In short, affective development is not left purely to chance. It is considered as important as academic aspects in good early childhood programs and well-trained and sensitive teachers are viewed as critical.

Potential Allegations of Sexual Abuse

An issue frequently raised by educators in providing nurturance to children and satisfying their affective needs has been the increasing number of allegations of sexual abuse leveled against adults who interact with children. A number of wrongful accusations have resulted in many early childhood programs taking a defensive posture, which has led to taboos against any hugging, patting, or touching and thereby shortchanging children in the process. To get around cutting out this essential aspect of a school program and also to protect educators from precarious positions, it has been suggested that the need for a warm, caring relationship between the teacher and children be fully communicated to parents and the community; children should be instructed in "good touch, bad touch" presentations; and the hugs, touches, and short personal conversations that are so necessary in a nurturing climate be delivered only when others are visible (Currie, 1988, 90).

Meeting the Needs of Special Children

Inclusion of special needs children into early childhood programs has been met initially with mixed reaction by professionals unfamiliar with children who have disabilities. With respect to supporting their emotional development, these children are similar in many respects to children without disabilities. They need and want affiliations with others, nurturing relationships, and stimulating and enjoyable classroom experiences. Like other children, they need protection from "the harsh realities of their environments . . . and freedom from violence, abuse, neglect and suffering" in order to develop good ego strength. Most of all, they need teachers who "value all young children, whatever their respective abilities" (Wolery and Wilbers, 1994, 3).

Character Education

Nothing in education today is as controversial as active attempts by professionals to include character education (otherwise known as moral education or values education) in the curriculum. The debate is usually centered around the purpose of education. Is it only to train children in the academic skills and fundamental information needed to function in a work place, or is it also to develop the skills and values necessary to live and thrive in a supportive social order? As stated elsewhere in this text, developmentally appropriate education calls for attention to the whole child. In this case, effective teachers model the kinds of behaviors they wish children to develop. They provide planned lessons and materials that focus on moral dilemmas, decision, choices, and discussion about right and wrong. "Like it or not," says Dennis Doyle (1997) "schools shape character." He cites the inherent capacity for good in every child, as well as the potential for dreadful behavior. Thus, he believes there is a need for schools to take an active rather than a passive role in the shaping of character that is likely to result in socially necessary traits and dispositions such as honesty, observation of rules, self-discipline, responsibility, respectful use of materials, and helpfulness to others.

Acquisition of Self-Esteem: Can It Be Taught or Must It Be Earned?

A major issue in the affective domain is the misconception that self-esteem is something that is provided for children—that simply giving children everything they want, frequently telling them how special they are, and engaging them in 15-minute sessions of self-esteem building endows them with healthy dollops of self-esteem that they can then draw on when needed during future challenges. This does not work. In fact, such an approach may work at odds in having children understand the relationship between hard work, true accomplishment, and feelings of self-worth. Nongenuine praise and ignoring a lack of effort have the capacity to diminish motivation in children. Young chil-

dren are in process of developing an internalized sense of others' values, and they will eventually compare or evaluate their own worth against that standard. In order to create a context in which good self-esteem is nurtured, adults must take the time each day to observe children's real accomplishments and comment on them. They need to provide the guidance children need to develop internal control and make healthy choices. This must take place in an atmosphere in which adults demonstrate warmth, respect, acceptance, authority, and empathy (Kostelnik et al., 1998).

Evaluating Emotional Growth

Measuring and evaluating affective development also seem to be problematic for many classroom teachers. This can be accomplished by using a variety of strategies. Criterion-referenced checklists can be developed directly from the curricular objectives that follow. Teachers can also use these checklists as a reminder about the need to structure a growth-producing environment and activities in the classroom. Other data sources might include a series of anecdotal records of particular behaviors such as offering assistance to another child, documentation through participation charts, notations about unstructured play and work partnerships formed, and structured and informal observations of the child's affective statements and behaviors. More specific strategies related to assessment and evaluation can be found in Chapter 17.

GOALS AND OBJECTIVES

The ultimate goal of the affective domain is for children to regard themselves as valued and capable persons. For children to make progress toward this goal, they must perceive the classroom as a psychologically safe and supportive environment and have a variety of experiences that promote growth of emotional health, self-awareness, and positive self-esteem.

Intermediate Objectives

As children progress toward the ultimate goal, they will demonstrate the following:

1. Learn that school is safe, supportive, predictable, interesting, and enjoyable.
2. Demonstrate that they have a feeling of belonging in the school environment.

3. Engage in affectionate relationships beyond the family.

4. Demonstrate growing ability to care for themselves and meet their own needs.

5. Independently begin and pursue a task.

6. Control their own behavior without external reminders.

7. Gain experience and demonstrate independence in using age-appropriate materials and tools (writing implements, cutting tools, measuring instruments, the computer, tape recorder, cassette player, etc.).

8. Complete a task they have begun.

9. Assume responsibility for caring for their personal belongings and classroom materials.

10. Contribute to maintenance of the classroom (e.g., caring for classroom pets, watering plants).

11. Experience the pleasure of work.

12. Recognize factors that contribute to quality work (e.g., time, care, effort, responsibility).

13. Make reasonable attempts to master situations that are difficult for them.

14. Become aware that criticism should be about ideas, not persons; learn to give criticism in a constructive manner.

15. Value their own gender, family, culture, and race.

16. Engage in a full range of experiences, not limited to stereotypes related to gender or background.

17. Increase their knowledge, understanding, and appreciation of their own cultural heritage.

18. Develop cross-gender competencies of various kinds.

19. Identify the characteristics and qualities that make each of them unique.

20. Identify their own emotions.

21. Explore similarities and differences among people to gain personal insight.

22. Make choices and experience the consequences of personal decisions.

23. Demonstrate increasing awareness of and ability to evaluate their accomplishments, as well as to set new standards and goals.

24. Understand the concept of possession and ownership.

25. Evaluate and describe their competencies.

26. Experience success.

27. Learn how to effectively express and clarify thoughts and feelings about emotionally charged situations, problems, and crises.

28. Learn satisfying and effective strategies for coping with personal emotions and tensions.

29. Learn to accept both positive and negative emotions as a natural part of living.

30. Become familiar with the situational circumstances that influence personal emotions.

31. Learn how to act deliberately to affect their own emotions.

32. Learn how to recover from setbacks.

33. Imagine and speak of future potential for themselves.

TEACHING STRATEGIES

1. *Create a positive classroom climate.* Structuring a positive classroom climate is essential in creating learning contexts in which children build a strong sense of feeling valued, confident, and competent. This requires that teachers be knowledgeable about and sensitive to variations in personality, as well as children's successes and failures in forming attachments to others. We need to assess and determine whether they are achieving competence or mastery, inner control and assertiveness, and prosocial behaviors to minimize developmental risk (Brentro, Brokenleg, & Van Bockern, 1990).

Today's lack of civility is seen as a serious and worsening problem and one that contributes to growing social aggression and violence in America. It can be remedied in part by professionals at every educational level creating a climate of classroom civility, which has to do with civic responsibility and the way we view and treat one another (Kauffman & Burbach, 1997). In such contexts, children have opportunities to develop personal insight about appropriate and inappropriate responses when involved in emotionally charged situations with others. Ernest Boyer's (1995) Basic School concept includes climate and commitment to character as two of four priorities for providing quality education for every child:

To support learning, schools must be organized in patterns to fit purpose, such as small classes, flexible teaching schedules, and flexible grouping arrangements. Resources must be available to enrich learning; and support services for children, including basic health and counseling and summer enrichment programs, must be provided.

The fourth priority is a commitment to character. The Basic School is concerned with the ethical and moral dimensions of a child's life; the core virtues of honesty, respect, responsibility, compassion, self-discipline, perseverance, and giving are promoted. Finally, children are encouraged to apply the lessons of the classroom to the world around them by living with purpose. (Greenberg, 1996, 51)

Use a variety of strategies to build a sense of community and promote children's development away from egocentrism and excessive individualism. In order to foster cooperative relationships and mutual respect, actively build rapport and team spirit. Impress on children that they need others in order to feel belonging, liked, valued, cared for, and in union with others. In order to develop a sense of community in the classroom, begin on the first day of school to develop social bonds and a sense of being a team among the children, using cooperative learning strategies. Encourage children to reinforce each other's efforts and to support one another in a respectful way. Provide activities that will sensitize them about the fact that we feel worthwhile not only when we achieve something but also when we display positive behaviors toward others and behave with kindness, courtesy, trustworthiness, and responsibility.

2. *Establish a low-stress and emotionally supportive environment.* As discussed earlier in Chapters 3, 4, and 5, the classroom teacher is a key person in helping young children make a smooth and comfortable transition to school and also in developing and maintaining their enthusiasm for working and playing with others. Establish a predictable schedule, and provide a daily overview of the day's activities, including any changes in routine, notice of visitors, and so forth. Monitor the pace at which the program moves and decide whether a distinction is being made that work is dull and play is the only thing to look forward to. Evaluate whether your sense of humor is alive and well, making the classroom a pleasurable place to spend time. Familiarize yourself with information about children's fears, and provide a safe and supportive context for children to gradually work through them. Teachers will want to examine their own self-esteem and how they model stress and conflict management to children when they are under pressure themselves.

3. *Assess the physical makeup of the room and use of space and materials.* Establish a stimulus-reduced area where children who are seeking quiet can work.

Balance quiet and active experiences so that children are not emotionally or physically overloaded. Evaluate the room for visual and auditory overstimulation, as well as noise levels, lighting, and temperature. Make space available where children can store their individual belongings and where their work can be prominently displayed at their eye level. Make available some materials that children can select for themselves, and take time at the beginning of the year to make sure children understand how to use them. Follow through to see that they return materials to proper storage.

4. *Work collaboratively with parents, building effective, continuing home-school partnerships.* Handle the separation process from home to school with sensitivity and respect for children's individual needs. Provide, if possible, opportunities for a gradual introduction to the school setting. Comfort anxious children and parents, and provide information to parents about how to ease children's transitions from home to school. Develop a system with parents to share knowledge about events at home or school that may be emotionally upsetting to a child.

5. *Monitor school materials and routines to avoid reinforcing stereotypes, and create activities that challenge stereotypes and prejudice.* An important first step for professionals is to evaluate the content and source of our own prejudices and to determine how these might influence our beliefs about children and their families (Haberman, 1994). Also, we need to survey the kinds of activities and materials used in the classroom. According to Boyer (1990, 63), educators should include at least 25 percent representation of minority groups in materials used, with particular attention to math materials, which are especially problematic. Portrayals should be positive. Provide children with opportunities to interact with adult members and other children of their own and other cultures. Plan visits to a variety of work sites, and invite people to explain a variety of occupations, including nontraditional ones.

6. *Promote children's emotional development and sense of worth.* Talk with children about their emotions, and structure activities and experiences specifically to build awareness of situations and events that influence emotions. Brewer (1998) suggests some general guidelines for these:

Have children dramatize situations in which anger or frustration are handled appropriately.

Use puppets to model appropriate responses to emotions. For example, with younger children, use puppets to model the use of language rather than hitting to express anger. With older children, model different responses to frustrations, such as not winning a race or a game.

Help children learn to acknowledge and label their feelings as they participate in classroom activities.

Choose literature in which the characters respond to emotions appropriately, and discuss how they felt and acted.

Provide empathy for children's fears and concerns. These may be imagined (fear of monsters), realistic (fear of someone making fun of them), or learned (apprehension about visiting the doctor). Because they are all real to the child, adults can help by acknowledging the child's discomfort and offering physical or verbal consolation (Kostelnik et al., 1998).

Allow children to share their humor: appreciate the growth of their sense of humor.

Primary children may be helped to express their feelings through writing. Select examples of literature that illustrate how children have written about their frustrations or stresses and learned to cope more effectively with them through writing.

Praise children's accomplishments, and, in order to build self-esteem, use genuine praise and more reinforcement than negative criticism. Give children adequate time and encouragement to finish tasks for themselves.

Never shame or compare children with others or label them with derogatory words. In classrooms with a lack of basic respect, children will not engage intellectually or emotionally, no matter how well developed the curriculum is (Wagner, 1996). Develop a ready bank of reinforcing and encouraging phrases, such as the following (remember to be specific so that praise doesn't become meaningless):

You worked so hard to figure that out. I'm proud of you!

I'm happy to see you cooperating like that.

It's such a pleasure working with you because you try so hard.

That's really an improvement!

Hey, I can see that you've been practicing and that it's paying off.

You are really burning those old neurons today!

Now that's what I call a terrific job.

You've remembered your homework every day this week. Good for you!

That was a friendly and very caring thing to do.

Wow! You've got it figured out, haven't you?

You have to feel really proud of . . . . It took meeting the problem head on, and you did it!

Accept and respect temperamental idiosyncrasies, providing support where needed for children who adapt more slowly to change. Avoid using children's names to mean "No," "Stop," or "Don't!"

Never ignore difficult behaviors or problems such as lying, stealing, or cruelty to self or others (see Chapter 6). When children demonstrate a pattern of difficult behaviors and are unresponsive to your attempts to modify them, seek help by working with other professionals who have more specific expertise.

Develop a sense of belonging and connectedness for each member of the class. Have the class send cards to children who are sick. Model and let children know that your motto is "We're a team; we respect and take care of one another."

7. Promote children's competence. Competence is the ability to meet age-appropriate expectations at a reasonably high standard. Be patient in helping children modify their behavior. View children's inappropriate behavior as a gap in their knowledge or skills. Rather than expecting immediate change, identify steps in progress, giving children reinforcement when you see them trying to correct a particular behavior.

Use subtle cues to remind children that their behavior is close to exceeding limits. Whenever possible, allow children opportunities to assess the situation, figure out what should be done, experience consequences, and modify their own behavior in a positive direction.

Set effective limits with clearly defined expectations. Involve children in structuring classroom rules, and apply natural and logical consequences consistently when rules are not observed. (Refer to Chapter 16 for further information regarding rules and consequences.)

Help children find satisfying ways to express their emotions to others. When an emotion has been

Provide opportunities for children to describe their emotions.

expressed inappropriately, recognize a child's feelings about the situation before moving ahead with helping the child correct the situation or learn new skills.

For children who have difficulty controlling impulsivity because of neurological disorders that manifest themselves behaviorally (e.g., attention deficit disorder, autisticlike disorders), use such approaches as nonpunitive separation to remove the child from an overstimulating situation. Use scaffolding and work completion strategies to help such children better organize their day. Provide reinforcement for keeping on task as well as frequent goal-setting sessions and helpful, concrete suggestions for more appropriate behavior.

Protect children's growing sense of autonomy by giving them frequent choices. Offer these only when you are willing to accept children's decisions. Be careful about providing too many choices or overloading children with decision-making "opportunities" that are meaningless or are better made by adults.

When children focus on the negative, accept their statements and then ask, "How do you wish it were different? What could you do to change it?" Help students set goals for what they can change and be more accepting of what they cannot. Teach children to be competent and responsible workers.

Involve children in planning, implementing, and evaluating some class activities and decisions. Set aside a portion of each day for children to engage in free-choice, self-initiated activities.

Design activities in which the primary purpose is to teach children to use various classroom tools. Give children opportunities to carry out classroom jobs. Encourage them to clean up after themselves whenever possible and also to assist others who need help.

Encourage children to evaluate the decisions they have made by looking back at how well they defined the problem, whether they thought about all the alternatives, whether they persisted long enough, what turned out well, and what they might do differently the next time. Also, invite children to evaluate their accomplishments. Conference with them and provide task-specific feedback and questions to help them focus on what they have learned and the next steps to enhance their learning. Guide them toward self-examination of their own growth and work rather than relying only on the teacher's or their parents' evaluation. Involve them in producing self-appraisal reports prior to parent conferences (see Chapter 16).

Support children in their efforts to try new or uncomfortable tasks. Verbally recognize their efforts, and praise courage and determination to try in the first place, not just the results. Include scaffolding strategies here; gauge the amount of support and challenge necessary for optimal growth, slowly decreasing support as the child moves toward increasing autonomy (Bedrova & Leong, 1996).

8. *In working with children with disabilities, avoid tendencies to overprotect them in order to develop their*

autonomy as much as possible. Assist children only when needed. Whenever possible, encourage children who are not disabled to seek help from children with disabilities. This helps both the child with the disability and the nondisabled child to build a perception that an existing disability should not be the central focus when evaluating another person's abilities.

ACTIVITY SUGGESTIONS

✎ Toy Land Relaxation

Objective 28   For children to learn satisfying and effective strategies to express and cope with personal emotions and tensions.

Materials   Hinged toy figure, flexible cloth figures, taped musical selections for marching and relaxing, tape player

Procedure   To help children become familiar with and contrast feelings of bodily relaxation and tension, talk with them about how our bodies are hinged together. Help them discover where these "hinges" are located (neck, wrist, fingers, ankles, toes, and waist) and how stiff and tight their bodies feel when the hinges are all "locked up." Contrast this with what happens when these same hinges are loose by having the children relax each locked body hinge, starting with the neck, then the waist, wrists, and so on, reminding them to sit down carefully as their body becomes increasingly limp.

To simplify   Demonstrate the process of locking up and loosening up with toys, such as stiff, inflexible robots and limp cloth dolls or animals.

To extend   To increase children's sense of contrast, use march music and practice being stiff robots; then switch to some peaceful, relaxing music, and encourage children to slow everything down and become completely limp and relaxed. Discuss with children other states they have experienced and how their bodies felt at the time, what their facial expressions may have been, what they may have said, or how they may have behaved (e.g., being angry vs. being happy and relaxed). For a follow-up activity, have children choose pictures from magazines that depict faces of people who seem "tight," angry, and hurried and those in which people seem "loose," happy, and relaxed.

✎ A Special Self Award*

Objective 25   For children to evaluate and describe their competencies.

Materials   Precut "award" shapes, labels, glue, ribbons, mirrors, blank booklets, markers

Procedure   Discuss the ideas of valuing yourself and liking things that you do well. Explain that awards are sometimes given to people to show what special things they do well. Ask the children to think of something they like about themselves and to design a special award for themselves. Provide a variety of precut shapes in colored, gold, and silver paper, ribbons, glue, and labels that say "I'm Special Because I _____."

To simplify   For children who have difficulty thinking of something, ask others in the group to help them by suggesting the things they do well.

To extend   Have children develop individual "I Am Special" booklets where they either dictate or write a sentence at the top of each page about a skill they have developed in which they take pride. Have them illustrate the process.

✎ Who's in Your Family†

Objective 21   For children to explore similarities and differences among people to gain personal insight.

Materials   Photographs of household members, blank booklets, markers, children's literature about families including a children's story in Spanish or another language, persona dolls

Procedure   Borrow and/or take photographs of all the people who live with each child and staff member. Make a bulletin board of "The People in Our Homes." Label each photo with the names and family relationships of each person.

To simplify   Talk with children about the similarities and differences in who lives together as a family.

To extend   Make a class book about "Our Families" with a page for each child and staff member, telling who

---

Note: Adapted from Kostelnik et al. (1991, 22)
†*Note:* Adapted from Derman-Sparks (1989, 59–60).

lives with each child and what work family members do in and outside the home. "This is Jamal's family. He lives with _____. His [mom, dad, grandma, grandpa, aunt, uncle] take care of him, work at . . . ." Be aware that some children's primary family members are temporarily or chronically unemployed. Focus on what they do, not on where they work. Let children take these stories home to read to their families.

Read children's books about families reflective of the ethnic groups in your class. Always read more than one book about each group. Talk about the differences and similarities between the children's lives in the book and the children from that ethnic group in your class. Discuss the books: "Is this how you do it in your family?" Expand on this with books about families from ethnic groups not present in the classroom. Include books about interracial and intercultural families (see resources listed in Derman-Sparks, 1989, 119–132).

Using persona dolls (those that represent a particular racial/ethnic group), tell stories about possible experiences or problems a child might have within the family, school, or neighborhood when belonging to that racial/ethnic group. For example, talk about a Spanish-speaking child's experience when beginning school, using a persona doll as a prop. Read a book in Spanish to the children, and talk about how they feel when they do not understand the words and how they think the doll felt. Tell a story where one of the dolls was teased for being Mexican; talk about how the doll felt and what the doll did to stand up for him- or herself.

✎ I Can Can

Objective 25   For children to evaluate and describe their competencies.

Materials   Large empty juice can, colored paper strips, markers, blank booklets

Procedure   Provide or have children bring in a large empty juice can that has been washed and checked for any sharp edges. Have them place a label around the can that says "I CAN!" and then decorate the can so that each is individual. As they learn and demonstrate a new skill, have them fill out a special colored paper strip, dictating or writing the skill and dating it.

To simplify   Watch for the child who fails to recognize his or her accomplishments. Remind these children that small gains also need to be recorded, and

help them identify some of these or set goals that can be accomplished.

To extend   At the end of each month, have the children transfer their "I CAN!" slips to an ongoing booklet, denoting the beginning of each month (e.g., "In November, I learned to do these things") and pasting in the strips following the heading. The pages could also be illustrated in some way. The booklets become a vehicle for children's self-assessment. They can also become one piece of a portfolio, shared with a portfolio buddy or the entire group, and shared with parents at conferences or open houses.

✎ I Can Get There All by Myself

Objective 11   For children to experience the pleasure of work.

Materials   Paper, markers, scissors, glue

Procedure   Demonstrate to children drawing a simple map from your home to the school. As you draw it, talk about several landmarks on the way. Draw them in and label them. Draw a clock by the house noting the time (on the hour or half hour) that you usually leave for school. After drawing the school, add a clock by it indicating (again, on the hour or half hour) what time you usually arrive. Tell the children, "This is a map of the way I come to school every day. The clocks indicate the time I leave for school and the time I arrive. Each one of you gets to school each day by walking or riding in a car or bus. That means you have to get ready to leave by a certain time and then get to this classroom by the time school is ready to start." Invite each child to construct a simple map showing their home, the school, and a route in between.

To simplify   Tell the children that you would like to construct a classroom map showing the school and the way to each one of their homes and that you need their help in drawing their houses. Have them make just a picture of their homes on individual pieces of paper and cut around them. Construct a very simple mural showing just larger cross streets, and help the children paste their homes east, west, south, or north of the cross streets.

To extend   Have the children also indicate the approximate time (half hour or hour) they leave their homes and arrive at school. Have them draw a more elaborate route between home and school on an individual basis.

Have them take part in constructing the classroom mural that integrates all of their homes in relation to the school.

✎ We're Learning to Do So Many Things

Objective 25 For children to evaluate and describe their competencies.

Materials Large precut hand on easel, markers, blank booklets

Procedure Tell the children, "Just think of how many things you do every day from the time you get up in the morning until you go to bed." Place a large precut hand on the easel. Tell the children, "Sometimes when someone is able to do a lot of different things, we say they are 'pretty handy.'" Ask them what they think the expression means, and discuss the many ways we use our hands in order to accomplish what we need to. Label the precut hand, "We are Pretty Handy." Encourage the children to think of skills they have developed, print them on the hand, and then have the group decide where to place it in the classroom.

To simplify For children who have a difficult time thinking of things they do, have the group suggest something they probably can do.

To extend Have the children construct an individual booklet that contains about ten pages titled "Learning to Be Handy." Have them work on completing the pages by drawing their hands on each page and then listing a separate skill they have learned on each of the fingers (e.g., "I brush my teeth," "I can count to 25," "I fix my own cereal," "I make my bed," "I feed my dog").

✎ Relaxing Our Bodies

Objective 28 For children to learn satisfying strategies to express and cope with personal emotions.

Materials Tape of relaxing music, tape player

Procedure One way to relax is through deep breathing. Even very young children can learn to do this with guidance. Have the children learn to assume a relaxed, comfortable position and be very quiet so that each of them can just listen to their breathing as they breathe in and out through their noses. As they relax, help them breathe more deeply and deepen their feeling of relaxation by having them try some of the following exercises:

❏ Imagine the air that comes to you is a cloud. The cloud comes to you, fills you, and then leaves you.

❏ Imagine your chest (or lungs) as a balloon. You may want to demonstrate this by putting your hand on your chest and then have them feel their own chests as they breathe in deeply. Tell them, "As you breathe in or inhale, your lungs expand like a balloon, don't they? As you exhale or breathe out, your lungs deflate like a balloon."

❏ As you inhale, say the word "in" to yourself. As you exhale, say the word "out."

To simplify Have the children learn to assume a comfortable, relaxed position. Put on some very relaxing music, and have them stretch slowly to the music, and then just lie quietly and listen to it. Use the works "relax" and "relaxing" to acquaint them with relaxation terminology.

To extend Have the children experience tensing specific muscle groups and then relaxing them. First be sure that they are familiar with all of the body parts that follow, and demonstrate any unfamiliar terminology used such as "clench" and "shrug." Then talk them through the exercise as follows:

Muscle	*Tensing Method*
Forehead	Wrinkle your forehead. Try to make your eyebrows touch your hair. Count to five. Relax.
Eyes and nose	Close your eyes as tightly as you can. Keep them closed and count to five. Open your eyes and relax.
Lips, cheeks, and jaw	Keeping your mouth closed, make as big a smile as you can. Keep the smile on your face and count to five. Relax. Feel how warm your face is.
Hands	Hold your arms in front of you. Make a tight fist with your hands. Squeeze them as tightly as you can while you count to five. Relax. Feel the warmth and calmness in your hands.
Forearms	Extend your arms out. Pretend you are pushing against a wall. Push forward with your hands and keep them against the invisible wall. Hold them there and count to five. Relax.

Shoulders	Shrug your shoulders up to your ears. Keep them there while you count to five. Relax.
Thighs	Tighten your thigh muscles by pressing your legs together as tightly as you can. Count to five. Relax your legs.
Feet	Bend your ankles toward your body as far as you can. Hold them there and count to five. Relax.
Toes	Curl your toes under as tightly as you can. Hold them there. Count to five. Relax.

Afterward, encourage the children to talk about how their bodies feel while they are doing the exercise. Tell them that some people like to relax their muscles when they go to bed by doing this exercise.

✎ We All Look Special*

Objective 15　For children to value their own gender, family, culture, and race.

Materials　Paint chip samples, paper, markers, skin-colored crayons

Procedure　Get paint chips from a paint store. In small groups, identify the ones closest to each child's skin tone, hair color, and eye color.

To simplify　Make a very simple graph using a range of colors and how many children have which color. Talk about how everyone has skin and the functions it serves for everyone. Provide skin-colored crayons that can be ordered from a number of companies such as Afro-Am Education Materials and Crayola. Help them choose the one closest to their skin color and then draw pictures of themselves. Mix paints so that each of the children has individualized color for painting pictures of themselves. Be creative in talking about the beauty of each shade.

To extend　In an all-white class, help children identify more subtle differences in skin shades, including freckles, and emphasize that skin color differences are desirable. In a diverse interracial/interethnic class, emphasize the theme, "Beautiful children come in all colors" and that the classroom is a wonderful mixture of colors. Make a rainbow from skin shade colors, eye

Note. Adapted from Derman-Sparks (1991, pp. 35–36)

colors, or hair colors and label it "We All Make a Beautiful Rainbow."

✎ Happy Faces

Objective 26　For children to identify their emotions and become more aware of facial expressions of happiness.

Materials　Paper plates with tongue depressor handles attached to them, yarn for hair, markers, crayons, glue, construction paper, facial features cut out of magazines (be sure to use magazines with pictures of many different races of children and adults)

Procedure　In the art center, spread out materials. Help the children use the materials to make puppets with happy faces, providing suggestions but not giving them a model to copy. Encourage them to talk about how they feel inside when they are wearing a happy face or how they feel when someone else looks at them with a happy face.

To simplify　With extremely young children, provide already prepared puppets and encourage them to discuss feelings that go along with happy faces.

To extend　Have older children write and/or stage their own puppet show about an especially joyous situation.

Extend children's ability to identify body language expressions of happiness. Have them hold the stick puppets in front of their faces as they march up and down repeating this chant in happy voices (to the tune of "Here We Go 'Round the Mulberry Bush."):

> This is my happy face, happy face, happy face. This is my happy face being worn at school today.
>
> This is my happy march, happy march, happy march. This is my happy march taking place at school today.

✎ We Get Angry When . . .

Objective 30　For children to become more familiar with circumstances that influence emotions.

Materials　Children's books about anger

Procedure　After you have discussed the feeling of anger with children in a large- or small-group situation and have read some books about anger (e.g., *Alexander and the Terrible, Horrible, No Good, Very Bad Day* by Judith Viorst; *Attila the Angry* by Marjorie Weinman Sharmat; *Let's Be Enemies* by Janice May Udry: *The*

Sorely Trying Day by Russell Hoban; *The Hating Book* by Charlotte Zolotow), have the children share examples of moments when they feel or have felt angry. Discuss ways the characters deal with the situations that help them get rid of the angry feelings. Talk about positive and negative strategies people use in trying to get rid of angry feelings.

To simplify   After reading the stories, talk about what made the main character angry or upset.

To extend   Write the title "We Get Angry When . . ." at the top of a large sheet of paper on the easel. List examples or write a class experience story as the children share their ideas. Older children could write and illustrate individual "I Get Angry When . . ." booklets.

SUMMARY

Young children have much to learn about themselves and the effect they have on others. And what they learn in the early years from significant others in their lives—particularly from parents, teachers, and peers—becomes vitally important in their later ability to form and maintain relationships, work and play well with others, and feel valued, confident, and competent in any number of situations.

The development of emotional strength and stability, a lifelong task, is interdependent with children's cognitive, physical, and social development. Because children spend major amounts of time in extrafamilial settings and because they are moving into these contexts earlier and earlier, good learning environments are those in which affective, physical, and social development are valued as highly as academic aspects of learning. Caring professionals who are able to structure positive learning climates, actively promote children's emotional development and sense of self-worth, and foster children's competence are key players in facilitating positive affective outcomes for young children. Also critical will be the sensitivity of caring adults to differences in personality, gender, ethnicity, and race in the children and families with whom they work.

✳ Applying What You Read in This Chapter

1. **Discuss**
   a. Review each of the opening questions in this chapter.
   b. In what way is the acquisition of self-esteem more dependent on internal than external factors?
2. **Observe**
   a. Arrange to observe an early childhood classroom to observe the following:
      (1) The overall affective climate in the classroom. What contributes most noticeably to it? What detracts from it?
      (2) Evidence that the teacher supports children on an individual basis as well as a cohort group. Cite specific examples of how he/she does this.
3. **Carry out an activity**
   a. Read Daniel Goleman's book *Emotional Intelligence* (1995). Find out what he believes is the cost of emotional illiteracy.
   b. Interview one or more principals of an elementary school. Ask to see how affective development is planned for in the curriculum. Ask,

"How is that translated to everyday instruction? Could you give me some specific examples?"
   c. Survey ten parents about character or moral education and whether they believe it should be part of the school curriculum or left for families to provide for their children. What are their reasons for their preference?
   d. Survey one child at each level, preschool through third grade, to find out how involved each is in terms of extracurricular activities. How much television does each child watch? How much leisure time does each have, and how do they spend it?
4. **Create something for your portfolio**
   a. Develop a lesson plan for the affective domain.
   b. Write a brief position paper outlining your beliefs about the importance of planning for affective development in the early childhood classroom.
5. **Add to your journal**
   a. How well is your own emotional intelligence or intrapersonal intelligence developed? Because this is a lifelong process, are there areas that need

attention? How can you address needed skill building?

b. When you feel overly stressed or overwhelmed, what strategies do you employ to reduce stress for the short term? For the long term? How do you react physically to undue stress? Psychologically? Behaviorally?

c. In what temperament category would you place yourself: easy, slow-to-warm-up, difficult, none of the three? What are some characteristics that make you believe that is an appropriate conclusion?

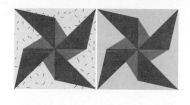

Chapter 10

The Cognitive Domain

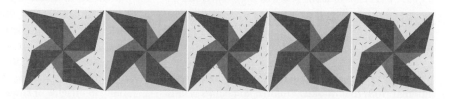

You may wonder:

How "smart" am I, and in what ways am I "smart"? What was the process of cognitive maturation that brought me to this point in my development?

What five subgroups make up a young child's developing knowledge base?

What exactly is meant by the term "scaffolding," and how does this take place most effectively in the early childhood classroom?

What should our goals be for effective science and mathematics education in the early years? Is hands-on activity enough to accomplish these goals?

How much emphasis should be placed on involving children with technology in the early childhood classroom? Does it enhance or deter early learning?

In this chapter on the cognitive domain, we present information to help you answer these questions.

In a discussion with a group of kindergarteners after reading It Looked Like Spilt Milk *by Shaw (Harper Collins), Ms. Linscott asks the children, "How do you think clouds stay up in the sky?"*

"They're stuck up there 'cause they're made out of white stuff . . . out of lots of white glue and stuff!" offers Kiley.

"And sometimes they fall down at night and the next day it's all sun and no clouds in the sky . . . just all sun!" adds Latonya helpfully.

That young children's thinking is dramatically different from that of older children and adults is illustrated again and again by the "cute" but inaccurate statements they make. Quite literally, they see the world from an entirely different perspective, and their fascinating journey toward more mature thinking will be a combination of inherent capacities, accumulated experiences, and the quality of their relationships with others who will accompany them on that journey.

Development in the cognitive domain—that is, the maturation of processes and products of the human mind that lead to "knowing" (Berk, 1996b)—is a complex process that impacts significantly and continuously on all other domains of development. At the same time, growth and increasing competence in other domains influence the qualitative development of cognitive capacities. For example, a young child's ability to imagine or fantasize what it is like to be another member of the family—mommy, daddy, or baby—

equips the child to take on such a role in a group of children playing "house." Interacting with other children as they play out their concept of "house" subsequently increases the child's knowledge and skill base in a variety of areas, for example, vocabulary, understanding of social do's and don'ts, one-to-one correspondence, and a sense of number as the children divide and combine materials. Also enhanced is their ability to manage conflict as they sort out roles and goal-directed behaviors. There is a growing understanding of cause and effect as they operate on objects, challenge and cooperate with one another, and figure out alternate ways to accomplish a variety of intended outcomes.

Because of the circuitous fashion in which the intellect evolves, promising new directions in early childhood education that support the integration of various learning domains through experiential learning have enormous potential. They are made even more effective when cognitive levels are matched carefully with classroom learning experiences and when professionals are sensitive to the negative effects of overchallenging or underchallenging the developing child.

COGNITIVE MATURATION

The Contributions of Neuroscience to Understanding Cognitive Development in the Developing Child

> A father comforts a crying newborn. A mother plays peekaboo with her ten-month-old. A child care provider reads to a toddler. And in a matter of seconds, thousands of cells in these children's growing brains respond. Some brain cells are "turned on," triggered by this particular experience. Many existing connections among brain cells are strengthened. At the same time, new connections are formed, adding a bit more definition and complexity to the intricate circuitry that will remain largely in place for the rest of these children's lives. (Shore, 1997, ix)

Gardner et. al (1996) and others have said that we have learned more about the human brain in the last two decades than in all of recorded history prior to this time. Since the 1970s, when anatomical study of the brain began in earnest, we have known that the human brain contains some 50 billion neurons at birth and that at least 10 billion of those neural cells continue a process

of connecting with one another in a series of plateau and acceleration periods. Males are generally 6 to 18 months behind females in moving into the acceleration stages in the preschool and primary years (see Figure 10.1). Because of a gene called CREB, which stimulates the number of connections made by each axon (see Figure 10.2), each of these cells has the capacity to connect with a thousand others, laying out the complex neural pathways for developing language, logical-mathematical understanding, social interaction, affective growth, and aesthetic intelligence. Shore (1996, 19) indicates that "among primates, only the human brain continues to grow at fetal rates after birth, and the frantic pace of this postpartum neural building boom continues for the first two years of life before it begins to show any signs of abating." By this time, children have developed half of all the neural connections they will make over a lifetime. Then begins a process of pruning or "weeding out" less-used synapses while continuing to build and strengthen other connections. The fatty myelin sheath that covers the nerves and allows smooth transmission of electrochemical impulses is fully formed in most children somewhere around 6 years of age, and neural development continues into adolescence, where the female brain is fully formed about two years before the male brain.

During acceleration periods of brain growth, myelinization and axon and dendrite growth in the brain is significant, enabling millions of new connections to form. Following each of the acceleration periods, children are able to experience more complex levels of learning. In the classroom, we see this in a child's excitement over finally "getting it," finally understanding a concept or mastering a skill that has been difficult in the past—managing to tie a paint apron without help, writing first words independently, or regrouping in math without assistance.

In forging new frontiers into how the mind works, neuroscientists have recently begun to document particular areas of brain activity in relation to environmental stimulation through in vivo PET (positron-emission tomography) scans. You may have seen TV presentations of this process where someone is given a task to do while areas of the brain are observed for increased blood flow. Scientists are then able to document how specific areas of the brain process information and any differences that exist in the way one person processes information as compared to another.

FIGURE 10.1
Plateau and Acceleration of Brain Growth According to Epstein (1978)

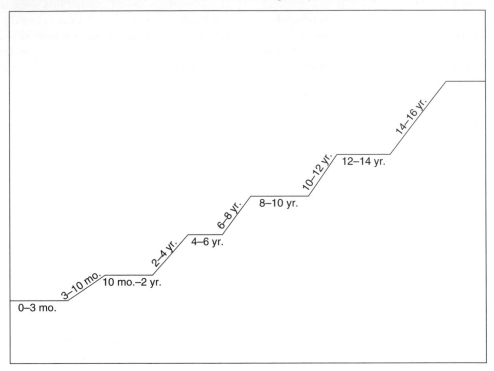

0–3 mo.
3–10 mo.
10 mo.–2 yr.
2–4 yr.
4–6 yr.
6–8 yr.
8–10 yr.
10–12 yr.
12–14 yr.
14–16 yr.

FIGURE 10.2
Neuronal Growth

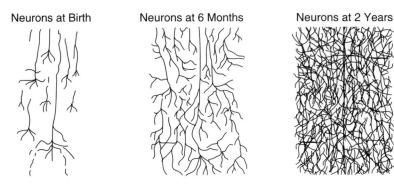

Neurons at Birth

Neurons at 6 Months

Neurons at 2 Years

Simplified Model of a Neuron

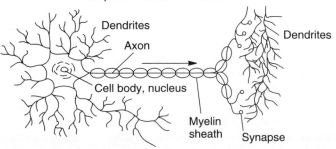

Dendrites

Axon

Cell body, nucleus

Myelin sheath

Dendrites

Synapse

This brain-imaging technology has sent us light years ahead in appreciating the value of early experiences in creating brain structures. In other words, a brain does not simply grow larger as do our toes and fingers; instead, it forms particular connections that are unique to each individual, depending on the quality and repetition of stimulating multisensory experiences encountered in the early years (Begley, 1997a). These repeated experiences strengthen specific synapses (brain connections) over time. In turn, they exert a critical influence on the kinds of pruning and neural connections (synaptogenesis) that ultimately produce the mature brain and corresponding abilities and capabilities in that child. Earliest evidence of this process is seen in the loss of some of the involuntary reflexes in the first 3 or 4 months, the appearance of earliest memory processes in the hippocampus around 8 months of age, thought and working memory in the prefrontal cortex in the second half of the first year, and burgeoning language in the second year of life.

There is evidence, also, that *particular* sensory experiences in the early years may have a dramatic influence on brain wiring. For example, if a child has a particularly "chatty" and nurturing mother, language is heightened; children exposed to music (particularly classical music because of the repetitive patterns) experience greater neural circuitry in areas controlling the spatial-temporal reasoning later connected to mathematics and engineering. Indeed, the peak learning years for human beings appear to be between the ages of 4 and 10, a time when children make huge leaps in language, logical-mathematical, and social discoveries (Viadero, 1996). Ultimately, the pruning, which becomes most aggressive around the age of 10, destroys the individual's weakest synapses, resulting in a more specifically patterned, efficient, and powerful brain (Begley, 1997a; Courtney et al.,1997; Nash, 1997).

Just as we know that high-quality, early environments set in motion positive trajectories for development, there is strong evidence that traumatic and chaotic environments negatively affect neural connections. Elevated stress hormones such as cortisol result in diminished brain growth in regions of the brain related to memory, learning, and emotional attachment; there is also increased arousal in other regions related to hyperactivity, anxiety, impulsive behavior, attention regulation, and self-control (Gunnar et al., 1996; Shore, 1997).

Moreover, although a child's environment might not be described as risky because of overt abuse or serious neglect, it may be one where the child is simply deprived of the kind of stimulating experiences that produce the most fertile minds. Previously, we had suspected that human development hinges strongly on the interplay between nature and nurture (Shore, 1997), but it was hard to convince professionals who believed that intelligence, school success, and the way we interact with the world are primarily the result of fixed brain structures at birth, with environmental experiences considerably less influential (Newberger, 1997). Research now removes any doubt about the effect of inadequate early experiences, yielding serious implications for parents, policymakers, and early childhood educators. Ironically, parents are more pressed for time than ever before (Nash, 1997, 51), and quality childcare for working parents remains problematic, both in terms of availability and cost. Too, although we have made inroads into providing a better match between children's cognitive levels and primary classroom experiences, there are still many children sitting in classrooms where a serious gap exists between professional knowledge and actual instructional practice. Susan Kovalik (1997), a well-known educator and advocate for Developmentally Appropriate Practice, has termed this gap a breach of morality in the profession. She reminds us that "[we] are the only species that creates the environment that creates us" and challenges all educators to provide the rich and flexible learning context that every child deserves.

Gardner's Multiple Intelligence Perspective

The possibility that strengths and outcomes in brain connections are also heavily influenced by *natural* inclinations has been offered as a theoretical perspective of intelligence by Howard Gardner (1993a, 1997), a Harvard University psychologist. Though preferring to think of intelligences as *human capabilities* or *talents* rather than some fixed phenomenon inside the head, Gardner sees the neurobiology just described resulting in "core information processing mechanisms" associated with particular intelligences. Making the claim for relatively autonomous intelligences, Gardner defines intelligence as "the ability to solve problems or fashion products that are of consequence in a particular cultural setting or community" (1993a, 15). As outlined in Chapter 2, he offers at least seven or more intelligences that account for the great variations seen in human beings within and across all cultures: linguistic intelligence, musical intelligence, logical-mathematical intelligence, spatial intelligence, bodily-kinesthetic intelligence, intrapersonal intelligence, interpersonal intelligence, and the possibility of a naturalist intelligence. He cites evidence for his theory from the many studies of breakdowns in specific mental functioning in brain-damaged persons and the intellectual profiles of special populations (eg., prodigies and savants) who demonstrate extraordinary development in one area but only minimal or even diminished capability in other areas. At the heart of his theory is his belief that humans come equipped with certain core mechanisms that are genetically programmed to be activated or "triggered" (e.g., syntactic ordering in language or pitch in music), but he notes that not everyone progresses to an expert end state in *all* areas (e.g., mathematics or music).

So far, the greatest influence of his theory has been felt in educational circles where children are challenged to round out their range of talents, encouraged to use a special strength to shore up a weaker area, and allowed to demonstrate performance competence in ways other than through traditional paper-and-pencil tests. Some of the diverse ways schools have devised to apply his theory have been "brilliant" and some have been "idiotic," Gardner has said (1994, 581). In response to criticism of his theory from his colleagues in psychology, notably Herrnstein and Murray (1994), Gardner has countered that he is put off by traditional intelligence testing and the Western practice of regarding only skills in language and logic as intelligence. He prefers to label the many diverse faculties he sees in human beings with the same term, one faculty being held in no greater esteem than another.

Hatch (1997, 26) cautions educators that there are many faces of the same "intelligence" and that a child may be both good and poor within the same intelligence. For example, in the interpersonal realm, children can show sensitivity and responsiveness to other people in significantly different ways. He suggests that instead of asking how much intelligence each young child has, we need to ask, "In what way does this child demonstrate intelligence" (i.e., labeling a child as "linguistic" is not as informative as noting the different ways in which he or she demonstrates particular language interests). Instead of tagging a child with a label, there is a need to balance a child's strengths and

needs and help children master more challenging content, skills, and concepts. Ernest Hall, a successful English entrepreneur, underscores the need to encourage children to stretch themselves:

> I discovered my interests (in music) before the crushing routines of my little school would have reduced me to a mere cog in a machine. Ability is not innate. It exists like a shadow of ourselves when we are willing to stand in front of a bright light . . . we must say to every child, "you are special. You are unique, but to develop your genius, you have to work at it and stay with it year after year." (Abbot, 1997)

THE THEORETICAL CONTRIBUTIONS OF JEAN PIAGET AND LEV VYGOTSKY

Though the theoretical conclusions of the Swiss epistomologist Jean Piaget are being reexamined in light of current research in the field, his contributions continue to be highly useful in understanding the qualitative cognitive changes that take place in the young child. As Gardner et al. (1996) succinctly stated it, "Piaget is important not because he got it all right, but because he was the first person to portray children's intellectual development in detail and because people continue to address the questions that Piaget himself first addressed." Because Piaget narrowly centered on the *commonalities* of intelligence that could be observed in *all* human beings, he neglected to address the differences that can be seen both within and across cultures. Nor did he apply his findings to intervening in any way in the cognitive development of human beings.

Piaget saw cognitive maturation as a progressive series of structurally defined stages, and it is this perspective that is currently drawing the greatest criticism by those who dismiss the idea of specific qualitative shifts in thought at particular times in the life span. However, his view that maturation evolves from the human organism's self-motivated efforts to adapt to and make sense of day-to-day experiences fits very well with current neurobiological findings and other current theories about cognition. In developing useful concepts, or schemes, children purposefully repeat certain acts again and again (e.g., dropping an object from the high chair, rhyming certain sounds or words, observing how someone ties shoelaces, drawing or scribbling, listening to a story, riding a trike, working a puzzle, or writing at school in a daily journal). These acts result in their "bumping into" new information that is either simply assimilated or produces a need for accommodation in terms of current functioning. When human beings cognitively assimilate experiential knowledge, they do so without feeling any need to adapt the way they think about a particular phenomenon or situation. However, there are other times when they become "disequilibrated," or thrown out of balance cognitively; this is because they have begun to notice something about a situation or phenomenon that no longer fits comfortably in their old way of thinking about it.

For example, a child may initially have only one concept for all vehicles and refer to them all as "cars." Later, as a result of new experiences with a number of wheeled phenomena and also structural maturation of the brain, it begins to dawn on the child that some vehicles *are* different from one another. As the child zeros in on how these newly noticed phenomena are different, the child also comes to understand that vehicles other than those initially catching his or her interest may also be different. If the child feels motivated to investigate these differences or pay more attention to them as encountered in everyday experiences, the child gains growing expertise related to vehicular phenomena, both in terms of vehicles in general and then in a horizontal fleshing out of vehicles in particular categories. As a result, the child comes to know not only that cars differ from buses and trucks but also that, within the category of cars, there are Fords and Volvos, sedans and coupes, convertibles and hard tops, sports cars and family cars. Now, instead of having one, incorrect mental "index card" for cars, the child has an expanded mental file for vehicles and a more mature scheme for understanding and interacting with the environment. These higher-order schemes are an outcome of both genetic, biological unfolding and experiences that catch one's attention and produce a field of disequilibration, creating the motivation to try a task over and over in order to "figure something out."

According to Piaget, there are four stages of mental operations used by children to make sense of events and phenomena, and these build epigenetically on one another. Hamachek's (1990, 469) summary of the basic intellectual abilities associated with each of the stages appears in Table 10.1. Ages connected to these stages are approximate, and children are continuously moving toward acquisition of higher-level processes while still showing evidence of characteristic limitations identified with particular stages. Early childhood educators working with young children can benefit greatly by understanding and respecting the characteristic modes of thinking within certain stages so that activities and experiences match cognitive levels and do not exceed a child's ability to gain from them.

CHARACTERISTICS OF PREOPERATIONAL AND CONCRETE OPERATIONAL THOUGHT

Because this text focuses on constructing effective learning environments for children from 3 to 8 years of age, characteristics peculiar to children in the preoperational and concrete operational periods deserve a closer look.

Centration, children's tendency to center on only one aspect of a stimulus rather than processing all available information and holding changes in two dimensions at the same time, is an important aspect of preoperational thinking. As children move toward the end of the period, they are not as easily fooled and are more able to decenter in situations or with materials familiar to them. Although their thought is perhaps still not as logical as that of the average 8- to 11-year-old, they are relying less on intuition and the appearance of things when they explain why things happen. Their understanding of cause and effect becomes clearer, and more mature preoperational children are also beginning to move away from the egocentrism that limits them from seeing other people's points of view. Children who have moved into the concrete operational stage still benefit from using real objects when problem solving but are now better equipped to deal with symbolic forms. Because their ability to decenter is more highly developed, they can focus on details while keeping the whole in mind, a skill necessary for understanding part-whole relationships involved in place value in mathematics or phonics in literacy.

Closely related to centration is a lack of ability to think in more than one direction. *Reversibility,* the concept that objects or actions can be structured, restructured, and then rearranged as originally structured, is limited in the preoperational child. Children under 5 years of age are influenced by perceptual salience; that is, their perceptions dominate their understandings, and seeing is believing. Thus, they do

TABLE 10.1
Overview of Piaget's Intellectual Stages

Stage	Age Range	Basic Characteristics
1. Sensorimotor	Birth–2	Infants learn that they are different from other objects and learn primarily through their senses and manipulations. There is a strong desire and need for as much stimulation as possible.
2. Preoperational thought	2–7	An essentially egocentric period insofar as children are unable to see things from others' point of view; they tend to classify in very simple ways (e.g., if a father is a man, then all men must be fathers).
a. Preoperational phase	2–4	
b. Intuitive phase	4–7	Children slowly begin to think in terms of classes, handle number concepts, and see simple relationships. Children are "intuitive"; that is, they are capable of making classifications even though they do not really understand why or how. They develop a gradual awareness of the conservation of mass, weight, and volume (e.g., they can see that the amount may remain the same even if transferred to a different size container).
3. Concrete operational thought	7–11	Children grow in ability to consciously use and understand logical operations such as reversibility (in arithmetic), classification (putting objects into hierarchies of classes), and seriation (organizing objects into a specified series, such as increasing size or weight).
4. Formal operational thought	11–15	Youngsters further develop the ability to comprehend abstract concepts (e.g., the ability to think about "ideals," understand cause-effect relationships, think about the future, and develop and test hypotheses).

Source: Adapted from Don Hamachek, *Psychology in Teaching, Learning, and Growth,* Fourth Edition. Copyright © 1990 by Allyn & Bacon. Reprinted with permission.

not automatically know what older children are coming to know—that number, mass, distance, volume, and area stay constant despite changes in appearance. Children in the concrete stage can be more reflective about such operations and also what it would require to undo an action. For example, at a summer camp craft class, 9-year-old Juana and her 3-year-old brother Carl had each created a sculpture from toothpicks and marshmallows. Each child had been given 20 marshmallows and 10 toothpicks to create whatever he or she wished. Carl, after completing a "spaceship" with his materials, began pestering Juana for more toothpicks and marshmallows to make a different one because he did not like the one he had created. "Just use the ones you have!" she responded testily. Carl looked down in a confused way at the unwanted creation, thought again about the other one he had in mind, and cried, "But they're all gone! I don't have no more!" Juana's point of view said it was possible to construct a new product from the materials available; Carl's said it was not.

It has been documented that, with coaching, children may be able to perform such operations somewhat earlier than Piaget believed they could and that early childhood educators and researchers need to be paying more attention to what preoperational children can do than what they cannot do, extending their learning from that point (Steinberg & Belsky, 1991). With the preoperational child, physical action and concrete materials are prerequisites to developing their understanding of particular phenomena. Also, they are often better able to express their feelings, thoughts, and conceptualizations through symbolic play than verbalizations. As they use varied strategies and trial and error to test possibilities and solutions, they become capable of more complex thinking and are able to use knowledge in increasingly sophisticated ways.

Lev Vygotsky's concept of the *zone of proximal development* (ZPD) is important here in terms of children's optimal learning. Vygotsky believed that development should not be viewed as a fixed entity but as a dynamic and constantly changing continuum of behavior, degree of maturation, or zone limited by behaviors that appear close to developing in the near future. He described two levels that form the parameters of development at any particular time: (1) the lower level of performance designated as *independent performance* (i.e., what the child knows and can *presently* do

without the help of someone more knowledgeable—an adult, a peer, an imaginary partner, or older children at higher developmental levels) and (2) a higher level designated as *maximally assisted performance,* which the child can achieve with support (i.e., clues, hints, rephrasing, demonstrations, explanations, specifically structured practice activities, etc.). This kind of external assistance (i.e., scaffolding) (Wood, 1989; Wood, Brumner & Ross, 1976; Wood & Middleton, 1975), was initially introduced in Chapter 4. You will recall that adults provide the social support that allows the child to move forward and continue to build new competencies. The adult's involvement is then reduced as the child grows in his or her ability to handle the problem or skill independently. At this time, a much more challenging task (i.e., a *new* ZPD) can be introduced (Gardner et al., 1996).

Subsequently, with assistance and practice, the assisted level becomes part of the child's independent performance, and advanced maturation occurs. Effective educators know that this concept of ZPD means that teaching should be aimed at the child's higher level of ZPD but that there are limits on how far a child can be challenged cognitively at any particular

Adults can facilitate children's higher-order thinking through scaffolding.

time. When skills or concepts too far above a child's ZPD are introduced, children will "tune out," ignore, fail to use, or use incorrectly that which is being pushed inappropriately (Leong & Bodrova, 1995).

Critical here, also, is Vygotsky's belief that "all higher mental functions are internalized social relationships" (i.e., that children continually make sense of and are drawn to learn more about concepts, skills, and processes because of their interactions with others). They learn what they are interested in learning or what they perceive as rewarding to learn. The bottom line is that knowledge cannot come in neatly packaged sets of understandings that can be passively given to children. When this happens, we risk short-circuiting in-depth or true understanding of phenomena in children because we cut them off from the intriguing and engaging work of concept formation. Piaget insisted that all knowledge, including the ability to reason logically, is constructed as children act on objects and people and try to make sense of their experience. Zahorik (1997, 30) claims this theory retains strong appeal—that knowledge results from disequilibrium, emerges from prior knowledge, and grows through experience and feedback. This is accomplished as children acquire the components of a fundamental knowledge base.

Developing a Fundamental Knowledge Base

To this point, we have focused on how children come to know things; now we will concentrate on what they *need* to know. A necessary knowledge base is made up primarily of five subgroups (DeVries & Kohlberg, 1990; Kindergarten Curriculum Guide and Resource Book, 1985, 25–34):

1. Physical knowledge—observable attributes of objects and physical phenomena: size, color, shape, weight, texture, tendencies under varying conditions (e.g., things roll downhill; snow is cold; sugar is sweet; spiders have eight legs).

2. Logical-mathematical knowledge—relationships between objects and phenomena deriving from observation; developing a logical organization to deal more effectively with incoming knowledge, including classification, patterning, seriation, number (counting, one-to-one correspondence, equivalence of groups of numbers, invariance of number), space in relationship to their own bodies (vertical and horizontal coordinates;

right and left, in front and behind coordinates; depth and distance coordinates; topological—closed or open shapes, inclusion/exclusion, proximity, order—and Euclidian—geometrical perspectives, including lines, angles, equalities, parallelism, and distance) and time, including order of events and length of events. Development in this arena is critical to the child's ability to organize a very complex and confusing world. White and Siegel (1976) perceive the process of getting "unconfused" as the essence of cognition, that is, beginning to recognize distinct and recurrent patterns that emerge from the stimulus flux surrounding the child.

3. Representational knowledge—imaginative expression of symbolic thought that represents the mental world of the child; manipulating images, art, symbols, language to stand for objects, events, and concepts (Steinberg & Belsky, 1991); competence in restructuring an experience in another way through symbolic representation (dramatic and creative play, rhythmic movement, imitation, construction of two- and three-dimensional models) and sign representation, which evolves through spoken language and then written language as follows:

Using names for objects in the environment.

Using words to identify the properties and functions of objects.

Using words to denote location in space and time.

Using words that describe relationships (comparing, describing differences and similarities, enumerating, measuring, and ordering).

Using words to relate physical knowledge.

Using words to relate social knowledge.

Using words to tell events and stories.

Using words to relate personal feelings and thoughts.

4. Social-conventional knowledge—cultural and societal conventions/rules/viewpoints transmitted to children by family, society, school, and peers to guide behavior related to other individuals, institutions, and the use of goods and services (e.g., 911 is a number to call if in danger; some families have more than one mother and father; many Jewish families celebrate Hanukkah; most people finish high school; farmers produce some of our food).

5. Metacognition—proficient strategies for monitoring their own thinking processes. Becoming an effective problem solver requires that children develop this unique cognitive quality that is activated and enhanced when we help them develop the requisite skills needed in critical and fair thinking, mental flexibility, organization of their ideas, and application of the many essential components of learning (McAfee & Leong, 1997). The use of Socratic questioning can move children away from fragmented, fuzzy, and inconsistent thinking by challenging as appropriate: "How do you know that?" "Where did you find that out?" "Why do you think someone would do that?" "When would that not be true? "Is there another way to think about that?" "How would you explain that to someone else who wanted to learn it?"

Expanded discussion of two aspects of this knowledge base, representational knowledge and social/conventional knowledge, can be found in Chapter 11 and Chapter 15. Two other aspects of children's knowledge base, physical knowledge and logical-mathematical knowledge, are considered in more depth in this chapter as we look at two major curricular vehicles for expanding children's conceptualization in these areas, science and mathematics.

Children are the best source of topics that interest them, and skillful teachers can best mobilize children's enthusiasm for learning when they design effective interdisciplinary "anchors" (i.e., complex problems that children think are worth solving and that capture their desire to learn a set of relevant skills and concepts). These can be invented or natural, as long as they fulfill the following requirements (Barab & Landa, 1997, 53): capture children's imagination; be perceived as important by learners; legitimize the disciplinary content they integrate; accommodate a variety of learning approaches, styles, and cultural experiences; require children to draw on concepts and skills associated with more than one discipline; and generate developmentally appropriate activities.

The Reggio Emilia and project approaches described in Chapter 1 are gaining popularity in the United States. These are just two examples of instructional approaches to teach *children* rather than teaching to a curriculum, and both use children's interests as worthwhile catalysts for skill and concept develop-

ment. For example, a primary teacher had children bringing in articles of interest from their local newspapers. The class showed more than passing interest in an article about the community's concern over an increase in roving packs of dogs. The children were guided toward thinking about the problem from a number of hypothetical perspectives and to web ideas that might be investigated. Included in their subsequent research was finding out about rabies and rabies treatment, the origin of humane societies, the cost of keeping dogs and other animals, and the duties and training of dogcatchers. They wrote stories about the situation from the dogs' perspective, investigated varieties of dogs and their histories and uses, drew pictures of dogs, and read stories about dogs. All during their study, children's interest remained high, as did their academic skill building and understanding of methods of finding information and organizing and communicating it to one another and to their teacher and parents.

It has been suggested that each child's brain is a "rich, layered, messy, unplanned jungle ecosystem" that probably thrives best in a learning context that includes many sensory, cultural, and problem layers closely related to the real world environment in which children live—the environment that best stimulates the neural networks that are genetically linked to it (Sylwester, 1995, 23). This speaks to one of the most important questions being asked today in early childhood education. Is it the role of teachers to directly teach children sometimes, or is it, rather, their role only to support them as they construct their own knowledge? A recent observation in an Oakland County, Michigan, kindergarten class at math time provides some insight to this dilemma:

Many of the children were actively involved with manipulatives while the teacher worked with a small group of youngsters on sorting. She passed a container filled with interesting objects around the group and asked each child to select two that were similar in some way. She then asked each child to tell the others how his or her objects were the same. Although every child was successful in choosing two objects that were similar in some way, not one child could verbalize the similar feature. It was clear that some children had an understanding of the salient characteristic as they attempted to show it nonverbally. One child, for example, who had selected a quarter and a plate, used his finger to trace a circle in the air. He did not, however, have a name for this characteristic. The teacher then complimented the children on their selections and excused them from the group.

Obviously, really effective teaching requires the early childhood educator to play many roles in the classroom, as described earlier in Chapter 3. In addition to being a facilitator and learning guide, the teacher must also be active in transferring existing knowledge that children cannot discover on their own. In this case, children needed vocabulary (social conventional knowledge) to help them articulate what they were trying so hard to describe. Although many thoughtful, well-meaning early childhood teachers are struggling with this issue, clearly direct instruction is an appropriate and necessary component in early childhood classrooms as we help children work on problems they find interesting to study.

The Young Child as Scientist

The purpose of science education is to provide the learning environment, the experiences, and the opportunities for discussion and reflection that will lead to interconnected, coherent, and articulated frameworks for understanding natural phenomena. (Howe, 1993)

Children are full of questions and expend a great deal of their energy in discovering how things work, what people do, and how they themselves can become more competent players in the general scheme of things. They have a driving need to learn: how electric outlets work, how toilets flush, how things open and close, where bubbles go, and how seashore waves "melt" sand castles.

Preschool children act on their intense curiosity through observation, trying out very simple operations, and questions to adults, over and over again. For these children, events simply happen or happen by magic. They turn on the TV and Barney appears. They ride with their family in the car at night, and the moon follows them—amazing! Later, as neural pathways mature and primary children gain additional experience and information, their understanding of cause and effect is more often correct, though still limited.

Based on Lind's (1997, 75) definition of science as a "process of finding out and a system for organizing and reporting discoveries," children who are in the process of observing, thinking, and reflecting on actions and events are doing science. When they are or-

ganizing factual information into more meaningful concepts, problem solving, and acting on their own curiosity, they are doing science. In trying to understand how the work of scientists is related to their own lives and investigations, they are doing science. They are *not* doing science when they are merely listening to someone talk about science, reading about it in a textbook, or learning facts and memorizing formulas. As we provide opportunities for them to be actively involved in the scientific process by forming hypotheses, collecting data, and formulating and testing their conclusions, we involve them in building the basic skills they will need for lifelong sciencing—multisensory observing, questioning, comparing, organizing, measuring, communicating, experimenting, relating (drawing abstractions from concrete data), inferring, and applying. In the early childhood classroom, we can increase the effectiveness of these opportunities by making sure that we respect children's present abilities and potential capabilities. Debriefing after each activity to evaluate the kinds of concepts children are forming will be a necessary strategy for building integrity into our instructional planning.

Nowhere is Piaget's view of children's developing intellectual capacities more useful than in understanding where we often go wrong in early science education! Because conceptualization in the early years is obviously unsystematic and intuitive, helpful adults want to guide children toward more complex, integrated modes of thinking and capability in organizing knowledge. The primary strategy for doing so is usually to supply manipulative materials and activities that allow children to "mess around"—observing, comparing, classifying, and measuring—believing that concepts will be learned in the process and that children can then easily move on to semiconcrete (iconic) and then abstract learning experiences.

Although the approach is reputably grounded in the constructivist approach of having children make their own discoveries in order to construct knowledge, Wright (1995, 1) and others have questioned the soundness of such an approach *if* teachers center on only one aspect of Piaget's theory (i.e., that children must construct their own knowledge) and forget an equally important aspect, that cognitive development occurs in stages along a continuum. For the preprimary and primary children who cannot think meaningfully about abstract things, manipulative materials are enormously important. They are of little value, however, if they are used to teach about concepts too far beyond the child's level of understanding, or ZPD.

Most problematic, note Kovalik and Olsen (1997, 6) are the study themes in early science education they term as "wildly age inappropriate." These center on concepts that are too highly abstract and not experienceable in any way, setting up a serious mismatch between content and cognitive capacity. An example they give is that of the solar system as a subject for second or third graders: "the ground on which we stand is spinning at hundreds of miles an hour, and the distances between planets are computed in millions of miles or even light years, a measurement that most adults can't relate to." The unfortunate result of these mismatches is that children are unable to apply or interpret deeper meanings of the content, lose interest in science, and develop more negative attitudes toward it (Lind, 1997).

Age-appropriate math and science concepts are those we would typically expect children to understand at particular ages, based on our knowledge of child development norms and also our experience with young children. Preschoolers probably function best when we provide science experiences spontaneously related to their outdoor play (spiders, insects, plants, soil, sand, and water) and natural interest in animals and animal homes. Very young children are also developing a basic understanding of some solar system concepts. We see this in some of their questions: "Where does the sun go at night?" "What are stars?" "Why does the moon change?" They note changes in the weather and seasons, delight in playing with shadows, and are structuring more sophisticated concepts about day and night.

As children move into the primary grades and progress in conceptual depth and complexity, teachers can have them doing a great deal more of the recording and written communication of their findings, building collections of natural materials, constructing dioramas, and using information books for guided study, focused reading, and vocabulary building. Science should continue to be primarily a hands-on activity, which can include gardening, hatching of eggs, the study of pond life, and so on. There are science curricula available that provide age-appropriate activity suggestions for elementary children, notably those that came out of such projects as the Elementary Science Study (ESS), the

Science Curriculum Improvement Study (SCIS), the Science-A-Process Approach (SAPA), and, most currently, the American Association for the Advancement of Science's *Benchmarks for Science Literacy* (1993).

Despite these resources, studies indicate that science teaching in the primary grades is still dominated by textbooks. Although texts have been revised to include more hands-on, process-oriented teaching methods, most still require a reasoning level and vocabulary beyond what most children have acquired in the primary grades (Howe, 1993, 226–227). Sometimes, however, we may find a small group of children who demonstrate conceptual levels not ordinarily seen in their age group? Some children move more quickly into representational and abstract concepts after a concrete introduction. Rather than providing age-appropriate activities for these children, we need to plan *individually appropriate* experiences. While these children still benefit by having experiences based on their near-environment interests, they may be ready for higher-level experiments, comparisons, and study of the ecosystem.

At the opposite end of this spectrum are children whose language, prior knowledge, motivation, lack of experiences, and other factors place them on a significantly lower operational level than might be expected (Howe, 1993). That we plan for the needs of the more advanced child as well as for the needs of a child still struggling with an age-appropriate experience is the essence of developmentally appropriate practice. It calls for carefully observing where individual children are in their thinking and capability and providing experiences *just slightly beyond* their present levels of functioning. Because developmentally *inappropriate* expectations foster a sense of incompetence in children when they cannot make sense of what we are trying to teach, it is wise to gear instruction toward age-appropriate concepts with a new group of children. We can then move into more or less sophisticated concepts that are individually appropriate after we have taken time to document that children are ready for a greater mental challenge or need additional support.

So that children can build a consistent picture of the physical world, educators must take into consideration their prior knowledge base (using the KWHLH process described in Chapter 2), relate new learning experiences to that base, and modify the presentation of new and subsequent experiences on an individual and small-group basis if children are to expand conceptually. This calls for evaluating any *misconceptions* children have about a particular phenomenon—and young children have a lot of them! For example, early research by Piaget (1965), Laurendeau and Pinard (1963), and Carey (1986) indicate that very young children believe that all things are alive. Later, they believe that moving things (e.g., a car, a person, or a cloud) are alive and that things that stay in one place (a house or a tree) are not alive. A marked shift takes place when children are about 10 years of age when the child considers the earlier misconceptions silly. Other early misconceptions include naive ideas about light and shadows, speed and movement, time and space relationships, and notions about the earth as flat instead of spherical and having its own gravity.

Although most inaccurate concepts involving physical and logical-mathematical phenomena are gradually restructured through experiences in the early primary years, some ideas are based in social conventional knowledge (e.g., the fact that the earth is not flat). Howe (1993) suggests that children naturally resist these ideas, which are counterintuitive and go against everything in their experiences, and says that teaching about them is wholly inappropriate in the preschool and primary grades. However, at some point, children must be directly taught this conceptual knowledge. She reminds us that Piaget delineated two kinds of scientific concepts: (1) "those that are spontaneous, which are developed mainly through the child's own mental efforts" and (2) "those that are not spontaneous, which are developed only through the influence or guidance of adults. . . . [W]ithout appropriate experiences and instruction, the naive concepts remain essentially unchanged" (Howe, 1993, 232).

Hagerott (1997, 720) insists that physics and other scientific knowledge *can* be taught to primary children if it is not "out of sync" with children's natural curiosity. For example, he notes that abstract physics concepts such as gravity, friction, inertia, and force can be connected to children's play and natural experiences on slides, monkey bars, swings, merry-go-rounds, bikes, and to such activities as the construction of paper airplanes—building their receptive vocabulary and burgeoning understanding of the concepts.

Teaching children about basic concepts in science is a natural catalyst for curriculum integration. For ex-

ample, when the children in Mr. Mishler's room became interested in the dandelions cropping up in a field near the school, their investigations led them to drawing and writing about their magnifications and dissections of the plants and roots of the plants, measuring and graphing lengths of stems they found, estimating and counting numbers of emerging plants, and painting the fascinating yellows and greens of the new plants and those that had already gone to seed. They classified the leaves of dandelions and other plants, discussed and formulated a definition for what constitutes a weed and what constitutes a flower, read and constructed poems about flowers and fauna, and performed for another class the silly song that Mr. Mishler had written about dandelions. They began using the correct term for the yellow substance that came off on their fingers and chins when handling the dandelions and discovered the purpose of the substance in the life cycle of plants. They experimented with creating a yellow dye and methods for removing it from swatches of material. Obviously, all curricular activity could spring from science; at the very least, good "sciencing" will require integration of activities and experiences from all other learning domains. The depth and breadth of children's learning will depend on opportunities to collect a wide variety of information and support in integrating that knowledge. Ideally, this calls for plenty of hands-on activity and supportive adults who provide "pertinent information at strategic times" and guidance in discussion (Schickendanz et al., 1990, 237).

It is important that children realize that science is more than a collection and an organization of already known facts and that the solution to problems or new discoveries can sometimes spring from intuitive feelings about a particular phenomenon as well as already documented laws, theories, and principles. Thus, children should be encouraged to think divergently and creatively as well as convergently in their problem finding and problem solving. These are cognitive skills that the American Association for the Advancement of Science's Project 2061 (Science for All Americans, 1989) notes are critical to living in a complex world.

Using a more in-depth, theme-repetitive approach toward science education that can lead to higher-order problem-solving skills rather than rote memorization should be a priority in good science teaching. Another is to help children make connections between science and real-world issues. Once children have developed the basic skills of observing, inferring, and experimenting, they should be encouraged to engage in scientific inquiry, a process that requires them to think about and interpret what they are gaining through the many sensory-experience activities in the early childhood classroom. Inquiry serves five essential functions according to Lind (1997, 83–84):

It assists in the development of understanding of science concepts.

It helps students "know how we know" in science.

It develops an understanding of the nature of science.

It develops the skills necessary to become independent inquirers about the natural world.

It develops the dispositions to use the skills, abilities, and habits of the mind associated with science.

Remember that teaching with a hands-on approach to science does not necessarily teach problem solving and inquiry. Also necessary will be the teacher's ability to use the strategies outlined earlier in Chapter 3—asking good open-ended questions and providing well-planned activities in guided discovery, problem solving, and social inquiry. For example, when Ms. Villareal asks children to use the paper bear tracks she has developed to measure the distance between the "bear den" and the dramatic play center, she is simply using a hands-on approach. However, when she tells them, "Find some way to measure the distance from the bear den to the dramatic play center and then report to the group on both your method and what you find out," she is engaging the children in inquiry. The first approach simply has children carrying out a process she has designed. The second encourages the children to figure out a way to gather data, organize their information, and articulate it to someone else.

The Young Child as Mathematician

Today, mathematics instruction is less about teaching basic computation and more about helping students become flexible thinkers who are comfortable with all areas of mathematics and are able to apply mathematical ideas and skills to a range of problem-solving situations. (Burns, 1993, 28)

For the young child, mathematics is everywhere! It is a natural and integral part of their world. They see numerals everywhere—on their house, on the clock, on the cereal box, on their play telephone, on the car, and in books. Gardner (1991, 75-76) notes that they want to count everything they see: "Often with surprising speed and ferocity, [they] see the world as an arena for counting: facial features in a drawing, beads, blocks, 'pounds,' candles, holes, tires, letters, lights." Many of their favorite finger plays, songs, and rhymes, which are used to encourage language also develop math vocabulary and concepts: Ten Little Monkeys Jumping on the Bed; One, Two, Buckle My Shoe; Eensy Weensy Spider; The Grand Old Duke of York (Smith, 1997). Favorite books such as Jon Scieszka and Lane Smith's *Math Curse,* Eric Carle's *Rooster's Off to See the World,* and *The Doorbell Rang* by Pat Hutchins help shape children's early perspectives about the relationships among different components of mathematics and their connection to every aspect of children's lives. At home, in preschools, and in elementary schools, young children sit at the computer, interacting with such characters as Zack the cabdriver and Chester the lazy raccoon, who take them through a variety of math activities in Infinity City or into fractions and decimals in a program called *Math Keys* (Macintosh/Windows). Some young children arrive at kindergarten able to count and understanding that a counting sequence represents increasingly larger quantities, an important concept for beginning arithmetic (Baroody, 1993); others can also identify objects to 10, recognize numerals, and identify coins and geometrical shapes; some can even solve simple addition and subtraction problems in their heads. Other children in the same classroom may never have seen a computer, and their math vocabulary may be limited to "big" and "little."

As pointed out earlier, conceptualization is somewhat limited by thinking parameters common to the preoperational period: centration, egocentrism, and irreversibility. This means that most children have a considerable amount of work to do before they will truly understand what "fiveness" is all about, as well as other logical-mathematical concepts. For example, although a child may be able to demonstrate "counting," there may be no true understanding of the hierarchical nature of counting. As with other mathematical concepts, children's understanding of counting moves through a sequence governed by a set of principles. As described by Gelman and Gallistel (1986) and Hohmann and Weikart (1997, 482), these include the following:

1. *The one-to-one principle.* Using one and only one number name (such as "one, two, three") for each number counted.
2. *The stable-order principle.* Using the number names in a stable order, such as "one, two, three" even though the order may be unconventional, such as "six, eleven, fifteen."
3. *The cardinal principle.* Using the last number name spoken to describe the number of objects in the set, "One, two, three . . . Three snakes!"
4. *The abstraction principle.* Counting part of a mixed set of items, for example, counting the red blocks in a building made of multicolored blocks.
5. *The order-irrelevance principle.* Recognizing that the order in which objects are counted is irrelevant. Six balls are always six balls no matter which one you count first.

Moreover, the child's logic may not yet be developed enough to know that a rearrangement of the same objects leaves the number or amount unchanged. For example, 4-year-old Chelsey was presented with two rows of five pennies each and asked to count each row. She did so, counting the pennies one at a time, and said there were five pennies in each row. When asked, "Are there the same number in each row, or does one row have more?" she methodically counted again and responded, "They're the same." As she watched, the pennies in the second row were spread further apart from one another. When asked, "Now is there the same number in each row, or does one row have more?" she quickly pointed to the second row and said with confidence, "This one has more!" Chelsey was obviously centering on the *length* of the two rows and was unable to think about the difference in spacing at the same time. With this kind of understanding, Chelsey does not yet have an anchor for making decisions in understanding the use of number.

Young children are eager to build on their basic concepts of logical-mathematical knowledge. Many of these, such as comparing, classifying, and measuring, are needed as the child grows conceptually in other developmental domains, including the affective, social, and aesthetic arenas. Similarly, concepts the child is de-

veloping in other areas such as science (observing, communicating, inferring, predicting, hypothesizing, defining, and controlling variables) and language (higher, slower, warm, hardest, longest, and juicier) will be important for logical-mathematical extensions (Charlesworth & Lind, 1995).

At first, a child's mathematical knowledge comes through *naturalistic* experiences completely controlled by the child; these are complemented by *informal, exploratory activity* with adults offering comments or asking questions. Eventually, this is replaced by primarily *structured acquisition*, consisting largely of preplanned activities conceived by the teacher (Ginsberg & Baron, 1993). Young children need a *prolonged* period of informal exploration to form basic concepts about shape, one-to-one correspondence, size, weight, texture, and amount. For the preschooler, this comes through such natural activities as building with blocks; pouring water; working with sand, puzzles, and playdough; cooking; matching, sorting, and seriating objects. In interacting with adults and one another during such activities, they also extend their foundational math vocabulary, picking up words for comparing, position, direction, sequence, shape, time, and number (Smith, 1997).

Primary children need opportunities for informal exploration. Given choices of a variety of investigations and chances to talk about them, primary children discover important patterns and relationships in the materials they are using. They learn to solve simple word problems, develop efficient counting strategies, attach meaning to basic symbols, and invent unique partitioning strategies for subdividing continuous quantities. These skills and connections are too often short-circuited when impatient teachers move too quickly to teaching algorithms and drilling children in number combinations (Baroody, 1993). Also diminished when formal instruction becomes the predominant teaching approach is the social interaction and exchange of ideas that occur in experience-based classrooms.

In the last decade, there has been a significant effort to reform the teaching of mathematics in the United States. "This new pedagogy has been driven largely by (1) changes in technology that require what is needed to do mathematics, (2) changes in society that have greatly extended the applications of mathematics and what constitutes basic survival skills, (3) evidence of educational shortcomings, indicating that traditional approaches to mathematics instruction are inadequate for preparing children for the future, and (4) cognitive research indicating that traditional approaches to instruction do not adequately foster the construction of mathematical knowledge" (Baroody, 1993, 155–156).

Much of the momentum for moving toward a more comprehensive, useful, and meaningful instructional approach has been provided by the leadership of the National Council of Teachers of Mathematics (NCTM), who formulated the 1989 *Curriculum and Evaluation Standards for School Mathematics* for grades K–4, 5–8, and 9–12. Overall goals of the *Standards* are to have children learn to value mathematics, become confident in their ability to do mathematics, become mathematical problem solvers, learn to communicate mathematically, and learn to reason mathematically. This document made it very clear that rote memorization is out. Students are to process information more actively, develop the kind of skills and understandings that will allow broad application in a number of fields, and learn to use tools such as calculators and computers for problem solving. Instruction should grow out of genuine problems of interest to children, and teachers are to engage children in small-group and paired activities. They are also mandated to follow up on classroom activity, discussing with children the methodologies they have developed for their problem solving and what they have learned (Kennedy & Tipps, 1994). Ongoing authentic assessment is the primary strategy suggested for documenting children's conceptual understanding and includes anecdotal records taken during observation and interviews and from work samples (drawings, graphs, sketches, and written work), inventories, and the child's self-appraisals collected in a portfolio. Assessment and evaluation should include strategies to determine a child's *conceptual* understanding of operations as well as his or her ability to work through problems by applying the "rules."

In kindergarten through grade 4, nine strands pertaining to the following topical areas of mathematics are to be included in the curriculum:

1. *Estimation* so that children can explore estimation strategies; recognize when an estimate is appropriate; determine reasonableness of results; and apply it in working with qualities, measurement, computation, and problem solving.

2. *Number sense and numeration* so that children can construct number meanings through real-world experiences and the use of physical materials; understand our numeration system by relating counting, grouping, and place-value concepts; develop number sense; and interpret the multiple uses of numbers encountered in the real world.

3. *Concepts of whole number operations* so that children can develop meaning for the operations by modeling and discussing a rich variety of problem situations; relate the mathematical language and symbolism of operations to problem situations and informal language; recognize that a wide variety of problem structures can be represented by a single operation; develop operation sense.

4. *Whole number computation* so that children can model, explain, and develop reasonable proficiency with basic facts and algorithms; use a variety of mental computation and estimation techniques; use calculators in appropriate computational situations; and select and use computation techniques appropriate to specific problems and determine whether results are reasonable.

5. *Geometry and spatial sense* so that children can describe, model, draw, and classify shapes; investigate and predict the results of combining, subdividing, and changing shapes; develop spatial sense; relate geometric ideas to number and measurement ideas; and recognize and appreciate geometry in their world.

6. *Measurement* so that children can understand the attributes of length, capacity, weight, area, volume, mass, time, temperature, and angle; develop the process of measuring and concepts related to units of measurement; make and use estimates of measurement; and make and use measurements in problem and everyday solutions.

7. *Statistics and probability* so that children can collect, organize, and describe data; construct, read, and interpret displays of data; formulate and solve problems that involve collecting and analyzing data; and explore concepts of chance.

8. *Fractions and decimals* so that children can develop concepts of fractions, mixed numbers and decimals; develop number sense for fractions and decimals; use models to relate fractions to decimals and to find equivalent fractions; use models to explore operations on fractions and decimals; and apply fractions and decimals to problem situations.

9. *Patterns and relationships* so that children can recognize, describe, extend, and create a wide variety of patterns; represent and describe mathematical relationships; and explore the use of variables and open sentences to express relationships (NCTM, 1989).

To promote optimal development of these concepts, effective teachers equip their classrooms with a wide variety of well chosen, interesting manipulative materials that invite exploring, sorting, combining, and experimenting. Minimally, these include interlocking counting cubes, linking materials in a variety of colors and shapes, measuring instruments, play money, geoboards, tangrams, geometric models, attribute blocks, collections (keys, buttons, shells, plastic animals, and bottle tops), beads, timers and clocks, base 10 materials, and probability devices (dice, spinners, etc.).

Effective teachers also structure many opportunities for children to hear the correct names for conventional tags again and again, especially those that cause children problems (e.g., in 11, there is no "teen" sound; in 20, there is no "2" sound), thereby promoting understanding, proficiency, and the language needed to describe operations. They involve children in activities especially contrived to promote a framework for mathematical thinking and problem solving. They monitor and nurture that understanding by posing good questions to help children notice discrepancies and come closer and closer to the correct answer. They encourage children to think about the relevant pieces of information needed to solve problems and challenge them to think of other ways to find an answer or defend their proposed solutions. Many of the experiences the children have are gamelike, including board games, dice, cards, bingo games, lotto, and measurement of real aspects of the near environment. Other experiences come naturally out of the everyday operation of the classroom, which helps children perceive mathematics as relevant and useful, rather than something to memorize and repeat (Brewer, 1997).

As with science, every aspect of the curriculum can and should be used to promote logical-mathematical conceptualization. Burns (1995) suggests that the integration of linguistic and mathematical thinking—having children write about mathematics—is an especially good technique for encouraging children to examine their ideas and reflect on what they have learned.

Age is not necessarily the key in a child's mathematical ability; rather, advances are probably more related to the quality of the child's classroom experiences—for example, being challenged to think about number relationships rather than simply being given an answer (Schickedanz, York et al., 1990). In this way, the child develops internal rules and principles to understand number and number relationships in our base 10 system of numbers. This internalized comprehension can then be used in other situations, such as those requiring understanding of multiple digits or place value. Children who are given the correct answer again and again do not necessarily discover why a fact is so. Thus, they are left with little ability to make use of the information without a helping adult continuing to do the "head" work. Teachers who encourage memorization of math facts without teaching some simple but helpful rules or "tricks" to remember produce children who "learn arithmetic at the expense of learning mathematics" (Baroody, 1987, 44).

CURRENT EDUCATIONAL ISSUES RELATED TO COGNITIVE DEVELOPMENT AND EXPERIENTIAL CONSIDERATIONS

Making sense of all of the information we currently have about cognitive development and experiential considerations is a complex but critical task for early childhood educators to tackle if children are to become effective, lifelong learners. Despite the extensive work to reform early learning contexts and ensure qualitatively better outcomes for children, a number of controversial issues persist. These include the following:

1. *The use of a Piagetian constructivist approach vs. a Vygotskian approach to instruction.* Educators continue to argue about how much focus should be placed on the child's "inner maturation, spontaneous discoveries, and independent construction of knowledge" versus emphasis on a sociocultural approach where the teacher takes a more active role in guiding children toward increasingly higher levels of understanding. Cobb's (1994, 17–19) analysis of this issue makes a great deal of sense: We should "give up the quest for a one-size-fits-all perspective, since the two views are complementary . . . each telling half of a good story." We can and should provide children with both kinds

of experiences. The introduction of new information should always be accompanied initially by children's "opportunity to construct their own relationships and share these with their peers and their teacher" (Charlesworth, 1997, 57). However, this approach takes place best in a social context that allows children to work with others on real projects and problems in which there is shared personal investment. Children should be encouraged to talk with one another and the teacher about their work to foster the development of conceptual understandings as well as their ability to calculate correct answers.

Some children, because of personality traits or cultural differences, may be less apt to try new experiences or take risks without encouragement to do so. Others, because of negative past experience with failure, may avoid activity that calls for higher-order thinking and skills—even when they are relatively ready for it. Instead, they persevere in areas where success is ensured. The teacher's role in moving such children along may include breaking more sophisticated tasks into manageable parts and helping children recognize how their past success and experiences can be used to tackle new challenges. Although all children benefit from genuine reinforcement for efforts to attempt more demanding tasks, those who noticeably avoid learning challenges must receive such attention and support in order to modify their attitudes toward approaching a more rigorous learning experience.

2. *The emphasis on* conceptual *knowledge to understand concepts versus the development of precise skills and* procedural *knowledge.* Piaget once remarked, "If the aim of intellectual training is to form the intelligence rather than to stock the memory, and to produce intellectual explorers rather than mere erudition, then traditional education is manifestly guilty of a grave deficiency." We make a mistake when we construct programs where one emphasis is favored over another. There is evidence that young children can develop highly efficient skills to solve math or science problems without ever really understanding what lies behind the process they have used. Although they can demonstrate expertise in getting the "right answer," they are often hard pressed to explain the procedure to someone else or transfer the discrete skills to other situations or problems. Because the brain requires a great deal of repetition in order to detect patterns,

concept formation is better ensured when children experience both variety and repetition in logical-mathematical activities and also the follow-up discussion that has been recommended for making sense of their findings. This means that professionals must develop classroom experiences that help children make meaningful connections through enriched, thematic, and real-life experiences rather than cutting off such connections by "bits and pieces" instruction (ASCD, 1991).

3. *The use of technology in the early childhood classroom.* Becoming knowledgeable about the growing number of technological tools available must be a requirement for today's learner. The questions related to their use include how early children should be introduced to them, how much time should be allocated to their use at the expense of other learning, and whether they should be allowed in "testing" situations or only as follow-up practice once conceptualization has been fixed.

Despite the widespread use of calculators, teachers and parents continue to resist their use in school. It is believed that children who are allowed to use them will fail to develop a conceptual understanding of mathematics operations. Research firmly disputes this, with more than 80 studies looking at the issue. Results indicate that using them in instruction and testing actually sharpens children's performance, problem-solving ability, and affective attitudes about mathematics (Kennedy & Tipps, 1994).

Although young children need to learn to estimate and calculate problems in their heads (mental math), they eventually must learn to do paper-and-pencil math and to use a calculator. Each of them should have access to a calculator, and Smith (1997, 22) has said that the ones they are given should have easy-to-read numbers found directly on the keys; easy-to-depress keys that move distinctly when depressed; a four-function calculator with automatic constant for addition; and solar power. Even very young children can use these in the dramatic play center and the math and science centers. Just as they are taught other skills with tools, they should be allowed to explore and practice with calculators, which are sure to become an increasingly important and helpful tool in their understanding number operation.

Similarly, computers can enhance learning and should be considered a necessary piece of equipment in the early childhood classroom, providing games and simulations that aid problem solving and also some fairly engaging tutorial programs for skill building and practice. Teachers need to be astute with respect to selecting software that is operationally easy to use. It should be not just entertaining but should actually teach a skill, process, or concept. Professionals will need to observe children carefully to see that they are actually able to understand the task involved and are not just pushing buttons. Kennedy and Tipps (1994, 87–88) provide a guide to selection of software:

> Where does it fit into the instructional design?
>
> Can it be used for informal introduction of a concept, for directed learning, or for investigation of math/science concepts?
>
> Will it add something unique to the program?
>
> Can it be used for independent, small-group, or whole-group instruction?
>
> How does its cost stack up against the need for other math learning aids?

They suggest a number of publications that offer technical, instructional, and practical aspects of computer programming with young children, including *Arithmetic Teacher, Child Care Information Exchange, School Science and Mathematics, Journal of Computers in Mathematics and Science Teaching,* and *Instructor Magazine*'s monthly feature on technology.

4. *The use of heterogeneous or homogeneous groups.* All evidence points to the value of structuring heterogeneous groups that are changed often enough to keep them dynamic, useful, and energetic. Children, like adults, are continuously scanning the environment to pick up information that will help them make sense of it. They watch what others do who are more or less skilled in accomplishing a task and then imitate, expand on, or modify what they see for use in their own problem solving, decision making, and leisure pursuit. Children on all points of a developmental continuum benefit from interacting with others who either need or can provide information or strategies for accomplishing a task. Research indicates that children who are grouped narrowly in homogeneous settings grow and develop but not at the rate they would if placed in a supportive, heterogeneous setting. Teachers can then structure one-on-one or small-group sessions to do miniworkshops in skill building or scaffolding. In this way, they can zero in on specific learning difficulties experienced by one of more children without denying those children the chance to learn from others.

5. *Coordination of an authentic assessment and evaluation package with what actually goes on in the learning environment rather than seeing standardized and end-of-unit tests in basal texts as the only acceptable and legitimate means for assessment and evaluation of children's conceptual understanding and progress.* More often than not, the latter perspective creates test-driven curricula and learning environments, which severely and negatively affect the development of qualitative critical thinking skills in the young child. Because the young child's cognitive development is *in process,* teachers must assess a child's approach to a task, stages and quality of a child's thought processes, and misconceptions as carefully as they assess outcomes and products. In addition, in order to build motivation and metacognition in children, they must be involved in self-appraisal, examining their own growth or lack of it. Strategies for assessing growth in conceptualization and skill building are outlined in Chapter 16.

Effective early childhood classrooms, then, are those in which children have many opportunities to express their thoughts, wishes, and ideas to one another as well as to adults. The best early childhood classroom exists in an active, well-prepared, workshop-like environment. It should contain familiar elements and also some that are slightly discrepant, which entice children to "actively explore, manipulate, transform and discover. They need opportunities both to initiate action and imitate action, to reflect and summarize their own actions for themselves and to hear the reflection and summarizations of others, to represent their ideas and thoughts and to encounter the ideas and thoughts of others" (Trepanier-Street, 1990, 197). A truly effective early childhood classroom must be carefully constructed by a professional who understands that young children are eager to learn and will respond responsibly when given the freedom, resources, and guidance necessary. Efforts should be undertaken to match what happens in the classroom as nearly as possible to what happens in the child's head. Moreover, in order to act effectively on a full range of later problems, children must maintain an appreciation of their own ability to think divergently, creatively, and imaginatively in addition to developing convergent modes of thinking. This kind of approach to information seeking and problem solving cannot result from learning a narrow set of learning strategies for information processing (Gardner et al., 1996).

Goals and Objectives of the Cognitive Domain

The ultimate goal of the cognitive component is for children to acquire, apply, adapt, integrate, and evaluate knowledge as they construct new or expanded concepts. There must be opportunities for children to develop physical knowledge, logical-mathematical knowledge, representational skills, social conventional knowledge, and metacognitive skills.

To help identify ways in which cognitive activities fit into the early childhood curriculum, selected intermediate objectives for this domain have been divided into three areas: (1) general cognition, including problem solving, critical thinking, and perception processes; (2) science; and (3) mathematics, both emerging and extended skills. Because cognitive processes pervade all aspects of learning, there are universal objectives that teachers should address each day. These are described in the general cognition section. More specific objectives traditionally associated with the subject areas of mathematics and science are listed separately.

Intermediate Objectives for General Cognition   As children progress toward the ultimate goal, they will demonstrate the following competencies:

1. Explore the observable properties of objects and the relationships among objects.
2. Discriminate similarities and differences among objects.
3. Organize objects and events via matching, classification (subclasses and supraclasses), sequencing, and patterning.
4. Attach meaning to symbols in the environment (e.g., signs and numerals).
5. Develop and refine their attending skills and ability to ignore irrelevant information.
6. Develop strategies for remembering (e.g., recording, creating personal rules, making associations, etc.).
7. Develop and refine their investigative skills by posing questions or problems to solve that involve collecting and analyzing information; using estimation, concepts of chance, and sampling to make better predictions; gathering information (questioning, experimenting, observing, and consulting); analyzing information, objects, and events; applying prior knowledge; and making inferences.
8. Develop organizational skills for arranging and using information more effectively by comparing, classifying, ordering, and representing (changing the form but not the substance of information).
9. Develop and refine their problem-solving skills by observing attentively; exercising divergent as well as convergent thinking; developing hypotheses; making predictions; developing plans; testing predictions; experimenting with ideas; connecting and combining information in an integrative manner; evaluating predictions; drawing conclusions; reviewing/summarizing experiences; generating alternative approaches to problems; and communicating findings.
10. Integrate knowledge and skills across subject areas and domains.
11. Generalize knowledge and skills from one situation to another.
12. Become aware of their own thought processes.
13. Acquire factual information to support relevant concepts.
14. Build more accurate, complete, and complex concepts over time.
15. Recognize and make use of diverse sources of knowledge.
16. Recognize that data come in many forms and can be organized and displayed in diverse ways.

Intermediate Objectives for Science   As children progress toward the ultimate goal, they will demonstrate the following competencies:

17. Examine natural objects and events using multiple sensory abilities.
18. Gather and arrange information through collecting, classifying, ordering, measuring, sequencing, and so on.
19. Learn the scientific process by predicting what they think will happen based on a hypothesis; guessing why certain things happen; carrying out experiments; talking about the results of their experiments; and formulating conclusions.
20. Participate in recording scientific data.

21. Explore firsthand a variety of cause-and-effect relationships.
22. Demonstrate an awareness of the interdependence of all things in the world.
23. Investigate differences, similarities, and patterns in natural objects and events.
24. Acquire scientific knowledge related to life sciences (characteristics of plants and animals, life cycles and basic needs, habitats, and relationships).
25. Acquire scientific knowledge related to physical sciences (change in matter; forces affecting motion, direction, speed, light, heat, and sound; physical properties and characteristics of phenomena).
26. Acquire scientific knowledge related to earth sciences (weather, space, ecology, and major features of the earth).
27. Explore a variety of scientific equipment, such as simple machines, magnets, and measuring instruments.
28. Use scientific equipment appropriately and safely.
29. Develop and use an accurate vocabulary to describe, name, and measure scientific events, objects, and processes.

Intermediate Objectives for Mathematics As children progress toward the ultimate goal, they will demonstrate the following competencies:

30. Connect mathematics with daily living and problem solving and use mathematics in other curriculum areas.
31. Increase their mathematical vocabulary.
32. Classify (group) or seriate (order) objects by common attributes.
33. Apply estimating in working with quantities, measurement, computation, and problem solving.
34. Develop number sense and an understanding of numeration system by extending their rote counting and rational counting abilities; constructing visual representations of given numbers using concrete numbers; associating the concept of quantity with the appropriate numeral; exploring properties of a given number; writing numerals; developing a concept of number invariance (one-to-one correspondence and conservation); developing ordinal concepts (first, second . . .); understanding place value; developing a concept of odd and even numbers; and developing an ability to count on (skip counting).
35. Extend their concept of whole number operations by adding and subtracting, using real objects; writing addition and subtraction facts symbolically; composing oral and written stories; and beginning to add and subtract with trading (regrouping, renaming).
36. Identify, reproduce, complete, extend, create, transpose, and utilize various patterns, concretely, pictorially, and as they exist in the environment.
37. Extend geometrical and spatial sense through handling, identifying, describing, drawing, classifying, combining, and subdividing shapes.
38. Expand their visual-spatial awareness of symmetry, balance, height, and directionality.
39. Compare lengths, masses, quantities, and volume.
40. Discover measurement relationships, using nonstandard and standard measuring tools.
41. Acquire concepts of time (calendar time, time terminology, clock time, and sequence of events).
42. Explain mathematical processes they have used.
43. Construct and interpret (predict, compare, and draw conclusions) graphs with real objects and symbols.
44. Use models, known facts, properties, patterns, and relationships to draw conclusions and justify their thinking about mathematics.
45. Extend their concept of parts of a whole to include fractions.
46. Name and correctly demonstrate the relative value of coins and how money is used in real-life situations.
47. Solve word problems that require reasonable proficiency with basic facts and algorithms.
48. Grow in their familiarity with and ability to use tools, such as the calculator and computer, to explore mathematical concepts.
49. Gain experience with data analysis (collecting, organizing, and describing data, and constructing, reading, and interpreting data displays) and probability (exploring concepts of chance).

TEACHING STRATEGIES

The most important thing to keep in mind during the preprimary and primary years is that the minds of young children are evolving—and if they are to build a solid and reliable cognitive base, we cannot do all the thinking for them. Teachers who fail to appreciate the young child's need to construct knowledge may, in fact, diminish potential development. On the other hand, teachers who go overboard in minimizing their role in the child's developing intellect, morality, and personality also err. Zahorik (1997) suggests that a teacher does not promote understanding by permitting student's constructions to stand even though they clash with experts' constructions. Rather than waiting for correct scientific entities and ideas to be constructed and validated, teachers find a way to provide developmentally appropriate experiences to challenge misconceptions.

What is needed in the early years are professionals who are knowledgeable about constructing environments conducive to learning. Instead of imposing their own predetermined goals, these teachers provide materials, activities, and suggestions that encourage initiative and independent pursuit, allowing children adequate time to explore, investigate, reflect, and ask questions. They differentiate effectively between teaching strategies that promote logical-mathematical and physical knowledge and those needed to extend social/conventional knowledge in young children (Kamii & De-Vries, 1977). This calls for, in the first case, refraining from giving the correct answer and challenging children to think about what it might be and then having them follow through to investigate and evaluate their own ideas. When extending conventional knowledge, good teachers respond to children's inquiries with correct information; if they are not sure what the answer is, they are honest about not knowing and then work with the child to obtain the information needed. Following are some additional ideas for structuring a fertile climate for learning:

1. Encourage intellectual autonomy in expanding children's general cognitive skills. The use of "long-term, multifaceted projects and themes that offer a broad and integrative framework for interaction" effectively sets the scene (Berk & Winsler, 1995, 145). The concept of hands-on experiences and activity in developing conceptual thinking on the part of the young child will be especially important. Teachers will want to introduce every concept with real objects first and to plan several related experiences to reinforce a given concept rather than present isolated activities at random. There should be an emphasis on the process rather than solely on the products of children's thinking.

Questioning used to stimulate their thinking or to find out why children have categorized, sequenced, or solved a problem in a certain way should be open ended. Children should be allowed to reach their own conclusions regarding cause-and-effect relationships, and the answers they offer should be accepted. When children make errors, teachers will want to plan further experiences or suggest other approaches that might help the children discover the right answer or have more success with individual tasks. When children are having difficulty with a concept or demonstrating proficiency, teachers will want to help them break a task into more manageable parts and introduce them to the next step in the sequence when helpful. Particular skills and facts should be taught in contexts relevant to children.

2. Develop children's ability to move out of a comfort zone with respect to inaccurate concepts. Cardellachio and Field (1997, 33–36) underscore the teacher's role in closing the gaps between children's "spontaneous constructs" and scientific constructs by providing the child with enough data to force them to challenge misconceptions and create strong, accurate conceptualizations. This can come through well-constructed activities used in conjunction with information books, resource persons, field trips, and provocative questioning. They also suggest the following seven strategies for encouraging cognitive development and divergent thinking:

a. Hypothetical thinking, a powerful technique to create new information. Einstein developed his theory of relativity by asking, "What would it look like to ride on a beam of light?" For example, a teacher might ask, "What would happen if you . . . ?"; "What if . . . ?"; The key is not in asking the organized question but in the follow-up questions such as "What if this had happened?" "What if this had not occurred?" "What if this were not true?" "What if I could do something I cannot do?"

b. Reversal, turning the current perspective upside down. For example, "What if you had your mother's role and she had yours?" "What if we slept during the day and stayed awake at night?" "What if we always ate our dessert before we ate the rest of our dinner?" "What if children ran the schools and teachers were students? What would it be like?" "What if we only had summer clothes to wear in the winter and winter clothes to wear in the summer?"

c. Application of different symbol systems. Instead of using words to tell something, have children create a song, act it out, or develop another set of symbols to use in place of a present one.

d. Analogy. Look for correspondences to create new insight about both elements in an analogy. What is like this? How is this like _____?

e. Analysis of point of view, determining why someone holds a particular opinion or belief. What harm might occur if we . . . ? What do you think one of your parents might think about that? Who would love it if . . . ? What if the wolf turned out to . . . ?

f. Completion. Give the beginning of a story and have children form the end; give the end of a story and have children form the beginning or middle.

g. Use of graphic organizers (charts, tables, webs, Venn diagrams, and flow charts). These promote children's comprehension and vocabulary development, eliminate oversimplification, and extend children's understanding of the complexity of relationships, events, and so on. They help to make relationships among concepts concrete and explicit.

3. Use teaming and cooperative learning often because it enhances children's ability both as learners and as persons who can teach something to others. This is especially important with children who come from cultures that accentuate the importance of cooperation rather than competition. Pairing children and placing them in small groups promotes the sharing of ideas, awareness of others, self-esteem, confidence, responsibility, self-control, extension of conceptual understanding, and movement away from egocentric perspectives.

Kennedy and Tipps (1994, 62) suggest that teachers structure groups that are heterogeneous with respect to talents, skills, and personalities. They recommend that the following rules and roles become an inherent part of cooperative grouping behavior (also refer to Chapter 3):

Rules

a. You are responsible for your own behavior.
b. You must be willing to help someone in your group who asks.
c. You may not ask the teacher for help unless all four of you have the same problem.

Roles

a. The lead investigator keeps the group on task.
b. The recorder takes notes on the group's ideas.

Pairing children in cooperative learning situations enhances concept building.

c. The materials manager picks up and returns materials.

d. The reporter summarizes the group's ideas (or findings) and verbalizes the group's responses to each task.

The spirit of these strategies can be adapted for younger children, and professionals will want to use fairly simple assignments for children who have not yet had experience with group work. As they gain experience, the teacher will want to build more autonomy in the children, making the tasks more open ended. Discussion about the process used to complete the task as well as what was learned in doing the assignment should always be part of the debriefing

4. Put more emphasis on children's understanding of concepts than on rote learning, and keep in mind that children's development of mathematical concepts follows a predictable pattern. Always begin the teaching of new concepts with concrete experiences. Provide a wide variety of manipulatives (real objects) to be used for sorting, classifying, comparing, estimating, predicting, patterning, graphing, measuring, counting, adding and subtracting, understanding parts and wholes, and gaining concepts of number, conservation of number, quantity, shapes, mass, and volume. When involving children in making mathematical equations, provide sets of real objects in addition to materials such as number stamps and number cards before paper-and-pencil tasks are introduced. Circulate among children, observing how they are approaching tasks and structuring brief miniconferences to check their understanding of the targeted concept.

After children have had numerous concrete experiences, introduce representational ones (e.g., pictures or drawn figures). Introduce abstract experiences last (e.g., abstract symbols such as $2 + ? = 5$). Allow children ample opportunities to explore a given material before asking them to use it in a prescribed way. Present the same mathematical concepts and skills on many occasions and in many different ways (e.g., drawing numerals in the air, in sand, in salt, in finger-paint, on the chalkboard, and on paper). Involve them in playing a variety of games utilizing cards and dice.

5. Integrate science and mathematical concepts and skills throughout all areas of the early childhood curriculum. Link logical-mathematical activities with social studies and language arts as well as with pretend play, affective, aesthetic, physical, and construction activities as often as possible.

6. Extend children's science and mathematical vocabulary. Use a wide variety of *accurate* terms when talking with children about their day-to-day experiences (e.g., number, mass, size, shape, position of objects in space, relations among objects, and changes in the functioning, position, or characteristics of objects).

7. Use everyday experiences in the classroom to help children connect science and mathematics to daily living and see it as useful and necessary. Capitalize on problems that occur naturally in the classroom, school, or community that can capture children's curiosity.

Incorporate mathematical tools into classroom routines (e.g., calendars, clocks, rulers, coins, scales, measuring cups, graphs, etc.). Practice addition and subtraction in natural settings without symbols, encouraging children to use "head work" to solve problems. Draw children's attention to aspects of daily work and play in the classroom that utilize mathematical concepts (e.g., durations of time—5 minutes until cleanup; 15 minutes for recess; and 2 weeks off for spring vacation).

Introduce scientific concepts by building on the everyday experiences in the lives of the children in your class. Make available a wide array of natural materials through which children can explore the physical world. Examples include collections of natural objects (shells, rocks, and bird nests), live animals (fish, guinea pigs, and insects), plants, and scientific tools (scales, magnifiers, and magnets). Take advantage of spontaneous events to highlight scientific ideas. Emphasize children's discovery of principles of cause and effect by allowing them to draw conclusions based on their experiences with real objects. Select scientific themes that include firsthand experiences for children and those with which children are already familiar.

8. Develop positive learning attitudes and practices in the classroom. Model an interested, curious, enthusiastic attitude toward science, and encourage children's curiosity by providing them with numerous hands-on scientific experiences and relevant demonstrations. Carry out scientific demonstrations with groups small enough that children can become actively involved and will feel free to ask questions about what they are observing. Help children to observe more carefully by first directing their attention to a particular aspect of an object or phenomenon and then

asking them to describe what they see (e.g., "Look up at the sky. Tell me what you see."). Encourage children to make predictions by asking them, "What will happen next?" and hypothesize and draw conclusions by asking them, "Why do you think that happened?" Convey only accurate scientific terms, facts, and principles to children, checking out any information about which you or the children are unsure. Help children recognize many sources of scientific information, such as their own experiences, books, and resource people.

9. Use collections as a way to extend and assess children's ability to categorize, classify, and display information. Give children individual or group opportunities to create collections of natural objects. Offer them guidance on collecting objects and what maybe appropriate or inappropriate to collect. Provide opportunities for children to display and tell about their collections.

ACTIVITY SUGGESTIONS

General Cognition Activities

✎ **Sniff Test**

Objective 1   For children to explore the observable properties of objects and the relationship among objects.

Materials   Two sets of small vials, each with a particular and unique smell (e.g., flower, perfume, lemon, orange, garlic, coffee, extracts), blindfold

Procedure   Have the children form a circle. Choose one child to be blindfolded in the center. Distribute one set of vials among children in outer circle. The blindfolded chid is given one vial from the second set and must use his or her sense of smell to move around the circle, find the matching vial, and identify what he or she is smelling.

To simplify   Have children individually match each container to pictures of the source of the scent.

To extend   Enlarge the variety of scents. Choose scents within categories (e.g., all flower scents, all fruit scents, or all coffee scents). Design a similar activity to test sense of taste.

✎ **Mystery Box**

Objective 5   For children to develop and refine their attending skills and ability to ignore nonrelevant information

Materials   Box; set of related objects

Procedure   "Hide" one or more objects in a box. Provide verbal clues to the children about what the objects are. Invite them to ask you questions about the object(s) to discover what is in the box.

To simplify   Place only one object in the box. Select one with which all the children are familiar.

To extend   Place several objects in the box that are different from one another but have one characteristic in common (e.g., all are articles of clothing). Have one of the children take on the role of "clue giver."

✎ **Balloon Race**

Objective 9   For children to develop and refine their problem-solving skills.

Materials   Balloons, straws, masking tape, easel paper, and markers

Procedure   Provide a set of inflated balloons of five different colors and individual straws for a group of five children. Have other children observe, telling them they will also have a chance to do the activity. Establish a starting line that has been marked off with masking tape. Tell the children that the object is to use their straws to blow the balloons as quickly as possible from the starting line to a designated wall.

To simplify   Have the children participate in the activity and then discuss what they think made the balloons go faster. Accept their answers. Prompt them to think about any differences that may have contributed to speed or direction of movement.

To extend   Before beginning the activity, explain the objective and then invite the children to develop hypotheses and make predictions about directing the balloons. Invite the children who are observers to watch carefully to see if they will do something differently when they participate in the activity. Prior to each "team event," have children offer ideas about what they think contributes to speed and managing direction. Afterward, have them evaluate their ideas and generate new ones. After every child has had a chance to participate, ask the children to produce an "advice sheet" related to the activity, listing tips (conclusions) they would provide to other teams of children (e.g., blowing in the middle of the balloon, not blowing down on or on the side of the balloon, or blowing steadily) who might want to try the activity in the future.

✎ Housing Costs

Objective 14   For children to build more accurate, complete, and complex concepts over time.

Materials   *This Is My House* by Arthur Dorros (Scholastic); catalogs and newspaper ads of housing items (furniture, appliances, etc.)

Procedure   After reading the book, guide a discussion with children about what their "ideal house" would be like and the items it would contain. With the children's help, make a webbing of categories of items (e.g., appliances, furniture, plumbing items, kitchen items, bedding and towels, accessories, etc.). In pairs or small groups, have children estimate what each webbed list of items might cost. Using catalogs and other price source information, have chidren check out the actual costs and the differences between their estimates and real prices.

To simplify   Limit activity to simply listing in large group the items they think are necessary in an ideal house. Encourage them to stretch their thinking by asking questions to elicit important items they have forgotten to include.

To extend   Very young children could cut pictures from magazines to make a "room." Other children may draw pictures of their ideal house. Have children individually list items they would include. Divide children into "research" groups to determine the exact cost of each category of items by taking a trip to local stores to check prices on the items and reporting back to the large group.

Science Activities

✎ Soil Samples

Objective 17   For children to examine natural objects and events using multiple sensory abilities.

Materials   Containers for gathering soil samples, trowels for digging, plastic wrap, magnifying glasses, pots and molds, water pitcher, paper, and markers

Procedure   Help children gather a number of different kinds of soil samples, such as sand, gravel, clay, and loam, placing each sample in a different container and covering with plastic wrap to retain moisture. Before the soil samples have time to dry out, place them on separate sheets of paper for examination. (*Note:* It is better to work with small groups of children so that subtle changes can be easily observed.)

To simplify   Invite the children to use magnifying glasses to observe differences in the samples. Have the children rub the samples between their thumb and forefinger to note differences in texture. Ask them to smell the samples to detect any differences in smell. Provide a number of pots and molds and suggest that they try to mold the samples. Discuss with them which samples seem to hold together better than others and why this might be so.

To extend   Examine the various samples to see how much air they contain by filling separate glasses with each of the soil samples and leaving some room at the top to add water. Slowly pour in the water and watch as it soaks in and displaces any air, helping the children to note the size and frequency of bubbles. Assign teams of children to each of the soil samples to carefully examine the pile for organic components, such as stones, insects, and leaves; have each team note the kinds of components they find, decide how to record their findings, and then report their findings to other teams. Place samples of each kind of soil in pots. Water to see if any weeds will sprout. Record findings. Place quickly sprouting seeds (one variety) in various samples to have children note which kinds of soil promote the best growth. In another experiment, have children test different growing conditions by altering light, water, and heat (Nickelsburg, 1976).

✎ What's the Solution?

Objective 19   For children to learn the scientific process.

Materials   Sand, salt, water, two clear jars, coffee filters, teaspoon measure, spoon for stirring

Procedure   Explain to the children that sometimes things mix together without changing. Sometimes the things being mixed turn into something new, which is then called a "solution." Have them fill one of the jars with very warm water, add 1 teaspoon of sand, and stir for 30 seconds. What happens to the sand? Then have them hold the filter over the mouth of the empty jar. Empty the first jar into the filter. What is left in the filter? What is left in the jar? Ask whether they have created a solution, reminding them of the definition of the term. Next, have them empty and clean both jars and then repeat their experiment, this time using a teaspoon of salt instead of sand. Stir for 30 seconds. Hold a filter over the mouth of the empty jar. Empty the first jar into the filter. What is left in the filter? What is in the jar? Where is the salt? What happens to the salt? Have they created a solution or not?

To simplify   Carry out the experiment using only the salt.

To extend   Have them experiment with other materials such as sugar, baking soda, coffee, corn starch (use $1/2$ c. cornstarch and $1/2$ c. water to produce an interesting goo!), dirt, gravel, beans, and tempera paint. Have children who are able record their findings in their science journals. Have children construct a chart differentiating materials that dissolve from those that do not.[*]

✎ In and Out of Balance

Objective 20   For children to participate in recording scientific data.

Materials   Balance scale, wood blocks, spoon, ping-pong ball

Procedure   Ask the children to carry out a series of experiments to see which weighs more: (1) a wood block or a ping-pong ball, (2) a ping-pong ball or a spoon, (3) a spoon or a wood block. Have them draw the results of each experiment in their science journals, numbering and dating each experiment.

To simplify   Have them discriminate between only two objects.

To extend   Have them choose other objects that are more difficult to discriminate visually, recording their predictions prior to the experiment and their actual findings.[†]

✎ Me and My Shadow

Objective 21   For children to explore firsthand a variety of cause-and-effect relationships.

Materials   One of the following for each child: piece of cardboard or stiff paper to make a cut-out of a shape or figure, pencil, thread spool, adhesive tape, large piece of white paper, crayons or markers

Procedure   After reading *Me and My Shadow* by Arthur Dorros (Scholastic), have children make a cut-out figure (person, bear, horse, etc.), use the tape to attach the cut-out figure to the eraser end of the pencil, and then stick the pointed end of the pencil in their thread spool. Ask them to predict what will happen when the figure is placed in the sun. On a sunny morning, have them go outside and place the figure in the center of a large piece of paper. Have them use different colored markers to trace the shadow on their paper at approximately 10:00 A.M., noon, and 2:00 P.M. Discuss with them how the shadows changed during the day.

To simplify   Supply already cut out figures.

To extend   Have the children figure out how to block the shadow made by the figure by using assorted materials (construction paper, waxed paper, plastic wrap, tissue paper, etc.). Have them describe what happens with each type of material. Have children measure the length of the shadows made at 10:00 A.M., noon, and 2:00 P.M. and describe what happens. Older children can write about the outcomes in their science journals. Provide information books about shadows and have children look up information about how shadows are formed. Have children construct drawings of the shadows formed at particular times of the days.[*]

✎ Magic Stars

Objective 23   For children to investigate differences, similarities, and patterns in natural objects and events.

Materials   Three varieties of apples, sheets of paper developed into two columns of three cells each for a total of six cells, markers

Procedure   In the left-hand column on the paper, have the children sketch the apples as they appear before being cut. Then place each apple sideways on a cutting board and slice through the middle, showing the "magic star" in the center of the apple to the chil-

---

[*]*Source:* Adapted from Scholastic's *The Magic School Bus.*
[†]*Source:* Adapted from Hein and Price (1994).

---

[*]*Source:* Adapted from Brainard and Wrubel (1993).

dren. Cut the three varieties of apples to see if all the varieties have stars or if the stars always look the same and have the same number of seeds. On the right-hand column of their paper, have the children draw the corresponding insides of the apples and the pattern and number of seeds inside. Have them label the name of the variety and date their work.

To simplify   Have predrawn pictures of the insides of the apples, labeled with the name. Have children match the apple after it has been cut to the appropriate picture.

To extend   Read *The Seasons of Arnold's Apple Tree* by Gail Gibbons (Harcourt Brace Jovanovich), a story of an apple tree's response to the four seasons.*

✎ Plants or Animals

Objective 24   For children to acquire scientific knowledge related to life sciences.

Materials   A variety of laminated pictures of foods (e.g., milk, fruit, vegetables, hot dogs, bread, cheese, hamburger, beans, etc.); two boxes, one labeled "plants" and another labeled "animals"

Procedure   Discuss with the children that all living things need food and that some food comes from plants and some from animals. Have the children sort the food according to their sources. Once the foods are sorted, have them make a list of the foods in each category.

To simplify   Just sort the foods without listing them.

To extend   Have the children find out how green plants get their food. How is that different from the way animals get their food? Ask if they can think of foods they eat that are a combination of plant *and* animal (e.g., spaghetti).

✎ Sticky Stuff

Objective 27   For children to explore a variety of scientific equipment, such as simple machines, magnets, measuring instruments.

Materials   Horseshoe magnets, one for each child; a variety of magnetic and nonmagnetic materials (plastic, aluminum, steel, paper, and wood); two boxes, one labeled "Magnetic" and another "Not Magnetic"

Source: Adapted from Brainard and Wrubel, 1993.

Procedure   Have children experiment with the magnets and materials, separating the materials into the two different boxes. Afterward, have them discuss what the magnetic materials seem to have in common that attracts them to the magnets and how those materials are different from the nonmagnetic materials.

To simplify   Have a chart available with predrawn figures and two columns, YES and NO, under which the children check their findings.

To extend   Have the children use their magnets to explore objects in the classroom to see which are magnetic and which are not. Have the children enter their findings into their science journals. Ask the children to write a letter to their parents describing their conclusions about the magnets.

Math Activities

✎ Grouping and Sorting

Objective 32   For children to classify objects by common attributes (size, shape, color, pattern, position).

Materials   Sets of objects that can be grouped on the basis of size, shape, color, pattern, or position

Procedure   Give children daily opportunities to classify a wide variety of objects. Remember that there are no right or wrong ways for children to classify. Instead, emphasize the process by which children reach their conclusions. Use the following script to guide your instruction:

> "Show me a way to put these into groups that are alike."
>
> "Good. You found a way to sort the objects."
>
> "Tell me why these things [point to one grouping] go together." Repeat for each grouping and accept the children's answer for each.
>
> "Show another way to sort the objects into piles."

To simplify   Have fewer numbers of objects with more obvious grouping possibilities.

To extend   Provide greater numbers of objects and ones with more than one common characteristic so that children will discover more sophisticated combinations (e.g., grouping all yellow objects that have something to do with transportation).

✎ **More or Less**

Objective 32 For children to seriate or order objects by common attributes.

Materials Sets of objects that may be seriated or ordered by size, shape, color, pattern, or position

Procedure Have children work in pairs, and give them daily chances to order objects from the most to least or least to most of a particular property. Vary the properties so that children have opportunities to order textures, colors, tastes, sizes, widths, and lengths. Following exploration of the materials, guided instruction might occur as follows:

> "Show me a way to put these in a line from more to less of something."
> "Good. You found a way to line up the objects."
> "Tell me how you decided what went where." Teacher accepts child's answer.
> "Show me a different way to put these in a line."
> "Tell me why you decided to line them up that way."

To simplify Have fewer objects with one characteristic in common and obvious differences in gradation.

To extend Have a greater number of objects with one characteristic in common but differences in gradation that call for greater observation skills. Have a number of objects that can be seriated by more than one characteristic (e.g., sticks that range in color hues and also length and/or width).

✎ **Pictorial Story Problems**

Objective 34 For children to develop number sense by constructing visual representations of given numbers using concrete materials.

Materials Pictorial scenes and sets of related objects, blank number strips, and markers

Procedure Give children individual pictorial scenes, such as an apple tree or a field, a barn and corral, or a seashore. Invite children to place selected objects on a particular scene and to tell an arithmetic story problem about what they have just depicted (e.g., "There were five apples on the tree, and three fell on the ground. How many apples were there in all?").

To simplify Use only a few objects. Demonstrate a very simple addition problem.

To extend Use more objects. Invite children to think of as many different combinations as possible. Have children develop written number strips for each combination after it is concretely constructed (e.g., $2 + 5 = 7$; $3 + 4 = 7$; $1 + 6 = 7$; $10 - 3 = 7$). Children may also work with partners, with one child thinking of and constructing the problem and the other child checking the work and developing a written number strip.

✎ **Count and Match**

Objective 34 For children to develop number sense and an understanding of numeration system by associating the concept of quantity with the appropriate numeral.

Materials Magazines, scissors, magnifying glasses, cards with numerals and representative symbols, blank cards, and glue or paste

Procedure Have the children gather pictures that clearly display a certain number of objects (e.g., number of teeth in a smiling face, number of birds flying in a flock, or number of boats sailing on a river). Have children pair up and tell them to look at the picture, count the objects, and then match the picture to a card with the numeral identifying the number of objects. Magnifying glasses can be supplied to help children more clearly distinguish the numbers of objects.

To simplify Use cards displaying only the numerals 1 to 5 and also including matching round circles or other graphics to represent the number indicated.

To extend Provide materials for matching numbers of objects beyond five. Have children hunt through magazines for pictures that can be matched with particular numeral cards. These can be pasted on cards, mixed up, and then sorted by children into appropriate piles coordinated with the appropriate numeral cards.

✎ **Fraction Fun**

Objective 45 For children to extend their concept of parts of a whole to include fractions (halves, quarters, thirds).

Materials Unifix cubes or bear counters in two colors, graph paper, markers in same two colors as cubes or counters.

Procedure   Have children line up six same-color cubes or bears. Ask them to make additional rows, substituting one more cube of the opposite color in each additional row until they get down to a seventh row made up entirely of the opposite color. Ask children what they notice (e.g., the colors look like stairs). Ask, "How many cubes are in the first row? What fractional part of our whole is the different-colored cube in the second row (1/6)? In the third row?" and so on.

To simplify   Begin with only four blocks in the first row, asking questions appropriate for the children's current understanding.

To extend   For older children, ask, "What fractional part of our whole is the different colored cube in the first row (0/6)?" Use ten blocks as a starter row. Have children make up fraction word problems to go along with their display (e.g., If there were ten apples, and Mother used eight of them to make a pie, what fraction of the apples is left?). Have children represent their two-color fractions on graph paper. Have children show and write their fractions. Ask, "What fraction is more of the bar, 2/10 or 8/10?" Note, "8/10 is bigger than 2/10. We show this as 8/10 > 2/10."

✎ Place Value Pocket Game

Objective 35   For children to extend their awareness of place value.

Materials   A series of laminated cards on which individual numerals 1–9 are written; pocket charts with six slots labeled (from right to left): ones, tens, hundreds, thousands, ten thousands, and hundred thousands

Procedure   In small or large groups, choose individual children to play the game. Hand a child two or three numeral cards (fewer cards for a child with a less-developed understanding) to form a two- or three-digit number. For example, hand the child the numerals 2, 3, and 6. Say, "Form a number that has 6 hundreds, 3 tens, and 2 ones (632). Now tell us the number you have made." Have children suggest any corrections if needed and tell why they are needed. Have the child select another to play the game. Vary the number of cards given to a child by matching to individual performance level. Children will build skills by watching higher degrees of performance demonstrated by other children.

To simplify   Demonstrate the game before asking children to play. Use only one or two places. Place numeral cards, noting the place for each, and then ask the children to tell the number you have made. Once they understand place value, place two or three numeral cards, and then ask whether they represent a number you are going to say to them.

To extend   When the children are ready, challenge them to play up to the hundred thousands place.

✎ Bulls Eye!*

Objective 48   For children to grow in their familiarity with and ability to use tools such as the calculator to explore math objectives.

Materials   A set of laminated cards with a numeral on each card between 1 and 100, a set of cards with a numeral on each card between 100 and 1,000, a set with a numeral on each card between 1,000 and 10,000, calculators, and paper and pencils or markers

Procedure   Using a set of cards selected according to children's abilities, pair three or four children together to play the game. Each child draws two to four cards (as agreed on by the group) and estimates in his or her head the sum of the numbers, which is written down. Each student then uses a calculator to find the sum and checks with the others. If correct (Bulls Eye!), the child receives a point. The child with the most points at the end of the time or after five rounds is the winner.

To simplify   Limit numerals to 1–50.

To extend   Have children use calculators to determine the difference between each sum and each estimate. The difference between the two numbers becomes a score. After five rounds, the group sums the scores for each player, and the player with the *lowest* sum becomes the winner.

SUMMARY

Cognitive development in the young child is a complex process. Outcomes depend on the quality of children's experiences both inside and outside of the formal classroom as they move through a series of psychosocial and neurobiological changes.

---

*Source: Adapted from Kennedy and Tipps (1994).

Children's ability to acquire knowledge and then use it effectively to plan, monitor, and evaluate their own capabilities is better ensured when they have developed and can maintain a measure of confidence in themselves and in others. This results when they are nurtured by adults who understand the critical interrelationship between cognition and all other areas of development.

Learning environments that stimulate optimal cognitive growth are those where curricular construction is guided by sensitivity to variations in development, where children are encouraged to be both independent and collaborative learners, and where high task involvement is motivated through the presentation of diverse and engaging activities that young thinkers and doers perceive to be personally useful.

Applying What You Read in This Chapter

1. **Discuss**
   a. How does Piagetian theory impinge on our choice of manipulative materials to introduce math and science concepts in the early childhood classroom?
   b. What are the differences in the way Piaget and Vygotsky thought about early learning contexts?
   c. What are the implications of our growing knowledge of neuroscience for our approach to educating young children?
   d. How does *inquiry* go beyond process learning? What are some strategies that encourage inquiry?

2. **Observe**
   a. Make an appointment to observe the classroom of an experienced early childhood teacher. What is her or his approach to the cognitive domain? What logical-mathematical materials are present in the classroom? How does the teacher use the outdoor environment? Are children encouraged to discuss their findings and how they arrived at their answers or simply involved in activity?

3. **Carry out an activity**
   a. Read about Piaget's conservation activities and replicate one of them (e.g., conservation of number, length, volume, mass, and area) to assess the conceptual level of children at different ages. How does a 3-year-old react to the experiment? A 5-year-old? A 7- or 8-year-old? Discuss the outcomes with each child to assess their levels of understanding.
   b. Identify upcoming specialized trainings or courses in manipulative math and/or hands-on science. Plan to attend one this year and try out at least five of the ideas with a group of young children.

   c. Keep a journal for one week. What kinds of problem solving were you called on to do that involved the use of the math or science concepts described in this chapter?
   d. With a small group of school-age children, ask, "Can you prove at least three things that happen or don't happen when water freezes?" How do they react? What do they say they will do to find the answer? Discuss how this approach might yield different results from simply asking them to fill a container with water, freeze it, and then explain what happens.

4. **Create something to put in your portfolio**
   a. Develop a math-based lesson plan based on the format provided in Chapter 3 of this text.
   b. Develop a science-based lesson plan based on the format provided in the text.
   c. Develop an activity for children to extend some aspect of their general cognition skills, using the lesson plan format provided in the text.

5. **Add to your journal**
   a. Think about your own early experiences with math and science. Did you take higher-level courses in secondary school and college? Were you encouraged to do so? Do you think your strengths or limitations in this area have had an effect on your professional development?
   b. How aware are you of the way you approach problem solving on an everyday basis? How adept are you at analyzing problems? How rational or logical are you in problem solving? How adaptable are you in your thinking? How fair-minded are you in judging others? Think of a specific example of your behavior for each of the questions posed here.

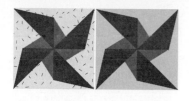

Chapter 11

The Language Domain

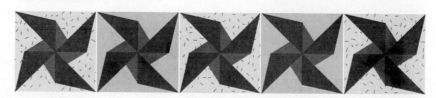

Some questions to think about before reading this chapter:

How do young children learn to speak?

If you had a 3-year-old child in your classroom who was not yet speaking, what steps should you take?

How do theoretical perspectives about reading readiness and emerging literacy differ?

What is meant by the term *whole language*?

Should we teach phonics to young children?

How do basal readers and workbooks fit into developmentally appropriate programs?

In this chapter on the cognitive domain, we present information to help you answer these questions.

Three-year-old John listens intently at his Head Start center as the dental hygienist explains why brushing our teeth is necessary to keep tartar from forming. He watches as she shows pictures of brownish tartar that has collected on some teeth. Later, he is playing with the family cat and exclaims, "Mom, look ! Snowball has tartar sauce on his teeth!"

Five-year-old Nancy draws a picture of herself as a ballet dancer. When her teacher asks her to write a story about the picture, she does so by drawing a series of round circles next to the picture, but no letters or words. She explains, "I can write, but it takes too long, so I make these."

Eight-year-old Eugene looks critically at a folder of written work he has produced over the past twelve weeks,
looking for three of his best pieces to place in a "showcase" portfolio. He is proud of the work he has done and is looking forward to sharing it with his parents at the upcoming student-led conferences.

All of these children are in varying stages of language and literacy development. The quality of that development will hinge on early and subsequent experiences in language exposure, interactions with others that focus on the use of print, and engaging opportunities to apply newly developing and higher-level understandings in a variety of situations. Development of both language and literacy are continuous in nature. Both are highly dependent on neural structures and also on culturally mediated learning experiences that drive children from rudimentary understandings to independent sophistication with language.

HOW LANGUAGE DEVELOPS

Alexander, at 2 years of age, is already attuned to three languages. His maternal grandmother has come to the United States from Hungary to live with the family and care for him while his parents work. Because she speaks little English, the language she and Alexander have come to share is Hungarian. His favorite playmate is a slightly older toddler who lives next door, Sarah Ho, whose primary language is Chinese. Recently, when crossing the street on the way to the playground with his grandmother, his friend Sarah, and her mother, he remembers and repeats his grandmother's warning of, "Vigyázz . . . kocsi! (Careful. . . car!)." At the playground, when he shares a sand toy with Sarah, her mother reminds Sarah to tell him, "Xie-xie (Thank you)." He looks thoughtful for a moment and then repeats the words over and over to himself softly as he fills his pail with sand, "Xie-xie, Xie-xie." That evening, when asked by his grandmother "Megfürdik? (take a bath?)," he shakes his head and responds, "Nem (No)" and then looks at his English-speaking father and says, "No!" just to be sure everyone understands that he isn't yet ready to begin his bedtime ritual.

Even with a variety of multicultural influences, Alexander's English language development at 24 months is right on target. His receptive vocabulary contains about 300 words (see Table 11.1), and he is learning many more words each day to express his needs and wants. At the same time, he is learning that he can use language to control the behavior of others, establish and maintain contact with others, ask questions and get information, inform others and assert himself, and express his imagination and ideas through words.

Because he is wholly unaware of language forms and structures, his creative ability to imitate and pick up on the patterns, rhythms, and meanings of language is believed to be primarily the result of innate tendencies. Noam Chomsky (1965), who believes that language "is a window to the mind," ascertains that children come equipped with a linguistic intelligence and what has been labeled a language acquisition device. However, it is the *environment* that ultimately determines the quality and content of their receptive and expressive functioning. By the time Alexander and Sarah are 6 or 7 years of age, they will have a remarkable, adultlike grasp of the grammar, syntax, vocabulary, noun phrases, meaning, and pronunciation that make up their primary languages.

All children, regardless of what language is being learned, follow a six-step sequence in language development (Gordon & Williams-Browne, 1995, 404–405):

1. *Infants' response to language.* Babies are sensitive to and attend closely to precursors of speech: changes in sound, rhythm, and intonation. Even at 4 days of age, babies are able to differentiate one language from another and will suck more vigorously when hearing their own language. By 6 weeks, they prefer faces that speak rather than those that do not, and by 3–4 months will notice when a speaker's words are not synchronized with their mouth movements (Dyson & Genishi, 1993, 123). When photographed in slow motion, a "dialogue" or communicative "dance" can

Sandbox Communication and Language Building

TABLE 11.1
Language Development: The First Three Years*

Age	Characteristics
0–2 months	Small throaty sounds; cooing by end of first month; communicates mainly by differentiated crying; vowel-like grunting such as "ooh-ooh" and "ahh-ahh"
3 months	Whimpers, squeals, chuckles, gurgles at back of throat; stimulated to make sounds by hearing others talk
4 months	May babble routinely to self and others; may raise voice as if asking questions
5 months	Watches mouths intently and tries to imitate reflections; may start to utter consonant sounds such as "m" and "b"
6 months	Learns to make new sounds by changing shape of mouth
7 months	May make several sounds in one breath; recognizes different tones and inflections; masters first language-like sounds of "eee-eee" and "ooo-ooo"
8 months	Starts to imitate a broader range of sounds; responds to familiar noises by turning head and torso
9 months	May respond to name and other words, like "no"; listens intently to conversation; may say "ma-ma" and "da-da"; likes to imitate coughs; first well-formed syllables appear
10 months	Adds gestures to words: waves when saying "bye-bye" or shakes head when saying "no"; first words appear at approximately 10–12 months
11 months	Imitates word sounds as well as actions; learns meaning of words by hearing them used in different situations
12 months	May babble short sentences that only he or she understands; shows more control over intonation and inflection; may say 2–8 words like "bow-wow" or "hi"; average number of words at 12 months is 3
13 months	May not say full words yet but gestures to complete ideas (e.g., says "ba" and points to ball or says "bow" and points to bottle)
14 months	Enjoys rhymes and jingles; expresses needs mainly through gestures; brings books to adults to read
15 months	May follow simple commands like "come here"; points to familiar objects when requested; recognizes names of major body parts
16 months	May say 6 or 7 words clearly; enjoys word games and singing songs like "Pop Goes the Weasel"
17 months	May start to use words to express needs; says "up" to be held; enjoys pointing at pictures; may understand more words than can say
18 months	Receptive vocabulary explodes; child starts learning as many as 12 words a day; "no" is chief word; points to own body parts or to pieces of clothing when asked; may refer to self by name; has average of 22 words; first word combinations begin by 18–20 months
19 months	Focuses on words and objects that are central to his or her life
20–21 months	Near end of second year, learns that everything has a name and constantly asks, "What's that?"; may combine two words like "All gone!"

TABLE 11.1
(continued)

Age	Characteristics
22 months	Enjoys listening to simple storiesmay take lead in conversation; and uses words to express feelings or ideas
23 months	May use words to express frustration or anger; at times, still relies on facial expression or an occasional scream to communicate feelings
24 months	By end of second year, some children have an average vocabulary of 272 words; mimics adult inflections and actions; first sentences occur
25–29 months	Vocabulary grows rapidly; child starts combining nouns with verbs to form 3- to 4-word sentences; begins to use pronouns such as "I" and "me" and other parts of speech; may begin to ask "why" questions; pays close attention to what others say, whether to him or her or someone else
30–36 months	May grasp two- or three-part command; can follow story line and remembers many ideas presented in books; rnay correctly name colors; at three, has average of 896 words

Source: Adapted from Lach (1997).

be seen between the young infant's motor movements and the rhythm of a speaker's voice (Stern, 1977).

2. *Vocalization.* Cooing and babbling are present by 3–4 months, with the babbling increasing with age and peaking between 9 and 12 months. The innate aspect of language can be seen in similar language development of deaf children up to this point and also the similar patterns across all cultures.

3. *Word development.* As children differentiate increasingly between speech and nonspeech noises, they begin to play and practice with speech sounds. They are then reinforced by responses from others around them when they repeat certain configurations of sounds and, as a result, a simple, primary vocabulary and more controlled speech develops. Cowley (1997) points out that each of the world's approximately 6,000 languages uses a distinctive assortment of phonemes to build words and that by 6 to 10 months of age, children have already begun to narrow their range. They have developed "magnets" that attract them to their own language and are already losing their ability to discern fine differences in other languages (ECS, 1996). For example, American children by the age of 7 months are accustomed to blends such as *tr* and *cl* but wholly unaccustomed to combinations such as *db, gd, kt, ts,* and *ng* that occur in other languages. By the time these children are adults, they will not even be able to *hear* such sounds ar-

ticulated in a nonfamiliar language, and highly accurate pronunciation of words in another language becomes difficult to attain.

Receptive vocabulary is always far greater than expressive vocabulary, and first words are likely to be about familiar people, foods, toys, and animals. These words are often "overextended" to entire categories (for example, "da-da" may mean all men), and single words are used as sentences (e.g., "milk" may mean "I'm ready for my bottle.").

4. *Sentences.* Two words constitute first sentences, which usually describe actions, possessions, or locations (e.g., "Go outside!"). Later, these telegraphic communications are enhanced with adjectives, changed verb tenses, or the use of negatives. Grammar is *not* a result of rule learning but imitating and internalizing what children hear again and again from others around them.

5. *Elaboration.* Vocabulary development in young children is a truly amazing phenomenon, and the young child moves from first words at about 10 months to as many as 6,000 to 20,000 words upon school entry. Those children who have been exposed to languaging experiences of all kinds and have had opportunities to practice their own developing skills with others are likely to be on the upper limits of development. As preschoolers, they occasionally surprise

adults by using words they would not be expected to know, and although they do not completely understand the meaning, they come close by associating the words to the context in which they originally heard them. Lauren, at age 3, shouted at her sister, "You're PAFETIC!" Reprimanded by her mother about the pejorative tone of the word, she was asked if she knew what the word meant. She responded confidently, "It means you're stupid!"

Conversely, those children who have had impoverished language experience in the early years are predictably less able to communicate their thoughts and feelings with others, and the emergence of reading and writing skills may lag behind. For example, children who enter school with little or no knowledge of nursery rhymes or print awareness have been shown to be significantly behind other children in reading even through grade three (Soderman, 1995).

6. *Graphic representation.* Children become aware of language as an entity itself somewhere around the age of 5 or 6. Their interest in what printed words "say" and how to write labels and messages to others is as naturally intense as was their earlier attention to verbalized language forms.

RED FLAGS IN SPEECH AND LANGUAGE DEVELOPMENT

By the age of 2, there are children who are noticeably behind the milestones presented in Table 11.1, most of them boys. Seventy-five percent of all expressive language delays resolve themselves by the time children enter school. A quarter of them, however, do not (Kalb & Namuth, 1997). These often signal more serious and long-lasting problems, such as those resulting from congenital or acquired hearing impairments or problems in the cognitive, sensorimotor, psychological, emotional, or environmental systems (e.g., poverty, nonverbal family, or bilingual home). Parents and caregivers of young children who are are not keeping up with their peers in language development frequently take a wait-and-see approach, rather than seeking intervention.

Mispronunciations are common in the preschool years, primarily due to a lack of auditory discrimination. A quarter of all children have difficulty untangling consonant sounds in their primary language even as late as 7 years of age, and this is often reflected in their spelling and articulation blunders. Thus, children

pronounce "then" as "ven" (see Figure 11.1) and "birthday" as "birfvay." "And" is often pronounced as "ad"; "spaghetti" is more frequently than not labeled "busketti," and words such as "trouble" and "tree" are heard and spelled as "chrubel" and "chree." Problems in dysfluency that frequently occur in 3- and 4-year-olds, such as primary stuttering, are often labeled "hesitant speech." This results from children having to focus cognitively on *how* they are communicating something, rather than what they want to say.

Many speech and language pathologists agree that much of speech or language therapy is unwarranted prior to kindergarten, particularly if the child is showing good comprehension and using gestures to communicate. To call the child's attention to a condition that will probably be outgrown is viewed as creating additional and unnecessary anxiety for the child. Others disagree, noting that young children who are frustrated at not being able to communicate their feelings and needs are in danger of developing behavior problems (Kalb & Namuth, 1997). Also, it is believed that children go through a "speech readiness period" beginning at approximately 9 months and extending until 2 years of age, in which they appear to be most receptive to learning language (Stinchfield & Young, 1938). Although apparent problems may seem to be resolved later, some experts believe that too much may be lost in the interim because language and developing cognition are so closely intertwined. Moreover, those children who are not speaking effectively by school entry often suffer from a lack of ability to interact successfully with others in the learning context. Red flags that may signal more serious long-term outcomes include the following:

0–3 months—child does not turn when spoken to or repeat sounds like coos

4–6 months—child does not respond to "no" or changes in tone of voice, look around for sources of sound like a doorbell, or babble in speechlike sounds such as *p, b,* and *m*

7–12 months—child does not recognize words for common items, turn when her name is called, imitate speech sounds, or use sounds other than crying to get attention

1–2—years child cannot point to pictures in a book that you name or understand simple questions

2–3 years—child cannot understand differences in meaning (e.g., *up* and *down*), follow two re-

FIGURE 11.1
Auditory discrimination that is not yet fully developed: "One day my daddy came home with a baby bunny. Then (Ven) it was time for my mommy and daddy to leave."

quests, string together two or three words, or name common objects

2–4 years—child does not answer simple "who," "what," and "where" questions, cannot be understood by people outside the family, use four-word sentences, or pronounce most phonemes correctly. If delays persist until kindergarten, most pediatricians recommend speech therapy (Cowley, 1997, 21).

The bottom line in determining the seriousness of abnormal speech and language development *prior* to the age of 5 seems to lie in making sure that from early infancy on, a child's *receptive* language is intact and that the child is demonstrating comprehension reasonably appropriate for his or her age level, good intelligibility, and a willingness to be engaged with others in his or her daily activities.

Both at home and in the early childhood classroom, children's speech and language thrive when the environment is rich in language opportunities, including conversation and the modeling of rich language, pretend play where children naturally expand their usual vocabulary in taking on the roles of others, singing, poetry, rhymes, chants, tongue twisters, a variety of shared reading experiences with others, listening games, and viewing experiences.

THE ACQUISITION OF LITERACY

Take a moment to reflect before continuing with this chapter. Can you remember learning to read? What specific memories and mental pictures are you *immediately* aware of related to the process?

When asked to reflect upon earliest literacy experiences, many of us today think about sitting in a formal reading group at approximately 5 to 6 years of age. A basal text is being used, and individual children in the group are being called on to read brief portions of the text. The teacher is there to correct mistakes and help the reader along.

How closely does this description match what flashed through *your* mind when considering the earlier questions? Usually forgotten or discounted are the many other experiences in infancy and early childhood that we had with pictorial representations, letters, words, and text before and in addition to formal reading instruction. These included leafing through cardboard picture books as infants, nestling down into a lap and being read favorite stories, watching programs such as Sesame Street, observing others reading and writing, playing "school" with other children, being challenged by an older sibling to name all the "B-buh" words we could think of, drawing pictures and scribbling with chalk on the sidewalk, excitedly sighting a favorite place to eat because we knew its name started with a huge M or B, and looking at newspapers and magazines. There were many other experiences—making our names and other words in fingerpaint or sand, figuring out secret codes from friends, looking at comic books, rhyming silly words, being fascinated with the sound and corresponding written version of certain words (even "naughty" words!), picking out specific letters on license plates while riding in the car, and the joy of identifying our first few sight words correctly without anyone else's help!

Even before children are able to read a single word, they already perceive reading experiences as delightful ways to learn about story characters, fantasy and reality, problems, turning points and solutions, settings, points of view, and styles of authors and illustrators. They come to understand that there are common elements among stories and that "those funny marks" indicate dialogue or what the characters "say." They can retell stories that have been read to them, outlining the details and main ideas with enough clarity to document they are deriving meaning from print.

Theoretical Perspectives About Literacy Acquisition

Despite an intensive campaign the last 20 years by reading association professionals to broaden perspectives about literacy, its beginnings and its complex, culturally interactive aspects, literacy continues to be equated primarily with formal reading ability—and formal reading ability with skill in decoding words. Also persisting are fairly rigid ideas that a "readiness" factor determines when a child is ready to read or write (at approximately ages 5 or 6) and that a "deficiency" factor (at about the end of first grade) exists when children have not yet learned to read. Given the documented variability in the development and experience of young children, these two factors wedge children into a very narrow and unrealistic window for acquiring literacy.

Charging that reading ability acquisition is greatly misunderstood, leading to extreme positions regarding literacy programs in the United States, Mason and Sinha (1993) note the lack of any agreed-upon theoretical perspective about how literacy is acquired. Gen-

erally, two major perspectives currently exist: (1) a reading readiness perspective, an "all-or-nothing" approach where maturation is seen as a precondition of the child's ability to read, and reading is seen narrowly as an ability to decode words, and (2) an emergent literacy perspective (Clay, 1979), which challenges the "neural ripening" (Elkind, 1981; Gesell, 1940) inherent in the readiness perspective and also the behaviorist theory for teaching reading skills that became attached to it.

The four components that define emergent literacy are as follows:

> Literacy emerges before children are formally taught to read.
>
> Literacy is defined to encompass the whole act of reading, not merely decoding.
>
> The child's point of view and active involvement with emerging literacy constructs is featured.
>
> The social setting for literacy learning cannot be ignored (Mason & Sinha, 1993, 141).

These authors suggest that, because the emerging literacy perspective has been well accepted but that many educators refuse to give up the contradictory readiness perspective, Vygotskian theory provides a highly useful framework for understanding how literacy is acquired. It is friendly to both readiness *and* emerging literacy perspectives in that Vygotsky (1929) differentiated between natural and cultural development. The first was targeted toward organic growth and maturation of the child, and the latter allowed for the cultural development in which the child's literacy learning involved the use of symbolic and abstract tools.

Stages in Literacy Acquisition

Moving through four stages of acquiring literacy, the child first begins to attend to the symbol and tools and then, with the continued help of adults or older children in a second stage, gains more experience with these and begins to remember them. For example, the child may practice readinglike behavior or write out a "menu" in the pretend play area. In the third stage, the child discovers how to put the symbols into practice but is still highly dependent on external aids (here, the child may write a story using invented spelling and words from the classroom word wall or ask a peer for help). Finally, in the most sophisticated stage, the child has acquired literacy to the extent that he or she has internalized the constructs necessary to be quite independent and confident in carrying out literacy tasks.

Promoting Literacy Acquisition in Young Children

The proposition of adopting Vygotskian theory in a developmentally appropriate approach to literacy in the classroom is an exciting one in that it allows for the differences we find in the young children with whom we are workir 3. It also advocates an interactive process in supporting the child's developmental progress rather than simply waiting for "readiness" to occur.

We know that there *are* a number of factors that predict or, when not well developed, deter literacy success. Many of these factors are developed naturally by the young child in the preschool years but can also be enhanced by activities structured for the early childhood classroom. For example, when parents or teachers take young children on a shape hunt to find as many triangles, squares, circles, and rectangles as they can, children are developing visual discrimination, awareness of whole-part relationships, memory to recall images and configuration, ability to differentiate and discriminate, ability to follow directions, and receptive and expressive vocabulary. With block and puzzle play, children increase visual discrimination, eye coordination, awareness of whole-part relationships, spatial relationships, memory to recall sequences and placement, and ability to attend to detail. Listening games where children have to attend closely in order to discover the secret object enhance memory, auditory discrimination, and ability to attend to detail and vocabulary. Watching big books as stories are being read or sitting in an adult's lap to listen to a favorite book heighten children's awareness of literacy conventions (left-to-right, top-to-bottom, page-to-page), vocabulary, reading for meaning, and eye coordination; subsequent games with familiar text increase the child's sight knowledge of words, growing knowledge of the internal structures of words (syllables, orthographic shapes of graphemes, grapheme-phoneme connections, visual discrimination, memory of configuration, and speed in differentiating between mirror images, for example, b/d, p/q, m/w, and 91/19). All of these skills serve as precursors for and enhance growing literacy.

A critical aspect of Vygotskian theory is his concept of a zone of proximal development (ZPD). This is "the hypothetical, dynamic region in which learning and development take place. It is defined by the distance between what a child can accomplish during independent problem solving and what he or she can accomplish with the help of an adult or more competent member of the culture" (Berk & Winsler, 1995, 5). Elsewhere, this help is referred to as "scaffolding" (Wood, 1989; Wood & Middleton, 1975) or "mediated learning" (Mason & Sinha, 1993), which involves modeling and coaching. More than a didactic approach of breaking down a task into subgoals or "smaller steps," scaffolding highlights the interactional, social nature of learning any task. It requires the teacher or mentor to help the child connect new understandings to already developed concepts (see Chapters 1, 4, and 10). Kay Clevenger, a superb kindergarten teacher at Miller Early Childhood Center in Brighton, Michigan, is this kind of scaffolder. Recognizing that one of the children doing a fair amount of good writing was ready for the next step—leaving spaces between his words—she challenged him to find a strategy. He decided he would put dots between each word to help him remember (see Figure 11.2). It did not take long to recognize that putting dots between the words took longer than just leaving spaces, and he quickly moved to a new level of understanding and capability in his writing.

In another setting, Mr. Hewlett can be seen "scaffolding" a small-group reading experience. Prior to beginning an unfamiliar story with new vocabulary, he leafs through the book, showing the children the pictures and challenging them to guess what the story is all about. Mr. Hewlett will probably take the time to ask the children about *their* experiences with the subject matter. Then, after writing some of the vocabulary words on a white board and asking the children to watch for the words in the story, he leads into the book, saying, "Let's find out how this situation turned out differently!" The emotional climate in any scaffolding situation should be not only warm and supportive but also one where the tutor constantly adjusts the amount of intervention to the child's needs and abilities. Most of all, the instructional nature of scaffolding should not be allowed to overtake the active engagement of the child in moving to a higher level of understanding (Berk & Winsler, 1995).

FIGURE 11.2
Scaffolding to move child to a higher level of emerging writing—no spaces between words to a strategy (teacher promoted but child selected) of placing dots between words as a reminder.

For adults to be effective in scaffolding *any* task, they must have expertise with respect to child development and also the sequences in which skills required for the task emerge, in this case literacy understandings. For example, in emerging writing, children will progress through the following stages:

Stage 1—Emergent

Preletter writing of marks, followed by differentiation of marks (see Figure 11.3)

Letterlike forms

Letters and letter strings: BuTERToWGlpR

Words written with fixed quantities

Single letters for words

Consonant level: Initial consonants (e.g., VKn for vacation)

Skipped endings

No spaces between words

Correct directional movement

Learning letter names and letter sounds

Approximations and invented spelling

Using some known words in correct spaces

Able to select own topic to write about

Stage 2—Early

Uses end sounds of most words correctly

Knows letter names and letter sounds

Alphabetic stage: vowels appear (e.g., vacashun for vacation)

Overcompensation of vowels (e.g., moashun for motion; ideeus for ideas)

Able to spell many difficult words correctly

Uses more correct spellings than approximations

Uses initial blends

Uses editing skills

Underlines approximations

Uses word sources to correct approximations

Uses capital letters in correct place

Writes a title

Varies topic choice

Stage 3—Fluency

Uses final blends

Uses suffixes correctly (e.g., -s, -ing, -ed, -ly)

Uses syllables

Uses editing skills

Compares own work with print in books and elsewhere

Correctly places quotation marks, question marks, apostrophes, and commas

Correctly divides story into paragraphs

Publishes correct articles of work

Varies sentence beginnings

Is able to sequence ideas

Writes in a variety of styles: Friendly letters, factual reports, imaginative pieces, retelling, and poetry

As adults use scaffolding to foster children's learning, it also has the effect of helping children to self-regulate their behavior and to self-direct their own learning. Children can often be seen doing this through *private speech*, which is overt in nature but clearly meant as self-talk. Piaget, a contemporary of Vygotsky's, labeled this self-talk in the preoperational child *egocentric speech* and viewed it very differently from the way his colleague did. Piaget viewed it as ineffective and immature social speech by the child. Vygotsky, on the other hand, theorized that private speech plays a critical role in child development and that its primary purpose was not a strategy used by children for communicating with others but a tool for thinking through their intended actions or for reorganizing already completed operations. He drew this conclusion by observing that children tended to use more private speech while working on tasks that were difficult for them. He noted, also, that it increased as the preschool child had more social interactions with others and then gradually became covert and internalized while continuing to be used as a way to self-organize (Berk & Winsler, 1995).

INTEGRATING LANGUAGE ACROSS THE CURRICULUM

The strength of the language domain is that it reaches naturally across the curriculum into every other domain. Literature of all kinds should be used to introduce "big ideas" to children, including those in science, mathematics, history, and social studies (Routman, 1996). Children should become as familiar with expository text as they are with narrative text, and they should be encouraged after the reading of a narrative text to do some follow-up work from expository texts when they have questions. For example, Ms. Rinker was sharing Eric Carle's *Very Hungry Caterpillar* (1981) with her first-grade class when DeMarco questioned the author's use of the term "cocoon." "My dad says that should be called a *chrystal*," he challenged. Knowing that DeMarco's father had probably used the term chrysalis, Ms. Rinker said, "I think DeMarco's fa-

FIGURE 11.3
Stage 1 in emerging writing: Lauren, age 4, trying to write a thank-you note to her grandmother, complained to her mother, "I don't know grown-up writing!" "Just write like a four-year-old," suggested her mother. Lauren drew lines on the page to make it "writing paper" and scribbled her message. When asked to read it back, she said, "I don't know what it says. I wrote it in French!"

ther is correct. How do you think your father knew that, DeMarco? Where do you think *we* can find out about that word?" An ensuing and very appealing "science lesson" took place, with a group of interested children taking a trip to the school library on a fact-finding mission. Later, they looked at differences between varieties of moths and butterflies, leading to the classification, labeling, painting, and drawing of a number of them. Another group of children looked with an interested parent on the Internet and discovered that Eric Carle had addressed the discrepancy and had also provided an explanation about continuing to use the word *cocoon*. A discussion followed about whether or not Mr. Carle should change the word after all, and a class letter was finally written to Mr. Carle letting him know that the children agreed with his decision and why they did so.

To reach across the curriculum, many teachers create what they call "literacy spinoffs," that is, activities in other curricular domains that seem to evolve naturally from the reading of a favorite narrative text. The book provides the children with a shared basis of understanding for the subsequent activities, which may take place over the span of a day, a week, or longer, and there is an effort to structure activities in all developmental domains. A group of second-grade teachers met to develop a set of spinoff activities that could be used with the text *This Is My House,* by Arthur Dorros (1992), a favorite of many of the children in their classrooms. In the book, children from many countries tell about their houses, typical of the kind found in their country. The diversity of homes is depicted, as well as how each is constructed, and a sample of the different languages people speak is provided as each child in the book proudly proclaims, "This is my house!"

As a connected reading experience, the teachers discussed with the children whether their lives would be similar or different if they lived in the other cultures depicted in the book. The children were assigned the task of interviewing an older family member or friend to find out what their house looked like when they were young and whether the house had changed while they lived there or afterward. The children worked together to construct a salt dough globe and labeled it showing the seven continents that were connected with the houses depicted in the book. They also constructed dioramas of the different homes to depict the climate and living conditions particular to that home and learned such terms as continent, equator, compass rose, hemisphere, foundation, adobe, thatch, yurt, houseboat, and shelter. Next, they graphed the kinds of dwellings they and their families lived in and, with the help of their parents, developed scaled floor maps of their home's layout. They found out about the various materials their homes were made of and researched how the materials were made. Inviting in a local contractor, they developed a descriptive listing of how much it would cost to construct a home of a particular size and estimated what it might cost to equip and furnish such a home, depending on the items selected. Small groups were assigned to take trips to a furniture store, an appliance shop, and a plumbing shop to check out their estimates and report back. Along with singing, "There was a crooked man who bought a crooked house" and after a discussion of the importance of measuring correctly when building and what would happen if the walls were not the same height, they drew crooked houses, constructed crooked houses from popsicle sticks, and made up poems about their creations to share with each other. When asked what would happen if the floor were slanted, they constructed inclined planes and watched and recorded the results when various items were rolled down them. Individually, they created essays about what houses and furniture might say if they could talk and shared their writing with one another during Author's Chair sessions. They made rubbings from the outsides of their homes and brought them to school for comparisons and discussion with their classmates. The spinoff naturally swung in the direction of animals' homes and, after some study of animal habitats and a listing of some questions they had, the classes took a joint field trip to the zoo to look at a variety of animals in habitats that simulated their natural homes. From these activities, the children greatly increased their overall vocabulary, their fund of knowledge, and their conceptual understandings across the entire curriculum.

Including print materials throughout the room, not just in the library corner, also increases children's attention to written language as it relates to learning in other domains (McGee & Richgels, 1990). For instance, one preschool teacher included books in every learning center in her classroom—books on machines, transportation, and building in the block area; cookbooks, telephone book, magazines, address book, and home construction books in housekeeping; books about artists, color, and design in the art area; and number books and books about nature in the math/science area.

It is natural to use literature to reach across the curriculum and, obviously, there are many ways to do it! To do so in the most effective way, however, calls for professionals to: (1) discard rigid ideas about time blocks that segment the day or week; (2) think creatively about how all curricular components relate to one another; and (3) involve the children, their families, and the community in the activities that take place inside and outside the classroom. Good planning is required to make sure there is a balance of activities, as are thoughtful evaluation strategies to provide the documentation needed to be sure children are making progress.

There are a number of publishers who have developed resources specifically for integrating emergent literacy with dramatic play, science, math, art, music, and geography. A few of these are included in the following listing by Walsh (1994, 4):

Abrohms, A. (1992). *Literature-Based Math Activities: An Integrated Approach.* New York: Scholastic.

Brainard, A. and Wrubel, D. H. (1993). *Literature-Based Science Activities: An Integrated Approach.* New York: Scholastic.

Davidson, J. (1996). *Emergent Literacy and Dramatic Play in Early Education.* Albany, NY: Delmar Publishing.

Kostelnik, M. J. (Ed.) (1991) *Teaching Young Children Using Themes.* Glenview, IL: Goodyear Books.

McCarthy, T. (1992). *Literature-Based Geography Activities: An Integrated Approach.* New York: Scholastic.

Moen, C. B. (1992). *Better than Book Reports.* New York: Scholastic.

Nyberg, J. (1996). *Charts for Children: Print Awareness Activities for Young Children.* Glenview, IL: Goodyear Books.

Schlosser, K. G. and Phillips, V. L. (1992). *Building Literacy with Interactive Charts.* New York: Scholastic.

Walsh, N. (1994). *Making Books across the Curriculum, Grades K-6: Pop Ups, Flaps, Shapes, Wheels and Many More.* New York: Scholastic.

EDUCATIONAL ISSUES IN EMERGING LITERACY

Today, unreasonable voices outside our profession are clamoring to tell us how and what to teach. People who have little idea how children learn to read and write are speaking out loudly, bombarding the media with simplistic "quick fixes" and loud criticism of sound educational practices. And we are letting them do it. . . . The cry of "back to basics," for a return to skills-based, phonics-based teaching, threatens much of what we know about the complexities of teaching and learning. We seem to be heading down the literacy track at higher and higher speeds with a derailment guaranteed unless we can take charge of steering the course. Routman (1996)

For almost a decade, Regie Routman, a language arts resource teacher in the Shaker Heights, Ohio, school district and a prominent author in the field of early literacy (*Literacy at the Crossroads: Crucial Talk about Reading, Writing and Other Teaching Dilemmas,* 1996; *Invitations: Changing as Teachers and Learners K-12,* 1991; *Transitions: From Literature to Literacy* 1988) has expressed concern about the misconceptions that exist relative to what constitutes good teaching. She is not alone! As many new teachers enter the field of early childhood education, they are often confused when they see colleagues in the same learning community who are at opposite ends of a philosophical continuum about guiding young children's emerging literacy. Some have no established philosophy at all, leaving them at the whim of any new idea that comes along or believing that "nothing is ever new . . . only recycled." When discussing issues related to curriculum, literacy instruction, or assessment, such individuals have a difficult time agreeing about a consolidated direction and, as a result, rarely effect productive change that supports a strong language arts approach for young children.

In other settings, staff form ongoing study groups around targeted issues to determine whether existing programmatic practice is, in fact, still the *best* practice or whether change is warranted because of new understandings in the field. Following a recent inservice to talk about new directions in early literacy, the early childhood professionals attending were invited to develop a list of questions that continued to bother them. The following questions represent the issues that surfaced quickly and seemed to arouse the hottest discussion:

Question: I have parents of toddlers asking me what they can do to ensure their child will be a reader. I'm concerned about the long-range, negative impacts of pushing young children. What do I tell them?

Answer: We know for certain that early readers are children who live with reading models. They are read to early and often from a variety of sources, including engaging narrative texts that are predictable and repetitive and allow for the child's active involvement. The fun and enjoyment that come from reading are emphasized over the necessity of skill building, and books are frequently given as gifts. Early on, these children know what books are for and also about print conventions. TV and video games are limited (for the whole family, not just the children), allowing family members to interact with one another. Conversations between parents and children about things that interest the child are important in that they build vocabulary, a characteristic that is predictive of first-grade reading ability (Snow et al., 1995). Actually, ensuring that a child becomes a competent and confident reader and writer is pretty simple: The child must see others who value and model reading and writing, and they must have subsequent opportunities to put these behaviors into practice. It works!

Question: I teach in a program that serves families from very diverse populations. A number of the children coming in do not speak English. Do you have any hints for the inclusion of these children, particularly in supporting their language and literacy acquisition?

Answer: NAEYC has recently developed a position statement for responding to linguistic and cultural diversity (NAEYC, 1996). Children enrolled in educational programs who are ESL (English as a second language), NEP (Non-English-proficient), or LEP (Limited-English-proficient) need the respect and active support of professionals and peers who will be helping them add English to their primary language. More than this, however, these children need a responsive pedagogy that considers bilingualism as a positive attribute rather than a linguistic, cognitive, and academic liability. These children come into the classroom already knowing a lot about language and, in the process of acquiring a second language, will be driven to higher levels of cognitive flexibility, metalinguistic awareness, concept formation, and creativity than is required of unilinguistic children in the setting (Garcia, 1993).

Professionals will want to examine the entire classroom structure: Is it a community of learners with an environment that promotes interaction of children with adults and peers? Are the opportunities for all children to speak, listen, read, and write (even in their native language) rich and varied? Are learning goals ("Let's see how much we can find out about this!") rather than performance goals and drill ("How much do you know about this?") emphasized? Is the active role the student brings to learning recognized and valued? How creative are instructional strategies? Is there sufficient repetition of activities and predictability so the child can begin to develop some comfort level? Are visual aids, toys, photos, and books from the child's culture included, as well as tapes, stories, rhymes, and songs? Are there opportunities for the child or the child's family members to share with others experiences such as a song or counting from the primary language? Are there authentic strategies for evaluating the child's progress?

Because the rate of acquisition of a second language (including reading and writing abilities) is highly related to proficiency levels in the child's primary language, every effort should be made to have the child continue gaining proficiency in his or her home language. This calls for encouraging parents to continue speaking and reading frequently to the child in their native language and recruiting someone familiar with the child's home language to participate in the classroom for at least a portion of the day. This person can be a parent, family member (perhaps a sibling), or person in the community who can not only translate in "sticky" situations but also scaffold language and literacy experiences for the child both in the home language and the language being acquired. Codeswitching, (i.e., the child's switching from one language to the other even within the same sentence) should be accepted without comment (Zentella, 1981).

When working with infants and toddlers, it is important to remember their intense need for language-rich experiences to promote linguistic development. If caregivers severely reduce their verbal interaction with the child because there is not yet a shared language or if they think the child will be confused, language development will be diminished. Caregivers will want to pay special attention to the child's nonverbal communication and also provide all of the verbal interaction they would with the rest of the children, singing to the child softly while holding him or her or changing a diaper, pointing out labels for objects and locations the child uses, labeling emotions and behaviors, and using other children's names frequently.

It does not take young children very long to acquire a second language. Within about three months in a supportive, secure environment, they will begin to demonstrate that they are making gains in second-language acquisition. For children whose primary language is developing typically, a second language is usually not a challenge.

Question: I've heard a lot of criticism of whole language. What exactly is it and, since controversy continues to revolve around it, should we be reappraising its effectiveness?

Answer: A number of myths exist about whole language, and these current misunderstandings may actually contribute to early childhood teachers

turning back toward traditional, teacher-directed instruction and away from concepts of continuous progress and emerging literacy (Mason & Sinha, 1993).

Whole language (see Figure 11.4) is language learning that is socially and contextually determined rather than compartmentalized instruction and rote learning (Mickelson, 1989). More than just a theory about how children do and should acquire literacy, however, it is a *set of principles* about what must happen in a developmentally appropriate classroom: that language learning is not fractured into pieces, destroying meaning, but maintains its integrity through integrated experiences that guide developing skills and concepts; that phonics skills are taught when appropriate but must be embedded in meaningful context rather than taught in isolation; that children should be often exposed to good literature rather than be "basal-and-worksheet-bound"; and that

FIGURE 11.4
Whole Language: Writing Across the Curriculum

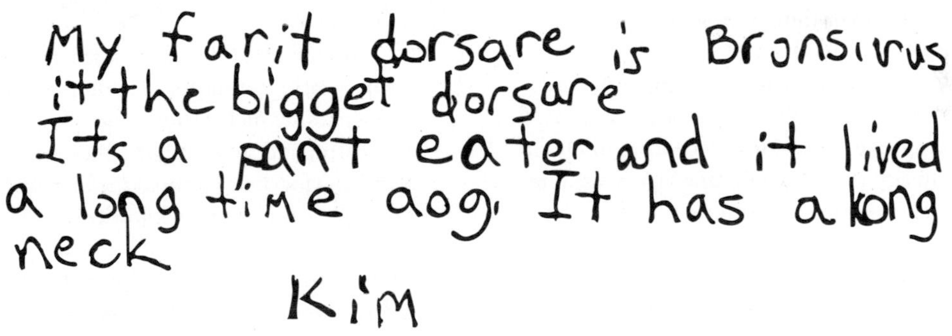

My favorite dinosaur is brontosaurus.

It [is] the biggest dinosaur.

It's a plant eater and it lived

a long time ago. It has a long

neck.

Kim

Grade 1

invented spelling is acceptable and appropriate as the child works toward conventional spelling.

Strongly underwritten in 1986 by the International Reading Association, the Association for Childhood Education International, and the National Association for the Education of Young Children, whole language encourages teachers to "focus on hands-on experiences to help children learn; to build instruction on what the child already knows about oral language, reading and writing, and to highlight worthwhile experiences and meaningful language rather than isolated skill development" (Jackman, 1997, 53). It does *not* mean that teachers can become haphazard about children's emerging literacy skills or leave phonetic and print awareness to chance, that spelling and grammar do not matter, that programs are less rigorous or children's products are unimportant, or that assessment should be ignored. Nor does it mean teaching only to entire groups of children rather than small groups or individuals. Routman (1996) suggests that the whole-language concept, which is research based, sensible, and child centered, has not failed us; we have failed it in that we have allowed it to become a scapegoat for everything that is wrong in education today.

In reality, what may be wrong with education in part today is that we do not have *enough* whole language classrooms. According to Dyson and Genishi (1993), whole language classrooms are in the minority and studies in various parts of the country indicate that workbooks and worksheets oriented toward the teaching of phonics dominate kindergarten and primary classrooms.

Question: People disagree about the best way to teach beginning readers about phonics. Some professionals advocate that direct, systematic teaching of phonics actually *hampers* learning to read, whereas others believe that trying to teach it in the context of a literature-based approach leaves too much to chance. I'm confused! Which camp is correct?

Answer: Patricia Cunningham, a recognized expert in early literacy and author of *Phonics They Use* (1996), describes her own struggle in determining the role of phonics in helping young children

progress in literacy. She is working hard to convince teachers, publishers, and others that phonics rules and skills describe the *system* of how our language is structured. Mistakenly, phonics are often isolated and taught to children and are what is *tested* (see any number of workbooks and elementary school report cards!), but they are not what children actually *do* when they come to an unknown word they must decode. Cunningham concludes the following (185–186, 192):

The answer to the question of whether phonics should be taught in a synthetic or analytic manner seems to be neither. Synthetic approaches generally teach children to go letter-by-letter, assigning a pronunciation to each letter and then blending the individual letters together. Analytic approaches teach rules and are usually filled with confusing jargon. Brain research, however, suggests that the brain is a *pattern detector*, not a rule applier and that, while we look at single letters, we are looking at them considering all the letter patterns we know. Successfully decoding a word occurs when the brain recognizes a familiar spelling pattern or, if the pattern itself is not familiar, searches through its store of words with similar patterns. . . . The kind of phonics instruction we need and for which we should advocate is not the "old phonics." It is not rules and jargon and worksheets.

Routman (1996) has much to say on this subject also, noting that children rely on sound sequences, visual patterns, graphophonic relationships, and meaning (in other words, familiar patterns) for their invented spelling, actually constructing their own knowledge of phonics. Teachers, in turn, rely on children's invented spelling to tell them what children are picking up relative to phonological awareness.

Phonological awareness activities connected with words children are already familiar with are extremely valuable when used in conjunction with frequent experience with good literature. For novice readers, a child's own name and other sight words are a good beginning, as are familiar songs, nursery rhymes, finger plays, and poems. These can help children learn letter names, match those names to the corresponding shapes, and then match the names and shapes to the corresponding sounds. They need to learn print conventions, that words can be categorized according to their beginning sounds (onsets) and rimes, that phonemes have corresponding graphemes, that there are patterns within words, and that there are particular endings to words—and they can learn all of this in the context of engaging activities with the print they love. Children also enjoy the fun of exchanging phonemes in word families and the many other awareness-raising activities that make learning to read and write as natural as speaking.

For the fewer than 5 percent of children who may have true neurological difficulties in reading without intensive remediation, a synthetic phonics approach may enhance abilities among those children who are visually dyslexic and need to focus more specifically on word parts as a decoding strategy; conversely, for children who have auditory dyslexia, such a teaching strategy would make matters *worse* because breaking an unknown word into letters and then trying to put it back together into a recognizable entity is nearly impossible for them.

Question: Can basal texts and workbooks be included in developmentally appropriate programming?

Answer: At least 75 percent of teachers today are using a published series at least part of the time for reading/language arts instruction, according to Routman (1996, 124). She notes that publishers are doing a better job in organizing mostly unabridged anthologies of literature for young children and admits that these can be helpful to ensure having text at different levels available for skilled and nonskilled readers (although a variety of grade-level texts are usually *not* unavailable in any particular classroom). Increasingly, publishers are supplying ideas for integrating language arts with other areas of the curriculum, and CD-ROMs and other supporting materials can be purchased to accompany the basals, including big books and accompanying smaller sets for shared reading and audio and video cassettes (Combs, 1996). Unfortunately, basals are more expensive than trade books; there is often an overfocus on "skills" and worksheets or workbooks with these published series, little integration of reading and writing, and a shortchanging of the reader with respect to picture cues that help to interpret the text and the other aesthetic and enjoyable aspects gained from handling "real" books (Routman, 1996). Before pro-

fessionals choose to use a basal series, they should decide the types of literacy experiences children need and subject the lesson plans and materials developed by basal authors to the same kinds of decision-making processes as those they create themselves for children (Combs, 1996). Also, children should have access to many other opportunities to enjoy good literature, both narrative and expository. In-classroom libraries should contain 100–150 different choices that children can use for silent and partner reading experiences and as aids during their writing activities.

Question There is a lot of disagreement in our program about "invented" or "temporary" spelling, with both parents and professionals unsure of its use. How can we be sure it isn't harming children's future writing ability?

Answer: Charles Sykes, author of *Dumbing Down Our Kids* (1996) says, "This (invented spelling) is the single cutting-edge issue in education reform," adding that when children come home with misspelled papers, parents' basic expectations of what education *should be* (Hellmich, 1996, 7D1) are violated. Conversely, proponents of temporary spelling claim that it allows children to think about how words are formed . . . and to push their own developing abilities rather than simply raising their hand and having a teacher spell the word correctly for them. Research indicates that when allowed to write freely in preschool through grade two, children take greater risks with their writing and are inclined to draw more sophisticated words from their receptive vocabulary (see Figure 11.5). When not allowed to use invented spelling, children are hampered by having to use only those words they already know how to spell or those they can get someone else to spell for them. Consequently, the content of their writing may be spelled correctly but of necessity quite dull and basic; despite the fact that they may have very rich words in their receptive vocabularies, they would be unable to use them because they have little experience seeing those words in print and are not yet able to use reference materials very efficiently.

As we work with young children, we should not lose sight of what writing is for—communication (Graves, 1994). Children's progress in moving

FIGURE 11.5
Temporary Spelling: "................................."

I'm in the ballet class.

Susan

Kindergarten

toward conventional spelling will depend upon their developing knowledge of phoneme/grapheme connections, visual memory, the amount of daily practice they have in seeing and forming words in print, and the quality of minilessons and writing activities that professionals or parents structure or model for them. We need to do a good job of sharing with parents this information, that temporary spelling really *is* only a temporary

tool. Children's writing progresses toward adult standards in stages much the same way they learned to speak, and parents need to be assured that we *are* guiding children toward that end. The best way to do this is to keep dated work samples of children's work to show parents how children are gaining in their ability to spell words conventionally (see Chapter 16). Increasing numbers of primary teachers are using the technique of having children write the same familiar nursery rhyme (for example, Humpty Dumpty) once a month to demonstrate progress.

Question: Should we be correcting children's writing in their journals?

Answer: No, but that does not mean you cannot have *them* editing their own writing. On an individual basis and after children have begun to write a number of words and sentences using invented spelling, have them begin to edit for targeted errors. For example, prior to their making their journal entry on Tuesday, ask them to go back to Monday's entry and underline just one word that was tough to spell and/or reread and then look it up on the word wall or in the classroom dictionary. Those children who still do not know the alphabetic sequence or are unfamiliar with the use of reference materials will need scaffolded assistance until they are able to use them independently. Another day, you can have children go back for two or three entries and make sure they have a capital letter on each of their sentences. This is an effective way of teaching composition with a contextual approach, just as long as the child is developmentally ready for this next step. Remember—the more *you* do the correcting, the slower the child will be in internalizing the error.

Question: What about the child who is not yet writing? Should I take dictation from individual children?

Answer: It depends on what your objective is. If the child is still in a stage where he or she does not yet know that speech can be captured with symbols on a page, then writing what the child dictates, reading it back to the child, and having the child read it back again is a valuable learning experience for the child. Once the child knows that combinations of letters represent words, that there are spaces between words, and that print communicates to others what we want to tell them, we need to back away from taking dictation from individual children so that their motivation to learn is not hampered. You do, however, need to write in front of children daily, taking time to name the letters for emerging readers and writers and pointing out configurations of particular words. Words that children need to use frequently in their writing can be placed on the classroom word

wall and walked through daily so that they become internalized. Once words go up on the word wall, children should be encouraged to refer to them and expected to spell the words correctly. Classroom dictionaries can be made for each child, with copies updated regularly with the children's help.

Question: What about teaching handwriting? Should we bother to do this at all and, if we do, what should be taught and when should it be taught?

Answer: First of all, penmanship is not truly a *literacy* issue unless the child's graphic production is so illegible that literate content cannot be understood. The National Council of Teachers of English (NCTE) considers the issue a motor production one and no longer includes penmanship in its curricular scope and sequence. Moreover, with the advent of computer use, there is widespread controversy about spending inordinate amounts of time to teach penmanship. Many school systems allow

Developmentally appropriate classrooms are joyful places in which children commit their ideas to paper with confidence.

children to choose a method that is most consistent with their fine motor development; thus, manuscript rather than cursive may continue to be the choice of a second grader, while a well-developed first grader who prefers cursive is allowed to practice and use it. If a district decides that cursive *should* be taught, the wisest choice is probably to introduce it in the second half of the second grade when 90 percent of children would be motorically ready to handle it. Because penmanship is a tool for communicating and not an end initself, children should be allowed to continue with manuscript if they choose to do so or even to edit final drafts of work on the computer. Final drafts of work should be as neatly produced as the child can manage, whatever method is preferred. Donald Graves (1994), who has been involved in writing research for over twenty years, notes that handwriting must be considered separately from content. Often, if handwriting has a poor appearance (again, more males than females), the content of the paper may be unfairly judged as poor or unimportant, whereas children whose penmanship is clear may mistakenly come to believe that what they have written is good simply because of its appearance. Children with major handwriting problems who are asked to reedit over and over "quickly learn to narrow their thinking and write as little as possible" (p. 246). We need to watch getting hung up on "what we've always done" and see graphic production primarily as a means for communicating our thoughts to one another, and there are many avenues for doing that (also see Chapter 12, for information about the physical aspects of handwriting development).

Question: Someone told me that young children should not be copying from the board. Why is that?

Answer: There is documented evidence that boys in kindergarten and first grade are significantly behind girls in their ability to track across print and not lose their place. For near-point containment tasks, this gender difference does not disappear until around the age of 7 (Soderman, 1995). Still, in the second grade, there are children who do not have fully developed visual abilities for scanning and focusing from a distance. The ability of the eye related to far-point convergence or switching frequently between near-point and far-point containment without tiring may also be somewhat problematic. There may be glare from the board, making it difficult to copy, and what is printed may be surrounded by lots of other distracting information or be too small to read without squinting. Children who are sitting at tables with their backs to the board may have difficulty simply from a positional standpoint. The children who are least developed will be the most highly penalized by this practice. Instead of having children copying from a blackboard, many teachers supply the information on laminated boards that can be erased and reused or on individual copies for children. These can be placed at individual tables for children so that unneeded strain and error making are reduced considerably.

GOALS AND OBJECTIVES

The ultimate goal of the language domain is to help children develop their innate capacities to share their thoughts and feelings with others and accurately interpret comunications they receive. The curriculum should include the following experiences:

Intermediate Objectives for Listening/Viewing   As children progress toward the ultimate goal, they will demonstrate the following competencies:

1. Participate in experiences that help them interpret nonverbal messages, including tone of voice and facial expression.
2. Enhance their listening skills.
3. Demonstrate courteous listening behaviors by:
   a. Looking at the speaker.
   b. Sitting relatively still.
   c. Waiting for a turn to speak.
   d. Responding to oral cues.
4. Increase their receptive vocabulary.
5. Identify and discriminate likenesses and differences among sounds (e.g., environmental sounds, letter-sound associations, and words).
6. Improve their ability to focus on relevant oral content and ignore distractions.
7. Develop their understanding of contemporary media (e.g., television, videos, and computer technology) and the impact of media on learning and values.

8. Demonstrate auditory memory by repeating in correct detail and sequence the messages they hear.
9. Demonstrate auditory comprehension and critical listening skills by
   a. Retelling in their own words the messages or stories they hear.
   b. Responding to oral language with relevant comments or questions.
   c. Verbally linking personal experience to what they have heard.
   d. Responding accurately to single- and multistep directions.
   e. Drawing logical conclusions.
   f. Distinguishing facts.
   g. Listening selectively for main ideas.
   h. Experimenting with and discussing different ways to express the same idea.
10. Identify and use resources to investigate a particular question or topic, including knowledgeable people, field trips, reference materials, and electronic media.

Intermediate Objectives for Speaking   As children progress toward the ultimate goal, they will demonstrate the following competencies:

11. Experiment with language sounds, rhythm, volume, pitch, and words.
12. Expand their abilities to
    a. Articulate intents, emotions, and desires.
    b. Describe events from the past, present, or future.
    c. Generate questions and demonstrate understanding of the answers.
    d. Demonstrate their level of comprehension of concepts and situations.
    e. Tell stories about pictures.
    f. Create and describe original imaginative situations.
    g. Persuade others appropriately.
    h. Rephrase or clarify their messages to others.
    i. Present information with clarity, becoming more fluent and coherent.
    j. Present conclusions based on the investigation of an issue or problem.
13. Use appropriate body language (eye contact, body position, and gestures) to alert a listener to their intent and convey emotion.
14. Note how their use of inflections, articulation, volume, intonation, and speed aids or hampers the listener in understanding their messages.

15. Increase their expressive vocabulary in size and precision.
16. Participate in conversations with others.
17. Participate in group conversations with others, with and without teacher guidance.
18. Demonstrate self-confidence and poise in group speaking and creative dramatics activities.

Intermediate Objectives for Writing   As children progress toward the ultimate goal, they will demonstrate the following competencies:

19. Observe others' purposeful writing, thus extending their awareness that writing transforms thoughts, ideas, and feelings into print symbols to communicate meaning.
20. Put their thoughts on paper, first through simple pictures and then progressing through the developmental stages of writing.
21. Utilize their own temporary versions of writing, working gradually toward conventional spelling, handwriting, punctuation, and format.
22. Write for a variety of purposes (e.g., list, inform, narrate, describe, and persuade), increasing the amount and quality of their writing over time.
23. Expand their writing vocabulary.
24. Increase their ability to select topics to write about.
25. Learn to organize their ideas in a logical sequence.
26. Begin to use writing strategies for organizing and planning writing, such as mapping, webbing, and clustering.
27. Express their ideas in complete thoughts.
28. Improve their ability to evaluate and edit their writing, preparing rough and final drafts, and publishing narrative, expository, and other text forms.
29. Describe their goals and challenges in writing to others.
30. Use reference materials to help them improve their writing, including electronic sources.
31. Explore and discuss differences in words, phrases, and language patterns used in spoken and written contexts within their own environment and from other cultures.
32. Identify and use correct formats for certain types of writing (e.g., personal letters, business letters, stories, and scripts).
33. Use writing to create original stories, poems, and informational pieces.

34. Use aspects of the writer's craft to formulate and express ideas, including dialogue, characterization, conflict, and logic.
35. Word process on the computer.

Intermediate Objectives for Reading   As children progress toward the ultimate goal, they will demonstrate the following competencies:

36. Enjoy shared reading experiences with varied genres of literature, including classic and contemporary literature.
37. Acquire an adequate reading vocabulary.
38. Practice readinglike behavior, moving from "pretend" reading to attempting to match the flow of their own language with book illustrations and with print.
39. Respond to written symbols in the environment (e.g., their name and the names of others, signs, advertisements, and labels).
40. Make predictions about what will come next in stories that are being read, based on the information in the text and/or their personal life experiences.
41. Discuss or demonstrate, either for listening or independent reading, how the characteristics of various narrative genre and story elements convey ideas and perspectives through
    a. Story sequence (first, next, last; beginning, middle, and end; before and after).
    b. Main ideas both at literal and inferential levels.
    c. Characters and character development.
    d. Setting.
    e. Plot development; cause and effect; problem and solution; logical conclusions.
42. Understand the relationship of reading to writing and thinking.
43. Tell or dramatize their own versions of stories to show comprehension of what they have read.
44. Create new endings for stories, drawing on logical elements of the original stories.
45. Read familiar or memorized nursery rhymes, songs, poems, and plays.
46. Distinguish between real and make-believe, fact and opinion, in written materials.
47. Read their own writing.
48. Expand their phonological and print awareness (e.g., identify upper- and lowercase letters, sight vocabulary, rhymes and rhyming words, segmen-

tation, common blends, vowel patterns, common contractions, common digraphs, and concepts about letter-sound relationships).

49. Develop a sight vocabulary and read simple lists and stories.
50. Read independently and construct meaning from both narrative and expository text, using decoding strategies (e.g., picture cues, context clues, phonic analysis, and syntax) to predict what makes sense.
51. Read fluently with expression and clarity.
52. Identify the parts of a book—cover (title, author, and illustrator), dedication page, table of contents, chapters, headings, and index.
53. Access print to seek information, ideas, enjoyment, and understanding of their individuality, our common humanity, and the rich diversity of our society.
54. Apply knowledge, ideas, and issues drawn from texts to their lives and the lives of others.
55. Become familiar with libraries as interesting places to find books and other materials for entertainment and information.
56. Evaluate their developing literacy skills, identifying their strengths and needs.
57. Use information gained from reading to compare/contrast/analyze/infer/express ideas and solve problems.

TEACHING STRATEGIES

To optimize language and literacy acquisition, teachers may utilize the following strategies:

1. *Structure a communication-rich environment.*

a. *Model appropriate, rich language usage.* Although you will not expect standard English usage from all children, you need to have a good command of it yourself. In addition, your diction needs to be clear and understandable to the children, with interesting vocabulary that stretches the children's understanding of and interest in the language.
b. *Listen to and talk with each child daily.* The school day is busy from beginning to end, and it is far too easy to neglect children who do not expect or demand attention. By making it a rule of thumb that every child will have a personal conversation with you each day, you are more apt to make individual attention a priority.

c. *Take advantage of spontaneous events to promote children's language development through discussion.* Some of the richest teaching moments occur unplanned. If you are too "scripted" by your teaching plans, you may not notice how something a child brings to the class, a change in the weather, or a serendipitous event can more effectively reach your immediate or long-range teaching goals.

d. *When a child states something, extend his or her phrase by repeating it using a new term or adding an appropriate clause.* Often, there is an opportunity to extend a child's vocabulary by repeating all or part of what a child says using an interesting synonym for a word or two or by adding a related idea.

e. *Plan the learning environment and the curriculum to provide opportunities for children to communicate informally with one another.* The activity-oriented classroom provides the natural environment for peer interaction. It is challenging to plan for children's purposeful conversations but very important for their continuing language growth.

f. *Plan activities each day in which the primary goal is for children to use language to describe events, make predictions, or evaluate phenomena.* Not all that you want to help happen in language development will occur

through activity centers. You need to plan particular small- and large-group experiences that stretch children's abilities to express themselves in particular ways. The challenge then is to see that each child in the group has enough opportunities to speak, and is developing the confidence and skill to do so.

2. *Structure a print-rich environment.* This should be one that integrates language development activities and quality literature throughout all areas of the early childhood curriculum. Because all subjects require language for learning, you will need to plan content around the language forms of listening/viewing, speaking, reading, and writing. High-quality literature uses language in its most crafted forms, and it is available at appropriate levels on nearly all topics of interest to children, so you will want to make a variety of literature central in your classroom. The literature will have important meanings for the children when you help them explore its relationships to, or its contrasts with, their own lives.

Consciously create an environment that highlights print in every area of the room (charts, bookmaking materials, labels, names, directions, recipes, menus, children's writing, etc.). The print that children see around them becomes their primary resource

Danielle has taken advantage of the paper and markers available in the block area to let others know she wants her road to remain undisturbed.

for their own writing and reading. In addition, make the environmental print serve real uses in your classroom. Put print materials at eye level for the children. Draw attention to print messages, pointing to letters or words and asking why the messages are important; refer to them at appropriate times. Model print concepts often by cueing left to right, top to bottom, page turning, and noting word and sentence formations (e.g., spaces between words, types of punctuation).

3. *Model and teach the importance of developing and using good listening skills.* Because our listening skills are used more than any other language skill (on average, nearly 50 percent of our waking hours), do not leave skill building in this area to chance!

a. *Model good listening behavior* by attending to the children and responding to their verbalizations. Modeling listening behaviors for children is often difficult to do because there are so many demands on your time. Stopping, looking at the child, and reacting probably will be the most important teaching of listening that you do.

b. *Give children appropriate cues* to help them listen better. Say, "Look up here" or "Watch me"; use voice inflections; change your volume appropriately for the small- or large-group setting. You cannot expect children to know how to listen well, although they often are more attentive listeners than adults are. Clues to listening behavior will be useful for them and lessen your frustration over inattentive listening behavior.

c. *Introduce sound discrimination* by using common environmental sounds (e.g., telephone or doorbell) and gradually alert children to interesting sound-symbol relationships in written language. Alerting children to the sounds in their environment calls attention to common experiences that are easily overlooked and creates understanding about hearing and sounds. When parents helped these children to learn to speak, they did not focus their attention on the individual sounds that made up the words they were learning. Sounds and the letters that represent them on paper are more readily understood when they are examined in the context of a song, poem, or story the children enjoy. Early, brief, and natural encounters with phonics, usually on a class chart or a whiteboard, ensures that sound-symbol relationships will not be overwhelming or confusing.

d. *Maintain children's attention* using props, gestures, proximity, and/or particular facial and vocal expressions but also gradually help children maintain attention without extra elements. A book, puppet, picture, or your special action is a useful attention getter; often, it visualizes for the children a concept that is difficult for them to conceive. But it is also important for the children to create their own mind pictures about the words they hear. You will need to plan listening experiences that develop the children's imaginations from verbal stimuli alone as well as with aids.

4. *Involve children every day in engaging reading experiences.*

a. *Read to the children* at least once every day, more whenever possible. Most teachers know that reading to children is important, and they love to share quality books with their classes. As those who understand the interdependence of language learnings, they know that listening to well-written prose and poetry has significant effects on children's developing reading and writing abilities and interests. Remember that children who may come from literacy-impoverished homes are in even greater need of read-aloud opportunities, including lap experiences.

b. *Utilize a variety of literary forms* when reading to children (picture books, poetry, folk and fairy tales, and factual books). Most teachers give children a read-aloud diet rich in stories. You will want to plan your oral reading time carefully so that you "tune your children's ears" to the ideas presented in a variety of genres and also to the vocabulary and sentence structures typical of different forms of writing.

c. *Draw attention to story* sequence and development, characters, cause and effect, main ideas, and details, but only when these discussions will not interfere with the children's enjoyment of the story. There are many opportunities when you are reading to children to teach them important concepts. You will want to do that on some occasions, but it is also important to preserve the continuity of what the children are listening to and the integrity of the overall meaning.

d. *Involve children* in songs, chants, poems, finger plays, rhymes, choral readings, and dramatic play. Dramatic activity is a natural learning mode for children. You will want to plan for the overt involvement of all the children as much as possible. Combining speaking or singing with reading the lyrics of these favorite songs or poems leads children into intuitively learning about reading.

e. *Plan for silent reading (book time) and shared reading experiences for children.* Even before children are reading, they can spend time looking through familiar books or picture books, putting their imaginations to work in rethinking what went on in the text. As they develop reading abilities, children can work with a reading partner, each of them reading a paragraph or page. Having to stop at a particular point draws children's attention to punctuation and capital letters, and the communicative aspects of print are enhanced.

5. *Involve children every day in enjoyable writing experiences.*

a. *Write in front of them every day.* Daily, in large group, have children take turns dictating a message. These can be centered on their own experiences and observations or even brief stories developed by the entire group. This allows the children to hear and see their own words in print, written in "adult language." As they dictate, they are able to concentrate on what they want to say without struggling with writing those ideas and words down. In this kind of activity, they are able to dictate longer, more complex pieces than they can get down on paper by themselves, and this models how messages are composed. Be sure to write what the childen say; they need to know that you value what is said and how it is said. Ideas can come from the group about how something might be "fixed" until everyone is satisfied with the message.

b. *Provide daily opportunities for children to write* and share their writing with peers and their teacher. Writing is learned by doing it. The daily play-based experiences chidren have putting their ideas on paper—usually first in pictures, squiggles, and letterlike approximations, and later in letters, words spelled in invented ways, and then in sentences—equate with the proess they went through learning to speak. Just as in learning to speak, much improvement comes naturally as children "practice." Children need access to a variety of materials for making their own print. Place writing materials in all centers of the room: order blanks for the pretend restaurant, sticks for making words in the sandbox, and so on. Provide reference materials, such as a simplified dictionary, in some centers so that children can readily use them.

c. *Allow invented spelling,* introducing editing as appropriate on an individual basis. Each child's level of performance in writing will depend on the opportunities he or she has had to write at home and in previous grades at school, understanding of the purposes of printed language, and the degree to which efforts have been accepted by others. Avoid drawing attention to words and letters as the children write so they can concentrate on the meanings they are trying to express. It has been a common school practice to spell words for children as they write or, before the writing session begins, to list on the blackboard words children think they might need, but these "helps" focus children's attention away from their thoughts toward correct form. At other, more appropriate times (such as morning message or daily news), point out similarities and differences in words, correct or unusual spellings, rhyming words, use of capital letters, and punctuation. Their enthusiasm for writing grows as they hear the responses of peers to their efforts. The children's writing can be shared through bulletin board displays or "published" books, or read by the child when he or she has a turn in the author's chair.

d. *Provide writer's workshop or minilessons* for teaching the appropriate elements of the writing process as is developmentally appropriate for the children with whom you are working: topic selection, drafting, and sharing drafts. In earlier stages of emerging writing, children write best and write most about the topics they know and care about. They often find it difficult and unpleasing to change their writing after it is on paper or to edit for mechanical errors. Gradually, young children will add additional words and sentences to their pieces or correct errors, and some young children may begin higherlevel revision strategies as they take increasing pride in what they have produced. You will want to take care not to push the children into revising or editing too soon for fear of diminishing their initial efforts in writing. Asking the child to read a piece to you or the other children often helps him or her see changes that need to be made.

6. *Plan literacy games, songs, and other play-oriented activities to enhance children's phonological and print awareness.* Children do need to develop letter-sound associations and phoneme-grapheme knowledge, and any activities structured to help them do so

should be carefully embedded in meaningful experiences. Call attention to letters individually and in words when reading charts of familiar poems, dictated writing, and so on. Highlight configuration of letters and familiar words by drawing around them and pointing out unique features of a particular letter or word. Draw children's attention, also, to various writing forms by providing examples (upper- and lowercase letters; manuscript, cursive and italic forms; contractions; boldface, etc.) when they appear in contexts interesting to children. Model strategies for figuring out how to read unfamiliar words.

7. *Accept children's risk taking in their listening, speaking, writing, and reading,* even when their efforts do not result in correct or useful production. Teachers sometimes are so anxious to have learning occur that they "take over" and provide the correct answer, when they should think instead about what the next small step is in the scaffolding process. Children's motivation to discover or remember how symbols work can be hampered when there is too much adult "help," thereby making the child more dependent on future help.

8. *Structure useful assessment strategies* to ensure that children are making progress in every area of the language domain. You will want to observe, record children's developing strengths and needs, save work samples that indicate progress, and involve children in the evaluation process (see Chapter 16 for specific suggestions).

ACTIVITY SUGGESTIONS

The following activities are structured to support children's growth in the language domain. Included are ideas for enhancing skills, processes, and concepts in each of the subareas of listening/viewing, speaking, writing, and reading. Clearly, more than one language objective is being supported in any of the suggested activities, and that is the hallmark of a well-designed activity. However, the *primary* purpose of each activity will be to focus on the objective specifically cited. This allows professionals to determine whether they are offering growth-producing experiences in each of the subareas and across the curriculum.

Because you may be dealing with children in any or all stages of emergent through fluent literacy and from 3 to 8 years of age, you will need to adapt these ideas to the developmental and experiential levels of the individual children with whom you are working. To aid that transition, suggestions are given for simplifying or extending each of the activities.

✎ Imitating Clapping Patterns*

Objective 11   For children to experiment with language sounds.

Materials   None

Procedure   Ask children to listen carefully while you clap a pattern (clap, pause, clap, clap, pause) to see if they can repeat it and move on to more complex and longer patterns as the children gain experience. Eventually have the children clap each other's patterns.

To simplify   Begin with very simple patterns

To extend   Move on to having them clapping the syllables in their names and other words.

✎ Song Writers†

Objective 12   For children to create and describe original imaginative situations.

Materials   None

Procedure   Sing songs with the children such as "Aiken Drum" and "Rig-a-Jig-Jig" for which they have to think of a key element (an article of clothing, a name of a person or animal, a color, a food, etc.) at certain junctures in the song. Encourage their participation and creative or original contributions.

To simplify   Sing only those songs with which the children are familiar.

To extend   Have children make up their own additional verses. Have children write out the songs individually and create their own elements.

Aiken Drum
(Traditional tune or chant)

There was a man lived in the moon,
Lived in the moon, lived in the moon.
There was a man lived in the moon,
And his name was Aiken Drum.

Source: Kostelnik et al. (1991).
†*Source:* Kostelnik et al. (1991).

Verse 1:

And he played upon a ladle,
a ladle, a ladle,
And he played upon a ladle,
And his name was Aiken Drum.

Change verses; for example:

And his coat was made of roast beef, etc.
And his buttons were made of strawberries, etc.
And his hair was made of spaghetti, etc.

Rig-a-Jig-Jig

(Tune: Let's All Sing Like the Birdies Sing)

As I was walkin' down the street,
down the street, down the street,
A (color) (animal)
I happened to meet,
Hi ho, hi ho, hi ho
Rig-a-jig-jig and away we go,
Away we go, away we go
Rig-a-jig-jig and away we go
Hi ho, hi ho, hi ho.
(Repeat with new color and animal).

✎ Listen and Dismiss

Objective 2   For children to enhance their listening skills.

Materials   None

Procedure   Once children have been together in a learning setting for several months, they begin to know one another's voices. This natural development can be used to help them focus their auditory senses in order to discover who is speaking to them without actually seeing the person. Model the listening game during large group by turning your chair around just before dismissing children and having one child at a time say, "Good morning, Mr. (Ms.) _____. How are you?" As you recognize the child's voice, respond by saying, "Very well, thank you, (*Child's Name*)," and excuse the child from the large group. As children listen carefully, they pick up on the nuances of the other children's voices. They can then participate by closing their eyes during dismissal and seeing if they can guess who is speaking to the teacher.

To simplify   Significantly reduce the number of voices that must be discriminated by designating only

four or five speakers in the large group before beginning the game, with the remainder of children being the listeners. The game may also be played in a small group of only four or five children, cutting down on the discrimination difficulty.

To extend   Individual children are chosen each day to play the role of teacher and be the dismisser.

✎ Going on a Sound Walk

Objective 6   For children to improve ability to focus on relevant oral content and ignore distractions.

Materials   None

Procedure   Tell the children they will be going on a walk (either inside the building or outside) to "collect" all the various sounds they can hear. Once on the walk, have the children stop every 25–50 steps (a good counting exercise, also!) and stand completely still, listening for 20 seconds to the different sounds they hear in that space. Before going on, ask the children what sounds they were able to hear, encouraging them to listen very carefully for unique sounds they may have never noticed before in that area.

To simplify   Practice "collecting sounds" while sitting in large group in the classroom by having the children be as silent as possible for approximately 20 seconds and then discuss the different sounds.

To extend   Upon returning to the room, record with the children on chart paper (or have children record in their journals) all the sounds they can remember hearing from the beginning to the end of the walk.

✎ Packing My Suitcase

Objective 8   For children to demonstrate auditory memory by repeating in correct detail and sequence the messages they hear.

Materials   None

Procedure   Seat the children in a circle. The teacher (or a child who has played the game previously) begins the process by saying, "I'm going on a trip, and in my suitcase I am taking a bathing suit."). The person to his or her right then says the exact same thing, adding an article (e.g., "I'm going on a trip, and in my suitcase I am taking a bathing suit and a towel."). The speaker must remember all of the articles in the correct sequence or is "out" of the game and moves inside the circle until there is one person remaining.

To simplify   It is important to eliminate the competitive aspect of the game with very young children. If they cannot remember the articles in sequence, have the group help them out. Go on only as long as the children seem to be enjoying the challenge of remembering the number of items and then move on to another activity. The game can also be made simpler by playing it with a smaller group of children so there is less to remember.

To extend   Have the children think of other categories. For example, they can go on a "trip" to a specific place and collect things found in that place. They may elect to go to a zoo and collect zoo animals, to a farm, to a country outside the United States, and so on. They may play the part of a community worker and think of different items that person needs to do his or her work (e.g., a police officer will need a police car, handcuffs, a gun, a walkie-talkie, and a badge).

✎ Viewing a Story through Different Lenses

Objective 7   For children to develop their understanding of contemporary media (e.g., television, videos, and computer technology) and the impact of media on learning and values.

Materials   Copy of children's book by Roald Dahl, *Charlie and the Chocolate Factory* (1988, New York: Puffin Books), video of *Willy Wonka and the Chocolate Factory* (available from Films Incorporated, 440 Park Ave. S., New York, NY 10016, 1-800-323-4222, Ext. 234), and VCR and monitor

Procedure   Using Dahl's book (or any other for which a video is available), read the story to the children (or have them read it independently), providing time for discussion after each section to talk about the way characters are portrayed and the plot developed. Following completion of the written story, have children view the story on video. Develop a Venn diagram with the children, looking at ways the book and video are similar and how they are different. For example, are the characters depicted differently? Is the story line the same or different? Which did they enjoy most and why?

To simplify   Choose a highly familiar text for emerging readers, such as *Goldilocks and the Three Bears,* so that children have a good sense of the characters and plot. Eliminate use of the Venn diagram in the activity.

To extend   Have the children role-play a familiar story and then create their own video.

✎ Puppet Drama

Objective 43   For children to tell or dramatize versions of stories to show comprehension of what they have read.

Materials   Children's storybook of *The Little Red Hen* (or another familiar story) and stick puppets of characters in the story

Procedure   Read the story to the children several times over a number of days, having brief discussions afterward to learn whether the children have a good sense of the characters and plot. Select a story narrator and supply other children with stick puppets of the characters. Have the remainder of the children act as the audience. Have the players reenact the story, encouraging those in the audience to listen carefully and applaud at the end. Switch roles so that all children have a chance to be either an actor or a participant in the audience.

To simplify   Supply all children in large group with a stick puppet. Have them stand when coming to that character, putting their puppet in the air and saying the character's line.

To extend   Have the children make the puppets from materials provided to them. Choose other familiar stories to have them play with puppets provided to them or ones they create.

✎ Favorite Character from *Goldilocks and the Three Bears*

Objective 12   For children to expand the ability to persuade others appropriately.

Materials   Drawings children have made of characters from the story "Goldilocks and the Three Bears" (or another familiar selection)

Procedure   Following the reading of several versions of "Goldilocks and the Three Bears," create a chart, listing the characters from the story. Have each child indicate on the chart which of the characters is their favorite and then have him or her create a drawing of that character. Explain to them that you are going to have them show their illustrations and try to persuade the others to change their minds about which character is the most interesting. Talk about the importance of what they *say* about the character, and tell them that the illustration is only to support what they say. Encourage them to have at least two reasons why the character is their favorite. Provide time for each of them to show the illustration they have produced and to talk about why the character is their favorite. Create a chart similar to the first one to see if anyone changes his or her mind about which character is their favorite. Compare the charts.

To simplify   Eliminate the illustrations and simply have children go up to the chart to make their mark, giving one reason why they have chosen that character.

To extend   Choose other persuasion topics (e.g., each child's favorite TV show, favorite food, favorite book, or the occupation they would prefer when they grow up).

✎ Just Like Mine

Objective 9   For children to demonstrate auditory comprehension by responding accurately to single- and multistep directions.

Materials: Bristle blocks or small unit blocks and a divider to separate person giving directions and person responding

Procedure   Construct a temporary divider on a table so that a child sitting on one side cannot see what the child on the other side is doing. Supply each child with the exact number and kind of colored blocks to make a structure. Challenge children to work together cooperatively to see if they can build the exact structures with one child first building something and then giving directions to the other child to reproduce the structure by only listening to the directions and not looking at the product. When they are finished, have the children remove the divider to see how well the one child was able to provide directions and how well the other child was able to follow them.

To simplify   Provide only a limited number of blocks. Have the children use colored blocks so they have more clues.

To extend   Provide paper and markers to the children. Have one child construct a drawing and then talk another child through reproducing the same illustration. Have them compare and discuss where the directions were clear or not so clear and difficult to understand.

✎ Book Making

Objective 20   For children to put thoughts on paper, first through simple pictures and then progressing through the developmental stages of writing.

Materials   Various kinds and colors of paper, markers, scissors, and glue

Procedure   Having very young children create their own books is one of the best activities to encourage them to write. A variety of books can be made, including "peek-a-boo" books, pop-up books, shape books (cover is in the outline of a particular animal or other theme), and accordian books (paper is folded accordian-style, with each section illustrating separate parts of the story), and flip books (cut into three sections, with head of person or animal on top section; torso on middle section; legs and feet on bottom section). Provide examples of differently constructed books. Explain the tools and techniques needed to construct them. Provide help as needed. Encourage children to draw different pictures on each page and to write as much as they are capable of under each of the illustrations.

To simplify   Provide very young children with a blank book that has already been constructed, having them complete the book as appropriate, given their fine-motor and literacy capabilities. Focus on only one type of construction at a time.

To extend   Challenge the children to come up with their own themes and shapes relevant to the content of the particular story they have written.

✎ Putting Humpty Together Again . . . and Again . . . and Again

Objective 21   For children to utilize their temporary versions of writing, working gradually toward conventional spelling, handwriting, punctuation, and format.

Materials   Paper and pencil or markers

Procedure   As an assessment and evaluation procedure, periodically have children illustrate and write the rhyme, Humpty Dumpty. Standardize the assessment by having the children spend only 15 minutes on the task. Have them use a date stamp to date their work sample, put their name on it, and place it in their portfolio for future comparisons. When the work samples are dated and saved, they become an excellent vehicle for the children to compare their earlier and later versions to see how they are growing in ability to represent detail through their drawing and qualitative movement toward conventional spelling, handwriting, punctuation, and format.

To simplify   At first, very young children may only be able to illustrate the rhyme and later add their first name. Later, they may use temporary spelling to reproduce some of the words. Do not point out children's errors at this time. Simply encourage them to do their best.

To extend   Once children are able to write all of the rhyme and have spelled many of the words correctly, have them begin to compare their samples with the original rhyme and make the corrections needed. Have them add an original story about why Humpty Dumpty could not be put back together and how it might be done.

✎ What's in a Name?

Objective 48   For children to expand phonological and print awareness.

Materials   Magnetic or moveable letters, paper and pencil or markers

Procedure   Have children work in dyads. Supply magnetic or moveable letters that are in each of their names. Challenge them to use the letters to make as many words as they can. Have them record the words as they find them and total up the number they get at the end of the time provided for the activity.

To simplify   Provide the 26 individual letters of the alphabet and encourage children to simply form any words they can from those letters.

To extend   Have older children work in groups of three or four, writing as many words as they can in a certain time period. Use as a math exercise as well by having them assign one point to two- or three-letter words, 2 points to four- or five-letter words, and 10

points to words of six or more letters. Have them write down the words they are able to make and total up the number of points they have been able to earn at the end of the time period. Second and third graders enjoy the competition in comparing their group results with those of other groups. Remember that *individual* competition is not appropriate; nor is group competition appropriate for children below grade two.

✎ Morning Message

Objective 19   For children to observe others' purposeful writing, extending awareness that writing transforms thoughts, ideas, and feelings into print symbols to communicate meaning.

Materials   White board or easel paper and markers

Procedure   Using a white board or easel paper, the teacher writes one to three sentences dictated by the children. The children are then asked to read the sentences back. As children become more familiar with the process, the teacher can put some "question word" reminders in the upper left-hand corner of the paper (e.g., how, what, who, why, when, and where). A child is selected to dictate a story about a personal experience while the teacher writes, purposely making some errors for the children to catch (e.g., ignoring some punctuation or misspelling some words). After each sentence is written, the children go back to the beginning to read what has been written so far. When the story is finished, the teacher works with the children to correct any errors they see in the text or make changes in the text to clarify or extend some points.

To simplify   Use only one sentence to begin with. As children's writing skills increase, the teacher makes errors that should be apparent to most of them. As he or she corrects the errors on the advice of the children, children at a less sophisticated level are picking up skills by watching what the children are catching and the teacher is correcting.

To extend   The teacher takes dictation (about three or four sentences) from the group and then goes back through each line of the text, asking if there are any errors that should be circled. As children call them out, the teacher circles them and then asks the children to write the message in their journals, individually making their own corrections where they believe they are needed.

✎ **What's the Question?**

Objective 33 For children to use the writing process to create original stories, poems, and informational pieces.

Materials Journals and markers or pencils

Procedure Stimulate the children to imagine what something looks like that cannot be seen (e.g., a leprechaun). Have them take out their journals and draw a picture of the thing on the left-hand page of the journal and write a question they would like to ask. The children leave their journals open to that page, and sometime after they leave the classroom and return the next morning, an answer appears on the right-hand page of the journal. Though children really know that the teacher is providing the answer, they love the fun of imagining the answer has really come from the leprechaun. Some teachers add to the fun by making small footprints across the page accompanying the answer.

To simplify Children at the prewriting stage may act as a group to dictate some of their questions on the left-hand side of paper on an easel. That evening, the questions are answered on the right-hand side. The next day, in large group, the teacher has the children help her read each question and answer.

To extend Challenge the children to illustrate and write to other imaginary or mythical characters (e.g., unicorn, fairy, or man in the moon) or real objects that are difficult to see (e.g., germs or a mouse that hides). When answering the question they have written, add a question they must answer in turn.

✎ **It's a Fact!**

Objective 50 For children to learn to read independently in both narrative and expository text.

Materials Expository texts containing facts and information about famous persons, 3 × 5 cards, pencils

Procedure Have children choose a famous person they would like to learn more about. Making available a number of expository texts at an appropriate reading level, have them search the books to find at least ten facts of interest about that person. Have them record only one fact on each card. Have children report to the rest of the class what they have found out about that person.

To simplify Have children work with a partner to find three or more facts about a particular person.

To extend Have children convert their facts into a set of questions and answers. These can be used by the children to set up a "Trivial Pursuit" or "Jeopardy" game to challenge one another about the facts. Some children may even enjoy making up and illustrating a board game using the facts they have gathered.

✎ **Secret Message**

Objective 48 For children to expand their phonological and print awareness.

Materials White board or easel paper and marker

Procedure Using a "Wheel of Fortune" approach, print out dashes where the letters for words in a "secret message" would be (e.g., _ _ _ _   _ _   _   _ _ _ _ _ _   _ _ _ _ _ _ !). Have children guess a letter, and, if it appears in the message, the teacher writes it in. If the letter appears more than once in the message, print it in all places as it is guessed. As letters are guessed, write them on the right side of the board so that children can see which have been guessed already. This is a valuable exercise because it is so engaging for children. They learn letter-sound associations and sight vocabulary as they see words produced from the letters (in this case, the message was "This is a secret message!").

To simplify Limit the number and complexity of the words. Put in the vowels to begin with and have children fill in only the consonants, which are easier for them.

To extend Extend the complexity of the message, using words that take letters less often seen (e.g., X and Z). Eliminate putting the guessed letters on the side of the board so that memory must be relied on more.

✎ **Find a Rhyme**

Objective 45 For children to read familiar nursery rhymes.

Materials Books of nursery rhymes

Procedure During silent reading, pair children up with a reading buddy. Give each set of children one or two books containing nursery rhymes. Have them take turns reading the rhymes to one another.

To simplify   Use a big book of nursery rhymes with a small group of children, having them read along with you. After reading each rhyme, see if they can tell you the pairs of words that rhyme.

To extend   Supply small white boards and markers to children and after they have read the rhymes to one another, have them find and write as many pairs of rhyming words as they can.

SUMMARY

A child's first word is a joyous experience for any family, signaling a lifetime of communication with others. Additional markers in the development of language are the child's first indications of interest in and emerging facility with symbolic language.

Although there are innate drives to develop linguistic abilities, the environment has a critical role in the quality of children's developing capabilities to use language effectively, imaginatively, and confidently. Adults are important players in this unfolding process. Their role is to model listening/viewing, speaking, reading, and writing skills and to help the child gain access to a balanced variety of well-designed experiences to enhance understanding and independent use of the language.

To be as effective as possible, early childhood educators must have expertise related to the emergence of language and literacy skills. Because of the many ongoing controversies surrounding the teaching of reading and writing skills, they must also have a well-researched theoretical perspective about the best practices in guiding children's progress and the capability of articulating it to others. They will need practical knowledge about structuring optimal learning environments that promote communication capabilities, an ability to draw the child's attention toward print in a variety of ways, and skill in providing the scaffolded experiences children need to move to new levels of understanding and use of language.

If we want children to be competent readers and writers, they must be involved in quality writing and reading activities on a daily basis. Their phonological and print awareness can be fostered and extended through well-designed, meaningful activities that support their individual acquisition of skills and concepts. All of this can take place most easily in a Developmentally Appropriate Program where educators appreciate the complexity of factors affecting language and literacy development, where language can be naturally integrated across other developmental domains, and where children's unique interests, strengths, and needs are considered.

Applying What You Read in This Chapter

1. **Discuss**
   a. Adding the information gained in this chapter to your own experience with young children, go back to the six questions that open the chapter and reexamine them.
   b. If you were interviewing for a position in a school district as a first-grade teacher and a search committee member asked you to talk about your philosophy in teaching young children to read and write, how would you respond?
   c. Name one of the strategies in this chapter that you feel confident about and another that seems more difficult to implement. Discuss why the second would be more difficult and what it would take to remove the barrier(s).

2. **Observe**
   a. Observe a classroom of children who are 3 years of age or younger, listening for examples of language and speech. Notice if there are any children who appear to have significantly less advanced or more advanced skills based on the developmental characteristics outlined in Table 11.1. Discuss your findings with the classroom professional.
   b. Make an appointment to observe the classroom of an experienced early childhood teacher. What evidence do you see that supports a print-rich environment or the need for enhancing that aspect of the learning environment? What strategies do you see that match or disagree with the

philosophical underpinnings about emerging literacy presented in this chapter?

3. **Carry out an activity**

a. Look at three different basal texts for a specific grade level. Is there a common vocabulary among the three? What approaches do the publishers support for making the reading experience developmentally appropriate? How viable are these suggestions based on your understanding of differences in young children at this age? Can you suggest two or three additional ideas that would enhance the use of a basal text for children in this age group?

b. Identify one issue presented in this chapter that you continue to be unsure about. Refer to the latest issues of several professional journals such as *Phi Delta Kappan, Educational Leadership, Young Children,* and *Reading Teacher* to see if you can learn more about resolving the issue. Write a one- or two-page position paper following your investigation.

4. **Create something for your portfolio**

a. Develop a language-based lesson plan based on the format provided in Chapter 3 of this text.

5. **Add to your journal**

a. Think about your earliest experiences with reading and writing. What were your favorite books? What can you remember about the process of learning to read? How much do you think your earliest experiences are related to your leisure-time literature choices as an adult?

b. Identify one goal you have for either extending your expertise relative to understanding children's emerging literacy or planning for more effective application of teaching strategies. What steps do you plan to take in order to reach this goal?

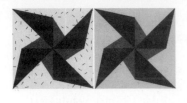

Chapter 12

The Physical Domain

You may wonder:

Is sending young children outdoors to play enough to support their physical development?

How do children develop the fine motor skills necessary for writing?

Are young children capable of learning health and safety information?

What kinds of motor skills are appropriate for children to learn?

How are perceptual motor development and motor development different?

What information do young children need to participate in their own safety and make healthy choices?

In this chapter on the physical domain, we present information to help you answer these questions.

PHYSICAL ACTIVITY

Mrs. Runningdeer scanned the room where small groups of 3- to-5-year-olds were engaging in large motor activities. Smiling, she watched three girls swinging a styrofoam mallets at soft foam balls suspended by strings from the dropped ceiling.

Carrie, who was not quite 3, held her mallet up and twirled it around and around. Sometimes the ball went swinging as her mallet contacted it from the front or the back. Her arm and wrist did not appear to move. Each hit appeared to be entirely accidental She was grinning joyously.

Jung Ji looked like she was really concentrating on hitting the ball, with eyes intently focused on it. Holding her mallet firmly with one hand, she swung it up and down from the shoulder and the elbow in a chopping motion. Occasionally, the mallet hit the edge of the ball, causing it to move. When the ball was moving briskly, Jung Ji missed her target every time. Eventually, she slowed down her strike attempts until the ball was still or nearly so.

Tabby, at 4$\frac{1}{2}$ the oldest and tallest of the three, was also focused on her ball as she swung the mallet from the right shoulder with her forearm partially extended, moving the right foot with a half rotation of her whole body. When she connected, the force was great, sending the ball swinging out fast in the full arc of the string. Sometimes Tabby did not move back fast enough, and the soft ball hit her. She struck the ball about once every three or four swings.

Mrs. Runningdeer recognized that Carrie was just exploring the mallet and hanging ball; Jung Ji was in the first stage of striking, and Tabby was further along in learning to strike the ball but was by no means at a mature skills level. Mrs. Runningdeer moved forward to encourage the play and to encourage Tabby to step into the strike using the other foot.

Mrs. Runningdeer is very knowledgeable about motor behavior for these preschool-aged children. Having arranged the equipment in the environment, she is providing encouragement and instruction as children play, with an understanding of each child's competence and what steps come next as they increase in skill.

Importance of Physical Activity

Children benefit from regular physical activity in many ways, a few of which are listed here (Seefeldt & Vogel, 1986, 1–2).

Physical activity does these things:

❏ Promotes changes in brain structure and function in infants and young children. Sensory stimulation through physical activity is essential for the optimal growth and development of the young nervous system.
❏ Assists in the development and refinement of perceptual abilities involving vision, balance, and tactile sensations.
❏ Enhances the function of the central nervous system through the promotion of a healthier neuronal network.
❏ Fortifies the mineralization of the skeleton and promotes the maintenance of lean body tissue, while simultaneously reducing the deposition of fat.
❏ Leads to proficiency in the neuromuscular skills that are the basis for successful participation in games, dance, sports, and leisure activities.
❏ Improves aerobic fitness, muscle endurance, muscle power, and muscle strength.
❏ Enhances self-concept and self-esteem as indicated by increased confidence, assertiveness, emotional stability, independence, and self-control.
❏ Effectively deters mental illness and alleviates mental stress.

Children obtain these benefits when they are able to participate in a variety of motor activities and are motivated to engage in regular vigorous play.

Because physical play is an integral part of the social life of childhood, competence as a participant enables children to interact with others, solve problems as they arise during play, and develop concepts of fairness. Over time, children also establish lifestyle patterns of food selection, eating, safety, and healthy daily life practices. They become participants in providing for their own safety, selecting their own foods, and engaging in health practices that many will maintain throughout their lifetime. As children begin to do more for themselves and learn how to keep themselves safe and healthy, they may have fewer contagious illnesses, sounder teeth, and avoid preventable injury. Meanwhile, adults remain substantially responsible for maintaining a safe and sanitary environment, providing adequate health services, as well as teaching young children what they can do for themselves.

Principles of Motor Development

Let us briefly review the basic concepts of directions of development, gross and fine motor development, and the roles of growth, maturation, and experience.

Developmental Direction   The body develops in an orderly way. *Cephalocaudal* development means that the child develops from the head to the foot, with strength and skill emerging first in the head and neck and finally to the feet. This also means that children will be able to move their upper arms and hands before engaging in complex dance steps. *Proximal-distal* development means that motor control begins at the midline of the body and moves to the extremities, with the ability to sit up with control coming well before the control of the fingers and thumb. For instance, youngsters scoop a ball with their arms and body before being able to catch it with their hands.

Gross to Fine Muscle Development   Few practical movements are entirely one or another (Payne & Isaacs, 1991). We generally recognize that *locomotor* movements (going from one place to another) require the use of the large muscles in the trunk, legs, and arms, whereas *manipulative* movements (with the hands) require the use of the many small muscles of the hands. Fine motor development of the feet is also possible for those who participate in dance and soccer, where such control is needed.

Growth, Maturation, and Learning   *Growth* is incremental change during childhood. Children gain weight and height in an orderly, predictable fashion when they are well nourished and healthy. Growth influences children's play as taller children run faster and are usually stronger than shorter ones. *Maturation* refers to qualitative changes in the individual that occur in a fixed progression from a lower to a higher functioning level. Rates of growth and maturation vary among individuals and are genetically determined. Children of the same age may be of various sizes and at differing levels of maturation, so it is unlikely that they would perform the same motor behaviors at the same time.

Learning is a more or less permanent change in behavior. Children learn the specifics of each motor skill once their bodies are mature enough. Instruction and practice of a motor skill before a child is sufficiently mature to benefit from it is ineffective (Gabbard, LeBlanc, & Lowy, 1987). Culture also affects what children learn: Sandlot baseball and American-style football are common in the United States but more rare in Africa, where other games are learned.

Maturation is required for the acquisition of the fundamental motor skills but by itself does not ensure the performance of the movement. Opportunities to move and learn specific skills are also necessary (Haywood, 1993). Because maturation and the prerequisite learning required for performance differ for different skills, children may be quite advanced in one skill while just beginning on the sequence of development of other skills. For example, walking and running appear much earlier than striking or kicking.

The principles of motor development, maturation, and learning apply to all aspects of physical activity: gross, perceptual, and fine motor skills.

Fundamental Motor Skills

After the first year of life, children learn to walk on their own, exploring their environment, manipulating objects, climbing on furniture, and moving about their near environments with curiosity and interest. Initial movements are short, with many falls. Gradually these skills improve qualitatively in a predictable sequence so that walking is more automatic as well as more mechanically efficient. Some gross motor skills such as walking or striking are *fundamental motor skills* that are the basic movements on which games or other more complex movements are formed. The early childhood period is the time when children become mature enough to acquire these movement competencies. Children may acquire the fundamental motor skills on their own or with adult guidance. Evidence suggests that if children do not acquire proficiency by the age of 6 or 7, they may never acquire it during the elementary years (Gallahue, 1993b; Seefeldt & Haubenstricker, 1986). Figure 12.1 is a summary of selected gross motor skills that most youngsters are capable of

FIGURE 12.1

Selected Gross Motor Skills to Be Learned Between Three and Seven Years of Age

Locomotor Skills

Walk	Run	Leap	Jump	Hop	Creep	Roll
Stop	Start	Dodge	Slide	Start	Skip	Gallop
Climb						

Manipulative Skills (Projecting and Receiving Objects)

Throw	Kick	Punt	Strike	Volley	Bounce	Roll
Dribble	Catch	Trap	Hug			

Nonlocomotor Skills

Bend	Stretch	Twist	Turn	Swing	Curl	Swivel
Whirl	Spin	Rock	Bend	Hang	Pull	Push
Lift	Sway					

achieving (Anziano et al. 1995; Gallahue, 1995; Ignico, 1994; Payne & Isaacs, 1991).

Most of the locomotor and manipulative skills listed in Figure 12.1 have inherent sequences that begin as exploratory movements and gradually evolve to more mature forms of movement. Several locomotor and manipulative skills are presented in more detail in Figure 12.2 to illustrate the predictable sequences that children go through while achieving competence. Additional skills are described in Table 12.1. Remember that children move through these sequences at different rates and that ultimate performance at the end of the early childhood period is determined by maturation, learning, and practice during this period. Note that many of these functions progress from the following positions: *bilateral*—usually forward facing, both hands at body midline; *unilateral*—one-sided, shift of body; *ipsilateral*—the foot, arm and body move from the same side, some rotation; and *contralateral*—across the body, the movement is diagonal involving both sides of the body and body rotation with stepping.

FIGURE 12.2
Developmental Sequence of Kicking, Catching, and Throwing

Developmental Sequence of Kicking

Stage 1
Little leg wind-up
Stationary position
Ball pushed forward by foot
May step forward or backward
    after contact to regain balance

Stage 2
Leg wind-up to rear
Opposition of arms and legs
Stationary position

Stage 3
One or more steps to approach
    the ball
Good opposition of arms and
    legs
Forward or side steps in
    follow-through

Stage 4
Rapid approach
• quick steps or run
• two airborne phases:
    1. leap before kick
    2. hop after kick
Backward lean in trunk during
    wind-up

FIGURE 12.2

(continued)

Developmental Sequence of Catching

Stage 1
Delayed arm action
Arms straight in front
Palms facing upward
No arm movement until contact
Attempt to secure the ball by
   holding it against the chest

Stage 2
Encircling arms
Feet stationary
Palms facing each other
Hug the ball
Arm action starts prior to
   ball-arm contact

Stage 3
Arms slightly flexed and extended
   forward
Arms "scoop" under ball to trap it
   against chest
May attempt to use hands upon
   failure to hold it
Securely, maneuver it to chest
Single step may be used

Stage 4
Flex elbows—arms in front
Ball is caught with *hands only*
Clean catch
One step may be taken

Stage 5
Catch with hands only
Body moves to catch—more than
   one step

(continued on the next page)

FIGURE 12.2
(continued)

Developmental Sequence of Throwing

Stage 1
Vertical (upward-backward)
    wind-up
Little or no weight transfer
No spinal rotation
"Chop" throw

Stage 2
Wind-up in horizontal or oblique
    plane
Straight-arm throw (sling) in hori-
    zontal or oblique plane
Block rotation with weight shift to
    opposite foot
Follow-through across body

Stage 3
High (upward-backward) wind-up
Forward stride with ipsilateral foot
Hip flexion, arm movement in
    vertical plane
Little trunk rotation
Follow-through across body

Stage 4
High (upward-backward) wind-up
Forward stride with contralateral
    foot
Trunk/hip flexion, arm movement
    forward, elbow extension
Limited trunk rotation
Follow-through across body

Stage 5
Low (downward-backward)
    wind-up
Body (hip-shoulder) rotation
Forward stride with contralateral
    foot
Sequential derotation for force
    production
Arm-leg follow-through

Source: Haubenstricker (1991a).

TABLE 12.1

Summary of Fundamental Motor Skill Stage Characteristics

Fundamental Motor Skill	Stage 1	Stage 2	Stage 3	Stage 4	Stage 5
Throw	Vertical wind-up "Chop" throw Feet stationary No spinal rotation	Horizontal wind-up "Sling throw" Block rotation Follow-through across body	High wind-up Ipsilateral step Little spinal rotation Follow-through across body	High wind-up Contralateral step Little spinal rotation Follow-through across body	Downward arc wind-up Contralateral step Segmented body rotation Arm-leg follow through
Catch	Delayed arm action Arms straight in front until ball contact, then scooping action to chest Feet stationary	Arms encircle ball as it approaches Ball is "hugged" to chest Feet stationary or may take one step	"To chest" catch Arms "scoop" under ball to trap it to chest Single step may be used to approach ball	Catch with hands only Feet stationary or limited to one step	Catch with hands only Whole body moves through space
Kick	Little/no leg wind-up Stationary position Foot "pushes" ball Step backward after kick (usually)	Leg wind-up to the rear Stationary position Opposition of arms and legs	Moving approach Foot travels in a low arc Arm/leg opposition Forward or sideward step on follow-through	Rapid approach Backward trunk lean during wind-up Leap before kick Hop after kick	
Punt	No leg wind-up Ball toss erratic Body stationary Push ball/step back	Leg wind-up to the rear Ball toss still erratic Body stationary Forceful kick attempt	Preparatory step(s) Some arm/leg yoking Ball toss or drop	Rapid approach Controlled drop Leap before ball contact Hop after ball contact	
Strike	"Chop" strike Feet stationary	Horizontal push/swing Block rotation Feet stationary/stepping	Ipsilateral step Diagonal downward swing	Contralateral step Segmented body rotation Wrist rollover on follow-through	
Long-jump	Arms act as "brakes" Large vertical component Legs not extended	Arms act as "wings" Vertical component still great Legs near full extension	Arms move forward/elbows in front of trunk at take-off Hands to head height Take-off angle still above 45 degree Legs often fully extended	Complete arm and leg extension at take-off Take-off near 45 degree angle Thighs parallel to surface when feet contact for landing	

(continued on the next page)

TABLE 12.1
(continued)

Fundamental Motor Skill	Stage 1	Stage 2	Stage 3`	Stage 4	Stage 5
Run	Arms-high guard Flat-footed contact Short stride Wide stride, shoulder width	Arms-middle guard Vertical component still great Legs near full extension	Arms-low guard Arm opposition—elbows nearly extended Heel-toe contact	Heel-toe contact (toe-heel when sprinting) Arm-leg opposition High heel recovery Elbow flexion	
Hop	Nonsupport foot in front with thigh parallel to floor Body erect Hands shoulder height	Nonsupport knee flexed with knee in front and foot behind support leg Slight body lean forward Bilateral arm action	Non support thigh vertical with foot behind support leg—knee flexed More body lean forward Bilateral arm action	Pendular action on nonsupport leg Forward body lean Arm opposition with swing leg	
Gallop	Resembles rhythmically uneven run Trail leg crosses in front of lead leg during airborne phase, remains in front at contact	Slow-moderate tempo, choppy rhythm Trail leg stiff Hips often oriented sideways Vertical component exaggerated	Smooth, rhythmical pattern, moderate tempo Feet remain close to ground Hips oriented forward		
Skip	Broken skip pattern or irregular rhythm Slow, deliberate movement Ineffective arm action	Rhythmical skip pattern Arms provide body lift Excessive vertical component	Arm action reduced/hands below shoulders Easy, rhythmical movement Support foot near surface on hop		

Source: Haubenstricker (1990).

The number of stages that a particular skill appears to involve also varies, with throwing and catching having five distinct stages and galloping and skipping only three. There does not appear to be carryover from one fundamental motor skill to another except for skipping, which is a combination of running and hopping. Obviously, a child who cannot hop cannot skip. However, children who can strike a ball using a stage three may only be able to throw it in a stage two. The same child may function at stage one of the long jump at age 8 if the opportunity to learn the skill has not occurred. Once the final stage of each of the fundamental skills is reached, children continue to eliminate extraneous movement, increase in power and strength, and may incorporate elements of style seen in very skilled players. There are many more gross motor skills than those defined as fundamental that children may develop as a part of ballet, horseback riding, or hunting with a spear, boomerang, or bow and arrow.

A verbal description of the characteristics of several fundamental motor skills is provided in Table 12.1. With conscientious reading, one can identify fine distinctions between stages. Children appear to need time to explore and practice movements in each of the stages before moving forward to the next. The length of time between levels one and two varies considerably, as is seen in Figure 12.3. The level of detail allows classroom teachers to determine what actions to encourage. Adults can plan for scaffolding that will permit the children to advance if they appear to need this level of support. Often more skilled children provide this for less skilled youngsters during informal play.

As Figure 12.3 shows, children also begin the sequences of development at different times, and the duration of time that it takes them to perform at mature levels also varies considerably. Throwing begins at age 1 for both boys and girls, and 60 percent of the boys demonstrate mature technique by age 5$^{1}/_{2}$, with girls

FIGURE 12.3

Age at Which Children Initiate Selected Fundamental Motor Skills and at Which 60 Percent of Boys and Girls Were Able to Perform at an Advanced Form

(Adapted from Seefeldt & Haubenstricker [1982].)

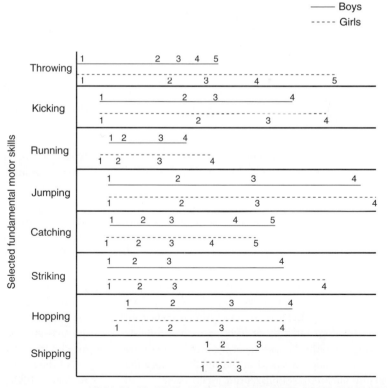

not showing this level of performance until much later. Catching does not start until around age 2, and both boys and girls show mature form by about age 7. At any age there are substantial individual differences.

Perceptual Motor Skills

Children always use all of their sensory capacities as they engage with the environment, explore, move, or handle objects. When professionals speak of perceptual motor development, they are usually referring to movement activities that will lead to academic or cognitive outcomes (Payne & Isaacs, 1991). There are, however, unclear distinctions between general physical activity and perceptual motor skills. Typically developing children use their sensory skills in every movement except when playing games like *Blind Man's Bluff*. In addition, movement is a portion of most social and communication events as gestures, approaches, and mutual activity. Therefore, the following discussion focuses on a few skills that appear to be distinctive and particularly useful for children to learn fully.

The perceptual process improves with practice, generally improving rapidly during the early childhood period (Williams, 1983). All modes of receiving sensation from the environment are involved: sight, audition, scent, taste, and touch. Frequently, multiple modes of sensation come from one source at the same instant, requiring sensory integration. For example, if a dog should approach a child, the child is likely to see (color, size, conformation, and demeanor), hear (footsteps, panting, or barking), and possibly smell the dog (breath or fur). These sensations are transmitted to the brain through the nervous system. The brain uses the current information, organizes it, and integrates it into previously learned concepts such as animals, brown things, or things that move with four feet. After a decision is made about a course of action, the brain transmits signals through the nervous system to initiate the desired movement. Finally, the movement is performed. A very young child may decide to run to an adult from fear, approach the dog cautiously, or even approach joyfully, depending upon the decision he or she makes. At last, relevant information is stored in the child's memory that will ultimately affect similar future experiences.

The perceptual process is rapid, continuous, and ongoing. The same set of events might constitute vastly dissimilar experiences for children. For example, if two children observed a large, inflated ball in the yard, one child might classify the ball as something to kick, whereas the other might see it as something to roll. Adults supervising children become aware of these differing understandings as youngsters disagree on how the play should go forward. Both children will enhance their concepts and skills as they learn to play successfully, using either or both responses. To the extent that perception of the environment is a steady component of living, all movement uses this capacity. There are five aspects of perceptual motor development that are of particular importance: balance, spacial awareness, figure-ground perception, temporal awareness, and body and directional awareness.

Balance   *Static balance* is the ability to maintain a posture while holding still. Standing on one foot, leaning forward with one foot in front of the other, or teetering on the edge of a stair with the toes only on the tread are examples of static balance. *Dynamic balance* is the ability to remain in a desired posture while moving. Walking a balance beam, hopping on one foot, running, and turning rapidly are all examples of dynamic balance. Balance is a component of most movements but is particularly important to complex movements in games or dance. Because children's center of gravity changes as they grow, youngsters require ongoing practice to adjust for changes in height and weight.

Spacial Awareness   Four-year-old Jeanne asked, "Why is my house little here and big when I get home?" as she looked out of the second-story window of the school. She had not yet learned that objects appear smaller when they are farther away. Young children understand their surroundings in relation to themselves. With more maturity and experience, they can describe locations using landmarks. In addition, an understanding of distance appears to increase with age. Inquiries such as "Are we there yet?" are typical of younger children at the beginning of a trip and occur later and less frequently with older youngsters, regardless of whether the children have made the journey before and regardless of the mode of travel: foot, bicycle, automobile, or airplane. Children also confuse distance with the time it takes to reach a destination. Thus, a six-block walk is longer than a two-mile drive!

In practical terms, youngsters may bump into each other during play because they misjudge the distance between themselves and another. Beginning writers often run out of room on the paper as they misjudge the amount of space they will need for all the letters. Most children in early childhood find it easier to get a needed item than to tell someone else where to find it in another room or a crowded cupboard. Experienced teachers learn that children are likely to be more appropriately separated for a dance experience if they stand with arms and legs outstretched and cannot touch another person than if they simply ask children to disperse so that they will have enough room to move. The space in the former strategy is defined by the child's body; in the second, their strategy depends upon a more abstract concept of their own and others' space.

Figure-Ground Perception   Determining what is in the foreground and in the background usually involves auditory or visual perception skills. The task in the visual modality is to find a specific object within a group. Three- to five-year-olds have difficulty selecting toys from very crowded cupboards. They will choose to play with one on the table or one that someone else is using. They will also find it challenging to locate a particular letter within a word.

Equally difficult is hearing the voice of a particular instrument in the background of an orchestra. Similar challenges occur in perceiving a particular consonant within a word. Skills develop over time so that primary-age children can "find" animals in drawings where the lines form other, more obvious, shapes. Early school-age children can discern directions spoken in an open classroom where several muted conversations are going on more readily than preschool children do.

Temporal Awareness   Time relationships are not fully developed until very late in the early childhood period or even into adolescence. However, the beginnings of the notions of speed and timing do begin to emerge. Rhythm is one aspect of organized time that most young children enjoy. Toddlers between 12 and 18 months will bob, bounce, or bend in time to music as an expression of their involvement. With guided practice, 2- to 5-year-olds may clap complex patterns and engage in increasingly challenging rhythmic activity.

Estimating speed is very difficult for 3- to 5-year-olds. You might observe that youngsters close their arms after the ball has already passed them. Many accidents occur on playgrounds because children do not accurately judge the speed of objects and other people. Their spacial awareness is not fully developed, and their sense of time and cause and effect are still immature (Frost & Sweeney, 1995). Children do improve with practice, but an approximate estimation of an object's trajectory and speed emerges during the primary years, with some 8-year-olds becoming quite adept at catching balls thrown at different speeds (Payne & Issacs, 1991).

Children who learn to assess their speed as slower or faster than their own previous performance experience pride and pleasure in their accomplishments. Premature competition generally is discouraging to all but the one child who is recognized as the winner. During the preschool years, the feeling of moving rapidly through space is exciting on its own. As children move into primary grades, noncompetitive running games are most appropriate as children are developing their competence in efficient running (Taras, 1992).

Body and Directional Awareness   *Body awareness* is a part of the conventional social information about the names and functions of the various body parts. For most children, the naming of the external body parts is primarily complete during the preschool years. Finger plays such as "Head, Shoulders, Knees, and Toes" or "Where Is Thumbkin?" can help familiarize children with the vocabulary. This vocabulary is most helpful to children as teachers give them suggestions such as "Billy, bend your knees when you land" while they are engaged in motor activity.

Directional awareness is a combination of the understanding of concepts such as up and down and front and back and the application of that information in a physical activity. Ideas such as left and right are related to a specific speaker and are much more difficult to understand than other concepts of direction or spacial relationships. For example, if two children are facing each other at a table and an adult asks them to point up, the children would be pointing in the same direction, yet if the direction were to point to the left, they would point in opposite directions. Most children master this idea by the end of the early childhood years.

Practice in perceptual motor learning continues throughout everyday life. Informed adults can support this informal learning through instruction and the provision of materials and equipment.

Selected movement concepts that include quality of movement and perceptual-motor ideas are listed in Figure 12.4 (Anziano et al., 1995; Graves, Gargiulo, & Sluder, 1996; Seefeldt, 1980; Werner, 1994). Young children can do all of these movements if they are provided with appropriate demonstrations, directions, and

opportunities to practice. Props such as ribbons or scarves often assist children with ideas such as *smooth* or *sustained* movement.

Music may also support children's understanding of qualitative distinctions of movement. The teacher selects combinations of these movement ideas and incorporates them into an activity. An obstacle course where children move through, around, under, and on top of objects at a slow pace until they reach a rug where they stop to rest would be an example of a large

FIGURE 12.4
Selected Movement Concepts

Effort
Strong   Firm   Light   Fine
Space
High (head & shoulders)   Medium (waist height)   Low (below the knees)
Time
Accelerate   Fast   Decelerate   Slow   Sudden   Sustained
Direction
Forward/Backward   Diagonal/Sideways   Up/Down   Lift/Lower   Rise/Fall   Reach/Collapse
Flow
Free (movements outward from the body)   Bound (movements constrained, close to body) Smooth (continuous)   Jerky (many stops and starts)
Pathways
Straight   Curved   Zigzag   Twisted
Percussive / Vibrate
Stamp   Pound   Punch   Shiver   Wobble   Shake   Flutter   Swing   Shudder Shake   Tremble
Stops
Freeze   Pause   Hold   Grip   Brake   Pull up   Rest
Relationships of Objects and People
Over/Under   In/Out   Between/Among   In front/Behind   Above/Below   Through/Around Mount/Dismount   Near/Far   Meeting/Parting   Expand/Contract

motor array of movements. Similar combinations may be made with moving smaller things with the hands. For example, Mr. Towl asked a few kindergarten children to draw diagonal lines on a tissue paper that they would later use to wrap around a shoe box, covering the inside and the outside of the box. Clearly, movement concepts apply to fine as well as large motor skills and require the use of perceptual-motor skills as well.

Fine Motor Skills

Using the hands to move objects precisely and accurately is the task most refer to as *fine motor skill*. As with gross motor skills, both maturity and practice are necessary for optimal development. The coordination of sensory information with the motoric action is also necessary. Control of head, trunk, shoulders, and arms is well established before hand and fingers attain more than rudimentary skill.

Throughout the preschool period, children fatigue easily, often feeling frustrated at their inability to accomplish tasks. Adult support and encouragement without pressure to perform to some external standard is quite helpful. An environment where the opportunities to use fine motor skills abound provide practice. Adults provide information and demonstration informally as the need arises.

Six- to eight-year-olds are generally quite independent in most manipulative tasks. They can do simple crafts including straight sewing, cutting objects reasonably skillfully with scissors, and stringing fine beads into simple patterns. They move to greater control, precision, and accuracy while refining earlier accomplishments. Girls tend to be more skillful in fine motor tasks earlier than boys, who appear to excel earlier in tasks requiring strength or power (Berk, 1996a). Many boys find penmanship challenging but may draw objects of interest to them in greater detail. Fine motor skills can be fostered in settings where the tools, children's experiences, and cultural expectations are supportive (Bredekamp & Copple, 1997). Cultural expectations in the home also affect the quality of drawing and writing observed in preschool settings (Huntsinger, Schoeneman, & Ching, 1994).

Children who have the maturity to do the tasks illustrated in Table 12.2 but not the experience in using the tools or engaging in the activities will begin their skills as much younger children do. For example, 4-year-old Emily had never been given writing implements of any kind at home. When she entered the children's program, she used a fist grasp on crayons and pencils first, learning quickly and with practice to use a more mature grasp. At age $3^1/2$, Vivian had always been fed by her parents to avoid a mess. Her use of spoon and cup in a childcare program was very immature for her age, but, in a climate of encouragement and support, she progressed quite rapidly. Heathy children do seem to catch up when their earlier experiences have not been conducive to the acquisition of skill. However, this requires time, patience, support, and instruction. Expectations of adults must be adjusted accordingly. Youngsters whose skills are first attempted between 2 and 3 years of age and brought to greater control and accuracy by age 7 are more likely to be more physically advanced than children who do not begin this process until age 4 or 5.

Handwriting as Graphic Production

Children learn about the written language much like they learn oral language. They first observe and then imitate it. Beginning attempts are so rudimentary that adults may fail to recognize that the child is beginning the process of handwriting. In environments where children see adults write grocery lists, letters, holiday greetings, or notes to family members, toddlers will attempt to participate in the activity as soon as they obtain access to a writing implement.

Gwen, about 18 months old, played near her mother's chair as the mother graded papers. When her mother left the room for a very few minutes, Gwen climbed on the chair, picked up a red pen, and marked every page of a stack of papers with a large mark. With mother's return, she smiled, pleased with herself for having completed this task so promptly!

The concept that meaningful messages may be written down has been discussed in Chapter 11. Handwriting, however, involves a progression of fine motor skills that entails maturation, learning, and practice.

Writing and Drawing Implements   Children use tools to write. At first, fingers are useful for drawing and writing in finger paint and sand, and these techniques remain the easiest method of leaving a mark on something.

TABLE 12.2
Expected Timing and Sequence of Fine Motor Skills for Children in Supportive Environments

Age	General	Targeting	Cut and Paste	Self-Help	Graphic Tools
2–3	Fatigues easily Undresses Carries small objects easily Precisely picks up small objects Uses door knob	Places one-piece knob puzzles accurately Puts shapes in appropriate holes Strings large beads on plastic tubing	Tears paper Large globs of paste may be put on top of the piece to be pasted instead of between the pieces of paper Snips with scissors Holds paper and scissors incorrectly Likely uses both hands with scissors	Eats with a spoon Drinks from a cup Undresses if fasteners are simple	Scribbles with pleasure Copies a cross or a circle May attempt simple capital letters such as H, V, and T May hold implement in fist
3–4	Opens doors, manages most latches Builds block towers Uses keyboard for simple programs Pounds, rolls, squeezes clay Turns pages of a book one at a time	Inserts large pegs into pegboards Strings large beads with a string Puts together simple puzzles with objects representing an object or a clear segment of an object (e.g., tail of a dog)	Uses large globs of paste Pours on lots of glue Uses index finger or paste brush to spread Cuts full length of scissors, may do two lengths Little directional control May not use correct grasp of scissors	Pours liquid from a pitcher into a container with increasing accuracy and control Handles velcro fasteners easily Puts on outdoor clothing but usually needs help zipping or buttoning Eats most foods independently	Tries three-point grasp of writing implement Is inconsistent and may grasp implement far from the point Uses circles, crosses, and horizontal and vertical lines in drawings May outline a scribbled shape of a rectangle
4–5	Builds complex structures with various construction materials May have problems with spacial judgments and directionality Practices to attain mastery of fine motor tasks With practice may be very adept at computer programs or video games	Uses pattern cards skillfully in placing small pegs in pegboards Laces Sews Multipiece puzzles may be mastered if they have color as well as shape cues Threads large needle with help Threads small beads on a string	Holds scissors and paper correctly Cuts straight lines and turns corners Places appropriate amounts of glue or paste in correct spot and speads with control	Dresses and undresses, buttons and unbuttons, zips haltingly Needs help starting coat zipper Uses a hanger if reachable Has complete toileting independence usually Eats with a fork Spills infrequently Washes and dries hands	Uses tripod grip on writing implement though position may still be high Draws sun and tadpole people and scribbles Paints with deliberateness Writes letters anyplace on the paper May write name or initials or portions of their names on their drawings

TABLE 12.2
(continued)

Age	General	Targeting	Cut and Paste	Self-Help	Graphic Tools
5–6	Sculptures with dough, able to do a pinch or coil pot Shows increased precision and control Does few if any false starts Pounds nails with accuracy Uses keyboard with increasing skill	Inserts increasingly small objects with ease Manages a 12–15 piece puzzle without dependence on color	Most children can cut on a curve, cut out interior shapes, geometric shapes, or magazine pictures Uses scissors easily and accurately Uses glues and paste skillfully	Organzies and takes care of own materials Combs and brushes hair, washes face and hands without getting wet Manages own clothing fasteners and ties shoe laces. Spreads with a knife and can do simple cutting with a table knife	Exhibits good control of pencil/marker Letters, both upper and lowercase, are crudely made but recognizable Makes inversions and reversals often Writes letters of name but not necessarily on a line or correctly spaced Draws cars, boats, houses, trees, and flowers with increasing detail Writes numerals
6–8	Has good basic skills Shows improvement in precision and accuracy Does simple crafts depending on interest	Does multipiece puzzles Uses shape and size to place pieces Places small objects more precisely	Shows good control and improvements in precision	Demonstrates mastery	97 percent of children make acceptable letters Spacing and placement of letters on the page acceptable Word, letter, and numeral reversals common, often self-correcting Drawings made with many media, increasing details

(Adapted from Allen & Marotz, 1989; Bredekamp & Copple, 1997; Cohen & Gross, 1979; Ignico, 1994; McAfee & Leong, 1997)

However, even very young toddlers use a variety of tools to write or make graphic designs. Paint brushes vary in diameter and length. Crayons vary in diameter and come with and without paper wraps. Pencils vary in hardness, diameter, and shape (round or many sided). Pens vary in the texture and materials in the point and diameter. Markers vary in diameter and point shape. All tools are available in many colors.

The least mature, least experienced child will more likely maintain interest in and explore writing implements such as markers, nylon-tipped pens, or #2 pencils. These implements create clear, often colorful marks with very little effort by the child and are responsive to the slightest movement. Children enjoy causing something to happen, and early success is very encouraging. With older, more experienced writers, pencils offer greater control. The general guide of experienced teachers is to move from larger to smaller diameter as the child matures and from implements where a mark is more easily made to one where greater control may be exerted. Apparently, however, preschool age children are as competent in managing a standard-sized pencil as they are a large one (Carlson & Cunningham, 1990). In the earliest phases of writing, the muscles of the head, neck, trunk, and shoulder are primarily engaged; later, the muscles of the elbow, wrist, and fingers are being brought into use as the child attains greater control.

Holding the Writing Implement   The mature tripod associated with adult writing is usually present by the age of 7 years. The progression from the earliest to more mature patterns is as follows:

❏ All four fingers and the thumb are wrapped around the implement with the thumb up (away from the point).

❏ The palm is engaged with a full-hand grasp, with the thumb toward the point of the implement. The implement is often grasped well away from the point. The arm and shoulder control the movement, which is usually very large.

❏ The hand moves closer to the point of the implement. Control of the movement of the pencil shifts from shoulder to elbow to fingers as the grasp moves toward the tip.

❏ Tripod positioning of the fingers with noticeable wrist movement and minimal finger control is often combined with the fingers bent and fingertips on the implement. (Children using this grip can tire easily, and their fingers may cramp.)

❏ The mature tripod, with the implement resting on the index finger, has rapid finger control of movements and is seen at about 7 years of age for most children.

❏ Refinement of the dynamic tripod occurs between 6 and 14 years, with the writing implement resting on the side of the index finger and infrequent use of fingertips to hold the implement (Payne & Isaacs, 1991).

The range of reaching a mature grasp is very wide, with some youngsters achieving this milestone as early as 3 years and others achieving it during middle childhood. Parental expectations and opportunities for

Early attempts at writing involve using large muscle groups and result in the formation of large, skewed letters.

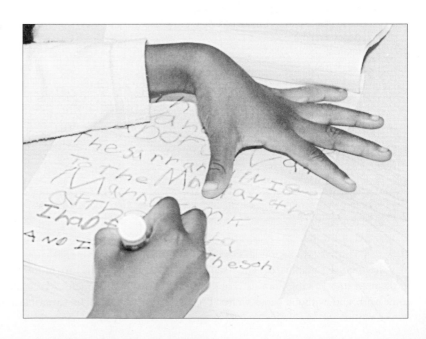

children to practice writing at home may account for such differences (Huntsinger, Schoeneman, & Ching, 1994).

Letter Formation　Practice with implements in drawing and painting occurs for most children in early childhood programs before children are encouraged to print. By the age of 4, they are usually capable of drawing letters but do not recognize the importance of the order or placement of letters on the page. Numerals and letters may be scattered, written vertically, sideways, or very slanted. By age 5, children generally are able to print their names with correct letter order. The letters are large and irregular in shape. By age 6, though the letters are still very large, they are smaller than those made by 5-year-olds and commonly include reversals.

Letters with one stroke remain easier than those with many; letters with diagonal strokes are the most difficult. Spacing remains a challenge through the end of the third and fourth grades (Cratty, 1979; Reimer, Eaves, Richards, & Chrichton, 1975). Incorrect letter formation in prekindergarten and kindergarten has been successfully used to predict later reading failure in first grade (Simner, 1988). It is not clear whether the children's early environments provided them an opportunity to encounter print or writing materials necessary to attempt to form letters early on. Difficulties with print formation may be the result of delay in the exposure to print and opportunities to use writing implements or even perceptual troubles. Environments that do not support letter formation may also not be supportive of other skills such as reading. This topic is more fully developed in Chapter 11.

The alphabet is one of the few artifacts of English language culture that changes meaning when rotated. A book, regardless of its position in space, is still a book. Children often find this confusing because letter groups such as *b, d, p,* and *q* are rotations of the same pattern in different positions. Similarities of other combinations such as *v* and *n* or *m* and *w* are also a challenge; *s* is a letter in one position, but the rotation is not a letter. Other principles related to drawing letters are as follows:

❏ Letters must be in a certain order.
❏ In English, writing goes from left to right.
❏ Capitalization rules require changes in size and shape of letters.
❏ Spaces are used to denote words and ends of sentences (Woodward, Ives, Levadi, & von Hippel, 1981).

Children need lots of practice with their hands before beginning to print letters, and they need opportunities to practice letter formation to develop the necessary motor skills. They learn to print from everyday experiences: observing adults print, observing letters and words in the environment, and during pretend play when they "write notes" of one type or another. Adults support this learning in the following ways:

❏ Starting at the upper left-hand corner when writing children's names on drawings.
❏ Using capitals and lowercase letters when appropriate.
❏ Providing writing implements and paper.
❏ Allowing children to observe them writing real things and using print to do so.
❏ Accepting children's explorations of handwriting: Adults recognize that children's initial attempts look more like waves than like letters.
❏ Encouraging children's attempts, focusing on the message, not the form.
❏ Telling children that it takes a long time to write like an adult and that everyone makes mistakes.
❏ Praising children's efforts, displaying their work, and providing an adult copy of the message on a separate paper below the children's work if necessary.

Handwriting is one example of a fine motor skill that has been closely examined. Other skills such as keyboarding, piano playing, sewing, or paper folding do not have sufficient research to support a similar discussion, but general principles might still be applied:

❏ The proximal-distal principle is applicable in most instances where the shoulder, arm, wrist, and then finger muscles are used in succession as children move to greater control.
❏ Maturation, learning, and practice are all significant factors in ultimate success; maturation alone does not lead to skillful performance.
❏ Children acquire knowledge and skill gradually and are heavily influenced by the presence of models in the environment.
❏ Mature performance is the result of years of practice.
❏ Growth, or the increase of the size of the hands, may contribute to the learning of some skills such as keyboarding and piano playing due to the reach required when using correct form.
❏ Children go through the same developmental sequences although there is a considerable variation in rates.

Children Who Have Special Needs

For many children who experience challenges in language and learning, physical play is an opportunity for more typical participation. Youngsters who are slower in learning may require more repetition to achieve success. However, for many children, vigorous play is one arena where they may participate successfully with their peers.

Safety may need particular attention when children do not hear or see well. The arrangement of equipment, the structuring of the activities, and the cooperation of other children usually suffice to enable most children to participate in large- and small-muscle activities.

Usually modifications in instruction are successful, such as gaining attention in the sensory modality that the child uses more typically to accommodate to particular limitations. Obviously, children who do not see cannot develop visual discrimination tasks. Instead, touch discrimination will facilitate eventual braille reading. Touching a youngster and then demonstrating a skill followed by pointing to the child is usually sufficient to give instructions to a hearing-impaired child. This is one domain where language may be optional in teaching.

Children with serious visual impairments are usually hesitant initially. Continuous physical contact, verbal encouragement, and direction may provide sufficient security for the child to try new motor tasks.

Some children have impairments in the physical domain. A report from the physical or occupational therapist is quite useful in identifying the strengths of the child and should be used as a guide by the general practitioner. If a child does not walk independently, walkers, wagons, or wheelchairs enable the child to move and even engage in some games as wheelchair control improves. Public schools now provide consultants to classroom teachers to assist them in adapting programs and activities for special needs children. Special interventions are necessary but not sufficient.

Heidi, a 7-year-old who wore braces on her legs, had sessions with the physical therapist once a week. She also went outdoors with the other children, one of whom was assigned to push open a heavy door. She was able to swing by herself and play catch with classmates, although her position was closer to a fence so the balls she did not catch did not roll too far. Her upper body strength was excellent, enabling her to hang from the horizontal ladder with ease. With encouragement and support during her primary years, she learned how to adapt many activities herself as she gained confidence and skill.

Most experienced teachers adapt to each specific child and build on what is easiest, safest, and most comfortable with consideration for the child's particular handicapping condition. They build on what each child can do, treating them with respect and expecting them to try what is possible. Specialists design equipment and educational experiences in problematic skills. For example, some very young children use computers to communicate by hitting keys with a stylus attached to the forehead if they do not have hands that work well. Increasingly, technology is helpful in enabling everyone to develop optimally.

Before children reach the age of 5, adults promote the development of basic skills before they incorporate technological resources. Tommy, who was very motorically involved as a result of cerebral palsy, could not roll over, sit up, or support his head when he entered the classroom for 3-year-olds. He did attain control of two fingers, his eyes, and some facial muscles early in life. He sat in a tilted support chair. When other children playing nearby had materials, they placed objects in his hand. He was initially frightened outdoors through lack of experience but eventually enjoyed lying in the grass and rolling on the hill with support. His 3-year-old peers pulled him in a wagon from time to time and would place a ball on the ground for him to roll to another child. He could drop a die, and a child helper would move his piece in a board game, which he watched carefully. Using support equipment to hold him upright, he could finger paint and engage in a variety of sensory experiences. During his time with more typically developing peers in this preschool program, his strength improved and his hand control increased. He also learned to talk, though speech continued to be difficult, slow, and infrequent. Even though some children have severe limitations, it is possible for all of the children in the group to have a measure of success.

HEALTH, SAFETY, AND NUTRITION

Children require safe and healthy environments in which to learn and play, both indoors and outside. Well-balanced meals are essential to growth. Equipment and facilities should be hazard free. Children require medical monitoring to ensure health and well-being (Hertel, 1992). These provisions are the responsibilities of parents, teachers, administrators, and the community. For certain elements of each of these facets, children themselves may take responsibility for their own well-being. During the early years of development, they can learn to make safe and healthy choices and develop lifestyle attitudes that predispose them to maintain healthy practices throughout their lifetimes.

Fitness

Physical fitness is a value more admired than pursued for young children. A reasonable aspiration would be that children enjoy physical activity and see it as an ordinary, permanent part of their lives as they grow (Branta, 1992). Both the length and the quality of their lives may be affected. Endurance, speed, strength, flexibility, and balance are part of being fit. Children increase in strength slowly between 3 and 5, with few differences between boys and girls (Malina & Bouchard, 1991). Gains in speed are rapid, as might be expected with the growth of their legs. Performance of tasks requiring agility, the long jump, and catching make notable improvement during the preschool years. Boys tend to excel in tasks that require power and speed, whereas girls excel in tasks that require balance, such as hopping. From 5 years of age onward, boys tend to excel in most of the fitness areas although the variability within each age group of children is generally greater than the difference between boys and girls.

Adults can design successful activities that engage preschool children in physical fitness endeavors. A group of 4-year-olds enjoyed a carefully structured 9-minute walk/run to improve their cardiovascular fitness. Adults "ran" along with children as they moved from one corner of a gym to the next, tapping helium-filled balloons as they passed the corners. All the children finished and appeared to enjoy themselves (Branta 1992).

Preschool-aged children generally are active, with the levels of activity decreasing as children attend elementary schools and engage in more sedentary activities. Preschool-aged children do tire easily, but they recover rapidly. Primary-aged children have better endurance, although they too benefit from opportunities

to shift from vigorous activity to quieter pursuits. Often an option of a quiet activity where they may come and go within a period of vigorous play gives them sufficient rest (Werner, 1994). During outdoor play, with most learning centers designed to support fitness or skill development, a center for sand play, which requires minimal exertion, would be suitable.

A minimum of 30 minutes of physical activity almost every day is recommended; however, 60 minutes of *accumulated* activity is an optimal standard for the early childhood period (Zaichkowsky & Larson, 1995). The accumulation includes moving up and down stairs, walking to and from school, vigorous play at home, and any other active pursuit in which youngsters may engage in programs or at home. Even elementary schools that have physical education as a planned component for every grade frequently do not have it often enough to meet this physical fitness standard. This means that after-school programs as well as classroom teachers must plan to contribute some time to fitness on a regular basis.

Children who are physically active maintain appropriate weight more easily than more sedentary youngsters. Unfortunately, increasing numbers of children do not have much opportunity to play outside at home, nor are they accumulating the necessary exercise in early childhood programs. Children in the United States are not as fit as their European counterparts (Zaichkowsky & Larson, 1995). In addition, the number of obese young children is increasing (Zaichkowsky & Larson, 1995). This may indicate the beginning of a cycle that is challenging to break. Some children gain weight as they move from a more active preschool level to the more sedentary school age. Being overweight may interfere with the development of additional motor skills and vigorous play. It is possible to be overweight and otherwise physically healthy and fit just as it is to be unfit at a normal weight. Any program designed to manage weight must also have an activity component for long-term success. Professionals are responsible for encouraging all children to enhance their motor skills and become or remain proficient in active physical pursuits.

Regular outdoor play is often a component of programs to promote physical activity and fitness. Free play is an effective part of the physical fitness program but is insufficient by itself to ensure it. Demonstrations provide appropriate modeling, and guided practice is necessary to ensure that all the children participate in the vigorous activity necessary for health. Some children as young as 3 have already developed the patterns of sedentary behaviors even outdoors. Many kinds of play occur outdoors, not only active play. When playgrounds are provided with age-appropriate equipment and are properly supervised by knowledgeable adults, children are likely to be safe in their active play. However, the climate and daily weather may require specific considerations for safety during outdoor active play.

Three- to five-year-olds are vulnerable to heat-related illness (Taras, 1992). Heat appears to have a greater impact on their smaller bodies, and this age group does not perspire as effectively as adults. Some youngsters appear to lack the instinct to drink and replenish their fluids when they play hard. When children engage in vigorous physical activity during high outdoor temperatures, adults should ensure periods of rest and monitor fluid intake to see that every child consumes some liquid. Hats, lightweight clothing, and light colors also diminish the possibility of heat stress.

Extreme cold—with the potential of frostbite—should be avoided even though the children are engaging in vigorous activity. Otherwise, children should spend some time outdoors every day, even in winter. Cold weather does not cause colds and flu; rather, close contact with ill people carrying the contagion is the cause. Children are less likely to catch cold outdoors than inside. Other considerations for health and safety are addressed through the health curriculum.

Comprehensive Health Curriculum

Even the youngest children participating in programs learn basic ideas about health, safety, and nutrition every day as a consequence of living and learning in an environment concerned with these issues and in which adults practice healthy behavior (Kendric, Kaufmann, & Messenger, 1988). In addition, adults teach specific knowledge that they know will help children to make safe and healthy choices. The *Michigan Model for Comprehensive Health Education* (George & Sellers, 1984) is an example of a written program that has content and materials to use with children in kindergarten through secondary school. An outline of the prekindergarten scope and sequence that is under development is shown in Table 12.3. This model includes some aspect of each

of the basic content divisions for children during the early childhood years (Macrina, 1995). Other completely developed curricula for the preschool years are available: *I Am Amazing* (1990), which was developed to coordinate with the Michigan Model, and *Here We Go, Watch Me Grow* (Hendricks and Smith, 1991) are commercially available, as are numerous other resources on specific topics.

Selected Health Topics

Do you recall if you washed your hands before and after the last meal you ate? Did you use the water splash and wipe with a towel, or did you do a thorough job? Do you routinely wash your hands before you enter into an interaction with children in the classroom and again as you leave? Think about these questions as you read the following section.

Hand Washing   The single most effective deterrent to contagious disease is the frequent and proper washing of hands (Newman, 1997). Adults may assume that children know the appropriate technique; however, that is not always so. For this reason, the directions are listed below (Kendrick, Kaufmann, & Messenger, 1988, 27):

Washing Your Hands
- ❏ Use soap and running water.
- ❏ Rub your hands vigorously.
- ❏ Wash all surfaces including wrists, backs of hands, between fingers, under fingernails.
- ❏ Rinse well from wrists to fingertips.
- ❏ Dry hands with paper towel.
- ❏ Turn off the water with the towel.
- ❏ Throw the paper towel in the basket.

Food Selection   Opportunities to influence eating practices and food choices abound in full-day programs and Head Start and in elementary schools where children eat together. Young children tend to eat foods with which they are familiar and reject foods that are new to them. When new foods are introduced slowly and always with other more familiar choices available, children become interested and actually learn to enjoy a greater variety. For example, every culture has a variation on vegetable soup. Pea pods are an ingredient in Chinese vegetable soup but not in minestrone. A child familiar with one might be inclined to try the other, especially when it is served with a familiar sandwich. Adults who plan educational content should take every opportunity to teach nutrition in every context, including the school lunch.

Additionally, children are often served differently in programs from the way they are served at home. When children are actually taught how to go through a cafeteria line or how to serve themselves family style, then they are more likely to be successful in having a relaxed meal and are able to eat in a less stressful climate.

Finally, adults who accept children's contributions to classroom discussions will find it helpful to learn the cultures of the classroom. For breakfast, some youngsters may have soup, rice, and seaweed with milk and fruit. Others might have dry cereal and milk and an orange, with some children having cold pizza and juice. The conventional "American" breakfast is not the only adequate choice. Combinations of foods rich in nutrients are all good choices.

CURRENT EDUCATIONAL ISSUES

In each domain, there are some recurring issues that adults must address in their practice. The physical domain is no exception.

1. *Why should I be concerned about teaching gross motor skills when they develop as a result of maturation?* Many parents and teachers take motor development for granted, assuming that children will automatically develop through everyday play. Young children are active, they explore their environments physically, and they may practice motor skills voluntarily when they have an opportunity to do so. Yet, we know that observation of skilled performance and instruction are the most significant factors in the acquisition of skill. Who, then, is to teach the skills that youngsters may practice on their own? Whom do they observe? Many children are spending at least $8^1/2$ hours a day in childcare or in a combination of childcare and school as their parents are employed. For safety reasons, latchkey children are often admonished to remain inside with the doors locked until parents return from work. Because of societal changes, opportunities for physical activity with older, more skilled children from the neighborhood become increasingly limited. Particularly when children are in age-segregated programs, dependence upon older children to model skills becomes even more problematic. Maturation of the body means that the child is capable of learning to move skillfully. Instruction and practice are required as well.

Knowledgeable parents who have the time and resources to do so provide their children with opportunities to develop motorically by teaching the youngsters themselves or by paying for after-school programs in the community. Many 3- to 8-year-olds engage in dance, swim, gymnastics, and other sports lessons in community programs, thus gaining some instruction while eliminating opportunities for informal practice. Less fortunate children do not have the resources for taking extra classes. In addition, fatigue and loss of family time should also be included when parents begin to consider when, where, and how a child is to learn the skills necessary for health and physical development.

Fundamental motor skills may not be acquired at all (Haywood, 1993); thus, otherwise normally developing persons may not be able to perform fundamental motor skills at mature levels as adults. Older children who cannot throw a ball with a mature throw are not included in ball games, thus limiting their opportunities for social interaction during the rest of childhood. In addition, children who lack some of the fundamental skills are severely limited in their choices of games and activites for remaining physically fit and healthy throughout their lives.

2. *Shouldn't motor skills be taught by specialists?* Physical education professionals have specialized knowledge of the development of motor skills, safety practices in teaching motor skills, and more experience in games. Physical and occupational therapists and specialists in adaptive physical education also have expertise to contribute to the early childhood field. Nonetheless, the basic program is usually delivered by the adult in charge of the children day to day.

Some programs hire these specialists to contribute to the whole program. They have classes with children on a regular, if infrequent, schedule. If their expertise is optimally used, they contribute to the programs delivered by generalists, assisting in developing objectives and suggesting strategies for working with the children. Even in programs where specialists are fully employed, there is usually insufficient time and space for them to take on the full responsibility of teaching motor skills and providing for the fitness of all the children in the program. Additionally, many elementary

TABLE 12.3

Scope and Sequence of the Michigan Model for Comprehensive Health Education Grades Prekindergarten Through Grade 2

Safety & First Aid Education	Nutrition Education	Family Health	Consumer Health	Community Health
Pre-Kindergarten				
Body rights & privacy/touch awareness Identifying/naming body parts Stranger awareness Strategies when lost Seeking help	Identifying foods & nonfoods Careful and varied food choices Food sources Body using food Introduction to nutrients	Family theme available as resource Family education activities/ newsletters Family involvement guidelines Seeking help/reporting problems to parents	Health helpers/roles Health product choices/functions	Environmental awareness Recycling Conserving
Kindergarten				
Fire safety rules for home and school Recognition of poison Safety rules: School, playground, bus, pedestrian, bicycle, dangerous objects Traffic signs and signals Seat belts Appropriate and inappropriate touch Learning to say "No" to inappropriate touch, telling adults	Varieties in food Food characteristics Snacks	Individual uniqueness Identification of a family Family roles Family members as health helpers	Health helpers and their roles	Health helpers: Roles and agencies Emergencies
First Grade				
Accident prevention/ seat-belt safety Safety signs & signals Safety hazards & prevention: Bus, pedestrian, bicycle, poisons, water, fire Emergencies Personal safety: Secrets, actions that promote safety, avoiding dangerous situations Definitions of sexual abuse	Examples of food groups Snacks from each group Variety of foods needed for good health Food as source of energy & growth	Recognition that offspring resemble parents Examples of families Family roles, responsibilities, & abilities Differences in family eating habits Recognition of need for adult care Changes affect families	Health helpers Effects of tobacco advertisement When to tell an adult	Personal medical procedures and instruments Immunizations Health checkups to prevent illness

Growth & Development	Substance Use & Abuse	Personal Health Practices	Emotional & Mental Health	Disease Prevention & Control
Body parts Senses Growth needs: own, plants, animals Introduction to body systems (heart, muscles, joints) Personal skills & choices	Definition of drugs Contrasts with medicines Care when accepting food from others Choosing not to smoke/stay around smokers Identification of alcohol/cigarettes as drugs	Protective equipment (helmets) Care of teeth, skin, hair Grooming tools and their uses Handling body wastes carefully; blowing nose Exercising for muscle, heart, strength, flexibility Dental health theme as resource	Individual similarities & uniqueness Emotions/feelings Making choices; problem solving Seeking adult assistance Self-help strategies	Introduction to use of medicines Health care professionals Handling body wastes Grooming and cleanliness routines/reasons Self-help strategies Appearance
Five senses Match body part with each sense Teeth	Definition of a drug Medicines as drugs Choosing not to smoke Poisons Saying "No" to drugs	Eye protection Eye function Primary & permanent teeth Care of teeth Tooth decay/tooth brushing Individual health practices Sleep, rest, and exercise Seatbelts	Making friends Likenesses and differences Naming and identifying feelings Ways to settle down Problem solving/ decision making Adult help: When to seek it Identification of dangerous or destructive situations	Prevention of spread of germs Medicine: Appropriate uses Recognizing systems Seeking adult help
Living and non-living Living and growing Identification of growth needs New growth Personal skills & abilities Abilities of differently-abled people External body parts Organs and their functions Body parts working together	Definition of drugs Identification of drugs Identification of alcohol & nicotine as drugs Harmful effects of tobacco & alcohol Poisons and medicines Saying "No" to drugs	Good health habits Exercises Protection of self and others when ill Health checkups and illness prevention Seat belts	Naming and identifying feelings Ways to settle down Mixed feelings that accompany change Showing courtesy Making friends Problem solving/decision making Adults to go to for help	Appearance and behavior associated with wellness and illness Factors changing health status/ symptoms of illness Prevention of germ spread Head lice Immunization Communicable diseases

(continued on the next page)

TABLE 12.3
(continued)

Safety & First Aid Education	Nutrition Education	Family Health	Consumer Health	Community Health
Second Grade				
Safety hazards and prevention: Pedestrian, bicycle, sun, water, dental	Review of food groups	Families are alike and different	Aids for visual and hearing impairment	Definition of environment
Traffic signs	Food choices	Each person is special		Definition of pollution
Safety belt	Need to develop regular eating habits	Family members are helpers		Noise and air pollution
Injury prevention	Combination foods	Changes affect families		Effects of littering
Personal safety: Dangerous situations, strangers, telling an adult	Healthy meals and snacks	Listening skills		Reduce, reuse, recycle

schools and most childcare centers rarely have access to specialists as a part of the teaching staff. The only realistic way to meet the children's needs is for the classroom teacher to become fully involved in direct instruction of physical activity as a part of the planned day.

3. *Won't teaching motor skills take time away from the "real" school subjects?* A child develops holistically. The body cannot be separated from the mind. The proper care of the human body is essential to all other learning. Additionally, physical fitness is a component of healthy functioning, mental well-being, and longevity. So when comparing the amount of time devoted to motor instruction—usually 15–20 minutes—to other activities, a quarter hour or so appears to be reasonable. Committed adults reduce the time children wait for routine events and incorporate exercises into opening and closing routines as well as planning for activities during outdoor play. In addition, children learn through action on things as they participate in learning activies in other domains. Good programs plan for gross motor, fine motor, and perceptual motor activity so that children acquire the skills that are prerequisites for other accomplishments. When motor development is incorporated into daily schedules, educating the whole child becomes a more achievable goal.

4. *Can't physical activity just be left as a choice since boys are more interested in physical activity than girls?* Both boys and girls benefit from physical activity. Boys have traditionally been rewarded for these interests; conversely, girls have traditionally been socialized away from physical activity at very young ages. The height, weight, and general size of boys and girls are about the same until puberty. In fact, maturation slightly favors girls over boys in the development of the central nervous system. Both male and female infants and toddlers enjoy physical action. However, adult expectations tend to be communicated to children, with girls being required to be more "ladylike" and boys encouraged to be more active. Both boys and girls profit from cooperative and, as they become older, competitive games; both may attain success in fine and gross motor skills areas.

5. *If a 4-year-old cannot throw and kick well, does that mean the child should be held back from kindergarten?* Difficulty in one area of development does not necessarily mean difficulty in another. In fact, many children show considerable unevenness in their development. Peter, at age 4, could identify each musical instrument as he listed to the orchestra play, but he could not go upstairs with alternating feet. His auditory discrimination skills were somewhat superior, and his

Growth & Development	Substance Use & Abuse	Personal Health Practices	Emotional & Mental Health	Disease Prevention & Control
Five senses	Medicines and other substances that contain drugs	Prevention of eye and ear injuries	Identifying feelings in self and others	Identification of eye problems
Function and compatibility of the senses	Effects of nicotine, caffeine, alcohol, secondhand smoke	Healthy behaviors	Ways to make friends	When to use medicine
Eye and ear development and function	How smoke enters the lungs	Self-responsibility and health status	Expressing appreciation, annoyance, and anger	Exercise and proper food for health
Eye and ear impairments and aids	Effects of alcohol on physical tasks or activities	Exercise	How to handle strong emotions	
	Saying "No" to drugs		Problem solving/decision making	
			Identifying personal skills and talents	

gross motor performance lagged somewhat behind. The teacher's task is to encourage the development of the motor skills while maintaining his interest in sounds, so she encouraged him to engage in dancing. Should this child be delayed for school entry? No, in fact, he did very well in kindergarten and subsequent years. There are a very few children who are extremely slow in both fine and gross motor development and whose central nervous system is not mature enough to help them acquire skills. As with other developmental delays, an assessment by specialists, using reliable instruments, usually provides accurate information to guide decision making. Parents and teachers should value fine and gross motor skills as they develop without attaching undue significance to the exact timing that children acquire these abilities.

In addition, kindergartens are open to all children who meet the state guidelines as a function of age. A developmentally appropriate program of instruction is likely to support the fine and gross motor development of *all* children.

6. *When should children begin to learn to write?* Children draw letters after they have learned to grip a writing implement and when they wish to communicate over distance or time. Experimentation with writing implements begins sometime in toddlerhood.

Adults frequently prevent 1- and 2-year-olds from experimenting due to concern about painted walls and wallpaper, where children are tempted to draw. By $2^{1}/_{2}$ or 3, young children may be given crayons in restaurants and at home when they are seated at a table. In the beginning, when children are scribbling and making large shapes, adults generally refer to the child as drawing. As children gain practice and observe adults write, their pretend writing becomes linear, with left-to-right progression and a few letter shapes randomly placed on the page. Children themselves begin to distinguish between the "writing" and the drawing, though adults may not be able to make this discrimination.

If children have appropriate samples of manuscript print available, they will try copying some of the shapes on paper. This is usually sometime between ages 3 and 4. The letters most often available to children are their names. Because these letters are often scattered in random order, tilted on the side, or otherwise distorted, adults may or may not recognize some of these representations. They are very large and frequently misshapen. The lines appear to be jagged because these young children are using large sets of muscles instead of their fingers to shape the letters. Providing writing implements and paper and displaying as much manuscript printing as possible is sufficient to encourage children to explore drawing letters. Premature adult standards for letter drawing are inappropriate until children have demonstrated a tripod grip and control of wrist and fingers in exploratory handwriting and drawing.

Informal instruction in short bursts when children ask "How do I make a *k*?" is always appropriate as the adult draws the letter. Asking children if they wish to write their own name or if the adult should write it on a painting is always appropriate as long as the adult accepts the child's approximation. The more exploration and practice the child gets, the more probable the skill will emerge. Age alone is not the best criterion. Youngsters who enter kindergarten and have never held a writing implement will need a lot of time using crayons, painting, and drawing with pencils before they have sufficient practice with muscles of the finger and wrist to produce credible approximations, whereas those with more experience may enter school drawing the letters of their name in a recognizable, though imperfect, form. If children's printing is decipherable, the focus of instruction should be on the message, not the mechanics. Second- and third-grade children who tire easily and whose handwriting is indecipherable may need individualized strategies that focus on posture, trunk, and shoulder stability, pencil grip, and correct form to improve (Soderman, 1991).

7. *Why aren't schools teaching penmanship as they used to?* Historically, beautiful cursive writing was the hallmark of the educated person. Penmanship was viewed as an art form of its own. Such refined skills take much time and practice over many years to perfect.

Educators are questioning the value of the time spent on penmanship as the range and depth of other content has increased over the years. Common use of computers may make touch typing the primary skill that children will need. Some children are taught to print, and cursive writing is omitted. Instead, children learn to print more accurately, smaller, and faster. Other children are given minimal instruction in penmanship with print formation in kindergarten and first grade, followed by cursive instruction in second grade only. With the exception of those who have not achieved basic letter formation, penmanship is not addressed again. Children are left to cultivate their own personalized form thereafter.

Touch typing on a computer must be taught as early as possible if it is to substitute for cursive writing. Availability for all children in all classrooms, however, is a resource issue. Children as young as two years of age are able to use a computer by the hunt-and-peck method. However, sheer hand size might become a major factor in early keyboard use because the hands of children 5 to 7 years old may be too small to use a standard sized keyboard successfully. Researchers will want to address this concern in the future.

8. *Will I offend the parents if I teach personal safety?* Preparing parents and involving them in discussions about personal safety is always a sound practice. Parents can be very effective at teaching personal safety to their own children and can integrate it with what they already know in the context of the family (Finkelhor, 1984; Wurtele, Gillispie, Currier, & Franklin, 1992). If parents believe that personal safety should be left to the family alone, then programs that train and support parents should be provided. Regardless, family instruction on child sexual abuse is relatively rare (Finkelhor, 1984). Feelings of discomfort with the topic, inadequate vocabulary to explain sexual matters to the young, and embarrassment in discussing sexual material with young children may prevent parents from getting started.

Childhood sexual abuse is a serious health problem and widespread. Sexual abuse is more likely to begin during the preschool years than at any other time (Finkelhor & Baron, 1986). Programs have been developed where either teachers or parents may be effective in teaching the basic concepts so that children are able to do the following:

❑ Know that they are the bosses of their own bodies.
❑ Locate their own private body parts.
❑ Distinguish between touching that is OK and touching that is not OK.
❑ Understand that touching an adult's private body parts is not OK.
❑ Say NO! and then run away and tell someone what happened.
❑ Understand that they are not at fault nor are they bad (Wurtele, Gissispie, Currier, & Franklin, 1992).

Professionals have had very mixed success with personal safety at the preschool level although older children appear to understand the concepts and can describe a course of action that should be taken. Some of the difficulty is related to the quality of the materials produced for this age group where materials do not take into account the learning style of very young children or the attention-getting strategies possible in media (Hulsey, Kerkman, & Pinon, 1997).

GOALS AND OBJECTIVES

The ultimate goals of the physical domain are for children to develop confidence and competence in the control and movement of their bodies and to develop the attitudes, knowledge, skills, and practices that lead to maintaining, respecting, and protecting their bodies.

Intermediate Objectives

As children progress toward the ultimate goal, they will be able to demonstrate the following competencies:

1. Gain confidence in using their bodies.
2. Develop awareness of the location of their body parts.
3. Develop spacial awareness (understanding of personal and general space and direction).
4. Develop temporal awareness (speed, timing, duration, and rhythm).
5. Improve total sensory awareness and integrate sensory information to solve movement problems.
6. Distinguish the foreground from the background visually and auditorially.
7. Engage in a variety of activities that require balance.
8. Engage in a variety of activities that require coordinated movements with large and small muscle systems.
9. Sustain a vigorous motor activity over time in order to develop endurance.
10. Engage in a variety of activities that require flexibility.
11. Engage in a variety of motor activities that require agility.
12. Use their whole bodies in appropriate activities to strengthen muscles and muscle groups.
13. Develop fundamental motor skills such as jumping, hopping, throwing, kicking, striking, running, catching, and climbing.
14. Coordinate wrist, hand, finger, finger-thumb, and eye-hand movements.

15. Control the movement of their bodies in relation to objects.
16. Use tools skillfully, including implements for eating, writing, dressing, and playing.
17. Develop a positive attitude toward their bodies; appreciate their own competence and that of others.
18. Learn practices that keep their bodies and their environments clean and sanitary.
19. Acquire attitudes, knowledge, and skills that predispose them to maintaining physically fit lifestyles.
20. Learn and practice sound nutritional habits and healthy, polite eating behaviors.
21. Learn and practice appropriate safety procedures for school, playgrounds, home, and neighborhood.
22. Discriminate good and poor health/nutrition/safety practices.
23. Learn how to apply health, nutritional, and safety knowledge in making choices in daily life.

TEACHING STRATEGIES

The two major components of the physical domain—skills and knowledge—utilize the strategies for teaching skills and social-conventional knowledge. Both types of learning are addressed in Chapters 3 and 4. Here are some specific strategies particularly useful for this content.

Gross and Fine Motor Skills

1. *Use learning centers to teach skills.* Young children have short attention spans, so movement from one activity to another allows them to participate in a variety of activities and maintain interest in as well as acquire and practice new skills. Depending upon the facility, a motor skill may be a center in a classroom with centers representing other domains, or, if a gym is available, four to five motor-skill centers may be set up at the same time. Usually classrooms are not large enough to contain more than one gross motor center and one writing center. Often several motor activities can be set up outdoors.

2. *Provide opportunities for children to explore equipment and try out physical behaviors suggested by the equipment or materials.* Children should have time to explore equipment and materials before instruction

begins. This promotes perceptual knowledge. In addition, adults have opportunities to observe what the children can do on their own. For example, in a preschool classroom, place pencils on a table with paper and watch how the children pick them up and hold them. Provide pencils of varying length and diameter. Place several large balls outside where they are convenient for children to get, and watch what they do. Younger children may need a lot of exploration time. By the time youngsters reach 6 or 7, only a few minutes may be necessary.

3. *Observe children's performance on each skill of interest.* To be effective and efficient, teachers must know where children are in their development to know what to do next. Just how does the child throw, kick, or catch? What new information will help the child to move toward the next level? Patience is always required because skills are acquired slowly. Most children will use the next stage of a skill and then move back to more comfortable levels before they move forward more or less consistently. Establish specific objectives that move just ahead of the children and that are an attainable challenge.

4. *Demonstrate the skill to be mastered.* Pick up a pencil and hold it in a tripod grasp if the grasp is the skill to be mastered. Scribble with it. Tell the child, "Look, this is how to hold the pencil," as you demonstrate. "You try it now." The child may or may not be able to imitate your behavior. Let the child continue with the approximation of the grasp to make marks on paper. Repeat demonstrations as often as necessary to support the child's learning. Similar strategies are used for large motor activities. For example, a teacher might say, "Watch me throw the ball. You try it now."

5. *Provide suggestions and strategies to support the child's learning.* Scaffolding for a large motor task might be as simple as placing a silhouette of feet on the floor where the child is supposed to stand in order to be in position to strike a ball. With a writing implement, slipping a grip on the implement usually denotes where the child is supposed to hold the shaft. A piece of tape might work as well on a paint brush. Frequently adults must ask the question, "What is interfering with the child's ability to do the task?" The answers are likely to be as varied as the learners as not all children stumble in the same place.

Large, soft balls rolled along the floor help this preschool child learn to secure the ball using only his hands.

6. *Intersperse guided practice with modeling.* We have described a several-year interval from beginning to success in acquisition of motor skills. Much practice is needed, as are intermittent demonstrations. Also provide many opportunities for the children to use their skills in free play with minimal adult guidance. Exploration of movement and creative use of the body often emerge as children experiment on their own.

7. *Emphasize qualitative movement over quantitative outcomes.* Form is important. When teaching the formation of letters to 5- or 6-year-olds, the position of the paper and the student's posture become important to the eventual speed and quality of handwriting.

With throwing, the orientation of the body, the step on the foot opposite the throwing arm, the rotation of the body, and the follow-through are very important to eventual success. The distance thrown or the speed of the ball will improve over time. The early childhood years establish basic skills and habits that last. As children grow and continue to learn, their skills become more refined; power and accuracy increase, and their motor activity will become more complex.

8. *Provide encouragement and feedback to children on their performance.* As discussed in Chapter 3, praise

children using specific descriptions when they are successful: "You took a step that time when you threw the ball!" Focus on the progress each child makes so that each experience is a success.

9. *Use problem-solving strategies to explore movement concepts.* After demonstrating high, medium, and low levels, ask children to show how they could move across the floor on the low level. Then ask them to find another way to do so. Use reflections to support individual children and to encourage creative movements. Vary the problems so that children explore the space near their bodies without moving their feet. Generally, this strategy works well with whole-group instruction because of the amount of space required. Music and rhythm may be added but are not necessary as youngsters begin to understand the movements.

10. *Combine the movements listed in Figures 12.1 and 12.4 to maintain interest and increase variety-of-movement options.* Use these concepts for fine and large motor skills where appropriate.

11. *Encourage suggestions from the children themselves.* You will be able to assess their movement vocabulary and concepts. Ask children to assist in constructing an obstacle course that includes a variety of object-person relationships: under, through, behind, and on top of. Remind the children of safety considerations if necessary.

12. *Establish guidelines for safety, level of participation, and respect for others.* Children must learn to be safe during physical play as well as develop a concern for the safety of others. Teach the signals directly and provide practice so that each child knows what to do. Remember that the youngest children have difficulty in stopping. In addition, because physical competence varies considerably across the group, each child should focus on his or her own competencies and offer encouragement to others. Here are a few suggested guidelines (Sullivan, 1982):

❏ Hard or sharp objects must be left in lockers or on the sidelines. Dangerous items should not be worn or carried.

❏ Children should be aware of their own personal space and avoid collision or pushing if possible. They may not hurt one another deliberately.

❏ Words of self-praise, encouragement of, or appreciation for others are appropriate. Children may not tease or ridicule one another.

❏ Children come to the adult promptly when they hear a prearranged signal.

❏ Children engage in the activities that are developmentally appropriate for them with some level of commitment. The "couch potato" pattern and the "I can't do it" pattern are not acceptable. (Adults, of course, must distinguish between real fatigue and a general pattern of no participation.)

❏ Children will "freeze" when called upon to do so. This allows the adult to call attention to competencies and interesting or creative postures. This is also a safety strategy.

Perceptual Motor Skills

13. *Provide opportunities to practice balance that are simple at first and move to more challenging ones.* Walking on a taped line on the floor offers children an opportunity to practice without the risk of falling off. Then move to the wide, low, balance beam and then to ones higher from the surface. Be sure to have mats under beams to absorb the force of falls. Children can incorporate a variety of nonlocomotor skills and locomotor skills such as slide, jump, and hop on the balance beam at the end of the early childhood period under supervised conditions. Always remain close to the children to support or catch them as they attempt new challenges.

14. *Incorporate concepts of spacial and time awareness into other domains as opportunities arise.* Various strategies using small- and whole-group instruction are effective in helping children become more aware of space and time. Yet it is probably as these concepts are imbedded in other ongoing activities that young children begin to understand the breadth of these concepts. All objects take up space. Problems with space occur in the blocks as a youngster shoves a long board along the floor, unintentionally interfering with another player. Sometimes adults and other children misinterpret a misunderstanding of the spacial concept as a disregard of another child's rights. Make every effort to use time and space concepts accurately. A 5-minute warning should be given as close to 5 minutes before the children put away materials as is possible. Young children have sufficient difficulty with estimating time that the intervals labeled as 5 minutes should not be someplace between 2 and 15 minutes.

15. *Select noncompetitive group games or modify familiar games to reduce or eliminate competitiveness.* Try to find games in which all the children play all the time. For example, assist children to stand in a circle. Give the group between one and three pillow balls (large, soft, cloth balls), and ask them to throw to someone across the circle. Instead of having an "out" as in dodge ball, tell children to catch or pick up the ball and throw it to another. The fun is in the throwing and catching. Children will have many opportunities to play competitively later.

16. *Use directional language in context daily including "left" and "right" for the older children of the early childhood period.* For preschool, modify dances such as "Hokey Pokey" so that you sing "put one hand in" instead of "left hand." This way all the children enjoy the dance and song and are capable of participating fully in it. Put a piece of yarn on the left hand of kindergarten children and other primary children whenever they need it and label it appropriately. Remember that some people have difficulty with the meaning of left and right into adulthood.

17. *Use accurate language for naming body parts.* Most 2-year-olds know head, knees, hands, arms, and legs because caregivers use these terms in dressing children. Other body parts such as chest, thigh, and forefinger are less frequent and can easily be introduced. The genitals should be labeled with correct terminology: penis and testicles for males, labia and/or vulva for the females. Sometimes children will surprise you with questions or comments. When an infant was being bathed by his mother during group time, one 3-year-old commented, "He's a boy 'cause he got balls." The teacher paraphrased the child's comment and responded using accurate language: "You noticed that he had testicles. All boys do."

Joking and laughing about private body parts is normal in informal settings for 6- to 8-year-olds even though their understanding may be inaccurate or incomplete just as 3- to 5-year-olds find comments related to elimination hilarious. Less appropriate behaviors generally diminish as children are provided with straightforward, factual information using accurate vocabulary.

18. *Provide safety information and guidance to prevent hazards as children explore their bodies' functions and capabilities.* Body awareness includes notions of what the body does. Body functions such as eating, drinking, eliminating, and sleeping are of interest as are the internal body parts (Fleer & Careen, 1995). Include appropriate information within meaningful contexts or through direct instruction.

Delighted by their strength and increasing competence, young children explore the environment. Due to less than accurate estimates of space, youngsters stick arms, legs, fingers, toes, and heads into apertures amazingly small and cannot get out again. For this reason, adults must always supervise this age group, pointing out hazards in matter-of-fact ways as children use equipment. As many parents and teachers know, children also experiment with stuffing objects into the orifices of their bodies. One teacher extracted five dried peas from a youngster's ear. The general rule is that food and water go into the mouth, but nothing is to be put into any other part of the body.

19. *With younger children, provide an uncluttered background for objects you want them to see.* High contrast in line, pattern, and color are easier to perceive than low contrasts. Place play and work materials on uncrowded shelves so children can find them. Point out relevant cues such as shape or color when the child is observing materials. Help children recognize how some plants and animals blend into the environment because of their shape and color. As children get older, they become more able to distinguish figure-ground relationships. When teaching children about handwriting, for example, use one letter or just a few letters on a whole page. Then the child can find and copy them. Usually the child's name is recognized first, but many youngsters focus on "their" letter—the initial of their first name. They are also aware of letters from the community, such as the *M* in the McDonald's sign. Using decorated or cute letters on the wall to stimulate interest in handwriting is not recommended because such decorations are too cluttered for the child to perceive the letter easily. Children often find it easier to see letters on the same plane that they are using to draw them.

Similarly, children hear rhythm and melody from instrumental music more easily than from a combination of instrument and voice. The tune of the music line is less complex and easier to imitate. Children need guidance in learning what to attend to and what to ignore. More information on this can be found in Chapter 11.

Health, Nutrition, and Safety

20. *Plan vigorous physical activity every day.* Incorporate stretching and moving opportunities as a part of group time and prolonged active play during outdoor time. Include motor skills instruction in daily schedules.

21. *Demonstrate a concern for your own fitness and health, for children imitate what you do.* Older teachers who have some difficulty with flexibility and stamina should tell the children this and do as much as they are able.

22. *Incorporate health and safety education wherever applicable.* Do not assume that children know it already. Statements such as "Walk with the scissors pointed away from you" or "Use a tissue once; then throw it away" provide children with straightforward guides for functioning with greater safety and health. More detail on developing appropriate rules is in Chapter 16.

23. *Communicate regularly with families.* Give them the health and safety information you are teaching children. When the home and the school talk the same language about the same topics, children learn better and remember more. In addition, you will be reminding families of the basic concepts. For example, when you teach what to do in case of a fire, send home directions for family fire safety inspections and evacuations. When you attempt to expose children to a greater variety of vegetables in a tasting experience, send the list of selections home so that the children can tell parents which ones they liked.

24. *Use mealtimes to teach nutrition and eating.* Children should learn to chew food slowly and eat a variety of foods. Each child can taste a tiny portion of a food (about one teaspoon) of those foods that are unfamiliar or disliked. Do not expect children to clean their plates every day. Meal time and snack time should be relaxing conversation time, not hurried. Teach socially polite behavior such as eating with the mouth closed and listening while chewing. Encourage children to drink plenty of fluids every day. When discussing what to eat for meals and snacks, focus on foods lower in fats and sugar and higher in other nutrients. For example, choose pretzels instead of potato chips. For the same volume of food, the child is better nourished with pretzels.

When children begin to participate in a school lunch program, rehearse the appropriate behavior with them at another time of day and then eat with them during the first few weeks and sporadically throughout the year. Many children do not know how to negotiate a cafeteria line or where to sit and are unfamiliar with the food. Children with free or subsidized lunches should always be indistinguishable from others. Help children to develop patterns of support and consideration by teaching them not to comment negatively on a child's food from home. Be alert to problems such as older children taking lunch money away from younger ones and ensure supervision as necessary. Children should not be denied their food for behavioral transgressions; instead they should have a supervised eating area where they may learn more appropriate behavior.

Mealtime should be a pleasant learning experience for children.

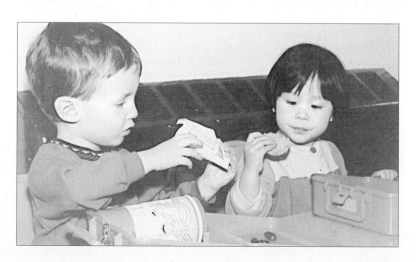

25. *When talking about food choices, use the term "a better choice" rather than "good foods" and "bad foods."* The term "bad food" is best reserved for decayed, moldy, or otherwise unsafe food. Care should be taken not to undermine parents and cultural patterns. For example, a quarter cup of salted peanuts is not the best choice for a snack but is an excellent meat substitute in many main dishes such as curries or stir-fried mixtures.

Most of the following activities are taught in small groups of children and then become self-sustaining with intermittent supervision as children practice skills. Some activities may be incorporated into whole-group sessions as a means for increasing physical activity in an otherwise sedentary experience. A few are for whole-group activities.

Activity Suggestions

✎ Fun on the Balance Beam

Objective 7   For children to engage in a variety of activities that require balance.

Procedure   Place a 2″–4″ balance beam between two foam mats or use an outdoor balance beam surrounded with fall-absorbent material. Demonstrate a walk across the balance beam at a slow, comfortable speed. Invite children to walk across the beam. If they are successful, suggest that they find another way to cross the beam. Stand nearby to support children if necessary. If they cannot think of any ways that are challenging, try some from this list: forward; backward; sliding; step sideways, step together; forward, turn around, then go backward; forward, bend knees, collapse, stand, then move forward; forward, hop, forward.

Safety   One person on the balance beam at a time. Children must be careful not to push or bump one another when they are on the beam.

To simplify   Tape two lines (2″–4″ wide) on the floor and have the children walk bewteen them with the suggested movements.

To extend   Use a narrower balance beam or a higher one. Some extensions on easy levels are suggested in the list of movements above.

✎ Indoor Striking

Objective 13   For children to develop fundamental motor skills such as jumping, hopping, throwing, kicking, striking, running, catching, and climbing.

Procedure   Hang three or more Nerf® or foam balls from the ceiling with string so that the balls hang approximately at child waist-height. Adjust the balls for the various heights of the children. They should hang 3 or more feet apart and be well out of the pathway of other people. (They can be clipped up when not in use.) Give each of three children styrofoam mallets the size of ping-pong paddles. Demonstrate how to hit the ball.

Safety   A hard strike sends the ball the full radius of the string. Soft balls will not injure a child, but being hit by a mallet during the strikers' follow-through may sting. Young children are not skilled in stopping in the midst of an action like this. For this reason, other players should remain outside the radius of the balls.

To simplify   Ask the children to strike the balls with their hands. Encourage striking the moving ball as well as the stationary ball.

To extend   After observation of exploratory hits, make suggestions about form so that the child moves from a straight approach with a chop to standing sideways to the ball to swing the mallet. If there appears to be any movement of the foot of the striking hand, encourage them to move their foot and rotate the body. If this is the appropriate stage in striking, demonstrate the step, strike, and follow-through typical of more mature form. See the description of stages in Figure 12.2.

✎ Move on Command

Objective 2   For children to develop awareness of the location of their own body parts.

Procedure   Children should sit in a circle or face the teacher. The teacher names a body part and a movement. The children then execute the movement of the body part. Demonstrate first saying, "nod head," and then do it. Ask them to do the next one, "lift arm." Use many different movements and body parts. Invite a child or children to contribute body parts or movements or both.

a. twist - - - - arms
b. stretch - - - - neck
c. raise - - - - elbow

To simplify   Say directions slowly. If children do not appear to know the body part, repeat the direction pointing to the part and do the movement. Then they can imitate the leader.

To extend Use all parts of the body and more complex movements such as rotate one shoulder, roll on your hip, or push on your abdomen.

✎ Moving Standing Still

Objective 3 For children to develop spacial awareness (understanding of personal and general space and direction).

Procedure Children need only their own personal space. This is the amount of space they can take up within kicking or stretched arm distance. Vary the movements, the body parts involved, and the tempo of the movements in the directions. Children are asked to stay standing on the same spot throughout the experience. Sample directions are listed as follows:

Bend one part of your body while stretching another part.

Stretch as many parts of your body as you can all at the same time.

Keeping your feet still, twist around as far as you can.

Find how many directions you can push. Think of all the body parts that can be used to push.

While standing, show all the body parts that can swing.

Swing fast. Swing slow.

Collapse to the floor slowly.

Pull something heavy as you rise.

To simplify Demonstrate so children imitate, and gradually repeat directions so they learn to do it without imitation. Use only a few directions.

To extend Increase the difficulty of the movements or the speed of transition from one movement to another or both.

✎ Mother/Father, May I?

Objective 10 For children to engage in a variety of activities that require flexibility.

Procedures This is fun to play outside. Invite children to arrange themselves in a line so that they will not touch anyone else as they move. The leader—mother/father—is in front facing a line of children. The starting line may be real, drawn in the dirt or grass, or imaginary. The leader presents the children with tasks that require flexibility as they move forward. The

leader may say, "Israel, bend down and put your hands on the ground and walk them forward."

Israel must respond, "Mother/Father, may I?"

Should the leader say, "You may," Israel may carry out the movement. Should the leader say, "No, you may not," Israel is expected to remain in place. If a child is caught moving without permission, then she or he goes back to the starting line. Some moves requiring flexibility are the following:

Put your hands behind your neck and take two steps forward.

Squat down and waddle four times.

Turn your body sideways and step sideways twice.

Swing your arms around and around and take three giant steps.

Sit down on the bottoms of your feet and stretch your arms forward as far as possible, and then move to where your arms reach.

To simplify Do this in a small group so each child does not wait very long for a turn. Younger children may need to practice the traditional steps before attempting the actions requiring flexibility. This alters the objective to Objective 13 (develop fundamental motor skills such as jumping, hopping, throwing, kicking, striking, running, catching, and climbing) although children do learn the rules to the game. They are as follows:

Baby step: toe to heel

Giant step: as big as possible

Banana splits: slide one foot forward as far as possible

Umbrella step: place forefinger on top of head and spin around once

Frog leaps: two-footed jump

Bunny steps: one-footed hop

Fire engines: run until "Mother/Father" says "stop"

To simplify further Use only forward and backward variations of step and jump.

To extend Older children may enjoy adding a "tag" game on the end. The child tags the leader, who then chases the child back to the starting line. If the leader tags the child, that person becomes the next leader.

Encourage children to become the leader and invent twisty ways to move. Make suggestions to encourage flexibility.

✎ Mastering Cutting Techniques

Objective 16   For children to use tools skillfully including implements for eating, writing, dressing, and playing.

Procedure   Provide magazines, pieces of scrap paper of various colors and textures, paste or glue, old sacks, classified ad pages, wallpaper scraps, and scissors. This opportunity for guided practice should be interspersed with demonstrations on how to use the scissors and should encourage children to attempt more challenging cutting tasks.

Draw lines on some of the scraps so that children cut increasingly difficult pieces:

No lines

Straight lines

Long wavy lines

Sharply curved lines

Corners

Zigzag lines

Children may paste pieces on other reused products such as newspaper or paper bags.

To simplify   Use unlined small papers of moderate weight or tear the paper.

To extend   Children who can cut all of the lines are capable of cutting on the line simple shapes that they draw themselves as well as cutting out the inside space of two concentric circles or two concentric squares or pictures from magazines.

✎ Puzzles

Objective 14   For children to coordinate wrist, hand, finger, finger-thumb, and eye-hand movements.

Procedure   Place a variety of puzzles in a puzzle rack or on the table where children can see them. Demonstrate how to take puzzles out by pouring puzzles of 50–100 pieces into a large tray or laying them out on a surface with the picture side up. Puzzles in frames should be removed one piece at a time and placed on a table. Do not flip them over because the pieces will slide and get lost on the floor or under furniture. Ask a child to look carefully at the picture, noting distinctive features. Guide the child as necessary to solve the problem. Point out curved and straight lines. Suggest tracing the edges of the shapes with a finger. Suggest looking for corner or edge pieces first because these usually have distinctive features.

To simplify   Select easier puzzles, one hole for each puzzle piece; 3–5-piece puzzles; 5–10 pieces with the cuts in logical places such as a tail or foot; 11–15 pieces.

To extend   Increase the numbers of pieces or the complexity of the picture. Three-dimensional puzzles are available and take a long time but provide great challenge.

✎ Pull a Friend

Objective 12   For children to use their whole bodies in appropriate activities to strengthen muscles and muscle groups.

Procedure   Outdoors, provide wagons, sleds, cardboard sheets with ropes making long bails, or tricycles that will carry passengers. Suggest that one child pull or push another in the conveyance. Demonstrate and suggest that another child take your place.

To simplify   Provide blocks or other objects for the children to transport that are lighter in weight.

To extend   Increase the weight being transported, or suggest they try the cardboard-and-rope combination. Due to friction, this is much more difficult, but it will work.

✎ Exploring Vertical Space

Objective 4   For children to develop temporal awareness (speed, timing, duration, and rhythm).

Procedure   Ask the children to spread out so that they cannot touch anyone else. Tell them to put their hands on their shoulders and then raise their arms overhead and say, "This is your high space." Then ask them to touch their shoulders and then the area joining the leg to hip and say, "This is your middle space." Finally, ask them to touch the floor and then their hip joint and say, "This is your low space." Demonstrate using your own body while providing directions and defining the meanings of *high, middle,* and *low* spaces.

Using a slow walking beat on a tambourine, ask the children to start at their high space and move their bodies to their low space. Using words such as *smooth, jerky, bent,* or *twisted,* and denoting speeds such as *very slow* or *fast,* continue giving children movement directions. Alter the rhythm on the drum to match your directions. Intersperse "freeze" or "stop" directions when children make interesting forms with their bodies and praise the performance.

To simplify   Demonstrate most of the specific moves with the language cues if the children do not know the vocabulary.

To extend   Give the children large balls to hold as they move through vertical space. Provide simple music and then ask children to suggest ways to move. Last, include locomotor directions. Remember that the more directions the child must include, the more difficult the activity becomes; thus, leaping smoothly while holding a ball in high space is very challenging indeed.

✎ Vegetable Tasting

Objective 20   For children to learn and practice sound nutritional habits and healthy, polite eating behaviors.

Procedure   Place a tray containing a variety of cooked and raw vegetables, tasting spoons, and/or toothpicks out where children can see them. Have small samples that you use to talk about and others that are used for tasting. Select combinations of very common and less common vegetables so that children are familiar with some and not with others. Keep portions tiny. One slender carrot coin or a kernel of corn is sufficient to explore the taste. Small soufflé cups are useful to prevent children from dipping used spoons into a serving dish. The adult may put a little in the cup, and then the child may eat it. Name the vegetables and encourage children to comment. Within the

context of this taste exploration, provide children with additional information such as "raw, crisp vegetables help keep your teeth clean" or "children should have several servings of vegetables every day to stay healthy." Maintain normal sanitary practices: clean hands, wash vegetables, and so on.

To simplify   Use fewer vegetables at a time, and repeat the process several times. Deliberately include vegetables common to all cultural groups represented in the classroom.

To extend   Increase the variety of vegetables to include those not commonly eaten by the children in the ethnic group being taught. Increase the information given so that children learn that some vegetables are really good or energy producing: potatoes of all kinds, corn, and peas. Groups of vegetables such as green leafy and yellow ones have specific vitamins (particularly A) that people need, and some are mostly fiber and are also necessary for good health.

✎ Snowperson Walk/Run

Objective 19   For children to acquire attitudes, knowledge, and skills about physical activity that predispose children to maintaining physically fit lifestyles.

Procedure   On brisk winter days, take the children outdoors and walk rapidly or run around the building. This is particularly effective after prolonged work at tables or quiet activities. Tell children that they are snowpersons in a hurry.

To simplify   Select a closer destination.

To extend   Gradually increase the length and speed of the walk. When returning inside, indicate how good you feel when you get out and really move!

✖ Applying What You Read in This Chapter

1. Discuss

a. If children are allowed to play on a playground daily, will all of them develop the fundamental motor skills by the end of the early childhood period? Explain your answer.

b. Ms. Cunningham wanted 2-year-old Phillip to be an athlete, so she showed him videos of tennis players and golfers, did infant massage, and engaged in many bouts of training in jumping,

kicking, striking, and throwing. What do you think was the outcome of all this effort and why?

c. Describe how a dance experience for 5-year-olds might be organized that would enhance their nonlocomotor movement skills.

2. Observe

a. Carefully watch two to five children engaging in gross motor activity. Using the information in Figure 12.2, try to determine the competence level in one of the fundamental motor skills for each child. Record your findings as best you can. List the difficulties you had in doing this.

b. Observe the fine motor skills of two children at least 12 months apart in age. Compare your observations with the descriptions in Table 12.2. Explore why there are differences between the description and the individuals you observed.

3. **Carry out an activity**

a. In pairs, try out the stages of each of the fundamental motor skills described in Table 12.1. One adult student should read the description while the other tries to do it. If you can do it yourself, you will understand what muscles are involved for the children.

b. Give a felt or nylon point pen and paper to a preschool child, and suggest that he or she write you a letter. If the child informs you that he or she cannot write, tell the child that it is not necessary to do grown-up writing, only children's writing or pretend writing. Describe how the child gripped the writing implement. Compare to the description in the text. Was there any apparent understanding of letters, left-to-right progression, or other aspects of written language?

c. Select a fine motor task such as sewing on a button, eating with chopsticks, or tying a fish lure, and write out step-by-step directions on how to do the task. Teach this task to another adult who is a novice and evaluate your effectiveness. Reflect on the strategies you used. What scaffolding was necessary, if any?

4. **Create something for your portfolio**

a. Write a lesson plan using the suggested strategies for any skill or movement concept. Prepare any visual aids that are necessary. Implement the plan if possible, and photograph a youngster carrying out the skill. Place these materials in your portfolio.

b. Photograph two children engaging in a fundamental motor skill, with fast multiple photos to catch the action. Write a short analysis of the stage that each child is in, and identify the next step necessary to advance the skill attempted.

5. **Add to your journal**

a. You are a teacher in a childcare program. Your assistant is a picky eater and really does not want to sit down with the children at lunch. When she does, she complains about the food selections, preparations, and stirs the food around indifferently. What are the health implications for the children in the group? What is your responsibility in this situation, and what actions should you take, if any?

b. Examine the curriculum suggested for substance use and abuse. Think about the choices you have made yourself. Considering the young children who will respect and emulate you, do you think you might reconsider some of your choices? Where does your personal freedom impinge upon your professional responsibility? What will you say when they ask, "Do you . . . ?" or "Did you ever . . . ?"

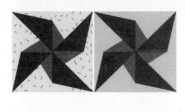

Chapter 13

The Social Domain

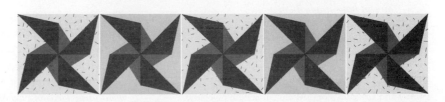

You may wonder:

How do children develop social skills? Are they important enough to teach in school?

Why are children's friendships important?

When children get into conflict, what can I do to help them resolve their disputes peacefully?

What is the relationship between social skills and the social sciences?

What kinds of activities will teach social skills as well as the social sciences?

In this chapter on the social domain, we present information to help you answer these questions.

From one corner of the preschool room comes the following interchange:

> *"I want that truck."*
>
> *"But I had it first."*
>
> *"I still want it."*
>
> *"You can have it when I'm done."*
>
> *"Be fast."*

This chapter was written by Laura C. Stein, Department of Family and Child Ecology, Michigan State University.

Ms. Roth's kindergartners are on their way to visit the local fire station. Their mission is to find out how the firefighters work and live and the ways in which they protect the community. The children have generated a list of questions they will try to answer through observations and discussion. One of their aims is to note diversity among the staff at the station. The children have brought paper, pencils, and markers in order to record, in any way they can, what they discover.

The first-grade class at the Greenleaf Elementary School embarks on a project to map the playground. Initially, they measure the space, choosing "footsteps" as their unit of measure. After much discussion, the children decide to create three-dimensional models of the playground equipment using boxes of various sizes and shapes. Small groups of children are taking responsibility for representing different areas of the schoolyard.

It is late October, and Mr. Hwang's second graders have been learning about the upcoming elections in their city, county, and state. The youngsters have demonstrated a great interest in voting, and lively discussions have arisen over issues of "fairness." When a guinea pig is offered as a class pet, the children ask if they can hold an election to choose a name for it.

Although these scenarios depict children of different ages in variety of school settings, they all represent a part of the social domain, which encompasses four essential aspects of children's development and education. The first of these, social skill development, deals with the ways children learn to interact with others. Socialization is the process by which children learn to understand and adapt to rules. Children's social responsibility is a measure of their respect for individual differences, care of the environment, and their ability to function as good citizens (e.g., by resolving conflicts peacefully). Finally, social studies or social science is the curricular area that focuses on the whole of human behavior, now and in the past. Because of its roots in the traditional social science disciplines such as anthropology, economics, human ecology, geography, psychology, and the like, social studies provides us with an organizing principle around which to plan programs for children. Thus, although each facet of the social domain is not the same as any of the others, they are inextricably linked.

There are many possible approaches to addressing children's social development and teaching social studies in the early childhood curriculum (Brewer, 1998). One strategy is to treat social studies as a separate content area with a body of knowledge to be learned through formal experiences. Proponents believe that children could be learning more specific knowledge than is traditionally taught to them. A second view is that the most important concepts of both social studies and social skills are best learned through the naturally occurring interactions within the classroom and that it is inappropriate to focus on specific content. This chapter will present a means for combining the best of these two so that children learn content related to social studies in ways that are relevant to them, while developing the social competencies they need through productive interactions with others.

Teaching within the social domain provides children with opportunities to develop knowledge and skills regarding themselves in relationship to people in their near environment and to extend this information to understanding human relationships in the larger world. The family is the foundation of these learnings, while the classroom is often the place where children are confronted with ideas and people both similar to and different from themselves. During the early school years, children are figuring out how to establish and maintain relationships with members of their group. As time goes on, they explore their contribution to the well-being of the group. Throughout this period, they are continually working out how to value others and how to understand and cope with the differences they encounter. Thus, the classroom functions as a "human relations laboratory" in which children explore social knowledge, concepts, and skills via daily interactions, routines, activities, and on-the-spot instructions (Reed, 1966). It is the place in which they assimilate values and attitudes about other people from listening to and watching the adults around them. It is also the arena in which they practice citizenship in its most basic forms. Through their social encounters and activities, children build their understanding of history, sociology, economics, and culture. These are by no means the only issues they face, but they are so important that teachers have to know how to address them.

To derive an understanding of the social domain, it is necessary to look at its individual pieces. We begin with a discussion of social skill development, including children's friendships and prosocial behavior, with an emphasis on the roles adults play.

SOCIAL SKILL DEVELOPMENT

Establishing relationships with others, learning to live within the bounds of societal expectations, and figuring out one's place in the group are all major tasks of early childhood and reflect aspects of children's social development. Indeed, as children mature, more of their time and energy becomes devoted to this area of their development. This is especially true as they move beyond their family and neighborhood and come into greater contact with community institutions, such as early childhood centers and elementary schools. In these circumstances, children encounter new sets of expectations to which they must adapt.

How well children perceive, interpret, and respond to the variety of social situations they meet is a measure of their social competence. A high level of social competence in our society means that a person exhibits responsible, independent, friendly, cooperative, purposeful, and self-controlled behavior. Youngsters with low levels of social competence, by contrast, act irresponsibly, timidly, hostilely, uncooperatively, or impulsively (Knopczyk & Rhodes, 1996). Children who display socially competent behaviors are perceived in more positive ways by society and are therefore treated in a more positive manner; the children thus experience more satisfying interpersonal interactions and are happier than their less successful counterparts. Furthermore, research demonstrates that children's social competence influences their academic as well as their social performance (Alexander & Entwisle, 1988). Finally, children who are socially competent experience high self-esteem, viewing themselves as worthwhile, capable people, which has positive effects on their social performance.

Children are not born knowing how to make friends and influence people, nor do they come into this world understanding the rules their society has established. It takes time as well as many varied experiences for them to master the skills necessary for them to master the skills necessary for successful functioning in society (Kostelnik & Stein, 1990). Children spend much of their early lives trying out a panoply of strategies in order to make sense of their social world. Through experimentation, they begin to figure out what works and what does not and under which circumstances. Once in school, their task becomes even more complex. Some of their actions may not lead to the same satisfactory outcomes as was true in former situations. For example, children may become bewildered when, after having been taught to work together with others on projects in preschool, their "team" efforts suddenly are viewed as "cheating" in higher grades. Or youngsters accustomed to talking openly with adults about transgressions of their playmates may be labeled "tattle-tale" by their peers in school. Thus, children still have much to learn about the two major aspects of social development—socialization and social skills.

Children's social development can be looked at as the foundation upon which other types of learning take place. Apart from nutrition and physical comfort,

the need for human association is basic (Maslow, 1970; Berk, 1997). This further implies that until individuals' essential needs, including positive association with others, have been met, they are unable to move beyond those realms into other areas of learning (i.e., academic, cognitive). Thus, instructional time spent on social development that heretofore has been regarded as "icing on the cake" must, instead, be treated as an essential ingredient of that cake.

There are several critical issues of children's social development that directly affect their lives at school that must be considered. The first of these primarily involves children's relationship with peers—that is, making and keeping friends and demonstrating prosocial behaviors, such as helping and cooperating. Another centers on children's interactions with adults, as they begin to figure out how to fit their behavior to adult expectations and rules. And, finally, learning to understand and appreciate differences in a diverse society and responding as a democratic citizen is a critical focus of youngsters' associations with both grown-ups and children as they develop.

Children's Friendships

Five-year-olds Bo and Casey are playing with dinosaur models in the dinosaur habitat. They are deeply engrossed in their activity, moving the figures from place to place and actively communicating with one another their ideas for the scenario. Jimmy walks over, picks up a dinosaur, and tosses it into the middle of the play area.

> *"Hey," says Bo, "you can't put it there. That's the water hole."*
>
> *"Yeah," adds Casey. "Besides you're not on our team!"*
>
> *"I am so, if I wanna be," Jimmy asserts, angrily standing up with his hands on his hips.*
>
> *"No, you can't," Bo responds*
>
> *"Teacher, they won't let me be on their team!" wails Jimmy.*

Until fairly recently, most educators assumed that making and keeping friends were aspects of life that some children were better at than others but that there was nothing much that could or should be done about it at school. They reasoned that it was most appropriate for children to deal with this issue on the playground or before and after school rather than allow instructional time to be used. At most, the playground supervisor was expected to deal with children who were having school problems. Those youngsters having persistent difficulty were referred to the school counselor or administrator. We now are more aware of the negative impact that disharmony in social relations has on children's abilities to concentrate on school subjects and, as a consequence, their school achievement. Furthermore, we also know that much can be accomplished by teachers and classroom aides in helping children become more successful in their friendship strategies (Asher, Oden, & Gottman, 1977; Kostelnik et al., 1998). To effectively assist children in improving their friendship skills, adults must understand the role that friendship plays in children's lives.

Why Friends Are Important   As they mature, children become increasingly interested in establishing friendships (Hartup, 1991). In fact, it has been documented that by age 7, most children find it almost unthinkable not to have a friend (Hendrick, 1997). Among other benefits, friends provide stimulation, assistance, companionship, social comparison, and affection (Parker & Gottman, 1989). Furthermore, within a friendship children can experiment with a number of social roles, such as leader, follower, risk taker, or comforter. In essence, children develop a sense of belonging and security through the special relationship with a friend.

Life without friends can appear fairly bleak. Although truly friendless children are few in number, there is evidence that poor peer relationships in childhood lead to difficulties later in life (Kupersmidt, Coie, and Dodge, 1992; Kupersmidt & Patterson, 1993; Hartup & Moore, 1990). For instance, adolescent delinquency and emotional instability have been linked to friendlessness in the early years. Naturally, just as in the case of adults, children vary in how many friends they want to have. Some are content with one "best" friend, whereas others seek a wide circle of friends. It is the quality of these relationships that counts more than the quantity (Stocking, Arezzo, & Leavitt, 1980).

Children's Changing Ideas About Friendship   Children's ideas of what constitutes a friend change as they grow older. Significantly, children at various stages of development view friends very differently from adults. It is valuable for adults to look as this developmental process in order to assess and facilitate children's relationships with one another more constructively.

In the early stages of friendship, children are preoccupied with their own emotions. They concentrate on youngsters who are available, as well as on their physical attractiveness or other outward characteristics and their material possessions (Selman, 1980). As part of their focus on the here and now, children between the ages of 3 and 7 are better at initiating relationships than sustaining them, and they may also inadvertently rebuff the advances of others because they are simply not very good at picking up friendship cues. They sometimes have difficulty entering an ongoing play situation or accepting others who wish to join, as illustrated in the example given earlier (Kostelnik et al., 1998). Adults who observe these difficulties often view these children as being heartless and inconsiderate instead of recognizing that they are experiencing a cognitive dilemma, that of centering on one way to carry out the play episode.

Somewhat later in their understanding of friends, between the ages of 4 and 9, children begin to look for pleasing behaviors from others. This may entail giving one another turns, sharing toys, or deliberately choosing to sit together. Although children seem content with their choices, some of these relationships may not always appear equal in the eyes of an adult. They worry when children select friends that seem to be uncongenial companions, ones that are bossy or overly compliant, for instance. It is difficult for teachers and others to stand by when children persist in these types of friendships. Parents and educators are often tempted to separate these youngsters forcibly. It is important to remember that children are deriving benefits from these relationships that are not always apparent to adults. For example, they may use their companion as a model for their own future behavior. Thus, the shy child may observe the bossy child achieve his or her aims through assertiveness and may ultimately try out a few of those strategies. Similarly, the bossy child may admire the more modest approach of his or her peer. If, as the children assume different behaviors within the friendship, their relationship flexes to accommodate these new variables, youngsters may continue to remain close companions. If it does not, they will lose interest in one another and try out new relationships. Adults must allow children themselves to decide when and if this change is to take place.

Children in this phase of friendship desire so much to have a friend that they often resort to bribery or threats. Furthermore, they still have difficulty having more than one close relationship at a time and are often heard to remark, "You can't be my friend—José is my friend." Adults are sometimes appalled at the tactics the children use toward one another. However, it is important to recognize that children are merely trying out strategies to get what they want and will soon learn from their peers how well they work; their aim is not to be deliberately mean or hurtful.

Because children at this stage actively seek friends that are like them, they are busy comparing themselves to others to determine likenesses and differences. They begin to choose same-sex and same-race playmates. This becomes even more pronounced at the next phase, which describes children between the ages of 6 and 12. Here, children are finally beginning to understand that their behavior must please another person, not simply the reverse. They are deeply involved in what is fair and not fair (as viewed from their special point of view). In this stage children want to be most like their friends, and so conformity in dress, speech, and actions reaches a peak.

Furthermore, friendships at this stage tend to come in twos; girls especially form close-knit diads, while boys travel in looser packs (Hartup, 1991). Both boys and girls are extremely possessive of their relationships, and conflicts and hard feelings often result. Adults express concern over the extremes of self-segregation by sex, race, and differing physical abilities that frequently occur at this stage (Hartup, 1991). Although adults cannot mandate friendships, there is much they can do to help children recognize similarities between themselves and others in spite of certain obvious physical differences. Some common ground between children might include cognitive skills, degree of sociability, interests, and attitudes (Bukowski, Sippola, & Bolvin, 1995). These issues are especially relevant when helping children develop nonprejudicial attitudes and behaviors. Adults must think of ways to take advantage of children's growing abilities to observe and reason in order to promote these values (Bergen, 1993; Deegan, 1993). (Strategies for helping children achieve a heightened awareness of similarity among people while recognizing and appreciating differences are presented in the activity section of this chapter.)

How children look at interpersonal relationships with peers over time is an important aspect of their growing capacity for friendships. Other crucial factors in their ability to make and keep friends are the skills they bring to the process. These skills can be divided into three distinct categories: establishing contact, maintaining positive relationships, and resolving conflicts (Kostelnik et al., 1998).

Friendship Skill: Establishing Contact   To start a potential friendship, one child must first approach another. If the friendship has any chance of success, the second person must respond positively. How this contact is carried out influences each child's perception of the other. If they have a good impression, the interaction will continue; if they do not, it will terminate at that point. Children who are cordial—that is, who smile, speak pleasantly, offer greetings, and seek information—tend to elicit positive responses from others (Hazen & Black, 1989; Ladd & Coleman, 1993). These replies can be cast in the form of responding to others' greetings and questions, offering information, and inviting participation. Another successful strategy for breaking the ice is imitation. Very young children feel flattered when others mimic their actions by playing nearby or using the same materials, and they tend to welcome more direct involvement of the imitator. Older children are more leery of this tactic and may become irritated at someone who is "copying." It may take some finesse on the part of the approaching youngster to recognize when he or she has breached the boundaries.

This kind of judgment may seem natural for all children to develop, yet there are many youngsters who fail to recognize that even the seemingly simple strategy of acting friendly will gain friends. They may have the right idea, but their timing is off, or their actions may be misapplied. These are children who benefit greatly from friendship coaching (Kostelnik et al., 1998). This involves pointing out the child's own behavior and its effect on other youngsters using specific observable terms rather than generalizations. Then the adult should demonstrate the appropriate skill and include a rationale explaining why it is effective. The next step is for the child to practice the skill and participate in an evaluation of how well it worked. Naturally, it takes a great deal of time and practice for children to learn to make themselves more appealing to others.

Friendship Skill: Maintaining Positive Relationships
The second level of friendship skills is to maintain positive relationships once they have been initiated. Children who speak directly to one another, are attentive to others in particular interactions, respond in an interested fashion, and offer suggestions are popular with others (Hazen & Black, 1989). In addition, these youngsters demonstrate cooperation and helpfulness and are comfortable expressing emotions such as affection, empathy, and joy in the accomplishment of their pals.

The children are able to sustain relationships because their behavior makes them fun and satisfying to be with. Children who lack these skills are far less successful in their abilities to sustain friendships over time. They annoy and antagonize their peers by showing off, being insensitive to people's reactions, becoming overly exuberant in their displays of affection, or taking over rather than being helpful or cooperative. Even though their intentions may be positive, their actions make it difficult for these youngsters to be viewed as potential friends.

Friendship Skill: Resolving Conflicts The most complex aspect of peer relationships is handling conflicts. Children's ability to deal with disputes in democratic ways such as recognizing and taking account of differences in another's viewpoint, compromising, bargaining, or suggesting nonviolent solutions to the problem is highly indicative of the future success of a relationship (Hartup, 1991). Children who forcibly demand that issues be decided their way or, conversely, who back down from establishing their legitimate rights lose the respect of their peers and tend to be rejected by them.

Thus, children who use constructive means of resolving disputes while at the same time satisfying their own needs are most successful in forming lasting relationships. The facets of this process are illustrated in Table 13.1 (Stocking et al., 1980).

Educators play an important role in helping children learn how to use these strategies. One way they can do this is by modeling the role of a conflict mediator in disputes between children. This involves being a nonjudgmental facilitator so that children learn to find peaceful solutions that are mutually satisfying.

The conflict mediation process consists of seven steps, summarized in Table 13.2. How to present this process so that children can practice the specific skills is discussed later in the activity section of this chapter.

Children vary widely in their abilities to engage in this form of resolving conflicts. Success depends on their age, understanding of relationships, communication skills, and experiences. The technique has been used productively with children as young as 3 who could communicate their wants. As children mature, refine their abilities to express themselves, and become more familiar with how it works, their capacity for

TABLE 13.1
Negotiating Conflicts

Strategy	Example
Expressing one's own rights, needs, or feelings	"It's my turn to use the stapler."
Listening to and acknowledging others' rights, opinions, and feelings	"Oh, you haven't finished yet."
Suggesting nonviolent solutions to conflict	"How about giving it to me in 2 minutes?"
Explaining the reasons behind the solution suggested	"That way we'll both get to use it before lunch."
Standing up against unreasonable demands	"No, it's not fair if you use it the whole time. I want it, too."
Accepting reasonable disagreement	"OK, I hadn't thought of that."
Compromising on a solution	"I can use tape now, and you can use tape later when I'm using the stapler."

TABLE 13.2
Conflict Mediation

Steps in the Process	Role of the Adult
1. Initiating the mediation process	Assumes mediator role Stops aggressive behavior Neutralizes object or territory
2. Clarifying perspectives	Solicits statements from each party Paraphrases perspectives Establishes own neutrality
3. Summing up	Defines problem in mutual terms
4. Generating alternatives	Solicits ideas from combatants and bystanders Suggests possibilities, if necessary
5. Agreeing on a solution	Summarizes points of agreement Identifies resolution
6. Reenforcing the problem-solving process	Praises children for developing solution
7. Following through	Helps children carry out terms of agreement

staying with the process increases. They shift from the belief that disputes are caused by one person against another to a more balanced view of shared responsibility. The mediation model presented here helps children move in that direction. They have opportunities to observe problem solving firsthand and experience the results of nonviolent solutions.

In addition, as the negotiation process becomes more familiar, the number of participating onlookers grow, which thus increases the involvement of more children. There is also promising evidence that not only does aggression diminish, but positive prosocial behaviors increase in groups where mediation is commonly used (Kostelnik & Stein, 1986). Furthermore, when adults take on this role, the number and duration of children's conflicts declines over time and children take over the peaceful management of their disputes (Stein & Kostelnik, 1984).

As stated earlier, the give-and-take of children's relationships with their peers has a profound effect on their success at school. Also important is their understanding of how groups of people can live and work comfortably and productively together. Being kind toward each other by behaving helpfully and cooperatively makes group living a more positive experience for all.

Prosocial Behavior: Acting Positively Toward Others

Prosocial behavior represents the most positive attributes of society. Acts of kindness such as helping, sharing, sympathizing, rescuing, defending, cooperating, and comforting benefit all persons, the givers as well as the receivers. When children and adults cooperate with one another by working toward a common goal or help someone by alleviating their distress or facilitating work or play, they contribute to an environment in which friendly interactions and productive group efforts abound (Gazda et al., 1995). Furthermore, in such an atmosphere routine or uninteresting tasks are easily handled, since no one person is burdened with them. In essence, then, a classroom in which prosocial values and behaviors are transmitted and encouraged tends to produce participants with a positive self- and group image. Further, they are likely to view themselves and others as competent and congenial (Kostelnik et al., 1998). Finally, children who learn to be kind tend not to be selfish or aggressive. It follows that providing instruction in prosocial behaviors within the classroom creates the kind of setting in which all learning is enhanced.

It was once believed that if people were taught to think prosocially, corresponding prosocial behaviors would follow automatically. Unfortunately, this correlation does not hold true. Good thoughts do not necessarily lead to good deeds (Bryan & Walbek, 1970). Although children can, on cue, proclaim, "We're supposed to share," all reason may go out the window in the midst of a race to get the red marker. Children must be helped to go beyond thinking and saying what is appropriate to doing what is right. To accomplish this, they must go through a series of steps. First, they need to recognize that help or cooperation is required, then they must decide whether or not to do something. Finally, they must perform a prosocial action that is appropriate to the situation at hand.

Prosocial Skills: Recognition, Decision, Action   Sensitivity to someone's cues for help or cooperation is the initial skill children must acquire to learn to be prosocial. The messages sent by others can be nonverbal (panting, crying, or sighing) or the more obvious verbal strategies of complaining or requesting assistance. Surprisingly, although these signals seem clear to most adults, some children appear to ignore them. Either these children misunderstand their meaning, or they do not think the signs are meant for them. Thus it cannot be assumed that just because children are in the presence of such cues they necessarily recognize them.

Once they realize a person is in need, children must decide whether to act. Several factors play a role in their decision. Youngsters are most likely to respond to people they know, like, or admire (Staub, 1978). If they are in a positive mood, they will more likely act than if they are upset or in a neutral frame of mind. In addition, they feel more responsible toward a person who has extended kindness to them in the past or from whom they hope to reap future rewards (Denhan, 1995). Older children and adults, in general, will respond independent of personal gain, as more generalized notions of justice play a role in their thinking.

Finally, a child must perform an action. How suitable the action is that they choose is influenced by their ability to take another person's perspective into account and by their instrumental know-how (McGinnis & Goldstein, 1990). At any stage of this process, children may experience difficulties. They may misinterpret cues or overlook them, they may miscalculate which behaviors would be appropriate, or they may act hastily or incompletely. As they mature and gain experience, their efforts will more likely meet with greater success.

Promoting Prosocial Behavior   As the primary conveyers of social values to children outside the family, educators play a key role in influencing prosocial behavior. Furthermore, educators have a profound effect on the degree to which children demonstrate prosocial behaviors in the classroom. They can increase children's kindness by creating an environment in which they themselves model the behaviors they expect of children, look for instances of prosocial behaviors and reward them, and teach children directly to think and act prosocially (Gestwicki, 1998; Kostelnik et al., 1998).

Additionally, children can be given many planned opportunities to participate in tasks and situations that allow them to rehearse prosocial skills. Children benefit greatly from these occasions and demonstrate a greater frequency of such positive behaviors in similar circumstances (Honig & Wittmer, 1992). This occurs because children can better remember both the appropriate behavior and the cues that signal which conditions apply in a given circumstance when they have had a chance to practice. (Specific techniques that combine verbal descriptions and explanations with practice are illustrated in the activity section of this chapter.)

The educator's role is significant in influencing children's prosocial actions. In the same vein, how educators teach children about expectations for behavior affects children's ability to understand and follow rules.

SOCIALIZATION: CHILDREN'S BEHAVIOR AND ADULT EXPECTATIONS

Much of children's interactions with teachers and other adults in school revolve around rules. Children are continually learning about what the rules are and how to act in accordance with them. This is not a simple process for children to master.

Educators often expect children to learn classroom and school rules within a few weeks and then be able to follow them consistently. Failure to do so has been viewed frequently as willfulness or resistance on the part of the child, and such youngsters develop reputations that follow them throughout their school career. Although teachers see it as important, they often resent having to take class time to teach children about the rules more than a few times. Furthermore, because following rules is an expected behavior, infractions are often noticed more than compliance. Learning rules and being able to follow them takes time. Just as in other areas, children vary both the rates at which they acquire the knowledge and skills and also the extent of adult intervention they require.

A major goal of early childhood educators is for children to be able to understand and then follow the rules even when adults are not present; in other words, for children to achieve self-discipline. How this can be achieved is such a vital aspect of children's social development that Chapter 6 has been devoted entirely to how children develop self-control and what the adult role is in the process.

SOCIAL RESPONSIBILITY

Many changes have occurred in the world during the past few decades, and more changes are to come. Families have become more mobile, special needs youngsters are being integrated in ever increasing numbers into classrooms, neighborhood boundaries are more permeable, and so children are exposed to a wider variety of people. In addition, the health of our planet has been brought into question. At the same time, educators have become aware that social attitudes are formed when children are young. Given these concerns, the question becomes how to prepare our young people to live in a pluralistic society in ways that uphold the democratic principles of fairness, equal opportunity, and justice. Thus we have come to understand that we must teach children about their responsibility to the world beyond their doorstep. This is the essence of encouraging children to become good citizens of their classroom, their neighborhood, and the larger society they will encounter as they mature. Through attention to social issues that are important to children's lives now, we are teaching them the attitudes and skills they will need to make reasoned decisions now and in the future. Through instruction in peaceful conflict negotiation, strategies for confronting bias, and the promotion of prosocial behaviors, we are giving them the tools.

Respect for Diversity

religion	ethnicity	gender role
race	age	family composition
language	abilities	lifestyle
interests	values	skin color

This list represents only a small fraction of the variations children encounter among the people in the school setting. Some of these differences are immediately apparent to children, whereas others take longer for them to discover. Children's attitudes about issues of diversity have their roots in childhood. Even before they are 3, children notice others' physical attributes and begin to compare these with their own. As their experiences broaden and their cognitive and language abilities develop, young people also become aware of and comment on more subtle distinctions (Alejandro-Wright, 1985; P. Katz, 1982).

Once it was thought that simply bringing children into contact with others who were different from them would lead to understanding and tolerance. Unfortunately, this hope has proven to be naïve. In some cases, already negative perceptions are strengthened rather than eliminated when diverse people are introduced into somewhat stable groups (Cohen, 1977). This occurs in part because adults neglect to take into account children's development and their own biases in teaching children positive responses to the differences.

The development of valid concepts of race, gender, and differing physical abilities appears to be age and stage specific, with older children displaying more accurate understandings than younger ones (Alejandro-Wright, 1985; P. Katz, 1982). As an example, children are not sure until about age 8 or older which physical attributes are constant and which will change with time. Furthermore, their rudimentary notions of causal relationships make it difficult for them to figure out what the process of change entails. They may conclude, for instance, that dark skin is dirty and, if washed, will turn white; that they may lose the function of their legs if they play with a child in a wheelchair; or that if a girl gets a short haircut she turns into a boy. Although there is some question as to the precise ages that children understand these issues, it is clear that it occurs during childhood.

Another developmental issue that comes into play here is children's continuing efforts to sort out likenesses and differences. In their attempts to figure out who is like them and who is not, their criteria may be based on obvious physical characteristics alone. At certain friendship stages, when children are seeking others who are like them, they may exclude children based on these external attributes unless other similarities are brought to their attention.

In addition to developmental considerations, how children evaluate differences and how they consequently behave are highly influenced by the adults around them, peers, and societal values as expressed in the media and other outside sources. Children's opinions of both their own and others' worth are affected by these forces, especially negative ones (Cross, 1985). Early childhood professionals must therefore pay attention to the messages they convey about diversity in the settings they create, the teaching materials they use, and the manner in which they respond to children's behavior and words.

Creating Inclusive School Environments   Inclusive school environments and teaching practices are those in which all forms of diversity are fairly and consistently represented. By virtue of the interpersonal interactions and planned activities that take place, the physical structure of the space, and the materials on walls and shelves, communities are created in which all people, adults and children alike, feel acknowledged, accepted, and valued (Sapon-Shevin, 1983).

One strategy for ensuring that diversity is valued is to make sure that classroom activities and materials represent different cultures, lifestyles, people with differing abilities, and men and women in non-sex-stereotypical roles. Deliberate introduction and integration of diverse people into programs on an ongoing rather than special basis should be done. Furthermore, all materials used in the educational setting must be examined so that stereotypical portrayals of groups are not unconsciously displayed or categories of people are not left out. In addition to the obvious (e.g., Native Americans shown with feathers in their hair or only at Thanksgiving), more subtle cues should be explored. For instance, classrooms and school hallways that feature only Christmas trees in December send the message to non-Christians that their holidays and traditional practices are not important. Furthermore, cultural awareness should focus on how people live today in our country, not only on cultures and people in other nations. Thus the focus of teaching should be on Asian-Americans, African-Americans, and Hispanic-Americans rather than on people's countries of origin (Derman-Sparks & and the ABC Task Force, 1989).

Adults have a responsibility to help children sort out valid conclusions from those based on incomplete or erroneous information. They can do this by pro-

viding accurate data for children to work with as well as deliberately setting up experiences that confound children's stereotypical assumptions. Answering children's questions honestly and carrying out frank and open discussions about the differences children observe is another way to help children gain important knowledge about others.

An additional strategy is to help children recognize the effects of their actions and words on others (Kostelnik et al., 1998). Pointing out instances of kindness and explaining how that made another child feel encourage further prosocial behaviors. In addition, it is important to confront children directly when they show evidence of overtly biased behavior or opinions. Letting children know that insensitive remarks made someone feel hurt or angry is the first step in changing their behavior in a more socially responsible direction (Derman-Sparks & the ABC Task Force, 1989). The adult must be sure to indicate a positive alternative to the child as well as determine any appropriate acts of restitution.

Changing the Curriculum   Several stages of curricular reform have been identified as teachers struggle with issues of inclusion in their programs (Banks, 1988). Although these were originally designed to describe ethnic content, they can be generalized to encompass all areas of diversity. The first stage that teachers often go through is called the "contribution" approach. This focuses on heroes, holidays, and discrete cultural elements. For example, teachers introduce heroes into the program, treating their lives as exemplars with special abilities. They are not integrated into the curriculum, nor are the issues they confront as members of minority groups, such as discrimination, truly explored. Rather, their successes are promoted, and they are treated as exotic, exceptional human beings, not representative of their group.

The "ethnic added" approach is a second means teachers use to introduce content related to diversity into their programs. At this level, content, concepts, and themes are added without changing the curricular structure. That is, although important steps have been taken to integrate diversity, the curriculum is still based on a majority-centered view.

The third stage is called the "transformational" approach. At this level, teachers have infused various perspectives, frames of reference, and content into their curricula. The result is that students will come away with a greater understanding of the complexities of our society and how society itself is a result of a synthesis and interaction among the diverse elements that compose it.

Banks' (1988) final stage is called the "decision-making and social action" approach. The most sophisticated of all, this approach includes all elements of the previous stage but requires children to make complex decisions related to their study and take some action.

The paradigm set forth by Banks (1988) offers much in the way of information for the teacher. A blending of the approaches just described seems a reasonable way to tackle the difficult task of changing one's own thinking and practicing to be more inclusive. Professionals must examine their own attitudes and practices for evidence of prejudice. This is not an easy task, as bias may rear its head in numerous subtle ways and emanate from sources that relate to our own early life experiences and learnings. Thus, by monitoring their own behavior, as well as confronting children's stereotypical beliefs, reinforcing positive behaviors, and proactively teaching about the similarities and differences that make us all part of the human family, educators can help children make strides toward a bias-free society.

Environmental Awareness

Individuals on almost every side of every issue use a popular saying: "Think globally; act locally." In no area is this more apt than when teaching children about their responsibility for the indoor as well as outdoor environments in which they live and play.

Environmental ecology deals with the complex interrelationships among all living things and their surroundings (Schickedanz et al., 1990). Like most areas of study, awareness of the environment spans more than one domain. It involves principles from science and the broad goals of the social domain. In addition, affective development is involved because the problems of caring for the environment relate to how children's behavior affects others. Thus, although it is true that pollution in its most overt forms is a concept difficult for children to understand, youngsters can, and should, be made aware of the effects of their own actions on their milieu. Attention to the environment has some far-reaching consequences in the lives of

young children. Just as attitudes about differences are established at an early age, so, too, are one's attitudes toward the world. Adults, as we know, exert a powerful influence on children, and the behaviors they display are more significant in proclaiming their values than any words they profess. Thus, for children to become sensitive to the needs of the global community, adults must demonstrate their concern through their actions.

Specific planning within the classroom in terms of activities and routines is an effective way of conveying children's responsibility for their setting. Children can be taught to clean up their own mess, either individually or with help from others. They can be shown how to generate less waste in school and at home and find uses for scrap materials. A classroom recycling center is a way to prompt their excitement as well as create a hands-on, concrete demonstration project for other classes to emulate. An activity as simple as planting, caring for, and harvesting plants can make an important contribution to the classroom as well. Activities such as these reveal important causal relationships to children because they are able to experience directly the results of changes in their actions.

The beginnings of social responsibility come about through such simple activities as planting flowers to beautify the neighborhood.

In addition, children can be made aware of the conflicting needs of human beings for resources and society's concerns about the untimely depletion of those resources. The classroom can be a microcosm for learning how to resolve these dilemmas in democratic ways, through negotiation and compromise.

SOCIAL STUDIES

Social studies has been defined as the study of people in society, past and present, and their relations with each other and the world around them, both near and far (National Council for the Social Studies, 1989). Its goals focus on expanding children's horizons and teaching the elements of citizenship in a democratic society. The ultimate goal is to produce individuals who feel good about themselves and develop the necessary concepts and skills to make worthwhile contributions to society through thinking and decision making. Social studies curricula take their perspectives from a variety of disciplines, such as anthropology, economics, geography, history, human ecology, political science, psychology, and sociology. All of these are similar in that they focus on the understanding of human behavior; however, the key concepts of each make unique contributions to children's knowledge (Schickedanz, York, et al., 1990; Seefeldt, 1993 and 1995c; Sunal, 1993).

Anthropology is the study of human beings and their diverse cultures and lifestyles. Children begin to understand that people represent many cultures as they come in contact with others in their school and community. Even people who look the same may have different beliefs, different ways of celebrating holidays and festivals, and different family structures. Children also learn that people who seem unlike them may share similar ideas and values.

Economics informs us about how people produce and consume goods and services. Children can be made aware of the diverse kinds of work adults engage in by talking with and observing persons who fight fires, care for people, buy and sell goods, grow produce and livestock, work in factories and build useful products, and perform services for pay. Money exchange and the value of money is a topic that can be introduced to children at a young age. Consumer education, such as learning how to evaluate advertising, is critical for children to understand. One component of this is for children to be able to distinguish their needs

from their wants and to make informed decisions on the basis of the difference.

Geography illuminates the characteristics of the earth's environment and the relationship of that environment to the people who live in it. Where things are in children's near environment is important information to have as they move farther from their home. In addition, children develop a greater appreciation for the natural world and its resources when they learn to be responsible for the waste they generate and the ways in which they dispose of that waste. Geography also relates to how people get from one place to another and the reasons they choose to move.

History deals with the past, the concept of change, and the forces that influence it. Important to the lives of young children is their own personal history and that of their family. Every child has an ancestry, and becoming aware of one's forebears helps children develop a sense of belonging and pride. History also deals with the passage of time and the sequence of events. In the early childhood setting these elements are built into the structure of daily living. Bringing them to children's consciousness is the first step in their understanding of temporal relationships (National Center for History in the Schools, 1994).

Human ecology is the study of the interplay between the individual and all systems with which that person comes in contact, both directly and indirectly. So, for example, the child is a member of both the home and the school setting and is also indirectly affected by his or her parents' place of work. Communication among these systems is also a part of the human ecological perspective and underscores the importance of regular contact between the child's home and school. When children bring items or information from home to the classroom, and when messages are sent home about possible visitors or field trips, children are active participants in their social groups.

Political science relates to the management and governance of social units. This very much relates to teaching children about living in a democracy. Children have opportunities to practice aspects of democratic living when they learn to understand the rules that govern the classroom and when they become involved in making some of those rules themselves. Within the social studies curriculum, children learn that everyone has rights and responsibilities and that it is sometimes necessary to negotiate and bargain for the things they need. Furthermore, they participate in group problem solving about issues that are important to them. All of these experiences teach them how societies function for the benefit of all members.

Psychology reveals the internal workings of the mind—how people think, feel, and respond. Every time children approach an interaction, they are dealing with their emotions. They are busy learning to recognize what these emotions are, the variety of ways they are expressing them, and what the impact of that expression is on other people. As they develop and extend their prosocial skills, children are finding out more about the emotions and needs of others. Teaching children about the similar and different ways people respond to holidays, for instance, gives youngsters experience in understanding their own feelings and those of others.

Sociology helps us understand the social groups in which we live. Like adults, children belong to many social groups, such as their family, class, after-school activity group, and congregation. How people function within these different settings, as leaders or followers, initiators or passive observers, dependent or independent thinkers, provides a focus for discussion among children. Specific activities can be planned so that children will sharpen their awareness of the roles they and others play in their groups.

From its earliest inclusion in the early childhood curriculum, real experiences have been the appropriate vehicles for teaching social studies content and concepts (Bredekamp & Rosegrant, 1992). Children's active and direct participation in projects and activities is the necessary means of instruction, as it is congruent with what we know about children's development (Bredekamp & Copple, 1997). The classroom is an ideal arena within which children learn the social skills, values, and rules required for living in society. For young children, therefore, social studies is viewed as an extension of their social development. Understanding that children learn best that which is most important to them, educators can logically translate children's natural concerns about their relationships with others and the world around them into studies of the self, the family, the school, and the community (Ministry of Education, Province of British Columbia, 1988). Thus, the integrative nature of social studies promotes children's understanding of the society in which they live.

Goals of Social Studies

As with other curricular domains, the goals for social studies are grouped by knowledge goals, skill goals, and attitude goals (National Council of the Social Studies Task Force, 1989). *Knowledge goals* focus on concepts that reflect the content of social studies, such as the uniqueness of all people, the interdependence of people, the influence of environment on people's choices of habitats and work, and the function and operation of social groups. Other knowledge goals deal with the structure of the social science disciplines, such as what and how we learn about human history and how people make decisions. Additional knowledge goals reflect similarities and differences among individuals and groups and how people learn to live together. *Skill goals* focus on children's mastery of techniques related to the gathering of information, improving their interpersonal interactions within their group, and problem solving, both in terms of content and social relations. *Attitude goals* relevant to social studies emphasize respecting individuals both similar to and different from themselves, understanding and appreciating their own and others' culture and traditions, and caring for the world around them. These goals and their implementation across the early childhood age range clearly encompass the entire range of the social domain.

Social Studies in the Classroom

It is instructive to examine how a social studies curriculum might look in practice for children of different ages. Table 13.3 includes sample experiences appropriate for the youngest children (3- to 5-year-olds), somewhat older children (5- to 7-year-olds), and the oldest children (6- to 8-year olds). Children's maturity and prior access to the materials and activities will affect which are best suited to their needs. Therefore, the age range should be viewed as a guide.

Obviously, teachers have the responsibility to teach social studies directly, as well as help children learn to have positive interpersonal interactions. Clearly, this learning must take place in the context of the child's daily experience in the classroom. This is best accomplished when teachers carefully plan activities that relate to children's lives and take advantage of the spontaneous occurrences that are a natural part of group dynamics to teach important lessons. Active participation by children in the exploration of these issues ensures

TABLE 13.3
Implementing the Social Studies Curriculum in the Classroom

Social Science Discipline	Experiences for		
	3- to 5-Year-Olds	5- to 7-Year-Olds	6- to 8-Year Olds
Anthropology	Children are provided with a wok, chopsticks, plastic models of sushi, and plastic plates with Asian designs as normal props in the Family Living Center.	Children are taught two versions of a similar singing game, each with a different ethnic origin.	Children interview family members about their cultural heritage. They record on tape or paper a story that represents their heritage and share it with the class.
Economics	Children participate in a theme entitled "The Work People Do."	Children set up a store in the classroom. Classmates are allotted a limited amount of money with which to buy goods. They are encouraged to bargain or barter other goods and services to get what they want.	Children develop a plan for a class project to earn money for a special field trip.
Geography	After a walk in the neighborhood, children are encouraged to use blocks to reconstruct their experience.	After a walk through the neighborhood, children arrange photographs of features in the area in the order in which they observed them. Later, they make a return trip to check out their recollections.	After a walk in the neighborhood, children create a map representing the buildings and other landmarks near the school.
History	Children bring in pictures of themselves as babies and dictate stories.	Children bring in pictures of their parent(s) as youngsters. They write or dictate descriptions comparing their parents' past and present appearances.	Children create their individual family trees. They get the information by interviewing family members.
Human ecology	A local kindergarten teacher spends the day in the preschool classroom, whereas on another day, the preschool teacher teaches in the kindergarten room.	Children address envelopes to themselves, go to the post office to mail them, and trace their progress through the system by observing the sorting machines, seeing a mail deliverer in action, and so forth.	To conclude a study of the community, children create a diorama, depicting the the interrelationships among all the community service agencies, such as the post office, fire department, police station, and the like.
Psychology	Each child wears a badge during the day that reads, "I'm special because I ___" (child decides what the special attribute or skill is).	Each child works on an "All about Me" book. In it are favorite objects, favorite people, things they dislike, and other categories they choose.	On a table set aside for the purpose, children bring in favorite items from home. They display the items, along with guidelines that others must follow in examining them. Children describe the articles to each other and explain why they are special.

(continued on the next page)

TABLE 13.3
(continued)

Social Science Discipline	Experiences for		
	3- to 5- Year-Olds	**5- to 7- Year-Olds**	**6- to 8- Year Olds**
Political science	During interpersonal disputes, children participate in conflict negotiation, with the teacher as mediator.	Children establish classroom rules for the safe use of a microscope on loan from the museum.	Children hold a mock election for a "town council seat." A campaign gives children the opportunity to influence their "constituency."
Sociology	Children take turns conducting a rhythm instrument band.	Children participate in a theme on "friends and friendships," during which they identify and practice friendship-making skills.	Small groups of children work on solving a designated classroom problem (e.g., figuring out how to make sure children's possessions remain undisturbed). The groups present their solutions to the class, where they are discussed and evaluated.

that they will derive the meaningful knowledge, skills, and attitudes that are the foundations of a social studies curriculum. As a result, these children will demonstrate good citizenship in their school, their communities, and, ultimately, their world.

THE RELATIONSHIP BETWEEN THE SOCIAL DOMAIN AND COGNITION

Many practitioners may find it difficult to justify spending classroom learning time on improving children's social skills and helping them become more aware of the social world around them. In fact, while children are engaged in these pursuits, they are exploring and sharpening their physical knowledge, intuitive knowledge, representational thinking, social-conventional knowledge, language, and critical thinking skills.

Let us use as an example an activity outlined toward the end of this chapter: The People's Choice. To summarize, children are offered an opportunity to negotiate a conflict or a difference of opinion in a democratic way by voting. In the activity, the adult poses a problem for the children to solve—naming a classroom pet, for instance. Children examine the animal in an effort to understand its physical characteristics (physical knowledge). They may discuss its characteristics and thus

learn the appropriate descriptive vocabulary (language). Names are solicited from children, requiring them to link the physical object to an abstract idea (representational thinking) and to recognize that the names written on the chart represent the animal. Each child has the opportunity to vote for his or her favorite (critical thinking and decision making). Finally, children determine which name has the most number of advocates, first by viewing the groups of children and "guessing" and next, by one-to-one correspondence, as the groups line up next to each other (logical-mathematical knowledge) and finally, by counting (conventional social knowledge). Throughout the decision-making process, children must separate what they *want* from what they *think*. This requires a very high level of cognitive functioning.

This very brief examination of the relationship between cognition and the social domain illustrates that the two are inextricably linked and that one cannot delve into social issues and skills without engaging children's minds.

CURRENT EDUCATIONAL ISSUES

Teachers working with young children sometimes pose several questions in relation to social development and social studies. These questions represent key issues regarding the social domain and the early childhood curriculum.

The Relationship Between Social Development and Social Studies

To live productively in the world, children must have satisfying relationships with the people in it. This means knowing about and following societal expectations, making and keeping friends, working out interpersonal conflicts, being kind to others and accepting kindness from them, and recognizing and valuing diversity among people. As they become aware of the impact of their ideas and behaviors on others, children gain an awareness of their own point of view and an understanding of the perspectives of people different from themselves. They also appreciate their own culture and family history. In addition, children become increasingly aware of the complex interrelationships among all things, living and nonliving, in the world. Through numerous experiences, children can be made cognizant of the necessary interdependence of people in any society and the need for responsible behavior toward the environment. Teachers can help children develop the skills they need to live in a peaceful world and provide opportunities for them to practice democratic problem solving and decision making. This empowers children to affect the world they live in. As children's concepts broaden, teachers may introduce children to issues that go beyond their immediate concerns, through a focus on greater world issues, such as peace and war, homelessness and poverty, and vanishing species. Thus, the social realm requires children to look both within and outside themselves as they build their repertoire of social studies concepts.

Teaching Peace: The Classroom and Beyond

The definition of social studies includes aspects of how we live in our social world (Sunal, 1993). For children in formal settings, this includes the home, the classroom, and the school or community center in which they spend most of their waking hours. Teaching children to generate and carry out peaceful solutions to conflicts involves helping them develop interpersonal cognitive and behavioral problem solving. Many teachers have adopted the conflict resolution model illustrated in this chapter, or similar ones, as they work with youngsters in their individual classrooms. The

question has arisen whether these same strategies can be applied to larger groups of children—in whole-school settings.

Indeed, many schools have used a systematic approach to teaching children to make more productive decisions in handling conflicts. "Peer coaching" is one such method reported to have widespread success. Older elementary school children are trained as conflict mediators. They are identifiable by their peers and by younger children via armbands or T-shirts as they operate on playgrounds and lunchrooms to recognize conflicts as they occur and to assist children in reaching nonviolent solutions. Other strategies include using "peace tables," where children come together to settle differences before an argument has reached the boiling point. The "Peaceable Schools Model" developed in New York City is another example of a systemwide attempt at enriching children's social responsibility by giving them conflict resolution and mediation skills and an appreciation of cultures different from their own (Lantieri & Patti, 1996). This model is currently being successfully used in school systems in five states. "The conflict wall" is an effort by yet another district to assist children in learning conflict resolution skills. Here, a wall in the principal's office displays a "conflict escalator" chart and posters to remind children, for instance, what to do when they are angry (Phillips, 1997). Although this idea has been used with older children, it certainly could be adapted for use with younger ones.

In all cases, active student participation and involvement of the community as a whole and parents in particular have resulted in positive outcomes (Weissberg et al., 1997).

Embracing Diversity: Interpretations and Misinterpretations

Important goals of education are exemplified by children who demonstrate self-respect, display self-confidence, possess the skills necessary for mastery over ideas and materials, approach new ideas and problems creatively, develop their individual potential to its highest level, and are productive members of society. An essential value of a good early childhood curriculum is that children of all races, religions, home languages, family backgrounds, economic circumstances, and cultures be treated with understanding and consideration. These values of equality and respect reenforce the democratic foundations of the U.S. Constitution in our pluralistic society. How these ideas are implemented in actual daily practice varies enormously from program to program. Some educators interpret these guidelines to mean that differences among children are to be acknowledged if they come up in the normal course of play or conversation; others prefer to be proactive and to seek out and introduce the variations in children's lives to them and to plan discussions and activities that emphasize the uniqueness of individuals and social groups. A different interpretation is to practice democratic principles in the classroom by involving children in making choices about what they learn. Others extend this idea to include classroom governance as a mutual agreement between adults and children. Wherever they fall within the spectrum, such interpretations are consistent with the values and goals of a democratic society.

In the past several years, criticisms of these ideas and practices have surfaced from a number of sources. Some interpret the notion of embracing diversity as the elimination of standards and values that it is wrong to teach youngsters that differences have no distinctions and that no one culture is superior to another. Others misinterpret acceptance of each child's family structure as active promotion of homosexual lifestyles. Still others misinterpret the practices of offering choices to children and of democratic governance in the classroom to mean that children are being taught to flout authority, which, they believe, will lead to acceptance of criminal behavior. Still others object to including diverse ethnic festivities in schools, claiming they dilute traditional Christmas and Thanksgiving practices. Such interpretations claim to uphold family values and the "American way."

Misinterpretations of the goals and attributes of diversity education for young children may be addressed by looking at the practical outcomes for individuals and society. Building self-esteem in youngsters through acceptance of who they are and whence they come enables them to overcome adversity because they have the confidence to try again. Offering numerous opportunities to attempt solutions to problems, evaluate those solutions, and seek other pathways should those routes not be fruitful develops perseverance and creative thinking. This quality leads to the ability to hold a job later in life and to be responsible to one's family. In the same vein, practicing decision making as

a child allows one to more easily make productive decisions when the stakes are higher. Exploring ideas creatively, taking risks, not assuming there is a "right" answer, as well as understanding that a "right" answer may not exist has lead, for instance, to technological innovation. Practice in decision making, reaching compromises, and experiencing the consequences of decisions fosters increased involvement in governance on every level. Thus, expanding the possibilities for children to participate actively in their school lives is to be welcomed rather than feared and avoided. Finally, exposure to a wide variety of people, ideas, and customs enriches the individual as well as society. Learning to recognize and appreciate differences among people by embracing diversity is a key to more harmonious living for all.

How the Social Domain Fits in the School Day

Teachers have numerous demands on their time and resources during school. They are expected to plan for instruction in all the domains, as well as to fulfill many other responsibilities. Where, then, does teaching about the social domain fit?

One important factor to recognize is that social development is integral to every part of school life. It appears in both implicit and explicit forms. Fundamentally, teachers are conveying information and values related to social development in everything they do in the classroom. How they treat children both individually and in groups; how they interact with aides, volunteers, and parents; what disciplinary strategies they employ; and how they respond to diversity of all sorts within their school community directly impact children's social development. In addition, they influence children when they take advantage of spontaneous opportunities to make children aware of the effect of their behavior toward others and when they model, encourage, and promote helpful and cooperative behavior. Other ways in which implicit instruction is conveyed is when teachers set up routines and practices during which children are expected to care for their immediate as well as the school environment. In all of these areas, teachers are addressing important aspects of children's social development.

In addition to the subtle attention to social development, teachers can deliberately plan for the social domain's inclusion in their program. In New Haven, Connecticut, a districtwide project has, over the year, achieved exciting success (Weissberg et al., 1997). In contrast, it is not very effective to try to teach a social skill or improve children's prosocial behaviors by using a predigested, 15-minute "kit." These are not very useful teaching tools by themselves, because we now know that even when children can verbalize appropriate behaviors, they may not actually act in those ways without practice in real-life situations. A far better approach is to integrate social concepts throughout the day-to-day transactions of the classroom. They can also be highlighted within particular activities. Planning thematic units that revolve around social studies content, such as "Families," "People in Our Community," and "The Work People Do," is another way teachers can underscore these significant understandings and help children comprehend the relationship between what they are experiencing and the processes in the world outside themselves.

GOALS AND OBJECTIVES

The ultimate goals of the social domain are for children to develop successful patterns of interaction with peers and adults, gain internal control, acquire and practice prosocial values, demonstrate positive attitudes toward diversity, and build social studies concepts. For children to progress toward these goals, they must have opportunities to attain interpersonal skills, learn the expectations of school and society, learn about and practice prosocial behaviors, gain respect and appreciation for the wide variety of people in the world, and achieve understandings and skills that relate to social studies.

Intermediate Objectives

As children progress toward the ultimate goal, they will demonstrate the following competencies:

1. Develop play skills (e.g., initiate play, join a group at play, make suggestions, take suggestions, recognize ways to deal with unpleasant social situations and the emotions associated with them, learn to play productively alone).
2. Develop peer friendship relationship skills (e.g., how to initiate, maintain, and terminate interactions and relationships constructively).
3. Become aware of other people's opinions, points of view, and attitudes.
4. Learn to negotiate conflicts in democratic ways (e.g., compromising, voting, bargaining).
5. Develop empathy for others (recognize others' emotions, respect others' emotional responses).
6. Perceive adults as sources of gratification, approval, and modeling.
7. Learn how to conform to reasonable limits set on behavior, play space, use of materials, or the types of activities in which they are involved.
8. Identify the reasons for classroom rules.
9. Distinguish acceptable from unacceptable classroom behavior.
10. Use their knowledge of appropriate behavior in one circumstance to determine appropriate conduct in another.
11. Begin to develop skills related to self-control (e.g., impulse control, resistance, delay of gratification, and positive social actions).
12. Learn approved behaviors related to social and ethnic customs (e.g., manners and other respectful behaviors).
13. Learn how to cooperate (work with others toward a common goal).
14. Learn how to be helpful (share information or materials, give physical assistance, offer emotional support).
15. Develop awareness of and concern for the rights and well-being of others.
16. Develop positive attitudes about belonging to a group beyond the family.
17. Become aware of similarities and differences among people.
18. Develop positive attitudes toward people who are different from themselves.
19. Develop an awareness of and respect for the values, ethnic background, family traditions, culture, gender, differing abilities, and special needs of others.
20. Become aware of how people live together in families, neighborhoods, and communities.
21. Develop a sense of responsibility for the environment.
22. Develop knowledge related to social studies content in the following areas:
    - ❑ Anthropology (e.g., culture).
    - ❑ Economics (e.g., money, consumerism, work).
    - ❑ Geography (e.g., home and school environs).

- ❏ History (e.g., personal history, family history).
- ❏ Human ecology (e.g., child-school-home connection).
- ❏ Psychology (e.g., understanding one's emotions and those of others).
- ❏ Political science (e.g., democratic principles and practices, conflict resolution).
- ❏ Sociology (e.g., individuals and communities).
- (23.) Develop skills related to social studies content, such as collecting data, mapping, and decision making.

TEACHING STRATEGIES

1. *Help children make friends at school by using their names.* Children feel most comfortable interacting with those whose names they know. Thus, acquainting children with each other's names is a basic strategy for facilitating children's friendships. To accomplish this, use children's names frequently. Identify by name youngsters who are sitting near one another, working together, and playing with each other. Unfamiliar or uncommon names will seem less strange with frequent repetition. Be sure you know how to pronounce every child's name correctly.

2. *Help children make friends at school by promoting social interactions.* To help children become more aware of others in their group, you can deliberately pair children to work on projects. Choose children who have something in common. Remember to point out these common attributes, attitudes, preferences, or shared experiences so that the youngsters will become more aware of them. Shy children, in particular, benefit from this technique, but it is effective with others as well. For the benefit of all children, remember to provide numerous opportunities during the school day for children to interact with each other informally. Another related idea is to plan activities that require more than one child's participation. Observe how children behave with one another and use that information in future planning.

3. *Provide activities that allow children to practice social skills.* Use the suggestions following this section to create activities that focus on specific social skills. For instance, use skits to teach children numerous ways to let others know that they want to play. Carry out discussions during which children themselves generate alternatives and explore the effectiveness of different solutions. As a follow-up, create opportunities for children to practice the strategies in real-life situations. Then, provide them with on-the-spot information regarding their progress in applying their knowledge. This will help them figure out which techniques are successful and encourage them to eliminate those that are not. Other examples include deliberately setting out materials in such a way that children must ask, bargain, or trade in order to get what they want.

4. *Help children become more helpful and cooperative.* A necessary first step in this process is to recognize and acknowledge those times when children behave in positive or prosocial ways. Pointing out such instances increases the chances that children will repeat the acts of kindness. Another strategy is to plan activities in which children have opportunities to practice helping or cooperating. For instance, activities in which children must work together cooperatively to reach a common goal are far more supportive of children's prosocial behavior than those that pit child against child or group against group.

5. *Help children understand and follow expectations for behavior.* Use the guidelines outlined in Chapter 6 to establish appropriate rules. Promote the development of children's internalization of rules through the use of the positive guidance strategies outlined there.

6. *Help children develop positive attitudes toward diversity.* As is well known, familiarity with a wide range of people helps children be more accepting of differences. Therefore, it is valuable to present children with opportunities to interact with adult members of their own and other cultural groups, individuals who display varying physical abilities, older people, and younger people. Invite grandparents into the classroom, for example, to talk with children about what life was like when they were growing up. Ask them to talk also about the activities that they engage in at present to dispel stereotypical attitudes about old people being helpless. Have parents in the group come in to tell stories remembered from their childhood and, if possible, bring books in their language of origin. Send home a request to families to provide recipes from their culture. Finally, use neighborhood resources to acquaint children with people who are different from themselves. In sum, introduce and celebrate diversity

by connecting it to children's common experience in the classroom.

7. *Provide children with classroom activities, materials, and discussions that address the wide range of diversity.* Ensure that diversity education and awareness is an ongoing part of your classroom by planning multicultural activities that are integrated into the daily routines of the program rather than reserving them only for holidays or special occasions. Check the pictures, books, learning materials, and other classroom props for evidence of stereotypical portrayals of any group. In some cases, remove them; in others, use the biased depictions as springboards for discussions with the children. When appropriate, create new pictures that more justly represent the true diversity in the world. Finally, engage children in sending letters of criticism and concern to manufacturers who are producing and marketing toys and games that undermine a fair portrayal of an ethnic, racial, gender, or ability issue.

8. *Help children deal with stereotypical ideas.* The first part of this process is to provide accurate information about the differences and similarities that children

Indira's horizons have expanded through her relationship with Mrs. Anna, a classroom volunteer.

perceive. This means that you should respond openly and honestly to children's observations and to the questions they ask. Giving them chances to explore differences by providing direct experiences is an important component. For example, activities during which children compare and graph skin color or hair texture sharpens children's awareness while, at the same time, it presents variety in a positive light. Another aspect of this strategy is to build children's critical thinking skills so that they will become more attuned to evidence of prejudice—within themselves, in others, and as portrayed in the media. Increasing their prosocial attitudes will make it possible for them to respond to these situations in positive ways. Furthermore, the more prosocial the child, the more likely it is that he or she can come to the aid of a friend. The final step is to assist children in defending themselves against bias directed toward them. School personnel are an important influence on how children view themselves and can therefore be effective in teaching children coping skills. Work with youngsters in designing verbal responses to name calling. Allow them time in the classroom to practice with their peers in the safe haven of the classroom. Give them opportunities to talk about their experiences within school time.

9. *Help children learn to care for their near and far environments.* Give children practical experiences in cleaning up the classroom, the school hallways, playground, and other areas in which they work. Use activities such as those suggested in this chapter to alert children to the uses of materials they would otherwise discard. When engaged in picking up litter, readying the classroom for the next day, and so on, use music to lighten the burden. Have children perform these tasks in groups so that they feel a sense of group participation and camaraderie and further develop their repertoire of shared experiences. Base themes around the issue of recycling. For example, prepare projects for children to ascertain the recycling efforts of their community, and invite local groups with interests in these matters to give presentations to the class. Assist children in assessing what actions they, as young people, can reasonably take.

10. *Help children build social studies concepts by practicing democracy in the classroom.* Plan activities in which children have opportunities to identify, generate solutions for, and carry out solutions for problems

inherent in group living. One way to do this is for children to create some of their own classroom rules and designate the appropriate consequences for infractions of those rules. When there is work to be done in caring for the classroom, let children decide on the means of handling them. In addition, promote children's abilities to evaluate the techniques they choose and to redesign the strategies as needed. Some school policies can also be decided by children and teachers working together. (An example of this in operation is described in Chapter 6). An additional way to practice democracy is for teachers to model strategies for helping children solve interpersonal conflict peacefully. Follow the steps outlined in "Activity Suggestions" as you take on the role of mediator in the conflicts that arise in the classroom or on school grounds. Peer coaches can also be trained to assume that role. In either case, with experience and feedback, children develop skill in managing their own disputes and the conflicts of others in nonaggressive ways.

11. *Help children build social studies concepts through theme choices.* When deciding on themes for teaching in the classroom, choose some that focus on social studies content. Such topics as the self, the family, the community, the interdependence of people, and caring for the environment are subjects in which children are naturally interested because they are directly related to youngsters' lives and activities. Other aspects of social studies can be addressed, for example, when you teach children that people learn about the past from evidence left by others and that they, too, can leave records for others to study.

12. *Help children build social studies concepts and skills across the curriculum.* Social studies is truly an integrative area of focus. For example, teach historical understanding and literature comprehension through the use of modern and old versions of the same story. Another idea is to compare the ways of living of two families during different time periods in history, assessing both similarities and contrasts (e.g., *The Little House on the Prairie* books can be read alongside a modern story by Judy Blume). Assist children in relating mapping skills both to geography as well as to mathematics when they represent an area of their school in a diorama after having determined the unit of measure they will use. Combine political understanding with increased self-esteem as you aid children in expressing their needs and wants during a conflict negotiation session. These are only a small number of examples that illustrate the potentially pervasive nature of social studies.

ACTIVITY SUGGESTIONS

The following is a set of activities designed to encourage children to practice the social strategies outlined in this chapter. Each subarea of social development has been addressed by at least one activity. Thus, there are plans that touch on developing play and friendship skills, negotiating conflict, recognizing other points of view, establishing rules, cooperating, helping, recognizing similarities and differences between self and others, and solving problems of group living. These lesson plans are aimed initially at 5-year-old children, with suggestions for simplification and extension so that they can be used successfully with children 3 to 8 years of age. Easily obtained materials are listed for each plan, where appropriate.

✎ Using Skits to Teach Social Skills*

Objective 1   For children to recognize and understand social skills.

Materials   Two dolls, puppets or pictures of children; several small blocks or other objects

General information   A very effective strategy for introducing and reinforcing particular social skills to children is to use skits or short scenarios. Children enjoy watching these presentations and can learn a great deal about effective and ineffective ways to interact with others. However, simply viewing them is not sufficient. Adults must point out the pertinent features of the interplay as well as pose questions that help children clarify their understanding. Older children benefit from opportunities to reenact the scenes as well as generate their own. The following are some general guidelines for developing and presenting skits to children.

---

*Many of these ideas are based on skits developed for *Teaching Young Children Using Themes,* M. J. Kostelnik (Ed.), Glenview, IL: Goodyear Books, 1991.

Procedure

1. Select the social skill on which you wish to focus. This may be one of the friendship skills, such as initiating an interaction, maintaining contact, negotiating conflict, or an aspect of helping or cooperating. Be sure to concentrate on only one skill at a time so as not to confuse or overburden children with too much information.

2. Decide on the medium of presentation. Realistic props such as dolls and puppets or photographs that look like children are the most effective because youngsters can more easily identify with other humans than they can with animals or cartoon characters. Be sure the dolls or puppets represent both sexes (or are androgynous) and depict a variety of racial and ethnic groups and differing physical abilities. If you are using puppets, choose them with movable arms rather than mouths to make it possible to manipulate objects.

3. Outline a script that consists of five parts:
   a. Demonstration of skill
   b. Demonstration of lack of the skill
   c. Explanation by the adult
   d. Discussion by the children
   e. Opportunity for children to use the props

The best scripts are only a few lines long and make the point without too much elaboration.

4. Write out the statements and questions you will use to facilitate discussion. These discussions will revolve around which characters demonstrated the skill, which showed lack of skill, the reaction of each character, how viewers evaluated the behaviors and why, and what they think the characters could do to improve their situation. Be sure to include both effective and ineffective strategies. This is very important for helping children distinguish appropriate from inappropriate behaviors in a variety of different situations.

5. Rehearse the skit before introducing it to children. Using a mirror is a good technique for determining how well you are coming across. Be expressive with your face and voice, and use different voices for each character. Manipulate the figures to correspond with the dialogue. Keep practicing until you feel confident. Write cue cards with the question you wish to ask, if needed.

6. Present the skit to all or part of the group. Seat children in a semicircle facing you. Make sure everyone can see your face and hands and the space directly in front of you. If you are sitting on the floor, kneel so that you are more easily visible to the children. If you are sitting in a chair, use a low bench or table to display the props.

7. Use the following as an introduction each time you do a skit. This prepares children to listen to what is coming next. Change the names and ages, as appropriate. Say, "Today we are going to talk about friends. Here are two dolls. We are going to pretend that these dolls are real children just like you. Their names are Sarvesh and Cathy. They are 5 years old and go to a school just like ours. Watch carefully and see what happens."

8. After you have presented the skit, ask the questions you have prepared, adapting them to situations that arise. As children suggest ideas, paraphrase them and possibly write them down where all the children can see them. Accept all ideas regardless of originality, correctness, or feasibility. If children have difficulty thinking of ideas, prompt them by providing information: "Sometimes, when people want to play, they can say, 'Hi, I want to play,' or they can ask a question like 'What are you building?' This lets the other person know they want to be friends. What do you think Cathy could do?"

9. Once children have suggested their ideas, replay the scene using each suggestion, one at a time. Ask the children to predict how Sarvesh will react in each case. Play out the scene as they suggest. Provide further information as appropriate. "John, you said Cathy could help Sarvesh build. Let's try that." (Maneuver the dolls and provide appropriate dialogue.) "Tell me what you think Sarvesh will do now."

10. Help children evaluate how well their solution worked. For example, "Sarvesh still doesn't know that Cathy wants to be friends. Tell us another way that Sarvesh could ask Cathy to play." Continue trying out their ideas. As children find solutions, praise them for thinking of ways to help the friends figure out what to do. Summarize for them the ways that were tried and which ones proved more successful. As unfriendly solutions are suggested and role-played, point out that the results may be confusion, hurt feelings, sadness, and anger.

11. Later in the day, evaluate how well your skit got your point across. If it seemed children were interested and were able to generate relevant ideas, plan to present the skit another time. Make changes based on your assessment. Remember that children learn from repetition, so it is recommended that you present each social skill numerous times and in several different ways. Each time you do a new skit or repeat an old one, change the roles that the characters play so that particular behaviors will not be associated in children's minds with a specific figure.

To simplify   Carry out the activity with a very small group of children. Keep the scenarios short and simple. As children suggest solutions, act them out and point out the results.

To extend   Encourage the children to reenact on their own the scenario you demonstrated. Introduce open-ended scenarios in which a problem is posed but no solution (effective or ineffective) is modeled. Invite the children to create a solution and then evaluate it. Make dolls available to the children to role-play other scenarios of their own invention.

✎ Conflict Mediation*

Objective 4   For children to learn to negotiate conflicts in democratic ways.

General information   This activity is to be carried out during the course of a naturally occurring conflict between two children in the classroom or on the playground. The exact nature of the conflict will influence the specific words and phrases used by the adult. Be sure to follow exactly the steps of the mediation process.

Step 1: Initiating the Mediation Process   The adult in charge observes signs of a conflict taking place. He or she moves to the site and watches carefully. The adult takes action if children seem unable to resolve the dispute or if they behave aggressively toward one another. The teacher stops any aggressive behavior and separates the combatants, saying, for example, "Sookyong and Alonzo, you are both pulling the toy. It looks like you

both want it. You've got different ideas about how to use it. I'll hold it while we're deciding what to do. I'll give it back when we've figured it out." The adult then removes the toy; if territory is at issue, he or she safeguards it from being taken over by other children by declaring it "out of bounds." This procedure stops the children from continuing to hit or grab, helps them to listen, and assists them in approaching a highly emotional situation more calmly and objectively.

Step 2: Clarifying Each Child's Point of View   Ascertaining and paraphrasing each child's perspective vis-à-vis the conflict is the second part of the process. The adult asks each one, in turn, to tell his or her side of the story without interruption: "Alonzo, you think . . .," "Sookyong, you wanted. . . ." Then the adult paraphrases every statement as it is made. Demonstrate that children may need more than one chance to express their point of view. This step is critical. For the adult to be trusted not to make an arbitrary decision, he or she must establish neutrality. Thus, do not make any evaluation or comment on the merits of either position. This step in the process may take considerable time; do not expect inexperienced children to complete it quickly because they may require repeated chances to fully express their points of view.

Step 3: Summing Up   State the problem in mutual terms: "You each want. . . . We have a problem. It is important that we figure out what to do so each of you will be satisfied and no one will get hurt." The problem thus defined implies that both youngsters have responsibility for the problem and its solution.

Step 4: Generating Alternatives   The focus of the fourth step is for children to think of a number of possible solutions to the problem. At this point bystanders as well as the combatants can have their say. Every time a solution is offered, the mediator paraphrases it to the youngsters directly involved. Each is then asked for an opinion. It is typical for children initially to reject a solution they later find acceptable, so even repeat suggestions should be brought to the table. Make suggestions such as "Sometimes when people have this problem, they can decide to share or take turns" if children seem unable to come up with ideas on their own. However, in order truly to leave the solution up to the children, do not indicate by words or tone of voice that any one plan meets with your approval or disapproval.

---

* For a more detailed discussion of this strategy, see Kostelnik et al. (1998).

Step 5: Agreeing on a Solution   The ultimate aim of step 5 is to agree on a plan of action that is mutually satisfying. Help children explore the possibilities and find one idea or a combination of ideas that is acceptable. Make sure that the final agreement generally involves some compromise on the part of the children and so may not represent anyone's ideal. The mediator states the result: "You've agreed that you can take turns. First Sookyong will have it for 2 minutes, then Alonzo. It sounds like you solved the problem!"

Step 6: Reenforcing the Problem-Solving Process Praise children for their hard work in reaching a solution. Your goal is to demonstrate that what the solution turned out to be is not as important as the process of reaching it. Thus, children's emotional investment in the problem and the compromises that were made should be acknowledged as well.

Step 7: Following Through   Help the children carry out the terms of the agreement. This is especially important so that they will learn to trust that the mediation process is worth the time and effort they have put into it.

To simplify   Shorten some of the procedural steps if you see signs of boredom or fatigue, such as extreme restlessness, turning away, or yawning. Keep the dialogue short and simple.

To extend   Present a skit using the conflict mediation process. Involve children in determining how each step is to be resolved. At first, focus on issues of rights, territory, and possessions. Write scripts that focus on children's feelings as well as on more concrete issues. For instance, use name calling as an example. Model how you would mediate this kind of disagreement. In this case, the appropriate intermediate objective is for children to develop empathy for others by recognizing and respecting their emotions.

✎ **The People's Choice***

Objective 4   For children to have an opportunity to negotiate a conflict in a democratic way by voting.

---

*Many of these ideas are based on skits developed for *Teaching Young Children Using Themes*, M. J. Kostelnik (Ed.), Glenview, IL: Goodyear Books, 1991, and *Themes Teachers Use*, M. J. Kostelnik (Ed.), Glenview, IL: Goodyear Books, 1996.

Materials   Chalkboard and chalk or large writing paper, marking pen, and three to five $3'' \times 12''$ pieces of oak tag or sentence strips

Procedure

1. Introduce the activity by explaining that the whole group will select a name for a class pet, their favorite story, or whatever. Tell them they are going to vote, which means that each person will have a chance to choose a favorite name or story, and at the end they will figure out which choice most people liked best. That one will be the most popular because the most people liked it best, and it will be the one that wins.

2. Begin the process of choosing the alternatives. Limit the number of possibilities to three to five, enough that children can have a real option but not so many that the cluster of children for each group is too small. Explain the limit to the children. Solicit suggestions and write down the first ideas on the chalkboard or paper, reading each aloud. When the list is complete, read each entry, running your hand under the word as you say it so that children can "read" it.

3. Write each option on a piece of oak tag and place it in a corner of the group area, separate from each other. For younger children, place an adult with each tag.

4. Tell children they are going to vote. Explain that they will choose only one of the options, and then stand by the corresponding name. Say that they may not change their minds once they are in place, but assure them that there will be many opportunities to vote throughout the year. Ask each child in turn to pick a favorite from the list. You should read the list before each child chooses to remind him or her of the options and to minimize the likelihood that children will simply repeat the last person's selection. Write the child's name on the chalkboard next to the appropriate station. Children may abstain from voting. In this case, direct the individual to remain seated and offer another chance when everyone is finished.

5. Once the group has divided into areas, instruct children to look at the groups and estimate which has the most people (which choice is the most popular). Make sure everyone who wishes to has a chance to speak. Paraphrase and then summarize their ideas.

6. Tell children that there are several ways to find out which is most popular. Line up two groups and ask the children which line is longer.

7. Paraphrase children's responses. Compare another group's line with the longer line. Continue comparing until the longest line is determined. Then ask children which line has the most people.

8. With the children assisting, count the members of each group and record the number on the board or chart. Ask children which number is largest.

9. Explain again that the group having the largest number of members represents the most popular choice. Ask children to tell which entry "won the voting." Announce the result and mark it on the chart or board.

A child may insist that the name he or she has chosen is the most popular (even if this is not the case). Differentiate what the child "wants" to be true from what he or she "thinks" is true. Carefully review the evidence (counting again if necessary) until the child can accept the answer. Be patient. This is evidence of egocentric thinking, not stubbornness.

To simplify   Younger children may tire of the process before the final decision. If you detect signs of restlessness, move to the final step quickly (you may have to condense a few steps) so that the children experience closure to the activity. Limit the children's choices to two or three.

To extend   In the step in which children "vote with their feet," substitute using their names on the chalkboard to represent them. Have youngsters count these and compare quantities. If this is your plan, print the names clearly enough for children to see easily. If children are having difficulty, quickly move to the original procedure. At a later time, ask children to recap the decision-making procedure that occurred and discuss the results. After a period of days or weeks, revote and compare the results with the original outcome.

✎ **Rules of the Game**

Objective 7   For children to conform to reasonable limits set on behavior, play space, use of materials or the types of activities in which they are involved.

Materials   Large paper and marking pen for recording children's ideas

Procedure

1. Select an issue for children to make a set of rules about. These might include a play space that can comfortably hold a limited number of children, how to decide who should be first in line, problems involving safety, people's rights, or the preservation of property.

2. Assemble the group for a discussion. Pose the problem to them. Explain that when groups of people encounter such difficulties, they often make rules to help people live and work together more harmoniously.

3. Define a rule as "a guide for behavior," and be sure to highlight how the specific issue you have chosen affects one or another key element of safety, rights, and property.

4. Ask children to name some classroom or school rules and to give reasons why they think these rules were made. Find out what they think of the rule.

5. Elicit ideas from children about what rules could be made to solve the current problem. Write down all of their ideas on the paper. Urge them to state their rule in a positive rather than negative way. You may have to paraphrase to accomplish this. Repeat each idea as you write it. Acknowledge all ideas, even when they are repeats, by saying, "You also think. . . ."

6. Next, go over the list with the children and refine it. If, for instance, someone thinks that 100 minutes is a good amount of time for a turn in the spacecraft, help the children understand what that means (e.g., "That is as much time as we spend at group time, *and* free choice, *and* snack time everyday!"). Once the list has been pared down to a few items, rewrite it and post it in an appropriate place for all to see.

7. At a later date, review the rules and assess with the children how well they are working. Make changes, if children and adults agree it is necessary.

To simplify   Choose very basic issues, such as how to carry blocks or scissors safely. Keep the rules simple.

To extend   Have children generate consequences for rule infraction. Help them understand that these should be closely related to the rule itself. Focus on restitution wherever possible and on loss of access, when appropriate. Allow the group to make rules about an increasing number of issues in their school lives as they become more experienced.

✏ All Together Now

Objective 13   For children to learn to be cooperative.

Materials   Boxes, cartons, and containers of various sizes and shapes (these could be provided by the adult, or children could be asked to bring one or more to contribute to the project), glue, masking tape, staple gun, stapler, poster paint, brushes, newspapers, towels, sponge buckets, scissors, markers, crayons, glitter, fabric swatches, wallpaper. There should be a wide variety of materials but a limited supply of each.

Procedure

1. Establish small groups consisting of five to six children each. The groups will remain stable throughout the life of the project. Plan this project over several days.
2. Set up the activity prior to the children's arrival by placing all of the materials in the center of the project area—crayons in one bin, markers in another, scissors in another, and so on. This will encourage youngsters to share materials more than if each child had his or her own personal supply.
3. Introduce the activity by explaining that many people will work together to make a group sculpture; no one person will be in charge. Instead, everyone must work as a team. Explain that everyone will have jobs to do and that the finished project will belong to everyone. Tell children they will be planners as well as constructors. Point out the materials that are available, and say that children may use any of them they wish.
4. The first day is for planning. Help children as a group figure out if they want their constructions to represent something or simply to be a design. This step may take some time to complete. Mediate any conflicts that children are unable to resolve on their own. Point out instances of compromise, taking each other's ideas into account and other examples of prosocial behaviors that the children display. Make suggestions if they are needed to help children move toward closure. The theme children are studying is a good starting point. Allow children to take as much responsibility for their own project as they seem able to do.
5. The second day of the project is construction. Remind children again that this is a task in which everyone is to be involved. Children may choose to work individually or in pairs while contributing to the construction. Allow ample time so children do not feel hurried. Also, provide a safe spot for the project to be housed between work periods. Once you have set up the materials, step back and observe the children at work.
6. When the construction is completed to everyone's satisfaction, display it in the classroom or elsewhere in school. Let children report about the process to the rest of the class, highlighting who participated and how each person contributed to the whole.

To simplify   Pair children to work on a short-range project. This may be as simple as painting on one paper at the easel. Set up a mural (e.g., of trees) and allow children to contribute parts (leaves, birds, etc.).

To extend   Have children generate a list in advance of the tasks to be accomplished. Then let children volunteer for the various ones. Encourage children to evaluate the project once it is completed. They can also write or dictate guidelines for future similar endeavors.

✏ Helping Decisions

Objective 4   For children to recognize situations in which people need help and to determine appropriate ways of helping.

Materials   Eight to ten pictures selected from magazines that show people or animals who need help in some way or people who are being helped in some way. These should be large enough for four or five children to be able to see them 2 or 3 feet away and mounted on cardboard. Pictures should depict a diverse population and different situations.

Procedure

1. Select one picture at a time for discussion. Keep other pictures facedown.
2. Introduce the activity by saying, "I have several pictures here about helping. Look at this one: Somebody needs help."
3. Prompt discussion with questions and statements such as "Tell me who needs help. How did you know? Is there anyone in the picture who could help? What could they do? Who has another idea? What do you think this person will do if someone tries to help? Why might the person in need of help not want the person offering it to help? What

might you do if you had the same problem as the people in the picture?"

4. Paraphrase children's suggestions and ideas, and elicit reactions from other youngsters in the group.

5. Accept all the children's suggestions, and praise them for working so hard at figuring out who needs help, who could help, and what should be done.

6. Should the discussion falter, provide useful information by pointing out facial expressions or other salient features of the scene that might give children clues. Offer suggestions for possible helpful behaviors.

To simplify   Focus on physical assistance and comfort as being the most easily discernible instances of need.

To extend   Use pictures that depict people in situations in which the best way to help is to do nothing (e.g., a child with cerebral palsy struggling to feed himor herself).

✎ A Fair Deal

Objective 14   For children to learn to be helpful by sharing.

Materials   Three crayons or markers and paper, or three animal models; table with five chairs—one for the teacher, the others for children

Procedure

1. Place the markers (modules) in the center of the table. Say, "I have three markers (models), and there are four children who want to use them. Tell me how everyone can have a chance."

2. Listen to children's ideas; elicit suggestions from everyone. Clarify each child's perspective by paraphrasing his or her ideas to the group. Follow up with "And what do you think of that?"

3. Remain impartial throughout this process. Do not show approval or disapproval of any child's idea, regardless of its content; what may seem "fair" to a child may not seem so to an adult. Remember, it is the children who are to determine the outcome.

4. Remind children as necessary that the first step in playing is deciding how that will take place. Point out areas of agreement as they occur. If children become bogged down, make suggestions such as "Sometimes when people are trying to figure out how to share something, they decide that one person should use all the markers or that children should pass the markers around and everyone takes turns playing with them."

5. Acknowledge children's hard work and good ideas as they grapple with the problem. Remind them they are helping each other share.

6. Summarize the solution when it has been achieved, and help children carry out the terms of the agreement.

7. Repeat this activity another time using a different material but a similar central problem. Be sure every child in the group has an opportunity to take part eventually.

To simplify   Limit the number of children involved to two. Watch for signs of frustration and condense steps if necessary to make sure children actually have a chance to use the materials.

To extend   After children have been working for a while, have them evaluate their original solution. Allow them to make modifications as they choose. Ask children if they can think of other situations for which the same or a similar solution would be appropriate. Make arrangements so that they can implement their ideas.

✎ Alike and Different

Objective 17   For children to become aware of similarities and differences among people.

Materials   Standing mirror, paper and pencil for recording children's observations

Procedure

1. Invite children two at a time to look into a mirror at themselves and each other. Help them discover characteristics they have in common and things that are different. This is an ideal opportunity to pair children who may be different in physical ableness, sex, and appearance in order to help them discover similarities beyond the obvious.

2. Make two lists, one in which likenesses are indicated ("We are alike") and the other that records differences ("We are different"). Urge them to begin with physical appearance and to move on to other attributes, such as interests, ideas, preferences, skills, handedness, number of siblings, letters in their names, and so on.

3. Tell the partners that as they observe more things about themselves and each other, they can add to the list throughout the day. At this point, allow the children to continue the activity without interference.

4. At the end of the day, suggest that children review the list and count up all the things they discovered. Let them find out if they came up with more similarities or differences.

5. Repeat this activity, mixing up pairs until all the children have had a chance to be paired with each other. If there is time, repeat the activity later in the year and compare with the original lists. See if the categories have increased as children learn more about each other over time.

To simplify   Focus only on physical attributes, adding other dimensions as children mature.

To extend   Without naming the children involved, read some lists to the class and have them guess the pairs in question.

✎ We Are a Family

Objective 19   For children to develop a respect for the values, ethnic background, family traditions, culture, gender, differing abilities, and special needs of others.

Materials   Photographs of children and adults in the classroom and members of their families, a board on which to display these

General guidelines   Request photographs from each child's family well in advance (2–3 weeks may be necessary). Assure the families that their photos will be returned. Label the pictures with names and relationships of each person. When you have secured the pictures, mount them temporarily on a bulletin board or oak tag, taking care not to mar them. Label the pictures with names and relationships of each person. Numerous activities can then be planned using these family pictures.

Procedure

1. Over a period of time, allow each person in the class an opportunity to talk about his or her family. Respond positively to children's comments about any similarities or differences they notice in family structures. Avoid using terms like *only* when describing a child's family, as in "Judith has only a

grandma in her family." Talk with children about the range of possible family compositions.

2. Encourage children to write or dictate stories about their family, telling what they like to do together, how each person in the family works to help the family, how they celebrate special holidays or occasions, and so on. Tell children to read these to the other children. Elicit comments from children about these practices. Reinforce the idea that each family does things in ways that are meaningful to its members.

3. Instruct children to graph independently the various families in the group. These can be compared with one another as children identify which families are composed of many people, which fewer; which families include pets, which do not; which family members look like other members, which do not.

4. Put the pictures in a book called "The Families in Our Class." Include stories and other descriptions that children have written or dictated. Make the book available for children to "read."

To simplify   Focus on what children can see depicted in the photographs, such as family composition.

To extend   Delve more deeply into family traditions by asking children to bring in and talk about important family artifacts. Elicit information from families about favorite stories, jokes, and so forth. Write these out for children to see. Compare them with other versions.

✎ Match-Ups

Objective 18   For children to develop positive attitudes toward people who are different from themselves.

Materials   One set of pictures portraying people of different ages, sexes, culture groups, races, and physical abilities; one set of pictures of commonly used tools, household implements, or office equipment; two boxes, one for each set of pictures

Procedure

1. Mount the pictures on cards or tag board so they will stand up to repeated use.

2. Explain the procedure to children. Pair children or establish small groups. Say that they are to pick one picture from each container, decide whether that person could use the tools, and give a reason for their decision.

3. As they work, listen for indications of children's stereotypical thinking (e.g., that a person in a wheelchair could not work in an office or that a man could not, or should not, use a blender). Confront these erroneous notions directly at a later time by giving children accurate and relevant information. Ask other children who may be standing by for their ideas. Facilitate discussions between children on these issues.

4. If children persist in their opinions, plan to introduce activities or visitors into your program that will confound their assumptions. For example, invite an individual in a wheelchair to demonstrate his or her abilities, or do a cooking activity with the boys as well as the girls.

To simplify   Select pictures that depict a limited range of tools. Focus on one personal attribute at a time in your pictures.

To extend   Write children's ideas on a sheet of paper. Discuss them with the group as a whole. Help children figure out how they could find actual answers to the questions that arise.

✎ **Recycle-Ickles**

Objective 21   For children to develop a sense of responsibility for the environment.

Materials   Medium-sized plastic bags labeled with each child's name, safety pins to secure them to children's clothing

Procedure

1. Carry out a discussion with children about trash—what it is, how it is generated, what the effect is on the environment, and what people can do to recycle materials that are no longer wanted. Explain that each child will collect the trash he or she produces during a day and place it in the plastic bag. Tell children that at the end of the day they will examine their trash and make determinations about how to reuse it. Then allow children to proceed on their own.

2. Plan a time at the end of the day for children to examine the things they have collected in their bags. Ask each individual to state one way he or she can recycle the materials (include the collection bag, as well). Tell children that they are now "Recycle-

Ickles." Provide each child with a badge that says, "I am a Recycle-Ickle. I reuse my trash."

3. Set aside a recycling center in which to store the materials they have collected and encourage children to reuse it on the following day.

To simplify   Use a classroom collection bag rather than individual bags.

To extend   Carry out the activity over an extended period of time. Evaluate whether children are able to generate less trash as time goes on. Set this as a goal for the school year. Extend the activity to include a collection of schoolwide trash. Follow a similar procedure and acknowledge the efforts of each classroom as they cut down on the trash they generate over time.

SUMMARY

The social domain encompasses four essential aspects of children's development and education: social skills, socialization, social responsibility, and social studies. The most effective paradigm for integrating this body of knowledge and skills is through children's personal experiences at home, at school, and in the broader community in which they live.

Learning to get along with others, both children and adults, is a major task of childhood and is one on which children spend an increasing portion of their time and energy. Some children make friends easily, and some do not. Friendships are so vital to human beings that friendless children and those whose interpersonal relationships with peers are unsatisfactory lead unhappy lives. Developing friendship skills, such as establishing contact, maintaining positive relationships, and resolving conflicts, as well as how they view friendships over time, are important aspects of children's ability to make and keep friends. Youngsters who behave prosocially (e.g., helping, cooperating, comforting, and sharing) develop feelings of competence, enjoy many successful personal encounters, and respond positively to offers of prosocial actions from others. Sensitivity to someone else's cues, decisions to help, and taking appropriate actions are the facets of successful prosocial behavior.

How well children understand and enact the rules and customs of society is a measure of their socialization. Chapter 6 is entirely devoted to this topic.

Societal factors in our modern world make it imperative that children become aware of and share responsibility for the world beyond themselves—to become good citizens in their homes, schools, and communities. This requires that children learn to recognize and embrace diversity in all its forms and that they learn about and care for their immediate environment. Social studies is the study of people in society, past and present, and their relations with each other, both near and far.

Thus, the social studies encompass anthropology, economics, geography, history, human ecology, political science, psychology, and sociology. Knowledge goals of social studies reflect the uniqueness of people, their interdependence, the similarity and differences among people and groups, and the ways in which people have learned over time to live together in democratic ways. In addition, skill goals focus on children's mastery of tools and techniques, while attitude goals emphasize respect for all people and efforts to make the world a healthier and safer place to live. Social studies, then, is the framework within which all of the areas of social development are integrated.

✖ Applying What You Read in This Chapter

1. **Discuss**
   a. Based on your reading and your experiences with children, discuss each of the questions that open this chapter.
   b. Discuss the educational issue "Embracing Diversity: Interpretations and Misinterpretations" raised in this chapter. Do you agree with the positions taken in the text? Explain your reasons. Include personal experiences you may have had.
   c. Using Table 13.3, create an additional activity in each category that is appropriate for the children with whom you work.

2. **Observe**
   a. Observe a group of children for signs of prosocial and antisocial behavior. Tally the incidents of each and summarize the results. Be sure to include the ages of the children in your report.
   b. Watch a group of children at play. Figure out who is friends with whom. Give a detailed description of their relationship. Using the information about the characteristics of friendship in this chapter and your observations, decide at what level of friendship the children are.
   c. Observe an early childhood classroom. Determine the degree to which children have decision-making opportunities by recording the number and types of choices that are offered or group problem-solving experiences in which children participate.

3. **Carry out an activity**
   a. Write a script using the guidelines in the activity section of this chapter. Choose a prosocial or a friendship skill on which to focus your teaching. Practice the skit at home or with friends. Present the skit to the group, using dolls or puppets to create the characters and the situation. Hold a follow-up discussion with the children and, if appropriate, replay the skit using information gleaned from them.
   b. Set up a recycling center in the classroom. Collect all scrap paper and paper products during a single day and plan for children to use the paper on the following day for an art project.
   c. Carry out one or more of the activities you developed for the social studies chart. Evaluate the results.
   d. Carry out one or more of the activities listed at the end of the chapter. Evaluate the results in terms of your preparation and the children's responses.

4. **Create something for your portfolio**
   a. Videotape your presentation of a skit in which you focus on prosocial or friendship skills. Include the script with the tape. Make sure the tape is no more than 10 or 15 minutes long.
   b. Write a summary of the skit focusing on prosocial or friendship skills. Give a synopsis of the discussion that followed the skit and note any changes in children's behavior that you observed as a direct or an indirect result of the ideas presented in the script.
   c. Keep a weekly or monthly record of children's friendships. Compare their relationships before and after you have presented specific information to them by way of skits, discussions, or literature.

d. Document ways in which you have integrated social studies and social development into your curriculum. Use photographs, examples of children's writing or drawing, and anecdotal records you have kept over time.

5. **Add to your journal**

   a. What is the most significant thing you have learned about the social domain based on your reading and experience with children?

   b. Does the information presented in this chapter correspond to your personal and professional experiences in the field? Review consistencies and inconsistencies you perceive.

   c. Think about ways in which you will integrate social skill acquisition and instruction in prosocial behavior into your program.

   d. Based on what you have read, are there changes you would like to see made in the social studies curriculum used in your program? What are they, and how might they be implemented?

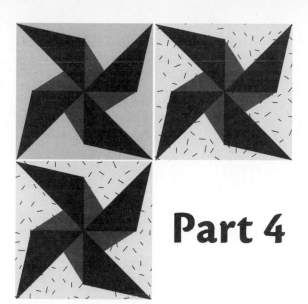

Part 4

Integrating Curriculum

Chapter 14

Integrating Curriculum Through Pretend and Construction Play

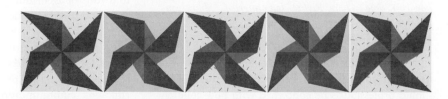

You may be wondering:

Isn't play just natural for children?

How can I convince parents or colleagues that play is important?

How do we account for the differences in the way children approach pretend and construction play?

How do children use construction to represent experiences or objects?

How do pretend and construction play relate to other aspects of development?

In this chapter on pretend and construction play, we present the answers to these questions.

Four first graders were talking intently in the bushes near the corner of the playground. "Let's pretend we're lost and all alone and have to build our house," suggested Alice.

"Yeah, we'll have to build it here. This could be a place to sleep," contributed Diane.

"And nobody knows where we are. No grownups. And no boys can come in here. Right?" Joan queried. "Shari, you get started on the kitchen. We gotta have a kitchen. To-morrow we can bring some food."

What are these children learning? Should this behavior be encouraged in educational settings? Why should professionals be concerned with how children play?

Teachers, along with much of the general public, take children's pretend play for granted and either do not think of it at all or assume that its place is in the home or on the playground.

Pretend play is the hallmark of the early childhood period. In fact, Piaget (1962) used simple pretend as one of the criteria for differentiating between the sensorimotor period and the more advanced preoperational period that encompasses children from 3 to 8 years of age. Adults recognize it immediately, frequently dismissing it as a trivial pursuit of young children. More recently scholars have recognized that pretend play has a formative function that enables children to adapt to the social and physical environment as well as an expressive function that facilitates children's communication with others about their thinking and feelings related to their understanding of the world (Bergen, 1988b; Frost, 1991). Early childhood educators have long perceived pretend play as a vehicle for integrating various developmental capacities. Growing increasingly complex during this period, children's pretend play allows for the practice of skills and the mastery of new challenges.

CHARACTERISTICS OF PLAY

In Chapter 2, the nature of all play is described. Play is fun, carried out for the pleasure of doing it, free of externally imposed rules, spontaneous, and voluntary. It requires the active involvement of the player as well as the suspension of reality. It is symbolic behavior that allows the player to treat objects as though they were something else. The spoon becomes the musician's baton; a block structure becomes a spaceship. Players assume roles as though they were performers or explorers and sometimes machines. Players establish rules consistent with the play theme and roles requiring each other to perform in patterns that fit the narrative. For example, any contribution to the establishment of a household, the protection of the group, or other survival topics would be appropriate to the scenario described at the start of this chapter. Extraneous events, comments, or behavior would be either rejected or ignored by the players or would cause the play to disintegrate. Reality is suspended, but the play is governed by rules; thus the play event itself has internal coherence. Children function in the enactive mode as they do simple make-believe, shifting to the iconic mode when they need to construct an object to further their play, and they utilize the symbolic mode in complex play scenarios. Thus, imaginative, abstract thinking, set within the play frame and composed of sequences of action events, is typical.

The Play Frame   The play frame describes the scope of the pretend play event. Inside the play frame are all of the people and objects that the children are using to enact their imaginative episode. The people, objects, and pretend narrative are all relevant to each other and the progress of the play event. If a photograph were taken of the pretend play episode described at the beginning of the chapter, the photographer would automatically move back to include all the players and relevant objects, even though other persons might be in either the foreground or the background of the photo.

Players within the frame are those who have a communication link and are engaged in the play. All of the other persons and objects without a relationship to the pretend narrative in progress are not in the play frame.

The frames of play may be established by a variety of modes (Sutton-Smith, 1986). Establishing the frame of the play allows children to communicate the theme, roles, and specific story to be enacted. Children might establish the frame by announcing it—"This is the house"—or by announcing a play role—"I'm the policeman"—or simply by acting on objects such as putting the train track together and running the train on it. Sometimes a smile and a gesture are sufficient between familiar players revisiting a common action sequence.

Recognition of play frames is important to educators because, although pretend play has its own internal logic with a unique imaginative quality, the player's behavior must be understood from that frame of reference. Usually, however, the "reality" described in the pretend play reflects the level of understanding shared by the children. For example, if children are pretending to be firefighters and they assign one of the players to set fires, they lack information about the causes of fires and the true functions of firefighters. Although everyone agrees that play within the play frame is not "for real," adults may gain insight into children's thinking by the content of the frames and skill with which they play.

Elements of Pretend Play

Pretend play is composed of a set of skills or elements that may be used singly (in less skilled players) or in combination (with players of greater skill). All players must be able to participate in *make-believe;* that is, they must be able to suspend reality, even momentarily, to engage in the simplest form of pretend play, which is pretending with an object. When children pretend with objects, they act as though a stuffed animal were a baby, as though bits of Play-Doh were food, or as though toy cars were real vehicles. Often the characteristics of the object itself suggest the make-believe scenario to the child. For example, a classroom computer might inspire a child to play airport controller, mission control for a space launch, or a worker with computers. Stuffed animals might suggest the pretend notion of a zoo, farm, or veterinarian in much the same way.

"...3, 2, 1, blast-off!" Charlotte has transformed the computer station into mission control.

When the needed object is not at hand, children engage in *object substitution.* This is straightforward representational thinking in which the child represents one object with another closer at hand (Raines, 1990). Whereas one child might use a pencil and paper to take an order in a "restaurant," another might substitute a hand for the paper and a finger for the pencil. Object substitutions are signaled by either actions or narrative. Three-year-olds can readily substitute one object in their play, and older children are capable of using more when playing alone. In addition, younger children are more likely to substitute objects that perceptually suggest the needed device. For example, a shell or a can is more likely to be substituted for a cup than is a string or a stick.

Primary-age youngsters may not need an object for the substitution. Instead, they use *object invention* and represent the needed objects solely through pantomime. A 7-year-old may open the door of a cupboard (that does not exist), remove a bowl (that is not there), place it on a real table, and begin to stir with an imaginary spoon. Measuring cups and ingredients may be represented either through the narrative or actions alone. Three- to five-year-olds find it very difficult to play with a variety of object inventions, although older children do it more easily. Additionally, all children

have difficulty when playing in groups with more than one imaginary person or object. They appear to need something as a placeholder to engage in shared imaginary objects. For example, three 6-year-olds who were engaged in playing out small-town life drew streets in the dirt with their fingers and used leaves for community buildings and small mounds for houses. One child had designated an empty area as the vacant lot early in the play, and later another started to construct a house on it. After much discussion, the children agreed to draw a ring around the vacant lot so that others would not forget what it was. The ring defined the vacant lot and became the placeholder for empty space. Frequently iconic representations of objects are used as placeholders with several players just to avoid the confusion these children experienced.

Children throughout the early childhood period play like someone or something. They take on *roles.* These roles may be based on TV or movies (Mighty Morphin and Power Rangers); functional roles (one who eats or uses a computer); familial or relational roles (husband/father, wife/mother); or occupational roles (nurse, robber). Obviously, children must be familiar with the roles they assume. Pretending to be oneself in another setting occurs between ages 2 and 3. Family roles predominate during the preschool period, with presentations of primary caregivers portrayed with emotional meanings (Garvey & Berndt, 1977). Nurturing roles may become very elaborate over time as children incorporate greater complexity into the action sequences they represent. Occupational roles emerge slowly in older preschool children as they become aware of the larger community. These roles are heavily influenced by children's experiences and their school curriculum. School-age children elaborate on earlier roles and include frightening fantasies and themes of victim and aggressor. Fictional roles, those developed in television, movies, or literature, generate high action, powerful roles particularly attractive to boys. Though these roles are fun, they may be somewhat flat, having limited dimensions of character. The sarcastic humor and the use of double entendres that are common in cartoons are not fully understood by young children, so they depend predominantly on action to interpret the character. Sometimes these portrayals lack the personal creativity the children are otherwise capable of demonstrating.

Children learn to *transform time, place, and setting*. These transformations enable them to pretend to be pioneers or space adventurers. The beach, stores, circus, or market might be places "visited" in the classroom play space. Time and place simply have no restrictions except those of information available to the players. For example, a 3-year-old who remains at home while family business is transacted would not have sufficient information to pretend banking or stores, whereas a second grader who had both a school social studies background and more community experience would be prepared to engage in these play themes with considerable elaboration.

Communications That Enable Play to Work   When children play make-believe together, they must engage in complex communications called *metacommunication,* which means a communication about a communication (Bateson, 1971). These communications tend to describe what is "play" and what is not. They may serve to construct the play frame ("Let's pretend to be hunters") or define roles ("We can be neighbors who don't like each other").

Metacommunication statements transform objects and settings. "This [puppet stage] is the post office window" or "I'm in a dark forest and lost" typically set the stage for continuing the play and provide the beginning narrative and context for continuing communication.

Additionally, children use metacommunications to extend their play and elaborate on characters' feelings or actions. In each case, cues for the content of continuing communication are provided: "This is a very dark forest, and I hope there are no monsters here" or "Pretend that you are a really mean bad guy."

Metacommunications also end the framed sequence. Children may deny the role ("I'm not the bad guy any more"), change the meaning of the props ("This window [puppet theater] is really a window out of a spaceship"), or redefine the setting ("Why don't we pretend we were rescued and put in the hospital?").

Metacommunications combine the basic elements of pretend play and the framing process so that all players in a cooperative play venture can participate knowledgeably. All of the preceding elements of pretend play may be engaged in alone; however, once more players are involved, metacommunications are necessary for the pretend sequence to be coherent.

Types of Pretend Play

Usually adults conceive of pretend play as unidimensional. Selected forms of pretend play are described here, but this listing is not intended to be definitive. The quality and complexity of the play and the setting are important variables among the types of play. The outcomes described in a later section are probably limited to the more complex sociodramatic play sequences, although skill in play can be developed in any form.

Make-Believe   Simple pretend is when a child takes on the characteristics of an object or a person and acts out a sequence. For example, 3-year-olds might pretend to be balloons who are being blown up by another child. Five-year-olds might walk down the hallway connected to each other to form a train and "chug, chug, chug" as they move. Eight-year-olds might pretend to be an airplane or a cloud moving over the mountains. Such episodes may be encouraged deliberately by the teacher or developed spontaneously by the children.

Pretend with Objects   Exploration of an object or any new material always precedes well-developed play sequences regardless of the children's age, skills, or familiarity with the material. In exploration a child discovers "What is the nature of this object?" whereas in pretend the child wonders, "What can I do with this?" Unskilled players may vacillate between pretend play and exploration while learning how to pretend with an object. For example, Rico, age 4, picked up a stethoscope and correctly identified it as a "doctor thing." He swung it around, talked into it, hung it on his neck, and used it to hit at Maria. Mark told him to put the earplugs in his ears and listen to his heart. Rico tried this. He listened to tables, a window, and a radiator before attempting to listen to another child. Then he engaged in a brief doctor episode while listening to a doll's chest. Alternating between listening to dolls, children, and other objects in the environment, Rico's play vacillated between pretending with an object and exploration. Older children may also pretend by themselves and focus on the object they are using. Children who have few playmates may be very skilled in developing a variety of pretend scenarios based on a single object. Over several play episodes, Allison used an old-fashioned wash basin for a doll bath, a helmet, and a cooking pot. Even in the most traditional classrooms, teachers are familiar with children's tendency to use anything for play: bits of paper, pencils, articles of clothing, science equipment, and so on.

Pretend with Art Materials   Some 3- to 5-year-olds are primarily concerned about the pattern, color, or form of their visual art experiences, whereas others typically have a story that the graphic portion represents. Children may verbally express the pretend story component as the child produces the graphic: "And the scary spider dropped down . . . to the ground. And he moved around. He went up and the wind blew him. Almost hit the boy." Thus, they use the "movements of play, the lines of drawing, and the sounds of language to represent the people, objects, and events that comprise their world" (Dyson, 1990, 50). Children may even share a pretend play sequence, talking and drawing at the same time. Five- to eight-year-olds may contribute the pretend portion of this creative experience but are more successful in doing so without speech than are the younger ones. Drawings incorporate more of the movement and more details of the pretend as children mature.

Pretend with Construction Materials   Probably the most complex of all play episodes are ones in which children construct the necessary play props to support their pretend theme or action sequence. In this case, the play shifts back and forth from construction to pretend play. In younger children, this is most frequently seen in the blocks with which a child might build a house or a barn and then use cars and small dolls to enact a scene. Older children may continue the same play action sequence for several days, building additional components as they go along. In one Indiana kindergarten, children reconstructed their own small town over a period of several weeks using clay, small cardboard boxes, and other discarded materials. Throughout the elementary school period, children build snow forts, treehouses, stores, and homes in which to engage in increasingly elaborate pretend play sequences.

Pretend with Miniature Buildings and People   Dollhouses, barns and animals, vehicles with passengers, and other miniature pretend settings are available to stimulate pretend play. Children provide the story and manipulate the characters suggested by the manufacturer. The big difference in this play is that children do not engage in the movement and cannot use facial expression or body action to convey ideas and feelings. They become the narrator; although they might portray many parts, they are not actors with their own bodies. Children from 5 to 8 usually have the capacity to use their voices to portray a variety of emotions. Younger children are likely to find some way to include larger movements, such as transporting farm animals in a truck.

Dramatic Play   During dramatic play the child carries out a sequence of events or actions that are related to one another. Pretend with object, place, time, and setting may all be utilized by the child in a particular episode. With younger children, the sequences are likely to be based on familiar routines—feeding and bathing a doll, putting the doll to bed—with other caregiving activities included as called for by the player. An older child might play a more distant role and pretend to be a bus driver or even a worker at mission control guiding spaceships (that are being constructed out of clay) in takeoff or landing sequences.

The play may be solitary or in the company of other children but not necessarily interacting with them except through observation or shared space. Seven- and eight-year-olds are able to pick up the play theme from day to day and continue, whereas three- to five-year-olds are more likely to start over. Such differences in skill and maturity influence the selection of the play topic and the duration and complexity of the play enactment.

Sociodramatic Play   This kind of play involves several children playing together for at least 10 minutes and engaging in the same narrative sequence. The story is negotiated, and the roles are established with directives on how to forward the play plan. Usually pretend with time, setting, and place are agreed on by the players as the play progresses and may be completely embedded in the script. "Gee, it's getting dark now" automatically calls for an evening sequence of actions by other players. A second child might respond, "Where will we sleep?" which draws the play into a housing or furnishing problem. The story line is shared by all the players, with any individual child both following others' leads as well as contributing new ideas. Children frequently prompt each other when factual errors are made in the play, such as one child whispering loudly, "The store man collects the money for the stuff. Doesn't pay someone to take it." Children of 4 to 5 rarely have more than one intangible object, if any, when playing in groups. It is difficult for several children to keep in mind objects that do not exist.

Theme-Related Play   This variation of dramatic and sociodramatic play is very goal directed and may center around a number of occupational themes: beauty shop, school, camping, hospital, restaurant, or fire station. When children are engaged in thematic instruction, some aspect of the theme is available for pretend play. Children may initiate it themselves (Fayden, 1997), or adults may instigate the play by providing the props, time, space, and information necessary for enactment. Sometimes even the action is suggested by supervising adults. However, once initiated, children should take it over or develop it themselves. Children who rarely participate in house play may readily engage in occupational or adventure roles that are more typical of theme-related play.

Detail and accuracy of portrayal increase with practice and maturity. In addition, children add problems that must be solved within the play. These frequently are reasonable for the setting, such as having a fire drill while playing school, running out of permanent solution in a beauty shop, or having a fire in a garage. Primary-age children may successfully incorporate themes from television, video stories, or literature within their play. Preschool children are able to play their most complex sociodramatic scenarios based on settings with which they are the most familiar, such as babies, families, and neighbors, although they sometimes also attempt fantasy characters.

Story Reenactment   Variously called *creative dramatics, thematic* or *fantasy play,* or *story reenactment,* this type of play involves children developing the skills of taking on a role and re-creating a plot they have heard in a myth, legend, poem, or story. Through story reenactment children are able to assume a variety of roles they otherwise would have no way of experiencing such as a princess or a space traveler. The scope of mood, setting, and plot structures in literature far exceeds what a small group of children can imagine without any additional sources. Older children may read-play-read again as they engage in the story enactment. Discussion of character and other elements of literature are possible and comprehensible as children dramatize a written or traditional story.

Write and Play or Writer's Theater   Children dictate or write a story and then enact it. In this case the creation of the story is with class members who become the author(s). Sometimes the story is started by the pretend play episode, sometimes by the story dictation. This form of pretend play builds on the skills of 6- and 7-year-olds for pretend play story plots and characterization. The additional transformation to word stories connects this form of play to learning in the language domain. Children also face the dilemma of written dialogue and begin to use grammar rules they otherwise would never attempt.

Fundamentally, children's story writing and their pretend play are blended so that the strength of one can foster the other. For example, a simple story written by a 6-year-old was only two sentences: "My baby brother got in my room. He made a mess." Several first graders were asked to think about this basic plot and pretend play it. The author was in the group and watched as various children played roles of baby, older brother, and parents. More than one pretend sequence was tried, and several solutions to the problem were explored as children acted out their roles. The author had the choice of incorporating some details, problems, and solutions into the story or leaving it alone. The advantage of this play form is that the connection between the familiar play and the new tasks of writing are clear, meaningful, and obvious.

Pretend play is the representation of ideas through the enactive mode. Children portray their ideas about events by what they do and say and use props to support their scenarios. This is the only enactive mode for representational thought. They also use the iconic mode when they represent their ideas through what they make. Objects that children construct represent processes, events, or other objects. By constructing a concrete representation, they gain greater understanding of their experiences. Construction play, though similar to pretend in that it represents children's interpretation of the world around them, has distinctive characteristics of its own. Both pretend and construction play may include symbolic modes of representation through written and oral language.

Construction Play

Four-year-old Kate spent several minutes studying a spider web in the fence of the play yard. When she returned to the classroom, she used Sticky Wickets, which are flexible, colored strips of plastic that stick to many surfaces, to reconstruct the spider web in a three-dimensional form. Then she drew the spider web on paper with crayon and announced, "I can make a spider web, too!" She was completely engrossed in her activity.

Aida was playing store with other kindergarten children. She seemed dissatisfied with simply pretending to offer money to the clerk and said, "I gotta get some real money to buy this stuff." Looking around the room, Aida walked to the paper supply shelf, selected a few sheets of green paper, carefully tore it into rectangles, wrote numerals on each piece, and returned to complete her purchases in the pretend store.

Mark, who had been participating in a unit on trees in his third-grade classroom, spent several days accumu-

lating leaves from the trees in his neighborhood on his own. Each leaf was mounted on a sheet of paper and labeled with its name. He carefully drew several trees with some details of the surrounding environment and labeled them "Tree in front," "Mr. McDirmid's tree," and "On the corner." Then he arranged them into a book of leaves in his neighborhood.

All of these children have demonstrated their ability to represent objects, events, or groups of objects that are meaningful to them in a concrete, physical way. All three children were able to bring together a variety of skills and concepts to be successful in their projects. For example, Kate demonstrated memory skills, imagination, perseverance, planning, and fine motor skills. She used her knowledge of materials, whole-part relationships, and concepts of line, direction, and space in addition to her obvious understandings of the spider web. Her emotional satisfaction was expressed in her comment. Aida, who could not pretend play comfortably with no placeholder for the symbolic money she needed, used her knowledge about money and good problem-solving skills to make "money" so that the play could continue smoothly. Mark, who is much older, was able to represent a group of trees, their location and environment, and their relationship to people and places familiar to him. He incorporated information that he had learned at school and used skills of observing, recording, and communicating his experience.

Construction is the transformation of an experience or object into a concrete representation of that experience or object. Children use materials to make a product. "Often these are symbolic products, such as drawings, paintings and three-dimensional creations that represent objects (e.g., house), ideas (e.g., friendship), or processes (e.g., war). Constructive and symbolic play can also be combined to create a poem, a dramatic production, a tape recording, or other visual or technological products" (Bergen, 1988a, 247). When a child constructs an object in many different ways such as a report, drawing, cardboard, or clay or wood model, the child must take into account previous representations as new ones are created. Each rendition takes a perspective that when passed on to the next media generates conflict, challenge, and change (Forman, 1996). Such multiple perspectives can be considered variations on the same system.

Children may use sound effects, vocalizations, or speech to explain or activate a construction. Most physical products are accompanied by children's commentaries as they are building. These comments complete the representation. For example, a child might name a particular block a "car" although it does not differ greatly from the block next to it. When children build machines, an adult may be able to identify them from the associated sound effects. Thus, auditory information may supplement the physical to represent the child's idea more adequately. Among the patterns of developmentally appropriate curriculum, perhaps construction play is the easiest for experienced traditional teachers to understand and emulate. To many it appears to be related to both play and work, and the outcomes are observable and understandable (Chaillé & Silvern, 1996).

Types of Construction Projects

Three broadly defined types of construction projects are "1) those resulting from a child's natural encounter with the environment, 2) those reflecting mutual interests on the part of the teacher and children, and 3) those based on teacher concerns regarding specific cognitive and/or social concepts" (New, 1990, 7). In all three types, the products emerge from an intense interest, an acute investigation, or a hands-on exploration of an object or event that appeals to the children. Constructions are children's attempts to solidify their own ideas or communicate ideas to others through imagery.

Projects Stemming from Natural Encounters   All young children are in the process of trying to understand their world. Often an ordinary object or some aspect of nature will capture a young child's interest. Drawings of people, houses, and animals are typical, as are modeling dough constructions of cakes, cookies, snakes, and bowls. Some constructions may be extremely simple, as when Sasha, age 3, watched raindrops flow down the pane and then painted the irregular vertical lines at the easel. At other times children's constructions are more elaborate. For example, when three children noticed the movement and seemingly purposeful activity of ants on the playground, their teacher suggested that they make something to help them remember what they saw. Other children joined

the discussion about the ants' behavior and were encouraged by their teacher to elaborate on their comments by making something with clay or illustrating their understanding of the ants using paper and chalk. This group of children continued to observe the ants and document what they saw.

Projects Stemming from Mutual Interests of Teacher and Children   This type of construction requires more advanced planning by the teacher, who often stimulates it by designing experiences based on common events in children's lives. For example, many young children are concerned about having a friend. Discussions of friendship enhanced with constructions of modeling dough or collages of magazine pictures representing children's ideas about friendship further mutual communication and understanding. Sometimes current events discussed at home or on television may stimulate both children and adults to read, discuss, and construct images related to the topic. For example, during the disintegration of the Soviet Union, one youngster illustrated the breakup by soaking manila paper in water and distributing bits of it over a piece of blue construction paper; another drew lines of people; still another painted the military tanks in the street during the coup. The teacher provides accurate information, ignites the children's creative thinking and questions, and supports the further examination of ideas. Often children's constructions provide cues that children have misinformation and misconceptions to which the teacher then responds.

Projects Stemming from Teacher Concerns Regarding Specific Concepts   The third type of construction focuses on ideas or concepts initially unfamiliar to children but perceived by adults as valuable for children to explore. They may be the subject of expressed interest or the outcome of the children's current experience. Such construction activities are embedded in a theme or unit in which children learn about other aspects of the social and natural world using a variety of the strategies described in previous chapters. For instance, children living in forested areas of the country are exposed to ideas related to oceans and deserts. Children living in a homogeneous community may explore ideas about people of various ethnic and racial backgrounds. Children may generate construction activities that emerge from topics in science, social studies, mathematics, health, literature, or music. Children listen or read, discuss, and then construct a representation of their understanding. Both the children and the teacher have opportunities to share insights into the thinking of others as the projects are examined and classmates communicate their interpretations (Gardini & Edwards, 1988). Constructions of this type are more typical of the primary child, although some 4- and 5-year-olds may attempt them.

Comparison of Construction and Other Related Activities

Object exploration, practice in fine motor skills, and craft projects are related to children's construction activities but are not quite the same. Each of these three activities involves knowledge or skills children use when constructing, but they do not require the level of representational thought and creativity associated with construction.

Construction Is Not Simply Object Play   Object play is exploration and investigation. A child attempts to discover the properties of an object or to answer the questions "What is this object like? How does it work?" The novelty of the object attracts the child's attention, and its complexity sustains interest. Behaviors such as repetitive actions, systematic examination, and attempts to use the object in a variety of ways are typical of object play. Thus, exploration and object play usually occur before construction becomes possible (Tribe, 1982).

When children stop investigating the nature of objects and begin using them to build something, they shift into construction. The contrast between object play and construction can be seen in the behaviors of two 3-year-olds. Jerry John arranged several blocks in front of him and engaged in snapping them together in various combinations. He seemed most interested in determining whether any combination could be snapped and unsnapped readily and answering the question "How does this work?" In contrast, Alexi selected only the units that could be fastened in a linear pattern and commented, "See my snake." He then arranged the snap blocks to represent the snake.

Three- and four-year-old children may spend substantial time exploring a material, creating a combination that reminds them of a familiar object, and

naming it, as Billy did in one of his rearrangements of the blocks: "Look here, I got this house." Sometimes youngsters are aware of this, as Dimitri was when he told an inquiring adult, "I'll know what this painting is when I've finished it." Regardless of age, all children move between object play and construction when they encounter new media or materials or ones they have not used in a long time. In general, however, as children mature, they spend less time exploring and more time using the materials to construct.

Construction Is Not Simply Fine Motor Practice The imitation and practice of hand skills such as holding a writing implement, cutting with scissors, sewing, weaving, and using various tools are addressed in Chapter 12. Something may be produced, but it is a by-product of the process and not intended to represent a child's idea or concept. Instead, it is the natural outcome of the process, such as fringe produced while snipping paper or a cutout of a pattern given to the child to practice cutting. Occasionally, preschoolers will name their by-products if they resemble a familiar object, such as labeling a spiral cut paper "snake" when they pull the ends apart. Primary children may have the basic skills and refine them during the construction process as the need arises. Clearly, children must control the materials and tools used for construction and apply their knowledge to tasks skillfully.

Construction requires that the child have an image in mind that she or he then represents using familiar processes. For example, Rebecca carefully cut along the lines of a pattern drawn for her. She focused her entire attention on the process of producing a smooth curve and turning corners neatly. In contrast, Marietta left a group of children looking at the visiting cat, walked to the center where materials were stored, and created a cat face by cutting into a paper plate to form eyes and ears and adding whiskers with a marker. Rebecca and Marietta both produced products, but only Marietta had a specific idea in mind when she engaged in the activity. The child's imagination is central to the reasoning process, and no activity is undertaken without some image of the result, whether his or her conception is accurate or not (J. Smith, 1990). As with object play, the skills with which to control the processes of construction are necessary but insufficient by themselves.

Construction Is Not Simply the Demonstration of Technique   Children must also learn techniques (N. Smith, 1982). For example, a child who wishes to adhere two pieces of paper must learn where to put the paste. Children also learn when to use which adhesive (e.g., white liquid glue, school paste, rubber cement, or a mixture of white glue and paste) that will adhere pieces of wood or cardboard. Skill in the use of tools and techniques generally precedes construction activities or is learned in the context of a construction project as the need arises. As children shift from one media to another, the demands for technical knowledge and skills increase.

Construction Is Not Simply Following Directions for a Project   In her kindergarten class, Diedra listened carefully as the teacher gave directions and demonstrated how to make a rabbit. Each piece had been reproduced on paper, and the rabbit would have movable legs. She cut, colored, and assembled the rabbit as directed, even though it did not quite look the same as her teacher's. Diedra used her language, memory, and motor skills to perform this task. In the kindergarten at another school, Fredrico had listened to the story of Peter Rabbit and studied several photographs of real rabbits. He constructed a rabbit from materials that he selected from those on the shelves. Fredrico also used language, memory, and motor skills to produce a rabbit. In addition, he made decisions about materials and used imagination and representational thinking to form his image of the rabbit. Both children created products, but only Fredrico was involved in the representational thought necessary for construction. However, Diedra might have produced a rabbit more appealing to adults by copying her teacher's image rather than creating her own.

Knowledge of necessary processes or step-by-step operations necessary to achieve a specific end is useful to the construction process but not a substitute for it. Does the child-drawn image of the human figure with a very large mouth and exaggerated hands mean that the child is unable to perceive the difference in length between fingers, arms, and legs? Of course not! The specific proportions of the human body are not necessary to convey the idea, and children between 3 and 8 have no difficulty in readily perceiving such contrasting lengths. Yet adults sometimes behave as though

children are functioning without sufficient information. The copyist theory of knowledge is that children learn by closely attending and that if the child were sufficiently skilled in perception, then he or she could accurately duplicate the idea (Forman & Kuschner, 1983). If children only followed the directions with care, the product, and incidentally the idea, would be replicated.

Unfortunately, imitation is not sufficient to develop a concept (Piaget, 1962). Children during the preoperational period do increasingly develop their abilities to perceive with accuracy. They also learn to use step-by-step procedures to achieve a specific outcome. Following directions, imitating, and copying enable children to acquire the techniques that provide them with the skills and procedures for carrying out their construction projects. For example, two 5-year-olds recreated their experiences with vehicles in the snow, using different media. One child drew a rectangle with circles on the side with a red crayon on blue paper, then neatly glued cotton balls around it. The second child used two paintbrushes held side by side and made parallel wavy lines across white paper to illustrate car tracks in the snow. Both youngsters demonstrated their abilities to use materials and fashion a concrete representation of an idea. Both used appropriate techniques for the medium selected and worked with care and deliberation. Imitation of the technique might be important, but once the technique is mastered, children construct the product according to their own ideas and interpretation. In fact, providing children with patterns to color in specific ways and expecting youngsters to replicate the teachers' models are likely to limit childrens' own abilities to make constructions of their own (Moyer, 1990). They may lose confidence in themselves if they must meet adult standards prematurely.

A second-grade teacher who had provided models and detailed directions for products in the past commented about a marked change in children's behavior when she altered her approach. "I have been really surprised. The children used to be concerned that their pictures looked just like their friends'; now they are trying to be unique in what they do."

Arts and crafts are favorites of young children and their teachers. When children make holiday ornaments from printed fabric and canning lids, decorate orange juice cans with macaroni and paint, or weave pot holders, they are participating in activities that have become traditional in some communities. These activities are legitimate exercises in fine motor control and may be useful in promoting perceptual development or listening skills. They have a place in the curriculum but do not substitute for genuine opportunities for children to construct something on their own. They have independent value but do not require the transformation of an idea into a product.

Construction and Materials of Choice

Construction opportunities are facilitated when children have access to a large array of materials. For example, one 4-year-old wanted a "cape." He examined butcher paper that was stiff but could be wrapped around and taped. He tried some lightweight tissue paper. Then he discovered some yarn and a piece of fabric. The texture of the latter made this his best choice for the purpose. Children can engage in this scope of problem solving to make successful constructions only in an environment where there is access to a supply of materials.

Various Blocks   Blocks abound in sizes, colors, and textures. Some fasten together and have pieces designed for wheels and axles. Others such as unit blocks are cut in regular, predictable intervals. Some sets have a color for each shape and provide a variety of angles in wedge-shaped pieces. Large hollow blocks may be used to build structures that children may enter.

Commercial Sets   There are numerous commercial construction sets with sections that children can fasten together using nuts and bolts or pieces that fit together when laid in place. These sets often have extender sets that include more complicated pieces and may even come with electric motors so that children can make more complex machines that run. Products that have many units and can be assembled in different ways provide for more diversity of construction than those with fewer units or those limited to some predetermined structures (Whiren, 1979). Older children frequently want their constructions "to work."

Carpentry Supplies and Tools   Woodworking benches with real hammers, nails, saws, drills, screws, screwdrivers, and other tools to enable a child to construct with

real wood are an alternative in many programs for young children. Tools should be of home-use quality. Most toy tools are impractical because they do not work. Some programs allow children to build with wood and later take the structures apart to reuse the wood for new projects. Soft woods are easier for children to use than hard woods. They are also less expensive and can be obtained as discards from local businesses.

Art Materials, Paper, and Common Discards   The scope of art materials was discussed in Chapter 8. Children use these materials to represent their ideas graphically. A multitude of papers that differ in color, texture, and size are available for purchase and as discards from businesses or families, such as old wrapping paper, commercial sacks, forms, used computer printouts, and even trim cuttings from printers. The numbers and colors available in paint and writing implements are considerable as well. In addition, a variety of three-dimensional materials such as egg cartons, packing material, meat trays, and other throwaway objects with interesting patterns, colors, or textures can be obtained for children to use.

Open-Ended Materials   Flexible materials such as sand, clay, plasticine, and Play-Doh can be used to represent a variety of ideas. Once they understand the properties of the materials and if they have supporting tools, children can create a wide array of representations. The advantage of these materials is that they are three-dimensional, with an undetermined shape in the beginning. With sand, children can try out their ideas and erase them without fear of making mistakes (Barbour, Webster, & Drosdek, 1987). Children can exert greater control over the medium at younger ages.

Natural Materials   Sticks, leaves, stones, mud, and other plant materials have long been used by children to create little worlds where pretend people carry out their lives. Snow is another excellent building material. These natural resources may be used outdoors or brought into the classroom as the occasion demands.

Materials Assembled with Specific Teacher Goals in Mind   Older children can create board games from file folders, poster board, or shirt boxes with assorted stickers, markers, and pieces to move (Castle, 1991). The child is required not only to construct a product but also to establish the rules of the game. The problems they encounter, such as how to have moving pieces that can be distinguished from one another or how to make the game challenging and fun, engage their creative interest as well as require access to an array of materials.

Independence of Materials From the Ideas They Represent

At times, children use the same materials to represent a variety of ideas. Painting and dough are particularly versatile. In one small group, children used dough to make nests and eggs, dishes, cups with handles, a ring, a long snake, and a cake. The diversity of ideas that individual children expressed expanded the vision of the entire group. Children see more and more possibilities as they practice with the material and modify them by using tools. In another group, children used paint to represent abstract ideas like friends, conflicts, or feelings in more concrete terms. On the other hand, some of the first identifiable drawings of people, vehicles, and houses are also made with paints (Kellogg, 1969). Whether or not children depict their ideas in realistic or abstract constructions, they tend to become more versatile when they are thoroughly familiar with the material and are in control of the process. Yet, each material also limits the content of expression and approach used to some extent (Forman, 1996; N. Smith, 1982). For example, it would be easier to represent the ocean using paints and paper or a paper collage than blocks.

Children often depict the same idea using a variety of materials. Children must use problem solving when they have a choice of materials for representing the same general idea. Different materials give different results, so the character or mood may vary from one depiction to another. Children also must solve a variety of problems relating to technique when materials are varied. Developing a theme of "Houses," the same child made houses using sticks, straw, and string; sugar cubes; blocks; crayons and paper; and paints and small boxes. The gravest technical difficulties were experienced when the child tried to use the straw, finally tying it at the top and sticking a finger in to make an interior. Various adhesives were tried, and the sizes of the houses differed considerably. The block house had an interior and an exterior. When given crayons, the child drew only the face of the house. These activities,

extended over several days, involved much peer cooperation and prosocial behavior. Children also compared their own work on the same idea from one medium to the next.

As children increase in their ability to represent objects and events, they are also better able to select the appropriate material to achieve their desired end. With practice, they become more confident, more skillful, and often more creative.

Accounting for Individual Differences in Children's Pretend and Construction Play

Maturity, family life experiences, style preferences, classroom context, practice, cultural background, and play quality all influence the content of pretend and construction play as well as the performance of the players (Mellou, 1994).

Maturity   Three-year-olds do not possess the vocabulary, life experience, or level of abstract thinking that older children demonstrate. Their play is usually solitary, beside another player who is playing similarly, or in short episodes of cooperative play. Frequently they are unable to express the metacommunication messages necessary for more elaborate pretend play. Younger children usually select content based on familiar roles, such as those of the family, rather than fiction.

A few children will begin true construction with regular materials as early as age 3. If the construction is not named by the child, it is difficult to tell if the child is involved in object play or simple construction. As children mature, their structures become more complex and have more parts (Reifel & Greenfield, 1983). Details of interest become elaborated and are often the subject of conversation among children. In addition, the intent of the child is much clearer, being either announced in advance or obvious from the context of the ongoing play. Four- and five-year-olds regularly engage in pretend play during the construction process. Six- and seven-year-olds may discuss in detail what they plan to construct and even determine the relationship among the structures before they begin. At any point in time children produce constructions that are more recognizable (drawing of a person) or abstract (whirling leaves in the wind). They may do this independently or as part of a larger, more complex, play frame. The developmental stages of block play are presented

TABLE 14.1
Developmental Stages of Block Play

Stage	Description
1. Object exploration	*Carrying blocks*—Children move blocks around and discover properties of the material.
2. Learning techniques	*Piling and laying blocks on the floor*—Children arrange both horizontal and vertical sets of blocks. Sometimes completed arrangements suggest a use, such as a "road."
3. Construction	*Connecting blocks to create structures*—Children make enclosures, build bridges, and design decorative patterns and layouts.
4. Advanced construction	*Making elaborate constructions*—Children create complex buildings, often with many parts, using curved as well as straight lines, around or over obstacles. This stage is frequently associated with pretend play.

in Table 14.1 because this is a very familiar and typical construction material. A more elaborate and complete description of block play can be found in *The Block Book* (Hirsch, 1984).

Family Life Experience   The general life experience of 3- to 8-year-olds varies considerably as well. Children from rural areas know more about farming than urban children and can pretend appropriate roles much earlier than their city counterparts of similar maturity. Some children have experienced police raids in the neighborhoods and have a working knowledge of street gangs by the time they are 5 years old, whereas other children of similar ages are completely ignorant of such occurrences. Ordinary things such as family composition, presence of pets, modes of typical transportation, and occupations of adults in the home provide some children with information that others do not have. Children tend to play out the scenes and scenarios with which they are most familiar. Therefore, for most teachers, variety in content and leadership is typical.

The "house" built by these 3-year-olds is a typical Stage 2 block construction.

Stage 3 constructions such as this "skyscraper" are common in kindergarten.

Cultural Differences   Many classrooms are composed of families from a variety of cultural backgrounds. The role of mother, for instance, is different in different families. This is true of the individual family culture as well as of nationality, such as Arabic, Japanese, or Spanish. Players of different backgrounds often need help in negotiating their play. Younger children generally do not realize that different people may come to the play with perspectives vastly dissimilar from their own.

Practice or Skill Differences   Children who do not have access to a wide variety of materials will not be as skillful as those who do, regardless of age. For example, although many 3-year-olds can cut simple straight lines, 5-year-olds who have just acquired access to scissors may still be figuring out how they work and so use them with less skill. High-quality construction play is dependent on the skillful use of the materials used in the process. Construction with blocks requires skillful placement and organization; with graphic materials, it requires control of implements.

Because pretend play begins very early, children often exhibit differences in learned skills. Smilansky (1968) was the first to note that skill development in the elements of pretend play was limited or absent in lower socioeconomic groups in Israel. This finding was later verified in studies in the United States (Fein & Stork, 1981) and modified by Eiferman (1971) to indicate that the deficiency was one of developmental delay rather than inability. This means that some children may not possess even rudimentary pretend skills at age 5 or 6 that other children exhibit at age 3. Children can

These second graders have constructed an elaborate Stage 4 movie theater, complete with screen, seating, concession stand, and parking.

and do learn the elements of pretend play with appropriate adult instruction in educational settings (Christie, 1986). Many children are skilled at pretend play by age 5, whereas others are just beginning to learn. These differences may be the result of parenting practice or of early childcare practices.

Classroom Context   The actual context of the classroom also accounts for individual differences among children in pretend play performance. First of all, the materials, equipment, and arrangement of these things in the classroom influence whether or not children engage in pretend play and even how many players play at one time (Dempsey & Frost, 1993). Even the subtle differences of play with hollow blocks and unit blocks appear to make a difference in play content and social structure (Rogers, 1985). Theme-related play is unlikely to occur without the necessary theme-related objects and sources of information (Booth, 1997; Fayden, 1997). The presence of peers with whom to play as well as the level of creativity and flexibility other players bring to the pretend play situation often influence the existence of play at all as well as its quality (Mohighan-Nourot, 1997). Experienced teachers who have had groups of youngsters whose pretend skills are minimal and groups with one or two "master players" capable of keeping the play going by altering play scripts, imaginative problem solving, compromising, and suggesting play elaborations are aware of how these differences influence other players.

The context also includes age range of the children, ability levels, and previous learning experiences of the same group of children. An integrated classroom of 6- and 7-year-olds who have been in a mixed-age group for at least a year with each other will appear different from a first-grade group that has just formed. In addition, the amount of time and space are also a part of this context as is the group's schedule of the day.

Play Style   Children seem to prefer one of two play styles: patterners and dramatists. Patterners tend to focus on form, line, color, design, and the general aesthetics of the construction. A 5-year-old with this style will build a more elaborate block structure, with turrets, corners, arches, and generally more blocks and space needed than a 5-year-old who does not predominantly prefer this style. The form, line, or design is

important. Patterners may be very interested in maintaining the structure for several days. In contrast, dramatists tend to focus on the narrative of the pretend play and might use only a few blocks as long as they represent the idea they have in mind. For a dramatist, the form is much less important than the function. As soon as the pretend sequence is complete, this child is finished with the materials and more readily returns them to the shelf. A youngster's characteristic style applies to all materials. Children can and should be encouraged to extend their constructions beyond the limits of the preferred so that dramatists pay more attention to form and patterners become more involved in the pretend play possibilities. More than a third of all children use either style with equal ease (Shotwell, Wolf, & Gardner, 1979).

Differences in style also appear in pretend play with some children very focused on the materials being used and others on fantasy (Grollman, 1994). One child might be very careful about the arrangements of the house, the neatness of the dishes, or the clothes the doll has on. Another, however, may use words and gestures to create a fantasy in the same setting that is stimulated by but not limited to the objects therein. Both children might be imaginative and creative, but in different ways.

Quality of Play   Finally, there are differences in the quality of play. These differences tend to center on the ability to maintain a group play theme over time and the inclusion of problems to be solved by the players in the theme (Roskos, 1990). Typical themes might be bakery, flea market, beach, school, or library. Children enact roles relevant to these settings. When they include a problem within the play, such as a fire starting in the library basement or an emergency patient entering the hospital, the narrative and enactment of the pretend play have more storylike qualities. There is (a) a beginning, (b) problem identification, (c) development of the plot, (d) resolution of the problem, and (e) an ending. Increased complexity of play is possible for 4- and 5-year-olds in environments that support their play and if they are skilled in all the play elements. Maturity is necessary but not sufficient to enable children to engage in high-quality play. Skill, supportive environments, practice, and time are essential to achieve the most advanced levels of pretend play.

PRETEND AND CONSTRUCTION PLAY RELATED TO OTHER ASPECTS OF DEVELOPMENT

Construction and pretend play are systematically related to other aspects of development. Though studies have been conducted independently of each other, they tend to be in the same direction. That is, pretend play and construction play are systematically related to positive developmental and learning outcomes. For clarity, they are separated for the discussion of cognitive development and are mentioned as distinctions in other developmental domains.

Cognitive Development

Pretend Play   Theorists have not always agreed about the role of play in cognitive development. Piaget (1962) assigned a consolidative role to pretend play, stating that play reflected the child's cognitive constructs and allowed for assimilating new feelings and experiences. Pretend play is a clear example of representational thought (Yawkey, 1987) in which the child transforms objects, situations, and events using make-believe (Piaget, 1962). Vygotsky (1967) viewed pretend play as being responsible for the emergence of abstract thought. The first abstract thinking that children demonstrate is in pretend play, using a stick for a spoon, for example. Whether pretend play mirrors children's cognitive processes or causes them is yet unclear. There is still ample evidence that pretend play is a significant factor in children's intellectual functioning.

Pretend play experiences result in improved problem solving (Dansky, 1980). Children are able to create new strategies applicable to novel situations (Bruner, Jolly, & Sylva, 1976). In pretend play children must invent as well as consider "what if" propositions in the normal course of the episode (Wolf, 1991). They try new roles and engage in experiences not otherwise available to them. Opportunities for problem identification and the generation of varieties of solutions to ordinary situations created in make-believe situations abound. Children simply can practice and consolidate their skills.

Children also construct cognitive prototypes or models for thinking about something in their play (Sutton-Smith, 1971). What is most remarkable is that children as young as 3 are able to think about a role at all. Although they cannot explain or define a role, they have little difficulty in observing, abstracting the outstanding characteristics of a particular role, and then portraying them. All the while, they are perfectly aware of what they are doing. Similar strategies are developed for other aspects of the pretend play process. Pretend play also results in improved creative thinking during which children can develop increasing numbers of divergent uses for objects (Pepler, 1982). This appears to be a by-product of the ability to "transform" one object into another.

Children may also acquire new information, although that is not the primary function of pretend play. It is most likely to occur when children of differing backgrounds and experience confront one another in the play setting. Players tend to require their peers to play consistently within the theme and behave appropriately to the role. To that end they may inform, coach, or direct other players and teach one another.

Construction   Construction activities provide opportunities for children to apply creative thinking skills. All creative efforts require two familiar elements of the active imagination: the generation of alternatives and a selection among these alternatives (J. Smith, 1990, 83). Children must choose among a variety of materials that may be suitable for their project. In addition, materials themselves may provide ideas for constructions. Given encouragement and time to think, children will propose many uses beyond the obvious for common materials such as paper (Tegano, Sawyers, & Moran, 1991). Even properly identifying the problem is a challenge for the very young, and the support and guidance of teachers even for older children may be necessary (Tegano et al., 1991).

Children also plan what they are doing (Casey & Lippman, 1991). They may do so briefly and casually at first, beginning with an idea or a goal. Once materials are assembled and implementation begins, children often start over or add and delete materials as they alter the direction of their work. Sometimes they comment on the criteria with which they judge their products. When Janet and Lanna, age 4, were building a house of blocks, Janet said, "We gotta get the bigger ones. These won't fit [across the roof]." Lanna replied, "Yeah, and get some little red and blue ones from the table to be flowers."

More mature creative efforts are never haphazard. Older primary children may plan a "fort" or "club-house" for several days before beginning construction. If allowed to continue, such constructions may be transformed repeatedly as children think of new alternatives.

In the process of construction, children use the concepts they already have as well as learn from others (Cartwright, 1987). Children need information about texture, size, shape, weight, flexibility, and translucency of materials to carry out their projects. They also learn about part-whole relationships as they construct complex forms having many components (Reifel & Greenfield, 1983). Position in space and the placement of objects in relation to one another are typical learnings of children during the construction process. Children may use their drawing constructions to facilitate memory of an important experience (Raines, 1990). The picture below is the painting of an 8-year-old child with disabilities shortly after she and her father built a snowman. The most complex construction that the child produced during the early years, this painting provided a source of many good memories as she grew.

Construction inevitably is an outcome of children's need to understand their social and physical world in their own very active terms by making things (Franklin, 1994).

Emotional Development

Pretend play has long been recognized as a vehicle for children to express their innermost thoughts and feel-ings. Although most play episodes are based either on immediate past observations and experiences or in response to cues from the physical environment of the school, children can and do enact play sequences that express their concerns. Children achieve mastery of their feelings when they rework a scene to a happier conclusion, can express repressed feelings, and can try out solutions to normal daily crises. All children experience fears about being accepted (and may actually be temporarily rejected by their peers) or may have concerns about family members. For example, two 8-year-olds played out marriage, separation, divorce, courtship, and remarriage over a period of several weeks. One child came from a stable two-parent family, and her best friend had already lived through the divorce process, with her father remarrying and a mother contemplating a second marriage. Through multiple play sequences the inevitable uncertainties that one child was experiencing were portrayed while the other learned about the social and emotional realities experienced by another. Pretend play is a normal process by which healthy children learn to cope with the problems of daily life.

Children gain self-confidence and demonstrate pride in their creations: "I did it!" "Look at mine!" "This, here, is my house!" Children have a sense of mastery as they work hard, solve problems, test their skills, and demonstrate patience and perseverance in the construction process. Such concentrated efforts lead to satisfaction (Cartwright, 1988). Construction play leads to a sense of confidence and competence as children have concrete evidence of their endeavors.

Anne Janette created this iconic construction to represent the snowman she had built the evening before.

Social Development

Social competence, or the ability to function effectively in society appropriate to one's age, is composed of several aspects (Eisenberg & Harris, 1984). Perspective taking, conceptions of friendship, interpersonal strategies, problem solving, moral judgment, and communication skills are all components of social behavior. Participation in sociodramatic play requires a high level of both social and cognitive abilities, including sharing and cooperation, appreciation of role reciprocity, and self-regulation of affect (Frost, 1991). Generally, increases in pretend play skills are associated with corresponding increases in all three aspects of social cognition:

❏ Visual or perceptual perspective taking—How does another person see the world?
❏ Cognitive perspective taking—What are other people thinking? What are other people like?
❏ Affective perspective taking—What kind of emotional experiences is another person having? (Johnsen & Christie, 1984, 109)

The spontaneous play of pretend scripts provides the context and the practice for children to learn negotiation skills and achieve social acceptance (Doyle & Connolly, 1989). Children, via the metacommunications that structure and direct their play, continually engage in social comparison and compare with one another their perceptions of a given situation. These checks are frequently in the form of tag questions ("You're not going to her house, right?") as a request for information. Correspondingly, they make requests for agreement ("Let's not play house today, OK?"), permission ("I need to make this street longer, right?" [moving into another's play space]), compliance ("You can put those babies to bed now, huh?"), verbal response ("You like to play cars, right?"), and attention ("This is a bridge, see?") (Chafel, 1986). As children initiate and respond to verbalizations that are essential to social play, they develop leadership skills (Trawick-Smith, 1988). In early childhood, children who are high in leadership are also high in following. They can contribute to the direction of play but do not dominate it.

The social skills developed and practiced during pretend play are also used in construction play. Cooperation and teamwork are required in a variety of construction activities: building with blocks, painting murals, or making a bus from a big box. When blocks are used, group murals are produced, or a cooperative project is deliberately planned, teamwork is required. Group work enables children to negotiate ideas, share information, cooperate, share space and materials, and compare their performance with others (Chafel, 1986). For example, because large hollow blocks are difficult to handle alone, they challenge 3- to 5-year-old children physically. Such blocks also afford opportunities for immediate holistic experiences requiring social organization and cooperation as youngsters build and later engage in pretend play (Cartwright, 1990).

Language Development

Research on the effect of pretend play on language development is extensive, with most studies finding positive relationships (Frost, 1991). In a detailed review of the literature, play was found to have the following specific effects (Levy, 1984, 167): Play stimulates innovation in language (Bruner, 1983; Garvey, 1977), introduces and clarifies new words and concepts (Chukovsky, 1971; Smilansky, 1968), motivates language use and practice (Bruner, 1983; Garvey, 1977; Garvey & Hagan, 1973; Smilansky, 1968; Vygotsky, 1962), and encourages verbal thinking (Vygotsky, 1962). Apparently, the relationship between symbolic play and language increases with age as the play becomes more abstract and independent of real objects as a source of shared meaning. Good players are more verbal during play. In fact, in kindergartners, examples of children's language at play were found to be better indicators of language ability than formal assessments such as the Illinois Test of Psycholinguistic Abilities (Levy, 1984). Language fluency and variety of language structures were even greater during block play than housekeeping (Isbell & Raines, 1991).

In the '80s and '90s, there has been a marked increase in the research relating emergent literacy to pretend play of children between 4 and 6 (Christie, 1990). When pretend or construction play is enhanced with appropriate materials, children incorporate literacy acts such as looking at a cookbook while preparing a pretend meal or writing labels on their constructions (Goldhaber, Lipson, Sortino, & Daniels, 1997). When appropriate teacher guidance is added, the variety and frequency of such acts is increased (L. Morrow, 1990). The free use of open-ended materials enabled children to play with the forms of written language as a part of their constructions, supporting emergent literacy (Miller, Fernie, & Kantor, 1992). Children also produce a variety of written language that is functional in nature. They write to (a) serve instrumental purposes (making a list of things to get), (b) regulate the behavior of others (preparing a "Keep Out" sign), (c) meet interaction needs (writing a phone number for a friend), (d) fill personal needs (putting their own name on paper), and (e) relay information (making a "telephone broken" sign) (Schrader, 1989; Stroud, 1995). Children also engage in conversations about literacy within the play context, which might include using literacy conventions, naming literacy-related objects, or even coaching one another in some literacy task in order to achieve a play goal (Neuman & Roskos, 1990). In addition, children may use similar representational mental processes in both symbolic play and literate behavior (Schrader, 1990) so that the enhancement and practice of pretend play is likely to facilitate the acquisition of reading competence.

INTEGRATION OF MULTIPLE DOMAINS

Construction and pretend play are integrative in nature. Children must synthesize ideas to enact or plans to build in this experience and utilize a variety of skills and abilities (Adams & Nesmith, 1996). The child is a meaning maker, the embodiment of knowledge rather than a passive recipient of it (Jalongo, 1990). One of the most salient characteristics of this play is that it facilitates the cross-fertilization of ideas and connections across traditional content areas (Chaillé & Silvern, 1996). Children have to employ logical-mathematical thinking about space relations, oral language skills, and techniques for negotiation and cooperation in order to build a fort and play in it. Like pretend play, construction play challenges children to use all that they know and can do to be successful.

To illustrate the amalgamation of curriculum goals more completely through pretend play and construction, Table 14.2 has been compiled to analyze the relationship of specific goals to a particular scenario in a primary classroom—post office. The opportunity to learn does not guarantee that all children will learn the same things. Participants must actively engage in the activity and take advantage of the opportunities provided.

Many intermediate objectives within the domains may be addressed during pretend play or construction; objectives may be combined as described in Table 14.2. The maturity of the children, their skills in pretend play and construction, their experience in playing with each other, and the topic of the pretend play are all relevant. For example, the goals addressed in cognition and language would not be as appropriate for 3- and 4-year-old children. In addition, the degree of the teacher's guidance and support would necessarily need adjustment for children of varying ages.

TEACHERS' QUESTIONS REGARDING PRETEND PLAY AND CONSTRUCTION

1. *Don't children get enough pretend play at home or on the playground?* For children who enter school without pretend play skills, the school is the only source of such information. If the parents of these children knew how to support pretend play, the children would have some of the skills when they entered school. In addition, few homes have the materials, information, and guidance techniques for developing a variety of play opportunities such as archeologist, scientist, or space explorer. Families may supplement what early childhood programs do if they receive information and suggestions.

Recess in most elementary schools is usually 15 minutes outdoors morning and afternoon. Some pretend play may occur in this setting, but it will not have the scope possible in a prepared environment or sufficient time to accrue the full benefits. This more casual approach to pretend play does not necessarily lead to the most complex play, nor does it necessarily lead to curricular integration.

However, the outdoor environment can be an excellent setting for planned play. Providing opportunities to implement curriculum outside makes a great deal of sense, especially in climates that have access to the outdoors most of the year. Even in colder climates, opportunities for pretend play can be managed. One group of second-grade children played weather forecaster as a part of a sequence of units during the year. They collected information on wind direction, temperature, and cloud formation; used weather maps, graphs, and other documents; and even researched

TABLE 14.2

Analysis of an Experience of Primary Children Creating a Postal Center

Domain	Intermediate Objectives	Immediate Objectives	Pretend Play	Construction
Aesthetic	Reflect on and discuss aesthetic experiences. Appreciate art as a means of nonverbal communication.	• Collect a variety of used postage stamps. • Discuss the images on the stamps. • Select stamps to use for pretend mail.	Children contribute stamps for the post office. Customers select stamps for their letters.	Use postage stamp designs as a part of the display in the post office. Place as appropriate to the structure.
Affective	Gain experience and demonstrate independence in using age-appropriate materials and tools. Assume responsibility for caring for classroom materials.	• Use pretend money with the cash register and scales. • Put away materials at the end of the daily play session. • Use hollow blocks and long boards appropriately.	Children will have scales to weigh the letters and packages, pretend money to purchase stamps, calculators to compute totals for multiple purchases, and writing materials for receipts.	Children build the postal center with blocks, boards, and furnishings.
Cognitive	Discover measurement relationships using standard unit tools. Add and subtract. Identify numbers.	• Base charges on actual weights using current postal rates. • Use a rate chart. • Calculate charges either by hand or with a calculator.	Most primary children can read the numerals for the postage stamps and charts. The challenge will be to figure cost per unit.	
Language	Demonstrate courteous listening behaviors. Demonstrate comprehension of spoken language. Use own version of writing. Respond to written symbols in the environment.	• Engage in polite exchanges between seller and buyer. • Ask appropriate questions in the pretend context. • Respond to written signs. • Write letters to classmates and others in the school; read own letters.	Maintain the flow of pretend play through metacommunications. Use enactment to supplement visual symbols and create the narrative that supports the pretend story. Use reading and writing within the play frame.	Make signs, envelopes, or other props using written language or pictographs.

(continued on the next page)

TABLE 14.2
(continued)

Domain	Intermediate Objectives	Immediate Objectives	Pretend Play	Construction«
Physical	Coordinate wrist, hand, finger, finger-thumb, and eye-hand movements. Maintain adequate levels of physical activity.	• Use pencils, pens, tape, and other adhesives. • Wrap/unwrap packages.	Children will be engaged almost continuously in fine motor activity as they write letters, put stamps on them, organize the post office, and use the tools and props provided. Post office play is active, with postal deliveries and general movement in the setting.	Children will be moving furnishings and blocks, requiring coordination during the construction process.
Social	Learn how to cooperate. Develop knowledge related to social studies.	• Make plans for building the postal station together. • Build the station. • Collect information about postal services from the community. • Use accurate information in play.	Many skills in play and social intercourse are required in complex thematic play in addition to those listed. Children must relate to each other in role-appropriate ways, settle disputes, negotiate roles, and use metacommunications to make the play move forward. Exchange with each other must be mutual and balanced.	Cooperation is required for children to build the postal station with large blocks and furnishings. Work must be organized, jobs assigned, placements agreed to, and then implemented. Objects must also be collected and placed and signs made.

These second graders are combining mathematic, language, and social skills as they pretend "store."

previous years' weather conditions for their make-believe weather reports on television.

2. *How can I incorporate pretend play in my classroom when I have neither the time nor the space?* Preschool and kindergarten teachers should plan for pretend play first and for other activities thereafter. (Various suggestions for the management of space are provided in Chapter 5.). For these youngest children, the development of play skills is critical for the emergence of abstract thinking and problem-solving abilities. Therefore, pretend play should be a priority. Teachers should ensure that all children in the earliest years have opportunities for extended time for pretend play.

The space in primary classrooms is frequently inadequate. However, teachers of older children have

been successful in incorporating pretend play in the following ways: using miniature materials and pretending in a small space, planning for pretend play twice a week for a longer period of time, involving children in moving equipment and setting up the play space, and including simple make-believe in a variety of other activities. One building with particularly small classrooms set up a separate classroom for all of the first-grade children to use for pretend play and established a schedule for use. Each day, children were allowed to go down to this room, which was supervised predominantly by volunteers.

Pretend play and construction need at least 20 minutes for full development and even longer for older children. If the time for pretend play is less than this, children usually do not even start. Therefore, it is better to have pretend play once or twice a week for a longer time, such as 25 to 40 minutes, than to try to have four 10-minute segments.

3. *What can I do without the proper equipment and materials?* Because pretend play for 3- to 5-year-olds is a priority, programs should allocate resources to this domain first. Quality unit and hollow blocks are expensive as an initial purchase. They last for 30 to 40 years with minimal upkeep that children themselves can undertake, so they are a relatively low-cost investment. In addition, a large set of each for all classrooms for the early childhood period provides many opportunities for learning across many curricular content areas.

Many of the materials for pretend play and construction are found rather than purchased. For example, teachers can gradually develop pretend play kits as described in Figure 14.1. The task of adding to and replacing materials in the pretend play kits may be shared among teachers. Parents, garage sales, flea markets, and discards from industry are sources of pretend play props. File boxes are often useful for storage, and schools may install near-ceiling shelving to hold them. Industrial and household discards make excellent resources for construction projects.

4. *How do I maintain control? I'm concerned that the children will just go wild.* Play is treated seriously by children. They become involved and focus their energies on what they are doing. They do have conflicts about roles, story direction, and use of materials, which they negotiate among themselves. Teachers may

FIGURE 14.1
Pretend Play Kits with Associated Teaching Themes

Unit Theme: Living in Homes

Pretend Play Theme: Real Estate

Props: Pictures of many kinds of homes, magazines, real estate brochures, desk, telephone, paper, pencil, chairs, "contract forms," "Real Estate" and "For Sale" signs

Moving Houses

Props: Wagons, small moving dollies, boxes with ropes, rags for wrapping goods, telephone, work order forms, pencils, child furniture, clothing, stuffed animals, dolls, "Moving Day" sign

Unit Theme: Clothing

Pretend Play Theme: Washing Clothes

Props: Doll clothes, a tub or water table with soap, clothesline and pins, plastic aprons

Dress Up

Props: Scarves, hats, curtains, coats and capes, shoes, mirror, dresses, ties, shirts

Unit Theme: Vehicles

Pretend Play Theme: Gas Station

Props: Gas pumps with hoses, windshield wash equipment, tires, tire pump, wrenches, fan belts, screwdrivers, cash register

Vehicle Showroom

Props: Many vehicles arranged, car sales brochures, ads, calculators, pencils, forms, price stickers, balloons

Unit Theme: Insects

Pretend Play Theme: Entomologist's Laboratory

Props: Insect pictures, specimens, tripod, magnifying glass, white coats, paper, pencil, insect books, dried insects, wasp nests, or other real things

Picnic Partners

Props: Dishes, pretend food, tablecloth, plastic or paper insects

Unit Theme: The Sky

Pretend Play Theme: It's Raining, It's Pouring

Props: Sand table village or miniature houses; rocks; seashells; twigs; miniature people for the houses; squirt cans; small drum for thunder; "Cirrus," "Stratus," "Cumulus," and "Nimbus" signs

Outdoor Slumber Party

Props: Sleeping bags or blankets, alarm clock, different phases of the moon to hang, stars, large pajamas (worn over clothes), stuffed animals

Unit Theme: Machines

Pretend Play Theme: Repair Shop

Props: Wrenches, screwdrivers, pliers, old clocks, radios, toasters, pencil, paper, do-it-yourself books, "Repair Anything" sign

Bike Repair

Props: Wrenches, loose spokes, cogs and sprockets (donations from local bike shop, cleaned), rags, telephone, pencil, paper, bikes or tricycles

Unit Theme: Storytelling

Pretend Play Theme: Storytelling Theater

Props: Chairs for seating, a "stage" marked off with blocks or tape, tickets, playbill, cash register, dolls for audience, dress-up clothes, hats, child-constructed costumes if desired, child-painted backdrops for older children

Measuring

Shoe Store

Props: Ruler or bannock device, shoes of various sizes, stickers to indicate size and price, "Shoes for Sale" sign, cash register, receipt book, pictures, and advertisements

---

Source: Adapted from material in *Teaching Young Children Using Themes* (Kostelnik et al., 1991).

need to assist them in the mediation process, but learning interpersonal skills is one of the chief goals in early education. One mistake that inexperienced teaches make is to do paperwork, leave the classroom, or engage in activities that result in lost attention to the children. Play activities deserve the same teacher supervision as any other learning event.

Loss of self-control, destructive behavior, or disruption of classroom processes will occur from some individuals regardless of the curricular design. In some ways, play may alleviate the frequency of the outbursts as children gain control of a medium for expressing their feelings acceptably.

A more practical problem is the misuse of materials by children who do not know how to play. If a child does not know how to make-believe, that child may have no idea how to function in a housekeeping area. Dishes may be crammed into purses, and dolls undressed and thrown around. This is symptomatic of children who need educational intervention. Once teachers recognize that the problem is one of knowledge, then teaching should follow. High-quality play is the outcome of learning and is not guaranteed by development alone. Most youngsters learn from their parents and siblings between 1 and 3 years of age; other children who have the developmental capacity to play but lack adult guidance and/or playmates may learn later in the school setting from teachers and classmates. Rarely does a classroom exist without some of the children knowing how to play pretend or construction. Children learn readily from each other, and the teacher may have to supervise the play carefully so that maximum advantage of this process can be obtained. Children's behaviors offer cues that they do not know what to do. Certain behaviors, then, may indicate that the child does not have a particular skill rather than that the child is being disruptive, disobedient, or uncooperative. Although the techniques for teaching skills are discussed in Chapters 3 and 4 and also later in this chapter, some common behaviors of children that concern teachers are listed, with possible very specific strategies for intervention, in Table 14.3.

However, teachers occasionally need to use guidance techniques to promote social responsibility and order. Procedures for setting and maintaining limits for children in groups are presented in other books as well as in Chapter 6 of this volume. All areas of the classroom and all functions of curriculum require quality classroom management skills. Reasonable limits should be set for the dramatic play, story reenactment, or other forms of play so that all children can profit from their learning experiences. Certain behaviors may indicate when a child is beyond these reasonable limits. Such a child may demonstrate play skills on other occasions but need adult guidance when she or he does any of the following:

❏ Engages in silly, unfocused, or irrelevant behavior.
❏ Grabs materials obviously to prevent others' access to them.
❏ Pushes, hits, or grabs and runs.
❏ Makes excessive noise unrelated to a role (e.g., there is a difference between being a fire engine and just shrieking).

Just because children are playing does not mean that "anything goes." On the other hand, the threat of potential chaos in groups of children is no greater in a developmentally appropriate classroom than in a setting where less appropriate programs are attempted.

5. *What is the teacher's role when the children are playing?* Pretend play usually occurs while other activities are also in progress. The teacher is responsible for setting the stage for play, providing materials, providing sufficient information to support the play activities, supervising the quality of play, and extending it as needed. Younger children are likely to need more support than older children because they have less information about the world and may be less skilled in negotiating differences. Older inexperienced children profit from direct instruction in how to play (Christie, 1986). In addition to teaching play skills, the adult may be called upon to provide instruction related to the cognitive domain, as is illustrated in the following experience.

A student teacher planned a unit on seeds and established a seed store as a sociodramatic play opportunity. Shelves, envelopes, pencils and paper, scales, a variety of seeds, money, and a cash register were available for the children to use. The 4-year-olds entered the play area and mixed up the seeds, throwing them around and otherwise demolishing the area. Intervening in this activity, the young teacher began to ask what the children knew about a seed store, only to discover that these urban children simply had no ideas they could easily apply to this activity. For the next few days the pretend play area became the scene of considerable instruction. The teacher addressed questions

TABLE 14.3

Common Child Behaviors Indicating Lack of Pretend Play Skills and Selected Teacher Intervention Strategies

Behavior	Teacher Intervention Strategy
Avoiding the pretend play area	Encourage participation directly. Assist the child in entering the area before others arrive.
Continuing a pattern of exploring materials without using them for play	Use open-ended questions: "What else do you think you can do with that?" "Show me how you might use that if you were a [role] policeman."
Manipulating play materials and discarding them	Engage the child in thinking about the materials: "Tell me about the _____." "How could that be used to_____?"
Misusing materials	Assess whether the material is appropriate for the age of child. If it has either too little or too much challenge, it may be misused. Ask children to tell you about an object. Some very young children may not "recognize" a common prop. Suggest appropriate object substitutions: "Pretend that the _____ is a _____."
Focusing on the reality aspects only; insisting that the stove will not cook something, for example	Explain that pretend play props are not supposed to work. Demonstrate pretend play with the object.
Regarding other players with amazement; watching, staring, and appearing confused (common among 3- and 4-year-olds)	Move close to this child and provide comments of what they are doing. "George and Alfie are pretending to be truckers. They are. . . ." Engage in pretend play with this child. Select another child with slightly better pretend skills, and encourage them to play together.
Either coercing others or participating very passively; not engaging in mutual theme or shared goal	Often 3- and 4-year-olds will work out patterns of leadership on their own, but if this goes on with older children or is persistent, play with the children and demonstrate mutual play. Discuss the play theme in a group, and explore possible ideas before children begin to play. Ensure that most of the children have the knowledge they need to play out the theme. In some instances intervene directly in the play and use the mediation strategies suggested in Chapter 6.

such as "What are stores for? What do store clerks do? What do customers do?" On the second attempt with the store, the only players allowed in the store area were employees. They sorted seeds, weighed and placed them in envelopes, labeled the envelopes, and wrote down prices. Flower seeds were in one display and vegetable seeds in another. Again the teacher provided direction, assistance, and instruction as needed. On the third venture into the store area, signs were placed and advertisements prepared. More discussion was held about what the customers would do with the seeds once purchased. Finally, the children were able to have their grand opening. Customers purchased seeds, some of which were later planted in peat cups. The seed store play continued successfully for another week. Children provided new players with information as they joined the activity.

Clearly, science and social studies concepts were taught within the structure or place usually set aside for pretend play. Children needed more information to use, which was quickly apparent in the first day of play. Once children had the information, the teacher focused her attention more on other activities and allowed them to proceed with adult observation, support, and supervision as needed.

6. *What do I do about superhero play and other play themes that make me uncomfortable? Sometimes it's violent.* Teachers are legitimately concerned about the level of violence in children's play. There are several sources of violence that might appear in pretend play, and each should be treated independently. First, there is violence that is simply the imitation of observed adult behavior at home and in the community. Second, there is violence portrayed as a result of events such as earthquakes, war, car accidents, and other catastrophes. Third, there is play that is related to children's inner needs to handle their feelings of aggression and helplessness. Fourth, children use pretend play toys and scripts from television, generally selecting only the action sequences and violent scenes for reenactment. Last, there is masked play in which the child engages in play for the purpose of behaving aggressively toward others without having to be responsible for the consequences of the aggressive act. Each source of violent play will be briefly considered here, one at a time.

Teachers of preschool children are likely to see youngsters enact events they have observed or participated in. Adults in some families have very little privacy, so children are likely to incorporate behaviors such as parental arguments, physical fights, and sexual intercourse into play sequences. Young children simply do not understand what should remain private and what is appropriate for play in school. Teachers who observe inappropriate play have found simple redirection to be most useful. Focusing on other activities that adult men and women engage in is usually suffi-

cient. Effort should be made to keep this redirection low keyed as children tend to imitate each others' outstanding play sequences. By first grade, youngsters usually can distinguish between public and private family information and are less likely to enact the latter. Frequent, repetitive, or excessively detailed play sequences of violent or sexual behavior may be an indicator that the child is living in an unwholesome situation that requires additional attention.

Children who experience a natural disaster such as an earthquake or flood and or witness serious accidents or violence on the street struggle with feelings of great fear, anger, and helplessness. In the process of enactment, the child can work out a variety of situations and solutions and perhaps master these emotions. Such play may take many repetitions for the child to feel safe. Teachers facilitate this process by providing accurate information and reassurance as children play out violent scenes. The content of the play is the violence itself and the fear, and other players often take on the roles of nurturer, rescuer, or comforter. Themes of family and friends, health care, and rescue workers of various sorts may be very useful should such incidents occur in a community.

Five- to seven-year-olds frequently are concerned with social position. Competent students and skillful players are accorded high status among peers. In some schools toughness or skill in fighting is another avenue to social position. Fighting has nothing to do with play and should be handled by adults as inappropriate behavior. However, children also are concerned about aggressor and victim roles in a more general sense, as in cops and robbers, good guys and bad guys. The roles of the players are designed to be oppositional. Opposing force pretend play may occur during children's recess or noninstructional time without real violence occurring. Frequently the bad guys are imaginary. If there are no injuries and no real violence, dealing with the forces of good and evil as a play theme may allow children to work out their ideas of right and wrong in an acceptable framework (Boyd, 1997). Play around issues of justice, right and wrong, and fairness are important concepts for children to explore.

The level of violence portrayed on television has increased over the past decade. Considering that young children are exposed to as much television as they are to schooling, it is not surprising that children reenact media episodes (Bergen, 1994). Working with parents to monitor television viewing may be the most practical solution to the least desirable programs (Boyatzis, 1997). Reenactment of film or video portrayals rarely entails more than the sequenced action scenes. With roles selected from commercial characters, children incorporate rough-and-tumble play into their pretend play. Enactment of fantasy heros of this type is much more common in casual play than in teacher-initiated or guided classroom play.

Rough-and-tumble play, consisting of laughing, running, smiling, jumping, open-hand beating, wrestling, play fighting, chasing, and fleeing, looks aggressive to many adults. However, children engaging in this type of play do not get hurt or cry. Frequently rough-and-tumble play is a transitional activity leading to games with rules, especially for popular boys (Pellegrini & Perlmutter, 1988). Aggression, which includes fixation, frowning, hitting, pushing, taking, and grabbing, is more likely to occur in relation to possessions than in the fast-moving superhero play typically seen on playgrounds.

Violent play rarely emerges from the carefully planned play opportunities provided by teachers as a part of the curriculum (Boyd, 1997). Acting out behavior, frequent violent outbursts, and excessive anger or hostility in a child may be symptoms needing special intervention and should be carefully assessed and referred to others. In the meantime, even distressed children can learn to behave appropriately in the classroom setting. See Chapter 6 for details.

7. *Won't children make a big mess if they are allowed to make things?* Sometimes they will, but then they can clean it up. The key to successful management is to have accessible storage that is labeled in a way children understand. In addition, children value their construction opportunities and tend to manage their time and materials to control the mess. Giving children advanced warning of when they must clean up enables them to achieve some closure on their project and then begin to put away materials themselves. Cleaning up must be planned for in the schedule and be allotted enough time for completion. Some primary teachers have managed this problem by having a substantial period of time one day a week for construction activities.

8. *What do teachers do when children say, "You can't play!"?* Children who are engaged in making a project, building a complex structure together, or are involved in an ongoing pretend scenario are likely to reject new players unless they contribute something unique to the activity. Sometimes they would be rejected anyway, or if accepted the play would disintegrate. In such a case, their inclusion would be similar to adding a fifth player to a partnered card game. On the other hand, individual children cannot control the materials from one day to the next. When teachers want particular children to engage in either a construction or a pretend episode, those children should begin the activity period in that area as part of the daily plan. Ideas for doing so are included in Chapter 5. When children do not know how to play, planning for moderately skilled players to engage with unskilled players is generally effective. As with other scaffolding tasks, the level just above the current level of performance is the goal for the less skilled.

Children may exclude on the basis of language, social group, race, ability, or sex. When this occurs, teachers should accept the opportunity to help children to understand biases better and develop together several rules based upon fairness. Typically, primary-aged children prefer to play in single-sex groups, which is both supportive to sex role socialization and acceptable. However, one first-grade teacher helped her group to develop the rule that space and materials had to be shared fairly but that individuals could choose with whom to play. Children understood the "fairness" issue and were cooperative.

9. *Should children use a pattern and follow the directions to get a realistic product to display, or should they make something of their own that does not look as good?* Developmentally appropriate classrooms display the work of all children and demonstrate respect for children's construction. Of course, it is infinitely easier to copy another's idea than to produce a more original object. However, even 3-year-olds are capable of selecting products to put in portfolios, hang on the wall, or acknowledge as the best work they can do. An adult-directed craft may appear more attractive to adults, but it is not a product of the child's thinking processes. When the learning and problem-solving process is explained to parents, they too value the children's own work.

Crafts that are undertaken for their benefits to children's motor coordination and social skills or that are related to other domains serve these functions, but they do not replace the need for opportunities for children to represent their own ideas concretely.

10. *What if the child has worked with blocks or wet sand and has nothing to carry home?* An instant photograph taken periodically to represent the child's construction is very useful. Although it is too expensive to do this frequently, the child might select one or two constructions to be preserved in this way. Occasionally, dough products can be taken home by youngsters when the dough needs to be replaced anyway. Children who produce music as a creative effort may consent to tape it if the teacher is unable to write the notation. Older children are often less concerned with carrying something home than they are with saving it from one day to the next. Block or box structures may be saved for a short time to maximize the opportunities for elaboration and expansion typical of these activities. Often the class as a group can establish its own ground rules and propose solutions.

11. *What will the parents think if children are playing in school?* Parents are very supportive of children playing in child-centered programs for 3- and 4-year-olds and generally believe that the time spent in play should decrease as children get older (Rothlein & Brett, 1987). However, parents do not indicate that play should be eliminated for 6-year-olds, merely that the amount of time should be less than for 3- and 4-year-olds. Parents, therefore, are likely to express their concerns and will have particular interest in how much school time is devoted to play. The value of play to the development of a competent child has considerable support in research and can be presented understandably to parents (Bergen 1988a; Nourot & Van Hoorn, 1991).

Research on the importance of play to development has been accumulating for the past two decades yet still receives limited acknowledgment by professional educators. Therefore, it is unreasonable to suppose that the general public would be better informed. As with any educational practice change, parents need basic information about the total program and how play is likely to benefit their children. When parents of primary-grade children see youngsters reading and computing, they are not as concerned with what else is going on in the classroom.

12. *How does pretend play relate to the real learning that is supposed to occur in the primary grades?* Extensive research on the effects of children's play concludes that play is critical for children's intellectual, social, physical, and emotional growth (Seeefeldt, 1995a).

For example, if birds are being studied, young children might pretend to be birds in the nest, and older children, scientists studying birds. Pretend play uses the information that children have to solve problems. In addition, teachers are able to assess the level of understanding children possess about the topic based on their play. If children are unable to incorporate information into pretend play sequences, they do not really understand it very well.

Furthermore, if properly structured, play may incorporate numerous literacy experiences and require children to use mathematical skills and ideas to further their own play goals. The guided play recommended and described by this text does relate to academic and developmental goals and is quite different from the casual, less focused play one might expect of children on their own in the neighborhood. It is the adult-initiated/child-initiated play that is effective (Sylva, 1993).

13. *Should second and third graders really spend school time in pretend play?* This very legitimate question for all primary teachers emerges as a result of widespread pressure for academic achievement as evidenced in standardized tests, where learning is equated with memorization. There is a place for memorization, for reading and writing in the goals of the language and cognition domains. There is also a need for other intellectual skill development in primary-age children. Teachers in rural areas provide more opportunities for play than their counterparts in suburban areas, who in turn provide more time than urban teachers (Newman, 1996). The practice of separating tasks down to skills and drilling them separately has not been a spectacular success (Peck et al., 1988). Skill instruction embedded in meaningful activity makes more sense to the children, and they are more likely to learn and use the skills. Thus, we might try strategies that make sense to children, building on what they already can do and then providing the skills instruction to expand their capacities. Including opportunities for play does not in any way preclude skills instruction.

If children have had appropriate early experiences, 7-year-olds will be skilled players. They are in the strongest position to do creative problem solving and to explore in depth a situation's possibilities. They add detail and substance to their play, which may continue, even though interrupted, over several weeks. Play is a strength of children that may be utilized to help them understand science, the humanities, and the world around them. Story reenactment is particularly useful in developing reading comprehension skills as well as in motivating children with more limited reading skills.

Teaching is more than telling and setting up drill experiences; it is more than going though textbooks, as a group of Iowa teachers discovered when they set aside all of their textbooks and shifted to unit instruction using developmentally appropriate goals (Barclay, Benelli, Campbell, & Kleine, 1995). For most teachers, a combination of unit instruction including play and some of the more traditional practices is more typical.

Integrating curriculum requires that a topic or focus be selected and then content introduced in a meaningful way. For example, a unit on machines can constitute a lesson in physics. Children read about machines, observe simple machines in action, make graphs and written recordings of their observations, and discuss the use of machines in society. They might construct simple machines such as wheels or levers to make a task easier. They may also pretend play a variety of themes, depending on their maturity, experience, and knowledge, such as hardware store, gas station, repair store, machine shop, or factory. Within the pretend play theme, children must use their knowledge and demonstrate their understanding. In addition, other players provide feedback and correction if necessary. A variety of pretend play theme kits are suggested, with the corresponding teaching units that might be present in many early childhood programs, in Figure 14.1.

PROMOTING PLAY SKILLS

As an infant grows into early childhood, play skills are learned from parents, siblings, and playmates. Some children enter programs with their abilities well developed, whereas other children are just beginning to gain preliminary proficiency. In this way, play skills are no different from skills in the six domains of the curriculum.

Providing an ample supply of materials, organizing them, and presenting them to children is usually sufficient to encourage exploratory, investigative, and testing play in 3- to 8-year-olds. The general ambience of the classroom is important for any kind of play (Chaillé & Silvern, 1996). To play productively, youngsters must be rested, free from hunger or other physical discomfort, and safe. They must feel comfort-

able and secure in the learning setting to engage appropriately in play and in other forms of learning. This means that adults let children know in many ways that child-initiated activity is acceptable. When adults show a lack of interest, fail to provide the materials necessary to support play, neglect assessment of skills, or criticize processes in play, the climate is not conducive to experimentation or exploration, let alone pretend play or construction.

Adults responsible for youngsters' development must attend to individual and group characteristics so that if children are not self-sufficient in this area, appropriate support and instruction are provided. The first step is to recognize what these skills are and then to examine how they can be taught. In Figure 14.2, specific behaviors are inventoried that are necessary for pretend play and construction. Strategies for actively supporting play are then described in the following section.

Customary Strategies to Enhance Play

The following strategies enhance play.

1. *Set the stage for children's play.* The teacher is responsible for establishing conditions that accept and encourage play. Suggestions for doing this are as follows:

❏ Incorporate make-believe into transitional times such as cleanup, dressing, or moving from one room to another as a group.

❏ Encourage pretend play in other aspects of the curriculum. Ask children to imagine what someone would feel like or how a setting would look or to pretend that they are the character in the story.

❏ Coordinate the theme of the dramatic play center to match other ongoing themes in your room. Provide theme-related props (see Figure 14.1) and materials for construction related to the theme. Add additional materials to the pretend play setup to expand the play as needed.

❏ Provide adequate space for play. This may occasionally mean moving furniture or making room for miniature play sets. Detailed suggestions are in Chapter 5.

❏ Provide enough time in any one segment for play to get under way.

❏ Pay attention to what children say and do during play. Watch carefully and concentrate. Listen for children's appropriate application of concepts or misinformation.

FIGURE 14.2

Skills Children Need to Engage in Pretend Play and Construction

Mimic in their play the behaviors that they have seen or experienced.

Engage in a wide range of experiences from which to draw their interpretations.

Use their bodies to represent real or imaginary objects or events.

Assign symbolic meaning to real or imaginary objects using language or gestures.

Take on the role attributes of beings or objects and act out interpretations of those roles.

Create play themes and engage in play themes created by others.

Experiment with a variety of objects, roles (leader, follower, mediator), and characterizations (animal, mother, astronaut, etc.).

React to and interact with other children in make-believe situations.

Maintain pretend play for increasing lengths of time.

Use narratives and metacommunications to structure the play.

Dramatize familiar stories, songs, poems, and past events.

Interpret events and reconstruct them in tangible ways.

Use diverse approaches and materials to represent objects or events by

> Representing a single object or event using different materials or techniques and
> Representing different objects and events using one material or technique.

Collaborate with classmates to construct a representative object.

Integrate new information into play episodes.

Integrate construction into pretend play episodes.

2. *Create conditions of acceptance and safety by what you say and do.* In a psychologically safe environment, children feel comfortable with and acceptable to their peers and adults and are unconstrained in wandering into unknown territory. Children then are able to risk being wrong or having a project not work out as they had hoped. Creativity is the outcome of challenge and risk taking. The strategies described here include behavioral reflections and questions initially described in Chapter 6. The concepts apply equally to pretend play and other forms as well, though for clarity, some specifics related to construction have been selected:

❏ Allow children to engage in their activity without intervention or comment unless they contravene safety, property, or social cooperation rules of the classroom. The play belongs to the children. Often acceptance, observation, and general support are sufficient.

❏ Ask about a project or pretend event when children are seeking information or assistance; do not assume you know what the intent is (Cassidy, 1989). You might be wrong. "Tell me about your drawing" or "I don't quite understand what you are trying to do here" are general statements letting the child know that you are not able to interpret his or her construction. "Did you have something specific in mind?" is more direct and is responsive to the child's questions or comments when the teacher is unable to respond because the representation is not clear. These and other strategies will help you to provide the help sought without taking over the project.

❏ Describe what you observe about the materials or technique being used or other specific characteristics of the project. Such statements should not be judgmental but might be comparative, such as "I see Harry has used all bright primary colors and George

TABLE 14.4
Respectful Commentary on Children's Block Constructions

Observation	Statement
Which blocks were used	"You found out that two of these make a half circle."
Where the blocks were placed	"You used four blocks to make a big square."
How many blocks were used	"You used all the blocks to make the building."
Whether the blocks are all the same	"All the blocks in your tower are exactly the same size."
How the blocks are connected	"All your blocks are touching."
How the blocks are balanced	"Those long blocks are holding up the shorter ones."

Source: Dodge (1991, 91).

chose the pastels." Describing specifically what the child has done models the appropriate language and also conveys respect for the unique characteristics of each child's work. Examples related to blocks are listed in Table 14.4. Similar statements could relate to other constructions or to pretend play events. Such observations may assist children in opening conversations about their constructions so that both adults and children may understand. Note that the statements are descriptions of the observation.

❏ Provide opportunities for children to share their projects with others. Display drawings, paintings, and sculpture regularly. Ask the child who made the construction to talk about his or her ideas at group time. Encourage relevant peer questions and comments. Color, line, mass or volume, pattern, shape or form, space, and texture are appropriate topics for discussion (Moyer, 1990). Demonstrate how to give feedback or ask questions about the construction. "You selected interesting colors for the [purple] cow" or "The size of this drawing is very small; tell us why you chose to do it that way" are statements based on observations of the construction as well as openings for explanation if the child wishes to provide it. Never use sarcasm; the child's feelings will be hurt, and no educational goal can be reached. Do not allow children to provide gratuitous negative comments without making them accountable. For example, if a child says, "That's ugly!" respond by saying, "You think that drawing is not attractive; tell us why you think that." If the child responds with detail, then discuss

how the same characteristics that appeal to one person may not be attractive to another.

❏ Support children who are feeling frustrated and angry when their work appears unsuccessful to them. Help them define the problem ("Tell me why you think this isn't going to work. What's wrong? What do you think you can do about it? Is there anyone else in the class who might be able to assist you?"). Children should be able to achieve their goal with their own actions when they work together (Tudge & Caruso, 1988). Occasionally offer assistance, but allow the child to control the decision making.

❏ Provide display opportunities to everyone. Keep the displays up a few days and then dismantle them. Avoid selecting the "best" construction for display. Sometimes the most appealing product does not indicate the most creative thinking.

❏ Teach children to respect each other's work. Help them to understand that it is because of respect that they do not kick down someone's blocks, make noise while someone shares a song, or jeer when someone hangs up a drawing (Kostelnik et al., 1998).

❏ Help other children focus on the play potential of the construction. If a child has made a particularly effective supplement to pretend play, then recognize his or her contributions. When children are working together on a construction, encourage them to discuss what they plan to do and how the construction will fit into their continuing play plans. Demonstrate respectfulness yourself. Make statements that recognize children's positive contributions to the ongoing play of their peers.

TABLE 14.5
Methods of Instruction From Least to Most Intrusive

Methods of Instruction	Example
Active onlooking	The teacher intently observes what children are doing and saying as they play.
Nondirective statements	"It looks like you're going to the beach" or "You're a cloud floating in the air."
Questions	"What do heroes really do?" or "When you go to the store, does the customer pay the storekeeper, or the other way around?"
Directive statements	"Tell me about the family that lives in the dollhouse" or "Think about the middle Billy Goat Gruff and show me how he crossed the bridge."
Modeling	"I'm your new next-door neighbor [Knocking at the pretend door.]," or the teacher picks up a stethoscope and says, "Is your baby sick?"
Physical intervention	The teacher adds or removes props during the play.

3. *Actively help children improve their level of performance in pretend play.* Table 14.5 lists procedures that increase in the level of intrusion and power exercised by the teacher. Usually, the teacher selects the least intrusive strategy that will accomplish the change. For example, either active onlooking or nondirective statements may facilitate the children's becoming more focused or starting to develop the theme for skilled children. Inexperienced youngsters may need stronger measures such as modeling and physical intervention (Wolfgang & Sanders, 1986).

Modeling is always done inside the play frame. The teacher becomes a player and assumes a role. Physical intervention during the play usually requires that the teacher enter the space of the play frame, if only briefly, to provide or take away materials. Removing materials is usually more effective if the adult assumes a role ("I'm the plumber and I have come to get the sink [full of water] for repair. You will get it back in a day or two."). This would be done only if there were sufficient reason to intervene—say, if children began adding real water to pasta the teacher had provided for pretend cooking. The water would ruin the pasta and make a sticky mess.

Nondirective statements, questions, and directive statements can quickly offer suggestions or assistance from outside the play frame. Usually the teacher watches, makes the verbalization, and listens to the children's response but would not move into the play directly. These strategies are effective before and after a

play sequence for assisting in the planning and evaluation process.

4. *Teach children the technical skills needed to use materials when engaged in construction activity.* Creativity is not impeded by showing the child how to use materials appropriately. On the contrary, lack of skill inhibits children's ability to do construction at all. For example, show children how much paste to use and where to place it; show them how to cut; demonstrate sewing; model the use of a wire cutter on potter's clay; and deliberately mix paints so they can see the effect. Then let them use the skills to implement their own goals (Cole, 1990).

Nondirective statements, questions, suggestions, and demonstrations that help the child to do what he or she has in mind are always appropriate. Discrimination between a statement that specifies an outcome and a technique that enables a child to achieve his or her chosen outcome is necessary. As in pretend play, use the least intrusive strategy necessary to support the child's activity.

5. *When possible, allow children to create their own sociodramatic play independently.* Prepare the environment, provide information and resources, and then allow the children to create their own scripts. If intervention is necessary, do it and withdraw promptly. Most 5-year-olds have all the basic skills and are able to elaborate on them within an appropriate setting; therefore, this is one center that may run rather smoothly for 5- to 8-year-olds with limited adult intervention.

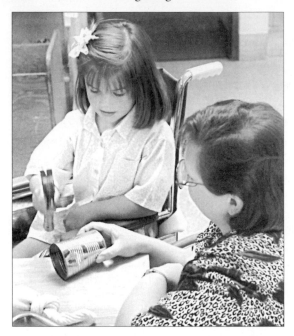

Learning how to use a variety of tools expands children's construction skills.

Encourage experimentation and creative problem solving whenever possible.

6. *Provide information relevant to the play theme.* Use picture books, field trips, videotapes, photos, and other sources of information so that children know what is supposed to occur in the pretend situation. For children with extremely limited skills, Lois Lenski's *Let's Play House* is effective in stimulating homemaking play. Although dated and illustrating traditional sex roles, this black-and-white picture book helps the least skilled child get some ideas of roles. Themes and topics from social studies, science, and literature support older children's knowledge needs and can be most easily incorporated into related pretend play themes. Identify information gaps and misunderstanding. If children pretend that firefighters set the fires before putting them out, then they need additional information on fire safety as well as community helpers! Strategies for providing information for pretend play work as well for construction.

7. *Provide a solid base of information and experience from which children develop their constructions.* Projects of investigation should be a regular part of the curriculum, not an add-on or an extra (Webster,

1990). Build on children's interest, and use the surrounding community as a source of information and assistance (Borden, 1987). Both field trips and visitors to the classroom enhance the information base established by the teacher. Some suggestions about how to do this are in Chapter 4. Projects and themes, which are described in the next chapter, are another good avenue to support construction.

8. *Support children in their problem solving,* and encourage them to expand the number and diversity of potential solutions (Casey & Lippman, 1991). (The corollary is that teachers should not arbitrarily announce "That won't work!" before a child has had a chance to think about their plan.) The following strategies will be useful:

❏ Attempt to grasp the child's intent. Direct observation sometimes works, but it may be necessary to ask ("It seems that you are trying to. . . ."). Honestly inquire if necessary ("I don't understand. . . .").

❏ Ask about alternatives children considered ("Tell me what you thought about doing. Anything else?").

❏ Inquire about the possible sources of information ("Has anyone done anything like this before? Might he or she help?"). Encourage the use of reference materials ("Where might you get a picture of the . . . ?" or "Is there anything else you might use to help you figure this out?"). In one instance a 4-year-old was attempting to build a pair of walkie-talkies. She had already nailed long spikes into the ends of two blocks of wood and was worried that "they won't work just like that." She had never seen a walkie-talkie up close but knew they had more than an antenna to make them receive and transmit. The teacher could have just handed her a walkie-talkie. Instead, she carefully engaged the child in a conversation until the child herself recognized the scope of the problem and then could quickly identify a potential solution.

❏ Encourage children to participate in the general planning and decision-making process. When a child enthusiastically asks, "Can we build a . . . ?" respond, "Yes, and what materials [space, time] will you need?" or "Yes, and how will you do this?" Avoid "Yes, but. . . ." Children cannot do everything just when they might like to. Older children are particularly sensitive to the competing needs for time and space. Involve them in making opportunities for carrying out as well as building projects.

❏ Actively involve children who are less likely to initiate construction projects (Tudge & Caruso, 1988). Some children have more confidence in themselves than others. Often the more timid child is left out of group constructions or does not initiate construction activities independently. Good ideas may be lost to the group and the timid child's abilities not acknowledged or recognized, even by the individuals involved. Watch for opportunities to suggest that the timid child participate in the group endeavor. Interact with the less forceful students, and encourage them to share their ideas with you and one or two others. Avoid telling them what to do or giving them solutions to problems. Standing by them (literally) when they approach other children is more likely to give them confidence and practice as well as helping them with the task at hand.

❏ Allow time for children to think and develop their ideas. Very few problems are solved spontaneously. Very little creative work happens on the spur of the moment. It sometimes takes more time to think about and plan a project than it does to carry it out. Rather than urging a child who is sitting quietly or abstractedly to "Get started on . . . ," offer a listening ear: "Would you like to share what you are thinking about? Maybe that will help."

9. *Encourage the flow among play, construction, and information acquisition.* Given the appropriate circumstances, experiences that are intended as basic information generate construction. Equally often the desire of children to construct something for their play motivates them to seek the information. Topical reference materials are essential to every classroom, even for the youngest children. Older children may look up information for themselves, and younger children can watch teachers who "don't know, but I'll find out."

10. *Evaluate the level of skill development.* Observe all the children and determine if each child is able to pretend play. If a child is able to do so, then check such qualitative aspects as posing problems to be solved, generating ideas, initiating play, following play, negotiating, allowing new players to enter the play, and creating objects to be used in the play. Check to see if children are using metacommunication skills to structure pretend play. Because play is often an area of strength, skills developed in this context may be transferred to other areas of developing competence. Recall that the highest level of play has a story structure with

a plot and a resolution of a problem. Higher levels of construction incorporate artifacts into pretend play or other areas of learning. Assessment is addressed more completely in Chapter 16.

The ten general tactics proposed to support pretend play and construction include approaches to creating an appropriate climate, instruction on interventions with less skilled children, methods for combining play and information, procedures for fostering cooperation and respect among the players, patterns of effective adult-child conversation, and recommendations for assessment. These are essential components to achieving desirable skills, yet there is more to be done. Adults must plan for play to occur, provide many opportunities for a variety of construction activities, and foster specific sociodramatic and theme play that enables children to make sense of their world.

Planning for Representation Through Pretend and Construction Play

In addition to the specific play ideas that have been included in the chapters on curricular domains, Tables 14.6 and 14.7 include several ideas that suggest how to implement pretend play and construction on a day-to-day basis. These suggestions should help you generate other alternatives as you make specific plans for a group of children.

You have already read how to set up learning centers for pretend play and construction in Chapter 6. Representational activities are so important for the integration of curriculum and the overall development of children that we recommend that pretend play and construction be a part of the daily plan for 3- to 5-year-olds and at least weekly for older children. We also recommend that one-third to one-half of the classroom space be available for pretend and construction activities for younger children. Older children may have to use space normally set aside for something else. Typically, desk and table tops are used for construction with smaller materials. Whenever possible, we recommend that between one-fourth to one-third of the classroom be dedicated to pretend play and construction for older children.

One advantage of planning for pretend play on a daily basis is that once the basic plan is made and the center is operating, it can continue as long as the unit of instruction continues. The teacher may add props or

TABLE 14.6
Activity Ideas to Support Pretend Play

Type of Pretend Play	Sample Activities
Make believe	Imagining what the clouds might be
	Pretending to be animals, autos, or simple machines
	Imagining how a character in a story feels
Pretend with objects	Hunt for props to support child-initiated activity
	Imagine an object if no placeholder is at hand
	Pantomime nursery rhymes, songs, or short poems
Pretend with art materials	Create stories as part of the drawing experience
	Illustrate told or written stories
	Listen to "pictorial" music selections while painting
Pretend with construction materials	Build or make a prop for pretend play
	Use blocks to build a setting for a pretend episode
	Use leaves, sticks, and other natural materials to build boats or houses.
Pretend with miniatures	Use models or replicas in enactments
	Dollhouse play
	Farm animals or miniature people with blocks
Dramatic and sociodramatic and thematic play	Enact occupational roles related to class themes
	Enact house, neighbors, and school play
Story reenactment	Perform a simple ballad with a clear story line
	Select and act out a traditional folk tale or folk song
	Dramatize a more modern story such as "Ask Mr. Bear" or "Caps for Sale"
Write and play	Ask children to pretend they are the characters in a story that a classmate has written and act it out
	Once children have engaged in a sociodramatic play set for several days, ask them to write a story based on their play

materials occasionally or encourage children to bring household discards from home to supplement school supplies. The teacher's task is to encourage, guide, and assess children's accomplishments.

Construction activities may be short term for younger children or may involve weeks of work with primary children. Variety of materials and represent-

ing the same objects and events with different media enhance children's understanding. Often construction and pretend play are a part of the same episode or activity. When children make their own props to enact a story with a problem and a resolution, they are involved in a very complex, intellectually demanding activity.

TABLE 14.7
Activities to Support Construction Play

Type of Construction Play	Sample Activities
Projects stemming from natural encounters	Using tissue paper, adhesives, egg cartons, scissors, and so on to make worms, flowers, or bugs
	Build houses using hollow blocks
	Construct a village using unit blocks and miniatures
Projects stemming from mutual interests of teacher and children	Prepare a creation station as a learning center and allow children to make anything they want
	Allow children to report on another learning activity by making something related to it and explaining what they did and why
Projects stemming from teacher concerns	Transportation unit: Build paper airplanes, boats from assorted materials, or cars using wood, saws, and nails
	Energy unit: Build a circuit board with batteries, bells, lights, and so on; make a magnet using a nail and another magnet
	Holiday unit: Create a collage depicting the many ways people celebrate
	Nutrition unit: Make "food" of papier-mâché and paint to be used in pretend play

SUMMARY

At the beginning of this chapter you were asked a number of questions that you should now be able to answer readily. Play has unique characteristics that distinguish this behavior from all others.

Children integrate their understanding of experience through pretend play and construction and learn other things on their own. The relationships between specific areas of development and play were illuminated as were the areas where expectations for individual differences could be anticipated. When teachers understand this, they are better prepared to plan for play experiences.

We suggested both general strategies to support play and ideas for planning appropriate learning centers and projects. When themes are incorporated into pretend play and construction, much learning is consolidated in the minds of the children. As you learn how to develop themes and projects in the next chapter, keep in mind the role that pretend play and construction might play in each theme.

✖ Applying What You Read in This Chapter

1. **Discuss**
   a. What makes an activity playful or not playful? How can you tell the difference?
   b. Why is there resistance to play in many public school settings, and what role might you play as a member of the teaching team in one of those settings?
   c. Describe what you might expect to see in (1) a classroom where guided play was a part of the curriculum and (2) a setting where the teacher simply let children play if they wanted to and treated it as a time filler until dismissal.

2. **Observe**
   a. Observe children at play with materials that can be used for construction and find (1) a child exploring or investigating only, (2) one who appears invested in the design (patterner), and (3) one who appears to be pretending with what he

or she has made (dramatist). How is their play similar? What distinguishes these approaches? Do children change in their approach during the observation?

b. Observe a 3-year-old and a child who is 5 or older in pretend play. What skills does each child have in pretending with an object; pretending about time, place, or setting; object substitution; pretending with another child for at least ten minutes; maintaining an idea or topic in the play with another; and introducing a problem and resolving it in the pretend-play sequence.

c. Review Table 14.2. Organize a similar table for analyzing either pretend play or construction. Observe a group of children at play at least 30 minutes and identify the specific intermediate objectives in each of the six domains that their play suggests. You will be inferring the relevant objectives from what the children do and say. You may not recognize all of the learning potentials in each of the domains on any one occasion. This observation activity is a very challenging one.

3. **Carry out an activity**

a. Examine the play ideas in Tables 14.6 and 14.7. Select one activity from each of them, and write a long form lesson plan to implement it.

b. Participate in the block area of a program. Use the strategies to support block construction suggested in the section on promoting children's play skills.

4. **Create something for your portfolio**

a. Using the information in the chapter, prepare a checklist to assess pretend play and/or construction play skills.

b. Write a newsletter for parents explaining why you will include pretend play in the classroom. Explain briefly how this will contribute to the children's learning. It should be well written and no longer than two pages single spaced.

c. Review Chapter 3, and select four teaching strategies that support pretend play and construction.

5. **Add to your journal**

a. Describe in detail one very memorable play experience from your own childhood in a program setting. Include details of what made this so memorable. Then review the chapter and reflect on the content in terms of your personal experience.

b. After interacting with a group of children who have had some opportunity to engage in pretend play or construction, contemplate your own performance in terms of the suggestions offered by this chapter. Where were you more or less successful? What questions do you still have regarding childrens' performance?

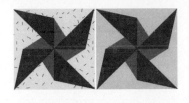

Chapter 15

Integrating Curriculum Through Theme Teaching

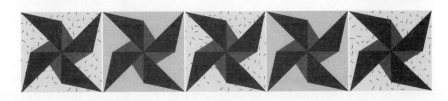

You may wonder:

What is theme teaching?

What are the benefits of theme teaching?

What kinds of themes are most suitable for preschoolers? for school-age children?

What are the steps involved in creating a theme from start to finish?

What are the pitfalls to avoid in theme planning and implementation?

How will I know if the theme is contributing to children's learning?

In this chapter on themes, we present information to help you answer these questions.

The children have been gathering a variety of rocks for their collection. With the aid of their teacher, they create a graph depicting differences in the color, size, and shape of the rocks.

The children use smooth, round rocks as tools to grind corn into a coarse powder. Later, they make fried mush from the cornmeal.

The teacher reads a story about an artist who makes rock sculptures. Next, she helps the children recall the sequence the artist used to create the sculpture. Later, the children use props to act out the events in the order they remember.

A lively discussion takes place when the teacher asks the children to predict what will happen to two large rocks

when one is placed in the shade and the other in the sunshine. She records the group's predictions, and after the experiments are carried out, the children compare their ideas with the actual results.

The children create a classroom book in which they draw, dictate, or write descriptions of rocks found on a recent rock hunt.

The children transform the pretend play area into a "rock shop" in which they pretend to buy and sell rocks and minerals to people at a mall.

These are typical activities you might see in any early childhood classroom from preschool through the second grade. All involve hands-on experiences for children and provide them with information about rocks. They also give children opportunities to observe, compare, count, predict, remember, role-play, express ideas, and develop fine motor skills.

In one classroom, these activities might be dispersed throughout the year; in another, they are offered within the framework of a multiweek theme focusing on rocks. Children experiencing either approach will probably profit from the activities and increase their knowledge. However, youngsters involved in several rock-related activities concentrated within a month-long theme have the added advantage of being able to make connections among those activities that could be harder to make were the lessons more spread out over time. The creation of such linkages is the essence of theme teaching (Kostelnik, 1996).

WHAT IS THEME TEACHING?

Theme teaching involves creating an array of educationally sound activities planned around a central idea. These activities are integrated into all aspects of the curriculum and take place within a concentrated time frame, ranging from several days to several weeks. This creates a common thread among activities that facilitates children's generalization of knowledge and skills from one experience to another (Eliason & Jenkins, 1994; Machado & Meyer, 1996). Early childhood educators who successfully implement themes incorporate into their teaching the principles of developmentally appropriate practice described throughout this volume. Such practices form the foundation for effective theme teaching.

HOW THEMES CONTRIBUTE TO CHILDREN'S CONCEPT DEVELOPMENT

Using themes to organize young children's educational experiences is not a new idea. It has been a popular teaching method since Dewey first proposed that curriculum be related to children's real-life experiences. Since then, educators have looked to themes as a way to help children gain an overall sense of direction and consolidation in their learning. Through participation in a theme, children form connections among individual bits of information. These connections contribute to children's concept development and are the most important reason for advocating a theme-oriented approach to teaching (Bredekamp & Copple, 1997).

Conceptual Development

Concepts are the fundamental ideas children form about objects and events in the world. They serve as the cognitive categories that allow children to group together perceptually distinct information, events, or objects (Deiner, 1993; Welman, 1988). As such, concepts serve as the building blocks of knowing, thinking, and reasoning.

Children form concepts through firsthand experiences (Berk & Winsler, 1995; Lawton, 1987). Each time they act on objects or interact with other people, they extract relevant bits of meaning from the encounter. They combine the new information with previously acquired knowledge and perceptions to clarify or modify current understandings and later to construct new ideas (Deiner, 1993; Hunt, 1961). By mentally cataloguing a growing number of experiences and making finer discriminations as well as more abstract connections among them, children build, adjust, and expand their concepts over time.

The Link Between Concepts and Themes

The natural process of mentally connecting bits of information into more unified ideas is enhanced through children's involvement in thematic instruction. As children engage in activities permeated by a theme, it is easier for them to link what they have learned in one activity to what they have learned in another. In this way, theme teaching provides children with opportunities to integrate learning across the curriculum (Freeman & Sokoloff, 1996). For instance, participating in theme-related aesthetic, language, or cognitive activities enables children to combine the individual elements of the curriculum into a cohesive whole. Similarly, when they carry out math, science, or social studies activities linked by a theme, children go beyond the bounds of traditional subject matter to form more holistic, comprehensive understandings (Schickendanz, Pergantis, Kanosky, Blaney, & Ottinger, 1997). These understandings represent increasingly elaborate concepts. Because young children are continually striving to make sense of their environment, the early childhood years are ones of rapid concept development (Eliason & Jenkins, 1994). Consequently, educators have become increasingly interested in helping young children make conceptual connections through an integrated curriculum that also provides concept organizers such as themes and projects (Bredekamp, 1991; Kovalik, 1997).

ADDITIONAL BENEFITS FOR CHILDREN

In addition to enhancing children's concept development, themes provide other advantages to young learners. First, they offer children a means for exploring a central pool of information through many different avenues. Regardless of whether children prefer small- or whole-group activities, more or less active modes of interaction, or auditory, kinesthetic, visual, interpersonal, or intrapersonal experiences, they can gain access to a topic in ways that suit their individual needs. If one activity is unappealing or does not match their learning style or fails to fit their capacities, children have other options for learning about the concept. They may pursue alternate activities instead, gaining similar insights. This is not the case when ideas are presented only once or in only one way.

Themes also encourage children to immerse themselves in a topic. As youngsters become interested in an idea, they often want to know *all* about it. Exploring a theme-based concept satisfies this desire. It also enhances children's disposition to become mentally absorbed in pursuing ideas (Katz & Chard, 1989).

Keeping the early childhood curriculum varied and interesting is another value of theme teaching. Both children and teachers experience a sense of novelty with each new topic. As themes change, so do props, activities, and room decorations, which reinvigorates daily routines. Not only do new themes spawn original activities, but the same or similar activities are given a fresh emphasis when they are used to support different topics.

Group cohesiveness is promoted when several children focus on a particular topic simultaneously. Children who have experiences and knowledge in common develop a nucleus of mutual interests that provides a natural context for cooperative learning. As children discover classmates whose interests match their own, their social circles widen. Their perceptions of one another broaden also because with each theme change, different children act as novices and experts; youngsters who are leaders for one topic may be followers for another. Thus, their patterns of interaction vary, allowing each youngster an opportunity to experience different social roles.

Finally, children's changing interests are accommodated year-round through theme teaching. As children become excited about new ideas, those ideas can be highlighted throughout the curriculum, conveying to children the message that their ideas are valuable and worth exploring. Also, themes developed in response to the expressed interests of some children in the class may spark the curiosity of their peers, enlarging children's notions of what is worth investigating.

TEACHERS BENEFIT, TOO

By acting as a focus around which to plan, themes help practitioners organize their thinking, encourage them to choose relevant activities and vocabulary to support theme-related goals, and enable them to locate resources prior to unit implementation. All of these factors tend to increase teachers' confidence in planning an integrated array of educational activities for young children (Cummings, 1989; Deiner, 1993).

Another advantage is that theme teaching enables early childhood educators to address topics in sufficient breadth and depth to ensure that each child has had a chance to learn something new. Both of these dimensions are enhanced by having multiple theme-related activities in a variety of curricular domains. Such cross coverage allows teachers to structure the presentation of concepts more coherently and devise sequential plans that gradually challenge children's thinking (Eliason & Jenkins, 1994).

Additionally, teachers who approach theme planning appropriately research each topic, generating a pool of factual information on which to build instruction. This increases their knowledge base as well as the accuracy of the information they provide to children. Further, it allows practitioners to consider in advance how to handle sensitive issues associated with the theme and prompts them to think of original activities, a process that teachers find intellectually stimulating. The collegiality that sometimes arises when they collaborate with fellow staff members on developing thematic units is also pleasing. Brainstorming theme-related activities, problem solving in relation to the theme, sharing props, and swapping written plans are timesaving, invigorating activities that teachers find rewarding.

Themes also provide a unifying framework for measuring children's progress. An important teacher responsibility is to continually assess children's grasp of concepts addressed by the curriculum (Bredekamp & Copple, 1997). Teachers do this by observing children and interacting with them individually and in groups. Attempting to evaluate children's concept development on a child-by-child basis, with no unifying framework within which to make judgments, is very difficult because it is so fragmented. These assessments are more easily accomplished when practitioners have a single concept on which to focus. Seeing and hearing many children within the group demonstrate varying interpretations of the same concept provides a context for the teacher's judgments. For instance, an adult is better able to determine whether children's incomplete or erroneous ideas are universal or particular to an individual. He or she can also gauge which of several activities enhances or detracts from children's grasp of a particular idea. This is harder to accomplish within a totally unrelated set of activities. For all these reasons, practitioners report that theme teaching is very self-satisfying (Hurley & Blake, 1997; Rosenbusch, 1994).

PROGRAM EFFECTS

As you can see, theme teaching enhances both children's and practitioners' education experiences. Themes also yield programwide benefits. First, theme teaching can be implemented across diverse program structures, among children of all ages, with youngsters whose needs differ greatly, and by teachers whose philosophies and styles vary, too (Bredekamp, 1991). This universal applicability provides a common bond between programs and increases the potential for collaboration among professionals. Conversely, because educators create themes with a specific group of children in mind, such instruction is very individualized and meets the autonomy needs of both children and teachers.

Second, family members who are kept informed of upcoming themes are better able to contribute their knowledge, expertise, and resources to children's educational experiences. It is often easier for them to envision how to participate in children's education with a particular topic in mind than to do so in terms of the more generalized instruction that takes place from day to day (Deiner, 1993; Kostelnik, 1991). Consequently, family support for the program may go beyond the traditional donations of discarded meat trays and toilet paper rolls. For instance, knowing the class is studying birds, a family may send in a bird's nest they found, a photograph of a

bird taken at their feeder, or a magazine article about birds. An older sibling may help the children build bird feeders, or a grandparent may show the children how to care for a baby bird fallen from its nest. This kind of family involvement promotes constructive home-school relationships and helps parents and other family members feel more involved in the education process.

The third and perhaps most important programwide impact of theme teaching is that it provides a tool by which content learning and process learning can be integrated within the curriculum. Often treated as mutually exclusive categories of knowledge, theme teaching is a means by which the two can be combined without violating the integrity of either one.

Focusing on Content

Content learning encompasses all of the factual information relevant to the theme. Learning content requires such mental abilities as attending, listening, observing, remembering, and recounting (Hendrick, 1997). Thus, a group of first graders studying wild birds might engage in a variety of experiences to learn the following facts:

- ❏ Birds live in a variety of places: in woods, meadows, plains, and deserts; near ponds, lakes, and oceans; and in cities.
- ❏ Each species of bird builds a nest characteristic of the species.
- ❏ Birds build nests to protect their eggs, which contain baby birds.
- ❏ Birds build nests of varying complexities.
- ❏ Different bird species build their nests in different places: on the ground, above the ground, in the open, or hidden.

As you already know, simple exposure to factual content such as this does not teach in and of itself. Only when children become physically involved in, talk about, and reflect on their experiences do they learn from them (Berk & Winsler, 1995; Elkind, 1988a). Children might gain access to factual knowledge about wild birds through firsthand activities such as going outdoors to watch birds fly, observing a nesting bird, recording the numbers and kinds of birds they see, or examining several different abandoned bird nests. Teachers might also give children make-believe wings and straw to use in acting like birds caring for their young, or they could work with children to construct a replica of a bird's nest. Throughout these activities, teachers and children would discuss which type of bird might build which type of nest, further extending children's content learning.

Focusing on Process

All of the aesthetic, affective, cognitive, language, social, and physical operations and skills that form the basis for children's experiences within the early childhood curriculum constitute process learning. Because they encompass the "whole" child, such processes range from imagining, creating, and performing, to grouping, differentiating, inferring, and concluding, to pretending, representing, and constructing. Just as with content learning, children gain proficiency in process learning through hands-on activities. In fact, the same bird activities cited earlier could provide the means for children to increase their competence and understanding in any domain.

Integrating Content and Process

Content and process come together in the activities teachers plan. These activities form the basis for instruction and offer children an applied means for experiencing the curriculum. Thus, two children acting out the roles of wild birds not only gain factual insight into bird life but also have opportunities to practice social and cognitive processes such as offering ideas ("You be the baby bird. I'll be the mommy"), reaching compromises ("OK, I'm the mommy bird first, and then you"), and drawing conclusions ("If we have two mommy birds, we'll need two nests"). In fact, during the early childhood period, often the content included in each activity is simply the medium through which children explore other, more process-oriented operations and skills (Hendrick, 1997). Consequently, even when children are involved in theme-related activities, it is not always the thematic content that captures their attention. They may be much more involved in the process learning represented within that experience. In this case, the children may eventually ignore the bird theme to concentrate on the dynamics of their social relationship. Even so, they are continuing to learn and benefit from the activity.

Furthermore, although teachers have a domain-specific goal for each activity they plan, children frequently proceed from that original aim to explore aspects of the activity related to other domains. Moving from content to process or from one process to another is a natural, appropriate way for children to expand their knowledge and skills. Such adaptations do not mean teachers should simply provide generic activities with no real content-learning or process-learning goals in mind. Rather, practitioners must be purposeful in their planning. This assists children in exploring facts and processes they might not otherwise experience and ensures a coherent, comprehensive set of activities from which children may choose. The integrative nature of such activities is well suited to the holistic manner in which children learn.

THE NEGATIVE SIDE OF THEME TEACHING

Considering all the pluses cited thus far, it may appear that theme teaching automatically translates into developmentally appropriate practice. Unfortunately, that is not always true. Themes can be enacted poorly (Freeman & Skoloff, 1996). For instance, some teachers may violate the principles of developmentally appropriate practice by failing to accommodate children's needs for movement and physical activity, social interaction, and independence. They may ignore certain domains or assume that theme teaching involves simply coordinating their ditto sheets around a single idea. Another pitfall arises when teachers, determined to get across the "facts," rely on reciting them to children rather than providing opportunities for children to engage in content learning through hands-on activities.

A second problem occurs when early childhood professionals select themes that fail to support children's concept development. That happens when topics are too narrow or when the links between the topic and the activities are contrived. This causes the theme to lack the depth and substance necessary to stimulate children's thinking. One such instance is exemplified by weekly plans centered around a letter of the alphabet, such as *g*. As children paint with green tempera at the easel, eat grapes for snack, and growl like lions, the teacher may confidently believe that youngsters are learning all about the letter *g*. In reality, the children may be focusing on the subject of their paintings rather than on the color, they may be thinking of grapes **as** fruit rather than a *g* word, and they may be more aware of the loudness or mock ferocity of their growling than the consonant sound they are making. Since *g* is not a concept and does not directly relate to children's real-life experiences, these are poor attempts at theme teaching.

Misdirected attempts at dealing with content are a third source of poor theme use. Some teachers value content over process so much that the integrated, child-centered nature of appropriate themes is lost. Others take the opposite position, ignoring content learning altogether. This happens when practitioners create a theme based on conventional wisdom, without researching carefully the factual information to support it. A similar outcome occurs when teachers assume that a few decorations and craft projects equal theme teaching. In both cases, not enough attention is paid to conveying accurate, meaningful information to children. As a result, children are not exposed to valuable content that could be interesting and valuable to them. Worse, they may even obtain inaccurate facts from teachers whose general store of knowledge is inadequate to support the theme.

Finally, some teachers assume they are theme teaching well when they simply relate several activities to a central prop, such as pockets (Cummings, 1989). Children may sing about having a smile in their pocket, hear a story about pockets, eat "pocket bread" for snack, and decorate paper pockets. Unfortunately, the factual knowledge attached to these experiences is minimal. Children are not learning much that is useful or interesting. The process learning involved is also perfunctory. Children are not being challenged to think, problem solve, expand their literacy skills, or develop their social and physical abilities. Although the activities may keep children busy or entertained, they fail to engage their minds and bodies in the excitement of real learning. Because this type of theme planning addresses neither content learning nor process learning, its educational value is poor.

PRINCIPLES OF EFFECTIVE THEME TEACHING

Effective theme teaching is much more complex and comprehensive than any of the misdirected approaches just described. It can be achieved without undesirable side effects when the following principles are incorporated into teacher's planning and implementation with children (Cummings, 1989; Jalongo & Stamp, 1997; Kostelnik, Howe, et al., 1996).

1. Themes must be age appropriate, individually appropriate, and socioculturally appropriate.
2. Themes should relate directly to children's real-life experiences, building on what they know and what they want to know more about.
3. Each theme should represent a concept for children to investigate. The emphasis in a theme is on helping children build theme-related concepts, not on having children memorize isolated bits of information.
4. Every theme should be supported by a body of factual content that has been adequately researched by the teacher(s).
5. Themes should integrate content learning (social-conventional knowledge) with process learning (physical, logical mathematical, representational, metacognitive, and other specific processes related to each curricular domain).
6. Theme-related information should be conveyed to children through hands-on activities that involve active inquiry.
7. Theme-related activities should represent all six curricular domains and promote their integration.
8. In teaching the theme, the same content should be offered more than once and incorporated into different kinds of activities (exploratory, guided discovery, problem solving, discussions, cooperative learning, demonstrations, direct instruction, small-group and whole-group activities).
9. Themes should lend themselves to the eventual development of projects that are child initiated and child directed.
10. Themes should provide opportunities for children to document and reflect on what they have learned.
11. Themes should include ways to involve members of children's families.
12. Each theme should be expanded or revised according to children's demonstrated interests and understanding.

When these principles are incorporated into theme teaching, the potential for negative outcomes is eliminated, and the benefits are maintained.

HOW TO CREATE THEMATIC UNITS

Sources of Ideas

Cats, gardens, art and artists, storytelling, people in our neighborhood, insects, measuring—all of these topics represent potential themes. As an early childhood educator, you will have to decide which topics are best suited to the children in your group. There are a lot of ideas from which to choose. These have many sources: the children themselves, special events, unexpected happenings, program-mandated content, and teachers and parents.

Children's Interests   The best source for thematic ideas is the children themselves. The things children frequently enact, discuss, or wonder about offer the most appropriate basis for selecting and implementing themes in early childhood programs. You will discover children's interests by talking with children informally, observing them, and listening as they talk with one an-

other. You may use more formal means to assess children's interests, such as interviewing children or using the KWHLH brainstorming strategy described in Chapter 4. Information from parents regarding upcoming events in children's lives or events at home provide additional clues about concepts that will be important to your class throughout the year.

For instance, you might decide to introduce the theme "machines" based on children's curiosity about the heavy equipment they observe at a nearby construction site. The birth of new siblings to one or more families in the class might prompt a unit on babies. Children's frequent discussions about who can play with whom could serve as the stimulus for a theme on friends. Ordinary events like these are important to young children, which is why they provide the strongest foundation for planning and implementing themes in the classroom. No matter what age group you are teaching, child-initiated topics are the most relevant ones around which to create themes.

Special Events   Occasionally, out-of-the-ordinary occurrences such as the program's annual farm trip, an assembly featuring leader dogs for the blind, or the celebration of Arbor Day also serve as a spark for theme development. Occasions like these, which teachers know about in advance, may be integrated into or serve as the cornerstone for related units of study such as "farm products," "working dogs," or "trees."

Unexpected Happenings   Sometimes unanticipated events stimulate children's thinking in new directions. This was the case for kindergartners intrigued by the habits of a grackle whose nest was in the eavestrough above their classroom window. The teacher responded to their curiosity by introducing a unit on wild birds, using the grackle as a firsthand example. Along similar lines, a sudden hailstorm prompted so many questions from children that a theme on weather evolved naturally.

Program-Mandated Content   In addition to child-inspired content, many school districts require particular subject matter to be addressed at given grade levels. This is also true for other early childhood programs in which certain topics such as dental care or fire safety are regularly mandated by the administrator or board of directors. Such required content can also

These visitors came because of the children's interest in animals and gave them firsthand experience with the "real" thing.

serve as a basis for thematic teaching. Social studies, science, health, math, or language arts concepts can be used as the core around which a variety of theme-related activities are created and integrated throughout the day. This approach has the advantage of ensuring that important but sometimes neglected subjects like science, social studies, and health receive adequate attention. Moreover, teachers gain the satisfaction of covering prescribed material in ways that are meaningful to children.

Teacher/Parent Interests   Theme ideas may also have their source in concepts that teachers and parents find exciting or valuable. A teacher enthralled by clouds may share his enthusiasm through a unit on the daytime sky. The teacher's desire to teach children constructive ways of working together could be the motivation behind the theme "cooperation." Apprehension expressed by parents regarding child sexual abuse might stimulate the development of a unit on personal safety.

With so many sources of themes and so many ideas to chose from, potential topics usually exceed the time available to teach them. Certain additional criteria will narrow your choices and help you pick the most appropriate themes.

Essential Theme Criteria

When finalizing an idea for a theme, consider five factors:

1. Relevance of the topic to children.
2. Ability of the theme to involve children in hands-on activities.
3. Diversity and balance across the curriculum.
4. Availability of theme-related props.
5. Ability of the theme to inspire child-initiated projects.

Relevance   Of the five criteria, the most important is relevance. Themes are relevant when the concepts they represent are directly tied to children's real-life experiences and support their interests. If relevance has been properly considered, themes become age appropriate, individually appropriate, and socioculturally appropriate. Relevant themes highlight concepts with which children have initial familiarity and provide new insights into their daily experiences. Themes

such as "self," "home," "family," "foods," "plants," or "night and day" are pertinent to preschoolers and early elementary-aged children because they help them understand their lives and the world around them. Some themes are inappropriate for this age group. "Life in ancient Rome" or "penguins" are too far removed from most children's day-to-day living to be relevant. Gravity and electricity are too abstract to constitute an entire theme, especially for children younger than 5 years of age.

Naturally, themes are most meaningful when they match the needs and interests of particular groups of children. Locale as well as family and community resources or traditions will influence which aspects of the concept are most pertinent. For instance, the theme "plants" has relevance for most children no matter where they live. However, it makes sense for children growing up close to a marsh to focus on cattails, marsh grass, and milkweed as examples of plant life, whereas youngsters living in an arid region would find it more relevant to study desert vegetation such as cacti, sagebrush, and yucca plants. Likewise, the relevance criterion makes backyard birds more appropriate for most children than exotic varieties with which they have had no experience. Moreover, entire topics that are relevant to one group of young children may be irrelevant to others. For example, studying tidal pools could be a significant learning experience for children living in Kennebunk, Maine (which is near the ocean), but not so for those in Lansing, Michigan (which is land-locked). Having never seen a tidal pool, the Michigan group would benefit from studying a more familiar water habitat, such as a pond.

In each of the preceding examples, relevance is determined by the suitability of the subject. Timeliness is another factor to consider. Timely themes build on children's current interests. What are children talking about? What has piqued their interest? The answers to these questions should shape your choice of themes. Consequently, effective theme planners do not plan a year's worth of themes in advance. Instead, they create a few themes at a time that reflect children's expressed curiosity or concerns. Timeliness may also prompt teachers to substitute one theme for another to take advantage of current events or to respond to shifts in children's needs and interests. The reasoning behind early childhood professionals' decisions to change themes is illustrated in the following situation.

A group of first graders attending the International School in Hong Kong were deeply engrossed in a theme on folktales. During that same time they learned that a dinosaur skeleton had been found in the Gobi Desert of China. While discussing these events, several children wondered whether the dragons they heard about in Chinese stories were based on real dinosaurs, a notion that elicited much interest among the group. Capitalizing on their excitement, the teacher substituted a dinosaur theme for the poetry unit she had originally planned to come next. Delaying attention to dinosaurs or ignoring children's hypotheses would have resulted in missed learning opportunities. The timeliness of the dinosaur theme in relation to the children's expressed interest made it quite relevant to these youngsters.

Hands-On Activities   A second criterion for theme selection is how well the content lends itself to the creation of related hands-on activities. Only themes whose content children can experience through the direct manipulation of objects are suitable for children 3 to 8 years of age. This hands-on instruction *must* include firsthand experiences but may also involve some simulations. Both forms of hands-on instruction could be offered through exploratory activities, guided discovery, problem solving, discussions, cooperative learning, demonstrations, and direct instruction activities. However, the emphasis must be on exploration and inquiry if children are to truly expand their concepts over time.

Firsthand experiences are ones in which children become directly involved with the actual objects or phenomena under study. These are real, not analogous or imaginary experiences. Consequently, they give children opportunities to derive relevant bits of information from the original source of the concept. For instance, youngsters engaged in the theme "pets" would gain firsthand insights into the life and activities of pets by observing and caring for pets in the classroom. A visit to a pet shop to see the variety of pets available or a trip to a veterinarian to see how pet health is maintained are other examples of real-life experiences. Simply looking at pictures or hearing about these things could not replicate the richness or stimulation provided by firsthand involvement. Firsthand activities are so essential to children's concept development that teachers should avoid themes for which few such

lessons are possible. In other words, when teachers know that children have had no direct experience with the theme and that related firsthand activities cannot be provided in the program, they should consider the theme inappropriate for their group.

Simulations are another hands-on activity type. They approximate but do not exactly duplicate firsthand experiences. Providing make-believe ears and tails so children can enact life as a pet or working with children to construct a replica of a veterinarian's office using toy animals are examples of simulations. In each case children act directly on objects or carry out activities that resemble the real thing. Although one step removed from the original concept, simulations give children access to data that, for safety or logistical reasons, they have no other means to discover.

Once you have determined that a theme suggests a wealth of potential hands-on activities, consider also the *variety* of hands-on experiences children will have. For example, themes that prompt many craft ideas but are not well suited to pretend play, games, or problem-solving activities are best rejected as too limited. A more appropriate topic would encompass a wider range of learning opportunities for children.

Diversity and Balance Within and Across the Curriculum   Throughout the year, it is desirable for children to experience a broad array of themes. As teachers contemplate potential themes, diversity across the curriculum and balance within it become other criteria for consideration. For example, some themes are primarily scientific in nature (seasons, machines, leaves, insects, and fish); others reflect a social studies emphasis (families, friends, occupations, and the neighborhood); still others highlight language arts content (storytelling, poetry, and writers); some focus primarily on mathematical ideas (stores, measuring, numbers, and numerals); and some are more health oriented (foods, dental hygiene, and fitness). Furthermore, many topics can be adapted to fit one or more of these foci depending on what intrigues the children and what the teacher chooses to emphasize. A unit on stores, for example, could stress the mathematical content of money and counting, the more social aspects of employees working together toward a common goal, or the health-related focus of safety in the store. Teachers can deal with these ideas separately, sequentially, or in combination.

In selecting themes, teachers should choose a cross section of topics in which all of the preceding content areas are eventually addressed. Over time, children have opportunities to expand their concepts and skills across a wide range of subjects, with no one topic predominating. The teacher has in mind both diversity and balance when, in response to second graders' fascination with the space shuttle, she plans a natural science unit on the sky to be followed by a theme on space exploration in which social cooperation is the primary focus. In this case children initiated the original idea for the themes, and the teacher influenced their direction.

Resources   Availability of props and other support materials is a fourth consideration in determining what themes to select (Kovalik, 1986). Because children need objects to act on, it is best to choose themes for which several real items are obtainable. Relevant materials may be accumulated over time as well as solicited from families, community resources, libraries, museums, and so forth. Also, when early childhood colleagues pool or trade props, the number and variety of materials at their disposal greatly increase. Themes for which no real objects are available for children to use should be dropped from consideration. This is also true for themes that depend on one spectacular prop, such as a hang glider or spinning wheel, which, if suddenly unavailable, would spell ruin for the entire theme. Better themes are those for which a variety of props are easily accessible.

Project Potential   Projects offer an exciting way for children to expand their understanding of the concept represented by the theme. The best thematic topics are ones that have project potential. This includes most themes that incorporate the criteria of relevance, hands-on learning, balance and diversity, and access to resources. Projects are open-ended activities in which youngsters undertake, over a period of days or weeks, the in-depth study of some facet of the theme. Ideas for projects to pursue emerge as children gain experience with a concept and become curious about particular aspects of it (Katz & Chard, 1989). As children's interests evolve, individual or small groups of children, in consultation with the teacher, plan and then carry out a relevant project. For example, children involved in a pet theme might decide to create a catalog of all the different pets owned by children in the class and then use it to create graphs, stories, and displays related to their investigation. Building a model of an animal hospital following a visit to one is another possibility. Small groups of children might choose to examine different aspects of the real setting and then take responsibility for re-creating it in the classroom. Project work requires sustained effort and involves learning processes such as exploring, investigating, hypothesizing, reading, recording, discussing, representing, and evaluating. Consequently, projects give children many chances to plan, select manageable tasks for themselves, apply skills, represent what they have learned, and monitor their own progress. More structured than spontaneous play and more self-determined than teacher-planned instruction, projects provide a bridge between the two. They offer children strategies for exploring topics in ways that are *individualized* and therefore more personally meaningful.

Because projects are such a valuable learning tool, the authors invited Judy Harris Helm, a noted expert on the project approach, to offer a brief description of why projects benefit young children and how they can be implemented in early childhood classrooms.

The Project Approach

Judy Harris Helm
Best Practices, Incorporated

The project approach is an example of developmentally appropriate, active, engaged, and meaningful learning. A *project* is an in-depth study, over an extended period of time, of a topic that is of high interest to an individual, a small group, or a whole class (Katz & Chard, 1989). Goals of the approach include thinking about content and learning specific content knowledge, applying intellectual and social skills, developing positive dispositions toward inquiry and investigation, and developing skills in using resources. The method encourages children to become intensely involved in investigating, asking questions, visiting sites, interviewing experts, and representing what they are learning. The project approach complements other parts of the curriculum.

The project approach is not new to elementary and early childhood education. It was part of the Progressive Education movement and was called the *project method* (Kirkpatrick, 1918). The British Infant Schools further developed the project method during the 1960s and 1970s. Interest has increased as documentation exhibits from the schools of Reggio Emilia, Italy, have revealed extraordinary understanding and representation by young children involved in projects. Research on brain development has also spurred interest in approaches that challenge children to think.

The project approach is similar to thematic teaching in the way content is integrated. A project on an ice cream store may involve reading stories about ice cream (literacy), surveying and graphing favorite flavors (math), or learning how ice cream becomes hard (science). The project approach is different from thematic teaching in the emphasis on child investigation and problem solving. In the process of investigating an ice cream shop, children might become interested in freezers—how they look, what they do, and where they come from. They might choose to interview an "expert" on freezers and refrigerators. Then they might decide to build a replica of a freezer, solving construction problems as they build. Because children follow their interests and answer their questions, they become emotionally involved and develop positive dispositions toward intellectual inquiry.

Projects begin with the selection of a topic. Topics emerge spontaneously from children's interest or are suggested by the teacher and then refined by the teacher working with the children. Before discussing the topic as a possible project, the teacher brainstorms and records her own knowledge of and experience with the topic. Selection of a topic is critical. Topics need to be relevant to children's lives, worthwhile, related to curriculum goals, and capable of firsthand exploration. Experts and field sites need to be available locally.

Phase 1

Once a topic has been identified, the project enters Phase 1, Beginning the Project. The teacher determines what children already know about the topic and what they want to know. A children's web is developed. Parents are alerted that a project is about to begin, and resources and materials are gathered.

Phase 2

In this phase, Developing the Project, the children do field work, interview experts, investigate real objects, and consult books and other research materials. Groups of children may investigate different aspects of the topic. For example, one group may do a survey of favorite ice cream flavors. Another may study signs in the store. When the class visits an ice cream shop, children are prepared to gather information through asking prepared questions, sketching, photographing, and bringing back artifacts to study. Class discussions keep everyone aware of the progress of the groups. Topic webs are updated with new knowledge.

Phase 3

During Phase 3, Concluding the Project, the children tell the story of their project. There may be a parents' night, demonstrations of play environments, class-made books, or an exhibit. A project lasts weeks or even months.

The teacher's ability to provide comprehensive, good-quality documentation is key to the success of this approach (Helm, Beneke, & Steinheimer, 1997). Documentation enables assessment of the knowledge and skills gained from the project experience. Careful and systematic recording of the project through notes, photos, journals, and videos enables the teacher also to evaluate and improve the project as it develops. Documentation captures for the teacher, parent, school administration, and the public a vision of the intellectual development and strengthening of the variety of intellectual and social dispositions that occur while children are involved in project research.

Engaging Children's Minds (Katz & Chard, 1989) provides an excellent introduction to projects. Sylvia Chard (1997) has two manuals, *Practical Guides to the Project Approach, I and II. Windows on Learning: Documenting Young Children's Work* (Helm, Beneke, & Steinheimer, 1997) includes documentation of the Mail Project in a prekindergarten classroom from first topic introduction to culminating event.

From Judy Harris Helm's description, it is clear that projects can be carried out independent of a theme. However, we suggest that projects also be treated as an extension of theme planning, wherein children truly become the source of instruction—determining thematic goals and direction. Projects that come about in this way usually evolve after children have had some exposure to the theme. As a result of participating in teacher-planned activities and group discussions, children begin to suggest related topics they would like to examine. These investigations become their projects. As children carry out projects, the teacher's job is to promote their learning using many of the teaching strategies found in Chapter 3 such as reflections, scaffolding, questions, and silence. Teachers also help children document their work and prompt them to reflect on what they have discovered.

Creating an Information Base

The core of every theme is the factual information on which it is founded and which is embodied in a comprehensive list of terms, facts, and principles (TFPs) relevant to the theme. These are similar in form to the TFPs you learned about in Chapter 3. Although the TFPs embody the theme, adults do not formally recite them to children. Instead they provide hands-on activities through which children derive factual information, learn relevant terminology, and engage in theme-related conversations with peers and adults. Through such experiences, youngsters gain meaningful insights that enlarge their concepts.

To be useful, TFPs must be accurate and thorough. Five steps are suggested for creating a suitable listing.

Step 1   Select a theme. Keep in mind relevance to children, hands-on activities, diversity and balance in the curriculum, the availability of theme-related props, and project potential.

Step 2   Use reference books, trade books, program-adopted textbooks, children's books, or other people as resources. From these, generate a master list of TFPs. Begin by writing down every item that seems relevant to the theme. At this point, do not worry about differentiating terms, facts, or principles.

Step 3   As the list grows, if subtopics become obvious, group the TFPs accordingly. For instance, a unit on cats might include the subtopics depicted in Figure 15.1. Brainstorm logical subtopics for the theme first, and then look up TFPs to support each one.

Step 4   Based on your understanding of the children's interests and abilities, decide whether a general overview or a more in-depth study of one of the subtopics is best suited to your class. If the former is true, choose a few TFPs from each of the subcategories; if the latter is your choice, focus primarily on one subset of TFPs.

FIGURE 15.1
Initial Topic Web for "Cats" Theme

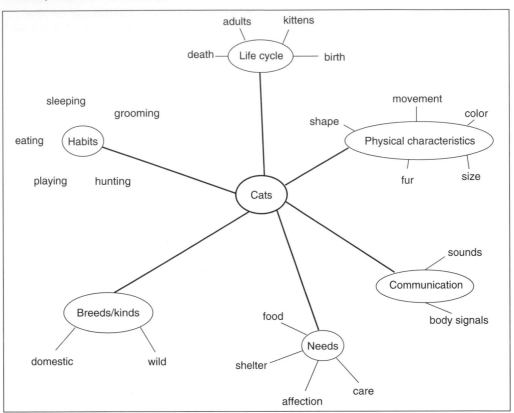

Step 5 Pick 10 to 15 TFPs on which to focus directly. Use the others simply as background information or as a guide in responding to children's questions regarding the topic.

Developing Activity Ideas

The steps for developing appropriate theme-related activities are straightforward and not nearly as time-consuming as those required to create TFPs.

Step 6 Brainstorm activities for each of the 10 to 15 TFPs you selected. Go through the TFPs one at a time, generating at least two or three activities per TFP. Do this with a colleague or in a small group to enhance the richness and variety of the activities generated. For instance, you might want children to learn that "People who own cats are responsible for providing them with food, shelter,

attention, and medical care." Sample activities to support this information could include (1) having children take care of a visitng cat for a day or week, (2) having children take care of pretend cats in the housekeeping area, (3) reading books about cat care, (4) visiting a veterinarian's office to witness cat care, (5) inviting a cat owner to visit the class to talk about how he or she takes care of a cat, and (6) creating collages that represent the different things people do to care for their cats.

Step 7 Assign each activity to one of the six curricular domains described in this text, making sure to have no less than one activity per domain per week. You might have a different number of theme-related activities in each domain. However, you should strive for some balance among them.

Depending on how you structure it, the same activity could be adapted to more than one domain.

Thus, a collage designed to help children represent different ways cat owners care for their cats takes on a social focus if children are asked to cooperate as a group to create one large collage. On the other hand, giving each child his or her own collage to work on, along with several different cutting tools, emphasizes the fine motor aspects of the activity, making it more physical in nature. Alternately, if the structure of the collage activity emphasizes children following step-by-step verbal directions, the focus shifts to listening skills (the language domain). With this example in mind, you can use the same activity to teach more than one thing on the same day or on different days.

Step 8 Make certain that the activities represent varying types of instruction as listed in Chapter 3 (i.e., exploratory activities, guided discovery, and problem-solving opportunities). If you become aware that the activities are dominated by watching or listening, redesign them to include more hands-on involvement.

Making a Plan

Once the TFPs and activities are fully developed, you can assemble them into a thematic plan. Such a plan typically covers no less than two week's instruction and may be extended for several weeks after that. The following steps outline the actual planning process.

Step 9 Commit your ideas to paper, incorporating several theme-related activities into your lesson plans. Some teachers plan each day on separate sheets of paper; others put an entire week's activities on a single sheet. Consider what time of the day certain activities will take place and whether each will be presented once or over several days. Design additional nontheme-related activities to fill in the rest of the instructional time and give children some respite from the theme. Remember, it is better to have fewer well-developed theme-related activities than to contrive to make activities fit. A daily plan for first graders engaged in a "cats" theme is offered in Figure 15.2.

Step 10 Check your plan to ensure at least three theme-related activities are included every day and that by week's end all of the domains have been included.

Step 11 If you are working with specialists such as art or music teachers, tell them the content of your theme. Explore with them ways they might support or complement children's concept development in their time with the class.

Step 12 Consider classroom management issues such as availability of materials, numbers of adults available to help, and special events. Adjust your plan as necessary. For instance, if you have scheduled easel painting and tie-dying for the same day and time but have only three smocks in your room, move one of these activities to another time in the day or to another day altogether so you will have enough smocks for children at both areas.

Step 13 Plan a portion of a group time to focus on the theme each day. Such whole-group activities allow children to become aware of certain concept-related information simultaneously, which provides a common foundation for exploration. Carried out at the beginning of class time, circle activities serve as an introduction to the day's experiences. Conducted at the end, they give children a chance to review and summarize their current understanding of the theme.

Step 14 Make a final check of your written plan, focusing on how well you have addressed the TFPs. Tally how often you have used each one. Refer to your original brainstorming list if you need a reminder of which activities relate to which TFPs. Verify that each TFP receives attention at least three or four times during the week. Also make sure that individual TFPs have been addressed within different domains across the plan. If you notice that some domains are seldom theme related or that certain TFPs are always addressed within the same domain, revise your plan to achieve better integration. In addition, if some TFPs have been left out or are underrepresented, either add a few related activities or extend the theme another week, focusing on these TFPs as well as some additional ones to give the children more time to explore the concept. In this way you will create two-, three-, and four-week units.

Step 15 After your plan is complete, gather your materials and create any props you will need. To minimize preparation time, use some props for more than one activity.

FIGURE 15.2

Daily Plan for First Graders Engaged in a "Cats" Theme

8:30–8:40 Arrival/Greeting	Greetings, attendance, lunch count, introduction to day's activities, and brief discussion of "home" cats
8:40–8:55 Journals	Each child keeps a journal. They may or may not choose to write in their own words about cats.
8:55–9:25 Large Group	Songs and movement; teacher reads "Freida the Wondercat!"; children retell story in their own words
9:25–10:30 Free Choice	Children select from the following activities; however, they must choose the reading group or study buddy activities sometime during this period.
Reading Group	Children meet the teacher for small-group reading. "Pretend You're a Cat" and "Cloudy the Cat" are the choices; groups are flexible/heterogeneous.
Study Buddies	Children work with a "study buddy" on an assigned activity.
Art Area	"Cat's Eye View" materials (black, white, and gray markers, pencils, charcoal, chalk, and paper), plus other free-choice art supplies
Blocks	Unit blocks, small plastic animals, including cats, measuring tools to measure cat habitats made from blocks
Book Corner	Selection of fiction and nonfiction books including several related to cats, listening center, peer reading, vocabulary cards
Math and Science	Cat classification, calico cat patterns, computer, eye color graphing, pulleys and gears, Numeral Bingo, counting to 100 activity cards, cause-and-effect science booklets
Pretend Play	Toy cats, cat beds, cat care books, cat toys, empty boxes of cat food, and water dishes added to the housekeeping area
Writers' Corner	Cat care booklets and other free-choice writing materials including several reference books

These activities are available for more than one day. The teacher adds and subtracts materials according to the group's needs.

10:30–10:50 Recess Outdoors	Children engage in physical activities; they may make cat movements as well as use the equipment and materials available
10:55–11:20 Story	Teacher reads from a chapter book; children are asked to recall events from previous chapters
11:25–12:00 Special	Music, art, library, or gym as assigned on the school's master schedule (time includes transition)
12:00–12:40 Lunch and Recess	

FIGURE 15.2
(continued)

12:40–1:00 Author's Chair/ Author's Circle	Children who have written and published books may read the work aloud, or children may read each other's books to the group
or	
Drop Everything and Read (D.E.A.R.)	Children and teacher get various reading materials and find a comfortable place to read quietly for 20–30 minutes
1:00–1:30 Whole-Group Math	Introduction to math/science activities; science available in centers later in the afternoon; may include demonstrations as well as children practicing a skill in small groups
1:30–2:30 Free Choice	Children select from center activities; however, they must choose the math/science center sometime during this period. Cat cookery (recipes from literature) added to math/science center after introduction at whole-group math time. Regrouping with manipulatives; children work in pairs. Other centers are similar to those in the morning. Children may work on their projects during this time as well.
2:30–2:40 Classroom Aerobics	
2:40–3:10 Group Projects	Children pursue self-selected projects, many of which will relate to the theme (e.g., creating a cat breed reference book, making a wild cat diorama, etc.)
3:10–3:20 Review and Departure	

Step 16   Create a thematic atmosphere in your classroom. Post theme-associated pictures at children's eye level. Choose CDs, videotapes, audiotapes, books, finger plays, and/or songs related to the topic.

Implementing the Theme

Once you have a sound plan, implement the theme. Let the following steps guide your actions.

Step 17   Carry out your plan. Also, take advantage of spontaneous events to further children's understanding of the concept they are exploring.

Step 18   Assess children's understanding of and interest in the theme through observations, interviews, group discussions, work samples, and constructions. Make note (mentally and/or through written anec-

dotes) of times when children talk about the theme, when they exhibit theme-related behaviors and knowledge, and when family members mention incidents illustrating children's awareness of and reactions to the topic. During the free-choice or learning center portion of your day, keep track of the activities children choose and the amount of time they spend there. A participation chart can help maintain this type of record (described in Chapter 16).

Step 19   Help children reflect on their understanding of thematic content and processes. Invite them to make drawings, graphs, murals, maps, constructions, journal entries, paintings, charts, and reports to represent what they have learned. Take photographs of the children's work. Keep work samples and include them in portfolios or display them for children to refer to.

The children's interest in a theme on tools has led them to examine rocks found near their school.

Step 20   Extend the theme if children's interest remains high. As children demonstrate understanding of and curiosity about the subject, introduce additional TFPs in subsequent weeks.

Step 21   Talk with children about what they want to know more about. Help them develop projects to address their questions and areas of curiosity.

Step 22   Establish two-way communication with families about the theme. Provide theme-related information to them through newsletters. Invite family members to contribute materials or their talents to the classroom. Suggest ways for family members to support the theme at home. Create opportunities for family members to share in the children's discoveries.

Step 23   Evaluate your implementation of the theme using the theme-teaching checklist presented in Figure 15.3. Write down the changes you made and how you might alter your plan if you decide to repeat it later.

Apples in the School Yard Prompt an Apple Theme

All of the steps involved in theme planning are illustrated in the following example of an "apple theme." As you read through this approach, consider how to adapt the theme for your children.

Step 1   The 4- and 5-year-olds in Hannah Solomon's preschool class noticed that two apples trees in the play yard were heavy with fruit. Eager to pick them, the children watched each day as the apples grew riper. Hannah decided that a theme about apples would interest the children and would also promote their observation skills and problem-solving abilities. Because the children lived in a community known for its apple orchards, she also thought it would be a good chance for them to become more aware of resources in their environment.

Steps 2 and 3   She prepared for the apple theme by looking up information about apples and making a list of terms, facts, and principles related to the concept. By not simply relying on her own knowledge, she discovered some facts about apples she had not known previously. As the list grew to around 25 items, she divided it into the following subsections: varieties of apples, physical characteristics, apples as food, apples' development from blossom to fruit, apples' journey from orchard to home, and apples as a cash crop.

Steps 4 and 5   Next, she narrowed the list to include 12 TFPs that would provide a general overview for the children to explore for at least two weeks. Here are 5 of the 12 she chose:

1. There are many kinds of apples.
2. Apples vary in size, shape, color, texture, smell, and taste.
3. People eat apples in many forms.
4. Apples grow on trees.
5. Apples are the fruit of the apple tree.

Step 6   Hannah brainstormed activities to go with each TFP. See how her ideas compare with yours. Would you add others to this list?

❏ *There are many kinds of apples.* ACTIVITIES: Select different varieties of apples at an orchard or a store, match the different apple types to their name, look at paintings that include apples, create apple paintings, look through seed and fruit catalogues that show various kinds of apples

❏ *Apples vary in size, shape, color, texture, smell, and taste.* ACTIVITIES: Examine different kinds of apples, make a chart graphing apple differences, generate a list of words that describe apple characteristics, create apple books with one page for each variety—list the

FIGURE 15.3
Theme Teaching Checklist

Purpose: To help teachers assess the effectiveness of theme implementation in their classrooms

Directions: Put a 1 by each item that accurately depicts the classroom being observed. Total the items to achieve a final score.

Score	Level of Effectiveness
23–25	Excellent use of themes
20–22	Good use of themes; minor additions could make it better
17–19	OK start; gradually address missing items in order to improve
16 and below	Poor use of themes; major revisions necessary

Theme-Related Activities

❏ 1. The theme planner can convey the relevance of the theme to children.
❏ 2. The theme-related information is accurate.
❏ 3. The theme-related information is meaningful to children (of interest to them and age appropriate in vocabulary and detail).
❏ 4. Two or more theme-related *firsthand experiences* are available each week.
❏ 5. At least two theme-related activities are available every day.
❏ 6. Theme-related activities take place at different times throughout the day.
❏ 7. Every week at least one theme-related activity is included for each of the six domains.
❏ 8. Children have opportunities to apply, synthesize, and summarize what they have learned about the theme throughout the week.

Child Involvement

❏ 9. Children are talking about the theme (offering information, asking questions, conversing with peers and adults).
❏ 10. Children are pretending in relation to the theme.
❏ 11. Children are creating theme-related products of their own invention.
❏ 12. Children report discussing or playing the theme at home.
❏ 13. Children demonstrate linking the theme to their past or current experiences either motorically or verbally.
❏ 14. Family members report that children have discussed or played the theme at home.
❏ 15. Children continue to refer to the theme or demonstrate knowledge of its content after the unit is over.

Classroom Environment

❏ 16. TFPs are posted or otherwise available for adult reference.
❏ 17. Children's own theme-related creations (projects, writings, etc.) are displayed in the room.
❏ 18. Theme-related props are available to the children each day.
❏ 19. Theme-related pictures, songs, poems, books, and so on are used to create a thematic atmosphere.
❏ 20. One circle time each day is theme related.
❏ 21. The theme-related purpose of the circle time is made clear to the children.
❏ 22. Theme-related circle time activities include active child participation.

Family Involvement

❏ 23. Family members receive information about the theme.
❏ 24. Family members are invited to contribute to the theme.
❏ 25. Family members receive feedback regarding children's interest and participation in the theme.

characteristics, sort apples, taste apples (seriate the apples from sweetest to most sour; seriate the apples from juiciest to least juicy), select favorite apples

❏ *People eat apples in many forms.* ACTIVITIES: Examine different apple products (raw apple, apple sauce, apple juice), make an apple product such as apple sauce, create a lotto game using apple product pictures or labels, create a grocery store in which children pretend to buy and sell apple products

❏ *Apples grow on trees.* ACTIVITIES: Examine an apple tree, examine apple leaves, do a bark rubbing, trace or paint with apple leaves, read fiction and nonfiction books about how apples grow, create a make-believe orchard in which children pretend to pick apples, go on a field trip to pick apples, read a book about how apple trees appear during the different seasons, construct apple trees out of art materials, make apple tree puzzles

❏ *Apples are the fruit of the apple tree.* ACTIVITIES: Examine seeds inside apple, examine dried apple blossoms, read a story about how the blossom becomes fruit, predict how many seeds will be in the different varieties of apples

Steps 7 and 8   Hannah could see that she had a wide array of firsthand activities to support children's learning. Next, she assigned the activities to different domains referring to the intermediate objectives for each one. For TFP 1 she developed the following list:

❏ Select different varieties of apples at an orchard or a store—affective (focus on the choosing process)
❏ Match the different apple types to their name—language (focus on language labels)
❏ Look at paintings that include different kinds of apples—aesthetic (focus on the color and design elements of the art)
❏ Create paintings that include different kinds of apples—aesthetic (focus on color and design elements while painting)
❏ Look through seed and fruit catalogues that show various kinds of apples—cognition (focus on the social-conventional knowledge related to the names of different varieties)

Hannah repeated this process for each TFP. She looked over the complete list to make sure she had included many exploratory, guided discovery, and problem-solving activities as well as some demonstrations, cooperative learning, discussions, and directed instruction activities. Convinced that she had a good selection of activities, she began to commit her ideas to paper.

Steps 9 through 14   Hannah created the weekly plan presented in Figure 15.4. She made adjustments to make sure she did not have too many "star" activities (ones involving a lot of adult supervision) on any one day and that there were both theme-related and non-theme-related activities daily. She also paid attention to the sequence of thematic activities throughout the week, so that certain activities could lead up to or build upon others. For instance, in the art area on Tuesday, Hannah hung three still-life paintings of apples by different artists in different styles for the children to enjoy. Over the next few days she drew the children's attention to the paintings, especially their color and design. The following week, Hannah provided a bowl of apples of different varieties along with watercolors and poster paints for the children to make their own still life arrangements and paintings. In this way, she used the Week 1 art activity to lead to another activity planned for Week 2.

Steps 15 and 16   Hannah gathered relevant materials and prepared the classroom. She asked families to contribute any materials they might have (such as favorite stories or songs) and invited a parent who was an orchard grower to visit the class.

Steps 17 through 19   Hannah implemented the theme pretty much as indicated on her written plan. However, on Tuesday a child brought in two pieces of fruit that resembled apples but which were actually Korean pears. Intrigued by their similarity, some children spent much of the free-choice time comparing the fruits and graphing their similarities and differences. In the second week, they created pictures, paintings, and charts of their experiences.

Steps 20 and 21   After two weeks, Hannah conducted a circle time in which she and the children talked about what they had learned, what they still wanted to learn, and how they might go about doing so. Several children were interested in finding out more about how apples from Oregon went to stores all

FIGURE 15.4

Sample Weekly Plan, Apple Theme, Week 1, Introduction

Time/Routine	Area	Monday	Tuesday	Wednesday	Thursday	Friday
8:30–8:45 A.M. Greeting Time	Group-time rug	Children arrive,	Greetings, job chart,		Introduction to	Day's activities
8:45–10:00 Free choice	Art area	Making play dough; tools available include apple cookie cutters and apple shapes to trace	Easel painting on apple shapes / Apple still-life pictures to enjoy		Sponge painting with apple shapes and red, yellow, and green paint (1,2,3)	Cooperative color mixing
	Blocks	Unit blocks with	vehicles		human figures	cardboard trees
	Library	Apple catalogs	Apple posters / Flannel board: "The Apple and the Worm"		*How Do Apples Grow?* by B. Maestro. *The Seasons of Arnold's Apple Tree* by G. Gibbons	Big Book: *Down the Road* by Alice Shertle
	Writer's nook	Class surveys	Apple adjectives		Apple books	
	Fine motor	Making apple tree puzzles with a friend / Lacing apple shapes	Cutting activity		Peeling apples for snack	Cutting activity
	Math and science	Numeral bingo / Pulleys and levers / Apple sorting	Magnets / Apple seed estimates		Ramps with rollers / Seriating apples by taste, touch, smell, size, and look	Counting apple seeds / Making apple sauce
	Open snack	Apple juice, crackers, and peanut butter	Dried apples, toast, and low fat cheese cubes	Snack at orchard	Tasting three kinds of apples	Charting apple favorites (juice, sauce, raw)
	Pretend play	Pretend orchard— trees, apples, bushel baskets, cash register materials for sign making plus house-keeping	Add pie-making materials to house		Add props to orchard as suggested by children	

Field trip to the orchard

(continued on the next page)

FIGURE 15.4
(continued)

Time/Routine	Area	Monday	Tuesday	Wednesday	Thursday	Friday
9:55—Warning for cleanup		Pairs of children clean up			Children self-select cleanup area and decide what needs to be done	
10:00–10:10 cleanup						
10:10–10:30 Large group	Group-time rug	Flannel board: "The Apple and the Worm" Two little apples hanging on a tree	Preparation for Orchard field trip Discussion		Thank-you note to orchard–group writing experience and reflection on trip	Book: *Down the Road* by Alice Shertle
10:30 to 10:35 Transition outdoors						
10:40–11:20 Outdoor time	Playground 1	Apple tree investigations—materials for bark rubbings, magnifying glasses, small plastic bags for collecting apple tree items, chart paper for recording observations	Musical hoops	Return from orchard during this time—transition to playground if weather is good	Apple tree investigations—materials for bark rubbings, magnifying glasses, small plastic bags for collecting apple tree items, chart paper for recording observations	Wheeled carts
11:20–11:30 Transition indoors	Bathroom handwashing					
11:30 A.M.–12:00 P.M. Lunch	Classroom	Set a place for a friend			Set a place for a friend	
12:00–12:15 Transition home	Saying farewell to friends					

Items listed here are provided in addition to the standard materials always available to children indoors and outside.

Tally of Theme-Related Activities: Aesthetic Activities = 3, Affective Activities = 2, Cognitive Activities = 6, Language Activities = 6, Physical Activities = 3, Social Activities = 4 over the country. Others were interested in finding out people's favorite apple recipes. Some children wanted to know if people had apples everywhere in the world. Hannah and the children carried out investigative projects over several days to answer these questions.

Step 22   Throughout the time the children were involved in learning about apples, Hannah communicated with families through individual notes home and a classroom newsletter. Family members provided favorite apple recipes for the class and were also invited to join the field trip to the orchard. As the theme neared a conclusion, children, teachers, and family members gathered to hear what the children had learned and to sample apple butter made by the class.

Step 23   Hannah formally evaluated the theme using the theme-teaching checklist and individual performance checklists in some activity areas each day. She also kept a journal to remind herself of things she would want to consider in future renditions of the theme. Here are two sample entries.

September 20: *The children enjoyed making apples to put on the trees in the pretend orchard. It was exciting to see them consult the catalogues to determine which variety to make. Having several different catalogues on hand was a good idea. Albert and Johan argued about whether two different kind of apples could grow on the same tree. This will be important to follow up on at the orchard.*

Hint for next time—Don't use the paper punch. Its holes are too large, and the brass fasteners pull through. Get a different, smaller punch, or have the children poke holes in the (paper) apple stem with a sharp pencil point.

October 6: *I found two apple cookie cutters in a kitchen store. They came with three cookie recipes: Sour Cream, Chocolate, and Gingerbread. The gingerbread won when we voted on our choice. I invited three family members (two moms and a dad) to come and help with the small groups. I acted as the gofer. We used all the tables in the room and covered them with split-open garbage bags. The children loved this! They mixed the ingredients and proudly accompanied their cookies to the kitchen for baking. The results were yummy. This was the first time I tried having all the children carry out the same small-group activity simultaneously. They were happily absorbed. No one wandered off or got bored. There was a*

lot of structuring involved in getting this together, but the sense of community and the children's pride in having measured all the ingredients themselves was worth it.

Hint for next time—Send a copy of the recipes home in the newsletter. I did, and families were pleased.

Although the apple theme was drawing to a close, Hannah made a note to herself to periodically take the children out to observe the apple trees in the play yard throughout the late fall, winter, and spring. She believed that ongoing observation would promote their interest in the seasonal cycle of the apple trees and in how the trees provide shelter and food for various animals and insects.

The next theme the children in this class undertake could be a spin-off from the apple theme, such as "trees," "insects," or "stores." In this way, one theme leads to another, providing conceptual links among several topics and a sense of intellectual coherence for children and teachers. On the other hand, the class's interests may move in an entirely different direction. "Poetry," "pottery," or "physical fitness" may be topics that intrigue them next. What prompts the development of each new theme will be unique for every group.

Now that you have seen a sample theme described from start to finish, let us consider the most common questions teachers have about theme planning, implementation, and evaluation.

COMMON QUESTIONS ABOUT THEMES

How Can I Ease Into Theme Teaching?

At first, follow these suggestions:

❑ Choose familiar topics for themes.
❑ Plan theme-related activities in the domains with which you feel most comfortable.
❑ Plan two or three theme-related activities each day.
❑ Incorporate theme-related materials during the portions of the day easiest for you to plan (e.g., large-group time, free-choice time, or outdoor time)

As your theme teaching skills increase, consider these suggestions:

❑ Branch out; select themes less well known to you.
❑ Gradually increase the domains in which you plan theme-related activities until all six are included.

❑ Increase the number of theme-related activities you plan each day, working toward a goal of four or five.
❑ Incorporate the theme into several parts of the day.

Must Every Activity Relate to the Theme?

As noted, effective daily and weekly plans include both theme-related and nontheme-related activities. However, this is such a commonly asked question that the answer bears repeating. Although it is important to have several theme-related activities each day, it is preferable to create a mix of theme- and nontheme-oriented activities each week. In half-day programs, the minimum number of theme-related activities is three or four, with one of these taking place during a group time. For full-day programs, an average of three activities in each half day works reasonably well. At least some portion of a group time should also be devoted to an aspect of the theme.

If the class is saturated by a given topic or the theme goes on too long, the subject loses its appeal for children and teachers alike. Moreover, the link between activities and the concept becomes contrived rather than obvious and real. Some nontheme-related activities interspersed throughout your teaching plan will provide a respite from the topic and enable you to address necessary skills unrelated to the theme. Reprising children's favorites, reviewing past experiences, and including subject-based activities whose content is mandated by the program curriculum are appropriate alternatives. Take time also to create activities that introduce children to new content that might be expanded upon in the future. These activities will allow you to gauge children's interest in and knowledge of untried topics.

Is It OK That When I Get an Idea for a Theme, I Immediately Think of Related Activities and Start to Plan?

As soon as you settle on a topic, it is natural to start thinking of activities that could fit into a theme on that subject. Although it is tempting to create an entire theme this way, it neglects the essential step of linking activities to the specific information you want to convey to the children. The result may be activities that lack breadth, depth, balance, or cohesion. For instance, you could end up generating activities that focus on a narrow range of content while inadvertently overlooking aspects of the theme that are useful for children to explore. Another outcome might be activities that are entertaining but not necessarily educational. Avoid these pitfalls by working from the TFPs to the activities rather than the other way around or skipping the TFPs altogether. The steps for theme planning always proceed in the following order:

$$\text{Concept} \longrightarrow \text{TFPs} \longrightarrow \text{Activity Ideas}$$

If you neglect the TFPs or address these three steps out of sequence, your theme is *not* likely to be effective.

How Long Does a Typical Unit Last?

It depends on the children's needs and interests and how you have structured the topic. Although some themes may last only a week or two, most others will last much longer. For instance, several days on "pumpkins" might cover the topic nicely. On the other hand, three or four weeks devoted to "seeds" may barely scratch the surface of possible information or children's curiosity about the topic. Similarly, one class could find two weeks devoted to the "kitchen" to be plenty. Another group of children might be so intrigued by the kitchen and what goes on there that they will choose to carry out a variety of projects regarding this important place in their center. The less experience children have with a concept, the more time they need to explore it. For example, youngsters who have had many opportunities to go to their local library or bookmobile may find that three weeks is enough time to learn more about them. On the other hand, children who have few books at home and have never visited a library may enjoy and profit from several weeks focusing on these related ideas.

Exercise judgment in determining the most fitting approach for your class. Many teachers report that two- to three-week themes (with an optional follow-up week) work well. If you anticipate that children will become involved in projects as a result of the theme, even more time will be necessary.

In addition, you should *beware of teaching an entire year of themes that last only one week each.* One-week themes are too brief to do more than survey a few bits of information. The short time frame denies children opportunities to become absorbed in a topic, conduct personal investigations into the concept it represents, and come away with new understanding.

Different weekly themes also force teachers to shift gears too quickly to put together a cohesive, well-considered set of plans.

Is There a Difference Between Planning Themes for 3- and 4-Year-Olds and Planning Ones for 6- to 8-Year-Olds?

The process of planning and implementing themes is the same regardless of children's ages. Selecting a topic, creating the TFPs, generating activity ideas, planning the unit, and carrying it out are steps required for every theme. However, themes vary in terms of TFPs selected and the concepts chosen for study based on the children's ages and their prior experience with the theme. To make age-appropriate and individually appropriate differentiations, divide the TFPs into two categories: simple and advanced.

Simple TFPs consist of terms or facts that can be observed or experienced by the children directly through their own activity (although they might not be able to put them into actual words). Existing in the here and now rather than the future or past, simple TFPs do not require teacher explanations. Adult talk may reinforce children's self-discoveries, but it is never a substitute for direct experience. Principles, because they often involve abstractions, are not identified as simple. For example, the theme "clothing" could be supported by the following simple terms and facts:

Terms Specialized names for certain articles of clothing are poncho, helmet, yarmulke, kimono, vest, kilt, turban, kaftan, and so on.

Facts Certain articles of clothing go on certain parts of the body. Clothes have different fasteners: buckles, buttons, snaps, zippers, ties, and Velcro. Clothing comes in a variety of sizes, shapes, colors, patterns, and textures. People wear clothing for different reasons.

Children engaged in activities and routines in the classroom could incorporate all of these terms and facts into their concept of clothing based on actual experience.

Advanced TFPs, on the other hand, are ones children often learn about through representational experiences such as pictures, models, or discussions. Advanced TFPs may refer to past or future events or events that take place outside the classroom and may also require children to envision something mentally in order to comprehend them. That cows have four legs is a simple fact because it is readily observable both in real cows and toy cows in the classroom. The fact that cows have multiple stomachs is advanced because it must be represented by a picture, diagram, or discussion and requires children to envision the internal workings of a cow without experiencing them directly. Advanced TFPs consist of more elaborate or enigmatic vocabulary and more complicated facts and principles. Because of these TFPs' complexity or abstractness, children generally need more opportunities and time to grasp them than is usually true for simple TFPs. Advanced TFPs related to the theme "clothing" are given in the following examples:

Terms When two pieces of fabric are sewn together, the joining point is called a *seam. Natural* fibers are made from animals or plants. *Synthetic* fibers are made from chemicals.

Facts People make leather from the skins of various animals. People created synthetic fibers for many reasons: strength, durability, ease of care, and so on.

Principle In choosing clothing they like, people may be influenced by advertising or other's opinions.

This designation of simple and advanced TFPs will help you to identify which category of TFPs to emphasize when working with a particular group of children. Simple TFPs should be used with 3-, 4- and 5-year-olds and older children who have little experience with the theme. Advanced TFPs are more appropriate for kindergartners who know the theme well and for children in the early primary grades as well as youngsters beyond the early childhood period. This stratification makes it possible to choose a subset of TFPs that best corresponds to the needs of your class. Depending on the concept to be addressed, the subset may be composed of TFPs representing either or both levels of difficulty.

The criteria that differentiate simple TFPs from advanced ones may also be applied to concepts overall. Concepts that deal with the here and now and that youngsters can explore through numerous hands-on experiences are most suitable for young children. Examples are clothing, water, plants, textures, books, and people at school. Children can explore all of these topics in the near environment of their classroom, play yard, or neighborhood. They do not rely on a one-time field trip or visitor as the children's only real experience with the concept. Neither must children try to remember or mentally envision something they have never experienced directly in order to think about the concept meaningfully. Concepts dependent on these latter forms of experience are more abstract and would be considered advanced. Samples are the circus (dependent on children remembering or envisioning a circus experience), communicating (focuses on actions rather than tangible objects), and the eye (focuses on representations such as models and diagrams to illustrate how the eye functions). Advanced concepts are better used with children toward the latter phases of the early childhood period and beyond.

How Do I Fit in Theme Teaching With So Much Required Content to Cover?

Theme teaching is not an add-on. It is not another strand to be incorporated into the day's instruction, nor is it an additional layer to be added to an already bursting curriculum. Teaching from themes is a strategy for breaking away from rigid compartmentalization of subject matter and the traditional use of designated time blocks.

Because time is limited in early childhood classrooms, efficient teachers do not confine subjects only to certain slots in the day. Teachers who attempt this find they run out of time without having adequately addressed all areas of the curriculum. In particular, we have learned over the past decade that knowledge, processes, and skills related to science, social studies, health, and the arts suffer most in this regard (Jalongo, 1990; Malecki, 1990). Yet the concepts associated with these subjects are essential to children's understanding of their experiences and the world around them. In response to this dilemma, professionals in a variety of disciplines are advocating a more holistic, interdisciplinary approach to educating children at all grade levels and across all subjects (Freeman & Sokoloff, 1996; Heibert & Fisher, 1990; Hurd, 1990; Kovalik, 1997). Consequently, it is a good idea to create some themes each year focusing on concepts generally associated with underrepresented portions of the curriculum. Also, by using required content as a source for themes and the

development of related TFPs, you can combine previously isolated subjects or skills (e.g., science and writing; social studies and math; health and reading; speaking, reading, and writing; or art and critical thinking). This makes the day less fragmented, allowing children and teachers more time to explore topics in depth.

Aren't Themes Too Time Consuming for Most Teachers to Prepare?

Theme planning does take time. However, as with any skill, practice leads to greater speed and mastery. The most time-consuming element in developing any theme is generating an accurate list of TFPs. Once that is accomplished, the rest of the planning steps take only an hour or two. One shortcut that saves time is to use commercially prepared thematic units as a base for creating your own. A few that include TFPs or similar factual content to get you started follow.

Themes Teachers Use, Marjorie J. Kostelnik (Ed.). Scott, Foresman, and Company, 1996.

Creative Resources for the Early Childhood Classroom, Judith Herr and Yvonne Libby. Delmar, 1995.

A Practical Guide to Early Childhood Curriculum, Claudia F. Eliason and Loa T. Jenkins. Merrill-MacMillan, 1994.

Teaching Young Children Using Themes, Marjorie J. Kostelnik (Ed.). Scott, Foresman, and Company, 1991.

Resources for Creative Teaching in Early Childhood Education, Darlene S. Hamilton and Bonnie M. Flemming. Harcourt Brace Jovanovich, 1990.

Early childhood professionals report that working with colleagues is more efficient than working alone, especially in the beginning. Start by collaborating with one or more teachers on the same theme. Brainstorm ideas and create props you all can use. Later, move to an arrangement in which you each plan different themes. Generate TFPs, activity ideas, and props to share. This reduces the number of themes you have to create from scratch. In subsequent years, revise already developed themes but continue to add new units to your collection to better address the needs of different groups of children.

Educators find working together on theme ideas satisfying and stimulating.

Is It Ever Appropriate to Repeat a Theme During the Year?

It is, but also remember that concept learning does not stop simply because a particular unit ends. Children will continue to explore and apply related knowledge and skills within subsequent themes. Although they will do this spontaneously, it is useful for teachers to plan some activities throughout the year that call for children to retrieve content and processes explored previously.

Second, some concepts are greatly enriched when they receive formal instructional attention for several days at different times of the year. As a good example, a leaf theme could be introduced in the fall and then repeated in the spring, building on what children learned earlier as well as contrasting leaves and leaf growth during two different seasons. Likewise, some teachers begin the year with a unit on friends, the primary aim of which is to help children "discover" one another and create a sense of cohesiveness within the class. Later in the year they return to the concept "friends" as a means of reinforcing social harmony and addressing more advanced TFPs that the children, now more thoroughly acquainted, are ready to explore.

What About Repeating Themes From One Program Level to the Next?

Sometimes teachers and family members worry about children revisiting certain themes as they move from

the 3-year-old room to the 4-year-old class or from kindergarten to first grade. Thinking children may get bored or will not learn anything new, they need to remember that children learn through repetition. Having opportunities to explore familiar concepts further is not only worthwhile; it is the best way for children to expand their understanding by building on what they already know. Each time children participate in a given theme, they glean new insights and skills from the experience. No one period of investigation is ever complete or offers children all they want or need to know about a topic. Consequently, repeating some themes from one year to the next is an effective instructional strategy.

On the other hand, simply rehashing the *exact same* material year after year may not provide enough stimulation to hold children's interest or enhance their concept development. To avoid this problem, teachers within the same program can plan similar themes to draw children's attention to different facets. They can also use multiyear themes to help children move from focusing on simple TFPs to more advanced ones. For instance, dinosaurs, a topic beloved by children throughout the later early childhood period, is one they often request. It may be covered two or three years in a row, which makes it an ideal vehicle for collaborative planning among teachers at different levels of the program. Such a plan could be formulated, keeping in mind that 6-year-olds are fascinated by the terms associated with dinosaurs, especially their names. Simple facts regarding dinosaurs' physical characteristics are also appealing to them. Second graders, already familiar with dinosaur names, continue to be intrigued with the physical attributes of dinosaurs as well as where they lived and how they protected themselves. By third grade, children who have experienced the theme twice before tend to be no less enthusiastic about dinosaurs, but they may have moved into exploring more advanced facts (e.g., why dinosaurs became extinct) as well as considering principles (e.g., attributes of the jaw and teeth are what distinguish meat eaters from plant eaters). Creating a programwide plan that incorporates this developmental progression from simple to complex and from concrete to more abstract supports children's interest in the theme. It also gives each teacher a chance to offer children opportunities for new insights. Obviously, the more often teachers within the same program talk to and collaborate with one another regarding theme planning, the more likely it is that they will complement rather than duplicate one another's efforts.

Is There One Best Way to Cover Particular Concepts?

Every theme can be approached from a variety of angles with potential benefits for children. To illustrate this point, a unit on storytelling could be carried out in either of the following ways.

Option 1

Week	Content
1–2	Fictional stories
3–4	True stories
5	Children as storytellers
6	Children select projects
7	Children's projects continue this week and the next two or three weeks if appropriate

Option 2

Week	Content
1	Story of the week (e.g., "Three Bears") or author of the week (e.g., Ezra Jack Keats, Barbara Cooney)
2	New story or new author or previous author continued
3	Children select projects
4	Children's projects continue.

Another approach is to choose a major concept like "the pond" or "people living together" to guide your planning for several months or even all year. These overarching concepts provide a unifying mechanism that not only permits choice but also creates a link from one theme to another. Thus, children and teachers together might choose "insects," "frogs and toads," "waterfowl," "aquatic plant life," and "water," all as part of the comprehensive concept of "the pond." In this fashion, one teacher planned an entire year around the idea of "life beneath, on, and above the Earth's surface." At the beginning of the year, she and the children chose "soil," "rocks," and "worms," —themes they associated with life beneath the surface of the Earth. By midyear, their investigations had moved above ground. "Mapping," "water," "plants," "animal habitats," and "human habitats" were topics they explored. As the year came to a close, children and teacher turned their attention to life in the sky as they explored "clouds," "air transportation," "birds," and "sky legends."

Obviously, more than one way is effective in approaching thematic teaching. Your own personal preferences as well as children's interests, their prior knowledge, availability of props and other support materials, and resource people will influence your choices.

What About Having All My Themes Revolve Around Holidays?

A common preprimary and elementary practice is to formulate themes that highlight the holiday of the month. Weeks at a time center around Halloween, Christmas, St. Patrick's Day, Washington's Birthday, Groundhog Day, and so forth. For some programs, holidays are the core of the curriculum, yet a number of potential problems are inherent in this approach.

First, such themes run the risk of being little more than a convenient backdrop for children's participation in numerous craft projects, with minimal attention paid to either content or process learning (Kostelnik, 1996). Youngsters usually come away from these units without having increased their skills or expanded their conceptualizations.

Second, when children spend an entire month focusing on Halloween or St. Patrick's Day, those times come to dominate children's lives. They take on a disproportionate importance in comparison to the more common and relevant phenomena that constitute children's real-life experiences.

A third risk is the inadvertent teaching of cultural or religious stereotypes. For instance, in many schools across the country, November marks the time when children hear about pilgrims and Native Americans. All too often, Native Americans are depicted as wearing feathers in their hair, dancing, and war whooping while their real contributions helping the pilgrims are overlooked (Hendrick, 1996). Moreover, Thanksgiving is presented as a time of universal celebration and feasting. Although true for many people, some Native Americans fast at this time and view the day as one of mourning in remembrance of the many tragedies suffered by native people following the arrival of the first white settlers (Heinrich, 1977; Little-Soldier, 1990; Ramsey, 1979). Equitable treatment of the subject demands a balanced point of view that would be too abstract for most young children. Yet, promoting the traditional stereotypes, assuming they will be altered or undone when children are older, is risky, because such corrections may never happen.

Similarly, a theme that promotes children's creation of Easter baskets, Easter rabbits, parading in Easter finery, and playing Easter bunny math games presupposes that every family celebrates this particular holiday or that such items and activities are nonreligious symbols of spring. Both notions are erroneous. These practices trivialize the day and violate the principle of respect for religious differences, making it inappropriate.

Finally, because there is so little time in formal group settings to cover every important topic, it is best to omit ones that focus on social-conventional knowledge to which children are heavily exposed outside the classroom. Holidays fall into this category and thus are not the worthiest topics for large chunks of instructional time. Having fewer holiday themes allows more opportunities to explore concepts for which program support adds richness, variety, and a dimension not so easily obtained elsewhere (Deardon, 1984).

Eliminating holidays as the *sole* basis for theme planning does not mean ignoring them altogether. Instead, teachers may incorporate these special times into the context of a larger concept such as "celebrations" or "family traditions." Both of these themes, for example, could support a wide array of TFPs, as illustrated in Figure 15.5. Such concepts tend to be inclusive rather than exclusive in nature. They support children's

growing awareness and appreciation of similarities as well as differences among people.

Additionally, integrating Valentine's Day into the more global theme "friends," using Halloween to pique children's interest in "costumes and masks," or exploring and comparing rituals in the home associated with Christmas, Hanukkah, and Kwanza through a unit on "families" or "homes" are all ways to acknowledge and enjoy holidays as they occur, while making more relevant connections to children's lives.

Finally, holiday customs need not be confined only to holiday times. Instead, a variety of observances could be highlighted within such generic themes as "clothing," "seasons," "storytelling," or "healthy foods" and could be carried out at any time of the year, incorporating rituals, games, props, and foods associated with various holidays.

How Do I Know That Children Are Developing More Sophisticated, Complex Concepts?

Children reveal their conceptual understandings through play, conversations with peers and adults, questions, errors, methods of investigating objects and events, products, and representations. To find out what children know, observe and talk with them about the concept. Give children opportunities to talk and interact with their peers, and provide open-ended activities through which they can explore the concept in their own way. Encourage them to represent what they have learned through drawings, charts, writings, dictation, and so forth. Make notes about what you see and hear using the assessment techniques described in Chapter 16.

Should I Expect Every Child to Demonstrate the Same or Equal Levels of Understanding?

First, presume that children come to your program already possessing rudimentary concepts about themselves and the world in which they live. Assume, too, that because each child's experiences are unique to him or her, the exact makeup of these concepts will differ from child to child. Youngsters may have some conceptual understandings in common, but they will also exhibit gaps in their knowledge that do not exactly

FIGURE 15.5
Terms, Facts, and Principles: "Family Traditions"

---

1. A family tradition is an activity families repeat in much the same way time after time.

2. Traditions are an important part of family life.

3. All families have traditions, such as special songs, celebrations, foods, activities, stories, recollections, routines, rules, beliefs, and values.

4. Family celebrations are often influenced by tradition:

   - Particular foods may be prepared.
   - A certain sequence of events may be followed.*
   - Special clothing may be worn.
   - Special songs may be sung.
   - Special stories may be told.
   - People may have special roles within the celebration.*
   - Special activities may be carried out

5. Families vary in the traditions they observe.

6. A family's religious and/or cultural heritage influences the traditions they adopt.*

7. Traditions help family members feel close to one another.

8. Some family traditions have been carried out for many years, and some are relatively new.*

9. Some traditions are very elaborate; others are quite simple.

10. Sometimes outsiders are invited to participate in a family tradition, and sometimes only the family participates.

11. Every family has stories or anecdotes about how certain traditions developed or how certain family members were involved in family traditions.

12. Photographs, home videos, or cassette recordings are often used to record traditional family events.

Source: These TFPs were developed by Laura C. Stein, M. S., Specialist, Department of Family and Child Ecology, Michigan State University. Those marked with an asterisk are advanced.

match one another's. As children participate in theme-related activities, they will take away meaning that is relevant to them. Again, the insights children experience will vary. Your role is to help them expand or alter their concepts in ways that are personally meaningful to them by using the teaching strategies in this text.

SUMMARY

Coordinating activities around a central theme has long been a tradition in early childhood education.

The benefits to youngsters, practitioners, and programs are many. Nonetheless, the greatest value of theme teaching lies in its use as a concept organizer. As young children engage in activities permeated by the same basic idea, they connect individual bits of knowledge and perceptions and form more comprehensive, accurate concepts. Such positive outcomes, however, result only when practitioners keep in mind principles of developmentally appropriate practice as well as those of effective theme teaching. The latter include relying on children's interests and capacities to influence theme selection and direction; focusing on the conceptual nature of thematic teaching; using an accurate, thorough body of factual information to support the theme; emphasizing firsthand learning as well as real objects in carrying out the theme; and integrating thematic activities across domains, subject areas, and parts of the day.

Creating thematic units involves several steps. The first is to select a topic. Ideas for themes most often come from the children but may also be initiated by special events or unexpected happenings in the program, school-mandated content, or teacher/family interests. In addition, potential topics must be screened for relevance to children and conduciveness to many hands-on experiences. How well each theme contributes to diversity and balance across the curriculum, the availability of theme-oriented resources, and the theme's potential to engage children in projects of their own choosing are other factors to consider when choosing themes.

Once an idea has been settled on, the next step is to create an accurate information base to support the concept under study. To do this, practitioners research relevant terms, facts, and principles (TFPs), which serve as the basis for activity development. Thus, each theme-related activity has its source within the factual base for that theme. This link between content and experience increases the accuracy of the information and elevates theme teaching beyond mere entertainment. To increase their educational value further, activities related to the theme also represent a variety of domains and learning modes.

Making a plan is the third phase of theme teaching. It involves distributing theme-related activities throughout your weekly lessons and across all parts of the day. Although it is important to have several theme-related activities included in the plan to make the links among them easier for children to grasp, not every activity in a day or week must focus on the theme. In fact, children and adults benefit when some theme-independent activities are offered. Such experiences give participants a break from the theme, help ensure that activities are not contrived, and enable teachers to address important knowledge and skills that do not match the central topic.

The last phase of theme teaching involves implementing, evaluating, and revisiting the theme as children become engaged in the topic. Within this chapter, a theme teaching checklist has been provided as a tool for assessing theme implementation in classrooms as well as children's theme-related learning. Educators' potential questions regarding theme teaching have also been posed and answered.

In sum, theme teaching is a valuable instructional tool when used properly. Practitioners who have never engaged in this kind of teaching may find it time consuming at first. Nevertheless, as their familiarity with the process increases, so will their speed and efficiency in carrying it out. Collaboration among colleagues is another way to make the process easier and richer. Moreover, as children come to the program eager to know "what we're talking about this week" and make connections between the information and processes they experience, educators will sense the rewards of this kind of teaching. Helping to make sense of what could otherwise be fragmented educational events is a plus both children and teachers will enjoy.

✖ Applying What You Read in This Chapter

1. **Discuss**
   a. Based on your reading and your experiences with young children, discuss each of the questions that open this chapter.
   b. The children in your classroom are excited about the new apartment building under construction across the street from the early childhood program building. What thematic ideas does this suggest? How would you plan a theme based on what you have learned in this chapter?
   c. Review the daily plan for the cat theme presented in Figure 15.2. How would you adapt this plan for 3-year-olds?
   d. Your colleague is planning to develop a theme about the circus. Is this a developmentally appropriate theme for 3-year olds in your community? Is it a developmentally appropriate theme for 7-year-olds in your community?
   e. Using the apple activities generated by Hannah Solomon for the children in her preschool class,

create a one-week overview of activities for a class of children you know. Add or subtract activities as necessary. How does your plan compare with Hannah's? What is the rationale behind your plan?

2. **Observe**

a. Observe a group of children for no less than 30 minutes. Based on what they talk about and seem greatly interested in, what themes or projects might this suggest for this group?

b. Observe a group of children in a classroom that uses theme planning. What do you notice about the children's involvement in the theme? What implications do your observations have for your approach to theme planning?

c. Observe a group of children carrying out a project. What do you notice about their involvement with the project? What implications do your observations have for your approach to facilitating projects?

3. **Carry out an activity**

a. Read an article on theme planning or the project approach. Summarize the primary points the author makes. Describe the extent to which the article supports or disputes what you have read in this chapter.

b. Interview two early childhood educators who work with children of different ages. Ask them to describe some of the topics their students are most interested in learning more about. Ask them

to talk about how they incorporate children's interests in their teaching.

c. Participate in a classroom in which thematic teaching or projects are offered to children. Describe how you supported children's involvement with these topics.

d. Using the guidelines in this chapter, choose a thematic topic for a specific group of children. Explain why you selected the topic, and discuss how it is age appropriate, individually appropriate, and socioculturally appropriate for these children.

e. Using the guidelines in this chapter, create a thematic unit for a specific group of children in which you identify a topic, TFPs, a week's activities, and methods for evaluating the plan's effectiveness.

4. **Create something for your portfolio**

a. Take pictures of and record children's reactions to a theme or project you supervised.

5. **Add to your journal**

a. What is the most significant thing you have learned about themes and projects based on your readings and experience with children?

b. What is your initial reaction to the idea of theme planning or project implementation with young children?

c. List the most pressing concerns you have about planning and implementing appropriate themes or projects for children. Describe how you will address your concerns.

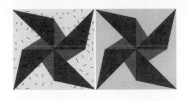

Chapter 16

Integrating Curriculum Through Authentic Assessment

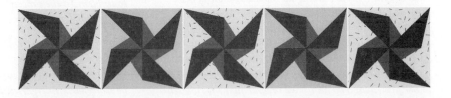

You may wonder:

Why is it necessary to assess young children? What do we need to know about them?

What part should standardized tests play in evaluating children's development?

What are some of the difficulties involved in testing and assessing young children?

What are the characteristics of "authentic" assessment? How can it be implemented appropriately?

How can data about children's progress be organized for evaluation and reporting purposes? How can information related to assessment be shared effectively with parents?

I n this chapter on the assessment and evaluation of young children, we present information to help you answer these questions.

Carolyn Afree has been teaching second graders for 12 years. She has become increasingly concerned about evaluating the progress of children in her classroom. Although she feels she is well aware of each child's general strengths and limitations and able to match learning tasks appropriately with children's varying abilities, standardized and "end-of-unit" tests are taking up more and more of her time. She notices that some of the children seem highly stressed in the formal testing situation; others seem to attach too little importance to it, rushing through carelessly and making mistakes they do not ordinarily make when participating in classroom activity. She has spoken about it to her principal, who said, "We need to quantify children's progress somehow if we are to be accountable. Until we

come up with a reasonable alternative, I'm afraid you'll have to go along with the present structure."

In a local school district, an early childhood education committee has been given the task of structuring a district-wide portfolio and student-led conferencing process. The facilitator is summarizing a list of concerns that have been raised by committee members: Will parents accept the new process? Should standardized and unit testing be continued? Should all teachers be required to implement the process? How involved should the children be? What products should be saved and included?

Tommy Nishilda's parents are meeting with his preschool teacher. Because he is considerably younger than some of his classmates, they are concerned about whether he will be ready for kindergarten in the fall. "Isn't there some kind of test he could take?" they ask hopefully.

Appreciation of the need for and value of well-designed assessment and evaluation in early childhood education is growing. In addition to learning more about how individual children think, learn, develop, and behave over time, we also need information to make decisions about instruction, to identify children who might benefit from special help, and to report to parents, other professionals, funding or regulatory agencies, boards of directors, school boards, legislators, and citizen groups (McAfee & Leong, 1997).

In this chapter, we look at the issues and practices related to standardized assessment, general practices related to the assessment and evaluation of young children, responsibilities of professionals conducting early childhood measurement, and evaluation guidelines for developmentally appropriate assessment. We also outline the basics of more authentic data gathering and evaluation for the early years and suggest effective strategies for organizing and sharing data and children's products.

ISSUES RELATED TO STANDARDIZED TESTING

On the day of the test (to qualify for entry to a prestigious elementary school), Sam, a vivacious, articulate 3-year-old boy, bounced into the office of an I.Q. examiner on the Upper West Side and in his most social fashion declared, "My, isn't this a blustery day?" Strolling over to the windows, which were outfitted with an expensive view, the child continued, "I see something familiar—the Hudson River!" It was a performance worthy of a precocious child actor on TV—the perfect prelude, his father thought, to the I.Q. test that Sam was about to take and, presumably, to ace. A few days ago, Sam's parents got a terse form letter with a percentile score almost carelessly scribbled into a blank. It condemned Sam, the apple of their eye, the boy who charmed strangers and wowed every preschool teacher, to a perfectly average intelligence. Nothing special. (Hartocollis, 1997, A-17)

Standardized testing is big business in the United States! According to recent reports, approximately 93 to 105 million standardized tests of achievement, competency, and basic skills are currently administered each year to fulfill local and state mandates, identify or qualify children for compensatory or special education programs, screening and placement for prekindergarten and kindergarten, Graduate Equivalency De-

gree (GED) tests, college admission, and National Assessment of Educational Progress testing (Neill & Medina, 1989; Puckett & Black, 1994). Think about how many you have taken in your own educational career so far!

Prior to 1950, standardized testing, as we know it today, was fairly rare in school systems and, before 1965, even less frequently seen in preschools and the early elementary grades. Because of an influx of federal dollars during the 1960s to stem poverty and the accountability requirements that accompanied these dollars, standardized testing became an accepted and increasingly prominent feature of public education. Largely, it was a quick and easy method of documenting that programs were "working." Eventually, however, these tests took on a life of their own, shaping the very programs, educators, and children they were designed to evaluate. In some measure, they continue to do so today.

Constance Kamii (1990), a noted early childhood educator, charges that the current overemphasis on standardized testing in the United States is the result of grown-ups playing a series of damaging games aimed at looking good politically and maintaining jobs. The "guilty" have ranged from legislators, governors, and school board members to superintendents, principals, classroom teachers, and parents. Pressure to achieve greater "educational accountability" has gradually spawned widespread approval of such practices as teaching to the test (if not the actual test itself) and placing heavy emphasis on worksheets, drills, and other inappropriate teaching strategies in early childhood classrooms. All have been designed to raise scores because it is erroneously assumed that high scores on standardized tests equal high rates of learning in the children taking the tests.

In addition to the problems already described, weaknesses and limitations of standardized tests include cultural bias in those selected; limited test content; inaccurate or inadequate norms; inappropriate use of results; and the harmful educational, economic, and societal tracking of children (Wortham, 1995).

By 1987, average test scores in all 50 states were found to be above established norms. Did that mean American children were smarter? Or were they simply becoming smarter at taking tests? It appears that a growing number of educators are now willing to admit that the latter is true and that standardized testing as it is carried out today must be curbed and should even be eliminated in the primary grades as a general practice. A call to do so has been supported by such national organizations as the Association for Childhood Education International, Association for Supervision and Curriculum Development, National Association for the Education of Young Children, National Association of Early Childhood Teacher Educators, National Association of Elementary School Principals, National Council of Teachers of English, and the National Council of Teachers of Mathematics (Kamii, 1990; Wortham, 1995).

This does not mean, however, that all screening, assessment, and evaluation of young children should be scrapped, nor should standardized testing and alternative assessment of children be viewed as oppositional methods for gauging children's progress. Standardized testing and the classroom strategies that follow later in this chapter should be seen as different but complementary means of gathering and interpreting information, each serving a different purpose (Birrell & Ross, 1996).

Very different philosophies and theories direct assessment (Seefeldt, 1990b). One group of educators is interested in what they call *idiographic* assessment, which is directed toward learning more about individual children and the settings, situations, and interactions that affect development. The most useful assessment methods for doing that include observations, case studies, interviews, and other methods that focus on the uniqueness of the individual. Another group of professionals, the empiricists, find idiographic methods too imprecise, personal, and general to be of use in meeting their goals; instead, they value *nomothetic* assessment, which is geared toward the study of representative samples, the development of normal curves, and the use of large numbers in order to understand how children develop in general. Methods include standardized and intelligence testing, standardized achievement tests, and screening and diagnosis procedures. Indeed, screening and diagnosis continue to be necessary and important factors in the early identification of the at-risk child. Diagnostic assessment intended to determine conclusively whether a child has special needs requires multiple types of data and sources (Meisels & Provence, 1989). Thus, carefully constructed and valid standardized tests are legitimate tools to consider. They may provide a more complete understanding of a child's strengths and weaknesses by comparing performance with an established standard. This procedure can help document the pre- and postintervention status of groups of children who may be considered at risk because of socioeconomic factors or the geographical context in which they are reared. The tests are not intended to provide in-depth information about the ways children learn or to ameliorate learning handicaps (Sattler, 1992). However, in a relatively limited amount of time, a sample of behavior can be obtained to measure developmental status and changes or effects of remediation. The challenge is to find reliable and valid measures, obtain a typical response from the child, and then use the data only in conjunction with other relevant information to evaluate a child's physical, intellectual, social, or psychological abilities and functioning. The Michigan Department of Education curriculum and evaluation guidelines for 4- to 8-year-olds describe the following criteria for minimizing the limitations of standardized tests when used:

1. They must be designed to be individually administered. An assessment instrument designed and normed for large-group administration is not appropriate.
2. They should require child responses that are mainly motoric or verbal or responses to auditory stimuli (e.g., point, construct, sort; name an object or picture; answer a question; follow directions; discriminate sound). Concrete materials and pictures should be the main media for obtaining responses. Paper and pencil should be used only as a check of perceptual motor functioning (e.g., copy a shape, write one's name).
3. They should be broad in scope. A variety of developmental domains should be covered, including emotional, social, physical, intellectual, aesthetic, language, and sensory functioning.
4. They must be relatively short to administer. Testing should take a maximum of 25 minutes.
5. They should be administered by an adult known to the child.
6. They should provide useful information for curriculum planning.
7. They should be normed on a large representative sample of children so that the norms match well with the children being tested.
8. They should be statistically valid and reliable.

LABELING AND TRACKING YOUNG CHILDREN ON THE BASIS OF TEST RESULTS

It is one thing to talk about the technical aspects of standardized testing. It is still another to consider that faulty decisions affecting children's futures are made because *too much* importance is attached to a particular test or score, even though the test is valid and reliable. If, for example, we were to interrupt your reading of this chapter right now, have you take a test on what you have read so far, score that test, and then compare your performance with a normed group of people very much like yourself (placing you somewhere on a normal curve), you might react in one of two ways. If your performance were better than average, you might come away from the experience with a very pleased feeling. Furthermore, if decisions about your professional life or future were based on your performance, you might feel quite relieved that your score was above the norm. However, if your performance on the one test rated *below* average, your reaction would be quite different. You might try to explain: "But I didn't take the test seriously. . . . I didn't realize what was hinging on the results. . . . I didn't feel well. . . . I know I'm better than the test indicates; in fact, I'm considered excellent in the classroom with children because I'm rather creative, and the test didn't measure any of that. The material we were tested on was presented in a boring way—I couldn't relate to it."

Fortunately, this is only a hypothetical situation, and your performance on such a test would not affect your job or future. Moreover, because you are an adult and capable of interpreting your performance in light of your actual strengths or weaknesses, you would no doubt be fairly assertive in articulating your concerns if any attempt were made to use the score inappropriately. Young children definitely do not yet have this ability, and many of their parents may not be confident enough to question decisions made by professionals, particularly when there are "real numbers" and evidence from a standardized test to back up such decisions. However, both standardized tests as well as those reported to have no established validity or reliability are regularly used to place children in special entry programs, resource rooms, and learning groups or to bar children from school entry for an additional year.

One principal proudly announced that, because of the screening methods being used in his district, staff had identified a number of children who were not yet "ready for kindergarten." Because the district had no other programs in place for such children, the children would have to wait another year to enter the system. Many of the parents were disappointed about the outcome but, for the most part, did not question the system. Instead, they accepted the decisions as valid and in the best interest of their children.

Gender- and Age-Related Issues

In the early years, males may be more vulnerable to such practices than females. Because they may be from 6 to 18 months behind their female counterparts in entering cognitive acceleration shifts, they are much more likely to be placed in resource rooms for the emotionally impaired and learning disabled (Soderman & Phillips, 1986) and recommended for developmental kindergarten placement, prefirst-grade rooms, or retention in kindergarten. Learning "deficits" or "disabilities" diagnosed in these children in kindergarten or first grade may very well be biological variations (i.e., the child simply needs more time to develop the necessary myelinization, neural pathways, and other biological maturation required to make sense cognitively of abstract material that has become increasingly commonplace in kindergartens and first grade).

Yale University findings (Shaywitz, Escobar, Shaywitz, Fletcher, & Makuch, 1992) suggest that the numbers of children diagnosed as dyslexic in first grade simply do not hold in third or sixth grade and that reading "problems" show year-to-year variability and may simply be the tail end of a normal reading distribution. They also suggest that because of such year-to-year variability, some children who appear to be functioning well at one point may, in fact, need extra support later on and not get it. Studies of eye development and reading accuracy rates in first-grade children indicate significant differences between males and females that tend to disappear by second grade (Soderman, O'Neill, & Linscott, 1996; Soderman, Beatty, Cooper, Cummings, Fleury, Darrow, Thompson, & Weber, 1995). Also relevant here is the research related to maturation of a child's brain and eyes to organize incoming retinal signals. Although controversial, findings suggest that early visual-perceptual (not visual acuity) problems contribute to letter reversal or letters that seem to "move about" and "run together" (Beauchamp & Kosmorsky, 1987, 1445).

Tracking and Grouping

The consequences of mislabeling children based on early developmental differences can last a lifetime. Evidence indicates that, despite our inclusion efforts, as few as 6 percent of children entering special education tracks ever move completely back into the mainstream. To guard against the inappropriate exclusion of children with disabilities from regular public school classrooms, Public Law 94–142, passed in 1975, stated that, to the maximum extent possible, these children would be educated in the "least restrictive" setting. While screening, assessment, and evaluation are important tools in providing supportive services to vulnerable children and families, no decision should ever be based on the score from one test; nor should a child be labeled or said to have a problem because of the child's performance on a test. Rather, as we stated earlier, results on any test should be considered *only* in light of other evidence accumulated, including that from a child's parents, preschool teacher, childcare provider, or other significant adults.

Unfortunately, the practice of providing homogeneous educational placements for young children has actually increased. When carefully examined, few of these have to do with the long-range best interests of the children. More often, they have more to do with our narrowing differences in children so that planning can be more precisely targeted on specific outcomes to prove statistically that children are progressing. Also, children who have more difficult problems (i.e., out-of-step rates of learning, learning modalities, or reasoning processes) and require more of a teacher's time are placed with special educators or resource persons so the regular classroom teacher can spend time with other children. Consequently, these children are spending time in settings more highly restricted than might be necessary, which goes against the intent of PL 94–142; moreover, regular classroom teachers in these settings lose confidence in their ability to handle such children.

In most cases, children consistently benefit from spending time interacting with peers who have a broader range of skills. When the classroom climate is built on respect for individual differences and activities allow for cooperative learning, high-quality interactive experiences, sequential learning, and active involvement of the teacher, all children are more highly motivated to grow. They observe what is going on in the group, pick up skills to be more like other children they admire, and contribute to or obtain help from other children in learning concepts and skills. This is not possible, of course, in early childhood education settings in which children are closely grouped depending on what we believe they know before they ever participate in a particular setting.

To the extent that the norm in an early childhood classroom is finding a correct answer and drawing on previously established facts rather than arriving at an answer after investigation, heterogeneous grouping will be less successful. In such settings, both the teacher and the children focus on avoiding wrong answers or "looking bad."

This is not to suggest that every child should always be included in the regular classroom setting. Children with significant organic attention deficit or psychological difficulties that would preclude their success in a regular classroom would benefit from a setting in which they gain more specific one-on-one attention from the teacher and less negative stimulation from peers. This is what broad-based evaluation is all about. Appropriately used, it is education's comprehensive response to each child's uniqueness (Cryan, 1986). Inappropriately used, it can lead to a qualitatively poorer education for some children and, consequently, fewer opportunities to achieve in the regular classroom. Increasing evidence suggests that early academic and social differences in children are no better addressed by separating these children from their chronologically older and/or more mature peers because most differences equalize by third grade (Creager, 1990). This is not to say that the developmental kindergartens so popular in the 1980s were not more comfortable placements for children less apt to achieve success in rigorously academic kindergartens. It does present proof, however, that early differences tend to disappear, and developmentally younger children can ultimately be successful when placed with children who score higher on entry measures—*if* the contexts in which they are placed are developmentally appropriate.

Conducting Responsible Early Childhood Evaluation

Those who **are** implementing evaluation procedures greatly affect **the** outcome—by design or default. That is, assessment and evaluation will be effective only to the extent that attention is paid to (a) the relative subjectivity/objectivity and skills of the evaluator, (b) the state of the child at the time of evaluation, (c) properties of the evaluation setting, (d) timing of evaluation, (e) appropriate selection of data collection tools and strategies, and (f) thoughtful application of outcomes. Assessment and evaluation findings should never become conversational fodder for the teacher's lounge or other public gatherings, and negative comments about a child (i.e., points of weakness) should be considered only in light of how corresponding strengths or modifications in instructional strategies can help minimize the limitations discovered.

Subjectivity/Objectivity and Skills of the Evaluator

Perhaps nothing is as dangerous in the evaluation setting as evaluators who (a) are unaware of their own personal traits, values, and expectations and (b) lack evaluation know-how. The latter would include a lack of knowledge about child development as well as the ability to structure and apply appropriate evaluation strategies. Because we are advocating that evaluation in early childhood settings be carried out primarily by the classroom teacher, we have little control over any effects related to differences in the teacher's and child's gender, race, ethnic background, and personality other than to ensure that the valuating teacher is aware that establishing good rapport with individual children is a necessary prerequisite to good evaluation. Teachers must also examine as objectively as possible the expectations they bring into the situation and avoid providing verbal and nonverbal reinforcement to one child that is not given just as freely to other children.

Obtaining the Child's Best Response

Young children are notoriously difficult to test. They have no concept of the importance attached to an assessment and are inexperienced with paper/pencil formats. They tire easily, are easily distracted, may have little interest in doing well, may be wary of the evaluator if unfamiliar, and may simply refuse to cooperate. English may be a second language for some children, and their cultural background can also affect their performance. Every effort should be made to obtain several samples of the child's best work, performed when the child is at ease, healthy, and motivated, which will then be evaluated. Many of these problems, of course, can be almost completely eliminated in early childhood classrooms

in which evaluation procedures become a normal and less intrusive part of everyday activity.

Choosing an Evaluation Setting

Ideally, early childhood classrooms, where evaluation should take place, are pleasant environments with adequate ventilation, light, space, pleasing aesthetic qualities, minimal distractions, and modified noise levels. Realistically, of course, these factors are not always optimal. When they are not, both children's learning and evaluation may be negatively affected. These factors should be considered when planning classroom activities that will serve as a basis for evaluation. Children should not be removed from the classroom to unfamiliar settings for evaluation of activity and events that normally occur in the classroom. However, every effort should be made to see that the classroom setting itself and ongoing activity in the room at evaluation time do not distract from the children's best efforts.

Timing of the Evaluation

Teachers need to consider two aspects of timing. One is the *consistency* in the scheduling of skill and behavior sampling. The other is the *assessment itself.* Some forms of assessment, such as vision and hearing testing and obtaining health records and family profiles, are most helpful when secured as early as possible before interaction with the child begins. Evaluation should be both formative (i.e., ongoing) and summative. Teachers should build into their programs ongoing methods of collecting daily work samples and opportunities for planned observation and discussion with children; they must also use more formal measures such as scoring oral reading tapes at specified periods during the year. Assessment of skills and behaviors should not be attempted until the teacher has established rapport with children and children have had adequate opportunity to practice the skills and behaviors to be assessed. Assessment should also not be undertaken at certain times of the school year and school day when children are more likely to be distracted, less able to concentrate, or likely to feel rushed (e.g., right before recess, on the day of a Halloween party, or after returning from vacation).

Selection of Data Collection Strategies and Tools

When we think of testing situations, we usually envision people sitting quietly taking paper-and-pencil tests in group situations. That scenario in early education spells disaster and is developmentally inappropriate. Errors on such a test would most likely result from a lack of skill in recording rather than lack of knowledge in the content area being evaluated. Moreover, young children are developing their ability to respond to direction and may become confused in a group setting about what they need to do. Their confidence in alerting an adult to problems they are having in the situation will depend on the rapport established with the attending adult. Such a methodology does not match children's everyday integrated experiences in good early childhood classrooms and lends itself more to the testing of isolated skills. Tests that fall in this category are the Early Prevention of School Failure Test, Metropolitan Readiness Test, Iowa Test of Basic Skills, Stanford Early School Achievement Test, Brigance K and 1 Screen, California Achievement Test, and Cognitive Skills Assessment Battery (Kamii, 1990).

Before deciding what kind of strategies or tools are needed, teahers should determine the purpose of the assessment. What do we want to know about this child and how specifically? Is diagnostic information needed? How will the data be used? Who else will need to see and use the data? If a federal or state granting or funding agency will be involved, will they accept only standardized test results, or are teacher-constructed measures considered as valid? What is there about the child or the testing situation itself that affects our decision? How much time can be spared for the evaluation, and when and where should it take place? Will just one child be looked at or a group of children? Should a direct strategy be used that involves the child, or can an unobtrusive measure work just as well so the child is unaware of being tested?

Once the basic purpose and related details have been considered, teachers can select a number of good evaluation methods. Because standardized tests have limited use with young children other than for diagnostic or research purposes, the focus in this last section of the chapter is on more *authentic* measures the classroom teacher can utilize in natural settings where children work and play.

The Concept of Authentic Assessment

Effective assessment and evaluation is more than tests and measurements and calls for comprehensive, continuous, and/or periodic appraisal of children's progress and performance (Phenice & Griffore, 1990). When evaluating children, someone makes use of a *variety* of data, *over time,* to gauge a child's developmental progress against an expected range of maturational behaviors, skills, readiness levels, and concept formation. Authentic assessment, which has been defined as "the process of observing, recording, and otherwise documenting the work that children do and how they do it as a basis for educational decisions that affect those children" is exactly what is needed! Its essential characteristics are as follows:

- ❏ Authentic assessment celebrates development and learning.
- ❏ Authentic assessment emphasizes emerging development.
- ❏ Authentic assessment capitalizes upon the strengths of the learner.
- ❏ Authentic assessment is based on real-life events.
- ❏ Authentic assessment is performance based.
- ❏ Authentic assessment is related to instruction.
- ❏ Authentic assessment focuses on purposeful learning.
- ❏ Authentic assessment is ongoing in all contexts.
- ❏ Authentic assessment provides a broad and general picture of student learning capabilities.
- ❏ Authentic assessment is collaborative among [family members,] teachers, students, and other professional persons as needed (Puckett & Black, 1994, 22).

Important advantages can accrue to early childhood professionals when they systematically and professionally document children's progress in order to facilitate learning and development. The National Association for the Education of Young Children (NAEYC, 1996a) has indicated that to provide an accurate picture of children's capabilities, teachers must observe children over time and use their findings to adjust curriculum and instruction. In addition, assessment is not to be used to recommend that children be eliminated from particular programs, retained, or assigned to segregated groups based on ability or developmental maturity. Principles set out by NAEYC to guide practitioners in assessment procedures for children ages 3 through 8 are as follows:

1. Curriculum and assessment are integrated throughout the program; assessment is congruent with and relevant to the goals, objectives, and content of the program.
2. Assessment results in benfits to the child, such as needed adjustments in the curriculum or more in-

dividualized instruction and improvements in the program.

3. Children's development and learning in all the domains—physical, social, emotional, and cognitive—and their dispositions and feelings are informally and routinely assessed by teachers' observing children's activities and interactions, listening to them as they talk, and using children's constructive errors to understand their learning.

4. Assessment provides teachers with useful information to successfully fulfill their responsibilities: to support children's learning and development, to plan for individuals and groups, and to communicate with parents.

5. Assessment involves regular and periodic observation of the child in a wide variety of circumstances that are representative of the child's behavior in the program over time.

6. Assessment relies primarily on procedures that reflect the ongoing life of the classroom and typical activities of the children. Assessment avoids approaches that place children in artificial situations, impede the usual learning and developmental experiences in the classroom, or divert children from their natural learning processes.

7. Assessment relies on demonstrated performance during real, not contrived, activities, for example, real reading and writing activities rather than only skills testing (Engel, 1990; Teale, 1988).

8. Assessment utilizes an array of tools and a variety of processes including, but not limited to, collections of representative work by children (artwork, stories they write, tape recordings of their reading), records of systematic observations by teachers, records of conversations and interviews with children, teachers' summaries of children's progress as individuals and as groups (Chittenden & Courtney, 1989; Goodman, Goodman, & Hood, 1989).

9. Assessment recognizes individual diversity of learners and allows for differences in styles and rates of learning. Assessment takes into consideration children's ability in English, their stage of language acquisition, and whether they have been given the time and opportunity to develop proficiency in their native language as well as in English.

10. Assessment supports children's development and learning; it does *not* threaten children's psychological safety or feelings of self-esteem.

11. Assessment supports parents' relationships with their children and does not undermine parents' confidence in their children's or their own ability, nor does it devalue the language and culture of the family.

12. Assessment demonstrates children's overall strengths and progress, what children can do not just their wrong answers or what they cannot do or do not know.

13. Assessment is an essential component of the teacher's role. Because teachers can make maximal use of assessment results, the teacher is the *primary* assessor.

14. Assessment is a collaborative process involving children and teachers, teachers and parents, school and community. Information from parents about each child's experiences at home is used in planning instruction and evaluating children's learning. Information obtained from assessment is shared with parents in language they can understand.

15. Assessment encourages children to participate in self-evaluation.

16. Assessment addresses what children can do independently and what they can demonstrate with assistance, because the latter shows the direction of their growth.

17. Information about each child's growth, development, and learning is systematically collected and recorded at regular intervals. Information such as samples of children's work, descriptions of their performance, and anecdotal records is used for planning instruction and communicating with parents.

18. A regular process exists for periodic information sharing between teachers and parents about children's growth and development and performance. The method of reporting to parents does not rely on letter or numerical grades but rather provides more meaningful, descriptive information in narrative form (NAEYC, 1996a, 15–16).

Strategies for Authentic Assessment in the Early Childhood Classroom

In keeping with the concept and principles of authentic assessment, we can employ a number of useful strategies to gather the information we need to determine whether children will need special services and whether they are benefiting from the kinds of learning activities we have planned for them.

Screening Procedures   One area that educators are struggling with is the effective assessment of incoming kindergarten children to see if they are "ready." Many school districts have spent thousands of dollars training professionals to evaluate children's readiness and/or need for further diagnostic assessment using measures such as the Gesell, DIAL R, Denver II, Brigance, Early Screening Inventory, and other standardized and nonstandardized tools. Meisels and Provence (1994) note the need to differentiate between screening (sorting out children for whom diagnostic assessment is the "definitive next step") and "readiness" (testing that looks at already acquired skills determined to be prerequisites for success in particular instructional programs).

Currently, many school districts are reassessing these earlier scrambles to identify weaknesses in children and, instead, are turning their energy toward training professionals who can cope with a wider range of skills in children. As a result, children in those districts are having a more positive first experience with school. Instead of taking a test, they are invited to come into an early childhood classroom once or twice in the spring for one hour just to enjoy the materials and developmentally appropriate activities planned for them. This is surely a better beginning! Parents can meet with the school principal and other professionals during this time to become better acquainted with school policy and ways in which they can work together with educators to support their child's successful orientation to school.

In addition to providing a more positive experience for children, the process just described has the advantage of allowing seasoned professionals—preprimary and kindergarten teachers, Chapter I supervisors, elementary counselors and principals, speech teachers, school social workers, and psychologists—to observe the children at work and play. For instance, some districts have the speech teacher interact purposefully with each child for a brief time during this period to get a speech/language sample. Vision and auditory screening are also scheduled to make sure these primary learning modalities are intact.

It is rarely difficult to spot the child who may have problems working with other children, adults, or materials. For those children, additional assessment is structured in addition to a private meeting scheduled with the child's parents to learn more about his or her history and present strengths and limitations.

Structured and Nonstructured Observation   One of the most underrated evaluation tools for use with the young child is observational assessment. As we have noted, the objective and experienced eye of someone who is knowledgeable about child development is invaluable. Observational assessment has much to offer: It is nonintrusive where the child is concerned; it yields instant, credible information that has on-the-spot utility for improving interactional and instructional strategies with children; it has heuristic value for formulating hypotheses to evaluate at a later date; it is a technique that can be used virtually anywhere people

are behaving; and it allows the professional to capture in natural settings important data that could not be obtained by other methods.

Goodwin and Driscoll (1980) define observational measurement as "the process of systematic recording of behavior as it occurs, or of a setting as it exists, in ways that yield descriptive and qualitative measures of individuals, groups, and settings" (p. 110). They indicate that formal observational measurement is more often used in research studies. Included here are such strategies as specimen records (continuous documentation of everything a subject does during a given time period), time sampling (noting selected behaviors or setting variables during intermittent but uniform time segments), event sampling (recording previously identified events of interest), and trait rating (subsequent rating of observed behaviors or underlying traits). Teachers frequently utilize trait rating when assessing and reporting behaviors such as cooperating and taking responsibility.

In a more informal sense, behavioral observation serves a number of valuable functions in the assessment process (Sattler, 1992) by providing a picture of a child's spontaneous behavior in everyday life settings (classroom, playground, hospital ward, or clinic playroom); information about the child's interpersonal behavior and learning style; and a systematic record of child behaviors that can be used for planning intervention or classroom instruction. In addition, behavioral observation allows for verification of others' reports regarding the child's behavior and comparisons between behavior in formal and more naturalistic settings. It affords us with an opportunity to study the behaviors of children who are developmentally disabled and are not easily evaluated by other methods.

Young children are particularly good subjects for observations because they have not yet learned to mask their feelings, thoughts, and behaviors very well. The technique also has great utility because it avoids the limitations of paper-and-pencil methods and, being fairly unobtrusive, requires no cooperation on the part of the child. One 4-year-old who was moving through a screening process for kindergarten entry had everyone believing her name was Melissa (her name was Kate, but she preferred Melissa). She refused to answer any of the questions until her mother noted what was going on and intervened, telling her that she had "better take things seriously and quit fooling around!" The teacher who was relating the story said, "She might have been one of our kids tagged for further diagnosis if her mother hadn't clued us in. As it was, Kate turned out to be an exceptionally bright kindergartner."

Observation of children can be seriously flawed when bias or misinterpretation by the evaluator results in "the halo effect" or "the leniency factor." For example, if a teacher observing Kate's earlier performance interpreted the behavior as a tendency to lie, she may subsequently allow that to negatively color future observations of Kate. If, however, she viewed Kate's performance as the funny stunt of a highly creative child, she may tend to see Kate *more* positively in subsequent situations than might be warranted. The leniency phenomenon distorts observation in quite a different way. This observer would tend to rate not only Kate more highly than would be indicated but *all* subjects more highly; this is the phenomenon we see occurring in grade inflation in secondary and postsecondary education in which entire classes of students receive a 4.0, despite distinct differences in performance.

Informal observation methods most useful to early childhood educators include the use of anecdotal records, frequency counts and charts, checklists, rating scales, and participation charts.

Anecdotal Records Anecdotal records (see Figure 16.1) are on-the-spot descriptions of both typical and unusual behaviors in a child. These single observations, which are most conveniently written on stick-on notes or index cards to be filed, contain sufficiently detailed descriptions of a particular behavioral event that can

then be used with subsequent observations to formulate hypotheses or conclusions about a child's behavioral functioning. Included is necessary information about the event, any known stimulus, persons involved, direct quotes if important to understanding the situation, and behavioral responses of the child. Unusual behaviors of any kind are noted. Any subjective inferences or interpretations may be noted but must be kept separate from the observation itself. Some teachers focus directly on four or five children per day, taking time after the end of the day or session to note behaviors of interest.

Frequency Counts Frequency counts are simply behavior tallies of specified behaviors as they occur (see Figure 16.2). Sometimes we have a feeling that a particular behavior is either increasing or decreasing on a day-to-day basis with a child. Occasionally, we may want to collect baseline information before beginning purposeful intervention to alter behavior. Frequency counts can help us document whether our intuitions about a situation are correct and can then be charted to display the effects of instituted treatment (see Figure 16.3). For example, a behavior of interest might be a child's aggressive interaction with other children, and a frequency count could document maintenance, increase, or decrease of the behavior following intervention.

Checklists and Inventories Checklists can range from formal criterion-referenced lists of developmental behaviors and skills to teacher-constructed inventories

FIGURE 16.1
Anecdotal Record

> **Child's Name:** Gary Denzell   **Observer:** B. Miller
> **Date:** 10/16/97   **Setting:** Kindergarten Classroom
> **Time:** 10:17 A.M.
>
> Children were asked by Ms. Sharpe to complete a worksheet identifying like and dissimilar objects. Gary continued to play with unit blocks until reminded by Ms. Sharpe to take his place at the table and begin working. He looked up but still did not move. When she moved toward him to get him to comply, he kicked down the block structure he had been making and walked to the table. Ms. Sharpe noted, "That's better." Gary did not respond.
>
> *Interpretation:* Gary balked when asked to do seatwork. He clearly preferred playing with blocks, trucks. Would there be a better way to "teach" logicomathematical concepts than forcing him to complete ditto sheets, which he continues to have difficulty with?

FIGURE 16.2
Tally of Aggressive Interactions

Child's Name:	Gary Denzell
Behavior:	Aggressive interaction with other children–biting, hitting, spitting, kicking
When:	During center activity (9:10–10:15)
Where:	Ms. Johnson's room
Observer:	B. Miller
Dates:	November 16–November 20, 1997

Days	Tally	Total
1	//////	6
2	////	4
3	///	3
4	/	1
5	//	2

FIGURE 16.3
Charting Aggressive Interactions

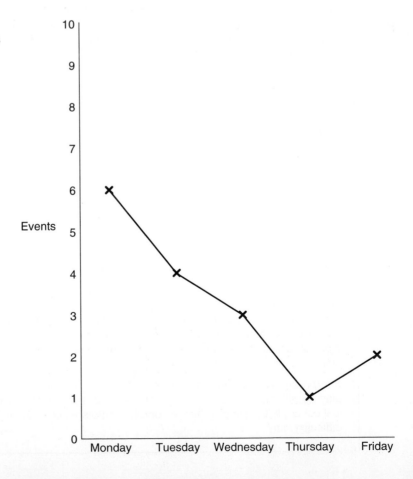

listing behaviors of interest to the educator. They note both individual and group achievement and usually require a simple check (√) indicating that the skill or behavior has been noted (see Figure 16.4). Teachers interested in documenting observation more than once may note the first observation by making a horizontal mark (-), the second with an added vertical mark (+), and additional crosses for subsequent observation of the skill (* *).

Rating Scales and Rubrics   Rating scales are similar to checklists in that lists of behavioral variables are made. They differ in that an *evaluative* component is attached that qualifies behavior or skill acquisition (see Figure 16.5). Such scales can be color coded for easier interpretation (e.g., 1 = green; 2 = blue; 3 = yellow;

4 = red). Evaluators may choose from a variety of predetermined categories or ranges of behavior, extremes, or opposites. These may be represented by a numbered continuum attached to a specified criterion (e.g., choosing from 0–10, in which 0 = low and 10 = high) or an open continuum (e.g., Extroversion □ □ □ □ □ □ □ Introversion). Obviously, objectivity cannot be ensured and can be problematic (Martin, 1994).

To increase the objectivity of rating a product, behavior, or skill, rubrics can be developed. These are scoring tools that list clearly-defined criteria to articulate gradations of quality from excellent to poor, high to low, and so on. The criterion to be evaluated is given at the left, and gradations of quality are then listed. For example, a rubric for evaluating the quality of a

FIGURE 16.4
Example of Self-Help Checklist

CHILDREN'S SELF-HELP CHECKLIST	Robert	Joanna	Jerry	Larue	Donna	Gavin	Laura	Paul	Rosalie	William
Knows telephone number	√			√	√	√		√	√	
Can give full address	√				√	√				
Buttons with no help	√	√		√	√	√	√	√	√	√
Zips	√			√	√		√			√
Can tie shoes	√			√		√				
Puts materials away without being reminded	√		√		√			√		
Follows directions	√		√	√	√	√		√		
Cleans up after self	√				√			√		
Asks for help when needed	√				√					

Date: 11/29/97

Teacher: Mrs. Gonzalez

FIGURE 16.5
Example of Rating Scale

SOCIAL SKILLS RATINGS SCALE

Date: _____4/10/97_____

Teacher: _Mr. Lofy_____

1 = Skill well developed; color code green
2 = Practiced often but not always; color code blue
3 = Working on; color code yellow
4 = Rarely observed; color code red

	Juan	Jim	Sandra	Jason	Kelly	Amy	Diedra	Eric	Taylor	Regina	Elizabeth	Kerry	Ervin
Developing friendship skills	3	3	1	3	3	1	1	1	3	1	1	3	4
Initiates play/work with others	4	1	1	2	4	2	2	2	4	1	1	3	4
Makes suggestions	4	1	1	3	1	1	2	1	1	1	1	1	4
Takes suggestions	1	3	2	2	3	1	1	2	3	2	2	2	3
Negotiates conflicts (compromises)	3	3	2	3	2	1	2	1	3	2	1	2	4
Is cooperative and helpful	2	2	1	2	3	2	2	1	4	2	2	2	3
Shares materials	2	3	2	2	1	2	1	1	4	2	2	2	3
Gives assistance to others	3	4	2	2	1	2	3	2	4	2	1	2	3
Respects others and their property	2	2	1	2	2	1	2	2	3	2	1	1	3
Conforms to reasonable limits	1	2	1	1	3	2	1	1	2	1	1	1	2
Demonstrates self-control	1	2	1	2	2	2	1	2	2	1	1	2	3
Adapts to new situations	3	3	2	2	3	1	1	2	3	1	2	2	3
Terminates interactions in socially acceptable ways	2	3	1	2	1	1	2	1	3	2	1	3	3
Interacts with new people	3	3	2	3	4	1	1	1	4	1	1	2	4

student-led conference by second graders could be written so that a child could self-evaluate his or her performance (see Figure 16.6). The rubric is shared with and explained to children *before* implementing the project, thereby serving a double purpose: (1) it is a performance *guide*, letting children know what is expected prior to the event and (2) it is a device they can use afterward to appraise their performance.

Participation Charts   Time-sample participation charts are useful for recording where children are at a particular time during the school day and who they interact with most often. Following the preparation of a coded form for documentation purposes, an observer simply notes the location of each child at a designated time. In Figure 16.7, for example, all areas of the classroom have been coded (A-J). Areas assigned to the two supervising adults in the room (Mr. Tanamato is the teacher, and Mrs. Gross is his aide) are identified. Names of children have been recorded down the left side of the form, and designated times when observations are to be made are recorded across the top. In a matter of seconds, the observer can document each child's location at that particular time. These can then be examined after a number of observations to look for patterns in children's interaction with other children and adults, as well as their involvement or noninvolvement in certain activities. For example, using the participation chart in Figure 16.7, a one-week time sample that documents where 15 children are at five different times during the morning's scheduled center activity, a teacher could obtain answers to the following points of interest:

1. You have had the feeling that too many children (more than five at one time) are in the art area. Do you need to structure a rule about this?

2. You suspect the boys rarely visit the language arts center. Is this true?

3. The children seem to avoid Brian (or vice versa). Is this happening?

4. Mr. Tanamato reports that Sam spends too much time in the bathroom. Does he?

5. You suspect a couple of the children may be coming to school without breakfast. Who are they?

6. What percentage of the children are visiting the science area each day?

7. The children appear to be avoiding one of the adults. What can you learn about the situation?

8. Some of the children are being dropped off late; you feel you need to document this to talk to parents. Which children are noticeably tardy and not arriving by 8:00?

9. Three boys are best friends. Who?

10. You found whole rolls of toilet paper in a toilet in the bathroom on Tuesday and Friday. Who may need to be watched more closely?

By examining the data collected over the five days in Figure 16.7, you might draw the following conclusions in response to previous questions:

1. No rule seems to be needed about too many children in the art area. Only one incident was recorded.

2. Yes, few boys appear to be working in the language arts center—only Brian every day and Michael on Monday. What can be done to stimulate their interest?

3. Yes, observation indicated that Brian and the other children are not interacting—he is often at lockers or in the bathroom or language arts center, where there are few other children. This needs to be observed more carefully to establish cause.

FIGURE 16.6
Rubric for Evaluating My Performance in the Student-Led Conference

Criterion		Quality	
Shared the important features of my work with my parents	Yes, I shared enough to give them a good sense of my work in all subject areas.	Yes, I shared some but left out some key work samples.	I shared very few samples of my work.

FIGURE 16.7
Time-Sample Participation Chart

	Monday					Tuesday					Wednesday					Thursday					Friday				
	8:15	8:30	9:00	9:15	9:30	8:15	8:30	9:00	9:15	9:30	8:15	8:30	9:00	9:15	9:30	8:15	8:30	9:00	9:15	9:30	8:15	8:30	9:00	9:15	9:30
Brian	A	B	F	J	I	B	A	I	J	J	I	J	J	B	I	H	A	H	I	B	I	J	J	A	I
Amy	C	A	H	D	G	H	A	D	C	C	A	B	H	D	D	D	C	C	A	I	C	C	A	B	D
Kevin	—	—	I	E	E	—	A	I	B	D	—	—	F	E	E	—	B	A	D	D	—	B	E	E	A
Amanda	C	B	D	A	C	C	C	D	E	E	A	F	F	D	D	C	C	C	D	D	D	D	F	F	A
Jenny	A	I	H	D	D	A	H	D	D	F	G	A	C	C	C	A	D	D	C	D	A	G	G	G	E
Joey	—	E	D	D	E	—	—	—	A	F	F	E	E	D	I	H	A	D	F	D	—	I	—	F	D
Bill	D	D	C	C	G	D	B	F	A	C	D	D	B	G	G	A	D	I	F	F	G	G	G	H	D
Sam	D	B	C	C	G	D	B	F	A	C	D	D	B	G	G	A	D	I	F	F	B	G	G	H	D
Sarah	G	G	A	D	D	D	D	C	C	H	—	A	F	F	F	C	C	G	C	G	D	D	C	C	A
Erin	G	G	A	D	H	F	F	D	A	B	A	D	I	H	B	D	D	F	E	I	B	A	D	D	C
Tamera	G	A	D	D	D	D	A	C	C	C	—	A	C	C	C	E	F	F	G	D	A	C	C	D	G
Julio	A	D	C	B	G	D	A	B	F	A	D	D	B	G	G	A	D	I	F	F	A	G	G	H	D
Ahmad	G	G	D	E	E	G	E	F	F	A	—	—		—	B	D	D	A	F	A	D	G	E	E	E
Randi	D	I	A	G	G	E	G	D	D	A	—	A	C	H	C	F	C	F	C	D	A	B	C	C	—
Michael	B	J	D	E	E	—	—	I	A	F	—	—	I	D	D	D	D	A	F	F	B	F	D	F	F

A = snack*
B = bathroom
C = dramatic play
D = art center
E = blocks/trucks**

F = manipulatives
G = large motor**
H = science*
I = lockers
J = language arts center

*Mr. Tanamato, MWF; Mrs. Gross, TTh
**Mrs. Gross, MWF; Mr. Tanamato, TTh

4. Cannot tell whether Sam is spending too much time in the bathroom from this set of observations. Try event sampling for this question.

5. Jenny and Julio may be coming to school without breakfast. This needs to be followed up immediately by talking to the children.

6. Only 20 percent (3) of the children visited the science area last week.

7. Boys are avoiding areas where Mr. Tanamato is stationed, even M, W, and F snack (also science on M, W, F and blocks and large motor on T, Th). Need to follow up.

8. Kevin was tardy on M, T, W, Th, F. Joey was tardy on M, T, F; Michael tardy on T, W.

9. Bill, Sam, and Julio appear to be best friends and travel from activity to activity together.

10. Kevin and Sam are the only boys who were in the boys' bathroom on both T and F. This bears closer watching!

Oral Reading Tests: Running Records   As some school districts move to a literature-based approach to reading in the primary grades as an alternative to basal texts, many of them are looking for a quantitative method to document that children are making progress in reading accuracy and their ability to recognize and correct mistakes without help. A literature-based method for obtaining samples of children's oral reading at several times during the year has been suggested (Kamii, 1990). The strategy is to offer children a selection of stories they have been introduced to in the classroom (e.g., Leo Lionni's "Fish Is Fish"), have them read one into a tape recorder, and follow up by discussing with an adult what they believe the story was all about.

The teacher, using a photocopied or typed version of the story, then listens to the tape to evaluate the quality of the child's reading, noting mistakes, number of words read, self-corrections, words omitted, words added, and words reversed (see Figure 16.8). Notes are

FIGURE 16.8
Analysis of an Oral Reading Sample

Name: Juana Perez
Date: April 4, 1997
Evaluator: Mr. Lofy

Fish is Fish

	Word Total
AT THE EDGE OF THE WOODS THERE WAS A BIG	10 / X
POND, AND THERE A MINNOW AND A TADPOLE	18 X
SWAM AMONG THE WEEDS. THEY WERE INSEPARABLE	25 X
FRIENDS.	26
ONE MORNING THE TADPOLE DISCOVERED THAT	32 X
DURING THE NIGHT HE HAD GROWN TWO LITTLE LEGS.	41 X
"LOOK," he said triumphantly. "LOOK, I AM A FROG!"	50 / X
"NONSENSE," SAID THE MINNOW. "HOW COULD YOU BE	59 X
FROG IS ONLY LAST NIGHT YOU WERE A LITTLE TINY FISH,	70 / /
JUST LIKE ME!"	73
THEY ARGUED AND ARGUED UNTIL FINALLY THE	80 X
TADPOLE SAID, "FROGS ARE FROGS AND FISH IS FISH	89
AND THAT'S THAT!"	92
IN THE WEEKS THAT FOLLOWED, THE TADPOLE GREW	100 /
TINY FRONT LEGS AND HIS TAIL GOT SMALLER AND	109
SMALLER.	110

FIGURE 16.9
Scoring the Oral Reading
Sample in Figure in 16.8

Name: Juana Perez

Date: April 4, 1997

Evaluator: Mr. Lofy

Literature Category: Level 3

A. Words read: 110
B. Mistakes (X): 8
C. Self-Corrections ($/$): 5
D. Meaningful mistakes (/): 0
E. Total corrected/meaningful mistakes (C + D + B)

Accuracy Score (A − B) ÷ A
    (110 − 8 ÷ 110) = .93

Self-Correction Rate: (C + D) ÷ E
    (5 + 10) ÷ 13 = .38

Comprehension (1 = fragmentary to 4 = full)**: 3

Comments: Juana's self-correction abilities are increasing (score on 2/27/97 = .22, score on 4/4/97 = .38). Comprehension was good, and she enjoyed reading to me. According to accuracy rate, literature category is still too difficult. Retest in May.

made on comprehension, fluency and expressiveness in reading, and the nature of the child's mistakes.

Scoring (see Figure 16.9) consists of establishing an accuracy rate, meaningful mistake rate (mistakes that do not destroy syntax or meaning; e.g., *house* for *home*), self-correction rate, and a comprehension score that ranges from fragmentary understanding (1) to full and complete understanding of the story (4). Such scores, over time, indicate whether the child is improving in accuracy and the ability to self-correct and whether more or less difficult material would be more appropriate. A summary of the process appears in Figure 16.10.

Teacher/Child Miniconferences Brief, one-on-one conferencing sessions between teacher and child about particular aspects of the child's work is an evaluation method that can be used to further follow up any of the methods described to this point. The teacher may ask questions to probe the child's thinking about the products, clarify concepts that are still fuzzy in the

child's mind, and learn more about what the child is interested in working on in the future. Information-gathering is most effective when teachers offer open-ended requests such as, "Tell me how you figured this out" or "This part is especially interesting. Tell me how you thought of that." Discussions that take place in small- and large-group meetings between children and the teacher also yield information about children's conceptualization that can be useful for more in-depth planning and assessment.

Self-Appraisal by the Child Children are rarely challenged to evaluate their own progress, yet it is important that they do so. Besides conferencing with the teacher periodically about their work, they can learn to document involvement in the classroom by using checklists that have been developed in many of the domains. For example, skills in a certain area (e.g., physical development, social-emotional development, or emergent writing) may be listed (see Figure 16.11),

FIGURE 16.10
Analyzing and Scoring Oral Reading Tapes

Analysis

1. Listen to the tape the child has made.
2. Underline *all* mistakes, writing above printed word what reader actually said.
3. Do not count the same mistake twice.
4. Indicate self-corrections by putting a C above the word and underlining it.
5. Circle any words omitted.
6. Put a caret (^) in space if an extra word is added, writing extra word above.
7. If letters or words are reversed, mark with horizontal S ($\sim$).
8. Make notes on retelling, comprehension, particular qualities of reading, or problems.
9. In the right margin
   a. indicate a meaningful mistake (does not destroy syntax or meaning) by a slash (/).
   b. indicate self-corrected mistakes by underlining a slash ($\underline{/}$).
   c. indicate mistakes not corrected or those that destroy meaning or syntax by a crossed slash (x).

Scoring

1. *Use the following designators:*
   A = Count total numbers of words read.
   B = Add total uncorrected mistakes (X).
   C = Add self-corrections ($\underline{/}$).
   D = Add meaningful mistakes (/).
   E = Total all mistakes (C + D + E).

2. *Obtain accuracy score.* From total words read, subtract uncorrected and nonmeaningful mistakes. Divide the resulting number by the total number of words read. Thus, use the following formula: [(A − B) ÷ A].

Note: If accuracy rate is below 95 percent, the child is likely to flounder and lose ability to use strategies ordinarily at his or her disposal. Try an easier text. If 100 percent accuracy, suggest a more difficult text to child.

3. *Obtain self-correction rate.* Divide number of self-corrections (C) by total of all mistakes (E). Thus, use the following formula: [C ÷ E].

Note: The self-correction rate assesses a child's determination to make sense of what is being read. The higher the percentage, the more the child is gaining meaning from reading.

4. Determine comprehension or retelling score, using the following criteria:
   1 = fragmentary understanding
   2 = partial understanding
   3 = fairly complete understanding
   4 = full and complete understanding; ability to make inferences on what is read

Note: Oral reading tapes may be passed on from one grade to another in order to assess a child's reading progress over time. It is important to use only one tape for each child, date each entry, and use the same scoring criteria across a school district so that interpretation of children's scores will be valid. Also, a school district should establish a "literature difficulty index" or category by using suggested lists such as that published in Routman's (1987) *Transitions*. It should be noted when a child is moving to a more difficult level of reading material, for it is expected that a child's accuracy and self-correction scores will fall temporarily until the child increases skills at the new level.

Tabita is marking how he spent his time at school and will evaluate whether his day was terrific, good, OK, sad, or terrible.

with spaces that can be dated by the teacher or student and then colored in by the child as a skill is achieved. As the year progresses, children are reminded about maintaining the skill every time they make entries and are also reinforced as they see the number of skills adding up on the checklist.

Teachers will want to produce self-evaluation checklists that have a range and number of skills so that every child will be able to check or color in at least a couple of skills right at the beginning. Skills still to be acquired should be reasonably within a child's reach,

given more time and practice. For children who are progressing more slowly, a checklist that breaks the skills down more finely and recognizes smaller gains in development should be drawn up. For younger children, pictographs and a rebus are helpful.

The Ecomap Finding out about the child's world outside the classroom can enhance assessment, particularly when done early in the year, perhaps in preparation for the initial fall conference between teachers and children's parents. The ecomap (see Figure 16.12) is a

FIGURE 16.11
A Form for Child's Self-Appraisal

Date:	9/27	12/5	2/14	4/12	5/10	6/12
I can zip.						
I play and work with others.						
I share with others.						
I help clean up.						
I put materials away after using them.						
I try new things.						
I am helpful to others.						

FIGURE 16.12
Ecomap: The Child's Developmental Contexts

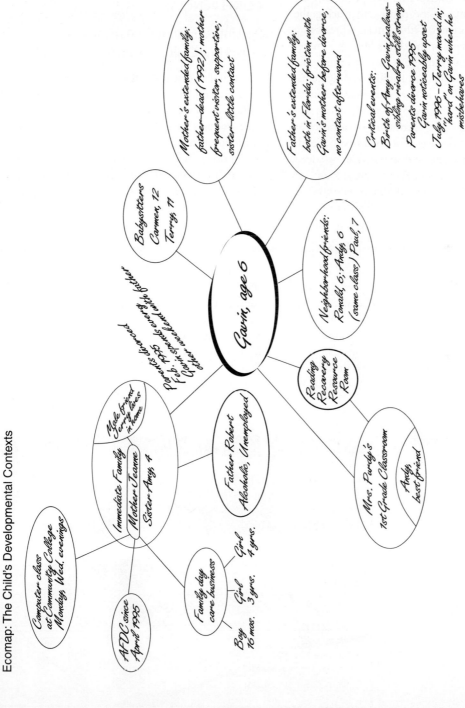

paper-and-pencil exercise designed to provide a simple, visual overview of the child's experience in the family and community. The teacher invites the parent(s) to sketch out the child's ecomap, beginning with drawing a circle in the middle of the paper and placing the child's name in the center. Other circles representing the most salient systems in the child's life (e.g., immediate family members living both in and outside the household, as well as extended family—grandparents, influential aunts, uncles, etc.) are then placed around the center circle and connected by lines. Other connections related to health care, recreation, extracurricular activities, parents' workplaces, the child's best friends outside of school, childcare, and so forth can be added to provide more information. As the connections are drawn, the teacher may elicit additional information about any connections that seem to be highly problematic or supportive for either the child or parent. In this way, the teacher becomes acquainted with the way children spend their time and energy outside the classroom. Also revealed is the qualitative nature of the various contexts, which provides a better understanding of a child's special needs or life events that may be affecting the child's classroom performance. Parents who have participated in the exercise have reported that it allowed them to establish better rapport and feelings of collaboration. Others have said the process made them more aware that even a very young child's world can be fairly complex.

ORGANIZATION AND USE OF ASSESSMENT AND EVALUATION DATA: PORTFOLIOS AND STUDENT-LED CONFERENCES

Portfolios: Matching Assessment With How Children Learn

There is no better method for organizing and displaying children's documented academic growth and "generative shifts in understandings in comparison to their younger selves" (Perrone, 1991, 59) than the portfolio. Having children save work samples and other classroom artifacts that document their growth is one of the most enjoyable aspects of working with children. When children show their dossier, portfolio, or process-folios of work to others, teachers are able to share in their obvious mixture of pure delight and heavy seriousness as children select their personal best.

The purpose of structuring portfolios is threefold: to make sense of children's work, to let others know about their work, and to relate the work to a larger context (Grace & Shores, 1991). Samples may include a child's drawings, paintings, video- and/or audiotapes, maps, graphs, descriptions and photographs of projects and friends, charts, webs, and written work—in short, anything that meaningfully depicts their progress. The process promotes developmentally appropriate instruction in that it requires professionals to

Portfolios are useful in noting development over time in a variety of domains.

plan performance-based evaluation activities from which products can be collected intermittently during the school year and to allow children adequate time and guidance to work on relevant artifacts for their portfolios.

The most compelling feature of portfolios is that they focus more on what children *can* do, whereas traditional assessment focuses primarily on what they *cannot* do or not do very well. Beginning as general collections of their work, portfolios are then reduced to selections the children feel are representative of their progress. Coexisting portfolios at any one time include the following (Tierney, 1991):

1 *An individual portfolio* in which the child stores dated work samples from his or her daily work as artist, reader, writer, problem solver, and scientist (Stone, 1997). When introducing the process, consider bringing in professionals who keep some sort of portfolio (e.g., photographers, models, architects, artists, journalists, or educators) to lead a discussion with children about what can be developed in each area of the curriculum. Because a sense of ownership will be important, children should brainstorm and have input about what kinds of representative samples to save. When children are working on pieces for the portfolio, the teacher will want to remind them about qualitative aspects of the work and the importance of their best effort.

Storage for easy access is important. Some teachers have obtained large, individual pizza boxes in which children store their work. Others have had children make them out of large pieces of sturdy tagboard. With large classes of children, two or three places can be established in the room for folder storage so that children do not have to wait in long lines to place daily work in their portfolios.

2. *A showcase portfolio* intended to be shared with others. It contains a *specified* number of carefully selected pieces the child feels are the best examples of his or her work. These may be negotiated with the teacher or remain wholly the choice of the child. At the time of selection, the child communicates to the teacher the *reasons* he or she considers a particular piece a good choice. These should always be arranged in chronological order to indicate growth. For very young children, there may be just three to five pieces. Primary children can be helped to select samples of work from *each* curriculum area and to categorize the material for the

viewer. If able, children may also construct a preface, table of contents, or labels to tell the reader how the materials were developed or organized.

Decorated or personalized showcase portfolios can be very simple or quite elaborate, depending on the skill and motivation of the children. Encourage children to customize them as creatively as possible and to take pride in the uniqueness of their personality or work style. As soon as children are writing, they can include a statement of purpose or an introduction for the portfolio. One child wrote, "Dear reader: My portfolio contains art work, journals, center work, writing pieces, and spelling sheets. This is work I adore, so please try not to rip it" (Soderman, Gregory, & O'Neill, 1999).

3. *A teacher portfolio,* usually a manila folder, with selections or copies of work from the student portfolio and also checklists and inventories of skill development, anecdotal notes, and any other data the teacher feels is particularly illustrative of the child's academic and personal growth. The teacher may want to include items that children may not have selected for their showcase portfolios but depict particular strengths or limitations of the child. These are not shared at student-led conferences but may be useful if parents wish to confer later with the teacher or if the teacher needs to confer with other professionals who are involved in educational planning for a child.

4. *An institutional portfolio* that contains a *specified* collection of the child's work over the period of time the child is in the school. The contents are a brief number of particular items agreed upon by the staff that are to be collected at each grade level for all children at consistent times during each year. For example, at the kindergarten level, children may be asked to draw a self-portrait at the beginning and end of the year. Also included may be a social skills checklist, a self-appraisal checklist, and an ecomap. In first grade, the child's self-portraits at the beginning and end of the year are again included, along with two samples of the child's best writing (the spring one might be a simple math story problem), and K-5 inventories of literacy and math progress are begun and entered. A picture of the child at each level, perhaps with special friends, should be included. These portfolios are collected at year's end (unless the child will be staying with the same teacher) and sent on to the next year's teacher. Some elementary schools hold a celebration evening for children who will be going on the next

year to a middle school and present the children and their families with these longitudinal, comprehensive collections of their work. They are highly valued because they paint a picture of significant growth by children as they move through the elementary years. One child who was looking back at some of the earliest entries grinned broadly and remarked, "I was such a baby then!" When schools are implementing new instructional practices, the portfolios help determine whether children's skills are improving over time.

Student-Led Conferencing: Bringing Parents and Others Into the Process

Producing a good piece of work is enormously satisfying, yet our satisfaction is expanded considerably when we share it with others. That is what student-led conferencing is all about. It encourages children to reflect on what they have produced and think about future goals. It is a celebration in which parents and interested others can view a child's accomplishments firsthand, make supportive comments and suggestions, exchange information, and be actively involved in the work world of the child (Stone, 1997). Instead of cutting the child *out* of the process (as in traditional parent/teacher conferencing), the child is not only brought *into* the process but, appropriately, takes center stage. Instead of the teacher relating simple scores or grades to parents and telling about work that was *not* produced, the onus is put on the child to present evidence of growth and achievement during a specific period of time. It is their party!

Student-led conferencing comprises three stages: (1) a preparatory period, (2) implementation of the actual conference, and (3) a debriefing period.

Getting Ready for the Big Event At specific times during the school year, anywhere from once to quarterly, teachers and children plan for a portfolio conference. The teacher sets a convenient time for parents to attend (one that does not conflict with other events in the community or with parents' work schedules), helps children to select and organize materials, sends out written invitations, plans for pictures to be taken, organizes childcare and transportation if necessary, and informs the parents about the process. Schedules can be drawn up to ensure that the teacher has adequate time to meet each family. An optimal structure is to

have four or five families in the room at one time for 20 to 30 minutes, depending on the size of the class. Preprimary and kindergarten teachers who have two different classes per day will want to schedule two separate evenings to accommodate parents comfortably.

The teacher will want to stress the importance of parents' remembering to be only positive because the work they will be viewing is their child's personal best at that particular time. If parents are inexperienced with the process, professionals can provide examples of questions parents may ask children during the conference (e.g., "Which piece is your favorite? Why?" "What are your goals for the next work period?" "What do you feel is the most important thing you've learned this year?" "What do you enjoy most about school this year? What do you find most difficult?").

In addition to selecting pieces for their showcase portfolio, children may practice communicating about their work by showing their portfolios to a classmate (a portfolio buddy) and to someone else in another class before the actual conference. They may role-play introducing their family members to the teacher, write invitations, and plan with the teacher how to restructure the classroom environment for the evening. For example, children can make posters celebrating the event, table decorations, and decorated paper tablecloths. They can make a parent guest book for written feedback, make refreshments, make a welcome sign for the door, and help select soft, instrumental music to be played in the background. They may also help clean and organize the classroom for the event. Children also discuss with their teacher the activities that might be of special interest to their parents: favorite books to share (and to show off their improving reading skills!), centers to show parents and involve them in classroom activities, journals, group projects, videos showing children at work in the classroom, and a bulletin board loaded with pictures of the children and teacher both inside and outside the classroom.

Celebrating Because of their extensive involvement in the preparatory phase, children are very excited about the celebration itself—perhaps even a little nervous! Like the artist, photographer, architect, writer, and scientist, the work in which they have so much personal investment is about to be viewed and evaluated by others. Even very young children can be encouraged to introduce their parents to the teacher and then to read a favorite book with their parents, engage a parent in a favorite classroom activity or game, share their journal, and look through the portfolio. Obviously, as children mature, student-led conferencing can become more sophisticated. However, the evening should maintain an air of celebration and be as enjoyable as possible for all.

In many school districts where attendance at parent/teacher conferences has been extremely low, administrators report that nearly 100 percent of parents attend student-led conferencing because they find it so enjoyable. Moreover, non-English-speaking parents do not experience the extreme language barriers that kept them away from parent/teacher conferences because their own children are the presenters. Because the focus is on what the children *did* accomplish and they feel grown up in taking on the role of presenter, most children share the feelings of one second grader who exclaimed to her teacher the next morning, "That was fun! When are we going to do it again?"

Debriefing: How Was It?   A written follow-up to thank parents for attending and to find out what they enjoyed or did not enjoy about the conference is important in order to improve future portfolio celebrations. A brief survey sheet can be included in the thank-you note, including such questions as What did you like about the conference? Is there anything you would like to see changed? How has your child responded to the student-led conference? Would you like to see this type of conference format continue in the future? Why or why not? A place for comments and suggestions can also be included (Soderman et al., 1999).

The teacher will want to schedule time with individual or small groups of children to discuss their reactions to the conference and even have those children who are writing fill out evaluations. Eric, a first grader, drew a picture of himself playing a board game with his parents, all three with huge smiles on their faces, which said a lot about his experience. He titled his page, "CONNFORNS (CONFERENCE)" and wrote, "I like when I plad games. I like when I sode (showed) my Mom & Dad my fobler (folder). I like when I sode them the room." Children may discuss their favorite aspect of the conferences, what they will plan to do differently the next time, and suggest changes to make for the next conference during the preparatory or implementation phases.

Portfolios and student-led conferencing empower children, teachers, and parents. In organizing their work and articulating to others what they have done to produce that work, children grow in their ability to make decisions and to take responsibility for their achievements (Batzle, 1992). Portfolios help them connect schoolwork with real purposes for learning skills, help them recognize their strengths and weaknesses, and see learning as sequential and connected with effort—life skills that are every bit as important as the academic skills being evaluated.

Teachers take on a different role, one that rids them of a "boss mentality" and instead equips them to become facilitators, consultants, and more knowledgeable guides in children's learning. They gain greater expertise in a wide range of developmental skills and become creative rather than prescriptive in structuring classroom learning experiences (Tierney, 1991). Parents are brought intimately into an interactive evaluative process that is more meaningful, more pleasurable, and more productive in terms of understanding and appreciating their child's growing abilities. The portfolio process is more effective when it includes student-led conferencing and when schools and school systems have institutionalized the practice over the entire period of children's school careers.

SUMMARY

Developmentally appropriate early childhood evaluation is necessary for documenting the growth of young children and providing sound information for program planning in the primary grades. Formulating an effective evaluation strategy to measure children's progress requires the following:

Early childhood educators with a solid understanding of the many facets of child development

Formulation of developmental objectives in all learning domains of interest, based on child development research and theories

A planned range of appropriate performance-based activities and experiences for children keyed directly to developmental objectives and children's abilities and interests

Appropriate and authentic evaluation strategies to measure children's engagement in activities and developmental progress over time

Thoughtful timing of individual, small-group, and large-group evaluation (time of day, spacing over school year)

Effective use of evaluation data to improve the quality of each child's educational experiences and growth

A useful structure for organizing and sharing obtained formative and summative information with relevant others (i.e., the children, parents, other educational staff working currently or in the future with the child and administration)

Although standardized tests can help us understand and plan for the child with special needs, information gained from them should be used only in conjunction with other equally valid sources. Single scores on standardized tests should never be used in isolation to direct or redirect the lives of young children; nor should they be used to structure children into homogeneous settings when they could better be served in regular programs and with their peers. In general, standardized testing in preschool through second grade is largely unnecessary. Alternative evaluation methods are preferred, including the observation and collecting of a variety of valid work samples.

Findings from evaluating children's work should, first of all, be used. Although that may seem obvious, testing and evaluation often do not go beyond collecting scores in order to assign grades or make comparisons across classes or schools. The process should always culminate in a plan by the teacher to structure learning experiences for the child. Results may also help the professional to note the strengths and weaknesses of classroom instruction and/or guidance. Findings should be considered in the context of the teacher's knowlege of the child and influence the timing and nature of the next evaluation.

All assessment findings should be carefully catalogued for future use, and information should be kept confidential except when used to support the educational experience of the young child. In the hands of professionals knowledgeable about child development, curriculum planning, and early childhood assessment, effective evaluation can become one of the tools needed to plan advantageous beginnings for children and the kind of classroom experiences that will lead to sustained curiosity and a desire for lifelong learning.

❋ Applying What You Read in This Chapter

1. Discuss

a. Return to the questions that opened this chapter. Based on your reading and experiences, discuss each of them in detail.

b. If you were interviewing for an early childhood teaching position and a member of the interviewing team asked you what you know about authentic assessment and how you would implement it, how would you answer?

2. Observe

a. Arrange to view the portfolios of a class of first and third graders in a local elementary school that utilizes student-led conferencing. Ask for permission to observe implementation of the process. Determine the following:

(1) What products were kept in the portfolios? How does this differ between the first graders and the third graders?

(2) During the conferencing, what role do the children play? What role does the teacher play? In what ways is the process an effective way to share information? In what ways could it be improved?

3. Carry out an activity.

a. Refer to the discussion about participation charts on page 551. Using the example provided, work through the exercise to answer the ten questions. Then identify a preschool classroom and construct a participation chart and several questions to be answered. Follow through with an observation in the setting to collect participation data. Analyze the data to obtain answers to your questions.

b. Carry out a reading accuracy test with a second grader, utilizing the process described in the chapter. Use Leo Leonni's "Fish Is Fish" as the text. What is the child's accuracy score? Self-correction rate? How would you score the child's comprehension? Summarize what you learned about the child's literacy skills.

c. Utilizing the information you gained about ecomaps on pages 556–558, ask to interview the parent of one or more children in a nearby early childhood education setting. What can you find out about the child that might be helpful in working with that particular child in an educational context?

d. Read a book about implementing portfolios in the early childhood classroom. Talk to at least two teachers who are currently using portfolios and student-led conferences. What additional tips can they give you that you did not find in the book? Find out how two sets of participating parents feel about portfolios and student-led conferencing.

4. **Create something for your portfolio.**

   a. Develop a position statement about the need for more authentic assessment of children in the early childhood classroom. Give reasons why it supports developmentally appropriate educational practices.

b. Create a subsection on your *ability to assess and evaluate the progress of young children.* Include a listing and brief description of a number of authentic methods. Carry out as many of these methods as you can with a child of the appropriate age. Summarize the results of each of the assessment procedures and attach a copy of the child's work.

5. **Add to your journal.**

   a. What are your earliest memories of taking tests? How well do you do today when taking tests? What are your strengths and limitations?

   b. How confident do you feel about implementing authentic assessment and evaluation strategies? Where do you need more information and/or practice?

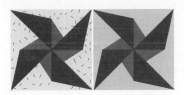

Appendix:
Sample Lesson Plans

SAMPLE GUIDED DISCOVERY PLAN

Domain: Cognitive   **Activity Name:** Sea Life Observations

Intermediate Objective: The children will examine natural objects using multiple sensory abilities.

Content

1. People learn about objects in nature by examining them closely.
2. Some ways to examine an object include looking at it, touching it, smelling it, and listening to it.
3. The more senses people use in their investigations of natural objects, the more they learn.
4. People improve their investigation skills through practice and by thinking about how they will remember what they observed.
5. People record their observations so they can refer to them later.

Assumptions

1. Children have handled natural objects, such as rocks, leaves, or shells, before.
2. Children have the vocabulary needed to describe what they see.
3. Children have the physical skills to make marks on a paper.

Intermediate Objectives

The child will

1. Examine an object using multiple senses.
2. Talk about what he or she discovered.
3. Record his or her observations for future reference.
4. Describe how he or she examined the object.

Materials: One large, dead starfish; a Dungeness or other hard-shelled crab, preserved on ice; strands of wet seaweed on a tray; a horseshoe crab shell free of insects; paper towels that cover the objects prior to use and that the children can use to wipe their hands as necessary; pads of paper for the children to use and pencils or markers.

Procedures

Examine and Talk

1. Gather the children in a large circle. Begin the activity with a discussion about all the different ways that the children have been examining objects during the week. Remind the children of some of the strategies they have used.
2. Divide the children into four small groups, each assigned to a different table.
3. Give each group a towel-covered tray that holds a natural object. Explain that everyone will have a chance to examine the natural object very closely. Make sure that the children know that the objects are safe to touch. Invite the children to examine the object *before* taking off the paper towels. Ask this question: "What did you find out?" Paraphrase the children's comments.
4. Ask the children, "How did you discover _____?" Paraphrase the children's comments.
5. Tell the children to remove the towels and continue their investigation. Ask open-ended questions to prompt the children's use of various senses. Paraphrase the children's discoveries. Add factual information if the children desire it.

Record

6. After several minutes, give each child a piece of paper and ask him or her to make a mark on the paper as a reminder of what he or she discovered. Such marks could take the form of pictures, words, or symbols. They need have no meaning to anyone other than the child.

Describe

7. Invite the children to return to the large group area with their marked papers. Conduct a discussion of what the children found out. Create on chart paper a master list of the children's discoveries. Post this where the children can refer to it and add to it throughout the day. During this discussion, continually refer to the investigative methods the children used and how they used them.
8. Tell the children that all the trays will be in the science/math center so they can explore items they did not have a chance to investigate.

Simplification: Divide the large group of children into small groups; give each group a specimen of a similar object (e.g., give all the groups a starfish).

Extension

1. Have the children examine a different object each day, keeping a journal of the properties of the object.
2. Ask the children what they would still like to know about the objects that they have not discovered yet. Brainstorm with them about how they could find out.

Hint for Success: Keep the objects to be examined covered until you are ready to begin to enhance the children's curiosity. Allow a bit of each object to be seen around the edges.

Evaluation

1. What properties were the most common among the children's observations?
2. What different strategies did the children use to investigate the objects?
3. What different ways did the children use to record their observations?
4. How might you revise the activity in the future and why?

SAMPLE PROBLEM-SOLVING PLAN

Domain: Affective   **Activity Name:** Making Plans

Intermediate Objective: The children will make a plan and carry it out.

Content

1. A plan is a guide for decision making and action.
2. A goal is something a person wants and tries to reach.
3. A goal can be better accomplished when we have thought about a plan of action to reach the goal.

Assumptions

1. Children are capable of manipulating the materials.
2. Children can communicate their ideas about a plan.
3. Children have explored the materials previously with no set agenda.

Intermediate Objectives: The child will

1. Establish a goal.
2. Create a plan for meeting the goal.
3. Carry out the plan.
4. Evaluate the plan.

Materials: A wide array of art materials; scraps of wood or cloth; glue, paste, and other fasteners; scissors, markers; crayons, and paint

Procedure

1. Invite the children to look at the materials available.
2. Tell the children they will have a chance to make something of their own choosing.
3. Ask each child to think of something he or she would like to make from the materials. This can be an object, such as a car, or something abstract, such as a collage.
4. Ask the children what they would have to do first, second, and third to make their projects. Write their ideas, making a sample plan.
5. Have the children implement their plan.
6. After the children have made something, review their plan with them and ask them if they kept to their plan or changed it.

Simplification: Work with the child to scaffold a two- or three-step plan.

Extension: Invite the children to make plans of four or more steps.

Hint for Success

1. Use open-ended questions aimed at metacognition: How did you decide?
2. Use open-ended questions to help the children think through their plan: "Then what?" "What will you do next?" "How will you know when you are finished?"

Evaluation: Complete the following evaluation sheet by putting a check beside the objectives that each child demonstrated. Note how many steps each child included in his or her plan.

Children's Names	Established a Goal	Created a Plan	Carried Out the Plan	Evaluated the Plan	Number of Steps in the Plan
Alonzo					
Cathy					
David					
Dwayne					
Hallie					
Jorge					
Mark					
Maureen					
Olivia					
Rita					
Talia					
Veronica					
Vincent					

SAMPLE DISCUSSION PLAN

Domain: Social   **Activity Name:** Rules for the Block Area

Intermediate Objective: The children will identify the reasons for classroom rules.

Content

1. A rule is a guide for behavior.
2. People make rules to protect property, to protect people's rights, and to ensure safety.
3. People in groups agree to follow certain rules to help them get along with one another.
4. People discuss things to better understand them and to reach agreement about them.
5. In a discussion, sometimes people talk, and sometimes they listen.

Assumptions

1. Children are capable of sitting in a group for approximately 15 minutes.
2. Children have been involved in open-ended group discussions in the past.
3. Children are able to communicate their ideas.

Intermediate Objectives

The child will

1. Participate in a group discussion about classroom rules.
2. Identify reasons for classroom rules.
3. Suggest an idea for a rule.
4. Provide a reason for his or her rule.

Materials: Easel and easel pad; dark, thick-tipped marker

Procedure

1. Open the discussion by talking about some of the current problems in the block area (people running, blocks all over the floor). Introduce the idea of rules as guides for behavior.
2. Invite the children to suggest ideas for rules that might involve play in the block area.
   a. Paraphrase the children's ideas.
   b. Use questions to stimulate the children's thinking.
3. Guide verbal turn taking.
   a. Remind the children to listen carefully when another child is speaking.
4. Record the children's ideas on a large sheet of easel paper.
   a. Restate each idea after it has been written.
5. Draw the discussion to a close by summarizing the children's rules.
6. Post the children's rules in the block area.

Simplification: If the children cannot think of ideas, offer suggestions to get the discussion started.

Extension: After a week, ask the children to evaluate their rules and revise them as necessary.

Hints for Success

1. Keep the discussion time short.
2. Remind the children of the topic often.

Evaluation

1. Who contributed to the group discussion?
2. Which the children met which objectives?
3. What surprised you about the discussion?

SAMPLE DEMONSTRATION PLAN

Domain: Cognitive   **Activity Name:** Body Patterns

Intermediate Objective: The children will reproduce patterns.

Content

1. A *pattern* refers to the ways in which colors, shapes, or lines are arranged or repeated in some order.
2. The way that the elements of a pattern are organized determines the pattern's design or how it sounds. A pattern can be a set of repeated actions.
3. The same elements may be organized in a variety of ways to create different patterns.

Assumptions

1. The children have participated in repetitive movement activities before, such as the song, "Head, Shoulders, Knees and Toes" and the game, The Hokey Poky.
2. The children have sufficient perceptual skills to discriminate differences in body movements.
3. The children are physically able to move.

Intermediate Objectives

The child will

1. Explore a variety of body movements.
2. Imitate simple body movement patterns consisting of two elements.
3. Imitate complex body movement patterns consisting of more than two elements.
4. Suggest/create/demonstrate a pattern of their own to the rest of the group.

Materials: None

Procedures

Explore

1. Invite the children to participate in the activity. Gain their attention by asking them to explore different ways to move their bodies.
2. Encourage the children to imitate a single motion that you or another child makes.

Imitate Simple Patterns

3. Invite the children to watch you as you show them a body movement pattern. Create a simple pattern of movements and words involving two body parts and single motion. For instance, tap your body and say the word for the body part in a rhythmic fashion: "Head, head, shoulders, shoulders, head, head, shoulders, shoulders."
4. Using a "do-it" signal, have the children respond by imitating your actions.
5. Repeat steps 3 and 4 using two different body parts and different number combinations. Keep the numbers the same for each body part, such as two taps and two claps.

Imitate Complex Patterns

6. Gradually increase the complexity of the patterns by increasing the number of body parts and motions (tapping, your head, clapping your hands, and stomping your feet). Another way to increase complexity is to vary the number of motions (two taps, three claps, one stomp). Have the children imitate the pattern you create.

Simplification: Use simple patterns slowly. Use major body parts such as head, hands, and feet.

Extension

1. Increase the complexity of the pattern and the speed of your movements using body parts such as wrist, neck, and ankles.
2. Demonstrate a repetitive movement. Ask the children to predict what comes next, and then do it.

Hints for Success

1. Use humor so that the activity is fun.
2. Once the children seem to have the idea of how patterns are created, have them take turns creating patterns for others to imitate.
3. Warn the children when the game is about to end: "We have time for one more person to make a pattern." Avoid an abrupt ending.

Evaluation

1. Which children participated in this activity?
2. What objectives did each child achieve?
3. Was the procedure carried out as described here? If so, what was the result? If not, what did you change and why?

SAMPLE DIRECT INSTRUCTION PLAN

Domain: Cognitive   **Activity Name:** Earthworm Facts

Intermediate Objective: The children will acquire scientific knowledge related to life sciences, specifically animal life.

Content

1. Earthworms are cylindrically shaped, segmented animals.
2. Earthworms have a mouth (no teeth), a headed end, and a tailed end (the head is more pointed than the tail).
3. Earthworms have no ears, eyes, legs, or skeleton.
4. Earthworms live and burrow in the soil.
5. Earthworms move by waves of muscular contractions traveling along the body.

Assumptions

1. The children have seen earthworms in the past.
2. The children have sufficient vocabulary to describe some of the physical characteristics of earthworms.
3. The children are able to follow simple directions.

Materials: A shovel full of soil in a bucket or in the water table; worms; a large picture of an earthworm depicting its segments, specifically, head end and tail end; a children's reference book about earthworms that includes pictures and simple facts about earthworm movement and habits; a clean piece of white paper on which to place an earthworm to watch its movements more easily; paper on which to write and markers or pens; cheesecloth

Procedures

Preparation: To prepare for this activity, dig up some large earthworms or buy some at a bait store. Keep the soil moist and covered with cheesecloth prior to asking the children to participate.

Learning Phase	Immediate Objectives	Adult Does	Adult Says
Explore	Given a shovelful of soil containing some earthworms, the child will	Invite the children to participate.	Hi. Look at what's in this water table. It's not water! Today we have some soil dug out of our yard.
	1. Gently pick through the soil searching for earthworms.	Remind children to be gentle.	Look carefully through it and tell me what animals you find
Acquire	2. Talk about the earthworms as he or she observes them.	Ask children what they are noticing about the earthworms.	Tell me what you see.

Learning Phase	Immediate Objectives	Adult Does	Adult Says
		Paraphrase the children's comments.	You noticed that some of these worms are red and some are black. You see skinny worms. The worm in your hand is very thick all the way around.
	Given an opportunity to observe and handle an earthworm while hearing an adult describe some of its features, the child will	Provide information to the children as they examine the earthworms. Talk about the shape, size, and movements of the earthworms.	Earth worms have a mouth at the head end of their bodies. Look for the mouth on your earthworm.
	3. Differentiate the head end from the tail end of the worm.	Ask the children to look for the earthworm's mouth.	Earthworms move head first. Look at that worm. Show me the head end.
		Refer to the picture of the earthworm to help children know at which end to look.	Look at this picture. See if your earthworm has segments on it like this.
		On a piece of paper, record the parts of the worm the children are able to identify.	So far, we have found heads and tails on these earthworms. Let's write that on our earthworm facts chart.
	4. Identify body parts earthworms do not possess.	Ask the children to tell you what body parts people or other animals have that they do not see on the earthworms they are examining.	Look to see if your earthworm has legs. Look at this picture; this earthworm has no ears. Look to see if that's true for your earthworm.
		Ask simple questions to help children focus on the body parts earthworms don't possess.	
		Provide correct information to children who have erroneous ideas.	You think your earthworm has eyes. Those dark colors on the tail aren't eyes.

Learning Phase	Immediate Objectives	Adult Does	Adult Says
	5. Describe ways the earthworms move.	Show the children how the earthworms move by contracting their bodies. This may be done in the soil and on a clean piece of paper where the worm's undulating motion is easily seen. In addition, the worm will leave a faint imprint on the paper that will show the wavy way in which it propels itself.	Let's look closely at how these earthworms get from place to place.

Tell me what you see.

Notice how the earthworm pulls in and then stretches out to move. |
| Practice | 6. Observe and talk about earthworms outside on the playground throughout the week. | Guide the children's attention to earthworms outside.

Review what the children discovered earlier in the week.

Add new information to the chart the children had dictated. | Let's see if any earthworms are out here today.

You remembered that earthworms come in different colors.

You discovered that earthworms have tiny bristles on the underside of their bodies. Let's add that to our list of earthworm facts. |

To Simplify: Focus primarily on color and shape and the variety among earthworms.

To Extend: Have the children compare earthworms to garter snakes, identifying similarities and differences.

Hints for Success

1. Give the children ample time to observe the earthworms prior to introducing specific information.
2. Keep the soil moist but not soaked.
3. Earthworms usually move head first; that's the end where the mouth is.

Evaluation

1. What strategy was most successful in engaging the less assertive children in the activity? the more assertive?
2. Which children achieved which objectives?
3. What did the children seem to know about earthworms in the exploration stage? What erroneous information did the children possess? About what were they most curious? What new facts did the children acquire over the week?

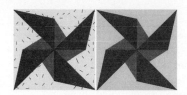

References

Abbot, J. (1997, March). To be intelligent. *Educational Leadership, 54*(6), 6–10.

Abrams, H. (1985). *The Museum of Modern Art, New York.* New York: Harry Abrams, Inc.

Abrohms, A. (1992). *Literature-based math activities: An integrated approach.* New York: Scholastic.

Adams, P., & Nesmith, J. (1996). Blockbusters: Ideas for the block center. *Early Childhood Education Journal, 24*(2), 87–92.

Adventures of Sherlock Holmes. (1939). 20th Century Fox Studios.

Albrecht, K., & Plantz, M. (1991). Developmentally appropriate practice in school-age child care programs. (Available from the American Home Economics Association, 1555 King St., Alexandria, VA 22314)

Alejandro-Wright, M. N. (1985). The child's conception of racial classification. In M. B. Spencer, G. K. Brookins, and W. R. Allen (Eds.), *Beginnings: The social and affective development of black children* (pp. 185–200) Hillsdale, NJ: Erlbaum.

Alexander, K. L., & Entwistle, D. R. (1988). Achievement in the first two years of school: Patterns and processes. *SRCD Monographs, 53*(2).

Anderson, J. A. (1988). Cognitive styles and multicultural populations. *Journal of Teacher Education, 29,* 2–9.

Andersson, B. E. (1992). Effects of day care on cognitive and socioemotional development of thirteen-year-old Swedish children. *Child Development, 63,* 20–26.

Anger and aggression: What we hope children learn. (1989, January-February). *Cornerstones, 1*(1), 1–8.

Anziano, M. C., Bilman, J., Kostelnik, M. J., & Soundy, C. S. (1995). *Approaches to preschool curriculum.* New York: Glencoe, McGraw-Hill.

Ard, L., & Pitts, M. (Eds.) (1995). *Room to grow: How to create quality early childhood environments.* Austin, TX: Texas Association for the Education of Young Children.

Arnold, L. (1995). High hopes. On *Sing along stew.* Hollywood CA: A&M Records.

Asher, S. R., Oden, S. L., & Gottman, J. M. (1977). Children's friendships in school settings. In L. G. Katz (Ed.), *Current topics in early childhood education* (vol. 1) (pp. 33–61). Norwood, NJ: Ablex.

Association for Supervision and Curriculum Development (1991, November). Teaching to the brain. *ASCD Update, 33*(8), 1–8.

Axton, H. (1995). *Jeremiah was a bullfrog.* Cypress, CA: Youngheart Music.

Balaban, N. (1985). *Starting school.* New York: Teachers College Press.

Ball, J. (February, 1989). The national PTA's stand on corporal punishment. *PTA Today, 14,* 15–17.

Bandura, A. (1989). Social cognitive theory. In R. Vasta (Ed.), *Annals of child development* (vol. 6) (pp. 1–60). Greenwich, CT: JAI

Banks, J. A. (1988, Spring). Approaches to multicultural curriculum reform. *Multicultural Leader, 1*(2). Edmonds, WA: Multicultural Materials and Services.

Barab, S. A., & Landa, A. (1997, March). Designing effective interdisciplinary anchors. *Educational Leadership, 54*(6).

Barbour, N. H. (1990). Flexible grouping: It works! *Childhood Education, 67*(2), 66–67.

Barbour, N., Webster, T., & Drosdeck, S. (1987). Sand: A resource for the language arts. *Young Children, 42*(2), 20–25.

Barclay, K., Benelli, C., Campbell, P., & Klein, L. (1995). Dream or nightmare? Planning for a year without textbooks. *Childhood Education, 71*(4), 205–11.

Baroody, A. J. (1993). Fostering the mathematical learning of young children. In B. Spodek (Ed.), *Handbook of research on the education of young children* (pp. 151–75). New York: Macmillan.

Baroody, A. J. (1987). *Children's mathematical thinking.* New York: Teachers College Press.

Bartels, J. (1990). Swinging on a star. On *Sillytime magic.* Van Nuys, CA: BMG Music.

Bateson, G. (1971). The message "This is play." In R. Herren and B. Sutton-Smith (Eds.), *Child's play.* New York: Wiley.

Battle Creek Public Schools (1990). *Primary curriculum: Kindergarten through second grade.* Battle Creek, MI: Author.

Batzle, J. (1992). *Portfolio assessment and evaluation: Developing and using portfolios in the classroom.* Cypress, CA: Creative Teaching Press.

Bauer, A. (Ed.). (1995). *Selecting educational equipment and materials for school and home.* Washington, DC: Association of Childhood Education International.

Baumrind, D. (1995). *Child maltreatment and optimal caregiving in social contexts.* New York: Garland.

Baumrind, D. (1988). *Familial antecedents of social competence in middle childhood.* Unpublished manuscript.

Baumrind, D. (1983). Rejoiner to Lewis's reinterpretation of parental firm control effects: Are authoritative families really harmonious? *Psychological Bulletin, 94,* 132–42.

Baumrind, D. (1978). A dialectical materialist's perspective on knowing social reality. In W. Damon (Ed.), *Moral development* (pp. 349–73). San Francisco, CA: Jossey-Bass.

Baumrind, D. (1977, April). *Socialization determinants of personal agency.* Paper presented at the biennial meeting of the Society for Research in Child Development, New Orleans, LA.

Baumrind, D. (1973). Current patterns of parental authority. *Developmental Psychology Monographs, 4,*1

Baumrind, D. (1967). Child care practices anteceding three patterns of preschool behavior. *Genetic Psychology Monographs, 75,* 43–88.

Beardsley, T. (1997, August). Trends in neuroscience: The machinery of thought. *Scientific American, 277*(2), 78–83.

Beauchamp, G. R., & Kosmorsky, G. (1987, December). Learning disabilities: Update comment on the visual system. *Pediatric Clinics of North America, 34*(6), 1439–47.

Becher, R. M. (1984). Parent involvement: A review of research and principles of successful practice (Report No. 400–83–0021). Washington, DC: National Institute of Education. (ERIC Document No. ED 182–465).

Begley, S. (1997a, Spring/Summer). The brain. *Newsweek,* sp. ed., 28–31.

Begley, S. (1997b, February 3). How to build a baby's brain. *Newsweek Special Report,* 28–32.

Begley, S. (1996, February 19). Your child's brain. *Newsweek,* 55–62.

Beilin, H. (1989). Piagetian theory. In R. Vasta (Ed.), *Annals of child development* (vol. 6) (pp. 85–131). Greenwich, CT: JAI.

Bellemere, E. (1991). [Results of a five-year longitudinal study comparing developmentally appropriate and developmentally inappropriate classrooms in the Scarborough, Maine, public schools. Personal communication.]

Bergen, D. (1994). Should teachers permit or discourage violent play themes? *Childhood Education, 70*(5), 302–3.

Bergen, D. (1993). Teaching strategies: Facilitating friendship development in inclusion classrooms. *Childhood Education, 69* (4) 234-36

Bergen, D. (1988a). *Play as a medium for learning and development.* Portsmouth, NH: Heinemann.

Bergen, D. (1988b). Using a schema for play and learning. In D. Bergen (Ed.), *Play as a medium for learning and development* (pp. 169–80). Portsmouth, NH: Heinemann.

Berger, E. H. (1995). *Parents as partners in education: The school and home working together.* Upper Saddle River, NJ: Merrill/Prentice Hall.

Berk, L. (1997). *Child development* (4th ed.). Boston, MA: Allyn & Bacon.

Berk, L. (1996a). *Infants and children: Prenatal through middle childhood* (2d ed.). Boston, MA: Allyn & Bacon.

Berk, L. (1996b). *Infants, children and adolescents.* Upper Saddle River, NJ: Prentice Hall.

Berk, L. E., & Winsler, A. (1995). *Scaffolding children's learning: Vygotsky and early childhood education.* Washington, DC: National Association for the Education of Young Children.

Berns, R. M. (1996). *Child, family, community.* New York: Holt, Rinehart, & Winston.

Beverly, C. (1995). Providing a safe environment for children infected with HIV. *Topics in Early Childhood Special Education, 15*(1), 100–9.

Biber, B., Shapiro, E., & Wickens, D. (1977). *Promoting cognitive growth: A developmental interaction point of view* (2nd ed.). Washington, DC: National Association for the Education of Young Children.

Bickart, T. S., Dodge., T. D. & Jablon, J. R. (1997). *What every parent needs to know about 1st, 2nd, and 3rd grades.* Naperville, IL: Sourcebooks.

Bierman, K. L. (1987). The clinical significance and assessment of poor peer relations: Peer neglect versus peer rejection. *Journal of Developmental and Behavioral Pediatrics,* 8, 233–40.

Birrell, J., & Ross. S. (1996). Standardized testing and portfolio assessment: Rethinking the debate. *Reading Research and Instruction, 34*(4), 285–98.

Bloom, B. (1984). *Taxonomy of educational objectives: Handbook of the cognitive domain.* New York: Longman.

Bly, R. (1988). *A little book on the human shadow.* San Francisco, CA: Harper & Row.

Bobbitt, N., & Paolucci, B. (1986). Strengths of the home and family as learning environments. In R. J. Griffore and R. P. Boger (Eds.), *Child rearing in the home and school* (pp. 47–60). New York: Plenum.

Bodrova, E., & Leong, D. (1996). *Tools of the mind: The Vygotskian approach to early childhood education.* Upper Saddle River, NJ: Merrill/Prentice Hall.

Bogart, J. (1994). *Gifts.* Richmond Hill, Ontario, Canada: Scholastic Canada.

Bollin, G. G. (1989, Summer). Ethnic differences in attitude towards discipline among day care providers: Implications for training. *Child & Youth Care Quarterly, 18*(2), 111–17.

Boneau, C. A. (1974). Paradigm regained: Cognitive behaviors restated. *American Psychologist, 29,* 297–309.

Bongiovanni, A. (1977, February). *A review of research on the effects of punishment: Implications for corporal punishment in the schools.* Paper presented at the Conference on Child Abuse, Children's Hospital National Medical Center, Washington, DC.

Booth, C. (1997). The fiber project: One teacher's adventure toward emergent curriculum. *Young Children, 52*(5), 79–85.

Borden, E. (1987). The community connection—It works. *Young Children, 42*(4), 14–23.

Bowman, B. (1994). The challenge of diversity. *Phi Delta Kappan, 76*(3), 218–25.

Bowman, B., (1991). Educating language minority children: Challenges and opportunities. In S. L. Kagan (Ed.), *The care and education of America's young children: Obstacles and opportunities. 90th yearbook of the National Society for the Study of Education* (pp. 17–29). Chicago,IL: University of Chicago Press.

Boyatzis, C. (1997). Of power rangers and v-chips. *Young Children, 52*(7), 74–79.

Boyd, B. J. (1997). Teacher response to superhero play: To ban or not to ban? *Young Children, 74*(1), 23–27.

Boyer, E. (1995). *The basic school: A community for learning.* Princeton, NJ: Carnegie Foundation for the Advancement of Teaching.

Boyer, J. B. (1990). *Curriculum materials for ethnic diversity.* Lawrence, KS: University of Kansas Center for Black Leadership Development and Research.

Bracey, G. W. (1987). Measurement-driven instruction. Catchy phrase, dangerous practice. *Phi Delta Kappan, 68,* 683–86.

Braddock, J. H. II, & McPartland, J. M. (1990). Alternatives to tracking. *Educational Leadership, 48*(7), 76–80.

Brainard, A., & Wrubel, D. H. (1993). *Literature-based science activities.* New York: Scholastic.

Brandt, R., & Epstein J. (1989, October). On parents and schools: A conversation with Joyce Epstein. *Educational Leadership,* 24–27.

Branta, C. F. (1992). *Motoric and fitness assessment of young children.* In C. Hendricks (Ed.), *Young children on the grow: Health, activity, and education in the preschool setting* (pp. 89–108). Washington DC: ERIC. Teacher Education Monograph No. 13.

Brazelton, T. B. (1992). *Heart start: The emotional foundations of school readiness.* Arlington, VA: National Center for Clinical Infant Programs.

Bredderman, T. (1982, September). What research says: Activity science—The evidence shows it matters. *Science and Children 20*(1), 39–41.

Bredekamp, S. (1991b). Guidelines for appropriate curriculum content and assessment in programs serving children ages three through eight. *Young Children, 46*(3), 21–38.

Bredekamp, S. (1987). *Developmentally appropriate practice in early childhood programs serving children from birth through age 8.* Washington, DC: National Association for the Education of Young Children.

Bredekamp, S. (Ed.). (1986). *Developmentally appropriate practice in early childhood programs: Servicing children from birth through age 8.* Washington DC: National Association for the Education of Young Children.

Bredekamp, S., & Copple, C. (1997). *Developmentally appropriate practice in early childhood programs.* Washington, DC: National Association for the Education of Young Children.

Bredekamp, S., & Rosegrant, T. (Eds.) (1995). *Reaching potentials: Transforming early childhood curriculum and assessment* (vol. 2). Washington, DC: National Association for the Education of Young Children.

Bredekamp, S., & Rosegrant, T. (Eds.) (1992). *Reaching potentials: Appropriate curriculum and assessment for young children* (vol. 1). Washington, DC: National Association for the Education of Young Children.

Brendtro, L. K., Brokenleg, M., & Van Bockern, S. (1990). *Reclaiming youth at risk: Our hope for the future.* Bloomington, IN: National Educational Service.

Brewer, J. A. (1998). *Introduction to early childhood education: Preschool through the primary grades.* Boston, MA: Allyn & Bacon.

Briggs, N. R., Jalongo, M. R., & Brown, L. (1997). Working with families of young children: Our history and our future goals. In J. P. Isenberg and

M. R. Jalongo (Eds.), *Major trends and issues in early childhood education.* New York: Teachers College Press, 56–69.

Brody, G. H., & Shaffer, D. R. (1982). Contributions of parents and peers to children's moral socialization. *Developmental Review, 2,* 31–75.

Brody, J. (1984, October 24). Program reverses unhealthy trend in children. *The New York Times,* p. 14.

Bronfenbrenner, U. (1993). The ecology of cognitive development: Research models and fugitive findings. In R. H. Wozniak and K. W. Fischer (Eds.), *Development in context* (pp. 3–44). Hillsdale, NJ: Erlbaum.

Bronfenbrenner, U. (1989). Ecological systems theory. In R, Vasta (Ed.), *Annals of child development* (vol. 6) (pp. 187–249). Greenwich, CT: JAI.

Bronfenbrenner, U. (1977, September). *Who needs parent education?* Paper presented at the working conference on parent education, Mat 1 Foundation, Flint, MI.

Bronson, M. (1995). *The right stuff for children birth to 8: Selecting play materials to support development.* Washington, DC: National Association for the Education of Young Children.

Brooks, M., Fusco, E., & Greenon, J. (1983, May). Cognitive levels matching. *Educational Leadership,* 4–8.

Brophy, J. (1987). Synthesis of research on strategies for motivating students to learn. *Educational Leadership, 45*(2), 40–48.

Bruner, J. S. (1983). *Child's talk: Learning to use language.* New York: Norton.

Bruner, J. S., Jolly, A., & Sylva, K. (Eds.). (1976). *Play, its role in development and evolution.* New York: Penguin.

Bryan, T., & Walbek, N. (1970). Preaching and practicing generosity: Children's actions and reactions. *Child Development, 41,* 329–53.

Bukatko, D., & Daehler, M. (1995). *Child development: A thematic approach.* Boston, MA: Houghton Mifflin.

Bukatko, D., & Daehler, M. W. (1992). *Child development: A topical approach.* New York: Houghton Mifflin.

Bukowski, W. M., Sippola, L.K., & Bolvin, M. (1995, March). *Friendship protects "at risk" children from victimization by peers.* Paper presented at the meeting of the Society for Research in Child Development, Indianapolis, IN.

Bundy, B. F. (1991). Fostering communication between parents and schools. *Young Children, 46*(2), 12–17.

Burns, M. (1995). W*riting in math class.* Sausalito, CA: Math Solutions.

Burns, M. (1993). *About teaching mathematics: A kindergarten through eighth resource.* Portsmouth, NH: Heinemann.

Burton, R. V. (1984). A paradox in theories and research in moral development. In W. M. Kurtines and J. L.

Gewirtz (Eds.), *Morality, moral behavior and moral development* (pp. 193–207). New York: Wiley.

Burton, R. V. (1963). The generality of honesty reconsidered. *Psychological Review, 70,* 481–99.

Burts, D. C., Hart, C. H., Charlesworth, R., DeWolf, D. M., Manuel, K., & Fleege, P. O. (1993, Fall/Winter). Developmental appropriateness of kindergarten programs and academic outcomes in first grade. *Journal of Research in Early Childhood Education, 8*(1), 23–31.

Burts, D. C., Hart, C. H., Charlesworth, R., & Kirk, L. (1992). Observed activities and stress behaviors of children in developmentally appropriate and inappropriate kindergarten classrooms. *Early Childhood Research Quarterly, 7*(2), 297–318.

Burts, D. C., Hart, C. H., Charlesworth, R., & Kirk, L. (1990). A comparison of frequencies of stress behaviors observed in kindergarten children in classrooms with developmentally appropriate versus developmentally inappropriate instructional practices. *Early Childhood Research Quarterly, 5,* 407–23.

Cardellichio, T., & Field, W. (1997, March). Seven strategies that encourage neural branching. *Educational Leadership, 54*(6).

Carey, S. (1986). Cognitive science and science education. *American Psychologist, 41*(10), 1123–30.

Caring for our children: National health and safety standards: Guidelines for out-of-home child care programs (1992). Washington, DC: American Public Health Association and Elk Grove Village, IL: American Academy of Pediatrics.

Carle, E. (1981). *The very hungry caterpillar.* New York: Putnam.

Carlson, K., & Cunningham, J. L. (1990). Effect of pencil diameter on the graphomotor skill of preschoolers. *Early Childhood Research Quarterly, 5*(2), 279–93.

Carman-Ainsworth Community Schools (1986). *Stepping stones to early learning.* Carman-Ainsworth, MI: Author, Instructional Program Committee.

Carnegie Foundation for the Advancement of Teaching (1988). *The conditions of teaching: A state by state analysis.* Princeton, NJ: Author.

Carta, J., Schwartz, L., Atwater, J., & McConnell, S. (1993). Developmentally appropriate practices and early childhood special education: A reaction to Johnson and McChesney Johnson. *Topics in Early Childhood Special Education, 13*(3), 243–54.

Cartwright, S. (1990). Learning with large blocks. *Young Children, 45*(3), 38–41.

Cartwright, S. (1988, July). Play can be the building blocks of learning. *Young Children, 43*(5), 44–47.

Cartwright, S. (1987). Group endeavor in nursery school can be valuable learning. *Young Children, 42*(4), 8–11.

Casey, M., & Lippman, M. (1991, May). Learning to plan through play. *Young Children, 46*(4), 52–58.

Cassidy, D. (1989). Questioning the young child: Process and function. *Childhood Education, 65*(3), 146–49.

Castle, K. (1991). Children's invented games. *Childhood Education, 67*(2), 82–85.

Castle, K., & Rogers, K. (1994). Rule-creating in a constructivist community. *Childhood Education, 70*(2), 77–80.

Cazden, C. (1976). Play and language and metalinguistic awareness. In J. Bruner, A., Jolly, and K. Sylva (Eds.), *Play: Its development and evolution.* (pp. 603–8). New York: Basic Books.

Ceci, S. J. (1990). *On intelligence . . . more or less: A bio-ecological treatise on intellectual development.* Upper Saddle River, NJ: Prentice-Hall.

Chafel, J. (1986). Call the police, okay? Social comparison by young children during play in preschool. In S. Burrows and R. Evans (Eds.), *Play, language and socialization* (pp. 115–30). New York: Gordon & Breach.

Chaillé, C., & Silvern, S. (1996). Understanding through play. *Childhood Education, 72*(5), 274–77.

Chance, P. (1979). *Learning through play.* New York: Gardner Press.

Chandler, L. A. (1985). *Assessing stress in children.* New York: Praeger.

Chang, H., Salazar, D., & Deleong, C. (1994). *Drawing strength from diversity: Effective services for children, youth and families.* Sacramento, CA: California Tomorrow.

Charlesworth, R. (1997). Mathematics in the developmentally appropriate integrated curriculum. In C. H. Hart, D. C. Burts, and R. Charlesworth (Eds.), *Integrated curriculum and developmentally appropriate practice: Birth to age eight.* Albany, NY: State University of New York Press.

Charlesworth, R., Hart, C. H., Burts, D. C., Thomasson, R. H., Mosely, J., & Fleege, P. O. (1993). Measuring the developmental appropriateness of kindergarten teachers' beliefs and practices. *Early Childhood Research Quarterly, 8*, 255–76.

Charlesworth, R., & Lind, K. K. (1995). *Math and science for young children* (2nd ed.). Albany, NY: Delmar.

Charlesworth, R., & Lind., K. K. (1990). *Math and science for young children.* New York: Delmar.

Chipman, M. (1997). Valuing cultural diversity in the early years: Social imperatives and pedagogical insights. In J. P. Isenberg and M. R. Jalongo (Eds.), *Major trends and issues in early childhood education: Challenges, controversies and insights.* (pp. 43–55). New York: Teachers College Press.

Chittenden, E., & Courtney, R. (1989). Assessment of young children's reading: Documentation as an alternative to testing. In D. S. Strickyland and L. M. Morrow, *Emergeing literacy: Young children learn to read and write* (pp. 107–20). Newark, DE: International Reading Association.

Chomsky, N. (1965). *Aspects of a theory of syntax.* Cambridge, MA: M. I. T. Press.

Christie, J. (1990). Dramatic play: A context for meaningful engagements. *Reading Teacher, 43*(8), 542–45.

Christie, J. (1986). Training of symbolic play. In P. Smith (Ed.), *Children's play: Research development and practical applications* (pp. 55–64). New York: Gordon & Breach.

Chubb, P. (1903). *The teaching of English.* New York: Macmillan.

Chukovsky, L. (1971). *From two to five.* Los Angeles, CA: University of California Press.

Clarizio, H. (1980). *Toward positive classroom discipline.* New York: Wiley.

Clay, M. (1979). *Reading: The patterning of complex behaviour* (2nd ed.). Auckland, New Zealand: Heinemann.

Clayton, M. K. (1989). *Places to start: Implementing the developmental classroom.* Greenfield, MA.: Northeast Foundation for Children.

Cliatt, M. J. P., & Shaw, J. M. (1992). *Helping children explore science.* New York: Macmillan.

Cobb, P. (1994). Where is the mind? Constructivist and sociocultural perspectives on mathematical development. *Educational Researcher, 23*(7), 13–20.

Coburn, C. (1991, June). If only we could use it! *Early Childhood News,* 11–12.

Cochran, M., & Henderson, C. R., Jr. (1986). *Family matters: Evaluation of the parental empowerment program.* Ithaca, NY: The Comparative Ecology of Human Development Project.

Cohen, E. G. (1994). Restructuring the classroom: Conditions for productive small groups. *Review of Educational Research, 64*(1), 1–35.

Cohen, E. P., & Gainer, R. S. (1995). Art: Another language for learning (3rd ed.). Portsmouth, NH: Heinemann. In M. R. Jalongo and L.N. Stamp, *The arts in children's lives: Aesthetic education in early childhood.* Boston, MA: Allyn & Bacon.

Cohen, M., & Gross, P. (1979). *The developmental resource: Behavioral sequences for assessment and program planning* (vol. 2). New York: Grune & Stratton.

Cohen, S. (1994). Children and the environment: Aesthetic learning. *Childhood Education, 70*(5), (302–3).

Cohen, S. (1977). Fostering positive attitudes toward the handicapped: New curriculum. *Children Today, 6*(6), 7–12.

Colbert, C. (1997). Visual arts in the developmentally appropriate integrated curriculum. In C. H. Hart,

D. C. Burts, and R. Charlesworth (Eds.). *Integrated curriculum and developmentally appropriate practice: Birth to age eight* (pp. 201–23). Albany, NY: State University of New York Press.

Cole, E. (1990). An experience in Froebel's garden. *Childhood Education, 67*(1), 18–21.

Coletta, A. J. (1994) *Positive discipline: Effective alternative practices.* Paper presented at the National Association for the Education of Young Children, Atlanta, GA.

Combs, M. (1996). *Developing competent readers and writers in the primary grades.* Upper Saddle River, NJ: Merrill/ Prentice Hall.

Connell, D. R. (1987). The first 30 years were the fairest: Notes from the kindergarten and ungraded primary (K–1–2). *Young Children, 42*(5), 30–39.

Consortium for Longitudinal Studies (1983). *As the twig is bent.* Hillsdale, NJ: Erlbaum.

Consortium of National Arts Education Associations (1994). *National standards for arts education: Dance music theatre visual arts: What every young American should know and be able to do in the arts.* Reston, VA: Music Educators National Conference.

Cost, Quality and Child Outcomes Study Team (1995). *Cost, quality, and child outcomes in child care centers* (public report). Denver: Economics Department, University of Colorado at Denver.

Courtney, S. M., Ungerleider, L. G., Keil, K., & Haxby, J. V. (1997, April 10). Working memory. *Nature, 386,* 608–11.

Cowley, G. (1997, Spring/Summer). The language explosion. *Newsweek: Your Child,* sp. ed., 16–22.

Crary, E. (1996). *Help! The kids are at it again: Using kid's quarrels to teach "people" skills.* Seattle: Parenting Press.

Crary, E. (1984). *Kids can cooperate: A practical guide to teaching problem solving.* Seattle, WA: Parenting Press.

Cratty, B. J. (1979). *Perceptual and motor development in infants and children* (2nd ed.). Upper Saddle River, NJ: Prentice Hall.

Creager, E. (1990, May 2). The test of time. *Detroit Free Press,* pp. 1F, 6F.

Crews, D. (1991). *Bigmama's.* New York: Trumpet.

Crosser, S. (1994). Making the most of water play. *Young Children, 49*(5), 28–32.

Crosser, S. (1992). Managing the early childhood classroom. *Young Children, 47*(2), 23–29.

Cross, T. (1995). The early childhood curriculum debate. In M. Fleer (Ed.), *DAP centrism: Challenging developmentally appropriate practice* (pp. 87–108). Watson, Australia: Australian Early Childhood Association.

Cross, W. E. (1985). Black identity: Rediscovering the distinctions between personal identity and reference group orientations. In M. B. Spencer, G. K. Brookins, &

W. R. Allen (Eds.), *Beginnings: The social and affective development of black children* (pp. 155–72). Hillsdale, NJ: Erlbaum.

Cruikshank, D., Fitzgerald, D., & Jensen, L. (1980). *Young children learning mathematics:* Boston, MA: Allyn & Bacon.

Cryan, J. R. (1986, May-June). Evaluation: Plague or promise. *Childhood Education, 62*(5), 344–50.

Cuban, L. (1984). *How teachers taught: Constancy and change in American classrooms.* New York: Longman.

Cummings, C. (1991a, February). *The components of developmentally appropriate practice.* Paper delivered at the Ingham Intermediate School District, Mason, MI.

Cummings, C. (1991b). [Results of the Carnegie Foundation elementary school survey and on-site visitation. Personal communication.]

Cummings, C. (1990). A look at kindergarten learning environments: Combining time, space, materials, media, people, and purposes. In J. S. McKee (Ed.), *The developing kindergarten: Programs, children, and teachers* (pp. 251–73). East Lansing, MI: Michigan Association for the Education of Young Children.

Cummings, C. (1989). *Translating guidelines into practice.* Saginaw, MI: Mid-Michigan Association for the Education of Young Children.

Cummings, C. (1986). *Teaching makes a difference.* Edmonds, WA: Teaching, Snohomish.

Cunningham, P. (1996). *Phonics they use* (2nd ed.). New York: Harper Collins.

Curran, J. S., & Cratty, B. J. (1978). Speech and language problems in children. Denver, CO: Love.

Currie, J. R. (1988, Winter). Affect in the schools: A return to the most basic of basics. *Childhood Education, 65*(2), 83–87.

Curry, M. (1982). Held back in kindergarten. *Early Years,* 3–27.

Curry, N. E., & Johnson, C. N. (1990). *Beyond self-esteem: Developing a genuine sense of human value.* Washington, DC: National Association for the Education of Young Children.

Damon, W. (1988a). *The moral child.* New York: Free Press.

Damon, W. (1988b). *Greater expectations.* New York: Free Press.

Dansky, J. L. (1980). Make believe: A mediator of the relationship between free play and associative fluency. *Child Development, 51,* 576–79.

Davidson, J. (1996). *Emergent literacy and dramatic play in early education.* Albany, NY: Delmar.

Dawson, M. M. (1987). Beyond ability grouping: A review of the effectiveness of ability grouping and its alternatives. *School Psychology Review, 16,* 348–69.

Day, B. (1988a). *Early childhood education: Creative learning activities.* Upper Saddle River, NJ: Merrill/Prentice Hall.

Day, B. D. (1988b). What's happening in early childhood programs across the United States. In C. Waiger (Ed.), *A resource guide to public school early childhood programs* (pp. 3–31). Alexandria, VA. Association for Supervision and Curriculum Development.

Deardon, R. F. (1984). *Theory and practice in education.* London, England: Routledge & Kegan Paul.

Deegan, J. G. (1993). Children's friendships in culturally diverse classrooms. *Journal of Research in Childhood Education, 7*(2), 91–101.

DeFina, A. (1992). *Portfolio assessment: Getting started.* New York: Scholastic.

Deiner, P. L. (1993). *Resources for teaching children with diverse abilities.* New York: Harcourt Brace Jovanovich.

Delpit, L. (1995). *Other people's children: Cultural conflict in the classroom.* New York: The New Press.

Delpit, L. D. (1991). Interview with W. H. Teale, editor of *Language Arts. Language Arts, 68,* 541–47.

Dempsey, J., & Frost, J. (1993). Play environments in early childhood education. In B. Spodek (Ed.), *Handbook of research on the education of young children.* New York: Macmillan.

Denham, S. A. (1995, September). Scaffolding young children's prosocial responsiveness: Preschoolers' responses to adult sadness, anger and pain. *International Journal of Behavioral Development, 18*(3), 485–504.

Derman-Sparks, L., & the ABC Task Force (1989). *Antibias curriculum: Tools for empowering young children.* Washington, DC: National Association for the Education of Young Children.

DeVogue, K. (1996, March). *Conflict resolution with children in grade school.* Presentation, Forest View Elementary School Teachers, Lansing, MI.

Devries, R., & Kohlberg, L. (1990). *Constructivist early education: Overview and comparison with other programs.* Washington, DC: National Association for the Education of Young Children.

Dinkmeyer, G., & McKay, G. (1988). *S.T.E.P.: Parents handbook.* Circle Pines, MN: American Guidance Service.

Dixon, G. T., & Chalmers, F. G. (1990, Fall). The expressive arts in education. *Childhood Education, 67*(1), 12–17.

Dodge, D. (1991). *Creative curriculum for early childhood.* Washington, DC: Teaching Strategies.

Dodge, D. (1989). Strategies for achieving a quality program. *Exchange, 67,* 43–45.

Dodge, D. T. (1995). *The creative curriculum for early childhood.* Washington, DC: Teaching Strategies.

Dodge, D. T. (1988). *The creative curriculum.* Washington, DC: Teaching Strategies.

Dodge, D. T., & Colker, L. (1996). *The creative curriculum for early childhood* (3rd ed.). Washington, DC: Teaching Strategies, Inc.

Doherty-Derkowski, G. (1995). *Quality matters: Excellence in early childhood programs.* Reading, MA: Addison Wesley.

Dowling, W. J., & Harwood, S. L. (1986). *Music cognition.* Orlando, FL: Academic Press.

Doyle, A., & Connolly, J. (1989). Negation and enactment in social pretend play: Relations to social acceptance and social cognition. *Early Childhood Research Quarterly, 4,* 289–302.

Doyle, D. P. (1997, February). Education and character. *Phi Delta Kappan, 78*(6), 440–43.

Doyle, R. P. (1989, November). The resistance of conventional wisdom to research evidence: The case of retention in grade. *Phi Delta Kappan,* 215–20.

Doyle, W. (1986). Classroom organization and management. In M. C. Wittrock (Ed.), *Handbook of research on teaching.* New York: Macmillan.

Dreikurs, R., & Soltz, V. (1964). *Children: The challenge.* New York: Hawthorn Books.

Duckworth, E. (1987). *The having of wonderful ideas and other essays on teaching and learning.* New York: Teachers College Press.

Dunn, L., Beach, S. A. & Kontos, S. (1994). Quality of the literacy environment in day care and children's development. *Journal of Research in Childhood Education, 9,* 24–34.

Dunn, L., & Kontos, S. (1997). What have we learned about developmentally appropriate practice? *Young Children, 52*(5), 4–13.

Durkin, D. (1990). Reading instruction in kindergarten: A look at some issues through the lens of new basal reader materials. *Early Childhood Research Quarterly, 5,* 299–316.

Duros, A. (1992). *This is my house.* New York: Scholastic.

Dyson, A. (1990, January). Symbol makers, symbol weaver: How children link play, pictures, and print. *Young Children.*

Dyson, A. H., & Genishi, C. (1993). Visions of children as language users: Language and language education in early childhood. In B. Spodek (Ed.), *Handbook of research on the education of young children.* New York: Macmillan.

Early childhood curriculum. (1992). Oakland Schools, Waterford, MI.

Eastman, G. (1988). *Family involvement in education.* Unpublished manuscript prepared for the Wisconsin Department of Public Instruction.

Eaton, M. (1997) Positive discipline: Fostering self-esteem in young children. *Young Children, 52*(6), 43–46.

Educational Productions (1988). *Super groups.* Portland, OR: Author.

Education Commission of the States (ECS) and the Charles A. Dana Foundation (1996). *Bridging the gap between neuroscience and education.* Denver, CO: Workshop.

Edwards, C., Gandini, L., & Forman, G. (Eds.) (1993). *The hundred languages of children: The Reggio Emilia approach to early childhood education.* Norwood, NJ: Ablex.

Egan, G. (1994). *The skilled helper.* Pacific Grove, CA: Brooks/Cole.

Ehlert, L. (1989). Eating the alphabet: Fruits & vegetables from A to Z. San Diego: Harcourt Brace Jovanovich.

Eiferman, R. (1971). Social play in childhood. In R. Herron and B. Sutton-Smith (Eds.), *Child's play* (pp. 270–97). New York: Wiley.

Eisenberg, N. (1986). *Altruistic emotion, cognition and behavior.* Hillsdale, NJ: Erlbaum.

Eisenberg, N., & Harris, J. D. (1984). Social competence: A developmental perspective. *School Psychology Review, 13,* 267–77.

Eisner, E. (1981). The role of the arts in cognition and curriculum. *Phi Delta Kappan, 63*(1), 48–52.

Eisner, E. W. (1970). Evaluating children's art. In E. Pappas (Ed.), *Art education.* New York: Macmillan.

Eliason, C., & Jenkins, L. T. (1994). *A practical guide to early childhood curriculum.* Upper Saddle River, NJ: Merrill/Prentice Hall.

Elkind, D. (1989, October). Developmentally appropriate practice: Philosophical and practical implications. *Phi Delta Kappan, 7*(2), 113–17.

Elkind, D. (1988a). Educating the very young: A call for clear thinking. *NEA Today 6*(6), 22–27.

Elkind, D. (1988b, October). The miseducation of young children. *Education Digest, 54,* 11–14.

Elkind, D. (1987). *Miseducation: Preschoolers at risk.* New York: Knopf.

Elkind, D. (1981). *The hurried child: Growing up too fast too soon.* Reading, MA: Addison-Wesley.

Elkind, D. (1976). *Child development and education.* New York: Oxford University Press.

Elkins, D. P. (Ed.) (1979). *Self-concept sourcebook.* Rochester, NY: Growth Associates.

Emde, R. N., Biringen, Z., Clyman, R. B., & Oppenheim, D. (1991). The moral self of infancy: Affective core and procedural knowledge. *Development Review, 11,* 251–70.

Epstein, J. L. (1998). *School and family partnerships: Preparing educators and improving schools.* Boulder, CO: Westview.

Epstein, J. L. (1986). Parents' reactions to teacher practices of parent involvement. *Elementary School Journal, 86,* 277–93.

Epstein, J. L. (1984, April). *Effects of parent involvement on student achievement in reading and math.* Paper presented at the annual meeting of the American Research Association.

Erickson M. F., Sroufe, L. A., & Egeland, B. (1985). The relationship between quality of attachment and behavior problems in preschool in a high-risk sample. In I. Bretherton and E. Waters (Eds.), *Growing points of attachment theory and research* (pp. 147–66). *Monographs of the Society for Research in Child Development, 50* (1–2, Serial No. 209).

Erikson, E. H. (1963). *Childhood and society.* New York: Hawthorn Books.

Essa, E. (1996). *Introduction to early childhood education.* Albany, NY: Delmar.

Evans, E. D. (1975). *Contemporary influences in early childhood education* (2nd ed). New York: Holt, Rinehart & Winston.

Faber, A., & Mazlish, E. (1995). *How to talk so kids can learn at home and school.* New York: Simon & Schuster.

Fabes, R. A. (1984). How children learn self-control. *Two to Twelve, 2*(5), 1–3.

Fayden, T. (1997). Children's choice: Planting the seeds for creating a thematic sociodramatic center. *Young Children, 52*(3), 15–19.

Feeney, S., & Kipnis, K. (1992). Professional ethics in early childhood education. *Young Children, 40*(3), 54–56.

Feeney, S., & Moravcik, E. (1987, September). A thing of beauty: Aesthetic development in young children. *Young Children,* 7–15.

Fein, G., & Stork, L. (1981). Sociodramatic play: Social class effects in integrated preschool classrooms. *Journal of Applied Developmental Psychology, 2,* 267–79.

Fields, M. V., & Boesser, C. (1994). *Constructive guidance and discipline: Preschool and primary education.* Upper Saddle River, NJ: Merrill/Prentice Hall.

Fields, M. V., and Spangler, K. L. (1995). *Let's begin reading right.* Englewood Cliffs, NJ: Merrill/Macmillan.

Finkelhor, D. (1984). *Child sexual abuse: New theory and research.* New York: Free Press.

Finkelhor, D., & Baron, L. (1986). High-risk children. In D. Finkelhor and Associates (Eds.), *A sourcebook on child sexual abuse.* Beverly Hills, CA: Sage.

Flavell, H. H., Green, F., & Flavell, E. (1986). Development of knowledge about the appearance reality distinction. *Monographs of the Society for Research in Child Development, 51* (1, Serial No. 212).

Flavell, J. H. (1977). *Cognitive development.* Upper Saddle River, NJ: Prentice-Hall.

Fleer, M. (1995). *DAP centrism: Challenging developmentally appropriate practice.* Watson, Australia: Australian Early Childhood Association.

Fleer, M., & Coreen, L. (1995). What do I look like on the inside? Developing children's understanding about their bodies. *Australian Early Childhood Association Resource Book Series, 2*(1). Watson, Australia: Australian Early Childhood Association.

Ford, S. (1993). The facilitator's role in children's play. *Young Children, 48*(6), 66–69.

Forest Hills Public Schools (1988). Curriculum guidelines, kindergarten through the second grade. Forest Hills, MI: Author.

Forman, G. (1996). A child constructs an understanding of a water wheel in five media. *Childhood Education, 72*(5), 269–73.

Forman, G., & Kuschner, D. S. (1983). *The child's construction of knowledge: Project for teaching young children.* Washington, DC: National Association for the Education of Young Children.

Foster, K. (1990). Small steps on the way to teacher empowerment. *Educational Leadership, 47*(8), 38–40.

Fox, C. L. (1993). *Let's get together: Activities for developing friendship and self-esteem in the elementary grades.* Rolling Hills Estates, CA: Jalmar.

Franklin, M. (1994). Art, play, and symbolization in childhood and beyond: Reconsidering connections. *Teacher's College Record, 95*(4), 526–41.

Franz, C. E., McClelland, D. C., & Weinberger, R. L. (1991). Childhood antecedents of conventional social accomplishment in mid-life adults. A 36-year prospective study. *Journal of Personality and Social Psychology, 60,* 586–95.

Freeman, C. C., & Sokoloff, H. J. (1996, Fall). Children learning to make a better world: Exploring themes. *Childhood Education, 73*(1), 17–22.

Freiberg, H. J., & Driscoll, A. (1996). *University teaching strategies.* Boston, MA: Allyn & Bacon.

Friedrich, L. K., & Stein, A. H. (1973). Aggressive and prosocial television programs and the natural behaviors of preschool children. *Monographs of the Society for Research in Child Development, 38*(151).

Fromberg, D. P. (1987). Play. In C. Seefeldt (Ed.), *The early childhood curriculum: A review of current research* (pp. 35–74). New York: Teachers College Press.

Frost, J. (1991). *Play and playscapes.* Albany, NY: Delmar.

Frost, J. L., & Sweeney, T. (1995). *Causes and prevention of playground injuries and litigation case studies* (pp. 60–88). Washington, DC: ERIC Clearinghouse, Ed. 394648.

Frost, L. (1992). *Play and playscapes.* Albany, NY: Delmar.

Frost, L., Talbot, J., & Monroe, M. (1990). Playgrounds. In L. Ard and M. Pitts (Eds.), *Room to grow: How to create quality early childhood environments* (pp. 149–60). Austin, TX: Texas Association for the Education of Young Children.

Froyen, L. A. (1993). *Classroom management: The reflective teacher-leader* (2nd ed.). New York: Macmillan.

Fry, P. S., & Addington, J. (1984). Comparison of social problem solving of children from open and traditional classrooms: A two-year longitudinal study. *Journal of Education Psychology, 76,* 318–29.

Gabbard, C., Le Blanc, E., & Lowy, S. (1987). *Physical education for children: Building the foundation.* Upper Saddle River, NJ: Prentice Hall.

Galen, H. (1991). Increasing parental involvement in elementary school: The nitty gritty of one successful program. *Young Children, 46*(2), 18–22.

Gallahue, D. (1995). Transforming physical education curriculum. In S. Bredekamp and T. Rosegrant (Eds.), *Reaching potentials: Transforming early childhood curriculum and assessment* (vol. 2). Washington, DC: National Association for the Education of Young Children.

Gallahue, D. L. (1993a). *Developmental physical education for today's children.* Dubuque, IA: Brown & Benchmark.

Gallahue, D. (1993b). Motor development and movement skill acquisition in early childhood education. In B. Spodek (Ed.), *Handbook of research on the education of young children.* New York: Macmillan.

Garbarino, J. (1995) *Raising children in a socially toxic environment.* San Francisco, CA: Jossey Bass.

Garcia, C. (1991). *A fieldwork study of how children learn fundamental motor skills and how they progress in the development of striking.* Unpublished doctoral dissertation, Michigan State University, East Lansing, MI.

Garcia, E. (1993). The education of linguistically and culturally diverse children. In B. Spodek (Ed.), *Handbook of research on the education of young children* (pp. 372–84). New York: Macmillan.

Gardini, L., & Edwards, C. P. (1988). Early childhood integration of the visual arts. *Gifted International, 5*(2), 14–18.

Gardner, H. (1997). *Extraordinary minds: Portraits of exceptional individuals and an examination of our extraordinariness.* New York: Basic Books.

Gardner, H. (1995). Reflections on multiple intelligences: Myths and messages. *Phi Delta Kappan, 77*(2).

Gardner, H. (1994). *The arts and human development.* New York: Basic Books.

Gardner, H. (1993a). *Frames of mind* (rev. ed.). New York: Basic Books.

Gardner, H. (1993b). *Multiple intelligences: The theory in practice.* New York: Basic Books.

Gardner, H. (1991). *The unschooled mind: How children think and how schools should teach.* New York: Basic Books.

Gardner, H. (1990). *Art education and human development.* Los Angeles, CA: Getty Center for the Education in the Arts.

Gardner, H. (1988). *Assessment in context: The alternatives to standardized testing.* Unpublished manuscript prepared for the National Commission on Testing and Public Policy, Berkeley, CA.

Gardner, H., Kornhaber, M. L., & Wake, W. K. (1996). *Intelligence.* Fort Worth, TX: Harcourt Brace.

Gartrell, D. (1997) Beyond discipline to guidance. *Young Children, 52*(6), 34–42.

Gartrell, D. (1994) *A guidance approach to discipline.* Albany, NY: Delmar Publishers.

Garvey, C. (1977). *Play.* Cambridge, MA: Harvard University Press.

Garvey, C., & Berndt, C. (1977). Organization of pretend play. *JSAS Catalog of Selected Documents in Psychology: 1.* (Ms. No. 1589).

Garvey, C., & Hagan, R. (1973). Social speech and social interaction: Egocentricism revisited. *Child Development, 44,* 565–68.

Gazda, G. M., et al. (1995). *Human relations development: A manual for educators.* Boston: Allyn & Bacon.

Gazda, G. M., et al. (1973). A general review of related research literature. *Human relations development: A manual for educators.* Boston, MA: Allyn & Bacon.

Geiger, K. (1991, March). President's viewpoint: An idea whose time has come. *NEA Today,* 2.

Gelman, R., & Gallistel, C. R. (1986). *The child's understanding of number* (2nd ed.). Cambridge, MA: Harvard University Press.

George, M. A., & Sellers, W. (Eds.) (1984). *Michigan model for comprehensive health education.* Mt. Pleasant, MI: Central Michigan University Educational Materials Center.

George, P. S. (1987). *What's the truth about tracking and ability grouping really?* Gainesville, FL: Teacher Education Resource.

Gesell, A. (1940). *The first five years of life: A guide to the study of the preschool child.* New York: Harper.

Gestwicki, C. (1998). *Developmentally appropriate practice: Curriculum and development in early education.* Albany, NY: Delmar.

Gestwicki, C. (1997). *The essentials of early education.* Albany, NY: Delmar.

Gestwicki, C. (1995a). *Developmentally appropriate practice: Curriculum and development in early education.* Albany, NY: Delmar.

Gestwicki, C. (1995b). *The essentials of early education.* Albany, NY: Delmar.

Gilbert, S. E., & Gay, G. (1985). Improving the success in schools of poor black children. *Phi Delta Kappan, 67,* 133–37.

Gilligan, C. (1982). *In a different voice: Psychological theory and women's development.* Cambridge, MA: Harvard University Press.

Gilligan, S. G., & Bower, G. H. (1984). Cognitive consequences of emotional arousal. In C. E. Izard, J. Kagan, and R. B. Zajonc (Eds.), *Emotions, cognition, and behavior.* Cambridge, MA: Harvard University Press.

Ginsberg, H. P., & Baron, J. (1993). Cognition: Young children's construction of mathematics. In R. Jensen (Ed.), *Research ideas for the classroom: Early childhood mathematics* (pp. 3–21). Reston, VA: NCTM.

Glasser, W. (1990). *The quality school: Managing students without coercion.* New York: Harper & Row.

Glasser, W. (1985). *Control theory in the classroom.* New York: Perennial Library.

Goetz, E. M. (1985, Fall). In defense of curriculum themes. *Day Care and Early Education, 13,* 12–13.

Goffin, S. G. (1989). Developing a research agenda for early childhood education: What can be learned from the research on teaching? *Early Childhood Research Quarterly, 4,* 187–204.

Goffin, S. G., & Tull, C. Q. (1985, March). Problem solving: Encouraging active learning. *Young Children,* 28–32.

Goldberg, S. (1997). *Parent involvement begins at birth.* Boston, MA: Allyn & Bacon.

Goldhaber, J. (1997). Books in the sand box? Markers in the blocks? Expanding the child's world of literacy. *Childhood Education, 73*(2), 88–91.

Goldhaber, J. (1994). If we call it science, *then* can we let the children play? *Childhood Education, 71*(1), 24–27.

Goldhaber, J., Lipson, M., Sortino, S., & Daniels, P. (1997). Books in the sand box? Markers in the blocks? Expanding the child's world of literacy. *Childhood Education, 73*(2), 88–91.

Goldman, C., & O'Shea, C. (1990). A culture for change. *Educational Leadership, 47*(8), 41–43.

Goleman, D. (1995). *Emotional intelligence: Why it can matter more than IQ.* New York: Bantam Books.

Goleman, D., Kaufman, P., & Ray, M. (1992). *The creative spirit.* New York: Penguin.

Gonzalez-Mena, J., & Widmeyer, E. D. (1997). *Infants, toddlers, and caregivers.* Mountain View, CA: Mayfield.

Goodlad, J. I. (1984). *A place called school.* New York: McGraw-Hill.

Goode, T. L., & Brophy, J. E. (1984). *Looking into classrooms.* New York: Harper & Row.

Goodman, K. S., Goodman, Y. M., & Hood, W. J. (Eds.). (1989). *The whole language evaluation book.* Portsmouth, NH: Heinemann.

Goodwin, W. L., & Driscoll, L. A. (1980). *Handbook for measurement and evaluation in early childhood education.* San Francisco, CA: Jossey-Bass.

Gootman, M. (1988, November/December). Discipline alternatives that work: Eight steps toward classroom discipline without corporal punishment. *The Humanist, 48,* 11–14.

Gordon, A., & Browne, K. W. (1996). *Guiding young children in a diverse society.* Boston, MA: Allyn & Bacon.

Gordon, A. M., & Williams-Brown, K. (1995). *Beginnings and beyond* (4th ed.). Albany, NY: Delmar.

Gordon, E. E. (1981). *The manifestations of developmental music aptitude in the audiation of "same" and "different" as sound in music.* Chicago, IL: G. I. A. Publications.

Gordon, J. (1990, April 23). Teaching kids to negotiate. *Newsweek,* 65.

Gordon, T. (1989). *Discipline that works: Promoting self-discipline in children.* New York: Plume Books.

Goth-Owens, J. (n.d.). *The stress connection.* East Lansing, MI: 4-H Youth Programs, Cooperative Extension Service, Michigan State University.

Gotts, E. E., & Purnell, F. R. (1986). Communication: Key to school-home relations. In R. J. Griffore and R. P. Boger (Eds.), *Child rearing in the home and school* (pp. 157–200). New York: Plenum.

Grace, C., & Shores, E. F. (1991). *The portfolio and its use: Developmentally appropriate assessment of young children.* Little Rock, AR: Southern Association on Children under Six.

Graves, D. (1994). *A fresh look at writing.* Portsmouth, NH: Heinemann.

Graves, D. H. (1983). *Writing: Teachers and children at work.* Exeter, NH: Heinemann.

Graves, S., Gargiulo, R., & Sluder, L. (1996). *Young children: An introduction to early childhood education.* St. Paul, MN: West

Greenberg, P. (1996, January). Ernest L. Boyer's legacy to children and families. *Young Children, 51*(2), 50–51.

Greenberg, P. (1992). Ideas that work with young children: How to institute some simple democratic practices pertaining to respect, rights, roots and responsibilities in any classroom (without losing your leadership position). *Young Children, 47*(5), 10–17.

Greenberg, P. (1989). Parents as partners in young children's development and education: A new American fad? Why does it matter? *Young Children, 44*(4), 61–75.

Greenman, J. (1995). Of culture and a sense of place. *Child Care Information Exchange, 101,* 36–38.

Greenman, J. (1988). *Caring spaces, learning places: Children's environments that work.* Redman, WA: Exchange Press.

Grezda, M. T., Garduque, L., & Schultz, T. (Eds.) (1991). *Improving instruction and assessment in early childhood education: Summary of a workshop series.* Washington, DC: National Forum on the Future of Children and Families, National Academy Press.

Griffore, R. J., & Bulbolz, M. (1986). Family and school as educators. In R. J. Giffore and R. P. Boger (Eds.), *Child rearing in the home and school* (pp. 61–104). New York: Plenum.

Grollman, S. (1994, September). Fantasy and exploration: Two approaches to playing. *Child Care Information Exchange,* 48–50.

Grusec, J. E., & Mills, R. (1982). The acquisition of self control. In J. Worrell (Ed.), *Psychological development in the elementary years* (pp. 151–86). New York: Academic Press.

Gullo, D. F. (1994). *Developmentally appropriate teaching in early childhood.* Washington, DC: National Education Association of the United States.

Gunner, M. R., Brodersen, L., Krueger, K., & Rigatuso, R. (1996). Dampening of behavioral and adrenocortical reactivity during early infancy: Normative changes and individual differences. *Child Development, 67*(3), 877–89.

Gunsberg, A. (1991, Summer). Improvised musical play with delayed and nondelayed children. *Childhood Education, 67,* 4.

Haberman, M. (1994, Spring). Gentle teaching in a violent society. *Educational Horizons,* 131–35.

Hagerott, S. G. (1997, May). Physics for first graders. *Phi Delta Kappan, 79*(9), 717–20.

Hale, J. E. (1994). *Unbank the fire: Visions for the education of African American children.* Baltimore, MD: John Hopkins University Press.

Halliday, M. A. K. (1975). *Learning how to mean: Explorations in the development of language.* London, England: Edward Arnold.

Halliday, M. A. K. (1973). *Explorations in the functions of language.* London, England: Edward Arnold.

Halverson, H. M. (1931). An experimental study of prehension in infants by means of systematic cinema records. *Genetic Psychology Monographs, 10,* 107–286.

Hamachek, D. (1990). *Psychology in teaching, learning, and growth.* Boston, MA: Allyn & Bacon.

Harlan, J. (1988). *Science experiences for the early childhood years.* Upper Saddle River, NJ: Merrill/Prentice Hall.

Harmin, M. (1994). *Inspiring active learning: A handbook for teachers.* Alexandria, VA: Association for Supervision and Curriculum Development.

Harris, J. A. (1978, September). Parents and teachers, Inc. *Teachers,* 85–87.

Harris, L., and Associates (1987). *The American Teacher, 1987: Strengthening links between home and school. The Metropolitan Life Survey.* Washington, DC: U.S. Department of Education. (ERIC Document Reproduction Service No. ED 289–841).

Hart, C. H., Burts, D. C., & Charlesworth, R. (1997). Integrated developmentally appropriate curriculum: From theory to research to practice. In C. H. Hart, D. C. Burts, and R. Charlesworth (Eds.), *Integrated curriculum and developmentally appropriate practice: Birth to age eight.* (pp. 1–27). Albany, NY: State University of New York Press.

Hartley, R. E., Frank, L. K., & Goldenson, R. M. (1952). *Understanding children's play.* New York: Columbia University Press.

Hartocollis, A. (1997, December 15). The big test comes early. Getting into a highly competitive public school. *The New York Times,* A-17.

Hartup, W. (1991). Having friends, making friends, and keeping friends: Relationships as educational contexts, *ERIC Digest.* Urbana, IL: ERIC Clearinghouse on Elementary and Early Childhood Education (ED 345-854).

Hartup, W. W. (1983). Peer relations. In P. H. Mussen (Ed.), *Handbook of child psychology* (vol. 4) (pp. 103–96). New York: Wiley.

Hartup, W. W. (1982). Peer relations. In C. B. Kopp and J. B. Krakow (Eds.), *The child development in a social context* (pp. 514–75). Reading, MA: Addison-Wesley.

Hartup, W. W. (1978). Children and their friends. In H. Mcgurk (Ed.), *Issues in childhood social development.* London, England: Methuen.

Hartup, W. W., & Moore, S. G. (1990). Early peer relationships: Developmental significance and prognostic implications. *Early Childhood Research Quarterly, 5*(1), 1–18.

Hatch, T. (1997, March). Getting specific about multiple intelligences. *Educational Leadership, 54*(6), 26–29.

Hatch, T., & Gardner, H. (1988, November/December). New research on intelligence. *Learning, 17*(4), 36–39.

Haubenstricker, J. (1991a, May). *Gross motor development in preschoolers.* Paper presented to Michigan Council of Cooperative Nurseries, East Lansing, MI.

Haubenstricker, J. (1991b). *Motor development as a biological imperative.* Unpublished manuscript.

Haubenstricker, J. (1990). *Summary of fundamental motor skill characteristics: Motor performance study.* Unpublished document, Michigan State University, East Lansing, MI.

Haubenstricker, J., & Seefeldt, V. (1986). Acquisition of motor skills during childhood. In V. Seefeldt (Ed.), *Physical activity and well-being.* Reston, VA: American Alliance for Health, Physical Education, Recreation and Dance.

Hayes, C. D., Palmer, J. L., & Zaslow, M. J. (Eds.) (1990). *Who cares for America's children? Child care policy for the 1990s.* Washington, DC: National Academy Press.

Haywood, K. M. (1993). *Life span motor development.* Champaign, IL: Human Kenetics.

Hazen, N. L., & Black, B. (1989). Preschool peer communication skills: The role of social status and interaction content. *Child Development, 60*(4), 867–76.

Heibert, E. H., & Fisher, C. W. (1990). Whole language: Three themes for the future. *Educational Leadership, 47*(6), 62–64.

Hein, G. E., & Price, S. C. (1994). *Active assessment for active science.* Portsmouth, NH: Heinemann.

Heinrich, J. S. (1977). *Native Americans: What not to teach. Unlearning "Indian" stereotypes.* New York: Racism and Sexism Resource Center for Educators.

Hellmich, N. (1996, June 5). Invented spelling: Creative or crippling to kids? *USA Today,* 7D.

Henderson, A., & Berla, N. (1994). *A new generation of evi-dence: The family is critical to student achievement.* Washing-ton, DC: National Committee for Citizens in Education.

Hendrick, J. (1997). *Total learning: Curriculum for the young child.* Upper Saddle River, NJ: Merrill/Prentice Hall.

Hendrick, J. (1996). *The whole child: Developmental education for the early years.* Upper Saddle River, NJ: Merrill/Prentice-Hall.

Hendricks, C. M., & Smith, C. J. (1991). *Here we go, watch me grow.* Santa Cruz, CA: ETR Associates.

Henniger, M. (1995). Supporting multicultural awareness at learning centers. *Dimensions of Early Childhood, 23*(4), 20–23.

Henry, T. (1990, July 29). Governors access education: Report asks states to redesign system. *The Burlington Free Press,* 1E.

Herberholz, B., & Hanson, L. (1995). *Early childhood art* (5th ed.). Dubuque, IA: Wm. C. Brown.

Herbert, E. H., & Papierz, J. M. (1990). The emergent literacy construct and kindergarten and readiness books of basal reading series. *Early Childhood Research Quarterly, 5,* 317–34.

Hernandez, D. J. (1995). Changing demographics: Past and future demands for early childhood programs. *The Future of Children, 5*(3), 145–60.

Herr, J., & Libby, Y. (1990). *Creative resources for the early childhood classroom.* New York: Delmar.

Herrnstein, R. J., & Murray, C. (1994). *The bell curve: Intelligence and class structure in American life.* New York: Free Press.

Hertel, V. (1992). Health assessment and intervention techniques for 3-, 4-, and 5-year-old children. In C. Hendricks (Ed.), *Young children on the grow: Health, activity and education in the preschool setting* (pp. 33–42). Washington, DC: ERIC Clearinghouse on Teacher Education.

Hess, R. D., Block, M., Costello, J., Knowles, R. T., & Largey, D. (1971). Parent involvement in early education. In E. Grotberg (Ed.), *Daycare: Resources for decisions* (pp. 265–98). Washington, DC: Office of Economic Opportunity.

Hildebrand, V. (1997a). *Guiding young children: A center approach.* Palo Alto, CA: Mayfield.

Hildebrand, V. (1997b). *Introduction to early childhood education.* New York: Macmillan.

Hildebrand, V. (1995). Guiding young children (4th ed.). New York: Macmillan.

Hinitz, B. F. (1987). Social studies in early childhood education. In C. Seefeldt (Ed.), *The early childhood curriculum: A review of research* (pp. 237–55). New York: Teachers College Press.

Hirsch, E. S. (1984). *The block book* (rev. ed.). Washington, DC: National Association for the Education of Young Children.

Hirsh-Pasek, K., Hyson, M. C., & Rescorla, L. (1990). Academic environments in preschool: Do they pressure or challenge young children? *Early Education and Development ,1,* 401–23.

Hitz, R. (1987, January). Creative problem solving through music activities. *Young Children, 42*(2), 12–17.

Hitz, R., & Driscoll, A. (1988). Praise or encouragement? *Young Children, 43*(5), 6–13.

Hoffman, L. W. (1984). Empathy, its limitations, and its role in a comprehensive moral theory. In W. M. Kurtines and J. L. Gewirtz (Eds.), *Morality, moral behavior and moral development.* New York: Wiley.

Hoffman, M. L. (1990). Empathy and justice motivation. *Motivation and Emotion,* 151–72.

Hoffman, M. L. (1983). Affective and cognitive processes in moral internalization. In E. T. Higgins, D. N. Ruble, and W. W. Hartup (Eds.). *Social cognition and social behavior: Developmental perspectives.* New York: Cambridge University Press.

Hoffman, M. L. (1970). Moral development. In *Carmichael's manual of child psychology* (vol. 2) (pp. 262–360). New York: Wiley.

Hoffman, M. L. (1967). Moral internalization, parental power, and the nature of the parent-child interaction. *Developmental Psychology, 5,* 45–57.

Hohmann, M., & Weikart, D. D. (1997). *Educating young children.* Ypsilanti, MI: High/Scope Press.

Hohmann, M., & Weikart, D. P. (1995). *Educating young children: Active learning practices for preschool and child care programs.* Ypsilanti, MI: High/Scope Press.

Holloman, S. T. (1990, May). Retention and redshirting. The dark side of kindergarten. *Early Childhood Education,* 13–15.

Holmes, C. T. (1990). Grade level retention effects: A meta-analysis of research studies. In L. A. Shepard and M. L. Smith (Eds.). *Flunking grades: Research and policies on retention* (pp. 16–33). New York: Falmer.

Holt, B. G. (1988). *Science with young children.* Washington, DC: National Association for the Education of Young Children.

Honig, A. S., & Wittmer, D. S. (1996). Helping children become more prosocial: Ideas for classrooms, families, schools and communities. *Young Children, 51*(2), 62–70.

Honig, A.S., & Wittmer, D.S. (1992). *Prosicial development in children: Caring sharing and cooperating: A bibliographic resource guide.* New York: Garland.

Howe, A. C. (1993). Science in early childhood education. In B. Spokek (Ed.), *Handbook of research on the education of young children.* Upper Saddle River, NJ: Merrill/Prentice Hall.

Howes, C. (1988). Peer interactions of young children. *Monographs of the Society for Research in Child Development, 53*(217), 1.

Hulsey, T. L., Kerkman D. D., & Pinon, M. F. (1997). What it takes for preschoolers to learn sex abuse prevention concepts. *Early Education and Development, 8*(2), 186–202.

Hunt, J. M. (1961). *Intelligence and experience.* New York: Ronald.

Huntsinger, C. S., Shoeneman, J. & Ching, W. (1994, May). *A cross-cultural study of young children's performance on drawing and handwriting tasks.* Paper presented at the Midwestern Psychological Association, Chicago, IL.

Hurd, P. D. (1990). Why we must transform science education. *Educational Leadership, 49*(2), 33–35.

Hurley, R. S., & Blake, S. (1997). Animals and occupations: Why theme-based curricula work. *Early Childhood News, 9*(1), 20–25.

Hyman, I. A. (1990). *Reading, writing and the hickory stick: The appalling story of physical and psychological violence in American schools.* Boston, MA: Lexington Books.

Hyman, I. A., & D'Alcssandro, J. (1984, September). Good, old-fashioned discipline: The politics of punitiveness. *Phi Delta Kappan, 66,* 39–45.

Hymes, J. (Narrator) (1980). *Hairy scary* [Film]. Silver Spring, MD: University of Maryland.

Hymes, J. I. (1974). *Effective home school relations.* Sierra Madre, CA: Southern California Association for the Education of Young Children.

Hymes, J. L., Jr. (1991). *Early childhood education: Twenty years in review.* Washington, DC: National Association for the Education of Young Children.

Hyson, M. C., Hirsh-Pasek, K., & Rescorla, L. (1990). The classroom practices inventory: An observation instrument based on NAEYC's guidelines for developmentally appropriate practices for 4- and 5-year-old children. *Early Childhood Research Quarterly, 5,* 475–94.

I am amazing. (1990). Circle Pines, MN: American Guidance Service.

Ignico, A. (1994). Early childhood education: Providing the foundation. *Journal of Physical Education, 65*(6), 25–56.

Inhelder, B., & Piaget, J. (1964). *The early growth and logic in the child.* London, England: Routledge & Kegan Paul.

Institute for Responsive Education (1990). *Schools reaching out.* Boston, MA: Author.

Integrated curriculum and developmentally appropriate practice: Birth to age eight (pp. 103–14). Albany, NY: State University of New York Press.

Isbell, R. (1995). *The complete learning center book.* Beltsville, MD: Gryphon House.

Isbell, R., & Raines, S. (1991). Young children's oral language production in three types of play centers. *Journal of Research in Childhood Education, 5*(2), 140–46.

Jackman, H. (1997). *Early education curriculum: A child's connection to the world.* Albany, NY: Delmar.

Jackson, P. W. (1997). Child-centered education for Pacific-rim cultures? *International Journal of Early Childhood Education, 2,* 5–18.

Jalongo, M. R. (1990). The child's right to the expressive arts: Nurturing the imagination as well as the intellect. *Childhood Education, 66*(4). 195–201.

Jalongo, M. R., & Stamp, L. N. (1997). *The arts in children's lives: Aesthetic education in early childhood.* Needham Heights, MA: Allyn & Bacon.

Javernick, C. (1988). Johnny's not jumping: Can we help obese children? *Young Children, 43*(2), 18–23.

Jenkins, E. (1991). Did you feed my cow? On P. Erickson (Prod.) & A. Seeger & S.I. McArthur (Dirs.), *Ella Jenkins live! At the Smithsonian* (videotape). Rounder Records.

Jenson, G. O., & Warstadt, T. (1990). *Ranking critical issues facing American families.* Washington, DC: U.S. Department of Agriculture.

Johnsen, E. P., & Christie, J. F. (1984). Play and social cognition. In B. Sutton-Smith & D. Kelly-Bryne (Eds.), *The masks of play* (pp. 109–18). New York: Leisure Press.

Johnson, D. W., & Johnson, R. T. (1991). *Learning together and alone.* Upper Saddle River, NJ: Merrill/Prentice Hall.

Johnson, P., & Winogard, P. (1985). Passive failure in reading. *Journal of Reading Behavior, 17,* 279–301.

Johnston, M. S. (1982). *How to involve parents in early childhood education.* Provo, UT: Brigham Young University Press.

Jones, E., & Reynolds, G. (1995). Enabling children's play: The teacher's role. In E. Klugman (Ed.), *Play, policy & practice* (pp. 37–46). St. Paul, MN: Redleaf Press.

Jorde, P. (1986). Early childhood education: Issues and trends. *Educational Forum, 50*(2), 171–81.

Kagan, J. (1997/1998). The realistic view of biology and behavior. In K. L. Freiberg (Ed.), *Human development annual editions.* Sluice Dock, Guilford, CT: Dushkin Publishing Group.

Kalb, C., & Namuth, T. (1997, Spring/Summer). When a child's silence isn't golden. *Newsweek: Your Child,* sp. ed., 23.

Kamii, C. (Ed.) (1990). *Achievement testing in the early grades.* Washington, DC: National Association for the Education of Young Children.

Kamii, C. (1985, September). Leading primary education toward excellence. *Young Children,* 3–9.

Kamii, C., & DeVries, R. (1977). Project for early education. In M. Day and R. Parker (Eds.), *Preschool in action* (2nd ed.). Boston, MA: Allyn & Bacon.

Kaplan, P. S. (1986). *A child's odyssey: Child and adolescent development.* St. Paul, MN: West.

Katz, L. (1996, March). *The essence of developmentally appropriate practice for children from birth to age 8.* Keynote address, Michigan Association for the Education of Young Children, Grand Rapids, MI.

Katz, L. G. (1988, Summer). What should young children be doing? *American Educator,* 28–45.

Katz, L. G. (1987). *What should young children be learning?* Urbana, IL: ERIC Clearinghouse on Elementary and Early Childhood Education.

Katz, L. G., & Chard, S. C. (1989). *Engaging children's minds: The project approach.* Norwood, NJ: Ablex.

Katz, L. G., Evangelou, D., & Hartman, J. A. (1990). *The case for mixed-age grouping in early education.* Washington, DC: National Association for the Education of Young Children.

Katz, L. G., Rath, F., & Torres, R. (1987). *A place called kindergarten.* Urbana, IL: ERIC Clearinghouse on Elementary and Early Childhood Education.

Katz, P. (1982). Development of children's racial awareness and intergroup attitudes. In L. G. Katz (Ed.), *Current topics in early childhood education* (vol. 4) (pp. 17–54). Norwood, NJ: Ablex.

Kaufman, J. M., & Burbach, H. J. (1997, December). On creating a climate of classroom civility. *Phi Delta Kappan, 79*(4), 320–25.

Keats, E. J. (1972). *Pet show.* New York: Macmillan.

Kellogg, R. (1979). *Children's drawings/children's minds.* New York: Avon Books.

Kellogg, R. (1969). *Analyzing children's art.* Palo Alto, CA: National Press Books.

Kendall, F. E. (1996). *Diversity in the classroom: New approaches to the education of young children.* New York: Teachers College Press.

Kendrick, A., Kaufmann, R., & Messenger, K. (1988). *Healthy young children: A manual for programs.* Washington, DC: National Association for the Education of Young Children.

Kennedy, L. M., & Tipps, S. (1994). *Guiding children's learning of mathematics.* Belmont, CA: Wadsworth.

Kenney, S. H. (1997). Music in the developmentally appropriate integrated curriculum. In C. H. Hart, D. C. Burts, and R. Charlesworth (Eds.), *Integrated curriculum and developmentally appropriate practice: Birth to age eight* (pp. 103–14). Albany, NY: State University of New York Press.

Kessler, S. (1991). Alternative perspectives on early childhood education. *Early Childhood Research Quarterly,* 7(2), 183–97.

Kibbey, M. (1988). *My grammy.* Minneapolis, MN: Carolrhoda.

Kilmer, S. J., & Hofman, H. (1995). Transforming science curriculum. In S. Bredekamp and T. Rosegrant (Eds.), *Reaching potentials: Transforming early childhood curriculum and assessment* (vol. 2). Washington, DC: National Association for the Education of Young Children.

Kindergarten Curriculum Guide and Resource Book. (1985). Victoria, British Columbia: Curriculum Development Branch, Ministry of Education.

King, M. L., & King, C. S. (1984). *The words of Martin Luther King, Jr.* New York: Newmarket Press, 92.

Klein, E. L., Murphy, K. L., & Witz, N. W. (1996). Changes in preservice teachers' beliefs about developmentally appropriate practice in early childhood education. *International Journal of Early Childhood Education, 1,* 143–56.

Klein, J. (1990). Young children and learning. In W. J. Stinson (Ed.), *Moving and learning for the young child* (pp. 23–30). Reston, VA: American Alliance for Health, Physical Education, Recreation and Dance.

Klein, T. (1981). Results of the reading program. *Educational Perspectives, 20*(1), 8–10.

Knapp, M. S., Turnbull, B. J., & Shields, P. M. (1990, September). New directions for educating children of poverty. *Educational Leadership, 48*(1), 4–9.

Knopczyk, D. R., & Rodes, P. G. (1996). *Teaching social competence: A practical approach for improving social skills for students-at-risk.* Pacific Grove, CA: Brooks/Cole.

Kohlberg, L. (1964). Development of moral character and moral ideology. In M. L. Hoffman and L. W. Hoffman (Eds.), *Review of child development research* (Vol. 1). New York: Russell Sage Foundation.

Kohn, A. (1996). *Beyond discipline: From compliance to community.* Alexandria, VA: Association for Supervision and Curriculum Development.

Kohn, A. (1993). Choices for children: Why and how to let children decide. *Phi Delta Kappan, 75*(1), 8–20.

Kontos, S., & Wilcox-Herzog, A. (1997). Teacher's interactions with children: Why are they so important? *Young Children, 52*(2), 4–12.

Kostelnik, M. J. (1998). Misconstructing developmentally appropriate practice. *The Early Years, 18*(1), 19–26.

Kostelnik, M. J. (1997a, October). *Spaces to learn and grow: Indoor environments in early education.* Paper presented at the Samsung International Early Childhood Conference, Seoul, Korea.

Kostelnik, M. J. (1997b, January). *The current state of developmentally appropriate practices in elementary programs in Michigan.* Paper presented to the Michigan Association of School Boards, Lansing, MI.

Kostelnik, M. J. (Ed.) (1996). *Themes teachers use.* Glenview, IL: Goodyear Books.

Kostelnik, M. J. (1993, March). Recognizing the essentials of developmentally appropriate practice. *Child Care Information Exchange, 73*–77.

Kostelnik. M. J. (1992). Myths associated with developmentally appropriate programs. *Young Children, 47*(4), 17–23.

Kostelnik, M. J. (Ed.) (1991). *Teaching young children using themes.* Glenview, IL: Goodyear Books.

Kostelnik, M. J. (1990, February). *Standards of quality for early childhood education:* Implications for policy makers. Keynote address, Michigan Department of Education Early Childhood Conference, Detroit, MI.

Kostelnik, M. J. (1989). Trends in K–1st. *Lansing City Magazine, 3*(8), 24–27.

Kostelnik, M. J., Palmer, S., & Hannon, K. (1987, November). *Theme planning in early childhood.* Paper presented at the National Association for the Education of Young Children Conference, Chicago, IL.

Kostelnik, M. J., & Stein, L. C. (1990). Social development: An essential component of kindergarten education. In J. S. McKee (Ed.), *The developing kindergarten: Programs, children, and teachers.* Saginaw, MI: Mid-Michigan Association for the Education of Young Children.

Kostelnik, M. J., & Stein, L. C. (1986, November). *Effects of three conflict mediation strategies on children's aggressive and prosocial behavior in the classroom.* Paper presented at the annual meeting of the National Association for the Education of Young Children, Washington, DC.

Kostelnik, M. J., Stein, L. C., Whiren, A. P., & Soderman, A. K. (1998). *Guiding children's social development: Classroom practices* (3rd ed.). Albany, NY: Delmar.

Koster, J. B. (1997). *Growing artists: Teaching art to young children.* Albany, NY: Delmar.

Kovalik, S. (1997, August). *Integrated learning: Integrated teaching.* Keynote address, Multi-Age Conference, Kalamazoo, MI.

Kovalik, S. (1986). *Teachers make the difference.* Oak Creek, AZ: Susan Kovalik and Associates.

Kovalik, S., & Olsen, K. (1997). *Integrated thematic instruction* (3rd ed.). Kent, WA: Susan Kovalik & Associates.

Kritchevsky, S., & Prescott, E. (1977). *Planning environments for young children. Physical space* (2nd ed.). Washington, DC: National Association for the Education of Young Children.

Krogh, S. L. (1997). How children develop and why it matters: The foundation for the developmentally appropriate integrated early childhood curriculum. In C. H.

Hart, D. C. Burts, and R. Charlesworth (Eds.), *Integrated curriculum and developmentally appropriate practice: Birth to age eight* (pp. 29–48). Albany, NY: State University of New York Press.

Kupersmidt, J. B., Coie, J. D., & Dodge, K.A. (1990). The role of poor peer relationships in the development of disorder. In S. R. Asher and J. D. Coie (Eds.), *Peer rejection in childhood* (pp. 274–308). New York: Cambridge University Press.

Kupersmidt, J. B., & Patterson, G. (1993). *Developmental patterns of peer relations and aggression in the prediction of externalizing behavior problems.* Paper presented at the biennial meeting of the Society for Research in Child Development, New Orleans, LA.

Lach, J. (1997, Spring/Summer). Turning on the motor. *Newsweek: Your Child*, sp. ed., 26–27.

Ladd, G. W., & Coleman, C. C. (1993). Young children's peer relationships: Forms, features, and functions. In B. Spodek (Ed.), *Handbook of research on the education of young children* (pp. 54–76). New York: Macmillan.

LaFrancois, G. R. (1992). *Of children.* Belmont, CA: Wadsworth.

Lane, M. B., & Signer, S. (1990). *A guide to creating partnerships with parents.* Sacramento, CA: California Department of Education.

Languis, M., Sanders, T., & Tipps, S. (1980). *Brain and learning: Directions in early childhood education.* Washington, DC: National Association for the Education of Young Children,

Lantieri, L., & Patti, J. (1996). *Waging peace in our schools.* New York: Beacon Press.

Larsen, J. M., & Haupt, J. H. (1997). Integrating home and school. In C. H. Hart, D. C. Burts, and R. Charlesworth (Eds.), *Integrated curriculum and developmentally appropriate practice: Birth to age eight* (pp. 389–415). Albany, NY: State University of New York Press.

Lauer, R. M. (1990, January 31). Self knowledge, critical thinking, and community should be the main objectives of general education. *The Chronicle of Higher Education,* Sec. 2, 1.

Laurendeau, M., & Pinard, A. (1962). *Causal thinking in the child.* New York: International Universities Press.

Lawton, J. T. (1988). *Introduction to child care and early childhood education.* Glenview, IL: Scott, Foresman.

Lawton, J. T. (1987). The Ausubelian preschool classroom. In J. L. Roopnarine and J. E. Johnson (Eds.), *Approaches to early childhood education* (pp. 85–108). Upper Saddle River, NJ: Merrill/Prentice Hall.

Lay-Dopyera, M., & Dopyera, J. (1993). *Becoming a teacher of young children.* New York: McGraw-Hill.

Lazar, I. (1981). Early intervention is effective. *Educational Leadership, 38*(4), 303–5.

Lee, L. (1997). Working with non-English-speaking families. *Child Care Information Exchange, 116,* 57–58.

Leeper, S. H., Witherspoon, R. L., & Day, B. (1984). *Good schools for young children.* New York: Macmillan.

Leong, D. J., & Bedrova, E. (1995, Fall). Vygotsky's zone of proximal development. *Of Primary Interest, 2*(4), 1–4.

Levy, A. K. (1984). The language of play: The role of play in language development. *Early Child Development and Care, 17,* 49–62.

Lewin, K., Lippitt, R., & White, R. (1939). Patterns of aggressive behaviors and experimentally created "social climates." *Journal of Social Psychology, 10,* 271–99.

Lightfoot, S. L. (1980). Families and schools: Creative conflict or negative dissonance? *Journal of Research and Development in Education, 9,* 34–43.

Lind, K. K. (1997). Science in the developmentally appropriate integrated curriculum. In C. H. Hart, D. C. Burts, and R. Charlesworth (Eds.), *Integrated curriculum and developmentally appropriate practice: Birth to age eight.* Albany, NY: State University of New York Press.

Lind, K. K. (1991). *Exploring science in early childhood—A developmental approach.* New York: Delmar.

Little-Soldier, L. (1990, January) *Anthropology in education.* Keynote address, Michigan Association for the Education of Young Children, Grand Rapids, MI.

Little-Soldier, L. (1989). Language learning of Native American students. *Educational Leadership, 46*(5), 74–75.

London Times. (1996, April 19). Sharp practice. Times Educational Supplement, p. B12.

Love, J. M., Ryer, P., & Faddis, B. (1992). *Caring environments: Program quality in California's publicly funded child development programs.* Portsmouth, NH: RMC Research Corp.

Lowenfeld, V., & Brittain, W. L. (1965). *Creative and mental growth.* New York: Macmillan.

Lubeck, S. (1994). The politics of developmentally appropriate practice: Exploring issues of culture, class and curriculum. In B. L. Mallory and R. S. New (Eds.), *Diversity and developmentally appropriate practices: Challenges for early childhood education* (pp. 17–43). New York: Teachers College Press.

Luria, A. R. (1961). *The role of speech in the regulation of normal and abnormal behaviour.* London, England: Pergamon.

Maccoby, E. E. (1984). Socialization and developmental change. *Child Development, 55,* 317–28.

Maccoby, E. E., & Martin, J. A. (1983). In E. M. Hetherington (Ed.), *Handbook of child psychology: Socialization, personality and social development* (pp. 1–101). New York: Wiley.

Machado, J. M. (1995). *Early childhood experiences in the language arts.* Albany, NY: Delmar.

Machado, J. M., & Meyer, H. C. (1996). *Student teaching: Early childhood practicum guide.* Albany, NY: Delmar.

MacLean, J. C. (1990). *Written schedule.* Dye Elementary School, Carman-Ainsworth School District, Carman-Ainsworth, MI.

Macon, R. A. (1992). Differential effects of three preschool models on inner-city 4-year-olds. *Early Childhood Research Quarterly 7,* 57.

MacPhail-Wilcox, B., Forbes, R., & Parramore, B. (1990). Project design—Reforming structure and process. *Educational Leadership, 47*(7), 22–27.

Macrina, D. (1995). Educating young children about health. In C. Hendricks (Ed.), *Young children on the grow: Health, activity and education in the preschool setting* (pp. 33–42). Washington, DC: ERIC Clearinghouse on Teacher Education.

Maeroff, G. I. (1991, December). Assessing alternative assessment. *Phi Delta Kappan, 272,* 281.

Magid, K., & McKelvey, C. A. (1987). *High risk: Children without a conscience.* New York: Bantam Books.

Malecki, C. L. (1990). Teaching whole science: In a departmentalized elementary setting. *Childhood Education, 66*(4), 232–36.

Malina, R., & Bouchard, C. (1991). *Growth, maturation, and physical activity.* Champaign, IL: Human Kinetics.

Mallory, B. L., & New, R. S. (1994). *Diversity and developmentally appropriate practices: Challenges for early childhood education.* New York: Teachers College Press.

Mangione, P. L., Lally, R. J., & Signer, S. (1993). *Essential connections: Ten keys to culturally sensitive child care.* Sacramento, CA: Far West Laboratory.

Mann, D. (1996). Serious play. *Teachers College Record, 97*(3), 446–69.

Manning, M. L., & Lucking, R. (1990). Ability grouping: Realities and alternatives. *Childhood Education, 66*(4), 254–58.

Mantzicopoulos, P. Y., Neuharth-Pritchett, S., & Morelock, J. B. (1994, April). *Academic competence, social skills, and behavior among disadvantaged children in developmentally appropriate and inappropriate classrooms.* Paper presented at the annual meeting of the American Educational Research Association, New Orleans, LA.

Marcon, R. A. (1992). Differential effects of three preschool models on inner-city 4-year-olds. *Early Childhood Research Quarterly, 7,* 517–30.

Marcus, S. A., & McDonald, P. (1990). Tools for the cooperative classroom. Palatine, IL: Skylight.

Marion, M. (1995). *Guidance of young children* (3rd ed.). New York: Macmillan.

Martin, S. (1994). *Take a look: Observation and portfolio assessment in early childhood.* Reading, MA: Addison-Wesley.

Maslow, A. H. (1954). *Motivation and personality.* New York: Harper & Row.

Mason, J. M., & Sinha, S. (1993). Emerging literacy in the early childhood years: Applying a Vygotskian model of learning and development. In B. Spodek (Ed.), *Handbook of research on the education of young children* (Chapter 10). New York: Macmillan.

McAfee, D. (1985). Circle time: Getting past five little pumpkins. *Young Children, 40*(6), 24–29.

McAfee, O., & Leong, D. (1997). *Assessing and guiding young children's development and learning.* Boston, MA: Allyn & Bacon.

McCarthy, T. (1992). *Literature-based geography activities: An integrated approach.* New York: Scholastic.

McDevitt, S. C., & Carey, W. B. (1978, July). The measurement of temperaments in 3-7 year old children. *Journal of Child Psychology and Psychiatry, 19*(3), 245–53.

McDonald, D. T. (1993). *Music in our lives.* Washington, DC: National Association for the Education of Young Children.

McDonald, D. T., & Simons, G. M. (1989). *Musical growth and development.* New York: Macmillan.

McGee, L. M., & Richgels, D. J. (1990). *Literacy's beginnings: Supporting young readers and writers.* Boston, MA: Allyn & Bacon.

McGinnis, E., & Goldstein, A. P. (1990). *Skillstreaming in early childhood: Teaching prosocial skills to the preschool and kindergarten child.* Champaign, IL.: Research Press.

McHan, J. (1986). Imitation of aggression by Lebanese children. *Journal of Social Psychology, 125*(5), 613–17.

McIntyre, E., & Pressley, M. (1996). *Balanced instruction: Strategies and skills in whole language.* Norwood, MA: Christopher-Gordon.

McKee, J. S. (1991). The developing kindergartner: Understanding children's nature and nurturing their development. In J. S. McKee (Ed.), *The developing kindergarten: Programs, children, and teachers* (pp. 65–119). East Lansing, MI: Michigan Association for the Education of Young Children.

McKee, J. S. (1990a). *The developing kindergarten: Programs, children, and teachers.* East Lansing, MI: Michigan Association for the Education of Young Children.

McKee, J. S. (1990b). Play-activity centers for the whole child: Invitations to play and learning engagement. In J. S. McKee (Ed.), *The developing kindergarten: Programs, children, and teachers* (pp. 25–61). East Lansing, MI: Michigan Association for the Education of Young Children.

McKee, J. S. (1986). *Play: Working partner of growth.* Wheaton, MD: Association for Childhood Education International.

McLaughlin, M. W., & Shields, P. M. (1987, October). Involving low-income parents in the schools: A role for policy? *Phi Delta Kappan, 156–60.*

McLeod, D. (1997). Self-identification, pan-ethnicity, and the boundaries of group identity. In F. Schultz (Ed.), *Multicultural education annual editions.* Sluice Dock, Guilford, CT: Dushkin/McGraw-Hill.

McNeil, D. (1966). Developmental psycholinguistics. In F. Smith & G. Miller (Eds.), *The genesis of language* (pp. 32–55). Cambridge, MA: M. I. T. Press.

McSwegin, P., Pemberton, C., Petray, C., & Going, S. (1989). *Physical best.* Reston, VA: American Alliance for Health, Physical Education, Recreation, & Dance.

Mechling, K., & Oliver, D. (1983, October). Who is killing young science program? *Science and Children, 21*(2), 16–18.

Medina, N., & Neill, D. M. (1990). *Fallout from the testing explosion: How 100 million standardized exams undermine equality and excellence in America's public schools.* Cambridge, MA: National Center for Fair Open Testing.

Meichenbaum, D. (1977). *Cognitive behavior modification: An integrative approach.* New York: Plenum.

Meier, J. H. (1978). Introduction. In B. Brown (Ed.), *Found: Long-term gains from early intervention.* Boulder, CO: Westview.

Meisels, S., & Friedland, S. (1990). Mainstreaming young emotionally disturbed children: Rationale and restraints. In M. Jensen & Z. Chevalier (Eds.), *Issues and advocacy in early education.* Boston, MA: Allyn & Bacon.

Meisels, S. J., & Provence, S. (1989). *Screening and assessment: Guidelines for identifying young disabled and developmentally vulnerable children and their families.* Washington, DC: National Center for Clinical Infant Programs.

Mellou, E. (1994). Factors which affect the frequency of dramatic play. *Early Child Development and Care, 101,* 59–70.

Mendler, A. N., & Curwin, R. L. (1988). *Taking charge in the classroom.* Reston, VA: Reston.

Mental Health Association of Michigan (1982). *I am loved…I am happy…I am worthwhile! The importance of self-esteem in children and some basic guides to it.* (n.p.) United Way.

Michigan Family Independence Agency. (1996). *Child care licensing regulations.* Lansing, MI: Author.

Michigan State Board of Education. (1992). *Early childhood standards of quality: Preschool through second grade.* Lansing, MI: Author.

Michigan State University Child Development Laboratories. (1997). *LPS parent handbook.* East Lansing, MI: Author.

Mickelson, N. (1989, April). *Perspectives on whole language.* Presentation at the annual meeting of International Reading Association, New Orleans, LA.

Midland Public Schools (1991). *Elementary curriculum: Focus 1991.* Midland, MI: Author.

Miller, D. F. (1995). *Positive child guidance.* Albany, NY: Delmar.

Miller, E. (1994). Peer mediation catches on, but some adults don't. *Harvard Education Letter, 10*(3), 8.

Miller, P. A. (1995, March). *Assessing empathy and prosocial behaviors in early childhood: Development of a parental questionnaire.* Paper presented at the biannual meeting of the Society for Research in Child Development, Indianapolis, IN.

Miller, R. (1996). *The developmentally appropriate inclusive classroom in early education.* Albany, NY: Delmar.

Miller, S. E. (1978). *The facilitation of fundamental motor skill learning in young children.* Unpublished doctoral dissertation, Michigan State University, East Lansing, MI.

Miller, S., Fernie, D., & Kantor, R. (1992). Distinctive literacies in different preschool play contexts. *Play and Culture, 5,* 107–19.

Milne, A. A. (1995). *Pooh's little instruction book.* New York: Dutton Books, 24.

Ministry of Education, Province of British Columbia (1988). *The primary program, Victoria, British Columbia.* Victoria, British Columbia: Author.

Minnesota Department of Education (1989). *Model learner outcomes for early childhood education.* St. Paul, MN: Author.

Mischel, W. (1978). How children postpone pleasure. *Human Nature, 1,* 51–55.

Moen, C. B. (1992). *Better than book reports.* New York: Scholastic.

Mohighan-Nourot, P. (1997). Playing with play in four dimensions. In J. Isenberg and M. R. Jalongo (Eds.), *Major trends and issues in early childhood education: Challenges, controversies and insights.* New York: Teachers College Press.

Mohighan-Nourot, P. (1995). Playing across curriculum and culture: Strengthening early primary education in California. In E. Klugman (Ed.), *Play, policy and practice* (pp. 3–19). St. Paul, MN: Redleaf Press.

Moles, O. C. (1982). Synthesis of research on parent participation in children's education. *Educational Leadership, 40,* 44–47.

Moog, H. (1976). *The musical experience of the preschool child.* London, England: Schott Music.

Moore, G. T. (1987). The physical environment and cognitive development in child care centers. In C. Weinstein and T. David (Eds.). *Spaces for children* (pp. 41–67). New York: Plenum.

Moorehead, G. E., & Pond, D. (1978). *Music for young children*. Santa Barbara, CA: Pillsbury Foundation for the Advancement of Music Education.

Moore, S. G. (1986). Socialization in the kindergarten classroom. In B., Spodek (Ed.), *Today's kindergarten* (pp. 110–36). New York: Teachers College Press.

Morado, C. (1990). A look at kindergartens: Past and present practices. In J. S. McKee (Ed.), *The developing kindergarten: Programs, children, and teachers* (pp. 5–24). East Lansing, MI: Michigan Association for the Education of Young Children.

Moran, J. D. III, & McCullers, J. C. (1984). The effects of regency and story content on children's moral judgments. *Journal of Experimental Child Psychology, 38*, 447–55.

Morrow, L. (1990). Preparing the classroom environment to promote literacy during play. *Children's Quarterly, 5*, 537–54.

Morrow, R. D. (1989, Winter). Southeast Asian child-rearing practices: Implications for child and youth care workers. *Child & Youth Care Quarterly, 18*(4), 273–87.

Moyer, J. (1990). Whose creation is it, anyway? *Childhood Education, 66*(3), 130–31.

Music Educators National Conference (MENC) (1994). MENC position statement on early childhood education. *MENC Soundpost, 8*(2), 21–22.

Musson, S. (1994). *School-age care: Theory and practice*. Reading, MA: Addison-Wesley.

Nash, J. M. (1997, February 3). Fertile minds. *Time Special Report*, 48–56.

National Academy of Early Childhood Programs (1991). *Accreditation criteria and procedures*. Washington, DC: National Association for the Education of Young Children.

National Association for the Education of Young Children (1996a). *Guidelines for appropriate curriculum content and assessment in programs serving children ages 3 through 8*. Position statement of the National Association for the Education of Young Children and the National Association of Early Childhood Specialists in State Departments of Education. Washington, DC: Author.

National Association for the Education of Young Children (1996b). *Guidelines for preparation of early childhood professionals*. Washington, DC: Author.

National Association for the Education of Young Children (1996c). *NAEYC position statement responding to linguistic and cultural diversity: Recommendations for effective early childhood education*. Washington, DC: Author.

National Association for the Education of Young Children (1995). *Quality, compensation and affordability*. Washington, DC: Author.

National Association for the Education of Young Children (1993). *NAEYC position statement on violence in the lives of children*. Washington, DC: Author.

National Association for the Education of Young Children (1986). *Early childhood teacher education guidelines for four- and five-year programs*. Washington, DC: Author.

National Association for the Education of Young Children (1982). *Early childhood teacher education guidelines: Position statement of the National Association for the Education of Young Children*. Washington, DC: Author.

National Association for the Education of Young Children & National Association of Early Childhood Specialists in State Departments of Education (1992). Guidelines for appropriate curriculum content and assessment in programs serving children ages 3 through 8. In S. Bredekamp and T. Rosegrant (Eds.), *Reaching potentials: Appropriate curriculum and assessment for young children* (vol. 1). Washington, DC: National Association for the Education of Young Children.

National Association of Elementary School Principals (1990). *Early childhood education and the elementary school principal: Standards for quality programs for young children*. Alexandria, VA: Author.

National Association of Music Educators (1994). *National standards for arts education*. Reston, VA: Music Educators National Conference.

National Association of State Boards of Education (1988). *Right from the start*. Alexandria, VA: Author.

National Center for History in the Schools (1994). National standards: History for grades K–4. Los Angeles, CA: Author.

National Council for the Social Studies (1984). In search of a scope and sequence for social studies. *Social Education, 48*, 249–62.

National Council for the Social Studies Task Force on Early Childhood/Elementary Social Studies (1989). Social studies for early childhood and elementary school children: Preparing for the 21st century. *Social Education, 53*, 14–23.

National Council of Teachers of English Committee on Elementary Language Arts Textbooks (1991). Guidelines for judging and selecting elementary language arts textbooks. *Language Arts, 68*(3), 253–54.

National Council of Teachers of Mathematics (1989). *Curriculum and evaluation standards for school mathematics*. Washington, DC: Author.

National Council on Family Relations (1990, January). *2001: Preparing families for the future* (Presidential Report) n.p.: Author.

National Forum on the Future of Children and Families (1991). *Improving instruction and assessment in early childhood education*. Washington, DC: National Academy Press.

National Research Council (1991). *Caring for America's children*. Washington, DC: National Academy Press.

Neill, D. M., & Medina, N. J. (1989). Standardized testing: Harmful to educational health. *Phi Delta Kappan, 46*(8), 688–97.

Neugebauer, R. (1994, January). Impressive growth projected for centers into the 21st century. *Child Care Information Exchange,* 80–87.

Neumann, D. (1972). Sciencing for young children. In K. R. Baker (Ed.), *Ideas that work with young children* (pp. 137–48). Washington, DC: National Association for the Education of Young Children.

Neuman, S., & Roskos, K. (1990). Peers as literacy informants: A description of young children's literacy conversations in play. *Early Childhood Research Quarterly, 6,* 233–48.

Newberger, J. J. (1997, May). New brain development research—A wonderful window of opportunity to build public support for early childhood education! *Young Children, 52*(4), 4–9.

Newman, B. M., & Newman, P. R. (1978). *Infancy and childhood.* New York: Wiley.

Newman, J. (1996). Teachers' attitudes and policies regarding play in elementary schools. *Psychology in the Schools, 33*(1) 61–69.

Newman, J. M., & Church, S. M. (1990). Myths of whole language. *The Reading Teacher, 44*(1), 20–26.

Newman, P. R., & Newman, B. M. (1997). *Childhood and adolescence.* Pacific Grove, CA: Brooks/Cole.

Newman, R. (1997). Learning healthful habits for a lifetime. *Childhood Education 73*(4), 234–35.

New, R. (1990, September). Excellent early education: A city in Italy has it. *Young Children, 7,* 4–8.

New, R. S. (1994). Culture, child development, and developmentally appropriate practices: Teachers as collaborative researchers. In B. L. Mallory and R. S. New (Eds.), *Diversity and developmentally appropriate practices: Challenges for early childhood education* (pp. 65–83). New York: Teachers College Press.

Ney, P. G. (1988, Spring). Transgenerational child abuse. *Child Psychiatry and Human Development, 18*(3), 151–55.

Nicholls, J. G., Cobb, P., Wood, T., Yackel, E., & Patashnick, M. (1991). Dimensions of success in mathematics: Individual and classroom differences. *Journal of Research in Mathematics Education, 21,* 109–22.

Nickelsburg, J. (1976). *Nature activities for early childhood.* Menlo Park, CA: Addison-Wesley.

Nourot, P. M., & Van Hoorn, J. (1991). Symbolic play in preschool and primary settings. *Young Children, 46*(6), 40–50.

Nyberg, J. (1996). *Charts for children: Print awareness activities for young children.* Glenview, IL: Goodyear Books.

Oakes, J. (1985). *Keeping track: How schools structure inequality.* New Haven, CT: Yale University Press.

Oakland Community Schools Early Childhood Committee. (1992). *Early childhood curriculum.* Waterford, MI: Oakland Community Schools.

Osborn, J. D., & Osborn, D. K. (1983). *Cognition in early childhood.* Athens, GA: Education Associates.

Paciorek, K., & Munro, J. H. (1995). *Notable selections in early childhood education.* Guilford, CT: Dushkin.

Palardy, M. J. (1996). Taking another look at behavior modification and assertive discipline. *NASSP Bulletin, 80*(581), 66–70.

Paley, V. (1995). *Kwanzaa and me.* Cambridge, MA: Harvard University Press.

Paley, V. (1988). *Mollie is three.* Chicago, IL: University of Chicago Press.

Palincsar, A. S., & Brown, A. L. (1989). Classroom dialogues to promote self-regulated comprehension. In J. Brophy (Ed.), *Advances in research on teaching* (vol. 1) (pp. 35–71). Greenwich, CT: JAI.

Palmer, J. M. (1990). Planning wheels turn curriculum around. *Educational Leadership, 49*(2), 57–60.

Palmer, S. (1991). [Ypsilanti public schools parent involvement strategies. Personal communication.]

Parker, J. G., & Asher, S. R. (1987). Peer relations and later personal adjustment: Are low accepted children at risk? *Psychological Bulletin, 102,* 357–89.

Parker, J. G., & Gottman, J. M. (1989). Social and emotional development in a relational context: Friendship interaction from early childhood to adolescence. In T. J. Berndt and G. W. Ladd (Eds.), *Peer relations in child development.* New York: Wiley.

Parker, W. C. (1991). *Renewing the social studies curriculum.* Alexandria, VA: Association for Supervision and Curriculum Development.

Patterson, G. R., & Stouthamer-Loeber, L. S. (1984). The correlation of family management practices and delinquency. *Child Development, 55,* 1299–1307.

Pattillo, J., & Vaughan, E. (1996). *Learning centers for child-centered classrooms.* Washington, DC: National Education Association.

Paul, R., Binkder, A. J. A., & Weil, D. (1990). *Critical thinking handbook: K–3rd grades.* Rohnert Park, CA: Foundation for Critical Thinking.

Payne, G. V. & Isaacs, L. D. (1991). *Human motor development* (2nd ed.). Mountain View, CA: Mayfield.

Payne, K. (1991, Spring). Principles of parent involvement in preschool classrooms. *National Organization of Laboratory Schools Bulletin, 18,* 8–9.

Payne, V. G., & Rink, J. (1997). Physical education in the developmentally appropriate integrated curriculum. In

C. H. Hart, D. C. Burts, and R. Charlesworth (Eds.), *Integrated curriculum and developmentally appropriate practice: Birth to age eight* (pp. 145–70). Albany, NY: State University of New York Press.

Pearsall, P. (1983). De-stressing children: Wellness for children. *Offspring, 25*(2), 2–9.

Peck, J. T., McCaig, G., & Sapp, M. E. (1988). *Kindergarten policies: What is best for children?* Washington, DC: National Association for the Education of Young Children.

Peery, J. C., & Peery, I. W. (1986). Effects of exposure to classical music on the musical preferences of preschool children. *Journal of Research in Music Education, 34,* 24–33.

Pellegrini, A. D. (1989). *Applied child study: A developmental approach.* Hillsdale, NJ: Erlbaum.

Pellegrini, A. D., & Perlmutter, J. C. (1988). Rough and tumble play. *Young Children, 43*(2), 14–17.

Pepler, D, J. (1982). Play and divergent thinking. In D. J. Pepler and K. H. Rubin (Eds.), *The play of children: Research and theory* (pp. 64–78). Basel, Switzerland: Karger.

Perkins, D. N. (1995). *Outsmarting I.Q.: The emerging science of learnable intelligence.* New York: Free Press.

Perrone, V. (Ed.) (1991). *Expanding student assessment.* Alexandria, VA: Association for Supervision and Curriculum Development.

Peters, D. L., & Kostelnik, M. J. (1981). Day care personnel preparation. In S. Kilmer (Ed.), *Advances in early education and day care* (vol. 2) (pp. 20–60). Greenwich, CT: JAI.

Peterson, P. L., Fennema, E., & Carpenter, T. P. (in press). Teacher's knowledge of student's mathematical problem solving knowledge. In J. E. Brophy (Ed.), *Advances in research in teaching: Vol. 2. Teacher's subject matter knowledge.* Greenwich, CT: JAI.

Peterson, R., & Felton-Collins, V. (1991). *The Piaget handbook for teachers and parents.* New York: Teachers College Press.

Petrakos, H., & Howe, N. (1996). The influence of the physical design of the dramatic play center on children's play. *Early Childhood Research Quarterly, 11*(1), 63–77.

Phenice, L., & Griffore, R. (1990). Assessment. In J. S. McKee (Ed.), *The developing kindergarten: Programs, children, and teachers* (pp. 373–97). East Lansing, MI: Michigan Association for the Education of Young Children.

Phillips, C. B. (1991). *Culture as process.* Unpublished paper.

Phillips, D., & Howes, C. (1987). Indicators of quality child care: Review of research. In D. Phillips (Ed.),

Quality in child care: What does research tell us? (pp. 1–19). Washington, DC: National Association for the Education of Young Children.

Phillips, J. L., Jr. (1975). *The origins of intellect: Piaget's theory.* San Francisco, CA: Freeman.

Phillips, P. (1997, May). The conflict wall. *Educational Leadership, 54*(8), 43–44.

Piaget, J. (1979). *Success and understanding.* Cambridge, MA: Harvard University Press.

Piaget J. (1965). *The moral judgment of the child.* New York: Free Press. (Original work published 1932)

Piaget, J. (1962). *Play, dreams and imitation in childhood.* New York: Norton.

Piaget, J. (1954). *The construction of reality in the child* (M. Cook, Trans.). New York: Basic Books.

Piaget, J. (1952). *The origins of intelligence in children.* Madison, CT: International Universities Press.

Pica, R. (1995). *Experiences in movement with music, activities, and theory.* Albany, NY: Delmar.

Plomin, R. (1989). Environment and genes: Determinants of behavior. *American Psychologist, 44,* 105–11.

Polloway, A. M. (1974). The child in the physical environment: A design problem. In G. Coales (Ed.), *Alternative learning environments.* Shoudsberg, PA: Dowdes, Hakkenson, & Ross.

Potter, S. (1992). *Portfolios and student-led conferencing.* Birmingham, MI: The Potter Press.

Powell, D. (1994). Parents, pluralism and the NAEYC Statement on Developmentally Appropriate Practice. In B. L. Mallory and R. S. New (Eds.), *Diversity and developmentally appropriate practices: Challenges for early childhood education.* (pp. 166–82). New York: Teachers College Press.

Powell, R. (1989). *Families and early childhood programs.* (Research Monographs of the National Association for the Education of Young Children, Vol. 3). Washington, DC: National Association for the Education of Young Children.

Power, T. J., & Bartholomew, K. L. (1987). Family-school relationship patterns: An ecological assessment. *School Psychology Review, 16*(4), 498–512.

Preston, C. (1991). *Implementation of a school-wide discipline Okemos policy—One year after initiation.* Unpublished manuscript. Okemos, MI: Okemos Schools.

Puckett, M. B., & Black, J. K. (1994). *Authentic assessment of the young child.* Upper Saddle River, NJ: Merrill/Prentice Hall.

Pulkkinen, L. (1982). Self-control and continuity from childhood to adolescence. In P. B. Baltes and O. G. Brim, Jr. (Eds.), *Life-span development and behavior* (vol. 4) (pp. 63–105). Orlando, FL: Academic Press.

Radke-Yarrow, M. (1987, April). *A developmental and contextual analysis of continuity.* Paper presented at the biennial conferences of the Society for Research in Child Development, Baltimore, MD.

Raffi. (1987). *One light, one sun.* Hollywood, CA: A&M Records.

Raffini, J. P. (1980). *Discipline: Negotiating conflicts with today's kids.* Upper Saddle River, NJ: Prentice-Hall.

Raines, S. (1990). Representational competence: Regarding presenting experiences through words, actions, and images. *Childhood Education, 139–44.*

Ramsey, P. G. (1979). Beyond "Ten Little Indians" and turkey: Alternate approaches to Thanksgiving. *Young Children, 34*(6), 28–52.

Readdick, C., & Bartlett, P. (1994). Vertical learning environments. *Childhood Education, 71*(2), 86–91.

Read, K., Gardner, P., & Mahler, B. (1993). *Early childhood programs: Human relationships and learning.* New York: Harcourt Brace Jovanovich.

Read, K. H. (1966). *The nursery school: A human relations laboratory.* Philadelphia, PA: W. B. Saunders.

Reed, D. F. (1991). Preparing teachers for multicultural classrooms. *The Journal of Early Childhood Teacher Education, 38*(12:2), 16–21.

Reifel, S., & Greenfield, P. (1983, Spring). Part-whole relations: Some structural features of children's representational block play. *Child Care Quarterly, 12*(1), 144–51.

Reimer, D. C., Eaves, L. C., Richards, R., & Chrichton, J. (1975). Name printing as a test of developmental maturity. *Developmental Medicine and Child Neurology, 17,* 486–92.

Reisman, B. (1996). What do parents want? Can we create consumer demand for accredited child care programs? In S. Bredekamp and B. Willer (Eds.), *NAEYC accreditation: A decade of learning and the years ahead* (pp. 139–48). Washington, DC: NAYEC.

Resnick, L. (1996). Schooling and the workplace: What relationship? *Preparing youth for the 21st century.* Washington, DC: Aspen Institute, 21–27.

Reuschlein, R., & Haubenstricker, J. (Eds.) (1985). *1984–1985 physical education interpretive report: Grades 4, 7, and 10.* Lansing, MI: Michigan Educational Assessment Program, Michigan Department of Education.

Revicki, D. (1982). The relationship among socioeconomic status, home environment, parent involvement, child self-concept and child achievement. *Resources in Education, 1,* 459–63.

Reynolds, E. (1996). *Guiding young children: A child centered approach.* Mountain View, CA: Mayfield.

Rich, J. M. (1985). *Innovative school discipline.* Springfield, IL: Thomas.

Richberg, J. (1991). *Intermediate results of a school-wide discipline policy.* Paper presented to the Okemos School Board, Okemos, MI.

Ritchie, F. K., & Toner, I. J. (1985). Direct labeling, tester expectancy, and delay maintenance behavior in Scottish preschool children. *International Journal of Behavioral Development, 7*(3), 333–41.

Rivkin, M. (1995). *The great outdoors: Restoring children's right to play outside.* Washington, DC: National Association for the Education of Young Children.

Roberts, E., & Davies, A. (1975). A method of extending the vocal range of monotone school children. *Psychology of Music, 4*(1), 29–43.

Rogers, C. R. (1961). On becoming a person. Boston, MA: Houghton-Mifflin.

Rogers, D. (1985). Relationships between block play and the social development of young children. *Early Child Development and Care, 20,* 245–61.

Rogers, F. Cited in Gestwicki, C. (1997), *The essentials of early education.* Albany, NY: Delmar, 135.

Rohde, B. (1996). Safety. In M. J. Kostelnik (Ed.), *Themes teachers use.* Glenview, IL: Good Year Books.

Rosenbusch, M. H. (1994, January/February). Preserve the rain forests: Integrating the social studies and a foreign language into thematic instruction for young students. *The Social Studies.*

Rosenthal, D. M., & Sawyers, J. Y. (1996, Summer). Building successful home-school partnerships: Strategies for parent support and involvement. *Childhood Education, 194-200.*

Roskos, K. (1990). A taxonomic view of pretend play activity among four and five year old children. *Early Childhood Research Quarterly, 5,* 495–512.

Rothlein, L., & Brett, A. (1987). Children's teachers' and parents' perceptions of play. *Early Childhood Quarterly, 2,* 45–53.

Routman, R. (1996). *Literacy at the crossroads.* Portsmouth, NH: Heinemann.

Routman, R. (1987). *Transitions.* Portsmouth, NH: Heinemann.

Rowe, M. B. (1974). Wait time and rewards as instructional variables, their influence in language, logic and fate control: Part one—Wait time. *Journal of Research in Science Teaching, 11*(2), 81–94.

Ruopp, R., Travers, J., Glantz, F., & Coelen, C. (1979). *Children at the center: Final results of the National Day Care Study.* Cambridge, MA: Abt Associates.

Russell, J. A., & Bullock, M. (1989). On the dimensions preschoolers use to interpret facial expressions of emotion. *Developmental Psychology, 22,* 97–102.

Rutter, M. (1983). School effects on pupil progress: Research findings and policy implications. *Child Development, 54,* 1–29.

Rutter, M., Maugham, B., Mortmore, P., & Ousten, J. (1979). *Fifteen thousand hours.* Cambridge, MA: Harvard University Press.

Rylant, C. (1985). *The relatives came.* New York: Bradbury.

Sacks, J., Holt, K., Holmgreen, P., Colwell, L., & Brown, J. (1990). Playground hazards in Atlanta child care centers. *The American Journal of Public Health, 80*(8), 986–91.

Safford, P. L. (1989). *Integrated teaching in early childhood.* White Plains, NY: Longman.

Salovey, P., & Mayer, J. D. (1990). Emotional intelligence. *Imagination, cognition and personality, 9,* 185–211.

Santrock, J. W. (1994). *Children.* Dubuque, IA: Brown.

Sapon-Shevin, M. (1983). Teaching young children about differences: Resources for teaching. *Young Children, 38*(2), 24–32.

Saracho, O. N. (1993). Preparing teachers for early childhood programs in the United States. In B. Spodek (Ed.), *Handbook of research on the education of young children* (pp. 412–26). New York: Macmillan.

Satir, V. (1975). *Self-esteem.* Millbrae, CA: Celestial Arts.

Sattler, J. (1992). *Assessment of children* (3rd ed.). San Diego: Jerome M. Sattler.

Sattler, J. M. (1988). *Assessment of children's intelligence and special abilities.* Boston, MA: Allyn & Bacon.

Scherer, M. (1997, April). Perspectives/Negotiating childhood. *Educational Leadership, 54*(7), 5.

Schickedanz, J. A., Hansen, K., & Forsyth, P. D. (1990). *Understanding children.* Mountain View, CA: Mayfield.

Schickedanz, J. A., Pergantis, M. L., Kanosky, J., Blaney, A, & Ottinger, J. (1997). *Curriculum in early childhood.* Boston, MA: Allyn & Bacon.

Schickedanz, J. A., York, M. E., Stewart, I. S., & White, D. A. (1990). *Strategies for teaching young children* (3rd ed.). Upper Saddle River, NJ: Prentice-Hall.

Schirrmacher, R. (1993). *Art and creative development for young children.* Albany, N Y: Delmar.

Schirrmacher, R. (1986). Talking with young children about their art. *Young Children, 41*(5), 3–7.

Schlosser, K. G., & Phillips, V. L. (1992). *Building literacy with interactive charts.* New York: Scholastic.

Schmidt, F., Friedman, A., Brunt, E., & Solotoff, T. (1992). *Peace-making skills for little kids.* Miami Beach, FL: Peace Education Foundation.

Schmoker, M. (1996). *Results: The key to continuous school improvement.* Alexandria, VA: Association for Supervision and Curriculum Development.

Schneider, R., & Barone, D. (1997). Cross-age tutoring. *Childhood Education, 73*(3), 136–43.

Schrader, C. (1990). Symbolic play as a curricular tool for early literacy development. *Early Childhood Research Quarterly, 5,* 79–103.

Schrader, C. (1989). Written language use within the context of young children's symbolic play. *Early Childhood Research Quarterly, 4,* 225–44.

Schultz, T. (1990, March). Testing and retention of young children: Moving from controversy to reform. *Phi Delta Kappan, 71*(2), 125–29.

Schwartz, S. L., & Robison, H. F. (1982). *Designing curriculum for early childhood.* Boston, MA: Allyn & Bacon.

Schweinhart, L. J., Barnes, H. V., & Weikart, D. P. (1993). *Significant benefits: The High/Scope Perry Preschool Study through age 27.* Ypsilanti, MI: High/Scope Press.

Schweinhart, L., & Weikart, D. (1980). Young children grow up: The effects of the Perry Preschool Program on youths through age 15 (Monograph No. 7 of the High/Scope Educational Research Foundation). Ypsilanti, MI: High/Scope Press.

Schweinhart, L. J., Weikart, D. P., & Larner, M. B. (1986). Consequences of three curriculum models through age 15. *Early Childhood Research Quarterly, 1*(1), 15–45.

Sciarra, D. J., & Dorsey, A. G. (1990). *Developing and administering a child care center.* Albany, NY: Delmar, 360.

Seefeldt, C. (1995a). Art—serious work. *Young Children, 50*(3), 39–45.

Seefeldt, C. (1995b). Playing with policy: A serious undertaking. In E. Klugman (Ed.), *Play, policy and practice* (pp. 185–94). St. Paul, MN: Redleaf Press.

Seefeldt, C. (1995c). Transforming curriculum in social studies. In S. Bredekamp and T. Rosegrant (Eds.), *Reaching potentials: Appropriate curriculum and assessment for young children* (pp. 109–24) (vol. 2). Washington, DC: National Association for the Education of Young Children.

Seefeldt, C. (1993). Social studies: Learning for freedom. *Young Children, 48*(3), 4–9.

Seefeldt, C. (1990a). *Teaching young children.* Upper Saddle River, NJ: Prentice Hall.

Seefeldt, C. (Ed.) (1990b). *The early childhood curriculum: A review of current research.* New York: Teacher's College Press, 183–236.

Seefeldt, C. (Ed.) (1987). *The early childhood curriculum: A review of current research.* New York: Teachers College Press, 144–97.

Seefeldt, C. (1985, November/December). Parent involvement: Support or stress. *Childhood Education,* 98–102.

Seefeldt, V. (Ed.) (1986). *Physical activity and well-being.* Reston, VA: American Alliance for Health, Physical Education, Recreation & Dance.

Seefeldt, V. (1980). Developmental motor patterns: Implications for elementary school physical education. In C. Nadeau, W. Halliwell, K. Newell, and G. Roberts

(Eds.)., *Psychology of motor behavior and sport.* Champaign, IL: Human Kinetics.

Seefeldt V., & Haubenstricker J. (1982). Patterns, phases, or stages: An analytical mode for the study of developmental movement. In J. A. S. Kelso and J. E. Clark (Eds.), *The development of movement control and coordination.* New York: John Wiley.

Seefeldt, V., & Vogel, P. G. (1986). *The value of physical activity.* Reston, VA: American Alliance for Health, Physical Education, Recreation & Dance.

Seigler, R. S. (1991). *Children's thinking.* Upper Saddle River, NJ: Prentice-Hall.

Seligman, M. E. (1995). *The optimistic child.* New York: Houghton Mifflin.

Selman, R. L. (1980). *The growth of interpersonal understanding.* New York: Academic Press.

Selman, R. L. (1976). Social-cognitive understanding. In T. Lickona (Ed.), *Moral development and behavior: Theory, research and social issues* (pp. 299–316). New York: Holt, Rinehart, & Winston.

Selman, R. L, & Selman, A. P. (1979). Children's ideas about friendship: A new theory. *Psychology Today, 13,* 71–114.

Sendak, M. (1963). *Where the wild things are.* New York: Harper & Row.

Seven styles of learning clip-and-save chart. (1990, September). *Instructor Magazine, 52.*

Shaffer, D. R. (1995). *Developmental psychology: Childhood and adolescence* (4th ed.). Pacific Grove, CA: Brooks/Cole.

Shaffer, D. R. (1994). *Social and personality development.* Pacific Grove, CA: Brooks/Cole.

Shaklee, B. D. (1997). *Designing and using portfolios.* Needham Heights, MA: Allyn & Bacon.

Shanab, M. E., & Yahya, K. A. (1977). A behavioral study of obedience. *Journal of Personality and Social Psychology, 35,* 550–86.

Shapiro, L. (1997). *How to raise a child with a high EQ.* New York: Harper Collins.

Sharp, C. (1987). *Now you're talking: Techniques that extend conversations.* Portland, OR: Educational Productions.

Sharpe, D. (1990). *Written schedule.* A hand-out for parents distributed by a teacher at Wilkshire Elementary, Haslett Public Schools, Haslett, MI.

Shaywitz, S. E., Escobar, M. D., Shaywitz, B. A., Fletcher, J. M., & Makuch, R. (1992, January). Evidence that dyslexia may represent the lower tail of a normal distribution of reading ability. *The New England Journal of Medicine, 326*(3), 145–50.

Sherman, C. W., & Mueller, D. P. (1996, June). *Developmentally appropriate practice and student achievement in inner-city elementary schools.* Paper presented at Head Start's Third National Research Conference, Washington, DC.

Shimoni, R., Baxter, J., & Kugelmass, J. (1992). *Every child is special: Quality group care for infants and toddlers.* Don Mills, Ontario: Addison-Wesley.

Shoemaker, C. J. (1995). *Administration and management of programs for young children.* Upper Saddle River, NJ: Merrill/Prentice Hall.

Shore, B. (1996). *Culture in mind: Cognition, culture and the problem of meaning.* New York: Oxford University Press.

Shore, R. (1997). *Rethinking the brain.* New York: Families and Work Institute.

Short, V. M. (1991). Childhood education in a changing world. *Childhood Education, 68*(1), 10–13.

Shotwell, J., Wolf, D., & Gardner, H. Y. (1979). Exploring early symbolization: Styles of achievement. In B. Sutton-Smith (Ed.), *Play and learning* (pp. 127–56). New York: Gardner Press.

Silvern, S. B. (1988). Continuity/discontinuity between home and early childhood education environments. *The Elementary School Journal, 89*(2), 147–59.

Simner, M. L. (1988, April). *Predicting first-grade achievement from form errors in printing at the start of pre-kindergarten.* Paper presented at the National Association for School Psychologists, Chicago, IL.

Sinatra, R. (1983, May). Brain research sheds light on language, learning. *Educational Leadership,* 9–12.

Slavin, R. E. (1990). Achievement effects of ability grouping in secondary schools: A best-evidence synthesis. *Review of Educational Research, 60,* 471–99.

Slavin, R. E. (1987). Ability grouping and student achievement in elementary schools: A best-evidence synthesis. *Review of Educational Research, 57,* 293–336.

Slavin, R. E., & Madden, N. A. (1989). What works for students at risk: A research synthesis. *Educational Leadership, 46*(5), 4–13.

Slobin, D. L. (1971). *Psycholinguistics.* Glenview, IL: Scott, Foresman.

Smart, M. S., & Smart, R. C. (1972). *Children: Development and relationships.* New York: Macmillan.

Smart, M. S., & Smart, R. S. (1982). *Children: Development and relationships* (rev. ed.). New York: Macmillan.

Smilansky, S. (1968). *The effects of socio-dramatic play on disadvantaged preschool children.* New York: Wiley.

Smith, C. A. (1982). *Promoting the social development of young children.* Palo Alto, CA: Mayfield.

Smith, C. A. (1979). Puppetry and problem-solving skills. *Young Children, 34*(3), 4–10.

Smith, J. (1990). *To think.* New York: Teachers College Press.

Smith, N. (1982). The visual arts in early childhood education. In B. Spodek (Ed.), *Handbook of research in early childhood education* (pp. 295–320). New York: Free Press.

Smith, R. A. (1992). Toward percipience: A humanities curriculum for arts education. In B. Reimer & R. A. Smith (Eds.), *The arts, education, and aesthetic knowing* (pp. 51–69). Chicago, IL: University of Chicago Press.

Smith, S. S. (1997). *Early childhood mathematics.* Needham Heights, MA: Allyn & Bacon.

Smith, T. E. (1988). Parental control techniques: Relative frequencies and relationships with situational factors. *Journal of Family Issues, 9,* 155–76.

Smith, T. M., Young, B. A., Bae, Y., Choy, S. P., & Alsalam, N. (1997). *The condition of education, 1997.* Washington, DC: National Center for Education Statistics, U.S. Department of Education.

Snider, M. H., & Fu, V. R. (1990). The effects of specialized education and job experience on early childhood teachers' knowledge of developmentally appropriate practice. *Early Childhood Research Quarterly, 5,* 69–78.

Snow, C. E., Tabors, P. O., Nicholson, P. E., & Kirkland, B. F. (1995). SHELL: Oral language and early literacy skills in kindergarten and first grade children. *Journal of Research in Childhood Education, 10*(1), 37–48.

Snow, M. (1982). *Characteristics of families with special needs in relation to schools.* Charleston, WV: Appalachia Educational Laboratory.

Soderman, A. (1997, August). *Multi-age classrooms: Accommodating gender differences among children.* Paper presented at the Michigan Multi-Age Conference, Kalamazoo, MI.

Soderman, A. K. (1995). Brownell Community School and Gundry Elementary School: Reading accuracy assessment: A baseline study of grades 1–3. East Lansing, MI: Michigan State University.

Soderman, A. (1991, May). *Facts about brain growth.* Unpublished paper delivered to the East Lansing public schools.

Soderman, A. (1985, July). Dealing with difficult young children. *Young Children,* 15–20.

Soderman, A., & Greenberg, B. (1988). Television and movie behaviors of pregnant and non-pregnant adolescents. *Journal of Adolescent Research, 3*(2), 153–70.

Soderman, A., & Phillips, M. (1986, November). Education of young males: Where are we failing them? *Educational Leadership, 44* (3), 70–72.

Soderman, A. K., Beatty, L., Cooper, P., Cummings, K. E., Fleury, J., Darrow, L., Thompson, C., & Weber, M. (1995). *Emerging literacy in Michigan first graders.* East Lansing, MI: Michigan State University.

Soderman, A. K., Gregory, K., & O'Neill, L. (1999). *Creating phonological and print awareness: developmentally appropriate Practices.* Needham Heights, MA: Allyn & Bacon.

Soderman, A. K., O'Neill, L. T., & Linscott, L. L. (1996, August). *Literacy assessment—Flint Gundry Elementary School, Brownell Community School and Mason North Aurelius Elementary School, grades 1–3. End of Year Report,* 1995–1996.

Spaggiari, S. (1987). *The hundred languages of children.* Reggio Emilia, Italy: Department of Education.

Spangler, C. B. (1997). The sharing circle: A child-centered curriculum. *Young Children, 52*(5), 74–78.

Sparling, J. (1996, February 19). Quoted in S. Begley, Your child's brain. *Newsweek,* 55–61.

Spear-Swerling, L., & Sternberg, R. J. (1994). The road not taken: An integrative theoretical model of reading disability. *Journal of Learning Disabilities, 27,* 91–103.

Spier, P. (1961). *The fox went out on a chilly night.* Garden City, NY: Doubleday.

Spivack, G., & Shure, M. (1974). *Social adjustment of young children: A cognitive approach to solving real-life problems.* San Francisco, CA: Jossey-Bass.

Spodek, B. (1986). *Today's kindergarten: Exploring the knowledge base, expanding the curriculum.* New York: Teachers College Press.

Spodek, B. (1985). *Teaching in the early years* (3rd ed.). Upper Saddle River, NJ: Prentice-Hall.

Spodek, B. (1973). *Early childhood education.* Upper Saddle River, NJ: Prentice-Hall.

Spodek, B., & Brown, P. C. (1993). Curriculum alternatives in early childhood education: A historical perspective. In B. Spodek, (Ed.), *Handbook of research on the education of young children* (pp. 91–104). New York: Macmillan.

Spodek, B., Saracho, O. N., & Davis, M. D. (1991). *Foundations of early childhood education.* Upper Saddle River, NJ: Prentice-Hall.

Sroufe, L. A., Cooper, R. G., DeHart, G. B., and Marshall, M. E. (1996). *Child development: Its nature and course* (3rd ed.). New York: McGraw-Hill.

Starky, S. L. (1980). The relationship between parental acceptance-rejection and the academic performance of fourth and fifth graders. *Behavior Science Research, 15,* 67–80.

Staub, E. (1978). *Positive social behavior and morality: Socialization and development* (vol. 1). New York: Academic Press.

Stein, L. C., & Kostelnik, M. J. (1984, Spring). A practical problem solving model for conflict resolution in the classroom. *Child Care Quarterly, 13*(1), 5–20.

Steinberg, A. (1990, May). Kindergarten: Producing early failure? *Principal,* 6–9.

Steinberg, L., & Belsky, J. (1991). *Infancy, childhood, and adolescence: Development in context.* New York: McGraw-Hill.

Steiner, J., & Whelan, M. S. (1995). *For the love of children: For people who care for children.* St. Paul, MN: Redleaf Press, December 29, 1995.

Stengel, S. R. (1982). Moral education for young children. *Young Children, 37*(6), 23–31.

Stephens, K. (1996, May). You can make circle time developmentally appropriate. *Child Care Information Exchange,* 40–43.

Sternberg, R. (1988). *The triarchic mind: A new theory of human intelligence.* New York: Viking.

Sternberg, R. (1985). *Practical intelligence and people skills. Beyond I. Q.* New York: Cambridge University Press.

Sternberg, R. J. (1997, March). What does it mean to be smart? *Educational Leadership, 54*(6), 20–24.

Sternberg, R. J. (1983). *How can we teach intelligence?* Philadelphia, PA: Research for Better Schools.

Stinchfield, S. M., & Young, E. H. (1938). *Children with delayed or defective speech.* Palo Alto, CA: Stanford University Press.

Stipek, D., Feiler, R., Daniels, D., & Milburn, S. (1995). Effects of different instructional approaches on young children's achievement and motivation. *Child Development, 66,* 209–23.

Stocking, S. H., Arezzo, D., & Leavitt, S. (1980). *Helping kids make friends.* Allen, TX: Argus Communications.

Stone, S. J. (1997). *ACEI speaks: Understanding portfolio assessment. A guide for parents.* Wheaton, MD: Association for Childhood Education International.

Stone, S. J. (1995). Wanted: Advocates for play in the primary grades. *Young Children, 50*(6), 45–54.

Stritzel, K. (1995). Block play is for all children. *Child Care Information Exchange,* 42–47.

Stroud, J. (1995). Block play: Building a foundation for literacy. *Early Childhood Education Journal, 23*(1), 9–13.

Sullivan, M. (1982). *Feeling strong, feeling free: Movement exploration for young children.* Washington, DC: National Association for the Education of Young Children.

Sulzby, E., & Barnhart, J. (1990). All our children emerge as writers and readers. In J. S. McKee (Ed.), *The developing kindergarten: Programs, children and teachers* (pp. 201–44). East Lansing, MI: Michigan Association for the Education of Young Children.

Sunal, C. S. (1993). Social studies in early childhood education. In B. Spodek (Ed.), *Handbook of research on the education of young children* (9th ed.). Upper Saddle River, NJ: Merrill/Prentice Hall.

Sunal, C. S. (1990). *Early childhood social studies.* Upper Saddle River, NJ: Merrill/Prentice Hall.

Surber, C. F. (1982). Separable effects of motives, consequences, and presentation order on children's moral judgments. *Developmental Psychology, 18,* 257–66.

Sutton-Smith, B. (1986). *Toys as culture.* New York: Gardner Press.

Sutton-Smith, B. (1971). A reply to Piaget: A play theory of copy. In R. E. Herron & B. Sutton-Smith (Eds.), *Child's play* (pp. 340–42). New York: Wiley.

Swick, K. J., & Duff, R. E. (1978). *The parent-teacher bond.* Dubuque, IA: Kendall/Hunt.

Swick, K. J., & McKnight, S. (1989). Characteristics of kindergarten teachers who promote parent involvement. *Early Childhood Research Quarterly, 4,* 19–29.

Sykes, C. (1996). *Dumbing down our kids.* New York: St. Martin's Press.

Sylva, K. (1993). Work or play in the nursery. *International Play Journal, 1*(1), 5–16.

Sylwester, R. (1995). *A celebration of neurons: An educator's guide to the human brain.* Alexandria, VA: Association for Supervision and Curriculum Development.

Szekely, G. (1990, Spring). An introduction to art: Children's books. *Childhood Education, 66*(3), 132–38.

Taras, H. (1992). Physical activity of young children in relation to physical and mental health. In C. Hendricks (Ed.), *Young children on the grow: Health, activity and education in the preschool setting* (pp. 33–42). Washington, DC: ERIC Clearinghouse on Teacher Education.

Tauton, M. (1983). Questioning strategies to encourage young children to talk about art. *Art Education, 36*(4), 40–43.

Taylor, B. (1992, January). Discipline practices: The influence of culture. *Central Michigan Association for the Education of Young Children Newsletter, 3.*

Taylor, B. J. (1995). *A child goes forth.* Upper Saddle River, NJ: Prentice Hall.

Taylor, B. J. (1993). *Science everywhere.* New York: Harcourt Brace Jovanovich.

Taylor, D. (1991). Family literacy: Text as context. In J. Flood, J. M. Jensen, D. Lapp, and J. R. Squire (Eds.), *Handbook of research on teaching the English language arts* (pp. 457–69). New York: Macmillan.

Taylor, S. I., & Morris, U. G. (1996). Outdoor play in early childhood education settings: Is it safe and healthy for children? *Early Childhood Education Journal, 33*(3), 153–58.

Teale, W. H. (1988, February). Developmentally appropriate assessment of reading and writing in the early childhood classroom. *Elementary School Journal, 89,* 173–84,

Tegano, D. (1996). Designing classroom spaces: Making the most of time. *Early Childhood Education Journal, 23*(3), 135–44.

Tegano, D., Sawyers, J., & Moran, J. (1991, Winter). Problem finding and solving in play: The teacher's role. *Childhood Education,* 92–97.

Thelen, E., Kelso, J. A. S., & Fogel, A. (1987). Self-organizing systems and infant motor development. *Developmental Review, 1,* 39–65.

Thomas, A., & Chess, S. (1984). *Origins and evolution of behavior disorders.* New York: Brunner/Mazel.

Thomas, A., & Chess, S. (1980). *The dynamics of psychological development.* New York: Brunner/Mazel.

Thomas, A., & Chess, S. (1977). *Temperament and development.* New York: Brunner/Mazel.

Thomas, A., Chess, S., Birch, H. G., Hartzig, M. E., & Korn, S. (1963). *Behavioral individuality in early childhood.* New York: New York University Press.

Thomas, R. M. (1995). *Comparing theories of child development* (2nd ed.). Belmont, CA: Wadsworth.

Thompson, C. (1990). "I make a mark": The significance of talk in young children's artistic development. *Early Childhood Research Quarterly, 5,* 215–32.

Thompson, C. M. (1995). Transforming curriculum in the visual arts. In S. Bredekamp and T. Rosegrant (Eds.), *Reaching potentials: Transforming early childhood curriculum and assessment* (vol. 2). Washington, DC: National Association for the Education of Young Children.

Thornton, T. P. (1996, July 13). If U Cn Rd This . . . *New York Times,* 15, 129.

Tierney, R. (1991). *Portfolio assessment in the reading-writing classroom.* Norwood, MA: Christopher-Gordon.

Tierney, R. J., Carter, M. A., & Desai, L. (1991). *Portfolio assessment in the reading writing classroom.* Norwood, MA: Christopher-Gordon.

Tisask, M. S., & Block, J. H. (1990). Preschool children's evolving conceptions of badness: A longitudinal study. *Early Education and Development, 4,* 300–7.

Toepfer, C. F. (1985). Suggestions of neurological data for middle level education: A review of research and its interpretations. *Transescence, 13*(2), 12–38.

Tompkins, G. E. (1990). *Teaching writing: Balancing process and product.* Upper Saddle River, NJ: Merrill/Prentice Hall.

Torgeson, L. (1996, May). Starting with stories: Building a sense of community. *Child Care Information Exchange,* 55–57.

Tough, J. (1977). *Talking and learning.* London, England: Schools Council Publications.

Trad, P. V. (1988). *Psychosocial scenarios for pediatrics.* New York: Springer.

Traverse City Public Schools (1987). *Early childhood curriculum guide: Kindergarten through 2nd.* Traverse City, MI: Author.

Trawick-Smith, J. (1988, July). Let's say you're the baby, OK? Play leadership and following behavior of young children. *Young Children,* 51–59.

Trepanier-Street, M. (1991). The developing kindergartner: Thinking and problem solving. In J. McKee (Ed.), *Developing kindergartens: Programs, children and teachers* (pp. 181–99). East Lansing, MI: Michigan Association for the Education of Young Children.

Tribe, C. (1982). *Profile of three theories.* Dubuque, IA: Kendall/Hunt.

Tudge, J., & Caruso, D. (1988). Cooperative problem solving in the classroom: Enhancing young children's cognitive development. *Young Children, 44*(101), 46–52.

Umansky, W. (1983, March/April). On families and the re-valuing of childhood. *Childhood Education, 59*(4), 259–66.

U.S. Department of Commerce (1996). Population projections of the United States by age, sex, race, and Hispanic origin: 1995 to 2050. Washington, DC: Author.

U.S. Department of Education (1986). What works: Research about teaching and learning. Washington, DC: U.S. Government Printing Office.

Vance, B. (1973). *Teaching the prekindergarten child: Instructional design and curriculum.* Pacific Grove, CA: Brooks/Cole.

Vandell, D. L., & Corasanti, M. A. (1990). Variations in early childcare: Do they predict subsequent social, emotional and cognitive differences? *Early Childhood Research Quarterly,* 5, 555–72.

Vander-Zanden, J. W. (1989). *Human development* (4th ed.). New York: Knopf.

Vasta, R., Haith, M. M., & Miller, S. A. (1995). *Child psychology: The modern science.* New York: Wiley.

Viadero, D. (1996, September 18). Brain trust. *Education Week on the Web* ^http: //www. edweek. org^.

Vogel, P. G., & Seefeldt, V. (1988). *Program design in physical education.* Indianapolis, IN: Benchmark.

Vygotsky, L. (1986). *Thought and language* (rev. ed., ed. A. Kozulin). Cambridge, MA: MIT Press.

Vygotsky, L. (1979). The genesis of higher mental functioning. In J. V. Wertsch (Ed.), *The concept of activity in Soviet psychology.* Armonk, NY: Sharpe.

Vygotsky, L (1978). *Mind in society: The development of higher psychological processes.* Cambridge, MA: Harvard University Press.

Vygotsky, L. (1967). Play and its role in the mental development of the child. *Social Psychology, 12,* 62–76.

Vygotsky, L. (1929). The problem of the cultural development of the child. *Journal of Genetic Psychology, 36,* 415–34.

Vygotsky, L. S. (1962). *Thought and language.* London, England: Schools Council Publications.

Wagner, T. (1996, October). Bringing school reform back down to earth. *Phi Delta Kappan, 78*(2), 145–49.

Waite-Stupiansky, S. (1997). *Building understanding together: A contructionist approach to early childhood education.* Albany, NY: Delmar.

Walberg, H. (1984). Improving the productivity of Americans' schools. *Educational Leadership, 41,* 19–30.

Walberg, H. J. (1985). Families as partners in educational productivity. *Phi Delta Kappan, 65*(6), 397–400.

Walde, A., & Baker, K. (1990). How teachers view the parent's role in education. *Phi Delta Kappan, 72* (4), 319–22.

Walker, L. J. (1989). A longitudinal study of moral reasoning. *Child Development, 60,* 157–66.

Walker, L. J., deVries, B., & Trevarthan, S. D. (1987). Moral stages and moral orientations in real-life and hypothetical dilemmas. *Child Development, 58,* 842–58.

Walsey, P. A. (1991). From quarterback to coach, from actor to director. *Educational Leadership, 48*(8), 35–40.

Walsh, D. J. (1991, April). Extending the discourse on developmental appropriateness: A developmental perspective. *Early Education and Development, 2*(2), 109–19.

Walsh, N. (1994). *Making books across the curriculum, grades K–6: Pop ups, flaps, shapes, wheels and many more.* New York: Scholastic.

Ward, S. (1986). *Charlie and grandma.* New York: Scholastic.

Weaver, R. L. (1990). Separate is not equal. *Principal, 69*(5), 40–43.

Webster, T. (1990). Projects as curriculum: Under what conditions? *Childhood Education 67*(1), 2–3.

Weikart, D. P., & Schweinhart, L. J. (1987). The high/scope cognitively oriented curriculum in early education. In J. L. Roopnarine and J. E. Johnson (Eds.), *Approaches to early childhood education* (pp. 253–68). Upper Saddle River, NJ: Merrill/Prentice Hall.

Weinstein, C. S. (1987). Designing preschool classrooms to support development: Research and reflection. In C. S. Weinstein and T. G. David (Eds.), *Spaces for children: The built environment and child development* (pp. 159–186). New York: Plenum Press.

Weinstein, C. S., & Mignano, A. J. (1997). *Elementary classroom management: Lessons from research and practice.* New York: McGraw-Hill.

Weissberg, R. P., Shriver, T. P., Bose, S., & DeFalco, K. (1997). Creating a districtwide social development project. *Educational Leadership, 84*(8), 37–40.

Weissbourd, R. (1996). *The vulnerable child: What really hurts America's children and what we can do about it.* Reading, MA: Addison-Wesley.

Welman, H. M. (1988). First steps in the child's theorizing about the mind. In J. Astington, P. L. Harris, and D. R. Olson (Eds.), *Developing theories of mind.* New York: Cambridge University Press.

Werner, P. (1994). Whole physical education. *Journal of Physical Education, Recreation and Dance, 65*(6), 40–44.

Wertsch, J. V. (1985). *Vygotsky and the social formation of mind.* Cambridge, MA: Harvard University Press.

Weston, D. R., & Turiel, E. (1980). Act-role relations: Children's concepts of social rules. *Developmental Psychology, 16,* 417–24.

Whiren, A. P. (1995, August). *Play and children's learning.* Paper presented for the Korean Association for the Education of Young Children, Seoul, Korea.

Whiren, A. P. (1991, May). *Children's play and learning.* Paper presented at the Kalamazoo Association for the Education of Young Children Conference, Kalamazoo, MI.

Whiren, A. P. (1990). The kindergarten teacher: Roles in the classroom. In J. S. Spitler McKee (Ed.), *The developing kindergarten: Programs, children and teachers* (pp. 275–301). Ann Arbor, MI: Michigan Association for the Education of Young Children.

Whiren, A. P. (1979). Tabletoys: The undeveloped resource. In L. Adams & B. Garbeck (Eds.), *Ideas that work with young children* (vol. 2). Washington, DC: National Association for the Education of Young Children.

Whitebook, M., Phillips, C. & Howes, C. (1993). National child care staffing study revisited: Four years in the life of center-based child care. Oakland, CA: Child Care Employee Project.

Whitebook, M., Sakai, L., & Howes, C. (1997). *NAEYC accreditation as a strategy for improving child care quality.* Washington, DC: National Center for the Early Childhood Work Force.

White, S. H., & Siegel, A. W. (1976). Cognitive development: The new inquiry. *Young Children, 31*(6), 425–36.

Wieder, S., & Greenspan, S. I. (1993), The emotional basis of learning. In B. Spodek (Ed.), *Handbook of research on the education of young children* (pp. 77–104). New York: Macmillan.

Wilcox, E. (1994). Unlock the joy of music. *Teaching Music, 2,* 34–35.

Williams, C. & Bybee, J. (1994). What do young children feel guilty about? Developmental and gender differences. *Developmental Psychology, 30*(5), 617–23.

Williams, D. L., Jr., & Chavkin, N. F. (1989, October). Essential elements of strong parent involvement programs. *Educational Leadership,* 24–27.

Williams, H. G. (1983). *Perceptual and motor development.* Upper Saddle River, NJ: Prentice Hall.

Williams, L. (1995, January 25). Can you read this? *New York Times,* C-1.

Williams, L. R. (1987). Determining the curriculum. In C. Seefeldt (Ed.), *The early childhood curriculum: A review of current research* (pp. 1–12). New York: Teachers College Press.

Wilson, R. (1995). Environmental education: Environmentally appropriate practices. *Early Childhood Education Journal, 23*(2), 107–10.

Winebrenner, S. (1992). *Teaching gifted kids in the regular classroom: Strategies and techniques every teacher can use to meet the academic needs of the gifted and talented.* Minneapolis, MN: Free Spirit.

Winfrey, O. (1996). About us: The dignity of children. Fred Berner Films and the Children's Dignity Project: CDP Films.

Wittmer, D. S., & Honig, A. S. (1994, July). Encouraging positive social development in young children. *Young Children, 4,* 4–12.

Wolery, M., Strain, P., & Bailey, D. (1992). Reaching potentials of children with special needs. In S. Bredekamp and T. Rosegrant (Eds.), *Reaching potentials: Appropriate curriculum and assessment for young children* (vol. 1) (pp. 92–11). Washington, DC: National Association for the Education of Young Children.

Wolery, M., & Wilbers, J. S. (1993). *Including children with special needs in early childhood programs.* Washington, DC: National Association for the Education of Young Children.

Wolf, D. (1991, July-August). Make believe: Why bother? *Exchange, 80,* 45–48.

Wolfgang, C. H. (1996). *The three faces of discipline for the elementary school teacher.* Boston, MA: Allyn & Bacon.

Wolfgang, C. H., & Sanders, L. (1986). Teacher's role: A construct for supporting the play of young children. In S. Burroughs and R. Evans (Eds.), *Play, language and socialization* (pp. 49–62). New York: Gordon & Breach.

Wood, D. J. (1989). Teaching the young child: Some relationships between social interaction, language and thought. In R. Olson (Ed.), *The social foundations of language and thought.* New York: Norton.

Wood, D. J., Bruner, J. S., & Ross, G. (1976). The role of tutoring in problem solving. *Journal of Child Psychology and Psychiatry, 17*(2), 89–100.

Wood, D. J., & Middleton, D. (1975). A study of assisted problem solving. *British Journal of Psychology, 66,* 181–91.

Woodword, V., Ives, W., Levamdi, B., & von Hippel, C. (1981). *Your child and writing.* Washington, DC: U.S. Department of Health and Human Services, DHHS Publication No. (OHDS) 81–31147.

Wortham, S. C. (1995). *Measurement and evaluation in early childhood education* (2nd ed.). Upper Saddle River, NJ: Merrill/Prentice Hall.

Wortham, S. C. (1984). *Organizing instruction in early childhood.* Boston, MA: Allyn & Bacon.

Wright, S. (1997). Learning how to learn: The arts as core in an emergent curriculum. *Childhood Education, 73*(6), 361–65.

Wurtele, S. K., Gissispie, G., Currier, L. & Franklin, C. (1992). A comparison of teachers vs. parents as instructors of a personal safety program for preschoolers. *Child Abuse & Neglect, 16,* 127–37.

Yawkey, T. (1987). Project P.I.A.G.E.T.—A holistic approach to early bilingual education. In J. L. Roopnarine and J. E. Johnson (Eds.), *Approaches to early childhood education* (pp. 197–212). Upper Saddle River, NJ: Merrill/Prentice Hall.

Yawkey, T. D. (1983). *Pretend play and language growth in young children.* Washington, DC: U.S. Department of Education.

Zahorck, J. A. (1997, March). Encouraging and challenging—Student's understandings. *Educational Leadership, 54*(6), 30–32.

Zaichkowsky, L., & Larson, G. (1995). Physical, motor, and fitness development in children and adolescents. *Journal of Education, 177*(2), 55–79.

Zavitkovsky, D. (1986). *Listen to the children.* Washington, DC: National Association for the Education of Young Children.

Zeece, P., & Graul, S. (1993, Summer). Grounds for play: Sound, safe, and sensational. *Day Care and Early Education, 23*–27.

Zemach, M. (1976). *Hush little baby.* New York: Dutton.

Zentella, A. C. (1981). Ta bien you could answer me en cualquier idioma: Puerto Rican code-switching in bilingual classrooms. In R. Duros (Ed.), *Latino language and communicative behavior* (pp. 109–32). Norwood, NJ: Ablex.

Zimmer, C. (1990). [Farmington Hills schools parent night successes. Personal communication.]

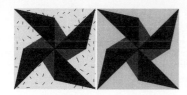

Author Index

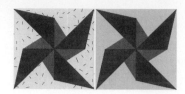

Subject Index